# Understanding Aesthetics for the Merchandising and Design Professional

**Ann Marie Fiore**
Iowa State University

**Patricia Anne Kimle**

Fairchild Publications
New York

Text design: Dutton & Sherman
Cover design: Dutton & Sherman



Library of Congress Catalog Card Number: 96-85915
ISBN: 1-56367-082-8
GST R 133004424
Printed in the United States of America

# Contents

## Part Three Aesthetics Related Skills and the Apparel Professional



## Part Four Application of Aesthetics Related Skills Used by Apparel Professional

# Extended Contents

## Part Four Application of Aesthetics Related Skills Used by the Apparel Professional

# Acknowledgments

We would like to acknowledge our colleagues in the Textiles and Clothing Department at Iowa State University for their support and suggestions. We would like to especially thank our departmental colleagues, Sara Kadolph, for her review, and Mary Littrell, Jennifer Paff, and Sherry Schofield-Thomschin for sharing their personal collections of photographs. Support and comments from graduate students and undergraduate students in the Textiles and Clothing Department are recognized. Colleagues from other academic institutions shared their expertise through readings written specifically for this textbook. Thanks to Ching-Yi Cheng (Fu Jen University in Taiwan), Josephine Moreno (University of Rhode Island), Gwendolyn O'Neal (The Ohio State University), and Nancy Rudd (The Ohio State University).

Sincere thanks to the textiles and apparel professionals who contributed their time and insight through personal interviews for Chapter 11 and Chapter 15 including Jaana Seppä, Anthony Fiore (yes, he's my brother), Natalie Perr, and Linda Tain. Additionally, the contributions of Lynn Amos, Lisa Norman Hendrickson, Pamela Holt, Christopher Kolbe, Brecca Farr, Sarah Rye, C. Shane Santi , and Lisa Williams Soltz (all graduates from the Textiles and Clothing Department at Iowa State) prove that we have some of the finest graduates.

Other readers selected by the publisher were also very helpful. They included: Dr. Jeanette J. Arbuthnot, Utah State University; Nancy Bryant, Oregon State University; Joan L. Chandler, University of California—Davis; Sheri L. Dragoo, Texas Women's University; Dr. Jane Lamb, University of Delaware; Traci May-Plumlee, UNC—Greensboro; Dr. Karen J. Robinette, California State University—Northridge; Dr. Cherry Searle; Diane Sparks, Colorado State University.

Without a doubt, Pam Kirshen Fishman and Olga Kontzias from Fairchild made the process of creating a textbook enjoyable for us through their positive comments, openness to new ideas, insight, and organizational and research skills. (Olga no longer has to explain to colleagues at work why she has a romance novel [used as a visual in the textbook] on her desk.)

On the home front, we would like to acknowledge our families for their support and understanding. Ann Marie Fiore would like to thank her fiancé, David Halstead, for not following through on the threat to nail the door to the office shut while she was endlessly working away in there; he knew she would come out sooner or later. And lastly, to Saber, for providing a requisite diversion of daily hikes.

1997

Ann Marie Fiore
Patrica Anne Kimle

# Message to the Reader

We believe the approach taken in this textbook is different from those of other textbooks you may have read. We wrote this book to foster understanding of aesthetics and how aesthetics applies to the roles of the apparel industry professional. We bridged the gap between textbooks emphasizing the "nuts and bolts" or basics of the apparel industry and textbooks based solely upon scholarly thought and research. Our textbook includes important information generated by scholars and researchers, but also addresses how this information directly relates to the development, selection, and promotion of apparel (and other textile) products.

You, as a student, should be intellectually challenged for growth and understanding to occur. Therefore, we did not "dilute" the information presented here to a level where the subject matter has the same weakness as a soup made from boiled socks. Contributions from many fields including anthropology, art and design, consumer behavior, marketing, philosophy, psychology, and textiles and clothing impart richness to this book. Apparel students need specialized knowledge about the apparel product. Students also require knowledge from many different fields or majors to understand the appeal for textiles and apparel products. The application of this broad knowledge base allows the textiles and apparel student to find employment in many aspects of the apparel industry and in other industries as well.

To help you understand and retain the information, visual examples and activities are interspersed throughout the chapters. Space in the book is provided in many of the activities for you to record your responses. We have also included readings from industry trade publications and popular magazines. Personal interviews with apparel industry professionals let the student hear about industry experiences. These articles and interviews provide insight into the importance of aesthetics from the apparel industry's perspective.

The importance of "learning by doing" and learning in an interactive classroom environment underlies the design of this textbook. It is designed to facilitate interaction among class members and the instructor; students should not

Similarity of swirls of frozen yogurt and swirls in apparel design.

(Left): NYT Pictures. Photo by Brian Diggs; (right): Zandra Rhodes, 1994. Photo by Justin Smith.

consider themselves passive recipients of information from the book, passed down through the instructor. In addition, students are not empty vessels to be filled with information by the instructor; students may have apparel industry experience and certainly have purchased apparel, which makes each student a source of insight and information.

While the book focuses on apparel, not all examples given pertain to aesthetics of apparel. This is a deliberate decision on our part for three reasons:

1. Attending to aesthetic qualities is a skill that is honed or sharpened by practice, like any other skill. Practice can take place with apparel or any object or event. Practice is practice.
2. Inspiration for apparel often comes from appreciation of qualities of the world around us. Thus, attending to the luxuriously smooth, silky swirls of frozen yogurt may inspire a designer to create a line of clothing from a similarly smooth fabric such as washed silk or micro fiber polyester (see photos above). One must be open to inspirational sources wherever they may lie.
3. The prevailing aesthetic preferences of apparel do not occur in a vacuum. In a (sub)culture, preferences for apparel are likely related to preferences for music, dance, food, etc. For example, in the U. S., popularity of "fusion cuisine," or combining ingredients from a variety of cultures in the same recipe, coincides with the trend of mixing garment styles and fabrics from a variety of cultures in the same ensemble. Therefore, understanding the aesthetic preferences of consumers in non-apparel objects can help forecasters and merchandisers identify trends in apparel.

To encourage awareness of the interconnectedness between apparel and other forms of aesthetic experience around you, Part one consists of a primer on aesthetics incorporating an array of products beyond apparel. Chapter 1 provides you with a broad definition of aesthetic experience, applicable to products or enviroments or events far beyond apparel. Chapter 2 continues the discussion of concepts introduced in Chapter 1 with a more detailed explanation of how apparel, the body, and their surrounding environment can contribute to aesthetic experience. Chapter 3 outlines benefits, including aesthetic experience, that influence the purchase of an array of products, including apparel. We then illustrate, in Chapter 4, that socio-cultural and individual differences of the person affect aesthetic preferences for everything from paintings to perfume. By the end of Part One, you will not only be able to speak cogently about the subject matter of aesthetics, but you will also be able to impress your friends and relatives with your ability to properly spell "aesthetics" without hesitation.

As you will discover, aesthetic experience is due to more than "what meets the eye"; it is a multisensory experience, where all the senses may contribute. Part two opens with Chapter 5 and a discussion of purely visual elements (color and lighting) affecting aesthetic experience. Chapter 5 continues with line and shape, elements that can be seen as well as touched. Chapter 6 focuses on texture, space, and kinesthetic; these elements are more strongly sensed by touch or "feel" of the body than the elements in Chapter 5. Chapter 7 introduces you to elements of sound and smell. These two sensory inputs have been largely ignored in the study of aesthetics of apparel. Yet, try to imagine a fashion show without music. Think about mall (the main) entrances of department stores. How often are fragrance and cosmetics departments located in these main entrance areas? Sound and smell are important elements in the study of aesthetics of apparel.

Understanding the individual elements of design in Chapters 5, 6, and 7 is important, but apparel professionals must also understand the effect produced when putting these elements together. Just as mint, orange, and chocolate are pleasurable by themselves, but quite unpalatable when mixed all together in equal proportions, the elements of design must be carefully "mixed" to produce an aesthetic textile or apparel product. Part Two provides considerations when combining the elements of design to create an aesthetic form. Creating a desired level of complexity and order is discussed in Chapter 8. Principles that affect level of complexity and order are presented in Chapter 9.

Parts Three and Four address a major concern of many college students today, application of their education to future professional activities. In Part Three, Chapter 10 outlines aesthetics related activities and skills required of a range of apparel professionals. In Chapter 11 you hear from apparel professionals, themselves, about their work experiences. The personal interviews in Chapter 11 stress the importance of aesthetics in a variety of apparel professions, divided into three groups: developers, gatekeepers (selectors), and promoters.

In Part Four, a sampling of the aesthetics related skills outlined in Chapter 10 are expounded. Chapter 12 details the steps in perceiving apparel on the body. Chapter 13 illustrates abstracting, or finding recurring similarities, across aesthetic forms. This chapter also catalogs recurring aesthetic similarities for a number of Japanese, French, Italian, and American designers. Chapter 14 discusses the process of trend forecasting, or identifying transitional changes in the aesthetic form across time. The final chapter, Chapter 15, depicts how visual and verbal messages can be used to promote textiles and apparel products within the firm or to the end-use consumer. This final chapter closes with advice on developing a portfolio, a promotional tool used routinely in job interviews by design students and becoming more common in interviews for merchandising and production positions as well.

We hope you find this book informative, useful, and enjoyable. The material presented in this book is not specific to one course or one profession, but is applicable to a number of courses and professions. Therefore, we hope you remember to use this book as a reference for other courses and refer back to this book during your professional endeavors.

# Understanding Aesthetics for the Merchandising and Design Professional

PART ONE

# A Primer on Aesthetics

CHAPTER 1

# Defining Aesthetic Experience

## Objectives

- Understand the importance of aesthetic aspects of the product or environment to consumers
- Understand the nature of aesthetic experience
- Understand how aesthetic experience affects the body, soul, and mind of the individual
- Recognize how form and content influence expressive and symbolic messages

Let's start with a riddle. If you walk down any shopping mall, you are likely to find a music shop, a candy or cookie shop, a cosmetics and perfume shop, and a sportswear shop. What do they all have in common? Yes, they all sell products and employ students such as yourself. Is there anything else in common? They all sell products *where pleasurable experiences are of primary importance in purchase of the products.* A consumer may purchase a new CD because it can be used to drown out the sound of the neighbor's barking dog, but chances are the CD was purchased because the music has a "sound" that is soothing or exciting and is pleasurable to the ear. The CD may also contain lyrics that lead you to imagine a pleasurable situation, such as love or romance. Gummi bears and chocolate chip cookies may be used to attract insects needed for your biology project, but we'll wager that these treats are purchased because they provide pleasurable sensations to the consumer's taste buds. Cosmetics beautify the look and feel of the skin and fragrance fills the air around the wearer with pleasurable, emotion-arousing particles. A consumer may purchase a jacket for its warmth. However, the decision to purchase a jacket will be affected by considerations such as, "Does the jacket make the wearer resemble an inflated rescue raft?" Another consideration may be, "Does the texture of the wool fabric feel smooth and rich or scratchy and harsh?" When was the last time you said,

"This garment makes me look horrible; I'll take two!" By now you should be getting a general sense of the types of pleasurable experiences that may come from products. These pleasurable experiences can be described as *aesthetic experiences.*

## IMPORTANCE OF AESTHETIC EXPERIENCE

Consumers report that aesthetic aspects of apparel are of primary importance in selection and purchase of apparel (Eckman, Damhorst & Kadolph, 1990). Aesthetic aspects are relevant to perceived quality (Fiore & Damhorst, 1992) and, ultimately, to satisfaction with the product. Apparel product features are not the only contributors to aesthetic experience. Aesthetic experience is also due to the promotional (shopping) environment. The experience provided by the promotional (shopping) environment has a definite influence on the consumer decision-making process.

Apparel professionals must understand aesthetic experience because this experience is integral to the successful development, selection, and promotion of apparel products. Apparel professionals should consider aesthetic aspects of apparel and the promotional environment to ensure consumer satisfaction and, consequently, the profitability of the apparel business. Because aesthetic experience is so important to consumers' purchase of and satisfaction with the apparel product, it is essential that we spend some time discussing aesthetic experience.

## DEFINING AESTHETIC EXPERIENCE

*Aesthetic experience can be defined as the sensitive selection or appreciation of formal, expressive, or symbolic qualities of the product or environment, providing non-instrumental benefits that result in pleasure or satisfaction.* Let us dissect this definition.

### Sensitive Selection or Appreciation

Aesthetic experience can result from *selection* of the product's design qualities, such as a designer selecting fabrics for a season's collection of garments or the wearer putting together her or his ensemble of garments in the morning. Aesthetic experience can also be derived from *appreciation* of what has been created by others, such as marveling at the deliberate synchrony between the beat of music and a model's gait during a fashion show.

An important point needs to be made here; aesthetic experience is not automatic, due to some mesmerizing power of aesthetic qualities. Instead, the individual is responsible for aesthetic experience. She or he must focus attention on the aesthetic qualities available in the object or environment. Two people can look at the same object (perhaps a sculpture or tuxedo), and one may be captivated by its elegance while the other may only attend to non-aesthetic features such as its price tag or weight (particularly if the person is appointed to pay for or carry the sculpture or tuxedo).

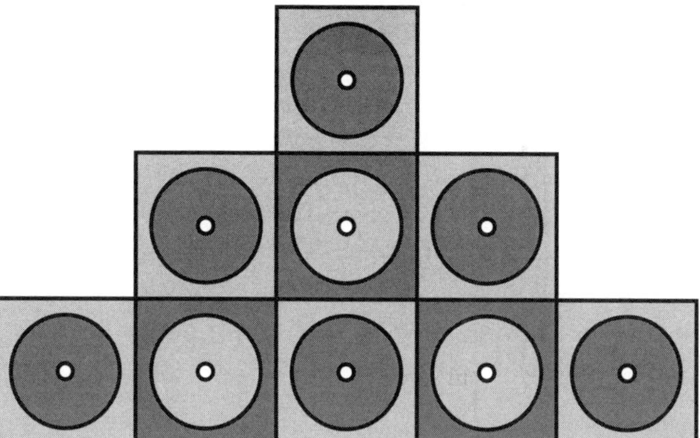

Figure 1.1. Ordered geometric pattern produced by a CD display.

Figure 1.2. Ordered geometric pattern found in a necktie display.

Sensitivity to aesthetic qualities requires training the senses and the mind to be sharply aware of (appreciate) these aesthetic qualities. To give an example, walking through that shopping mall again, you may attend to the aesthetic qualities of the window displays. You may appreciate the ordered pattern produced in a vivid window display of compact disks (Figure 1.1) or a similar pattern found in a necktie on display (Figure 1.2). Many objects can be seen as containing aesthetic qualities, but without the focused attention of the individual on these qualities they will be of little consequence aesthetically. This textbook will help train the senses and mind to be more sharply aware of aesthetic qualities. This awareness should make you a more effective apparel professional, able to distinguish aesthetic features leading to the appeal of apparel.

## Formal Qualities

In aesthetic experience, stimulation of the senses comes from attending to the *formal qualities* of the object or environment. Formal qualities *do not* refer to the casualness of the quality. **Formal qualities** refer to the perceivable features of the structural composition of the object or environment. For instance, the formal qualities of apparel include color, texture, line, shape, balance, rhythm, and proportion. These qualities are compositional features of apparel, just as pitch, tempo, dynamics (loudness), harmony, and melody are compositional features of music. Complete Activity 1.1; you will examine the importance of formal qualities of textile and apparel products.

## Expressive Qualities

Formal qualities (e.g., color, shape, balance) have the ability to express or evoke emotion, to allow the creator or appreciator to feel the emotion. **Expressive qualities** may represent the emotions of the creator and evoke emotion in the appreciator. There are two explanations for the expressiveness of form (1) expressiveness is *inherent* in the form or (2) expressiveness of the form is due to *learned* responses.

First, some believe expressiveness is inherent in, or part and parcel of, the form (Arnheim, 1972, 1986 Gibson, 1979; Lindauer, 1984). The inherent expressiveness of form may be due to the consistent effect that qualities of the form (e.g., color or shape) have on the body. For instance, intense colors (particularly red) excite the brain and raise blood pressure and respiration. Thus, high intensity colors may be perceived as exciting because of their associated physical responses of the body. The emotional feeling of music is partially based upon its tempo; tempos that are faster than the average heart rate of 70 beats per minute arouse the listener whereas slower tempos have a calming effect.

Expressiveness of form may be inherent because of underlying similarities of human experience, such as the feeling of warmth from the sun. The color yellow is experienced as warm because of the physical warmth felt when exposed to the yellow sun. Similar to the example of color, Arnheim (1988) proposed that visual composition is made up of a configuration of shapes, all generating forces. The constellation of forces reflect universal or shared human experience. For example, the ellipse is formed by interaction between two spheres of force (Figure 1.3). These two centers of energy coping with each other reflect a state of antagonism or tension.

Second, formal qualities may express or evoke emotion because of learned associations shared by a group. Certain formal qualities may symbolize ideas imbued with emotion. For example, feelings of loyalty may be expressed or evoked through the use of red, white, and blue for many Americans because these are the colors of the U.S. flag, a symbol of the country. These three colors may have less effect on the emotions of other groups, such as Italians, because their country's flag is red, white, and green. Explain expressive qualities in Activities 1.2 and 1.3.

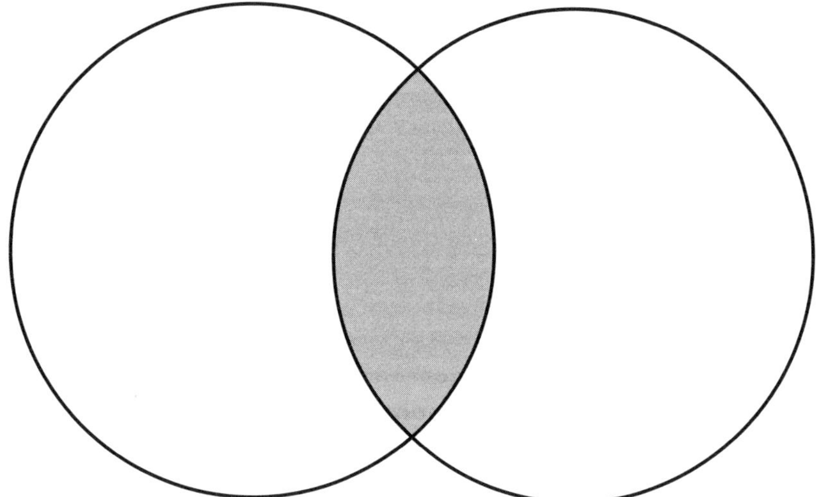

Figure 1.3. The ellipse, or overlap between two circles, expresses tension because of the pull between two spheres of force.

**ACTIVITY 1.1**

Take a moment to record 5 to 10 sensations from formal qualities that you have found to be pleasant in your apparel or home furnishings. For example: soft texture of stone washed jeans or plush thickness of a bath towel.

1. ______________________________
2. ______________________________
3. ______________________________
4. ______________________________
5. ______________________________
6. ______________________________
7. ______________________________
8. ______________________________
9. ______________________________
10. ______________________________

Your instructor may combine your list of pleasant qualities of apparel and other textile products with that of other students during a class activity. This activity will help identify some of the common aesthetic experiences that can influence the popularity and sale of apparel and other textile products among consumers similar to the class members.

**ACTIVITY 1.2**

Both inherent and learned associations can effectively evoke emotional responses in aesthetic experience. Here are exercises to test the expressiveness of form and the level of agreement. Your responses can be compared against other students during class to determine the level of agreement as well as the underlying similarities of form found to express emotion.

Imagine that you are in a culture where you do not know the language, but you want to communicate your emotions to members of this culture. As part of this culture, all women or men must wear dark veils over the face as a sign of respect, which means you cannot use facial expressions to communicate your emotions. You must use paper and pen to relay the information of your emotions. You can use different types of lines, shapes, textures, and colors arranged on the paper in any manner as long as the forms do not create a representation of objects that exist in the physical world. For example, "smilie faces" or birds cannot be used, because these are objects found in the outside world. There are no right or wrong answers to this exercise, but you may be asked to justify your drawings. These are the emotions you must express:

- Fear
- Joy
- Peacefulness
- Shock
- Happiness
- Anger

Once you have completed the task, determine which of the emotions resulted in similar formal qualities. Think about the nature of emotions expressed by similar formal qualities. Do these emotional experiences have anything in common? Can you draw any conclusions about the feelings expressed by particular formal qualities? For instance, do angled shapes express negative emotions better than curved shapes? Record three conclusions regarding feelings expressed by formal qualities:

1. ______________________________

2. ______________________________

3. ______________________________

Figure 1.4. Organic and geometric shapes.

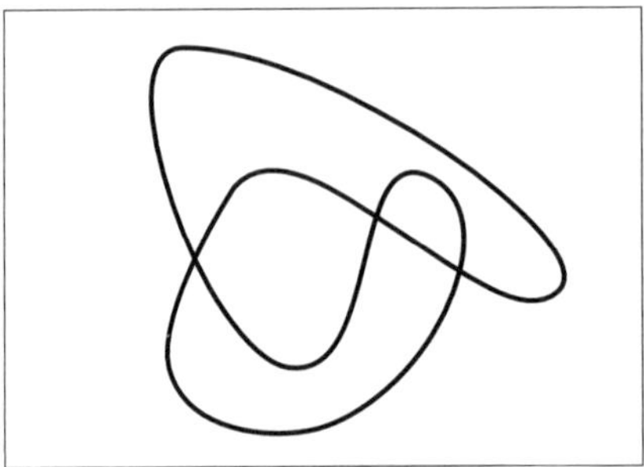

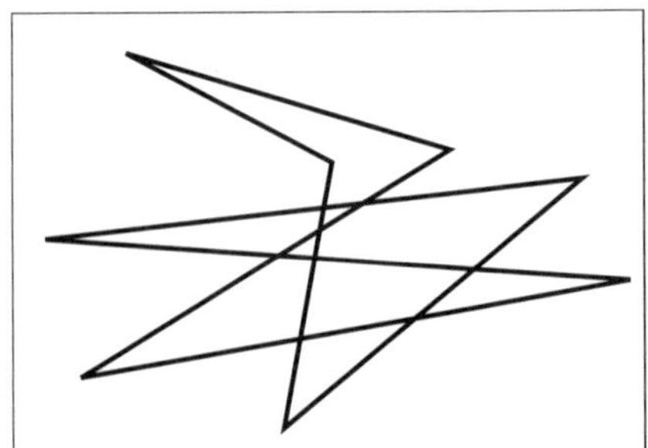

**ACTIVITY 1.3**

The next exercise involves coloring the two shapes in Figure 1.4. Use colors that best match each shape.

Were there significant differences among colors matched to these "nonsense shapes" in Activity 1.3? Your instructor may ask the following questions related to this activity. As a group, was there an overall similarity of intensity of color, lightness of color, or color family (e.g., red, blue, orange) selected for each shape? What are the reasons for similarities or differences in the group's color selections for each shape? Similarities may be due to inherent associations between formal qualities and expression. Differences may be due to learned associations as well, either common to a (sub)culture or unique to the individual. Researchers used this same activity with a variety of people and found that there were overriding similarities in color selections for these shapes (Lindauer, 1984).

### Symbolic Qualities

Creative use of symbols is said to be what separates human beings from other animals. **Symbols** are things that stand for or represent something else. Words, a "peace sign," a wavy "v" shape (to represent a seagull), a stick figure, a raised clenched fist, and mental images all are symbols that stand for something else. **Symbolic qualities** culminate in meaning or content, communicating an idea about the world. Pleasure can be derived from exercising the mind in creating or imagining one's own representation of the world, as well as understanding the ideas of others. Objects (e.g., paintings and clothing ensembles) and subjective mental images (e.g., fantasies) contain symbolic meaning that can lead to aesthetic experiences.

Symbols may have no physical resemblance to the ideas being expressed. For instance, the "peace sign" has no direct resemblance to the idea of societal peace. The artist or designer may depend on various levels of accuracy in depicting visual qualities of the object. The range moves from realistic representation to non-representation. Realistic images consist of an accurate depiction of visual qualities. Stylized images simplify the form and play up particular design qualities. Abstract images have less direct resemblance to the object, but captures the important essence of the object. Figure 1.5 displays levels of presentation in depicting visual qualities of "flowers." The messages sent by "flowers" are different to reflect the artists' or designers' intended messages. Complete Activity 1.4 to explore the meaning of flowers.

### Product or Environment

Aesthetic experience can come about from products or environments. **Products** are material goods with physical properties that can be repeatedly experienced during appreciation. These include such objects as paintings, perfumes, compact disks, and apparel. One can repeatedly see, smell, hear, or touch these goods. In terms of apparel products, aesthetic experience is the result of the interaction between the product and the consumer's body in many cases. The **environment** is the multisensory setting that surrounds and interacts with the (apparel) prod-

Figure 1.5. Three levels of presentation of "flowers": (a) realistic, (b) stylized, and (c) abstract.

(a) Iris: Van Gogh:
The Metropolitan Museum of Art; gift of Adele R. Levy, 1958.

(b) Japanese paper stencils for textiles. Tokugawa Period, 1613–1857.
The Metropolitan Museum of Art; gift of Clarence McKenzie Lewis, 1953.

(c) Black Iris III, 1926, Georgia O'Keefe.
The Metropolitan Museum of Art, Alfred Stieglitz Collection, 1969.

a

b

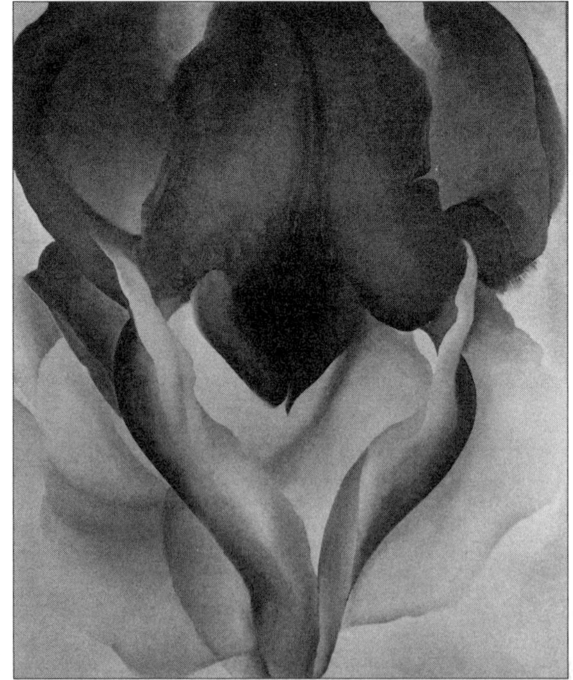

c

**ACTIVITY 1.4**

With the change in presentation comes a change in the meaning attributed to "flowers." This shows that symbolic meaning includes two facets: 1) *denotation* and 2) *connotation*. Denotation consists of the more explicit (obvious) meaning whereas connotation involves the more suggestive (subtle) meaning. The denotation of each of these is "flower," but your thoughts and feelings about flowers may differ.

What do you think the different images in Figure 1.5a, b, and c suggest about "flowers"? Flowers are:

a. ______________________________

b. ______________________________

c. ______________________________

uct (and the body). This setting has social as well as formal, expressive, and symbolic qualities. Environments, such as concerts, runway shows, and store settings can result in aesthetic experience for the participant. These environments have an influence on one's attitude toward a product. Retail environments are designed to produce special emotional effects in the consumer that enhance the probability of purchase (Kotler, 1973-1974). Thus, limiting attention to the actual product does not tell the whole story of the aesthetic experience that leads to consumer liking or purchase of the product. For example, the "free facial" becomes an environment offering a pleasurable experience that influences the purchase of beauty products.

Jeffrey Bleustein, the CEO of Harley-Davidson, humorously discusses the company's dramatic turn-around brought about by changes to the product and the store environment. The aesthetic qualities of the product had to be maintained, while the technological aspects of the motorcycle changed. Bleustein stated:

> And we've really changed everything on the bike except the look and the sound and the feel, because those are the things that people really wanted in a Harley.
>
> That created a pretty difficult design problem, because new technology changed everything and made everything work better, but we had to make it look the same and sound the same and make it have the same appeal . . . (Bleustein, 1995).

Changing the store environment added to the success of the product. Bleustein continues:

> [w]e did another thing in the marketing distribution area. That is, we encouraged our dealers to upgrade their stores, to make them a more attractive retail environment. We spent some money with a designer; we came up with a concept of a Harley-Davidson store; we just made it more modern in terms of getting the product out to the customer. When you shopped in most Harley-Davidson stores in the mid-eighties, if you wanted to buy something you would walk into the store and

there would be a lot of motorcycles all over the place, used, new, clean, dirty, and in the back of the store there was this big counter with three or four burly guys behind it and you had to guess which product you wanted to buy. You had to plead with one of these guys to go back and bring it out. That wasn't a very conducive retail environment. What we do now is bring the product out where customers could touch it, feel it, smell it, and buy it. What we found was the pay-back on this investment for most of our dealers was less than a year. In any business, a payback of that sort is very attractive. It's not just a one time thing. It continued to work for the dealers and our customers liked it as well.

We picked a dealer out and started to work with him on designing the store. His biggest fear was that he would alienate his traditional customers, people who were used to the oil and grease and felt comfortable in that environment. He said, "They feel comfortable in my store. I get carpet and this and that and they won't want to come." So we said he should give it a try, we were paying the money anyway so he could always get it back. He had his opening just before Christmas. He had a Christmas party and some of the traditional customers came in; now all of them put their cigarette butts out before they came in. He asked "Well, what do you think of my store?" He was really worried. He knew they would show up for the Christmas party (free eats and all that), but he wasn't sure that they would ever come back again. But what they said was, "You know, it's about time you did this." And that's the way it's been. The original customers have all liked it. Some of the dealers have gotten pretty exotic. It's been a competition between dealers: one dealer in one part of town would do his store and then the next dealer would follow with a more elaborate store. Some have been through this three or four times and every time they redesign and make it more elaborate, they get an incremental sales boost out of it. So it seems to be something customers appreciate (Bleustein, 1995).

### Non-Instrumental Benefit

One may distinguish the aesthetic from the non-aesthetic based upon the nature of reward provided by the object or experience. Appreciating aesthetic qualities is rewarding and pleasurable in itself. Non-aesthetic qualities are satisfying because they are instrumental in attaining external benefits such as social or economic gain (Berlyne, 1974; Holbrook, 1987). Instrumental or utilitarian qualities allow an individual to achieve some purpose or goal other than aesthetic pleasure. Aesthetic experience results from appreciation of the non-instrumental (Hirschman & Holbrook, 1982) or non-utilitarian qualities (Hirschman, 1983). Appreciating non-instrumental or non-utilitarian qualities is rewarding in and of itself and done for its own sake. An example will help clarify the difference between aesthetic and non-aesthetic. Attending to the color of a traffic light may be instrumental to the driver, because it signals when the driver can safely enter an intersection. This (safety) is a utilitarian concern. If, on the other hand, a driver is sitting at a red light and notices the brilliance of the illuminated red and how that red compares to the red of another light, then the driver is gaining an aesthetic benefit from the experience. Attending to differences in red lights is not benefiting the driver in any instrumental way; both red lights signal the same thing in terms of safety and traffic flow. (Differences in benefits may help explain the impatient driver's wise-crack to a fellow driver who does not respond quickly to the change of traffic signals, "Go—what shade of green are you waiting for?")

### Pleasure or Satisfaction

The result of aesthetic experience may be pleasure or, more broadly, satisfaction. Both **pleasure** and **satisfaction** entail gratification or fulfillment of desires. However, pleasure suggests a positive feeling, which may not accurately describe the state of emotional satisfaction. Both positive (e.g., joy) or negative (e.g., sadness) emotions may result in a satisfying experience. A film such as *Schindler's List* certainly evokes sadness within the viewer, but this experience may be seen as a powerful aesthetic experience that the viewer is glad to have gone through. People consciously expose themselves to emotionally "painful" movies, plays, and operas as a way to experience the emotion without having to live through the actual pain-causing experience (Hirschman, 1982). The same may be true of the use of apparel; products may be worn that express or evoke negative feelings. For instance, neckties may be printed with images of endangered species of animals. These neckties that stress the beauty and plight of endangered animal species may evoke feelings of distress for the wearer. Therefore, one must think broadly about the nature of aesthetic experience.

## INTERCONNECTIONS AMONG FORM, EXPRESSION, AND SYMBOLISM

Formal qualities have the ability to evoke or express emotion. For instance, one may feel the excitement created by high intensity colors, curving and diagonal lines, and asymmetrical balance. Symbols or representations are created from formal qualities. The same colors, lines, and balance may become representations of sails moving across the unsettled surface of a lake (Figure 1.6). Thus, symbolic content represented in the aesthetic form may communicate abstract ideas as well as emotion. For example, the dynamic feel from images of sailboats or the horror of war may be communicated. Designers and artists try to use the formal qualities and their expressiveness in the development of symbolic meaning.

## THE HOW AND WHY OF THE AESTHETIC EXPERIENCE

Aesthetic experience affects three aspects of the individual: the body, soul, and mind. Pleasure comes from *stimulating the senses* of the *body, arousing or expressing the feelings* of the *soul,* and *activating the thought processes* of the

Figure 1.6. Formal and expressive qualities used to represent the dynamic nature of sails.
The Image Bank, Magnus Rietz.

*mind.* The next section outlines "how" the human being is affected in each component of aesthetic experience and "why" affecting the body, soul, or mind results in pleasure.

Before moving on, we would like to explain why pleasure is an important response. Pleasure is the reinforcing mechanism in evolution that helps to ensure the survival of human beings. Evolution is nature's way of ensuring future survival of a species. Characteristics of a species evolve to adapt to the physical environment. Adapting permits the species to withstand or better utilize the environment. For instance, some species of birds evolved over the generations to have long thin beaks in order to better feed on (utilize) nectar-rich, tubular-shaped flowers. Other species of birds evolved to have short powerful beaks to crack open the husks of seeds. Along with change in the physical form of a species, pleasure and pain responses also help species adapt to their environment. Nature ensures the survival of the species by making beneficial behaviors pleasurable and harmful behaviors unpleasant or painful (Dissanayake, 1988; Tiger, 1992). For example, because sweet foods such as fruits were nutritious and poisonous foods were bitter, sweet tastes have become pleasant and bitter tastes have become unpleasant (Tiger, 1992). As we will discuss shortly, pleasure in aesthetic experience may be connected to the well-being of the human species.

## Stimulating the Senses of the Body

The simplest type of aesthetic experience results from stimulating the body's role in perception. In particular, this experience results from two steps of perception. First, pleasure can be due to *stimulation of sensory receptors* of the body. Second, pleasure comes from the *recognition* and *discrimination of those sensations* by the brain. Sensory receptors of the body such as eyes, ears, skin, nose, and mouth receive information about the formal qualities of the world around us. These receptors are attached to nerve fibers that transmit electrical signals to the brain for recognition and discrimination. For example, the eyes receive visual information in the form of light wave energy bouncing off objects. The nerve fibers attached to the eyes then electrically transmit the energy signals to the rear portion of the brain to decode the visual information.

The brain is responsible for recognizing (e.g., the color is red or the taste is bitter) and discriminating the information (e.g., the green is brighter than the blue, the taste is very bitter) sent by the sensory receptors. The interdependency of the receptor, nerves, and brain in the process of perception of sensory information becomes obvious when one thinks about loss of the senses. Blindness or the inability to process visual information may be due to damage of the eyes, the nerves, or the brain. (Anyone who has watched an hour of daytime drama would know this fact because it's a very popular story line—the beloved character bumps her/his head in an auto accident, injuring the brain, and thus is blinded. Rest assured, she/he always miraculously regains her/his sight.)

Stimulation of nerve fibers and the brain is pleasurable because this stimulation leads to proper development of the biological and psychological facets of the living organism. The need for sensory stimulation is most evident in infants. The infant deprived of physical touch struggles to survive and develops at a much slower rate than the infant who is caressed (Tiger, 1992). Many toys are now specifically designed to provide the sensory stimulation needed by the infant. *Discovery Toys* has developed a line of toys for infants that provide stimulation to many sensory channels. These toys provide the infant with sound, sight, touch, and smell sensations. The toys play music, are covered in vivid visual patterns and mixed textures, and are impregnated with a pleasant smell.

As the sensations reach the brain, the brain attempts to recognize and discriminate among the sensations. Pleasure comes when the brain is successful in recognizing or discriminating among the sensations. For instance, pleasure comes about when the brain recognizes the loftiness of a cashmere sweater. Pleasure may also come about when the brain discriminates between the loftiness of the sweater texture and the density of wool trousers when worn together. When the brain cannot recognize the sensations or create order out of the sensations, pleasure is diminished. Order is difficult to find because too much variety exists for the brain to decode, such as many colors used in an ensemble. As an apparel industry professional, your job includes creating the level of order desired by your consumer. Creating order may take several forms such as designing coordinated pieces of apparel (Figure 1.7) or selecting and arranging stock within a store or catalog. This allows the consumer to more easily see the relationships among the pieces of apparel.

However, there is such a thing as over-stimulation of the senses that leads to desensitization or destruction of the receptors (Coren, Porac & Ward, 1978). Over-stimulation occurs when the intensity of sensation is too high or the sensation is experienced for a prolonged period of time. Both overburden the nerve fibers and result in an unpleasant or painful sensation. For example, the tactile

Figure 1.7 Stock in catalog layout arranged by bright color, crisp edged shapes, and tailored fit to provide a pleasing order for consumers.

(touch) sensations of a back scratch may be wonderfully pleasant if performed with gently curved fingers, but painful if performed with a garden rake. The stimulation of a bright color may be very pleasant as a store accent but unpleasant when the entire store is painted "screaming" yellow. "Screaming" colors may be unpleasant for the same reason a screaming voice is unpleasant; both result in over-stimulation of the senses.

## Arousing or Expressing the Feelings of the Soul

Just as pleasure results from stimulating the body, pleasure can come from *arousing emotions* as well as *expressing feelings* (Robinson, 1994) of the soul (spirit). Just as a delicious dessert may "feed" the desires of the body, a piece of music may "feed" the soul.

The soul is different from the body. The soul refers to a non-physical entity, something that cannot be physically sensed. The body can be physically seen, touched, and smelled, making it a physical object. The soul (or spirit) cannot be scrutinized using the powers of the physical senses, even though phrases suggest otherwise: "the eyes are the windows to the soul," an experience "touches the soul" or "lifts the spirit," and (for *Nirvana* fans) "Smells like teen spirit." These phrases suggest that there is a depth to the spirit or soul and a strong connection to emotions or feelings. When one says, "the music lacks soul," one means that an aesthetic experience is limited because the music lacks a force or vitality that reaches in to arouse the emotions of the listener. Aesthetic experience comes about when feelings or emotions are aroused in the appreciator or when the emotions inside the individual are released.

Arousal of intense emotion through aesthetic experience is pleasurable or satisfying because these emotions make us feel alive, engaged with the world, and vibrant (Dissanayake, 1988, p.134). This arousal of intense emotion adds zest to life, which makes life worthwhile. The zest or enthusiasm for life guarantees the continuance of life (Dissanayake, 1988, p.70). The intense joy of a wedding or the excitement of a concert add to the pleasure of life. Appreciating the less intense but cumulative emotional experiences of everyday life are also important to the quality of life. For example, the thrill of winning a friendly video game of *Doom* or poker may not arouse intense emotions but is still enriching. Therefore, arousal of emotion in aesthetic experience has the most central biological function, survival of the organism and species.

As stated earlier, stimulation of nerve fibers and the brain is pleasurable because it ensures proper biological and psychological development. Similarly, expression of emotion can lead to pleasure or satisfaction because it too ensures this proper human development. "Bottling up" emotions can be harmful to one's physical and mental health. Crying and laughing are forms of emotional expression that release chemicals in the body which alleviate stress. Stress may adversely affect physical health (e.g., leading to cancer and heart disease) and biological development of human organisms. Stress can influence the rate at which children grow. Releasing intensely felt emotions is a natural response ("I'm so happy I could cry" or "I'm so angry I could scream"). Releasing emotions or feelings is therapeutic. Pleasure comes from expression of feeling, either through verbal expression or through the expressive nature of the arts and sports. Psychologists actually use the arts (e.g., painting, music, and dance) as a form of therapy for patients who cannot verbally express intense negative feelings bottled up inside (Winner, 1982).

Apparel can be an expressive outlet as well. For instance, the bold patterned and colorful nature of children's wear or active sportswear expresses the energetic nature of the wearers. Apparel professionals must take the expressive nature of apparel and the environment into account. Reading 1.1 shows that some consumers find arousal of intense emotion from skiing to be pleasurable. Capturing this excitement in bright colored products and photographs of daredevil skiers in a catalog evokes pleasurable arousal for these consumers as well.

## Activating the Thought Processes of the Mind

As discussed, pleasure can be derived from stimulating the body (sensory receptors and brain). Pleasure also comes from stimulating the mind. Both the mind and the brain co-habit the space between the ears. The *mind* consists of cognitive (thought) processes whereas the *brain* consists of physical (chemical and electrical) connections. The cognitive activity of the mind and the physical connections of the brain are interrelated. Biofeedback, for example, is the practice of consciously altering the body through thought processes. Thought patterns can produce a change in the chemical and electrical activity of the brain. Chemical imbalances have been linked to the suicidal thoughts of the severely depressed. Thus, the activities of the brain and the mind are enmeshed, but we have partitioned them into two separate components because the mechanisms leading to pleasure are different.

Pleasure from activating the brain, as we have explained, is the result of successful processing of sensory information about formal qualities of objects. These processes are identification and discrimination. Pleasure or satisfaction from activating the mind results from more advanced mental processes. These processes are *understanding* and *creating content or symbolic meaning*.[1] It's the sense of satisfaction represented by a spark of delight and the "I get it now!". For instance, satisfaction can be derived from understanding that a dress made from dish cloths is suppose to symbolize the traditional role of women, relegated to simplistic tasks in the household.

Why would nature make understanding symbolic meaning of aesthetic objects pleasurable? It may be because understanding symbolic meaning "is crucial to the cerebral [brain] evolution of the human organism . . . by which humans develop and extend their consciousness . . . (Dissanayake, 1988, p.67)." Cerebral evolution allows human beings to extend their understanding of the world through the use of symbols. For instance, physics requires understanding of symbols that represent concepts of force, inertia, and gravity. These symbols extend the understanding of the interactions among force, inertia, and gravity to determine what is actually required to propel a spaceship to the moon. Thus, understanding the symbolic meaning of these concepts gives scientists an increasing firmer grasp of the world.

Symbolic content of aesthetic forms may also provide ordinary folk a firmer grasp of the world. The symbolic content of aesthetic objects gives clarity to ambiguous human experience and a world in a state of flux. The softening of the shape of men's and women's business apparel helps give clarity to the current striving for balance between personal and professional life. A firmer grasp of reality aids interpersonal interaction (Miles & Leathers, 1984) and facilitates thinking about and acting upon the world (Fratto, 1978). Taking the dish cloth dress example, the symbolic meaning of the object may awaken the individual to the state of women's role in society and lead her or him to more equal sharing of responsibilities in and outside the home. Being creative and able to see in a new way through use of symbols helps ensure that solutions are found to problems faced by the individual and society.

Reading 1.2 shows how important the retail environment is as a source of aesthetic experience for the consumer and how this experience may affect the

[1] Pleasure can come from the creative activity in creation of formal aspects of aesthetic objects or experiences as well.

**LAB ACTIVITY 1.1**

To enhance awareness of form and content, collect twenty to twenty-five advertisements that contain the graphic art representations of apparel store names or designer names. These ads may come from newspapers, popular magazines, trade publications, or catalogs.

1. Sort these graphic art representations of store and designer names into piles based upon similarity of the formal qualities (e.g., color, texture, line, shape, balance, proportion) of the lettering. It is up to you to determine the number of piles. You should, however, have at least three piles.
2. Once these piles are created, give a description of the expressive message of each. For instance the piles may differ in terms of excitement. (Don't use this expressive quality unless it really applies.) The point is for you to feel the expressiveness of the form.
3. Then, describe the message communicated by each of the piles of store names and designer names. What images are the stores or designers trying to create? For example, does one pile communicate a message of snobbishness more than the others? (Again, don't use "snobbishness"; think of your own terms. Give at least three messages communicated by each pile.

success of the product. Notice how entertainment, or activating the thought processes of the mind, affects the consumer. Incorporating the pleasurable experience of entertainment is becoming increasingly important in the design of the retail environment.

## SUMMARY

The purpose of this chapter is to lay the foundation for understanding aesthetic experience. Aesthetic experience can be defined as the sensitive use or appreciation of formal, expressive, or symbolic qualities of the product or event, providingnon-instrumental benefits that result in pleasure or satisfaction. One must hone or sharpen the ability to perceive aesthetic qualities because aesthetic experience comes from sensitive awareness on the part of the creator or appreciator. It is im-portant to remember that pleasure or satisfaction is the result of stimulating the body, soul, and/or mind. This stimulation can come from products and/or environments. Aesthetic qualities are rewarding and pleasurable in themselves, not because they are instrumental in attaining external benefits such as social or economic gain. Once you understand the nature of aesthetic experience, you are able to apply this understanding to apparel, other textile products, and the promotional setting.

## KEY TERMS AND CONCEPTS

activating thought processes

aesthetic experience

arousing or expressing feelings

environment

expressive qualities

formal qualities

importance of aesthetic experience to professionals

interconnection among form, expression, symbolism

non-instrumental benefit

pleasure

product

satisfaction

sensitive selection or appreciation

stimulating the senses

symbolic qualities

symbols

## SUGGESTED READINGS

Dissanayake, E. (1984). Does art have selective value? *Empirical Studies of the Arts, 2*(1), 35-49.

Lindauer, M. S. (1984). Physiognomy and art: Approaches from above, below, and sideways. *Visual Arts Research, 10*(1), 52-65.

### For Advanced Levels

Holbrook, M. B. (1987). The study of signs in consumer esthetics: An egocentric review. In J. Umiker-Sebeok (Ed.), *Marketing and semiotics: New directions in the study of signs for sale* (pp. 73-121). New York, NY: Mouton de Gruyter.

## READING 1.1

# Degre 7 Puts Its Best Ski Forward

According to the judges, Degre 7, the gold-award winner in the Sporting Goods category, does everything right. "This book is such fun!" one of the panelists says. "I'm not even a skier, but I got so involved that I'm going to buy from it."

Degre 7 gets off to an enthusiastic start on its front cover with a dramatic action shot of a skier catching air in his Degre 7 skiwear. The company logo is in bright magenta at the bottom of the page. At the top left are the words "Powder perfect skiwear from France . . . and other essentials for life at altitude."

The back cover—a shot of a fearless skier hurling himself off a rocky precipice—is just as exciting. This time the logo is in smaller type at the top of the page so that the company can devote some space to selling the benefits of its exclusive line of "high-test clothes to match skiers' daring."

"The catalog makes excellent use of both covers," a judge says. "You simply have to open this book."

### Exhilarating presentation

On the opening spread, Degre 7 keeps the catalog's energy level high with another action shot of a dauntless heliskier and this vicariously thrilling passage: "A sparkling wind slips through the rock and ice chutes of the Pas de Chevre above Chamoix near dusk, whispering past our belay rope in a low moan of danger and escape. Behind lies peace. Ahead, the unknown. The rope tightens. One ski pushes forward. Like a particle of snow, we are circling, spinning, tumbling down in an unexpected rappel. Does our equipment matter now? Only as much as oxygen and adrenaline. Gear we love and trust frees our mind to act on instinct, unbound by fear, creating new moments of physical art and passion." "Brilliant!" a judge exclaims.

Degre 7's next spread, "What We're Made Of," explains the fabrics used in Degre 7's outer shells and inner linings. "You can't fool a frequent skier," Degre 7 says. "Either a ski suit works on your $5,000-a-week heliski vacation, or it doesn't. If it didn't keep you dry last time, or it didn't keep you warm, or it didn't make you look like a million bucks and attract powerful lust from the opposite sex, then you leave it at home. Case closed."

"Fabulous!" declares a panelist. "I'm hooked." The entire catalog is an exuberant combination of dynamic photographs and captivating copy. Each spread features an action photo of an intrepid skier wearing the featured clothing, large off-figure shots of the colorful skiwear with eye-catching call-outs to highlight special features.

"It's an absolutely first-rate integration of action visuals and presentation of the offer," a judge comments. "The printing and production are excellent, and the photography is outstanding."

But it's Degre 7's copy that most impresses the judges. As one says, "Degre 7 tells such a great story that I keep charging to the next page to read more." An excerpt from Degre 7's description of Seven (a men's snowboarding and powder suit), for example: "If you love a spring meadow full of daisies and hope, a late summer sky full of burnt orange and glory and a midwinter granite spire slick with moss and iced with challenge, then this is your suit. It's not for everyone. But for the few, the cocky, the ebullient, the mad, this ski suit will be a real find because it's different, brilliant and brash, swaggering on the outside but bulletproof on the inside. It'll find a home on the backs of powder hounds and mogul fiends who want to stand out from the crowd."

Another example, this time for Tim (a men's powder suit): "This is the suit you always take along, whether it's the middle of winter or the cusp of spring. Just ask Dr. Joseph Anis. The anesthesiologist from Dallas, TX, bought his version of this suit during a November squall at Alta when the wind was whipping around High Rustler at 50 m.p.h. and his instructor told him to get a new Degre 7 outfit or stay inside. He was unconscious the rest of the weekend, skiing in a new zone of warmth and style."

Reading 1.1 Degre 7 Puts Its Best Ski Forward, (1994, September). *Catalog Age,* pp. 117–118.

Photo captions, too, are loaded with charisma. "Danny Caruso gave up the life of international banking for one perfect afternoon of diving off cliffs at Snowbird," Degre 7 says. "This is his 450th try."

"This is better than reading a novel," one of the judges claims. "I just can't put it down."

Judges also have nothing but praise for Degre 7's merchandising. The fifty-six-page book contains a wide selection of ski suits, jackets, pants and accesories—all designed and manufactured by Degre 7—for men, women, and children.

"These are the clothes that good sport skiers want to ski in," a judge says. "They look expensive, and they are expensive, but you get the feeling that this skiwear is the best in the world, that it's worth saving for. The level of quality really comes through in the catalog."

"The clothes are gorgeous, too," another judge says. "Most skiwear is quite unattractive with no sense of color whatsoever, in my opinion, but this stuff is beautiful." Moreover, all Degre 7 pants and ski suits have three extra inches of fabric sewn into the hem of the snow cuff; this allows for growth in children and affords the taller-than-average adult skier a better fit.

## READING 1.2
## That's Entertainment

S. Reda

Incredible Universe shoppers sing along with karaoke and watch their performances on a giant screen television.

Warner Bros. customers stand in front of the massive video wall and take in a compendium of movie, television, cartoon, and music clips.

Planet Reebok patrons play games on interactive kiosks in hopes of winning a coupon for $10 off a future purchase.

Entertainment—the E-factor—has emerged as a critical element in the new paradigm of retailing.

In an overstored environment, where time is precious, price parity is endemic and non-store shopping options are blossoming, retailers and developers across the country are convinced that entertainment is the way to lure consumers out of their homes and into stores and malls. So they are spending millions to transform selling floors and shopping environments into interactive theaters complete with stages, coffee bars, and amusement park rides.

Skeptics say the bells and whistles of the E-factor explosion are an expensive distraction from the real business of retailing. The key to making store-based shopping a viable experience in the 21st century, they argue, will be the same as in the past—by selecting goods that people want and need and presenting them in exciting and attractive ways.

But both views beg the fundamental question: What do consumers want? A new study, conducted exclusively for STORES Magazine by America's Research Group, shows that a significant number of shoppers enjoy and are influenced by retail entertainment. But the E-factor is far from a universal solution to retailer's success equation.

The survey finds that 70 percent of shoppers who have experienced entertainment in a shopping center or store would return for another visit. Of that same group, three in ten shopped at an average of 4.5 stores during that visit—evidence that the more enjoyable the shopping experience is, the longer shoppers are likely to stick around.

The research, based on random telephone interviews with 1,000 shoppers in five major cities across the country, also reveals that 38 percent of consumers want more entertainment ideas to be added in the future. And 35 percent consider shopping a source of entertainment for themselves or their families.

Reading 1.2 Reda, S, (1995, October). That's Entertainment, *Stores*, pp. 16–20.

"Consumers keep saying that they have less time to shop, and our research shows that they are, in fact, shopping less," explains C. Britt Beemer, founder and chairman of America's Research Group, headquartered in Charleston, South Carolina.

"As consumers screen out which stores they're going to consider when shopping for electonics or sporting goods or apparel, the challenge for retailers becomes how to move their stores to the top of the list," Beemer says. "Merchants constantly ask, 'Will entertainment move me closer to the top of this list?' The answer is yes, but entertainment itself is not going to win the war."

Results at chains that are deeply involved in retail "show business" show that the E-factor is already paying dividends:

- At Incredible Universe, 20 percent of the people who visit a store will return within a month—a figure that is three to four times the industry standard. Repeat shoppers are helping to propel this three-year-old company toward the $1 billion mark in sales.
- Warner Bros.' Video wall and Space Rocket are encouraging shoppers to stay in the store longer and, according to president Peter Starrett, boosting the average transaction.
- A combination of sports memorabilia and high-tech audio/video equipment has enabled the four-unit Niketown chain to consistently achieve double-digit sales increases. Sales at the Orange County, California, location have advanced 25 percent over last year's figures.
- Blockbuster Music's interactive buying experience, where shoppers can preview their selections, has led customers to stay longer in the store and spend more on average at each sales transaction.
- At Mall of America, the gigantic Minneapolis-area center that has become a byword for retail entertainment, sales per square foot are twice the national average. Thirty-eight million people visited the facility last year, which includes the Knott's Camp Snoopy indoor amusement park.

The results of the survey conducted by America's Research Group reveal that a solid majority of shoppers, 73 percent, view shopping as an opporunity to see what's new. Sixty percent feel shopping should provide a break from their normal activities, while 54 percent enjoy looking for bargains.

Given those inclinations. It seems clear that the E-factor can have a positive effect on the total shopping experience.

"The Blockbusters and the Incredible Universes of today have developed a unique value proposition, namely entertainment," says Gene Wright, industry director of The Retail Place at Andersen Consulting. "That's what it's all about."

"We're at a crossroads," says Wright. "Retailing is either driven by replenishment or by entertainment in the form of information, ideas, or fashion. If you can't 'out-Target' Target or 'out-Wal-Mart' Wal-Mart, you've got to take another angle."

Entertainment can help to downplay some of the elements that make shopping stressful, says Bill Chidley, vice president Design Forum, a Dayton, Ohio–based design firm.

"Retailers can use entertainment to diffuse the risk of making a purchase. That's what Incredible Universe does by inviting shoppers to try out everything in their stores," explains Chidley. "Merchants can also use entertainment to help shoppers manage time. Supermarket shopping can be real drudgery, but put a few interactive kiosks in that offer meal/menu ideas and you've instantly managed the shoppers' time and made the experience more entertaining."

But even those retailers that have made a commitment to entertainment argue that it is still the merchandise that counts.

"We believe that retailing should be an enjoyable experience, so we have music playing, theatrical lighting and celebrity appearances. But, bottom line, it's the merchandise that's the star," says Rick Hollander, vice president and general merchandise manager at Incredible Universe.

"Entertainment can be a tremendous factor in achieving success, but product is No. 1," says Warner Bros.' Starrett. "Consumers spend money based on how they like the product."

Moreover, while some retailers are heavily emphasizing entertainment elements, at least one major department store chain has backed away from the grand-scale productions for which many of its stores became known in the 1980s.

"Today, the customer is the star and the spotlight is on the merchandise," says Robert Unger, chairman of Federated Department Stores' visual merchandising team. "We're creating the new theater in retailing—producing a user-friendly, open and exciting environment.

"Our emphasis is on creating an environment that highlights the merchandise, informing and communicating with the customer," Unger adds.

On the other hand, industry analysts also stress that a retailer does not have to have the vast resources of a Walt Disney or a Sony to create an entertaining environment.

"As we design new store prototypes today, we try to encourage retailers to have an entertaining focus," says Anne Brixner, director of marketing at the Retail Group, based in Seattle. "The word entertainment means to hold the attention of someone, to amuse them. Retailers need to think of that first, not necessarily of the bells and whistles."

Pet Food Warehouse, an eight-store chain recently redesigned by the Retail Group, features "paw call buttons" that bark when pushed for service, whimsical signs such as "Prices cut to the bone" and a photo booth for snapshots of customers and their pets.

"It's not Laurel and Hardy," says Brixnel, "but the entertainment elements that have been included contribute to making the total shopping experience more enjoyable."

While the E-factor has a place in many shopping environments, the entertainment must above all be appropriate to the store. "Whenever a subject gets as much attention as entertainment has recently, retailers rush to cash in. There are probably retailers out there right now who are building stages yet can't even make their margins," says Kate Murphy, vice president of Fitch, a Worthington, Ohio–based design firm.

"The key to incorporating entertaining elements is to make sure that what you're doing is appropriate to your image and matches the expectations of what customers expect to find," adds Murphy.

Observers also caution that entertainment isn't necessarily right for every retailer.

"If you're going to do entertainment, you've got to have square footage," says Beemer of America's Research Group. "At drug stores, where merchants are facing such short margins, introducing entertainment is virtually impossible."

The E-factor also doesn't figure very prominently at discount stores, Beemer suggests. "People tend to go there with specific objectives and they want to get in and out quickly. If you complicate the ability to get in and out, shoppers are going to get mad."

Another inherent problem with entertainment is that shoppers become accustomed to constantly changing and ever-more-stimulating excitement, putting demands on retailers to keep coming up with new things.

When Banana Republic introduced its entertaining store design a few years ago, recalls Murphy of Fitch, "Everyone talked about the jeep and the animals, but it got old very quickly."

"Retailers who choose to incorporate entertainment have to be acutely aware that it has to be regularly updated and upgraded, or shoppers will lose interest," she warns.

"Entertainment can be a trap," says Chidley at Design Forum. "Like the summer movie blockbusters, which seem to get bigger and bigger each year, the onus is on retailers to keep improving the experience. Entertainment can't become the headline at retail. If it does, that retailer is in trouble."

CHAPTER 2

# Apparel, Body, and Environment as Contributors to Aesthetic Experience

## Objectives

- Understand how apparel, the body, and the environment contribute to aesthetic experience
- Understand the sensory aspects of aesthetic experience from apparel, the body, and the environment
- Understand the emotional aspects of aesthetic experience from apparel, the body, and the environment
- Understand the cognitive aspects of aesthetic experience from apparel, the body, and the environment
- Develop a multi-sensory aesthetic experience considering apparel, the body, and the environment

As you recall from Chapter 1, aesthetic experience consists of sensory, emotional, and cognitive pleasure or satisfaction. **Products** *and* **environments** provide the formal, expressive, and symbolic qualities that foster aesthetic experience. For many consumers, aesthetic value derived from the product, body, and environment is a major contributor to consumer satisfaction. Consumer satisfaction is the goal of apparel professions because it helps ensure that the consumer will buy from your firm in the future. Research has focused upon the relationship between the product and consumer satisfaction. However, more attention is currently being given to the effect of the environment on consumer satisfaction. The present chapter will discuss the interrelationships among concepts of product, environment, sensory, emotional, and cognitive experiences introduced in Chapter 1.

## CONTRIBUTORS TO AESTHETIC EXPERIENCE

This chapter will outline the sensory, emotional, and cognitive (aesthetic) aspects of apparel, other body-related products, and environments that apparel professionals must consider. These aspects of products and environments affect the aesthetic experience offered the consumer and are influential in their buying decisions. We would like to emphasize that the *apparel product is not the sole contributor to aesthetic experience or aesthetic value.* If apparel were the only contributor to aesthetic value, the apparel industry would have little need for fashion models, retail (merchandising) directors, advertisers, display artists, and stylists. These professionals create an environment for the product. Whereas this environment may provide an aesthetic experience by itself, the goal of the apparel professional is usually to use the environment to enhance the aesthetic value of the product. These professionals create an environment that "sets the stage" for the product. Props and settings create or reinforce an image for the product. An example may clarify this point; a retail director may hire a classical pianist to perform in a large department store. As you try on shoes in this store, the elegance of the music fills the air and affects the gracefulness of your steps in these new shoes. As you saunter around the shoe department in these shoes, the music helps you envision wearing the shoes at a very elegant event. The music, its effect on your step, and the image of the future event influence your impression of the shoes as stylish and elegant. The shoes are sold!

We will now expand upon the contributors to aesthetic experience. Remember, these aspects all work together to create an aesthetic experience for the consumer. As you read each section you should consider your personal experiences that relate to the discussion.

### Apparel Products as Contributors

The most obvious contributor to the aesthetic experience is the apparel product. When consumers shop at a store, on TV, or through a catalog, they probably focus primarily on the product. For instance, one may pay attention to what's new in swimwear, neckties, or coats. A consumer may seek out specific aesthetic qualities of a product, such as searching for a suit in a specific shade of charcoal gray or infant sleepwear with little "Tasmanian devils" printed on it. Aesthetic experience and consumer satisfaction may be directly tied to the product's aesthetic qualities. The consumer may have to "settle" for a suit in a less appealing, lighter shade of gray, which may diminish the aesthetic experience offered by the product. The consumer who purchases "Tasmanian devil" sleepwear may be very satisfied because she or he enjoys the symbolic aspects of the little devils (it reminds the purchaser of her or his favorite cartoons or the instigation of the infant wearer). Even though consumers may focus on the product, this does not mean that they must seek out *specific* aesthetic qualities in order for aesthetic experience and consumer satisfaction to occur. You may have experienced "impulse buying" where you purchase a product even though you had no preconceived notion of purchasing such a product before you "laid eyes" on it.

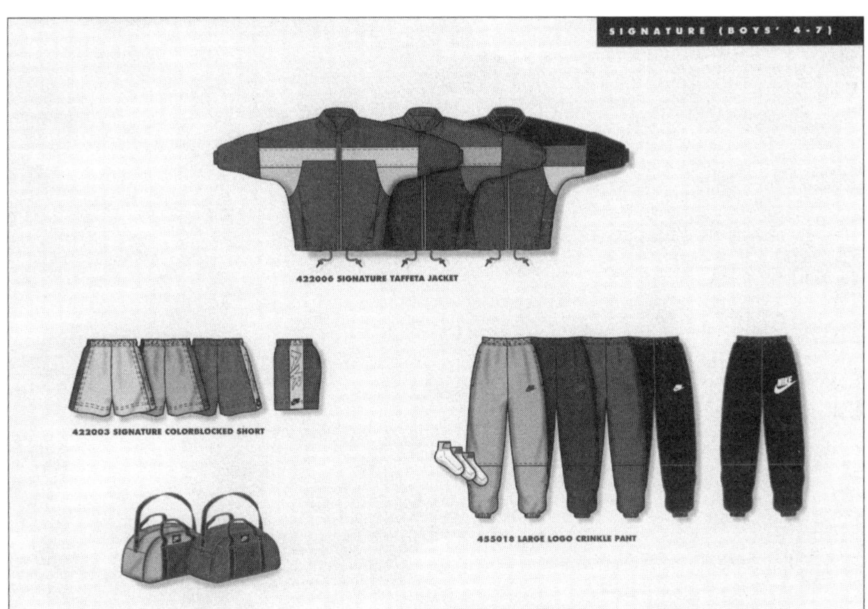


Figure 2.1. Line of boys' activewear. Design variations of shorts, pants, and jackets that coordinate across product categories.

A consumer may browse through a catalog and be captivated by a new style detail on a jean jacket that hadn't been seen before. For some consumers, this novelty or newness of the product is responsible for providing pleasure (Hirschman, 1984).

Let's look at two examples where aesthetics of apparel is important to the tasks of apparel professions. First, we will discuss the importance of aesthetics to *development* of the product. Designers and manufacturers offer lines of clothing (Figure 2.1). A **product line** (or assortment) is a group of products that have an underlying aesthetic similarity of formal, expressive, and/or symbolic qualities. A line may contain items that can be worn together or may consist of design variations of a product category (e.g., jackets or shorts) or both. Apparel lines serve consumers because they can create a complete ensemble or "outfit" that can be worn together. The coordinated outfit may be perceived as aesthetically pleasing and provide more satisfaction to the consumer than one product, alone, from that line. For instance, in Figure 2.1 the shorts and pants coordinate with the jackets. The colors, color blocked strips of fabric, and fabric textures provide the underlying similarity in the line of products, which allows the consumer to combine the pieces.

Developing product lines serves manufacturers because fewer garment patterns need to be made and similar production steps can be used across a number of style variations. Lines also allow the manufacturer to purchase a larger quantity of fabric, which may decrease the cost per yard. These are cost-saving measures that decrease the final cost of the product, making it more competitive with products of other firms. The combination of aesthetically similar products creates a more powerful impact, drawing the attention of consumers. However, an "aesthetic eye" must be used by merchandisers and advertisers in combining these products for presentation.

Figure 2.2. (top) Smooth transition in boxer short prints and colors adds to the aesthetic appeal of this J. Crew catalog display and the appeal of individual products.

Figure 2.3. (bottom) Computer-generated alteration to the J. Crew boxer short display. The smooth transition of the display is disrupted and the sensory and symbolic appeal of the products (e.g., "barn jacket" print) is diminished.

Second, aesthetics is important to *promotion* or presentation of products. Retailers benefit from stocking lines of apparel, because it leads to "multiple sales," where consumers purchase more than just one item. The way that products are grouped together for presentation may be appealing in itself and may enhance aesthetic qualities of the individual product. In Figure 2.2, the arrangement of men's boxer shorts is pleasing in itself because of the smooth transition from bright colored prints of large rounded shapes to more subdued colors and linear prints. This arrangement of boxer shorts also enhances the aesthetic qualities of individual designs. The casual and rustic "barn jacket" print looks rather dowdy next to the more wild and crazy dot print. The vivid nature of the multi-colored print drains the color from the more subdued "barn jacket" print, making it appear drab by comparison. When the "barn jacket" print is placed next to the more traditional, casual, subdued plaid in Figure 2.3, the "barn jacket" print makes sense; it's just a variation on the casual print theme offered by the striped and plaid boxers. The visual appeal of the more subdued colors is reinforced by the similar colors of the neighboring plaid boxers. Activity 2.1 gives you practice combining products of a line for presentation.

**ACTIVITY 2.1**

One of the easiest ways to offer consumers more aesthetic choices, but hold the cost on these variations, is to create a line by keeping the garment cut or style layout the same, but producing the style layout in a variety of colors or fabric patterns. This strategy is apparent in catalogs and in stores where, for instance, the same pullover sweater may come in five different colors and two knitted argyle patterns. Careful consideration must be given to how these items of the line will be grouped together for display.

Collect catalog displays of two garments that show different colors or fabric design. Each should contain at least four different variations of color or fabric designs. Record the order in which the items in each grouping were displayed, and what you think was used to organize these in an aesthetically pleasing way. Then cut these items apart. For one of the groupings, rearrange the items in the group in a new way that still offers a visually and symbolically pleasing arrangement (refer to the "barn jacket" print example if you are not clear on the idea). Now explain what you used to organize these items in the groupings.

For the last step, rearrange the remaining grouping together in a visually *displeasing* manner. Explain why this arrangement is displeasing.

### Body as Contributor

The human body consists of aesthetic qualities (form, expression, and symbolic meaning) that can be altered and appreciated, just as aesthetic qualities of apparel products can be altered and appreciated. Looking first at formal aspects, the body's aesthetic aspects include skin, hair, and eye color and texture. In addition, shape or three dimensional form of the body is a major contributor to aesthetic satisfaction with the body (e.g., Lennon, 1988). Why does a woman religiously follow the "buns of steel" exercise routine? What sort of chair does this woman sit on during the day that she needs to condition her glutei muscles to become "buns of steel"? Such exercise routines are probably not followed because mighty glutei muscles are needed to withstand physical stress. Rather, "buns of steel" are desired because a smooth, firm human form is perceived to be the aesthetic ideal within her culture. Consider the amount of time, money, and effort spent on just a few of the ways to enhance the aesthetic nature of the human body in various cultures: dieting, "fattening," exercising, weight lifting, hennas, perms, hair relaxing, shaving, bleaching of skin and hair, collagen injections, liposuction, body piercing, binding feet, scarifying, tattooing, and tanning. The huge expenditure of resources to enhance the aesthetic appeal of the human body supports the view that aesthetic aspects of the body are very important for many cultures.

Why is the desire for an aesthetically pleasing body form important to apparel professionals? The aesthetic ideal of the human form often guides the design of apparel. Apparel is many times designed to *enhance* or *reinforce* the aesthetic qualities of the human form. Consider the hot selling "Wonderbra" (Figure 2.4). The success of this apparel product is only partly due to the aes-

Figure 2.4. The success of the Wonderbra is due to its ability to enhance the female body form.

*Women's Wear Daily.*

thetic appeal of the product itself; the success is mainly due to its ability to enhance the female body ("maximum lift and volume" of the breasts). Also, there are shelves of popular press books that educate the reader on the use of apparel to enhance the body form, including *Looking Thin* (August, 1981) and *Breaking All the Rules* (Roberts, 1985; for enhancing the larger than average body form). Thus, the enhancing effect of apparel on the body is important to consumers when evaluating the product.

Apparel may also reinforce or accent a pleasing body. A black dress with a plunging neckline and side slit may expose the curvatures of the female form, while a cinched waist may accentuate an hourglass shape. A dark color fabric may create a striking contrast with a model's pale skin and may blend nicely with dark hair. Consumers judge the reinforcing effect of apparel on their own bodies and also make assumptions about this effect based upon the images found in promotional environments. If you have ever said to yourself, "but it looked so good on the model," you were probably making an assumption about the interaction of the product on your body based on the image of the model/product interaction in the promotional environment.

When was the last time that you saw an apparel product you liked and *didn't* try it on before you purchased it? Consumer satisfaction with apparel depends upon the *aesthetic appeal of the interaction between the body and apparel.* This helps explain why stores have mirrors in the dressing rooms as well as on the sales floor. Consumers judge the appeal of the product as it interacts with the body, "It looks great on you" is a more desirable compliment than, "The garment is beautiful, but it makes you look (. . . sallow, intimidating, or like Queen Elizabeth)." Research supports the importance of the interaction between clothing and the body in purchases. As female consumers entered and exited dressing rooms they were asked what determined if they would try on or purchase the garment(s) (Eckman, Damhorst & Kadolph, 1989). Model 2.1 shows you the results of this survey. It appears that aesthetic aspects of the apparel product are important to what consumers tried on, but the interaction of clothing on the body (appearance) is important to consumer purchases.

The expressive and symbolic aspects of the body are also important to the aesthetic appeal of the product. These aspects are particularly important in promotional environments. A fashion model's physical characteristics (e.g., height, size of facial features, or coloring) and expressive behavior (e.g., swagger or vocal inflection) can reinforce or influence the product image (Figures 2.5 and 2.6). Models have different "looks." Some models are more exotic, while others are more classic, still others are more "fresh and natural." A "fresh and natural" model, with soft body coloring, small facial features, and long flowing hair may reinforce the image of "outdoorsy" L.L. Bean sportswear. This same model would contradict the dramatic, blatantly sexual nature of a Versace design. Explore the expressive and symbolic aspects of the body in Activity 2.2.

**MODEL 2.1** Model of In-Store Selection and Purchase Criteria for Apparel. (From Eckman, Damhorst & Kadolph, 1989. Courtesy of International Textiles and Apparel Association.)

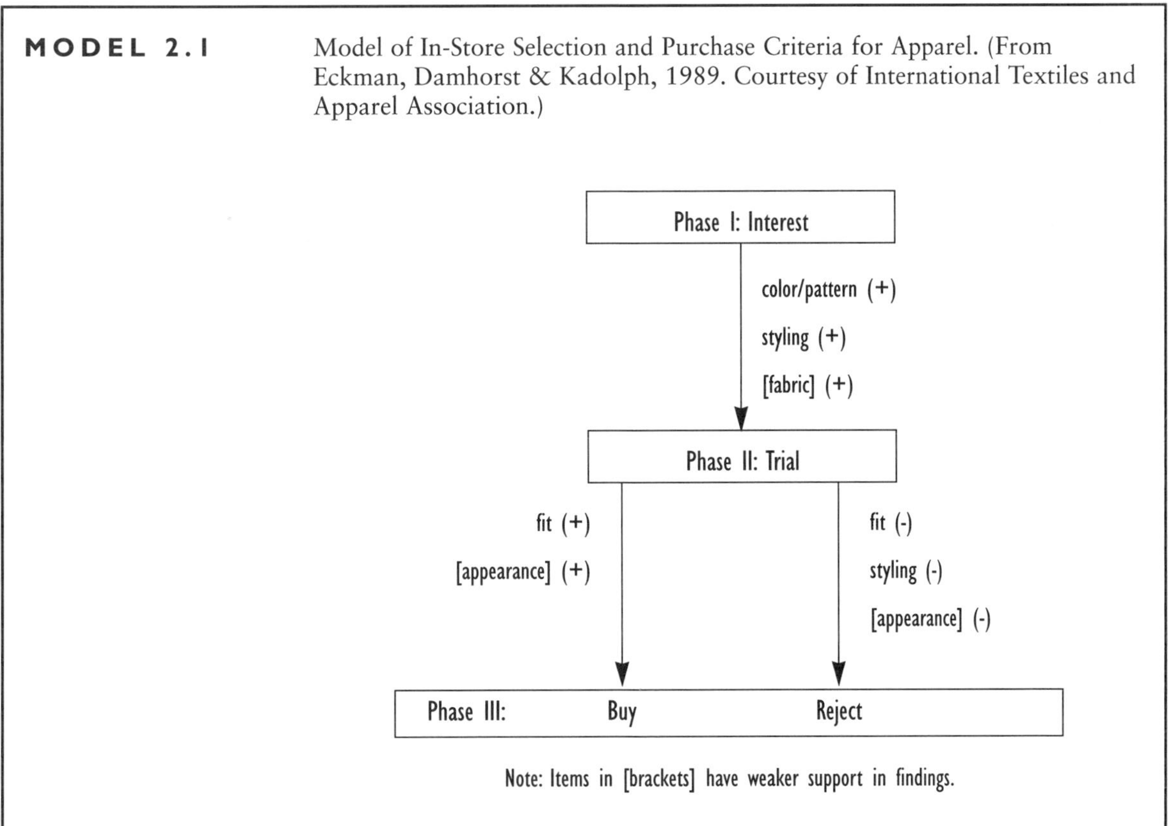

**ACTIVITY 2.2** Compare the differences in expressive and symbolic aspects of the two models in Figures 2.5 and 2.6. While both models are seated, their facial expressions and postures are quite different. Which of these do you feel expresses more energy? Which appears more natural and which appears more coy? Now try to switch the apparel—try to imagine the model seated on the bench wearing the vested ensemble and the model on the floor wearing the blazered ensemble. Does the expressive and symbolic nature of the model now "work" with the apparel? What is the effect on the expressive and symbolic content? This juxtaposition shows how important the expressive and symbolic aspects brought by the model are to the image of the apparel product.

Figure 2.5 (left) and 2.6. (right) Comparison of expressive and symbolic aspects of models in J. Crew and Liliane Romi ads, respectively.

## Environment as Contributor

The **environment** is the multisensory setting that surrounds and interacts with the apparel product (and the body). This setting consists of social as well as formal, expressive, and symbolic qualities. These qualities can be pleasing in themselves and can influence the appreciation of the apparel product (and interacting body). Thus, the environment is an important consideration for the apparel professional. For instance, the professional must consider the marketplace and the background of promotional events or promotional materials.

The marketplace or retail shopping environment can vary widely in level of formality and festivity (Sherry, 1990). **Formality** refers to how official, con-

**MODEL 2.2** Marketplace Environments Characterized by Level of Formality and Festivity. (From Sherry, 1990. Courtesy of Journal of Consumer Research.)

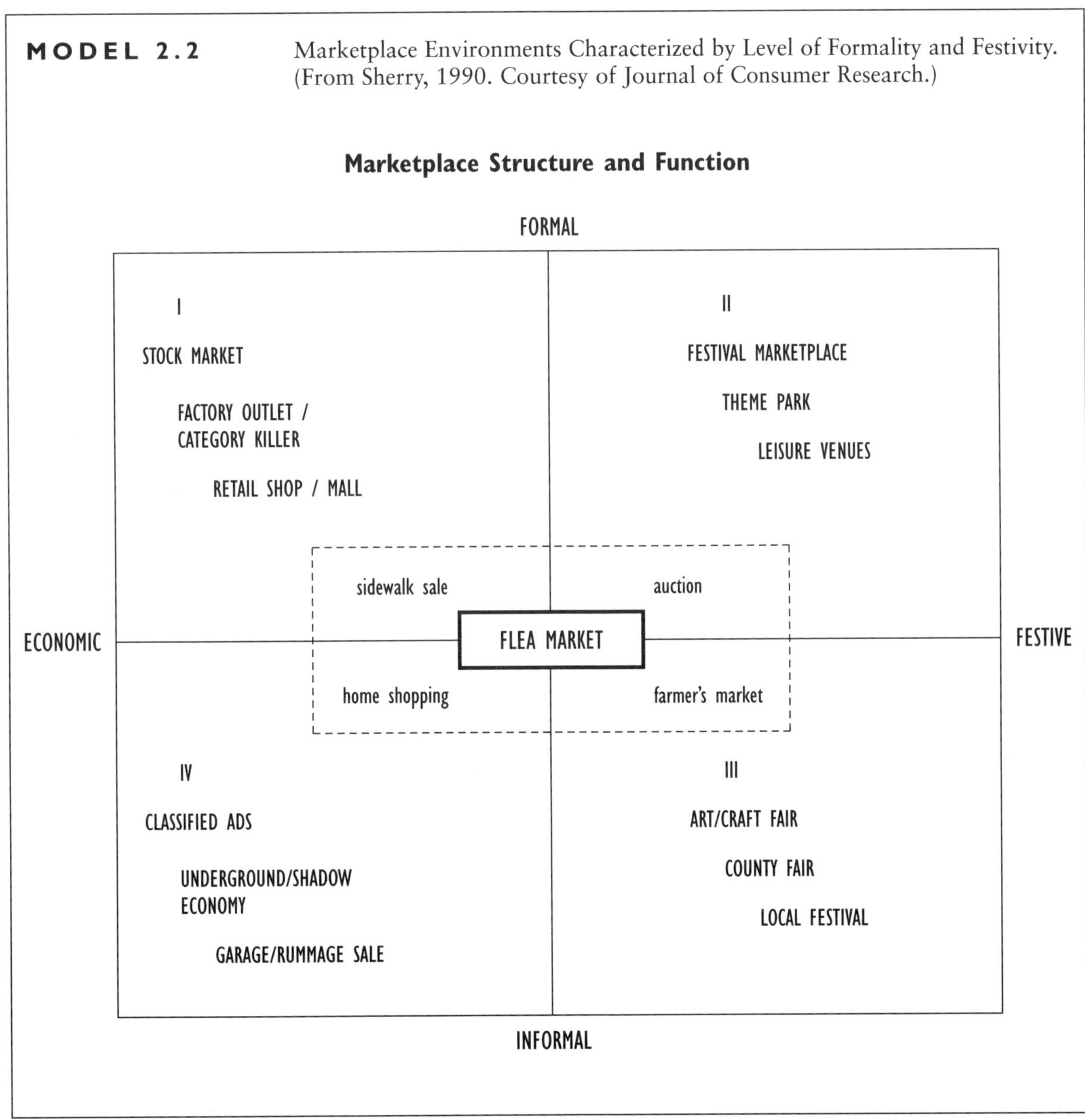


trolled, and institutional (permanent) the environment appears to be. Informal environments are less official, less controlled, and more transient. **Festivity** refers to the degree of practicality or utility of the marketplace experience. Festive environments are fun and pleasurable experiences. The opposite (economic) environment is characterized by ration concerns and usefulness.

Formality and festivity have been used to distinguish shopping environments (Model 2.2). The environment of a factory outlet or mall is labeled as more formal and less festive than flea markets and arts and crafts fairs (Sherry, 1990). The atmosphere of a marketplace environment can influence the aesthetic experience of consumers. For example, the festive and informal nature of flea markets have been shown to be a source of aesthetic experience for some consumers because of the energy and excitement. "The affecting presence and power of the sheer numbers of goods, of people, of smells and sounds, of big ticket cash transactions, of temperature extremes . . . are undeniable (Sherry, 1990, p. 25)." Other shopping environments that offer unique items in a less organized manner, such as overstocked surplus stores and "second hand" or vintage clothing shops, may provide environments similar to a flea market, also leading to aesthetic experience.

The design of the retail environment may not only be pleasing in itself, but also influence appreciation of apparel products. Some of these design features include display hardware, furnishings, lighting, and music. For instance, lighting has a large impact on store ambiance, as well as calling attention to and enhancing specific apparel items ("Lighting Design," 1992). White light with a warm yellow appearance suggests a feeling of intimacy, which could enhance lingerie products, but undermines the bold color intensity of active sportswear, such as team jerseys and athletic shoes. The persuasive nature of store design and merchandise presentation is discussed in the article by Serge Kingsley (Reading 2.1).

The backgrounds of promotional materials are important in internal "sale" of ideas to business associates within the firm, to wholesale buyers and in the promotional ads aimed at consumers. The environment becomes an important feature of presentation of pre-adoption designs and post-adoption styles. **Pre-**

Figure 2.7. Cotton Incorporated presentation board with environment used to reinforce trend ideas internally in the apparel industry.

**adoption designs** are design ideas presented internally in the firm for determining what should be produced (Glock & Kunz, in press). **Post-adoption styles** are designs that are selected for production (Glock & Kunz, in press). For example, much thought goes into the presentation of design ideas through storyboards to other members of the apparel firm. A **storyboard or presentation board** (Figure 2.7) is a visual presentation of ideas on a hardboard or computer screen to members within the apparel industry. Storyboards can be used to present a line or collection of textile and apparel products and/or design inspirations, or to present advertisement concepts. Post-adoption styles are presented to industry buyers through showing of actual products or promotional materials. For instance, a sales representative may show a design assistant an array of button styles arranged on large cards for consideration in the upcoming season's designs. Retail buyers also consider styles presented in buyer's guides (i.e., catalog of styles) when stocking the store with merchandise.

After in-firm and wholesale promotions of the new products, these styles are promoted to consumers through events such as fashion shows and advertisements. The environment is essential to fashion shows and advertisement of apparel products. For example, the Christian Dior advertisement (Figure 2.8) shows a model wearing a 19th century inspired dress. This environment contributes visual formal qualities that are pleasing and may affect perception of the clothed model. The irregular pattern found on the tree bark, foliage, and bare ground blend with the patterned fabrics used in the ensemble, but soften the pattern of the apparel product because of the stronger appearance of the environmental patterns. This environment also affects the symbolic content given to the clothed model. Placing the model in this outdoor setting harkens, or calls up, images of (perhaps) a romance novel heroine (Figure 2.9) or a damsel from times past wistfully longing for the arrival of her beau. Thus, the formal and symbolic qualities of the environment may encourage appreciation of the softly romantic apparel product.

The consumer also considers the environment when selecting apparel to purchase or wear. The environment in which the apparel product is worn by the consumer can affect the product's aesthetic value. You have probably gone through the ritual of determining what to wear for a special occasion. This ritual starts with pulling every piece of clothing from your closet, combining in a multitude of ways while envisioning your appearance at the event. These apparel items may have provided you with aesthetic pleasure in other circumstances, but they are not as rewarding in the setting of that specific occasion. So, as part of the ritual, you unearth the phone from the clothing strewn around the room and call to ask what your friend will be wearing. Of course, your friend has no sage advise to offer and actually *was about to call you with the same question.* You both begin to define the environment to better determine the appropriate garb for the occasion. "The setting is really dramatic; the lighting is soft, but there are large marble pillars and gilded furniture that add a sense of formality; the night will be filled with classical music and fancy morsels of food." From this description, you know that your autographed football jersey is definitely out. You eliminate the more casual items and settle on a black

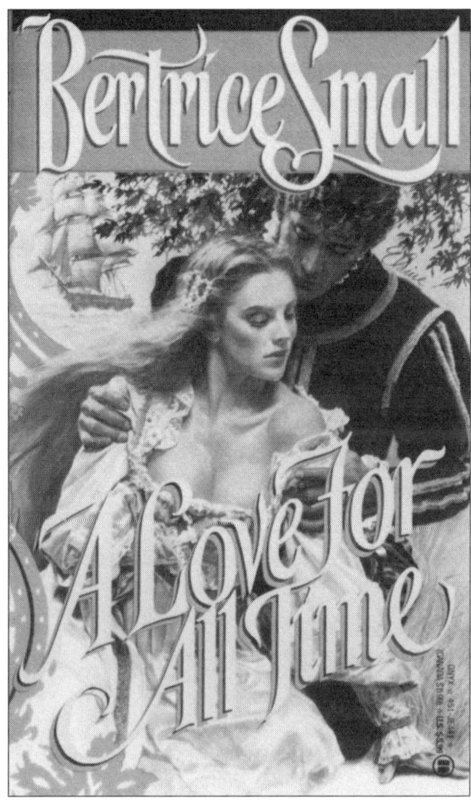


Figure 2.8. (left) Visual and symbolic qualities of the environment encouraging the appreciation of the softly romantic apparel product.

Figure 2.9. (right) Romance novel heroine portrayed on the book cover, harkened by the similar image created in the Dior ad.

worsted wool suit that has a clean line, but a dramatic shape because of the padded inner structure. You add polished gold accessories.

## Apparel, Body, and Environment as Total Experience

As we have seen thus far in this chapter, the body interacts with apparel and apparel interacts with the environment to affect aesthetic experience and consumer satisfaction. In actuality, *apparel, body, and environment all work together to affect aesthetic experience and consumer satisfaction.* We view our clothed bodies within an environment. The environment can affect the formal qualities of the clothed body. Consider the scary experience of trying on swimwear under the stark lighting of a dressing room. The vivid colors of the garment contrast sharply against the pale skin tone under the fluorescent lighting. Referring back to Figure 2.8, the texture of the skin appears smooth and soft compared against the fabric surfaces and surfaces of the environment.

In the present chapter we have suggested ways that apparel, the body, and the environment can contribute to the sensory, emotional, and cognitive aspects of aesthetic experience. We will now outline the components of sensory, emotional, and cognitive experiences. We will provide only a few examples for the components of apparel, the body, or the environment. However, each component can contribute to the aesthetic experience provided by apparel, the body, and the environment.

## SENSORY EXPERIENCES

### Multi-Sensory Experience

The majority of aesthetics literature focuses upon the visual qualities of the product, but scholars are becoming increasingly aware that stimulating other senses also leads to an aesthetic experience. Not only are these individual sensory inputs important, but these inputs combine to create a holistic (an organized whole) experience. Apparel, the body, and the environment *each* provide multi-sensory aesthetic experiences. **Multi-sensory experience** consists of all the sensory information available through sight, touch, kinesthetics, smell, hearing, and taste. New technology amplifies the multi-sensory qualities offered by apparel. Consider micro-encapsulated fabric finishes that emit a pleasant fragrance when the tiny cells of the finish are abraded. Or consider "virtual-reality" body suits of the not-too-distant computer future that will mimic the tactile stimulation generated by bodily contact with another person. The pleasant bandy (give and take) between a slim Lycra® skirt and the muscles of the wearer's legs, or the soothing nature of a rhythmic chatter of beaded fabric in synch with the movement of the body are examples of aesthetic experiences overlooked when the focus is on the observation of visual aspects of products.

A multi-sensory aesthetic experience can be fostered by the *interaction* of apparel, the body, and the environment. Observers expect an organized relationship between the visual and tactile aspects of a wearer's apparel and olfactory aspects of perfume on the wearer's body (Fiore, 1993). People who wear fabrics with certain visual and tactile qualities are expected to wear particular fragrances. (Reading 2.2 will provide examples of aesthetic experience from the interactions within apparel). This integration extends to the environment as well. For instance, one derives pleasure from body movements that are in synch with the beat of music. This is called a beat-for-beat rhythm and is very apparent in MTV videos in the late 1980s and early 90s performed by artists such as Michael Jackson and Paula Abdul.

Fashion shows are an excellent example of the importance of the interactions of apparel, the body, and the environment to the aesthetic experience. The formal, expressive, and meaning aspects of music are carefully selected to coincide with the these aspects of apparel products. Lighting and the model's coloring, texture, and body shape are selected to enhance the appeal of the apparel products. The model strolls down the runway in a manner to reflect the tempo of the music and expressive qualities of the clothing. Lighting and backdrop enhance the environment and reinforce the aesthetic qualities of the product.

### Visual

Before you read this section, complete Activity 2.3. Sight is probably the most obvious source of aesthetic experience for individuals from Western cultures. Western cultures depend heavily on visual sensory information for communication (Classen, 1993). These (literate) cultures depend upon written words in books, magazines, and newspapers for communication. People from these

**ACTIVITY 2.3**

List seven sensory qualities that you personally feel make someone attractive (e.g., size of feet).

1. ______________________________

2. ______________________________

3. ______________________________

4. ______________________________

5. ______________________________

6. ______________________________

7. ______________________________

Now label each of the seven with the sensory channel that receives this information (sight, hearing, touch, smell, taste). Tally up the count for each sensory channel. What did you find?

cultures also depend upon visual images ("seeing is believing"). Photographs are commonly found in printed and electronic media. Other (oral) cultures depend more on the spoken word and use other sensory systems for making sense of the world. For instance, some cultures of Latin America order the world on the basis of temperature; things in the universe (even colors in clothing) are thought to contain different qualities of heat or dynamic power (Classen, 1993).

The dependence in Western cultures upon the visual sensory input influences one's aesthetic appreciation of apparel and the body. Interpersonal interactions are susceptible to the visual appearances of others. We treat visually attractive individuals, those with more attractive apparel or bodies, better than we treat less attractive individuals. When defining attractiveness of others, visual qualities are of primary importance. Was this supported by your personal list in Activity 2.3? Other sensory cues such as smells are seldom expressed, but they do influence attraction and behavior towards others (Levine & McBurney, 1981).

If you look back to the Eckman, Damhorst, and Kadolph model of in-store consumer behavior (Model 2.1), you will notice the prevalence of visual aspects in consumer's criteria for selecting apparel. The importance of visual components to aesthetic appreciation of apparel is reflected in the prevalence of research examining the visual aspects of garment silhouette, proportion, pattern, and color (See Fiore, Kimle, Moreno, 1996, for a review).

### Tactile

Pleasurable experience can result from touching and from being touched. Humans have sensory receptors all over the body that register the sensation of touch. When researchers study touch and apparel, they focus on fabric "hand"

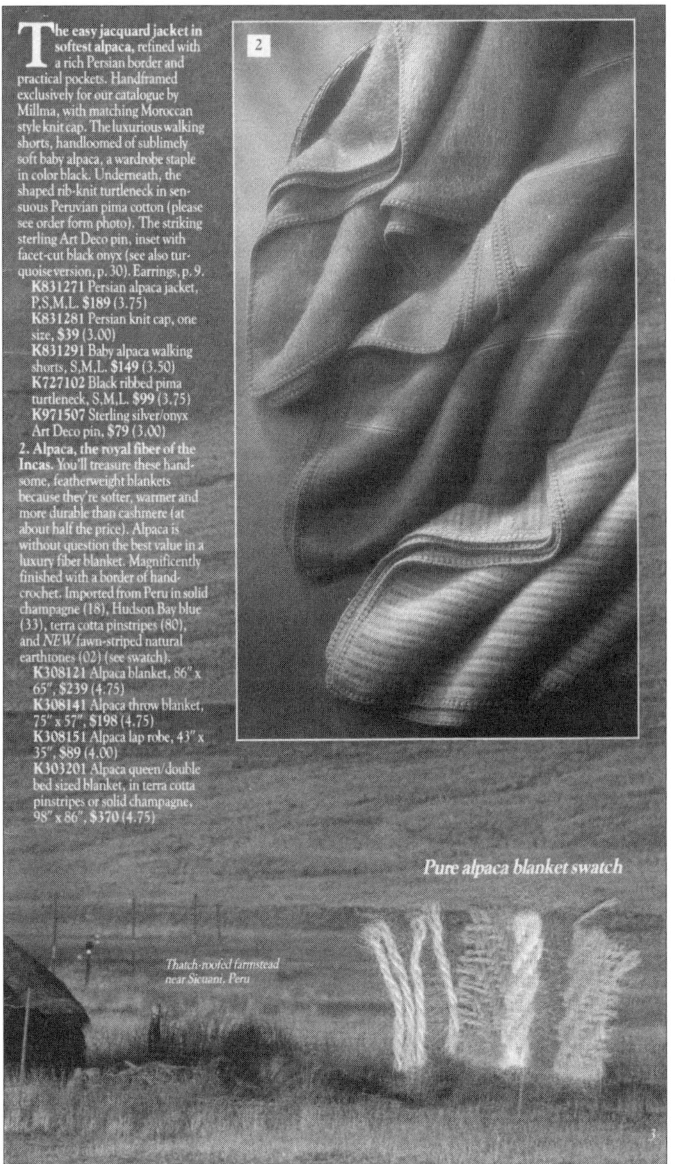
**The easy jacquard jacket in softest alpaca,** refined with a rich Persian border and practical pockets. Handframed exclusively for our catalogue by Millma, with matching Moroccan style knit cap. The luxurious walking shorts, handloomed of sublimely soft baby alpaca, a wardrobe staple in color black. Underneath, the shaped rib-knit turtleneck in sensuous Peruvian pima cotton (please see order form photo). The striking sterling Art Deco pin, inset with facet-cut black onyx (see also turquoise version, p. 30). Earrings, p. 9.

**K831271** Persian alpaca jacket, P,S,M,L. **$189** (3.75)
**K831281** Persian knit cap, one size, **$39** (3.00)
**K831291** Baby alpaca walking shorts, S,M,L. **$149** (3.50)
**K727102** Black ribbed pima turtleneck, S,M,L. **$99** (3.75)
**K971507** Sterling silver/onyx Art Deco pin, **$79** (3.00)

**2. Alpaca, the royal fiber of the Incas.** You'll treasure these handsome, featherweight blankets because they're softer, warmer and more durable than cashmere (at about half the price). Alpaca is without question the best value in a luxury fiber blanket. Magnificently finished with a border of hand-crochet. Imported from Peru in solid champagne (18), Hudson Bay blue (33), terra cotta pinstripes (80), and *NEW* fawn-striped natural earthtones (02) (see swatch).

**K308121** Alpaca blanket, 86" x 65", **$239** (4.75)
**K308141** Alpaca throw blanket, 75" x 57", **$198** (4.75)
**K308151** Alpaca lap robe, 43" x 35", **$89** (4.00)
**K303201** Alpaca queen/double bed sized blanket, in terra cotta pinstripes or solid champagne, 98" x 86", **$370** (4.75)



Figure 2.10. Page from Peruvian Connection mail order catalog that includes alpaca fabric swatch.

or the feel of fabrics. Many researchers examine responses to fabrics when literally felt by the hand. However, it should be remembered that when actually wearing apparel, the garment is interacting with other parts of the body (e.g., arms, thighs, and torso) that register touch sensations.

Fabrics can offer pleasurable sensations to the body. For instance, washed silk is pleasurable because of its light, soft, and silky feeling on the body. Alpaca is valued for its loft and delicate furry quality. The tactile sensation from fabric may be a major selling point and must be presented to the consumer for appreciation to occur and thus encourage sales. *Peruvian Connection,* which sells hand-made products from Peru, includes a swatch of the alpaca fabric used in their products in their mail order catalog to encourage sales (Figure 2.10). Some

**ACTIVITY 2.4** Partners are needed for this activity. Find a partner. The partners should face each other. Partner A should hold a pen vertical about fifteen inches from the (center of) partner B's face. Partner B stands on one foot as the partner A's pen is moved slowly two feet to the right and then back two feet past the center of partner B's face. Partner B must follow the pen, still standing on one foot, with the eyes and not rotating the head. What is the effect on partner B? Did partner B find this activity pleasurable (was she or he laughing)? This activity usually results in smiling and laughing and is an example of pleasure that results from one's own body movement. Here, the shifting of balance and the tension felt in the leg muscles is responsible for the sensations leading to pleasure.

labels sewn into garments have been likened to strips of cactus. The label is removed to eliminate unpleasant tactile sensations detracting from the pleasurable sensations of the product. Decisions made in production may also affect the pleasurable touch sensations of the product. The decision to use monofilament nylon thread may negatively affect pleasurable sensations, because the ends of the thread feel like barbed-wire against the skin, particularly for children.

Being touched by sales staff may affect the aesthetic experience and affect consumer behavior (Hornik, 1992). One of the authors found that a free hand massage was so pleasurable that she "shelled out" $45 for a small bottle of hand massage oil. This purchase was seen as unwise until receiving the massage from the sales consultant.

### Kinesthetic

**Kinesthetics** is the perception of one's own body movement. Muscle and tendons contain nerve fibers that register sensory input when the muscle is stretched or contracted. The inner ear is responsible for registering balance. Sensations from these sensory receptors can promote aesthetic experience. A simple activity (Activity 2.4) will exemplify this point.

Apparel can contribute to the kinesthetic experience; as mentioned before the bandy between a slim Lycra® skirt and the muscles of the wearer's legs can be pleasurable. A fabric floating behind the movement of arms can reinforce the feeling of graceful motion for a dancer. This feeling results because the fabric moves gracefully and without much effort from the dancer. The same feeling may be felt when wearing a loose shirt that moves freely with the movements of the wearer.

### Olfactory

When thinking about apparel one does not usually think of smell, but pleasant smells can have an impact on the aesthetic experience coming from apparel. Japanese fabric manufacturers are producing micro-encapsulated scented fabrics. These fabrics have a finish that contains minute cells of fragrance that are broken open through abrasion, releasing a pleasant fragrance. This idea of scenting apparel products to increase sales is not new; consumers in a study during the 1930s consistently selected the scented pair of women's hose over an identical pair of unscented hose. Consumers have placed pleasant smelling sachets in lingerie, shoes, and other apparel products for centuries.

Smell is a major factor in aesthetic experience offered by the body (Stoddart, 1990). Consider the number of products with a fragrance that are used regularly by consumers. Bathing, to eliminate any natural body odor, coincides with replacing natural odors with "bottled" scents. Look at the "typical" grooming routine: during the bath or shower a scented soap or bubble bath and fragranced shampoo and hair conditioner are used. This is followed by the application of scented shaving cream, powder, hair styling products, and body lotions. The teeth are brushed (or soaked) and the mouth rinsed with products that freshen the breath. To top it all off, the body is sprayed or dabbed with cologne or perfume. This regular routine for many consumers adds up to a $4 billion/year fragrance industry. This ritual pays off for many fashion houses; Chanel, Yves Saint Laurent, and Calvin Klein are just a few of the fashion companies that make a substantial portion of their profits from fragrance sales. This ritual also appears to pay off in terms of perceived attractiveness. Fragrance has a strong influence on perceived attractiveness of the wearer (Levine & McBurney, 1981).

"**Environmental fragrancing**" is the process of scenting an interior environment with a pleasant fragrance to help produce a change in the occupant's thoughts, mood, or behavior. Environmental fragrancing of retail environments successfully stimulates desirability and sale of a range of products (McCarthy, 1992, Mitchell, Kahn & Knasko, 1993). Retailers from Victoria's Secret to JCPenney are filling stores with pleasant, mood-evoking odors to successfully stimulate product desirability and sales (McCarthy, 1992). Reading 2.3 illustrates some of the retail establishments that have turned to environmental fragrancing.

### Auditory

Apparel occasionally offers aesthetic experience due to sound. A few examples may be the crisp snap of cotton sheets dried on the outdoor clothes line, the rhythmic chatter of beaded fabric in synch with the movement of the body, or the whispering rustle of a taffeta evening dress or Korean traditional dress. Because movement is needed to bring about the pleasurable sounds in apparel, sound frequently combines with kinesthetics to enhance aesthetic experience. One of the authors holds a black belt in Tae Kwon Do, a martial art. She finds the resulting snap of the uniform reinforces the pleasure derived from the kicks and punches in the art.

Sound filling the environment can facilitate aesthetic experience. This environmental sound, like environmental smells, may also influence consumer preference for apparel. Research showed that music influenced the preference of colored geometric shapes (Bierley, McSweeney & Vannieuwkerk, 1985) and actual products (colored pens) (Gorn, 1982). Respondents were shown slides of either beige or blue pens while listening to music they either liked or disliked.

| TABLE 2.1 | Pleasure (P), Arousal (A), and Dominance (D) profiles for emotions. (From Valdez, P. & Mehrabian, A. (1994).) |
|---|---|
| +P+A+D: | admired, bold, creative, powerful, vigorous |
| +P+A-D: | amazed, awed, fascinated, impressed, infatuated |
| +P-A+D: | comfortable, leisurely, relaxed, satisfied, unperturbed |
| +P-A-D: | consoled, docile, protected, sleepy, tranquilized |
| -P+A+D: | antagonistic, belligerent, cruel, hateful, hostile |
| -P+A-D: | bewildered, distressed, humiliated, in pain, upset |
| -P-A+D: | disdainful, indifferent, selfish-uninterested, uncaring, unconcerned |
| -P-A-D: | bored, depressed, dull, lonely, sad. |

Respondents in an experiment chose the color of pen that had been associated with liked music rather than disliked music. The effect of music on the apparel product may be found in retail store environments, fashion shows, and TV advertisements. The pleasurable effect of music conditions us to like the product shown while the music is playing. Fashion shows present apparel products accompanied by music that is perceived to be pleasurable to the audience. We don't think too many *Nine Inch Nails* cuts will be heard at conservative Bill Blass' couture show.

### Gustatory

Last and probably least important to aesthetic experience of apparel is taste. With the exception of "edible underwear" and the "candy necklace," taste has little to do with aesthetic appreciation of apparel. Other products that are used to enhance the body may have flavorings added to improve the product's appeal. Consider flavored lip glosses.

## EMOTIONAL EXPERIENCES

While stimulating the senses is one way of creating an aesthetic experience, arousing emotions and expressing feelings are also factors in aesthetic experience. Researchers (Havlena & Holbrook, 1986) found that emotion involved in consumption experiences, including aesthetic experience, can be described. The essence of the emotional experience is captured using three dimensions (pleasure, arousal, and dominance). This means one may describe the emotional experience provided by the product or environment using all these three dimensions. Pleasure (P), arousal (A), and dominance (D) can be high (+) or low (-). Profiles of emotions (see Table 2.1) are created through the combination of high or low value of the three dimensions (Valdez & Mehrabian, 1994). A holiday shopping experience may be pleasurable (+P), very exciting (+A), and overwhelming (-D) because of the wide selection of products, festive decorations, and energy of the crowd of customers. We will discuss each of these three dimensions separately, but remember that they all can describe the same product or environment.

### Pleasure

**Affect** is the evaluative dimension of emotion. **Pleasure** is a positive affect. Pleasure is good, preferable, and liked. These terms represent the positive end of a continuum of the affective dimension of emotion. The pleasure dimension is the easiest for individuals to recognize; you have probably said, "I don't like the feeling I get from (the garment or store), but I'm not sure why." This ease of evaluation and the difficulty in recognizing other dimensions can be frustrating when trying to identify underlying dimensions of consumer preference.

The goal of the apparel professional is to offer products and environments that create emotions that are perceived to be pleasurable, good, positive, or liked. Multi-sensory aspects of products and environments can affect pleasure (Mehrabian & Russell, 1974). Thus, the apparel professional must consider more than the visual appearance of the product or environment, as we explained above. One of the ways that the environment contributes to these feelings is through touch sensations. As stated above, being touched on the arm by the attending sales staff member in a retail environment affects consumer behavior (Hornik, 1992). This casual touch resulted in an increase of time spent in the store shopping and enhanced customers' *positive* feelings towards the store and the sales staff member. Casual touch also influenced purchase; purchase of a (food) product increased when customers were touched on the arm.

### Arousal

**Arousal** is defined as a feeling state varying along a single dimension ranging from sleep to frantic excitement. Just as multi-sensory aspects of products and environments can affect emotional pleasure, these aspects also affect level of arousal or energy (Mehrabian & Russell, 1974). For instance, color has been shown to affect level of arousal (Bellizzi, Crowley & Hasty, 1983). Bright (high intensity) colors are more arousing than dull (low intensity) colors. This may help explain why children (basically bundles of kinetic energy trapped in little human bodies) look more appropriate in bright blues, reds, and greens, than they do when dressed in gray or beige. How would you describe the ensembles in Figure 2.11? Which would you say is more arousing? What about the form do you think is responsible for your impressions of arousal?

The environment must also be considered. Warm hues (red, orange, and yellow) are exciting and arousing and produce elated mood states, while cool hues (green and blue) are less arousing and produce relaxed mood states. Hence, red and yellow store interiors were perceived by research participants as more tense than blue interiors (Bellizzi, Crowley & Hasty, 1983). Loud (more arousing) music decreased the time spent shopping; the aroused shoppers moved more quickly through the store.

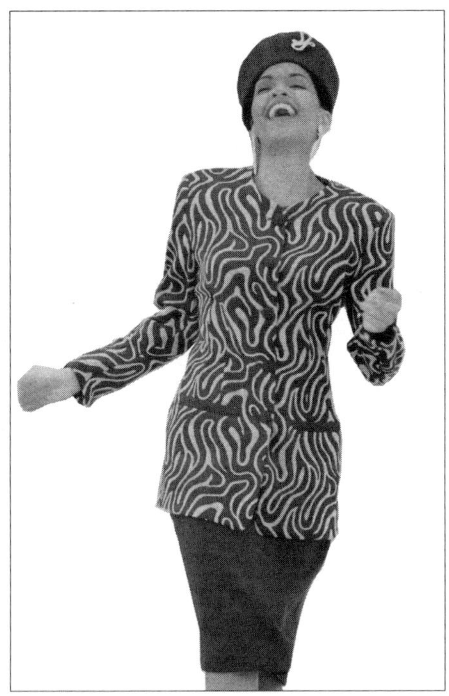

Figure 2.11. Examples of suits providing arousal.

### Dominance

The last of the three dimensions of emotional experience is dominance. **Dominance** is the feeling of being unrestricted or in control of the situation. Little research has examined dominance. Personal feelings of dominance may be expressed through apparel. The low dominance feeling of infatuation or love may be appropriately expressed by soft-edged, lacy, romantic apparel. Apparel may aid the wearer in feeling dominant. A bright colored, clean-line suit may aid the wearer in feeling in control of a business situation (Kimle, 1994). Explore the expressiveness of apparel in Activity 2.5.

The retail environment may be overwhelming, making the consumer feel less dominant. A consumer explains why she prefers to shop in the mall instead of at a flea market. "I don't like crowds, I don't want to be closed in. . . . I don't like to bump up against sweaty bodies. I don't like prices that change that

**ACTIVITY 2.5**

Collect three photographs of ensembles from catalogs, trade publications, or fashion magazines fitting each of the following descriptions of arousal and dominance:

1. high arousal and high dominance
2. high arousal and low dominance
3. low arousal and high dominance
4. low arousal and low dominance

For each of the four descriptions define at least two underlying similarities of formal characteristic of the apparel in the group.

quickly; it makes me uncomfortable. I feel like I'm *losing* (Sherry, 1990)." The chaos of the flea market limits the control of some consumers, who would rather shop in the orderly mall environment. One of the authors felt the same loss of control that decreased aesthetic experience when shopping at (finding my way out of) the maze called the Mall of America.

## COGNITIVE EXPERIENCES

As you remember from Chapter 1, cognitive pleasure or satisfaction comes from mental activity. This activity consists of understanding and creating content or symbolic meaning. One can create objects that contain the symbolic meaning for others to understand or the creation may only exist in the private recesses of one's mind. Both the apparel product and the environment can facilitate these cognitive activities leading to aesthetic experience.

### "Reality"

Communicating **reality** involves the use of the products or environments to represent a view of the world or "what is." Reality is our view or perspective of the world. Reality is a subjective matter that can vary from individual to individual. Because reality may vary from individual to individual, two people can listen to the same music or observe the same object and have very different subjective interpretations of what it means. Both of these interpretations are "real," because reality lies in the mind of the individual. Cognitive pleasure comes from representing one's own internal reality. Cognitive pleasure also comes from understanding another's insightful view of the world. Thus aesthetic experience comes from communicating and extending insight about the world around us.

The messages that are communicated may be very personal or may reflect views of larger social or political issues. For instance, the "Ex Libris" silk tie communicates a very personal message, one's passion for books and reading. The catalog copy cleverly support the message of the tie (Figure 2.12). Terry Niedzialek, a costume maker, communicates social and political messages about the relationship between humans, nature, and technology (Figure 2.13). Niedzialek simulates the world through hair as a way of communicating her perspective, the oneness of people and their environment (Boswell, 1992). Niedzialek stated, "Primitive cultures used to adorn their hair with twigs and other materials as a part of their ritual, spiritual life. My creations are more than the redefinition of beauty. They are intended to transform our level of consciousness about our own relationship to our environment (Boswell, 1992, p. 128)."

K. Ex Libris Silk Tie
If he's up to his neck in books, if the man just loves to read, he'll appreciate a tie that speaks volumes about his passion for the printed page. Screened in shades of rust and brown on a navy background, pure silk tie measures 3½" at its widest point. #32648...$32.50
K

Figure 2.12. "Ex Libris" silk tie and catalog copy that communicates one's passion for books.

### Fantasy

Aesthetic experience is facilitated by communicating reality or cognitive understanding of "what is." Aesthetic experience also comes from fantasies. Feeding **fantasies** involves the use of products or environments in envisioning "what could be." Apparel and the environment feed fantasies, fostering "what could

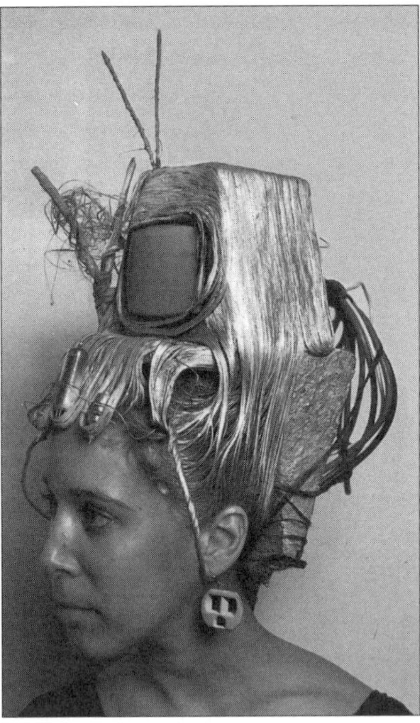

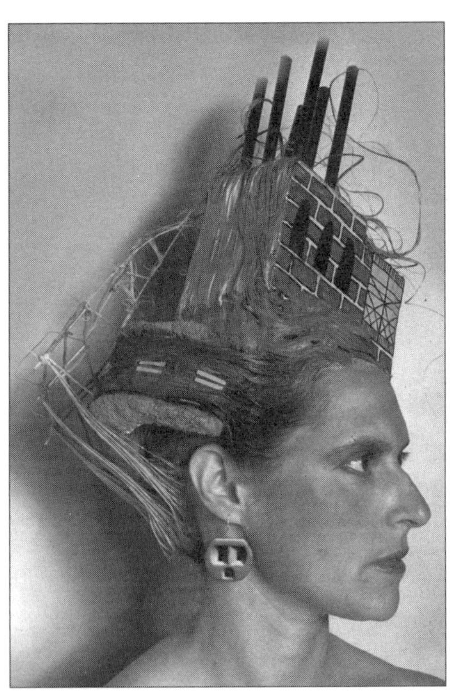

Figure 2.13. Hair designs by Niedzialek that communicate her perspective on the oneness of people and their environment.

be." This is done by *supporting* an alternative existence or through *envisioning* a pleasurable experience. Apparel (e.g., Halloween costumes, wedding gowns, and sports team uniforms) supports an alternative existence (e.g., becoming scary monsters, "fairy tale" brides, or sports stars). The environment also supports an alternative existence. An avant-garde designer may create a theatrical fashion show to help the audience catapult into a another reality, where the designs compliment this alternative existence.

The product may help the consumer envision a pleasurable experience. Products, such as books, CDs, and movies, are valued for their role in stimulating imagery. Apparel stimulates imagery as well. Value of the product is enhanced by the rewarding qualities of the envisioned fantasies involving the product (MacInnis & Price, 1987). The value of lingerie may be partially based upon the product's visual or tactile qualities. However, value of the lingerie may be augmented by pleasurable mental imagery involving the lingerie (the role of the lingerie in a fantasy about a perfect romantic evening).

## Entertainment

Apparel and the environment can be aesthetic because of the mental and emotional activity involved in entertainment. **Entertainment** involves seeking or finding something new, unusual, unexpected, or challenging. In other words, entertainment involves enjoying creative aspects of products or environments. Tops with clever slogans can be entertaining because they offer creative perspectives.

Shopping the flea markets (Sherry, 1990) or markets of other cultures while a tourist (Littrell, 1990) may provide aesthetic experience because these settings present new and unusual products and environments. Products and shopping experiences in other cultures may be unlike one's own, making them intriguing and exciting. Memories of the foreign adventure are attached to the product and add to the value of the product (Littrell, 1990). Walt Disney Company operates stores in its theme parks and across the country. These retail establishments, selling Disney character and theme park products, are outlets for shopping as a form of entertainment ("Disney World," 1991). More traditional retail outlets, such as mall stores can offer entertainment. Browsing any store may be an aesthetic experience because "seeing what's new" can be entertaining.

## SUMMARY

Products *and* environments provide the formal, expressive, and symbolic qualities that foster aesthetic experience. Apparel is not the only contributor to this aesthetic experience or value. Apparel, the body, and the environment all play a part in aesthetic experience. For many consumers, aesthetic value of the product or environment is a major contributor to consumer satisfaction, the goal of apparel professionals. In many cases, *apparel, the body, and the environment all work together to affect aesthetic value and consumer satisfaction.* This chapter suggests ways that apparel, the body, and the environment can all contribute to the three aspects of aesthetic experience. The three aspects are: (multi-)sensory, emotional, and cognitive experiences. Multi-sensory experiences consist of all the sensory information available from sight, touch, kinesthetics, smell, sound, and taste. Emotional experiences have three dimensions: pleasure, arousal, and dominance. Communicating "reality," feeding fantasy, and entertainment are the component parts of cognitive aspects of aesthetic experience.

## KEY TERMS AND CONCEPTS

affect

apparel, body, environment a total aesthetic experience

arousal

cognitive experience

reality

contributors to aesthetic experience

dominance

emotional experiences

entertainment

environment

environmental fragrancing

fantasy

festivity

formality

kinesthetics

multi-sensory experience

pleasure

post-adoption style

pre-adoption design

product line

sensory experiences

storyboard or presentation board

**LAB ACTIVITY 2.1**

This activity will give you a chance to *create a multi-sensory aesthetic experience*. You will *coordinate a small fashion show*. You should consider the formal, expressive, and symbolic qualities of the apparel, the body, and environment to create an integrated whole. The point is to have each component reinforce the other components, creating a multi-sensory whole with a unified expression or symbolism.

1. Collect twelve ensembles from catalogs, trade publications, or fashion magazines. These will be the apparel products for the show so they should be similar enough to organize into groupings. Cut the models from the photographs so that you are left with just the apparel.
2. Apparel: Organize the apparel products into groupings as you might see them walking down the runway. You should have no more than four groups.
3. *Body:* Find new models from other images found in the catalogs, and trade and fashion publications. When selecting models for each ensemble, consider the image you are trying to create for each grouping.
4. *Environment:* Select the music to be played during the show. This may have to be done outside of class if music resources are not available in class. You may select separate cuts for the different groupings or fewer cuts that reflect the overall feel of the show. Provide a sample of the music selected on a cassette tape.
5. Describe what you used to coordinate the apparel into groups. Then describe why you matched the apparel with the various models. Describe how the music fits with the groupings of apparel. You may coordinate these aspects of the show based upon sensory, expressive, or symbolic connections.

## SUGGESTED READINGS

Kotler, P. (1973-74). Atmospherics as a marketing tool. *Journal of Retailing, 49*(4), 48–64.

McCarthy, C. (1992, April). Aromatic merchandising: Leading customers by the nose. *Visual Merchandising and Store Design,* 85–87.

### For Advanced Levels

Burns, L. D. & Lennon, S. J. (1994). The look and feel: Methods for measuring aesthetic perceptions of textiles and apparel. In M. R. DeLong and A. M. Fiore (Eds.), *Aesthetics of textiles and clothing: Advancing multidisciplinary perspectives,* (pp. 120–130). Monument, CO: International Textiles and Apparel Association (special publication #7).

Fiore, A. M., Kimle, P.A. & Moreno, J. M. (1996). Aesthetics: A comparison of the state of the art outside and inside the field of textiles and clothing. Part two: Object. *Clothing and Textiles Research Journal, 14*(2), 97–107.

MacInnis, D. J. & Price, L. L. (1987). The role of imagery in information processing: Review and extensions. *Journal of Consumer Research, 13,* 473–491.

## READING 2.1
# A Grass Roots Approach to Presentation

S. Kingsley

A new store opens amidst the usual fanfare. Odds are a lot of attention has gone into store design and merchandise presentation. But what happens a month after opening day? If a retailer feels obliged to call again on an elite team of specialists to introduce new forms for the future, perhaps it's time to look into training one's own staff in order to make presentation an ongoing concern.

Just as a store that has neglected to invest in cash registers and cashier training is operationally crippled, an organization that has failed to see the value of a concentrated approach to merchandise presentation is incomplete. The investment neccesary to build a well-oiled merchandise presentation system is insignificant though no less important than the capital outlay for other expenses designed to maximize productivity, increase sales, and maintain a bank of skilled human resources at the field level.

Obviously, design isn't everything. Pretty displays, inventive fixtures, eyecatching signage, and elegant decor are well and good. But what retailer wants customers to be impressed with ambiance while not purchasing? Stores are in the business of selling merchandise, not creating showpieces where the environment is more memorable than the goods. The purpose of store design and merchandise presentation is to maximize the productivity not only of each square foot of selling space but every fixture within the square footage allocated.

That's not to say store design isn't important. Establishing well-defined traffic flow patterns and having innovative fixtures and decor are necessary concerns of retailers.

The alliance between store design, merchandise presentation, and training can result in:

- Improved perception of the selection and mix of merchandise in the customer's eyes;
- Improved self-esteem for sales associates;
- Improved application of merchandising principles;
- Average sales per customer improvement;
- Improved productivity;
- Improvement in gross margin through the selective predominance of high-yield merchandise.

One lesson employees can learn is to take into account customer motivation, physio-psychological characteristics, and behavioral traits.

For example, consider the field of vision of a customer. The field of vision, or focus, of an individual is relatively wide. When looking straight ahead, one's peripheral zone of vision takes in a radius of visual perception (object recognition) of approximately forty degrees. However, the zone of focal (intense) perception is limited to a mere one degree radius. Although in depth our vision can focus from either a close point to an infinite point, our perception is restricted to looking at one

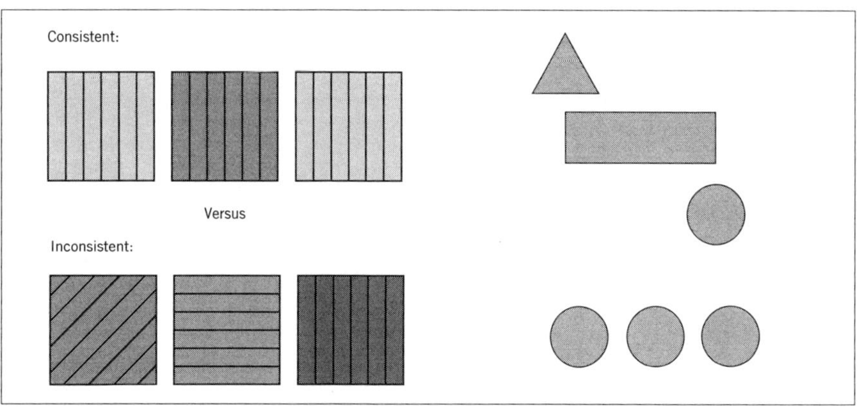


Reading 2.1 Kingsley, S. (1991). A Grass Roots Approach to Presentation. *Discount Merchandiser,* pp. 66–67.

specific point at a time. Taking this fact into account, we must recognize there are areas that will not be seen in focus by customers. Conversely, there are other areas such as facing main aisles and entrance or frontage areas on key traffic pattern aisles, that are highly visible by customers.

The customer wanders down the aisles and looks at products on the right and left without really focusing on all merchandise. However, we know that in order to finally reach a destination and avoid collisions, the customer does look straight ahead on occasion.

### Visual Persuasion

For this reason we know that products that are presented in areas at the store entrance or facing corridors will be focused on by the customer. Clearly, the possibility of encouraging impulse buying is conditional on focusing on a specific product.

We should, therefore, be selective in our choice of products for feature presentation. Our choice depends on the image we wish to project and on the products we wish to sell.

Other factors involved in the visual perception of customers center around the concept of the "eye in movement."

1. When looking at the three geometric patterns, one's optic system must be commanded to focus on one object at a time.
2. In comparison, the eye naturally, almost automatically, moves from one shape to another in the illustration below.

Our vision naturally follows a consistent visual approach more easily than it does an inconsistent approach.

Each time we establish a continuity of color, form, shapes, etc., the customer's vision is guided from one product to another product. Thus, the more merchandise seen in focus by the customer, the higher is the probability of generating an impulse purchase.

The experience of New Mercandising K.P., Inc., indicates that employees exposed to the principles and techniques of merchandising presentation need betwen six to nine weeks to fully assimilate the merchandise presentation training program and internalize it. The typical path of evolution after the assimilation period, with adequate follow-up, is a marked improvement in the standards of presentation during the following eighteen-to-twenty-four-month period.

The reason for the improvement is simply due to the increase of the employee's creativity within the basic principles comprising the merchandising program. This presentation-skill enhancement at the grass-roots level demonstrates that anyone provided with the proper tools and technical knowledge has the potential to excel in merchandise presentation.

## READING 2.2
## Clothing and Aesthetic Experiences

J. Kupfer

The aesthetic appreciation of clothing includes our interaction with it when worn. Clothing is an immediate environment, moving with and against us, like a second skin. When we wear clothing, others can appreciate the aesthetic of how we look in it better than we can. But the aesthetic of direct interaction is available only to the wearer. This interaction is, above all, sensuous; seeing, hearing, smelling, and feeling the clothing adorning us has great aesthetic potential. As we raise our arm, we notice the color and texture of our sleeve; looking down, we enjoy the cut and gleam of our shoes; standing up, we appreciate the shadows created by our pant's pleats. Some fabrics stimulate us auditorily: crisp crinoline, swishy satin, whispering cotton. Still other materials have distinctive odors. An important aspect of leather's aesthetic, for example, is its thick, inundating scent.

Especially significant is the way clothing provides tactile interaction, often missing in other dimensions of daily life. Consider the aesthetic differences produced by a stiff, constraining leather coat and a soft, yielding cashmere one. Depending on other garments, context, and interests, each could enter a rewarding aesthetic experience. The leather coat affords a sense of security in its resistance to our movement, defiance of wind, and armor-like impenetrability to rain or snow. The cashmere coat feels luxurious, caressing our neck and clinging to our legs as we stride down the street. This contrast indicates how opposite qualities can be aesthetically valuable in the appropriate context. Clothing that constrains or resists us may be as aesthetically rewarding as more pliable attire.

The same is true of weight and weightlessness. The sense of touch is compound. In addition to the surface affects on our skin are proprioceptive influence on our muscles and joints. Clothing can be heavy, weightless, and anything in between. When the experience of weight reinforces the clothing's tactile qualities, unity is increased. A dense, wool suit or coat that never lets us forget its presence can be coarse-textured so that we feel as if we are moving within a malleable shell. On the other hand, lack of pressure on our muscles can combine with gossamer surface sensations to create an easy, carefree quality, as in a lightweight silk outfit.

Forgetting what we are wearing or ever mindful of our garb—each can produce a valuable aesthetic of interaction. Still another possibility is contrast between surface tactility and proprioceptive pressure. For example, a slightly rough or scratchy cotton that is nonetheless weightless creates a disparity between surface awareness and muscle serenity. Conversely, a heavy but smooth sweater exerts pressure but with little stimulation of the skin.

When movement is involved, proprioceptive stimulation can translate into kinesthetic sensation as the clothing's pressure deepens our awareness of movement and bodily position. In the case of the light, airy outfit mentioned above, kinesthetic awareness is provided solely by our bodies. Heavier garments can supplement our sense of bodily movement. This kinesthesia can be general or localized in a body part or region. For example, walking in heavy boots through the snow, but wearing a lightweight, insulating jacket and cap, we may feel as though our head and torso are floating above our earthbound, hard-working feet and legs. Such contrasting sensations occurring simultaneously can add complexity to the aesthetic enjoyment of interacting with our clothing.

Sometimes when we move, our clothing moves against us—a winter coat flapping against our legs as we walk. The rhythm of the repeated, regular pressure provides a steady foundation on which transitory melodies of sight, sound, and smell may play. Some people enjoy the way a voluminous blouse or robe billows and wafts about them as they move, only to envelop them gently when they sit. This alternation also sets up a unifying rhythm, and even though we may not be aware of it, such rhythms inform our aesthetic attraction for certain garments and their combination.

Think of the feel of being snugly hugged by a wool watch cap. Its mild tightness and the warmth it contains is so different from the feathery feel of a barely noticeable Panama. The Panama's brim casts a cool shadow over our face and varies its pressure on our head as the wind catches it. Tactile cues such as the feel of a crease against arm or leg, the crispness of a starched shirt, or the constriction of elasticized undergarments punctuate our aesthetic interaction with clothing.

As several of the examples discussed indicate, the experience of wearing clothing occurs within our interaction with the environment. The clothing we wear often shapes this interaction, fostering or hindering aesthetic experience.

Reading 2.2 Kupfer, J. (1994). Clothing and Aesthetic Experiences, Section 3. In M. R. DeLong and A. M. Fiore (Eds.), *Aesthetics of Textiles and Clothing: Advancing Multidisciplinary Perspectives*, pp. 97–104. Monument: International Textiles and Apparel Association (special publication #7).

## READING 2.3
# Different Smells for Different Shoppers

D. Frost

Reading 2.3 Frost, D. (1991, January). Different Smells for Different Shoppers. *American Demographics,* pp. 10–12.

You're shopping in a store, and you're happy. Something in the air is making you relaxed and ready to buy. You're not sure of the source of these good feelings, but your nose knows. The sense of smell has a direct hookup to the part of the brain that controls emotion, and businesses are starting to tap its potential.

The Galleria, an upscale mall in a Minneapolis suburb, gave winter-weary shoppers a preview of summer last year. Tapes of nature sounds played instead of Muzak. Minnesota wildflowers bloomed in the common areas. A subtle fragrance, "Summer," was coated on light bulbs and soaked into cotton balls hidden throughout the mall.

"I would guess most people didn't notice," says Marilyn Garber, marketing director for Gabbert and Beck, the mall's owner. "We didn't want the place to smell perfumed."

Garber knows the six-week event was a hit with shoppers, but she doesn't know if the summer scent swelled sales. Dr. Alan Hirsch sees that potential.

"Smells that are totally dependent and unrelated to the object you're buying will be used to influence your decision-making process," says Hirsch, who directs the Chicago-based Smell and Taste Treatment and Research Foundation. "The olfactory lobe is in the part of the brain that generates emotion."

Certain smells can transport people to different times and places in their life, Hirsch says. Studies show that Easterners are carried back to childhood by the bouquet of flowers, while Southerners swoon at the redolence of pine-scented air. Midwesterners like the tang of hay and farm animals, and Westerners are turned on by barbecuing meat. The scientific name for this is "olfactory evoked recall."

Many Oriental perfumes are made with baby powder, Hirsch says, because this scent creates "a pure and safe environment. You won't smell it unless you sniff for it."

Different ethnic groups have different nasal talents. "What Korean Americans can smell, Japanese Americans can't even detect," Hirsch says. Black and white Americans are somewhere in the middle.

In an experiment at a Philadelphia jewelry counter, a floral scent made people linger longer, while a spicy scent had a more pronounced effect on men, Hirsch says.

"Different odors can impact different brain waves," Hirsch says. Jasmine boosts beta waves, which stimulate the brain, while a whiff of lavender increases relaxing alpha waves. This means that certain smells may increase worker productivity at video display terminals or help air traffic controllers stay more alert. In Japan, one brand of alarm clock sprays out an odor ten minutes before wake-up time to initiate alertness.

A pleasant aroma has always been a sales tool. Realtors bake bread in a house before showing it. An aerosol spray lends a new-car smell to a second-hand Chevy. Lingerie shops are steeped in potpourri.

But odor's subliminal uses can be misused, says Hirsch. If a scent is undetectable, it could have the same effect as flashing "popcorn" on a movie screen every fifteen frames. Public outcry led to the banning of such unfair uses of visual stimuli; Hirsch cautions that companies seeking to manipulate odors risk fueling a similar backlash.

And it could come. At Minnesota's Galleria, Garber was miffed at a news article headlined: "The Smell of Money."

"I don't think we ever want to get people to the point where they'll just open their pocketbooks and dump all their change on the counter," Garber says. "We're making shopping a pleasant experience. It's our job to do that."

CHAPTER 3

# Value Derived From Products and Environments

## Objectives

- Identify benefits or value of the product or environment affecting consumers
- Distinguish between aesthetic and instrumental value of the product or environment
- Recognize value from formal, expressive, and symbolic qualities of the product or environment

In order to have a more accurate view of what the consumer considers during product selection and purchase decisions, the chapter will discuss factors apart from aesthetics. Product selection and purchase decisions are complex. These decisions include the evaluation of the intricate mix of aesthetic or non-instrumental aspects of the products, body, and environment outlined in Chapter 2. In addition, product selection and purchase decisions are based upon instrumental or utilitarian benefits offered by the product or environment. Aesthetic and instrumental benefits are considered together by the consumer and both types of benefits are derived from the purchase, ownership, and use of the product or environment.

Before we outline the differences between aesthetic and instrumental benefits, think about the consideration expressed by two shoppers during the following purchase decision scenario. For Activity 3.1, imagine you are overhearing a conversation in a dressing room. Analysis of the conversation reveals the thoughts behind the purchase or rejection of products. A conversation may sound something like this:

**Shopper 1:** What do you think about this dress?

**Shopper 2:** It looks too tight on you; it makes you look like Ginger on *Gilligan's Island.*

**Shopper 1:** You're right, it feels too tight; I can hardly breathe.

**Shopper 2:** Breathing is important. You can't enjoy yourself if you pass out from insufficient oxygen to the brain. Forget that dress.

**Shopper 1:** What about this other dress?

**Shopper 2:** It's just not you.

**Shopper 1:** You're right. It looks like I should be herding sheep in the Alps or something. People would confuse me with the Heidi character in the children's book. One good thing though is the thickness of layers of petticoats; I'd be protected from injury if I ever fell down the stairs at work. Okay. Then how about this next one?

**Shopper 2:** I think you would get good "mileage" out of that dress. It would be appropriate for work. When the bottom front opening is buttoned up it looks professional, so you'll fit right in with the "sea of gray suits." Or you can look hot if you unbutton it up to here.

**Shopper 1:** The swinging movement of the hem is exciting; it makes me want to dance. Wait. There is a loose thread here. I'll try to break it off. OOPS. It just unraveled the side seam. Now it's a bit too revealing. I could sew it up.

**Shopper 2:** For that price!? If you're paying that much for a dress you should be able to wear the dress in a ground war without the seams ever coming apart.

**Shopper 1:** You're right. And I never seem to find the time to mend things. It's such a bother to set up the sewing machine, find the right color thread and proper needle size.

**Shopper 2:** What about this fourth dress?

**Shopper 1:** No way! It's made by that company exposed on *60 Minutes* for cheating its employees.

**Shopper 2:** I love the color combination of this other dress. It also brightens the color of your skin.

**Shopper 1:** The silk is wonderful against my skin too! It makes me feel like I'm floating as I move in this dress. Plus, it has the CK logo. That ought to impress the snobs in the office who "wouldn't be caught dead" wearing anything from a discount store. I'm going to buy this one.

**Shopper 2:** Why would they care what other people thought of them when they're dead?

**Shopper 1:** It's just a saying. But if they could have Giorgio Armani design their coffins, they probably would.

**ACTIVITY 3.1** In the first column, record the considerations expressed by the two shoppers in the purchase decision process. For example: "Too tight" or "Makes you look like Ginger on *Gilligan's Island.*" These comments will be analyzed later in the chapter.

| | Comment | Formal Expressive or Symbolic | Aesthetic or Instrumental | Value |
|---|---|---|---|---|
| 1. | | | | |
| 2. | | | | |
| 3. | | | | |
| 4. | | | | |
| 5. | | | | |
| 6. | | | | |
| 7. | | | | |
| 8. | | | | |
| 9. | | | | |
| 10. | | | | |

You will complete this chart in Activity 3.2.

## WHY WE BUY: VALUE TO THE CONSUMER

Evaluation and purchase decisions depend upon the product, body, or environment's ability to provide the consumer with desired or expected benefits. **Value** is the perceived benefit derived by the consumer from the acquisition (i.e., purchase), ownership, or use of the product or environment. Value can also be thought of as "what I get for what I give" (Zeithaml, 1988, p. 13). Enhancing attractiveness, saving time, and becoming the envy of one's peers are just some of the values affecting consumer decisions. The following statement in the trade publication, *Discount Merchandisers,* suggests that retailers recognize the importance of providing consumers with the mix of values expected from a product, "With fashion and safety key parent pleasers in today's value-conscious juvenile market, retailers plan to play up stylish prints and practical product features" (Pellet, 1993, p. 44). Apparel professionals must not lose sight of the value(s) desired by the consumer.

Aesthetic value, more than utilitarian (functional) value, is associated with U.S. consumers' willingness to pay more for apparel products (Morganosky, 1984).

However, consumers may differ in the benefits generally considered most important in the purchase decision process (Bell, Holbrook & Solomon, 1991). For some consumers, aesthetic value of apparel may be most important. For other consumers, functional benefits may be more important (Morganosky, 1987). In addition, the importance of the various benefits depend upon the product category (Bell, Holbrook & Solomon, 1991 Holbrook, 1994). A consumer may think most about aesthetic benefits when selecting a wedding gown, but think most about functional benefits of warmth and durability when purchasing work boots.

A product or environment offers a range of values concurrently (Sheth, Newman & Gross, 1991). Thus, two consumers may purchase the same product for different reasons. One consumer may purchase a hat because of its aesthetic value (frames the face nicely), whereas another consumer may purchase the same hat because of its utilitarian value (makes a good shelter for a pet snake). In addition, a consumer may evaluate the same product differently in different usage situations (Bell, Holbrook & Solomon, 1991). The utilitarian value of a hat may be positively evaluated for keeping the sun out of the wearer's eyes, but the same hat may be negatively evaluated for keeping the wearer dry in a driving rain.

## AESTHETIC AND INSTRUMENTAL VALUE OR BENEFIT

As you recall from the first chapter, aesthetic qualities are distinguished from instrumental qualities based upon the nature of the reward or benefit provided by the product or environment. Aesthetic qualities are non-instrumental, (i.e., rewarding and pleasurable in and of themselves). Non-aesthetic qualities are satisfying because they are instrumental in attaining external benefits such as social or economic gain (Berlyne, 1974 Holbrook, 1987). **Instrumental** or **utilitarian benefits** result from the achievement of some purpose or goal other than aesthetic experience. A product (Bell, Holbrook & Solomon, 1991) or shopping environment (Babin, Darden & Griffin, 1994) can offer both aesthetic and instrumental benefits. Both aesthetic and instrumental benefits are derived from the formal, expressive, and symbolic aspects of the product or environment. Chapter 2 provided a thorough discussion of the aesthetic aspects of the product and environment. The following values will be discussed in this chapter:

- **Formal and Aesthetic**
  - sensual pleasure
  - beauty
- **Formal and Instrumental**
  - physical comfort
  - physical protection and safety
  - quality
  - efficiency
  - attractiveness to opposite (or same) sex
- **Expressive and Aesthetic**
  - aroused emotion
  - creative expression
- **Expressive and Instrumental**
  - reflected emotion
  - elevated emotion
  - spiritual ecstasy

- **Symbolic and Aesthetic**
  - identity
  - alternative existence
  - cognitive challenge
- **Symbolic and Instrumental**
  - self-acceptance
  - status
  - social acceptance or affiliation
  - spiritual protection

## Formal Qualities and Aesthetic Value

**Formal qualities** refer to the perceivable features of the structural composition. Formal qualities include color, texture, line, shape, rhythm, sweet tastes, or odors. These qualities of products or environments may provide pleasure to the senses or may enhance beauty.

**Sensual Pleasure.** Formal qualities of the product may provide aesthetic satisfaction due to pleasure to the senses. Sensual pleasure from a musical melody, the smell of fresh coffee, the "ride" of a sportscar, a "coordinated" color combination, or a silky texture of ice cream on the tongue or velvet against the skin are a few examples. Sensual pleasure from the apparel product can have a major impact on selection and purchase decisions as shown in the in-store selection and purchase criteria model in the previous chapter. These sensations can be pleasant in themselves, not because they signal other values of the product. Pleasure will diminish with repeated exposure to a form. Fashion change ensures new formal qualities will be offered to continually create sensual pleasure. Pleasure can also come from the store environment. This pleasantness of a store environment may have a larger effect on consumers' intentions to patronize the store than does merchandise quality or general price level (Darden, Erdem & Darden, 1983). Store-induced pleasure also influences the consumer's willingness to spend time in the store and to spend more money than was originally planned (Donovan & Rossiter, 1982). Pleasantness of the store environment increased the actual time and money spent by consumers in the store (Donovan, Rossiter, Marcoolyn & Nesdale, 1994).

**Beauty.** Humans (males and females) around the world have a desire to beautify the body. Undergoing liposuction, bleaching one's skin, and wearing figure-enhancing apparel have a major similarity, the desire to make the body more beautiful. Products such as apparel and cosmetics (Figure 3.1) are developed and consumed with the value of enhancing the beauty of the wearer in mind (Vacker & Key, 1993). Environments may affect beauty. For instance, "warm" lighting added to a sterile environment, such as a nursing home or store dressing room, may enhance the skin tone of the occupant and the appreciation of the body. A recent trip to the mall revealed that a number of the stores have switched to a "warm" lighting that makes even the pallid look as if they have a golden tan. Manufacturers' of swimwear have tried to combat the fact that four out of five women who shop for a swimsuit leave empty-handed by making the experience less traumatic. To do this, rose-tinted mirrors have been installed in dressing rooms (Schiro, 1990).

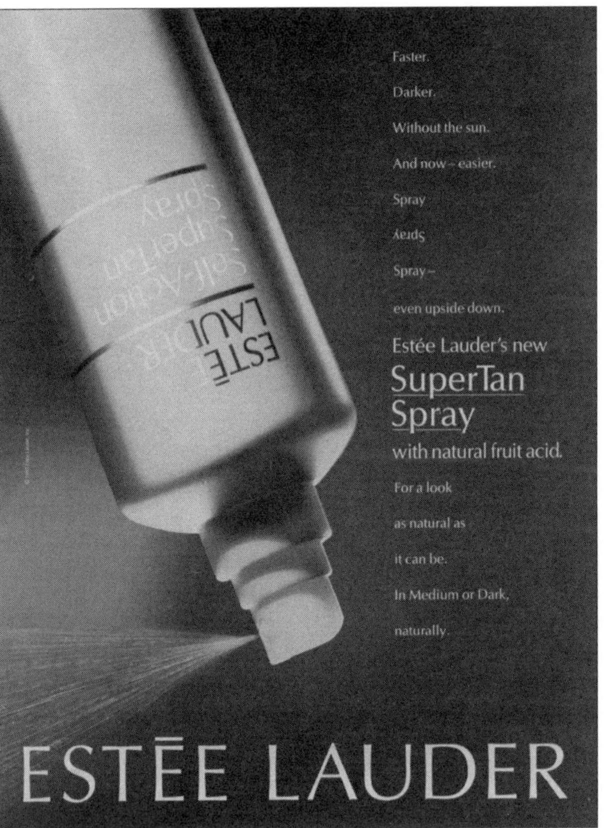


Figure 3.1. Estée Lauder ad espousing the ability of its product to enhance the beauty of the skin.

Beauty may satisfy the creator or wearer, but not necessarily impress others. The resulting beauty may not even be apparent to others, as is the case with figure-enhancing underwear worn under loose clothing. Beauty does not require sensual pleasure. In fact, beautifying the body may be quite painful. A "sausage casing" dress or constricting cummerbund are two examples of apparel that may be worn to beautify the shape of the body, but actually inhibit sensual (tactile) pleasure.

## Formal Qualities and Instrumental Value

Formal qualities may not only contribute to aesthetic experience, but may also contribute to the instrumental values of comfort, physical protection, quality, efficiency, and attractiveness to the opposite (or same) sex.

**Physical comfort.** Comfort is an instrumental component of formal qualities. Research confirms our logic of separating comfort from the domain of aesthetics; consumers differentiate between the concern for comfort and the concern for aesthetic qualities (Morganosky, 1987; Winakor, Canton & Wolins, 1980).

**Physical comfort** is separate from aesthetics, because it does not address enhanced pleasurable sensations. Instead, comfort involves a means to some

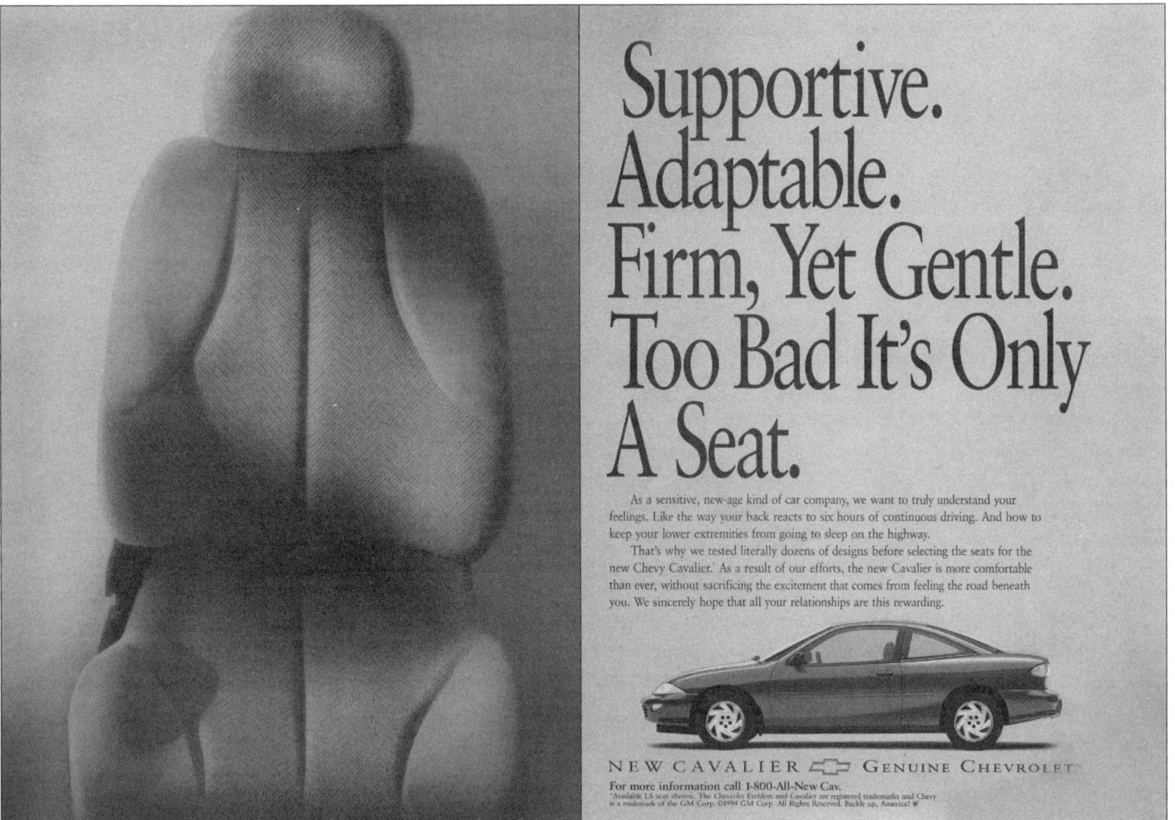


Figure 3.2. Chevy Cavalier ad stressing the comfort offered by the seat without sacrificing the sensual pleasure of the feeling of the road.

other goal or the avoidance of negative sensations (Hollies, 1989). For instance, the texture of thick-cushioned soles of running shoes may be purchased because the soles allow the wearer to reach the goal of completing the marathon. The utilitarian nature of comfort is apparent when one considers how negative sensations may distract the wearer from the task at hand. For instance, the shape of (pointy) shoes may "pinch" the toes and limit the wearer's ability to walk. A product may, however, offer both comfort and sensual pleasure (Figure 3.2). Formal qualities of the store environment may also create comfort. Sensations of temperature (warmth), humidity, and air freshness are controlled to provide a comfortable shopping environment.

**Physical protection or safety.** Formal qualities of the product may also offer a measure of protection. Sour smells or bitter tastes may warn that food has gone bad or is poisonous. Apparel may protect the wearer from physical harm. Reflective textures on active wear can illuminate the wearer in the dark to increase visibility to automobiles. The spongy texture of a neoprene wet suit may help a swimmer stay buoyant and warm during a triathlon swimming event. (And as one of the author jokes to her triathlon friend, the buoyancy also makes it easier for lifeguards to fish from the water the weak swimmers who cramp up during the race.) Figure 3.3 shows how the comfort and protective features of apparel may be major selling points.

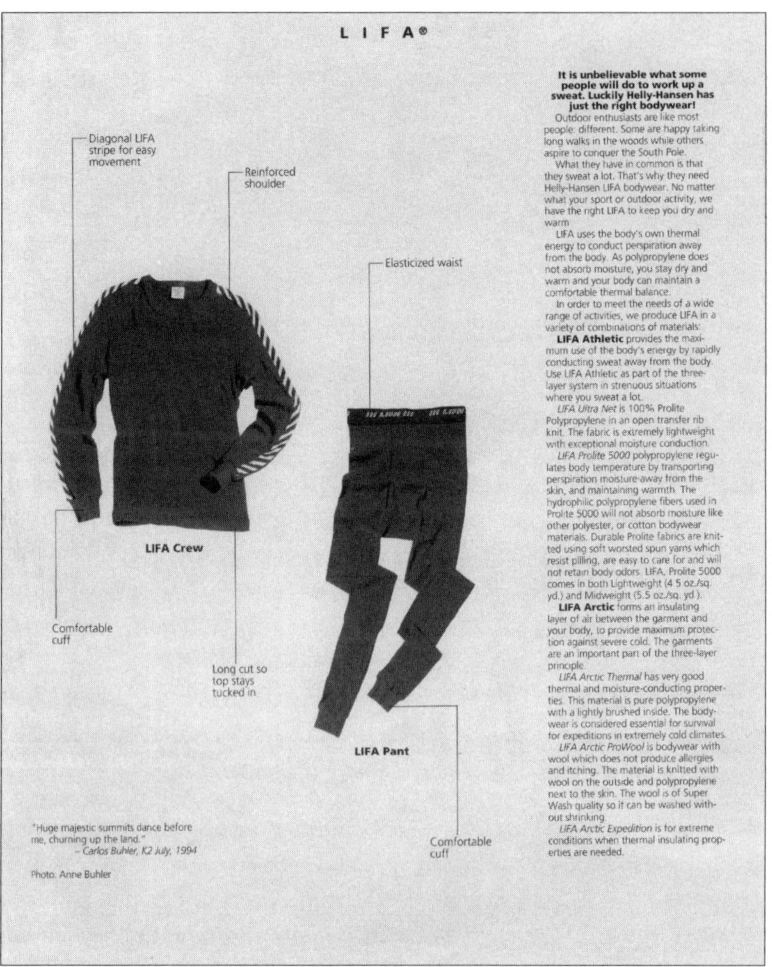


Figure 3.3. Helly-Hansen body wear that keeps the wearer comfortable and protected during outdoor activities.

**Quality. Quality** can be broadly defined as superiority or excellence (Zeithaml, 1988). Quality helps assure that the consumer made a wise purchase decision. Formal structure of an apparel product may signal level of quality for consumers (Fiore & Damhorst, 1992), particularly when these structural attributes are present at the point of purchase (Zeithaml, 1988). For instance, when color or flavor of a beverage are able to be sensed at the point of purchase, these attributes become important determinants of quality of the product. If these attributes are absent, then the consumer may depend upon other (external) cues to the product, such as the product's price, brand name, or level of advertising. The same may hold true for apparel. Brand name may be influential in estimating quality of products sold through a catalog, where the actual product attributes may be limited.

Many aspects of product quality are the result of excellence in production methods. Automobile companies (e.g., Ford and Saturn) commonly stress the quality of their products because of their production methods where all the workers are deeply concerned about the quality of the product. Some formal structures of apparel resulting from excellence in production methods include smooth seam lines created by proper stitching, consistent color matching of garment components (e.g., sleeves, bodice, collar), smooth surfaces uninterrupted by inner construction details (e.g., seam allowances, facings), continuous flow of stripes or pattern shapes across seams, self-supporting three-dimensional shape of the garment, and symmetry of details of the garment.

Durability is the mark of quality during product *use*. **Durability** is the ability of a product to wear well or withstand use without change in structure. Formal structures such as density or hardness of texture may signal durability for a variety of products including tires, mattresses, and apparel. Quality assurance testing for colorfastness is based on a visual measure of change in color value.

**Efficiency.** Efficiency is the ratio of outputs to inputs (Holbrook, 1994). Inputs include money, time, and effort. The efficiency of time and effort is convenience. "Microwave dinners" are convenient because the input of time and effort on the part of the cook is low in comparison to the output of the (somewhat) attractive, palatable, nutritious meal. Formal qualities may affect efficiency. For instance, the arrangement of coordinated ensemble units in an area of the store may not only make the area more visually appealing but also save the consumer time and effort when shopping for a wardrobe. Carpet patterns may contribute to efficiency by directing shoppers through the store to departments and customer service areas (Dayton Hudson: Design Excellence, 1992). The carpet may act as a visual and physical pathway for the customer just as an airport runway directs the pilot where to land, turn, and stop the plane.

Consumers may consider the input of money to the output of money when purchasing products. Products such as rare stamps and coins, fine art, wines, and antique furniture are many times purchased with this economic reason in mind. Reading 3.1 shows that fashion-forward designer clothing may also be purchased based upon considerations of input to output of money. Consumers of these resale items have an eye out for rarity of the piece and the future (increased) price the piece might fetch. Thus, these consumers are attracted to the aesthetic design of the product, but also purchase the product due to economic efficiency.

**Attractiveness to the opposite or same sex.** An instrumental outcome of beauty is attracting the opposite (or same) sex (Berscheid & Walster, 1974). Human beings, like many other species, use their physical appearance to attract a mate. The male peacock displaying its multicolored tail feathers is similar to the human male donning a tight tee shirt that contours his rippling muscles to attract the attention of females. Thus, one may enhance attractiveness of the body, itself or through the enhancing aspects of clothing, in the hopes of attracting a mate. "Dressed to kill" suggests the effect attractiveness can have on "bagging" a potential mate. Many ads use the value of sexiness or attracting a mate to sell products (Figure 3.4).

## Expressive Qualities and Aesthetic Value

In our discussion of expressive qualities in Chapter 1, we stated that pleasure may result from arousing emotions or expressing feelings of the soul. These expressive qualities may be part of the creation or appreciation experiences.

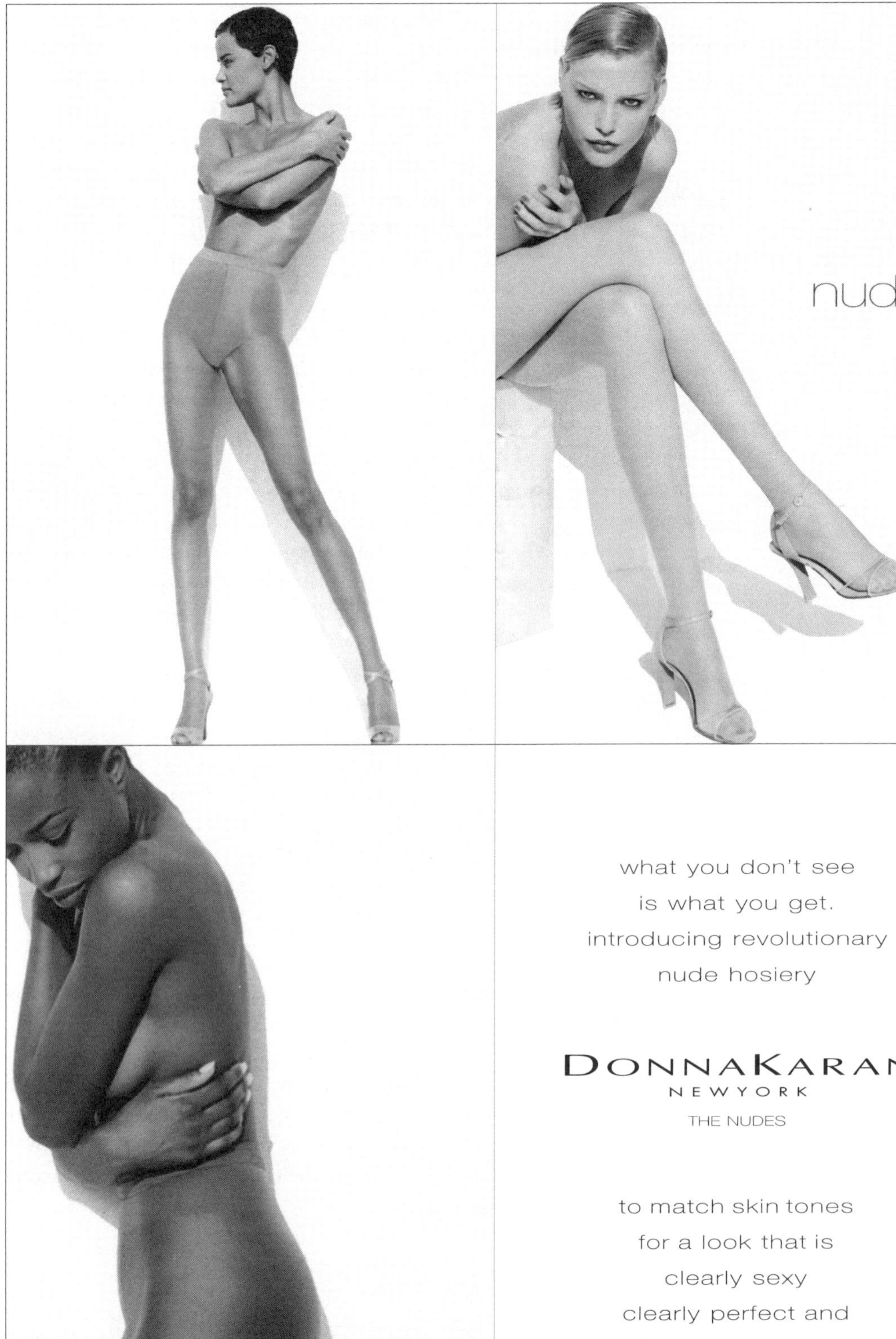
nude?
what you don't see
is what you get.
introducing revolutionary
nude hosiery
DONNAKARAN
NEWYORK
THE NUDES
to match skin tones
for a look that is
clearly sexy
clearly perfect and
clearly you

Figure 3.4. (facing page) Visual and verbal aspects of an ad for Donna Karan hosiery stressing sex appeal.

**Aroused emotion.** The aesthetic form may arouse the emotions of the appreciator. For instance, the vivid colors and bold patterns of pro-wrestling costumes may help arouse excitement in the spectators. The excitement enhances the experience of this and other spectator sports (Figure 3.5). The environment may also arouse emotion. The massive roof with the sweeping diagonal overhang of the airport looks as if it is in a precarious state of motion. This enhances the state of excitement felt by air travelers at this racetrack (Figure 3.6).

**Creative expression.** The release of emotion is an integral part of creative expression. Artists such as actors and musicians may feel "emotionally drained" after a performance. The artist is caught up in the emotional portrayal of a character or the emotions of the music. This release of emotion is seen as satisfying, just as an appreciator may find satisfaction in the emotional release from watching a sad film. The design of apparel or creating one's appearance may also result in emotional release.

## Expressive Qualities and Instrumental Value

The expressive qualities of products may be instrumental in elevating or reflecting emotions. Both aesthetic and instrumental benefits of expressive qualities

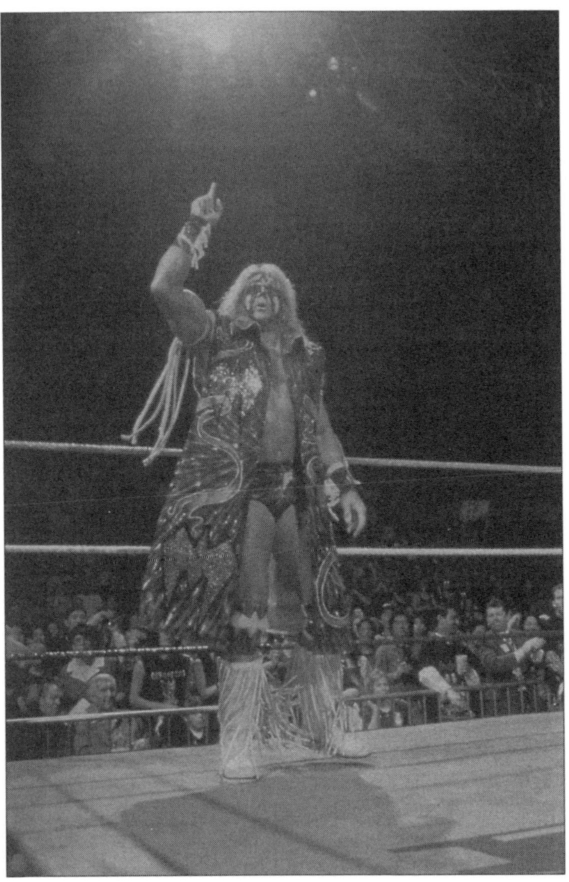

Figure 3.5. Vividness of pro-wrestling costumes add to the fervor of the event for the spectators.

Figure 3.6. Design of Dulles National Airport, Washington, D.C., by Eero Saarinen, adds to the excitement of air travel.
UPI/CORBIS-BETTMANN.

result in an effect on emotion that may be therapeutic. The difference in the two is that therapeutic effects are the *goal* of instrumental value. Apparel may also help the wearer express spiritual ecstasy.

**Reflected emotion.** Expressing emotions may be necessary for the psychological health of the individual. Products and environments may be used to reflect the appropriate mood of interpersonal interactions. Sharing the emotional experience through these interpersonal interactions enhance the therapeutic effect. For instance, one might purchase a black serge dress to reflect the morose nature of the family member's funeral. This appearance, along with environmental aspects such as music, will cue friends into the emotional state to be shared at the funeral, which will help the emotional healing of the bereaved.

**Elevated emotion.** The expressive qualities of products can help one attain the utilitarian goal of getting through a rough day. Products including apparel can be used to elevate mood. For instance, the smell and taste of fresh-brewed coffee, Mountain Dew, or music with a quick tempo and firm rhythm may be used to arouse the drowsy person in the morning. Individuals reported using clothing to lift them from their mild states of depression (Dubler & Gurel, 1984).

**Spiritual ecstasy.** Products and environments may help one attain the state of ecstasy associated with spiritualism. The awe-inspiring glory of a immense, ornately decorated cathedral or temple augments the spiritual experience of the worshiper (Figure 3.7). Amulets, healing crystals, and "first communion" dresses may assist the wearer in the belief of the higher power (Figure 3.8). This faith may lead to a state of spiritual ecstasy.

## Symbolic Qualities and Aesthetic Value

The aesthetic and instrumental values of symbolic qualities differ only in intended goals. Both involve communication of ideas about the person or the surrounding world. However, aesthetic communication has no motive other than pleasure from representing, understanding, and "playing with" ideas. Whereas instrumental communication has as its goal psychological comfort.

Figure 3.8. Children dressed in ornate white "first communion" dresses to mark the significance of this spiritual event and add to the emotional intensity of the participants.

MAGNUM Photos, Inc.; © Abbas.

Figure 3.7. Grand scale and ornamentation of the Saint-Basil cathedral facilitates the spiritual experience of worshippers.

MAGNUM Photos, Inc.; © Chris Steele-Perkins.

Figure 3.9. (left) Tool belt boxer shorts communicates a similar message about the wearer.

Figure 3.10. (right) Star Trek® sound effects key chain supports fantasies such as transporting oneself out of a boring meeting.

Symbolic qualities of the aesthetic product or environment also provides an intellectual challenge.

**Identity.** Aesthetic products can communicate identity, either something about the owner or the owner's views of the world. These ideas reflect one's view of reality. Possessions are seen as a major contributor to and reflection of one's identity (Belk, 1988). Boxer shorts with the printed impression of a tool belt may relay a message about the wearer (Figure 3.9). A Mr. Fix-It drill mug with a drill-like appendage for the mug handle may say something similar about the identity of the user. These products offer aesthetic value through self-expression, where the goal is *not* to enhance self-image or win the favor of others.

The (store or mall) environment may also communicate something about the identity or image of the retail establishment. This identity or image is partly based upon the communication of aesthetic aspects of the store environment (Langrehr, 1991; "Don't Make Store Design," 1991). The environment may have a significant impact on the success of the store, as is evident in Reading 3.2. The acceptability of the message affects the consumer's willingness to shop in the establishment.

**Alternative existence.** Aesthetic products and environments may also support fantasy or an alternative existence. One finds pleasure in fantasy, a desirable view of what could be. For instance, the Star Trek® sound effects key chain allows the user to fantasize about blasting a discourteous driver or transporting oneself out of a boring meeting (Figure 3.10). As mentioned in Chapter 2, apparel products such as costumes, wedding gowns, and football jerseys can support an alternative existence. Store displays and background scenery in advertisements help consumers envision themselves in a fantasy involving the product, which has been found to increase consumers' willingness to purchase the product (Fiore & Yan, in progress).

**Cognitive challenge.** Symbolic qualities of products or environments provide cognitive challenge because of their novelty, complexity, or unusual nature. A recent advertisement for a transparent vinyl purse in a Korean fashion magazine played up the novelty of the product by photographing the purse filled with tropical fish, a butterfly, cut flowers, and other objects not usually found in a woman's purse. Looking back to Chapter 1, Reading 1.2 discussed how store

Figure 3.11. Similarity of appearance among employees of a business.

MAGNUM Photos, Inc.; © Erich Hartmann.

environments offering entertainment can appeal to the consumer and bring the consumer back to the store.

## Symbolic Qualities and Instrumental Value

Ownership or use of a product may do more than provide aesthetic pleasure. The symbolic qualities of the product may provide psychological comfort. Psychological comfort is the freedom from self-doubt or worry. This comfort comes from enhancing self-acceptance, status, or social acceptance (Cialdini, Bordon, Thorne, Walker, Freeman & Sloane, 1976). Symbolic qualities may also provide psychological comfort by offering a measure of spiritual protection.

**Self-acceptance.** The symbolic qualities of a product or environment may affect self-acceptance. Self-esteem or self-acceptance is affected by evaluating one's personal character. Purchase or use of a product may symbolically reflect the depth of one's personal convictions. Thus, self-acceptance may result from the evaluation of one's consumer decisions. For instance, a consumer may like the taste of meat and admire the beauty of fur, but shun the eating of meat or wearing of fur for ethical reasons. The purchase of a faux fur may signal personal conviction of the consumer, and thus positively affect the consumer's self-acceptance. Purchasing "Made in the U. S. A." products or wearing organic fibers may, likewise, affect the self-acceptance of the consumer even though others may not be aware of the personal conviction behind the purchase.

**Status.** Self-acceptance doesn't depend upon the validating opinions of others, whereas status relies upon the validation of others. However, both may affect psychological comfort. The acquisition or purchase experience, itself, can affect perceived status. Compulsive shoppers feel that the purchase experience, being surrounded by attentive sales staff displaying new products, is a signal of the shopper's status. In order to maintain that status, the shopper must purchase to the point of financial ruin in many cases.

| Age | Trust | A Particular Look | Fashion/Style | Social Status |
|---|---|---|---|---|
| 18-24 | 49% | 73% | 73% | 46% |
| 25-34 | 57% | 62% | 56% | 32% |
| 35-44 | 64% | 64% | 58% | 26% |
| 45-54 | 60% | 56% | 54% | 18% |
| 55-64 | 70% | 68% | 66% | 34% |
| 65+ | 63% | 57% | 47% | 29% |

Graph 3.1. Value associated with brand name apparel vary by age of the consumer and likely influence purchase of the product.

*DNR* infotracs. November 1995, p. 13.

The symbolic image or actual rarity of a product may elevate status by separating the owner from others. Owning products may show the consumer's "exquisite good taste" or individuality. Advertising has a major impact upon the symbolic meaning ascribed to products. "Advertising is such a powerful mechanism of meaning transfer that virtually any product can be made to take virtually any meaning" (McCracken, 1989 in Kleine & Kernan, 1991). Thus, promotion of the product in terms of store displays or advertising is vital to the success of the product (Kleine & Kernan, 1991).

Brand image and store image are carefully cultivated because of their effect on consumer demand, perceived status, and resulting profitability. For example, the ad for Louis Vuitton stresses that these high priced bags are "Available *only* in Louis Vuitton shops and *select* department stores" A Louis Vuitton bag is not easily acquired because of its limited retail availability and high cost, potentially affecting the status of the owner of this product.

The products that enhance status vary. For a consumer in her/his 20s, owning an expensive, high-performance Japanese sports car may have a positive effect on perceived status. The same effect on status may not be true if the owner is in her/his 90s. The ownership of fine art created by the masters such as Van Gogh may be a means of status among the very rich, but inconceivable for most consumers.

**Social acceptance or affiliation.** Whereas elevating status is accomplished by distinguishing oneself from others, affiliation is generally accomplished by showing similarity to others within a social group. Wearing current fashion or identifying symbols (e.g., gang "colors," tribal markings, varsity jackets, village costume, nose rings) of a social group may lead to social acceptance or affiliation. The affect of clothing on social acceptance is particularly important among adolescents (Creekmore, 1980). The bellow of every child, "But all my friends are wearing it!" suggests the importance of similarity of appearance in the process of social acceptance. However, affiliation knows no age limit. Adults may dress similarly in business situations to be accepted within the organization. The unwritten dress code of the business organization may be quite apparent in the similarity of appearances of its employees (Figure 3.11).

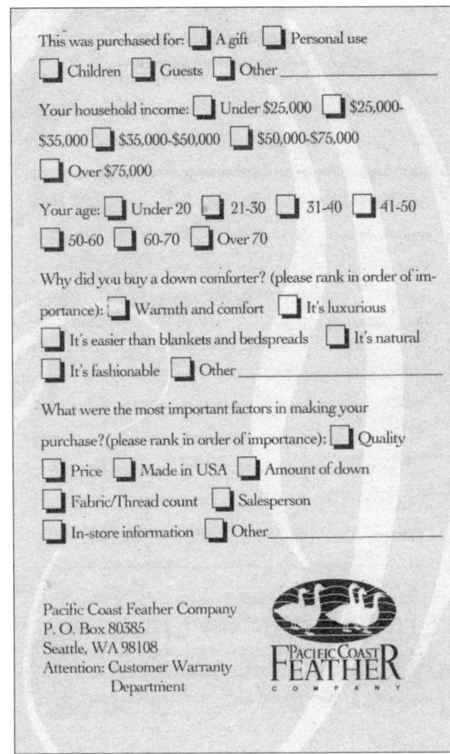

This was purchased for: ☐ A gift ☐ Personal use
☐ Children ☐ Guests ☐ Other ____________

Your household income: ☐ Under $25,000 ☐ $25,000-$35,000 ☐ $35,000-$50,000 ☐ $50,000-$75,000
☐ Over $75,000

Your age: ☐ Under 20 ☐ 21-30 ☐ 31-40 ☐ 41-50
☐ 50-60 ☐ 60-70 ☐ Over 70

Why did you buy a down comforter? (please rank in order of importance): ☐ Warmth and comfort ☐ It's luxurious
☐ It's easier than blankets and bedspreads ☐ It's natural
☐ It's fashionable ☐ Other ____________

What were the most important factors in making your purchase? (please rank in order of importance): ☐ Quality
☐ Price ☐ Made in USA ☐ Amount of down
☐ Fabric/Thread count ☐ Salesperson
☐ In-store information ☐ Other ____________

Pacific Coast Feather Company
P. O. Box 80385
Seattle, WA 98108
Attention: Customer Warranty Department

Pacific Coast Feather Company

Figure 3.12. (left) Magical figure from Kongo, Zaire to ward off evil.

The British Museum, London.

Figure 3.13. (right) Pacific Coast Feather Company survey of values important in the purchase of their comforters.

**Spiritual protection.** Many cultures use objects to ward off an evil presence (Figure 3.12). Crosses, garlic, and lucky mitts are perceived to offer protection from the devil, vampires, or bad luck on the ball field. Wearing these and other items can provide a sense of psychological comfort. You are now prepared to complete Activity 3.2.

Consumers make their purchase decisions based on the product's or environment's ability to fulfill the desired or expected values. Thus, to be commercially successful, product development, selection, and promotion must be concerned with the values desired or expected by the consumer. For example, Pacific Coast Feather Company taps the values seen as important in the purchase decision of down comforters through the survey sent along with the product (Figure 3.13). Graph 3.1 shows that values associated with a brand name product may vary by age of the customer. This is especially important to consider when designing promotions of apparel products for different consumer segments. Try your hand at analyzing values promoted in Figures 3.14 and 3.15 of Activity 3.3. The next chapter will discuss more of the personal differences, such as age, that may affect a consumer's selection of aesthetic products.

**ACTIVITY 3.2**

Now you are ready to complete the task started in Activity 3.1. Determine if the ten considerations expressed by the two shoppers in the purchase decision process focus on formal, expressive, or symbolic qualities. Then determine if the consideration reflects an aesthetic or instrumental value. Using the values described on pages 56 and 57 (e.g., efficiency, creative expression, elevating status), identify the underlying value of each of the ten considerations.

**ACTIVITY 3.3** Promotional activities such as advertising attempt to illustrate values of the product desired by the consumer. In Activity 3.3 you will identify the values presented in the verbal content (copy) of ads for two products—a watch and an automobile. For the ads in Figure 3.14 and 3.15, complete the same analysis as you have done with the shopper's considerations in Activity 3.2.

*figure 3.15 (watch)*

| | Comment | Formal Expressive | Aesthetic or Instrumental or Symbolic | Value |
|---|---|---|---|---|
| 1. | | | | |
| 2. | | | | |
| 3. | | | | |
| 4. | | | | |
| 5. | | | | |
| 6. | | | | |
| 7. | | | | |
| 8. | | | | |
| 9. | | | | |
| 10. | | | | |

*figure 3.16 (automobile)*

| | Comment | Formal Expressive or Symbolic | Aesthetic or Instrumental | Value |
|---|---|---|---|---|
| 1. | | | | |
| 2. | | | | |
| 3. | | | | |
| 4. | | | | |
| 5. | | | | |
| 6. | | | | |
| 7. | | | | |
| 8. | | | | |
| 9. | | | | |
| 10. | | | | |

Figure 3.14 (left) and 3.15 (below). Analyze values of promotional Breitling and Chrysler ads in Activity 3.3.

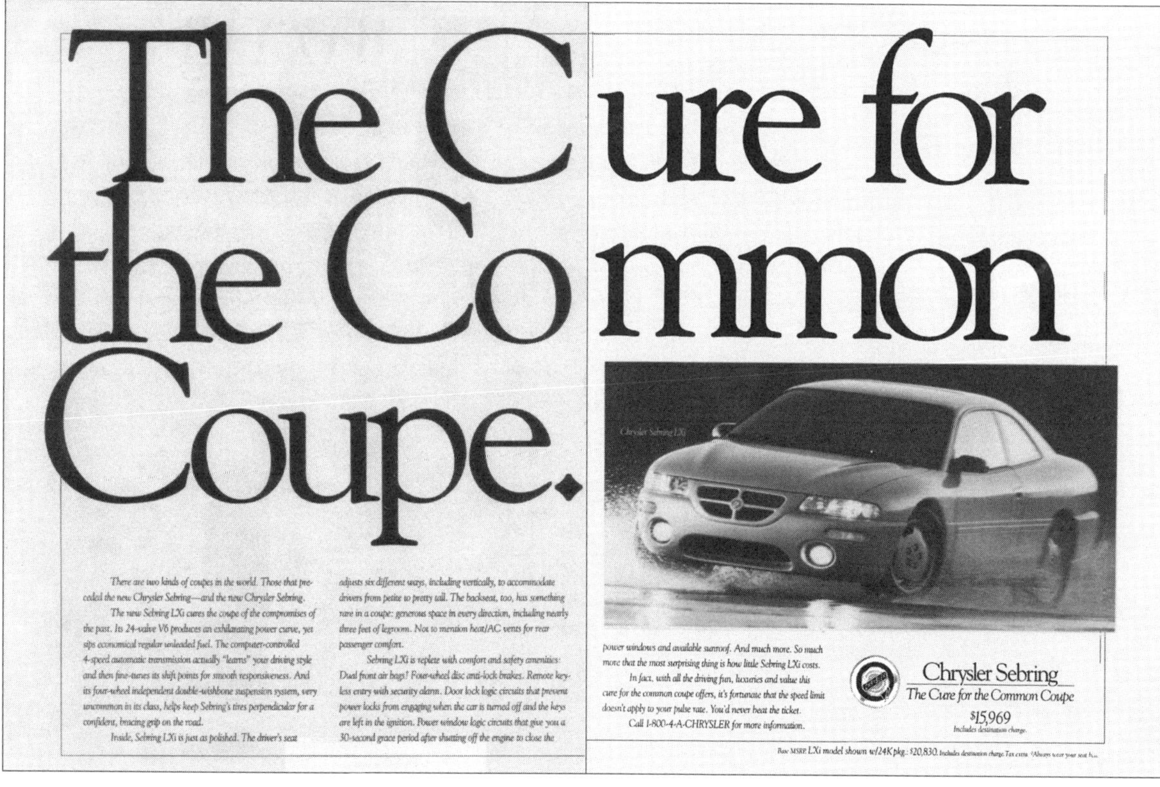

**LAB ACTIVITY 3.1**

The purpose of this activity is to develop an advertisement that stresses the values you feel are most important to the consumer of that product. You will develop the verbal copy and describe the visual images of the ad. You may use an imaginary product or an actual product.

The ad must stress at least three values (e.g., playing with ideas, status, sensual pleasure). The values should be stressed through the verbal and visual components of the ad. The ad must contain the following:

1. Product name.
2. Verbal content (i.e., copy).
3. Image of the product itself. Consider what style variation(s) you will present in the ad. How will it be positioned?
4. Model(s) or celebrity(s) to appear in the ad. What will they be doing? How will they be positioned or posed?
5. Props and/or background.
6. Explain how each component of the ad stresses the values important to the consumer for your particular product.

## SUMMARY

Evaluation and purchase decisions depend upon the environment's or product's ability to provide the consumer with desired or expected benefits. **Value** is the perceived benefit derived by the consumer from the acquisition (i.e., purchase), ownership, or use of the product or environment. Aesthetic qualities represent non-instrumental value (i.e., rewarding and pleasurable in and of themselves). Formal, expressive, and symbolic qualities can also be of value because they are instrumental in attaining external benefits such as social or economic gain (Berlyne, 1974 Holbrook, 1987). **Instrumental** or **utilitarian benefits** result from the achievement of some purpose or goal other than aesthetic experience. A product (Bell, Holbrook & Solomon, 1991) or shopping environment (Babin, Darden & Griffin, 1994) can concurrently offer both aesthetic and instrumental benefits. Both aesthetic and instrumental benefits are derived from the formal, expressive, and symbolic aspects of the product or environment. The values discussed are summarized on page 56 and 57.

## KEY TERMS AND CONCEPTS

alternative existence

aroused emotion

attractiveness to opposite or same sex

beauty

cognitive challenge

creative expression

durability

efficiency

elevated emotion

expressive qualities/aesthetic benefits

expressive qualities/instrumental benefits

formal qualities/aesthetic benefits

formal qualities/instrumental benefits

identity

instrumental or utilitarian benefits

physical comfort

physical protection

quality

reflected emotion

self-acceptance

sensual pleasure

social acceptance

spiritual ecstasy

spiritual protection

status

symbolic qualities/aesthetic benefits

symbolic qualities/instrumental benefits

value

## SUGGESTED READINGS

Fabricant, S. M. & Gould, S. J. (1993). Women's makeup careers: An interpretive study of color cosmetic use and "face value." *Psychology and Marketing, 10*(6), 531–548.

Sproles, G. B. & Burns, L. D. (1994). Changing appearances: Understanding dress in contemporary society. New York, NY: Fairchild Publications. (Chapter 8: Fashion adoption and the individual, pp. 179–216).

### For Advanced Levels

Vacker, B. & Key, W. R. (1993). Beauty and the beholder: The pursuit of beauty through commodities. *Psychology and Marketing*, *10*(6), 471–494.

Belk, R. W. (1988). Possessions and the extended self. *Journal of Consumer Research, 15,* 139–168.

# READING 3.1

# Glad Rags to Riches in the Resale Market

Amy M. Spindler

The sale of a Charles James couture evening dress at a William Doyle Galleries auction on April 24 for $49,450 was unprecedented for a designer from the second half of the 20th century. But as surprising to those who don't regularly wield a paddle was the Hermes bags, Chanel jewels and Judith Leiber clutches from the last decade that went for close to their original prices.

So, might there be such a thing as investment dressing after all? Outside the auction house, the recent rise of the resale store suggests there is.

The new version is hardly the mothball-redolent thrift shop of the past. Sheryl Crow is on the soundtrack, preferred-client lists are kept for designer favorites, and a hefty selection of designers names are on the racks. Depending on the day, there is as much Jil Sander, Prada and Chanel at Ina in SoHo, at Renate on the Upper East Side, at Out of Our Closet in Chelsea or at Allan & Suzi on the Upper West Side as there is at the average designer boutique. And resale today is a rarefied world: customers ask for a designer by name and for particular seasons, with a vast breadth of knowledge.

"They'll say: 'This is 1982 spring Gaultier. I've got to have it,'" said Ina Bernstein, who opened her store, Ina, at 101 Thompson Street (near Prince Street), three years ago.

Mary Kavanagh, who ran the Chanel boutique at Bloomingdale's and Bergdorf Goodman's personal shopping service, opened a resale shop, Kavanagh, in February at 146 East 49th Street, with antiques and "preowned" Chanel, Gianni Versace, James Galanos and Geoffrey Beene priced at less than $1,000.

"When you walk into my shop, it's like walking into a Madison Avenue boutique," Ms. Kavanagh said. "The whole environment, presentation and quality of what is being offered are changing."

Terin Fischer, a former buyer for Barneys New York, opened Out of Our Closet at 136 West 18th Street, a block from Barneys' Chelsea store, and her store mirrors the merchandise mix nearby. She even offers in-shop tailoring.

What has emerged from all these ventures, along with a new style of running the consignment business, is a vigorous resale market for designers who have reached cult status. These shops contend that people buy designer labels to wear as collectors buy art, monitoring the entry of each new piece on the market.

"It shows people are looking at fashion with a sense of connoisseurship, which I've always experienced working with the clothes at auction," Caroline Rennolds Milbank, William Doyle Galleries' couture specialist, said of the trend. "I think the fashion industry has such a low opinion of its client that that aspect has been missed. It's a very interesting change, because I think it shows loyalty to a designer in a different way than you would have seen before."

She compared it to that of billionaires in the technology business buying Mickey Mouse memorabilia instead of Impressionist paintings.

"It's people spending money on what it is they like," she said.

In a market in which designer labels are bought cautiously by retail stores, there is often a scarcity of signature looks. A resale shop may be the first place where a collector of favorites can find certain pieces by Comme des Garcons, Issey Miyake, Yohji Yamamoto, Jean-Paul Gaultier, Vivienne Westwood, Azzedine Alaia, Stephen Sprouse, Geoffrey Beene, Thierry Mugler, Chanel, Yves Saint Laurent, Romeo Gigli and Isaac Mizrahi. Most resale stores keep lists of clients who actively collect those designers.

Designer resale is a business born of customers who aren't as interested in trends as they are in designer vision. A 10-year-old piece by a designer they believe in is more valuable than the hot label of the moment. In addition, designer prices have given investment dressing a whole new meaning.

Reading 3.1 Spindler, A. (1996, June 4). Glad Rags to Riches in the Resale Market. *New York Times,* p. B7.

Terrin Fischer at Out of Our Closet.

Philip Greenberg / NYT Pictures.

"Investment dressing is terminology invented by retailers to justify our overspending and spending fortunes on our backs in the 1980's," said Sandy Schreier, a couture collector and appraiser. "I don't think people in the 90's find it as justifiable as they did then."

Ms. Schreier, who never wears her voluminous collection of couture, recently examined her closet full of designer ready-to-wear that she bought in the 1980's and decided she had to divest. She even opted to get rid of her lucky Karl Lagerfeld suit, in which she was photographed by Art and Antiques magazine. From her home in Detroit, she called a nationwide sampling of resale stores and found that those in New York and Los Angeles were the top buyers.

She is not alone in her quest for a good price at resale. New tax laws have made the Internal Revenue Service tough on once-lucrative deductions on clothes given to museums, fashion schools and charity. "As an appraiser, what I'm supposed to do is appraise them for fair market value," she said. "Those are the key words with the new tax laws. This has killed everyone."

A $3,000 suit for which donors would once give themselves a $2,000 deduction must now be appraised for its value at auction or for the amount it would bring a resale, she said. Consignment shops are profiting from people who don't want to take that meager deduction.

Ina, for instance, has rare finds like World's End shorts designed by Vivienne Westwood and Malcolm McLaren, a flowered Comme des Garcons trench coat with fabric by Junya Watanabe and a Pucci cashmere-and-silk dress. Ms. Bernstein regularly attends the William Doyle auctions, where it is not uncommon for Zandra Rhodes, Rudi Gernreich, Giorgio di Sant'Angelo or Halston to be on sale, even as they are in New York's resale shops.

Ms. Bernstein carefully edits her store, adding good vintage pieces in the mix. "Pre-edited is the new way to do resale shops," she said.

Ms. Milbank, of William Doyle, said there were two ways to buy for investment purposes.

"If people want their current wardrobe to be worth something, they should buy the great classics," she said. "If they're looking 30 years into the future, to sell their clothes for their children to pay for college, they should buy more unusual things."

Which is why she recommends investing in landmark collections, like Christian Lacroix's first for Patou.

It is perceived scarcity that drives much of the resale business.

"In the case of Moschino and Giorgio Sant'-Angelo, when they passed away, everyone was looking for that stuff," said Suzi Kandel, who owns Allan & Suzi with Allan Pollack. "They became like artists. They're the new Picassos."

Allan & Suzi, at Columbus Avenue and 80th Street, even have a local-access home shopping show, on Mondays at 9 P.M. on Channel 35.

After nine years in business, Mr. Pollack notes a big change.

"In the 80's, people would brag, 'I spent $5,000 for this Alaia,'" he said. "Now they brag, 'I only spent $100.' And this is from the upper echelon of our customers."

It is all proof, he said, that the long history of the powerful marketing of designers has succeeded.

"The designer label is more than still alive," he said. "The designer label means everything. It is an investment, for those who buy it now and can sell it again, and those who give it up."

## READING 3.2
## Don't Make Store Design Too Posh for Clientele

When upgrading the image of a store, the trick is not to make it seem so luxurious that it will intimidate the customers. This was the message of Mark Pucci, Senior vice president, Walker/CNI, delivered at one of the department/discount/general merchandise store seminars at SPECS. He specifically referred to the new Cachanilla store in Mexicali, Mexico, which won first place honors in the foreign category for the 1990 New Store of the Year competition sponsored by *Chain Store Age Executive*. Cachanilla is a unit of Dorian's, a chain of twenty-five department stores located in northern Mexico.

Walker Group was the consultant responsible for the design. Gregorio Goldstein, director of commercial operations, Dorian's, explained that the store is a departure from Dorian's past design, which is downscale, since most of its stores cater to a population of low-income people.

Although the store is not in an affluent neighborhood, Dorian's management decided to go with a more professional look and a better image to see what might result. The upshot, according to Goldstein, was that the store became the center of attraction of the town and beyond, and its sales per square foot of $160 are the highest for the chain. It's Mexicali's only full-line department store.

Pucci said the store is 180,000 sq. ft. on two levels, and is the largest Dorian's to date. It has a large atrium space in the center of the store where the cosmetics counters are located. Each department, he said, has logical sequences and adjacencies to make the search-and-find process easy for the customers.

In its attempt not to make the store seem too posh, the designers used no carpeting. Because few people in Mexicali are familiar with escalators, the store has stairwells next to the moving steps.

Lighting is fluorescent. Detail work in plaster and terrazzo was done by local artists.

Construction costs were less than $50 per square foot, including land, mainly because of the availability of highly inexpensive labor.

In a session on care and maintenance for new types of flooring, Walt Todoro, regional sales manager, Permagrain Products, said that before a retailer installs a floor, he should know what's required in maintenance care.

"Aesthetics are important to draw consumers in. But aesthetics are only part of the equation. You have to ask what the floor can and can't do. Is the floor a good choice for the area you have?"

He asked whether there were safety considerations associated with maintenance and

Reading 3.2 Don't Make Store Design Too Posh For Clientele. (1991, May). *Chain Store Age Executive*. 67(5), pp. 183–184.

what the slip-and-fall liability is. What are the local fire codes? Is test data independently verified? Does the manufacturer offer technical assistance?

The retailer/merchandise vendor collaboration session dealt with departments which focus exclusively on the coordinated product line of a single vendor, and how retailers and vendors can collaborate to foster mutual success.

In the session Frank Bracken, senior vice president, marketing, Haggar apparel, said that most retailers do not have enough sales associates to service all their customers. "In order to make self-service as pleasant as possible, more information must be provided through the displays," he said.

David Nafziger, director, visual merchandising, J.C.Penney, said his chain is embarking with Haggar on a twenty-store test of Haggar casual shops starting Aug.1. The program will include cooperative advertising. "There has been unbelievable growth in the notion of what co-opting can include," he said. "We welcome the idea of involving Haggar in the merchandising of their product line. Who should know their business better than Haggar?"

In a workshop on maintenance management software, Don Mechin, chief engineer, Strawbridge & Clothier, said that he has been trying to convince his top management of the need for a maintenance automation package for years. Finally, last month (April), a system was put in place in the chain's 1.1 million-sq.-ft. Center City store. "We feel this will be the key to getting away from breakdown maintenance," he said, "and into preventive maintenance."

Eli Katz, president, Maintenance Automation Corp., stressed that computerization is the key to performing maintenance procedures in an organized fashion.

"Chain and mall managers can combine the microcomputer hardware configurations with available software and their management know-how to obtain an optimum set of management tools for their facilities," Katz said.

They can use them to provide highest quality maintenance and services at lowest practical costs. They can have complete control and accountability while delivering the highest possible levels of service to stores and malls.

"There are two applications for mall management in regards to common area maintenance, or CAM," Katz said. "One is meeting legal fiduciary responsibilities, and the other is keeping the mall competitive at minimum costs for highest quality."

Katz explained that for tenants, there are also two applications, he said. One is monitoring a major variable rent component, and the other is being assured of quality mall services and environment at minimum costs.

CHAPTER 4

# Factors Influencing Aesthetic Evaluation or Preference

## Objectives

- Understand the importance of moving away from an egocentric view when determining aesthetic preferences of others
- Understand how products and environments reflect and reinforce the socio-cultural context
- Recognize how socio-cultural differences across cultures may affect aesthetic preferences
- Recognize how socio-cultural differences within a culture may affect aesthetic preferences
- Recognize how individual differences may affect aesthetic preferences
- Identify (differences in) preferences of consumer groups for apparel products

Chapters 2 and 3 presented qualities of the *product, body, or environment* considered during aesthetic evaluation and consumer evaluation of the product or environment. However, aesthetic evaluation (and the affect on consumer behavior) is not solely due to the product; it is a combination of product qualities and characteristics of the individual (Bell, Holbrook & Solomon, 1991). The present chapter will discuss how characteristics of the *individual* affect aesthetic evaluation or preference, influencing consumer behavior. **Aesthetic evaluation** is the appraisal of a product or environment's aesthetic qualities. *Aesthetic preference* is a comparative evaluation, where the aesthetic qualities of one product or environment are judged against others resulting in a preference for one product or environment over the other options.

An individual's socio-cultural and personal experiences affect evaluation of or preference for a product or environment's aesthetic qualities. For instance, a

British friend of the author's wears a steady stream of horizontal striped shirts. When asked about his aesthetic tendency, he posed that it's likely the result of a positive association with the stripes of rugby uniforms, his country's beloved sport. Thus, his socio-cultural experience affected his aesthetic preference. One of the authors spent eight arduous years wearing a green plaid parochial school uniform. This personal experience causes the author to break out in a cold sweat at the sight of similar plaids in fashion apparel.

## MOVING AWAY FROM AN EGOCENTRIC VIEW

An **egocentric view** of the world is taken when one evaluates all things from a personal point of view. It is natural for one's attitudes and beliefs to shape perception and interpretation of the world. For instance, if one owns a dog, believes dogs are companion animals, and loves the dog as if it were one's own child, one may find training dogs as attack animals to be offensive and see using dogs as food as down right inhumane. This is a totally valid point of view for the individual. The problem arises when one's view of the world is perceived to be the only legitimate perspective and generalizable to all others. Socio-cultural differences (e.g., geographic location) and individual differences (e.g., personality) may make for very different points of view among individuals. Each perspective may be equally valid given the socio-cultural and individual context. Another culture may not consider dogs to be companion animals, making dogs a potential food source, but may see the consumption of beef as outrageous given the religious significance of cattle in the culture. Individuals in the role of law enforcement may find it appropriate to train dogs as attack animals given the fear for their personal safety in the apprehension of criminals.

An egocentric view may become a problem when determining aesthetic preferences as well. One's aesthetic preferences may not be generalizable to others. A spandex dress may be the aesthetic preference of a teenage female in the United States, but inconceivable as the aesthetic preference of a seventy-five-year-old woman or a Muslim woman following the religion's rules of modesty. By the same token, one must not assume too much about differences in preferences. Reading 4.1 discusses how professionals in the fashion industry have moved away from the view that larger size women differed from misses' sized women in basic aesthetic desires. The industry is shedding the belief that larger size women care little about formal aspects of the product and about enhancing the body. Becoming more attuned to preferences of the ultimate consumer has had a positive impact on sales of larger size apparel. Thus, one should move away from an egocentric view when developing, selecting, or promoting products for consumers.

## PRODUCTS AND ENVIRONMENTS AS REFLECTION AND REINFORCEMENT OF THE SOCIO-CULTURAL CONTEXT OF THE INDIVIDUAL

Product developers do not create in a vacuum, nor do consumers make aesthetic selections in a vacuum. The **zeitgeist** or the "spirit of the times" is the dominant ideology or beliefs of a culture and historical period that surrounds the aesthetic

a

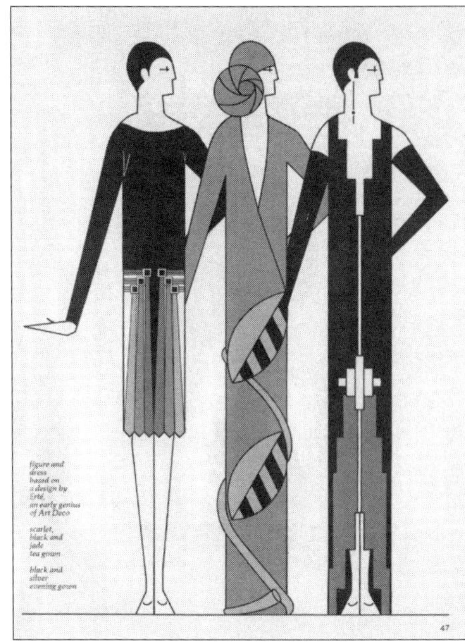


b

Figure 4.1 a and b. Cubist art (a) depicting the human body and Art Deco (b) reflecting the importance of mechanical technology of the Industrial Revolution. (a): Leger, Fernand. *Three Women (Le Grand Dejeuner)*. 1921.



decision. The zeitgeist or surrounding socio-cultural context shapes the individual's thoughts, beliefs, and feelings. In turn, these thoughts, beliefs, and feelings manifest themselves in the development, selection, and promotion of formal *expressive,* and *symbolic* qualities of the product and environment. For example, in the Western world the reverence for and fascination with mechanical technology during the industrial revolution was symbolized by the design and acceptance of geometric shapes of cubism and Art Deco in the 1920s and 1930s (Figure 4.1). The repetition of shapes in Art Deco designs, particularly mechanical shapes made with compasses, triangles, and straight edges, showed mass production methods applied to design (Hull, 1975). Development of the product *reflects* the socio-cultural context by communicating ideas central to the context. Selection of the product *reinforces* or gives credence to the context, as selection shows acceptance or approval of these ideas.

A structural-functionalism approach in the social sciences supports the idea that the aesthetic object or experience is a reflection and reinforcement of culture (Flores, 1985). In this approach, the formal structure of the aesthetic object or experience reflects the structure of society. The formal structure also has the function of symbolically reinforcing the structure of society. A positive aesthetic response results from a similarity between formal qualities of the aesthetic object and the organizational principles of the culture or group. For instance, in the dance of the Kono's of Sierra Leone, the overly expressive dancers are encircled (Figure 4.2). This use of space in dance parallels the Kono's containment (encircling) of antisocial forces in daily situations (Hardin, 1988). In industrialized Western societies, Victorian era chairs displayed differences in height. Men's chairs were higher than women's chairs reflecting and reinforcing the perceived lower status of women in society at the time.

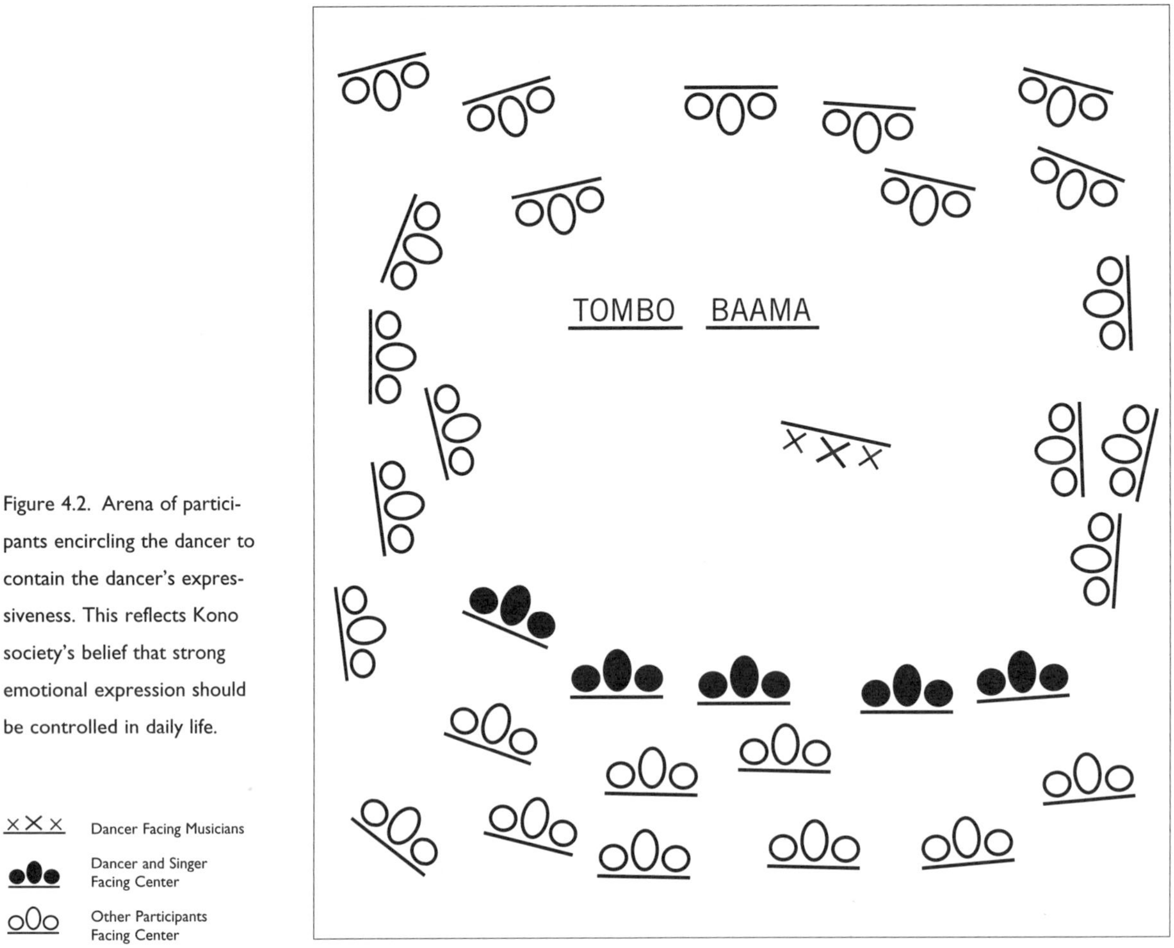

TOMBO BAAMA

Figure 4.2. Arena of participants encircling the dancer to contain the dancer's expressiveness. This reflects Kono society's belief that strong emotional expression should be controlled in daily life.

Dancer Facing Musicians

Dancer and Singer Facing Center

Other Participants Facing Center

## Contemporary Socio-Cultural Context: Modern versus Post Modern

The zeitgeist or "spirit of the times" is always in transition. Industrialized Western cultures presently appear to be in a state of transition between what is called "modern" and "post modern." Modern is marked by the industrial revolution, development of capitalist society, a linear sense of time, and concern for national issues. Post modern is marked by the information revolution, development of a global society, fast changing cyclic sense of time, and concern for world or local issues (Gitlin, 1989). One may find expressions of both modern and post modern in present day aesthetic forms, including architecture (Figure 4.3), music, store displays, and appearance (Figure 4.4) (Kaiser, 1990; Kaiser, Nagasawa & Hutton, 1991). Table 4.1 characterizes differences between modern and post modern appearances and means of creating these appearances. The different appearances can be found side-by-side on the street, in fashion publications, and possibly in your classroom (Activity 4.1). Appearances may range from modern to post modern, including combinations of both.

Figure 4.3. Example of post modern architecture by Frank Gehry with an unusual mix of surfaces and angles.

MAGNUM Photos, Inc.


**ACTIVITY 4.1** Look around the classroom and determine if examples of modern and post modern style elements exist. Identify the modern and post modern elements of appearances found in the class. Determine the retail sources providing the modern and postmodern elements of these appearances. Students who refer to fashion magazines, TV, movies, and retail store displays as main sources of inspiration for creating appearance are likely to emphasize modern elements. Students customizing their looks by wearing apparel found in vintage, surplus, and second-hand clothing stores and by wearing apparel of other cultures may be emphasizing post modern elements (Henderson, 1994). Are there differences between the retail sources used to create modern and post modern elements of the appearances?

## SOCIO-CULTURAL DIFFERENCES ACROSS CULTURES AND AESTHETIC PREFERENCES

Human beings are located within a specific socio-cultural context. They cannot be plucked out of this context for analysis of their aesthetic preferences. Instead, socio-cultural factors should aid understanding of these preferences. Differences in socio-cultural factors often lead to divergence in aesthetic preferences and consumer behavior.

First, variation in aesthetic preferences relates to the culture's definition of aesthetic experience. Many industrialized Western cultures (i.e., European and North American) believe that the aesthetic object *provides* the internal feelings and thoughts creating the aesthetic experience. Thus, aesthetic preference depends upon the impact of the formal, expressive, or symbolic qualities of the object. Some Eastern cultures (e.g., Japan) see the aesthetic object as a means to quiet self-reflection of inner feelings and thoughts (Deutsch, 1975). Aesthetic

Figure 4.4. Examples of modern appearances (top) and post modern appearances (bottom) in the same fashion publication.

Top: Gianni Versace, 1996 and Jil Sander, 1996. Bottom: Gucci, 1996 and Prada, 1996. *Women's Wear Daily.*

**TABLE 4.1** Differences between modern versus post modern appearances and means of creating these appearances. Based upon Morgado, M. A. (1994, October). *The Postmodern paradigm: An instructional guide to contemporary appearance codes.* Paper presented at the International Textiles and Apparel Association Conference, Minneapolis, MN.

| *Modern* | *Post Modern* |
|---|---|
| New styles are visible indicators of progress | Styles are recycled from past history |
| Rhythmic cycles of fashion change | Rapid and volatile style changes |
| Elite fashion inspires mass fashion | No distinction among elite, mass, and street fashions |
| Fashion originates from designers* | Fashion originates on the streets |
| A few styles dominate | Many diverse styles are popular |
| System of rules for combining design elements (e.g., color combinations) | Unstable and intentional changes to aesthetic code |
| Emphasis on unity and harmony of design | Disordered combinations; intentional destruction of harmony |
| Emphasis on simplicity and function | Emphasis on ornament and decoration to make special |
| Unequivocal relationships between body and garment structures | Disregard for body and garment relationships (trousers worn several sizes too large) |
| Traditional assumptions about how garments are worn | Challenges to tradition (e.g., men's garments are jockey briefs as hats) |
| Concern for the symbolic meaning of aesthetic aspects | Little concern with symbolic meaning of aesthetic aspects (e.g., religious significance of the cross) |
| Appearance codes suppress ethnic and subcultural distrinctions | Diversity of ethnic and subcultural style |
| Appearance codes based upon time, occasion, gender, race, and status | Codes distorted or intentionally undermined (e.g., wearing a mink coat with jeans) |

*Some major fashion designers, such as Christian Lacroix and Anna Sui, are considered to exhibit a post modern aesthetic.

experience is due to the thoughts and feelings of self-reflection rather than the thoughts and feelings conveyed by the aesthetic object. For example, Japanese rock gardens (Figure 4.5) may be preferred to Western floral gardens because rock gardens encourage quiet contemplation of inner states and thoughts. Individuals from industrialized Western cultures may find a rock garden to be nothing more than raked sand and rocks, lacking the intense sensory stimulation offered by vivid floral gardens of Western cultures.

Second, a culture also influences whether the formal, expressive, or symbolic aspect of the product is most important in aesthetic evaluation. U.S. consumers depend most on formal aspects in aesthetic evaluation of apparel (Eckman, Damhorst & Kadolph, 1990; Morganosky & Postlewait, 1989). Formal aspects were also more important than symbolic meaning in selection of wax print textiles by Ghanaian women of Africa (Littrell, 1980). Koreans,

Figure 4.5. A Japanese rock garden does not offer the sensory stimulation offered by traditional Western floral gardens. Instead its simplicity encourages self-reflection. A similar level of simplicity is found in the design of Japanese interiors.

MAGNUM Photos, Inc.
© 1983 Erich Hartmann.

however, evaluated the aesthetic appeal of traditional silk textiles based upon their symbolic qualities (Kwon, 1979). Yet, since 1945, emphasis shifted from traditional symbolism in woven pattern designs to patterned motifs with more formal and decorative arrangements. The same may be said about textiles products of Guatemala; historically, the symbolic qualities were central to the aesthetic evaluation of traditional Guatemalan costume (see Reading 4.2).

Third, specific aesthetic preferences and purchases may be a reflection of particular socio-cultural beliefs. For example, aesthetic preferences for fragrances are strongly tied to the socio-cultural context. The women's movement has taken hold in Spain. Young Spanish women prefer fragrances that are masculine with an herbal-woody scent rather than the traditional floral scents. Germans perceive anything linked to animals as unclean or primitive. Thus, the use of musk (an animal product) in fragrances negatively influences aesthetic appeal of the fragrance. Saudi Arabians believe it is appropriate to exhibit power and wealth. Saudi Arabian women exhibit this wealth through use of strong perfumes (LeNorcy, 1988).

Readings 4.2 and 4.3 examine how aesthetic aspects of apparel may reflect particular factors of a culture. A Central American culture and an Asian culture are discussed. Once unique in their aesthetics, the traditional appearances of these cultures are now being influenced by the aesthetic of Western cultures.

## SOCIO-CULTURAL DIFFERENCES WITHIN A CULTURE AND AESTHETIC PREFERENCES

There are differences within cultures, as well as among cultures. Socio-cultural differences *within a culture* affect aesthetic preferences. Socio-cultural differences affecting aesthetic preference include geographic location, ethnicity, religion, and sexual orientation. Retailers are successfully using differences in these socio-cultural factors to "**micro-market**" or tailor merchandise in individual stores to the (aesthetic) preferences of its patrons (Reading 4.4).

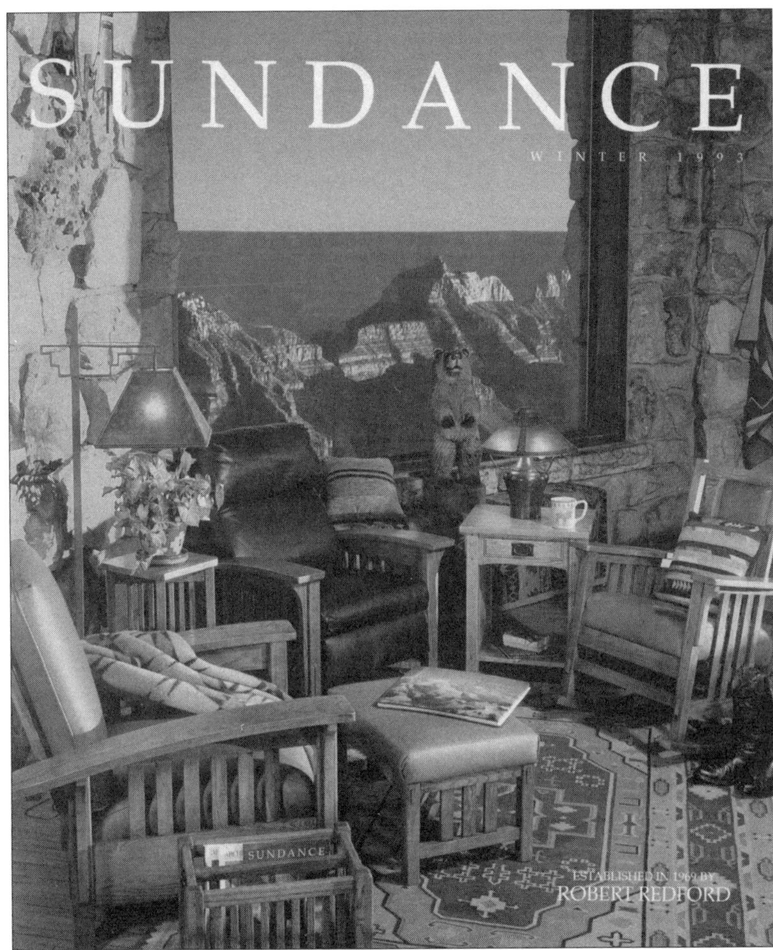


Figure 4.6. Interior and apparel items reflecting aesthetic of the southwestern U.S. Natural materials of leather and stone are used. Native American inspired geometric patterns are found in the textile items, pottery, and floor lamp.

## Geographic Location

Geographic location can influence aesthetic preferences. The difference may be due to the climatic conditions of the location, but are also influenced by factors such as physical environment, ethnic heritage, industry, and historical events of the area. For example, the Southwest U.S. was settled by Native Americans, ranchers, and miners who worked outdoors in rugged conditions. The Native American aesthetic of geometric pattern is popular for many interior and appearance-related products. The rugged conditions of the weather and land help shape the aesthetic for sturdy, natural materials such as leather and stone. Leather, a product of ranching, is used frequently for interior and appearance products. Stone, a plentiful yet beautiful material, is frequently used for exteriors and interiors of buildings and influences the preference for more blended colors (Figure 4.6).

Presently, differences in aesthetic tendencies can be found among the apparel products of the major design centers of the United States. For example, compare the contemporary, sporty, bright colored styles of California with the more conservative, professional, neutral colored styles of New York (Figure 4.7). Geo-

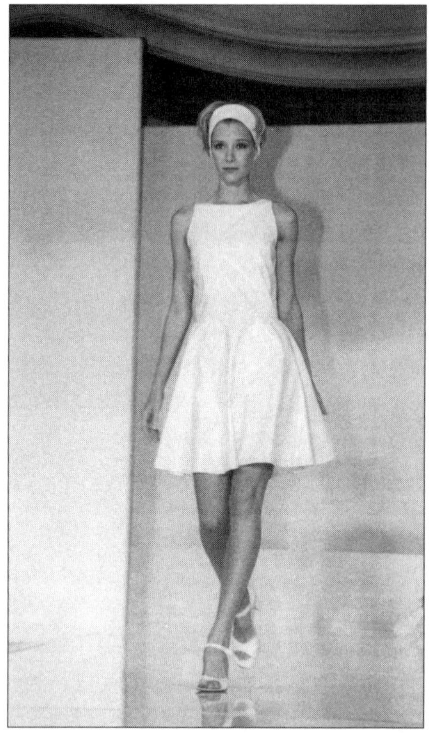

a

b

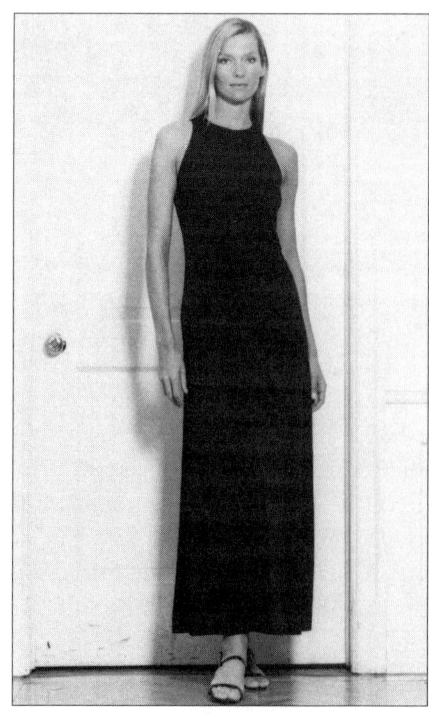

c

d

Figure 4.7. Differences in the styles from two apparel design centers in the United States. (a) Karen Kane and (b) Shelli Segal reflect the aesthetic trend of the California design center. Ralph Lauren (c) and Calvin Klein (d) represent the aesthetic trend of the New York design center.

*Women's Wear Daily.*

**ACTIVITY 4.2** Apparel designs of California tend to differ in aesthetic from designs of New York. Examine designs from these two design centers. *Women's Wear Daily* showcases the designs of these two centers. For instance, *WWD*, October 12, 1995, featured an article (pp. 1, 12–13) and special report (color supplement) on California designs. *WWD*, October 27, 1995, showcased New York designs (pp. 8–9).

1. Describe five differences in aesthetic for the two centers. Examples: interesting fabrics used or styles geared toward casual sportswear.

*California*

1. ______________________
2. ______________________
3. ______________________
4. ______________________
5. ______________________

*New York*

1. ______________________
2. ______________________
3. ______________________
4. ______________________
5. ______________________

2. Define five socio-cultural factors that may explain the aesthetic of California and New York designs. Example: Sporty look: Californians are much more active, participating in outdoor sports.

*California*

1. ______________________
2. ______________________
3. ______________________
4. ______________________
5. ______________________

*New York*

1. ______________________
2. ______________________
3. ______________________
4. ______________________
5. ______________________

Figure 4.8. An African-American aesthetic is found in the consumer product, Sparkle Baby Kenya dolls. Individual expression is encouraged in the styling of the dolls hair. Off-beat patterns and high affect colors are found in the apparel worn by the doll.

graphic location of the design center appears to have an effect. In Activity 4.2 define the socio-cultural factors that may influence the aesthetic tendencies among California (Los Angeles) and New York designers' apparel products.

## Ethnicity

An increasing number of products are designed and promoted to meet the preferences of specific ethnic groups or markets. Variations of products designed to cater to specific ethnic markets range from dolls ("The rainbow", 1995), books, cosmetics (Dunn, 1992), and apparel (Kissel, 1993). Whereas ethnicity may affect preferences, there are still differences within the group. A member may not identify closely with the ethnic group, diminishing the effect ethnicity has on preferences of the individual (Deshpande, Hoyer & Donthu, 1986). Reading 4.5 and Figure 4.8 provide examples of aesthetic preferences influenced by ethnicity. An African-American aesthetic is defined from the perspective of African-American women and underlying socio-cultural influences are presented.

### Sexual Orientation

Sexual orientation may be defined as an individual difference, but may also be considered the basis for a socio-cultural group (Freitas, Kaiser & Hammidi, in press). Sexual orientation, as with other socio-cultural factors, is perceived to define groups set apart from each other by their distinctive cultures. Sexual orientation may influence aesthetic preferences for certain apparel products and fragrances (Reading 4.6 discusses preferences of homosexual males). These aesthetic preferences may be due, in part, to the function appearance plays in interactions among homosexual men (Freitas, et al., in press). More work is needed in defining the homosexual market, because there are diverse variations within this group.

## INDIVIDUAL DIFFERENCES WITHIN CONSUMERS AND AESTHETIC PREFERENCES

Age, body image and body features, gender, level of art training or education, and personality are differences within consumers that affect aesthetic preferences. Such individual differences are particularly important when dealing one-on-one with a customer. These characteristics, considered demographic and psychographic variables, may be included in *marketing profiles* of consumers used in development and promotion of products. To develop a **market profile,** information about characteristics of consumers for a particular product or brand is gathered. Then underlying similarities of the characteristics are identified to create a consumer profile of the "typical" customer for the product or brand. Reading 4.7 provides an example of how the consumer profile is developed and implemented to sell a product offering aesthetic value. A promotional environment is created through advertising to reinforce the aesthetic value of the product.

### Age

Age has an effect on taste or preferences for many aesthetic products including music (Holbrook & Schindler, 1989), fragrance (Furukawa, 1995; "H & R Book," 1984), and visual appearance including apparel (Schindler & Holbrook, 1993) in Western culture. Age also has an effect on aesthetic preferences in non-Western cultures (e.g., textiles; Littrell, 1980).

Development of personal taste does not progress at an even pace throughout life. Instead, enduring tastes are formed in a critical period in a consumer's life. Taste for certain aesthetic forms is developed early in life and may influence preferences for a lifetime. Preferences towards popular music formed around age twenty-four will become the type of music preferred into old age (Holbrook & Schindler, 1989). Luckily, enduring preferences for personal appearance are formed later, around the age of 41 (Schindler & Holbrook, 1993). It's odd enough envisioning present day students turning seventy and rocking (pun intended) to current musical preferences such as Megadeth and Whitesnake without the added image of these seventy-year-old women wearing Doc Martens

**ACTIVITY 4.3** Before you come to class, collect information about preferences from people in various age groups. Your instructor may make this a group survey project where the group will select respondents from various locations on campus (e.g., entrance to the university library, campus cafeteria, campus administrative offices) at different times of the day. Respondents may also come from friends or relatives.

1. Each student or group needs to ask one person in the following age groups about their favorite musical group or band, fragrance (cologne or perfume), clothing brand or designer, car model, and movie star. Fill in the following chart:

| *Age* | *Music* | *Fragrance* | *Clothing brand* | *Car model* | *Movie star* |
|---|---|---|---|---|---|
| 31–35 | | | | | |
| 36–40 | | | | | |
| 41–45 | | | | | |
| 46–50 | | | | | |
| 51–55 | | | | | |
| 56–60 | | | | | |
| 61–65 | | | | | |
| 66–70 | | | | | |
| 71–75 | | | | | |

2. Once the survey is complete combine the information for each age group as a class.
3. Are there similarities within the responses for an age group?
4. Have preferences endured over the years for the age group? Explain why or why not.

boots and miniskirts. Activity 4.3 will let you examine whether preferences are formed early in life and endure over the years.

## Body Image and Body Features

**Body image** is the mental perception of one's body. Body image may influence general desire for aesthetic products. How people experience their bodies affects their pursuit of beauty and, consequently, their desire for products and services to enhance the body (Domzal & Kernan, 1993). An individual may formulate specific aesthetic preferences based upon their particular body features and perceptions of the body.

General experience of the body may be broken down into four types: disciplined body, particularizing body, communicative body, and mirroring body

(Domzal & Kernan, 1993). The disciplined body type is controlled, commonly through careful dieting and exercising. The disciplined body must be kept pure, so adorning it and dressing it in fashion are seen as inappropriate. This belief leads to negative evaluation and non-use of beauty products and services. The particularizing body is seen as an instrument to be used for social purposes, such as attracting a mate, acquiring a job, or winning peer approval. The particularizing body type uses grooming aids and apparel for these instrumental purposes. The communicative body is a set of symbols for the sake of aesthetic expression. The body is used to attract attention, to make a statement about oneself, or to convey an impression. The particularizing body and the communicative body are similar in their focus on the body as a symbol. However, the communicative body focuses on the non-instrumental nature of the experience. The communicative body sees the symbol as an accurate expression of the real person whereas the particularizing body sees the symbol as a sign of the desired role or status. The communicative body type constitutes a good market for attraction-enhancing products such as apparel, cosmetics, and jewelry. The mirroring body emphasizes formal embellishment and is in love with itself. The mirroring body type searches for products and services that make her or him glamorous, alluring, charming, fascinating, and beguiling. The body exists in order to be decorated, supporting the sale of a plethora of beauty products and services. Take a minute to determine which of the values discussed in Chapter 3 would be most important to the different "body types" described here.

Consumers may have troublesome physical body features, considered "special needs." These body features may affect their aesthetic preferences and functional needs for textile and apparel products. Reading 4.8 shows that while a body form may not be perceived as the ideal, it should not be assumed that the consumer is any less interested in the aesthetic appeal of appearance and the effect products have on enhancing appearance. Body features do, however, dictate the design features preferred by the consumer. This requires that the apparel professional must uncover the specific preferences of consumers with special needs.

### Gender

Female consumers may prefer particular aesthetic products that do not appeal to male consumers, and vice versa. Reading 4.7 shows that gender has an effect on the aesthetic preferences of consumers. The reading also discusses how symbolic qualities of the environment are developed in advertisements to intensify the aesthetic value of the product. Formal qualities of the environment should also be targeted towards a particular gender because these qualities may be perceived differently by females and males. For instance, loud music used as part of the environment in advertisements and in retail stores may have a negative effect on female consumers, who prefer softer volumes (Kellaris & Rice, 1993).

Differences in aesthetic preferences due to gender are readily apparent when walking through a department store (Figure 4.9). The store is divided into departments based on gender of the consumer. Aesthetic differences may be perceived between the products and environment of the "female" departments

a

b

Figure 4.9. Men's (a) and women's (b) departments of a retail store that shows variation in aesthetic preference by gender. Textures, colors, and shapes of the products and environment vary between the women's and men's departments.

(a): Bloomingdale's, Mall of America, Minneapolis, MN; photo by Dan DuBroff. (b): Marshall Field, State Street, Chicago, IL; FRCH Worldwide.

versus those found in the "male" departments. Perception of the same product may vary by gender. Women and men differ in their evaluations of images of apparel on the body (DeLong, Salusso-Deonier & Larntz, 1983). However, women and men are similar in the level of importance placed on aesthetic aspects of apparel. **Fashion risk** is defined as "the fear that a product will be unsatisfactory aesthetically or perhaps cause humiliation" (Winakor, Canton & Wolins, 1980, p. 46). Women and men have been found to have similar levels of fashion risk of apparel (Lubner-Rupert & Winakor, 1985). Both women and men are concerned that the apparel product should be aesthetically satisfying and not cause social humiliation. Women and men are also similar in their aesthetic judgments about silhouettes of female body forms (Douty & Brannon, 1984).

## Level of Training

In general, formal training in the arts raises the level of complexity an individual finds pleasing (Child, 1981). Trained individuals judge dynamic, complex elements, and innovative materials as pleasing (Purcell, 1984). Other studies corroborated these findings; trained individuals prefer complex visual figures over simpler figures significantly more than untrained individuals (McWhinnie, 1971). Trained individuals associate beauty and pleasure with complexity, power, and "interestingness" (Biaggio & Supplee, 1983). The positive connection between level of training and increased preference for complex forms applies to music (Burke & Gridley, 1990; Jones, 1991) as well as visual forms (e.g., Purcell, 1984), including apparel (Sailor, 1971). This connection between training and preferences for complexity may guide creation of environments. For example, a more complex environment may be appropriate if selling products to an upscale, educated consumer.

Training in textiles and apparel enhances perception and preferences of formal qualities of the product. Training affects analytical abilities (DeLong, 1977) including the ability to recall design lines in clothing (Baer, 1979). Those trained in textiles and clothing preferred style lines that created illusionary effects, such as two shorter separate lines creating a longer continuous line across parts of an ensemble (Sailor, 1971). Apparel professionals may be more sensitive than untrained consumers to the formal qualities of the product resulting in differences in preferences. However, advertisements, catalog copy, and wardrobe consulting may be effective tools in training the consumer to become more sensitive to aesthetic qualities by pointing out the aesthetic appeal of the product.

## Personality and Mood

**Personality** refers to the stable disposition or temperament of an individual, affecting behavior patterns. For instance, a person with an outgoing personality is more likely than a shy person to interact in a social setting. **Mood** is a more temporary disposition, also affecting behavior. Personality and mood have been shown to affect preference of aesthetic stimuli.

As discussed in Chapter 1, stimulating the senses is one of the ways to bring about the pleasure of aesthetic experience. This stimulation or arousal comes from novelty, complexity, variability, and intensity (Mehrabian & Russell, 1973) of the product or environment. For instance, red is seen as having the highest intensity of all colors (Berlyne, 1971). The *level* of stimulation needed to bring about pleasure is affected by personality and mood. High stimulation-seeking personalities prefer the color red, whereas the color blue is preferred by low stimulation-seeking personalities (Nelson, Pelech & Foster, 1984). Preferences for high arousal colors have been associated with other personality traits such as extroversion (Eysenck, 1981) and risk-taking (Nelson, Pelech & Foster, 1984). Preferences for high arousal colors have also been associated with mood. Preference for a high potential arousal stimuli (i.e., the color red) was found for those in a positive (high energetic arousal) mood versus those in a negative (high tense arousal) mood (Crane & Hicks, 1989). In terms of environments, high arousal seeking individuals seek out, explore, remain in, and prefer highly stimulating environments (Mehrabian & Russell, 1973; Raju, 1980).

Personality not only influences aesthetic response towards formal aspects, it also influences aesthetic preferences for expressive and symbolic content. There were similarities between expressive content of a painting and the ideal and the real personality attributes of the appreciator (Alexander & Marks, 1983). For example, the appreciator who enjoyed abstract expressionist paintings tended to be uninhibited, emotional, and imaginative. The strength of an individual's beliefs influences aesthetic preferences for symbolic content. Dogmatic persons, who cling to an established belief system, reject aesthetic objects that do not fit a preconceived ideal of pleasing content (Lee, 1987).

Personality affects preference of consumer products. For instance, level of stimulation-seeking and emotional stability affect preference for fragrance notes (Mensing & Beck, 1988). Figure 4.10 shows a personality based chart developed for use with female consumers. The chart is used to identify the type of fragrance note preferred through selection of preferred colored patterns, both found to be associated with certain personality traits (level of stimulation-seeking and emotional stability).

Another personality trait, self-monitoring, was found to significantly affect preference for furniture styles (Thompson & Davis, 1988). Self-monitoring is the awareness and control of one's public behaviors in response to situations. High self-monitors rated the importance of furniture characteristics such as beauty, attractiveness, distinctiveness, and "stylishness" higher than did low self-monitors. Lastly, gender consciousness is associated with fashion consciousness. Men who are more fashion conscious are higher in private gender-consciousness (inward consciousness of being a man or masculine). Women who are most fashion conscious tend to have higher levels of public self-consciousness (focus on themselves as public objects) (Gould & Stern, 1989).

Identifying (aesthetic) preferences is difficult because these preferences are affected by the multi-layered factors of socio-cultural and personal context. However, development, selection, and promotion of products have been helped greatly by understanding the socio-cultural and individual differences of the consumer.

## SUMMARY

Aesthetic evaluation, and its affect on consumer decisions, is not solely due to the product; it is a combination of product qualities and characteristics of the individual. An **egocentric view** of the world is when one evaluates all things from a personal point of view. Apparel professionals must move away from an egocentric view when determining a consumer's aesthetic preferences, because socio-cultural and personal experiences affect evaluation of or preference for a product or environment's aesthetic qualities. The present chapter discussed how characteristics of the *individual* affect aesthetic evaluation or preference. Socio-cultural differences *across cultures* affect how aesthetic experience is defined, including whether the formal, expressive, or symbolic aspect of the product is most important in aesthetic evaluation. Preferences for specific aesthetic qualities are influenced by differences among cultures.

Socio-cultural differences *within a culture* also affect aesthetic preferences. Socio-cultural differences include geographic location, ethnicity, religion, and sexual orientation. Retailers are successfully using differences in these socio-cultural factors to "micro-market", or tailor merchandise in individual stores to the (aesthetic) preferences of its patrons.

Age, body image and body features, gender, level of art training or education, and personality are differences *within consumers* that affect aesthetic

## LAB ACTIVITY 4.1

This activity will involve group participation spread out over a few class periods. A group of students will work together as a team of product developers and marketers. The assignment is designed to give you an opportunity to "develop" a line of products considering a specific consumer market.

1. Form a group of four or five students.
2. As a group, define a consumer group incorporating the socio-cultural and personal factors discussed in the chapter and any others you might think important. This group should reflect actual individuals your group will be able to interview about their preferences. Campus groups (e.g., international student groups, gay and lesbian groups, adult student groups, or service groups with connections to children or the elderly) may provide a starting point for consumer groups. Each team should define a different consumer group.
3. The team must decide how to divide the responsibilities for "developing" the products and for surveying the market. The responsibilities are divided this way: product developers will collect information about preferences of the consumer group, select visual or actual examples of products, and suggest changes to the products based upon the market information of preferences. Marketer will develop questions and gather and summarize information from actual individuals about their evaluation of the products.
4. All teams should use tops (e.g., blouses, dress shirts, sports tops) as the product category to be developed.
5. Gather information about preferences of the consumer group. The product developers may gather information from a variety of sources, including photos or articles from magazines or catalogs aimed at the group, articles in the popular press or trade magazines, actual products worn by members of the consumer group in the area, or information from sales consultants familiar with the consumer group.
6. Select five examples of tops that the team's product developers feel would appeal to the consumer group. These could be actual products, flats created by the developers, or color copies of visual images from magazines, trade publications, or catalogs. They should be in color.
7. The marketers should develop a line of questions to get to the consumers' evaluations of the five product samples. These questions should not only tap their liking of the product, but also identify the aesthetic features they would prefer.
8. The marketers should use the line of questions and samples to survey at least five consumers fitting the profile identified by the team.
9. Marketers should summarize the information about their consumer group.
10. The team should use the information to make changes to the products. These changes may be visually represented through drawings, new visual examples from print media, and/ or fabric swatches.
11. Describe the process undertaken by the team: identify the consumer group, discuss the initial consumer research sources and conclusions, show the original product samples, discuss why the team selected the original samples for the consumer group, summarize the questions and responses of consumers, display the redesigned products, and outline the changes made.
12. As a class, compare the products developed to meet the preferences of the various consumer groups. What are the major differences in preferences among groups?

preferences. Individual differences within consumers are important when dealing one-on-one with a customer. These characteristics, considered demographic and psychographic variables, are also included in marketing profiles of consumers used in the development and promotion of products offering aesthetic value.

## KEY TERMS AND CONCEPTS

- aesthetic evaluation
- aesthetic preference
- body image
- egocentric view
- fashion risk
- individual differences affecting aesthetic preference
- market profile
- micro-marketing
- modern socio-cultural context
- modern versus post modern appearances
- post modern socio-cultural context
- socio-cultural factors affecting aesthetic preference
- zeitgeist

## SUGGESTED READINGS


Dunn, W. (1992, July). The move toward ethnic marketing. *Nation's Business,* pp. 39–41.

Furukawa, T. (1995, October 6). Lighter fragrances, looser import rules spark sales in Japan. *Women's Wear Daily,* pp. 1, 4.

Henderson, B. (1994). Teaching aesthetics in a postmodern environment. In M. R. DeLong & A. M. Fiore (Eds.), *Aesthetics of textiles and clothing: Advancing multi-disciplinary perspectives* (pp. 39–47). ITAA Special Publication #7. Monument, Co: International Textiles and Apparel Association.

Kaiser, S. B. (1990, July). Fashion as popular culture: The postmodern self in the global fashion marketplace. *The World and I, 5*(7), 521-529.


### For Advanced Levels


Coote, J. & Shelton, A. (Eds.). (1992). Oxford studies in the anthropology of cultural forms. New York, NY: Clarendon Press.

Deshpande, R., Hoyer, W. D. & Donthu, N. (1986). The intensity of ethnic affiliation: A study of the sociology of Hispanic consumption. *Journal of Consumer Research, 13,* 214–220.

Morgado, M. A., (1996). Coming to terms with *Postmodern:* Theories and concepts of contemporary culture and their implications for apparel scholars. *Clothing and Textiles Research Journal 14*(1), 41-53.

Venkatraman, M. P. & MacInnis, D. J. (1985). The epistemic and sensory exploratory behavior of hedonic and cognitive consumers. *Advances in Consumer Research, 12,* 102–107.

# READING 4.1
## BAT Shows Potential of Plus-size Fashions

Nicole Simon

**Las Vegas**—The plus-size market is stepping up to the fashion plate.

A market that has traditionally offered customers low-priced goods with little, if any, reflection of current trends has evolved into a more fashionable source of better-priced goods.

Manufacturers at the eleventh Big and Tall Woman show at the Tropicana Hotel here said there is rising potential in plus sizes, with more specialty stores catering to large women. Consequently, more markets are focusing on niches in this market, like super-size apparel, from size 26 up.

Buyers at the show, which was held October 9–11, spoke enthusiastically about the number of new vendors and fashion options.

Betty Floura, an owner and designer of first-time exhibitor Coco & Juan, Los Angeles, said BAT had good exposure to new plus-size stores.

"Buyers were there to write orders, and it showed," she said. "We opened new accounts and increased business by 5 percent."

PFI, a Genoa City, Wisconsin, company that has been exhibiting at this event since its inception six years ago, reported its best show ever with a 75 percent increase in business over last year's show.

Cello, of Santa Monica, California, showed its line of skirts and novelty T-shirts for the first time and said it exceeded $30,000 in orders.

"The [plus size] industry is growing as the emphasis in America switches from dieting to accepting who you are," according to Liria Mersini, owner and designer of Cello. "And manufacturers need to understand the market before breaking into it."

"As a plus-size woman, I am perceived by manufacturers, buyers and the fashion industry as a whole as having no taste," said Mersini. "And that message is being sent to plus-size consumers by what buyers are bringing into their stores. Buyers are beginning to believe in our products. And that's a start."

She added that women want fashion options that fit, which is a key issue.

While some manufacturers think making plus-size garments means adding fabric, industry veterans argue that simply isn't true.

"Designers can't just add fabric to make a garment plus size," said Pat Hink, merchandise manager of the plus-size line at Denver-based Rocky Mountain Clothing Co. "We have built our reputation on fit, and it has nothing to do with whether our customer is junior or misses' size. It's not about age. It's about body shape."

The company offers four different fits in its jeans.

Lin Anderson, owner of More to Hug Fashions, a two-store chain in California's San Fernando Valley, concurred.

"There are too many misses' manufacturers entering the market," she explained, "and they just can't add fabric to compensate for size."

She admitted that she has been "burned" by manufacturers whose fit didn't measure up. Now, if a manufacturer can't provide line specs, Anderson doesn't buy.

Coco & Juan's Floura added: "The plus-size customer wants fashion, but some buyers have the mentality that plus-size women only want certain things, like big, bold prints. But that's just not true. She wants everything that is available to her peers in other markets, but she wants it to fit. Stores need to offer more fashion, every season."

Price is another key issue in the plus-size market.

Judith Mastera, owner and designer for Shane Lee, Murray, Kentucky, said retailers are pressuring makers for lower prices. She said 15 to 20 percent of its business is in large sizes.

"I find it difficult to make a quality garment that requires double the fabric at low prices," Mastera says. As a result, she sells to better department and specialty stores.

Reading 4.1 Simon, N., BAT Shows Potential of Plus-size Fashion. (1995, October 26). *WWD*, p. 14.

Some key items at the show included dresses; long bias-cut skirts in satin, printed satin, rayon crepe and distressed rayon georgette; double-layer floral georgette separates in taupe and smoke combinations, and drapable rayon separates in solids and prints.

Most specialty store buyers were upbeat about business.

Anderson of More to Hug spent $21,000 at this show and increased her open-to-buy by 25 percent. Crediting it as "the best show I've attended," she bought cotton dresses for spring, swim coverups, novelty items, sportswear, and lingerie.

Eliza Baker-Folk, owner of Eliza, a plus-size specialty boutique in Denver, increased her budget 50 percent.

"Prices were good and the quality was there. This show was better than the last two," said Baker-Folk, adding that she was happy to see more upscale manufacturers. She purchased specialty items like wide-calf boots, lingerie, and leathers.

Bill and Jill Ramage began JW Ramage, a catalog for plus-size women, about a year ago. Bill Ramage said the company began by sending 50,000 catalogs in the fall and spring. This spring, that will increase to 250,000 and he said he hopes to increase circulation to four times a year. The book includes lingerie, activewear, swimwear, dresses, and sportswear. Ramage increased his open-to-buy by 25 percent.

## READING 4.2

## Socio-cultural Influences Upon Aesthetic Preferences of Indigenous Guatemalan Women

J. Moreno

The indigenous men and women of the Central American country of Guatemala have long roots entwined with textile production that are reflected in contemporary dress. Referred to as indigenous or natives, these people are contemporary descendants from the Mayan civilization that flourished in what is now Southern Mexico and Guatemala from 250–900 A.D. (Altman & West, 1994). Since the sixteenth century, the indigenous people of Guatemala have made many adjustments with the onslaught of the Spanish who conquered them and their land at that time. Indigenous people are estimated to comprise approximately half of Guatemala's nine million inhabitants.

Many aesthetic preferences in indigenous dress today have pre-Spanish origins or have been garnered and translated from early Spanish forms. Indigenous female dress has remained relatively unchanged in form as compared to indigenous male attire which has practically been abandoned in favor of Western European dress. Called "traje" in Spanish, traditional costume for women is especially reflective of past and contemporary socio-cultural influences.

Formal aspects of female costume have strong ties to pre-Spanish forms such as the dominant use of rectangular garments straight from the loom that can be easily adjusted to accommodate a female's body (photo, top left). Blouses are often sleeveless and made from one to three rectangles or panels. Skirts are also rectangularly shaped and may or may not be sewn into a tube and wrapped tightly around the torso to be held in place with a long sash of varying widths. Indigenous women regularly use hair ribbons to construct elaborate coiffures from the wrapping or tucking of the ribbons around the wearer's head. Finally, a utility cloth or a shawl may be used to guard against the cold and to carry bundles or even children! Some indigenous women in Guatemala do wear more European tailored clothing such as blouses with sleeves and collars and skirts gathered on to waistbands, but the pre-Spanish forms are preferred to be worn when possible.

Reading 4.2 Moreno, J. (1995). Socio-cultural Influence Upon Aesthetic Preferences of Indigenous Guatemalan Women. Written by Moreno for this textbook.

(left) A Guatemalan weaver in Antiqua wearing traditional blouse and skirt styles made from simple rectangular pieces of fabric, similar to that being woven (right), featuring prominent symbolism, intense colors, embroidery, and patterned weaves.

Photos by Mary Littrell.

Additionally, color is an important component of traje in Guatemala. Intense, saturated colors dominate color palettes and background colors of white, red, and indigo are common with elaboration or decoration often using potent golds, greens, and purples (Altman & West, 1992). The importance of the color red is particularly salient as expressed by the Nobel Laureate, Rigoberta Menchu herself an indigenous woman of Guatemala,

> Red is very significant to us. It means heat, strength, all living things. It's linked to the sun, which for us is the channel to the one god, the heart of everything, of the universe. So red gives off heat and fire and red things are supposed to give life to the child. At the same time, it asks him to respect living things too. (Menchu, 1983, p.14).

Even with the introduction of brilliant acrylic and metallic yarns today, preferred color palettes have centered around saturated or luminescent colors ignoring the soft hues preferred in other countries. It is possible that preference for brilliant colors could be related to the historic use of brilliant natural dyes such as cochineal or how bright colors naturally complement the dark skin tones and hair colors of indigenous Guatemalan women.

Symbolic representation in female dress is common in both secular and religious forms. The use of not only clothing forms, but motifs and color combinations can be village specific identifying the wearer as belonging to a particular village, age group, marital status, and social class. Creativity in women's costume is confined within the boundaries of tradition with some variation allowed and the use of identifying marks (signatures if you will) woven into the design of a textile object (Adams, 1993). The continuance of village specific dress is said to have developed after the arrival of the Spanish (Altman & West, 1992).

Religious symbolism is inherent in dress through the use of particular design motifs and color combinations. The importance of weaving in religious beliefs of contemporary Maya continues today. Textile objects are important components of many festivals and life events such as births, weddings, and funerals (Altman & West, 1992). Certain motifs are particularly representative of Maya mythology and carry religious significance as to one's ancestors and role in the natural universe. Prominent symbols may include the sun and moon, the tree of life, a serpent, or a heavenly bird (photo, top right) (Altman & West, 1992). Additionally, female participation in religious brotherhoods is marked by the wearing of precise dress elements (e.g., item, motifs, colors) that symbolize devout membership and participation. Religious brotherhoods are comprised of indigenous men and women in Guatemala who have dedicated themselves to the care of a particular saint for, at times, more than a year (Asturias, 1985). Cofradia membership imparts a certain level of prestige and status upon cofradia members within indigenous communities.

Guatemalans wearing elements of traditional and Western dress.

Photo by Mary Littrell.

Present day socio-cultural changes in dress have affected how females wear traje; some of the changes are due to economic restrictions, recent civil war, personal preference, and the impingement of the outside world into once remote villages. Presently, more women are opting to wear dress elements from other villages and items made by machine rather than hand woven items because of the high cost to make or buy one's village specific costume. Also, recent civil war has forced the abandonment of traje for Western European dress so as not to identify oneself as belonging to a targeted village. Increasingly, young indigenous women in Guatemala are also choosing to wear traje from another village for solely personal preference of another's costume elements (Moreno, 1994). Finally, with the onslaught of world-wide travel, villagers in once remote areas in Guatemala are influenced by the wearing of Western clothing by travelers and visitors to their villages.

Contemporary indigenous women in Guatemala form their aesthetic preferences based on a synchronization of the past and present. While pre-Hispanic forms of dress have survived, post-conquest identification with a particular village also exists. Symbolic representations of both secular and religious factors play a prominent role in the selection of motifs, designs, and colors; yet, modern influences of the economics of production, political strife, personal preference, and global travel are influencing aesthetic components in dress for contemporary Maya.

## References


Adams, W.R. (1993). Mayan Indian weaving and its symbolism. In R.K. Jantzen, *Threads of life: Mayan clothing from Guatemala.* North Newton: Kauffman Museum.

Altman, P.B. & West, C.D. (1992). *Threads of Identity: Maya costume of the 1960s in Highland Guatemala.* Los Angeles: Regents of the University of California.

Asturias de Barrios, L. (1985). *Comalapa: Native dress and its significance.* Guatemala City, Guatemala: Ixchel Museum.

Menchu, R. (1983). *I Rigoberta Menchu: An Indian woman in Guatemala.* London: Verso.

Moreno, J.M. (1994). [Retailers as interpreters of textile traditions in Antigua, Guatemala]. Unpublished field notes.

# READING 4.3
# Chinese Aesthetics of Human Appearance

C. Cheng

Western (e.g., American) and Eastern (e.g., Chinese) cultures have different life styles, sex roles, religions, ideals, social customs, values, forms of government, and economics (Hsu, 1981). Differences between Western and the Eastern cultures can also be observed in art and fashion (Rowland, 1964; Sullivan 1989). Western art and fashion tend to attach more importance to object, form, or shape, while Eastern art and fashion tend to attribute more importance to modesty, moral principles, and ethics (Sullivan, 1989). Zehou (1991) indicated that "Chinese aesthetics, like Chinese philosophy, stresses not cognition or imitation, but emotion and experience. So the Chinese pay less attention to the object and substance and more to function, relationship and rhythm" (p.74).

Chinese art has rarely focused on the organic or athletic nature of the body as an object of physical loveliness (Rowland, 1964). Differences in perceptions of art between Western and Eastern cultures appears to influence perceptions of physical beauty between American and Chinese/Taiwanese college students (Cheng, 1994). Chinese/Taiwanese males and females tend to pay more attention to functional body items (e.g., reflexes, agility, and stamina) when determining both males' and females' physical attractiveness, whereas American males and females attribute more importance to the object parts (e.g., face, chest, legs, waist). Similarly, Eastern females attributed more importance to psychological traits (intelligence, kindness, confidence, etc.), whereas Western females place more importance on physical traits (e.g., eyes, hair, height, etc.) when judging males' physical attractiveness (Thakerar & Iwawaki, 1979).

## Chinese Aesthetic Concepts and Traditional Chinese Costume

Chinese aesthetics has an impact on the illustration of Chinese traditional costume. Western illustrations of women and costumes use lines and shapes to represent the three-dimensional nature of the object. Compared to this sculptural illustration of women and costume, Chinese illustrations stress vivacity, life and rhythm. Lines stress the continuous movement of the body or costume. Lines of the costume do not only contribute to formal pleasure but also express the inner beauty of emotion and spirit. The most important element for a successful illustration of Chinese traditional costume is expressing Chinese aspects including ch'i (the vital spirit or psychic energy), harmony, liveliness, and movement. Physical posture showing the direction of movement of the head, hands, and legs is very important in the expression of Chinese aesthetics of clothing. In addition to physical posture, lines are an important ingredient, because lines are the fundamental component of Chinese painting and calligraphy (Figure A). Successful lines reflect the rhythm and continuous ch'i inside the body to achieve the state of total harmony. Actual garment details such as broad sleeve and ribbon (Figure B) may create a rhythm of movement when walking or dancing.

Chinese aesthetics also affects the construction of traditional Chinese costume. Unlike the contouring of the body through construction methods found in Western costume (e.g., seaming, corsets, and bustles), traditional Chinese costume uses broad and flattened shapes. For thousands of years, traditional Chinese costume remained a flattened T-shape, disregarding the contour of the body beneath. Embroidered edging, decorated bands, embellishment on the shoulders, and sashes were often added as ornamentation to the relatively plain layout structure (Figure C).

The Ch'i-P'ao, a modified form of a traditional Ch'ing Dynasty fashion, is still considered representative of Chinese women's traditional dress. This garment was originally a flattened T-shape. However, during 1910s to 1930s, Western culture had an influence on Chinese costume. By 1925, the Ch'i-P'ao became a fitted sheath with slits on both

Reading 4.3 Cheng, C. (1995). Chinese Aesthetics of Human Appearance. Written by Cheng for this textbook.

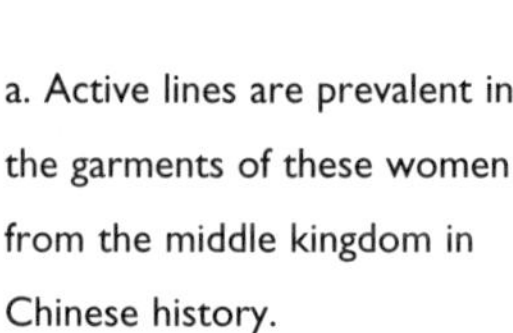

a. Active lines are prevalent in the garments of these women from the middle kingdom in Chinese history.

b. Traditional Chinese costumes with long flowing sleeves and ribbons.

a

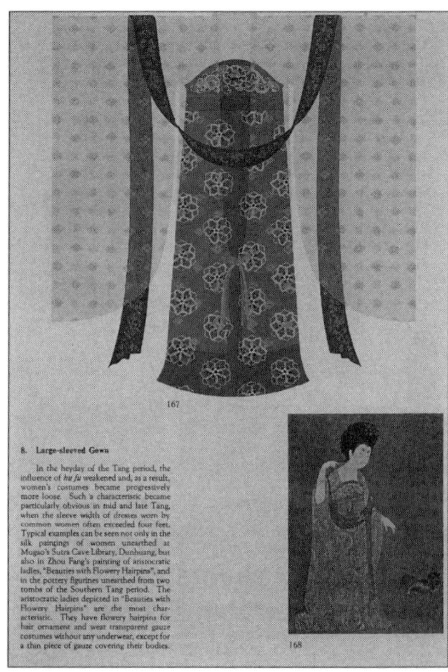

167

**8. Large-sleeved Gown**

In the heyday of the Tang period, the influence of *hu fu* weakened and, as a result, women's costumes became progressively more loose. Such a characteristic became particularly obvious in mid and late Tang, when the sleeve width of dresses worn by common women often exceeded four feet. Typical examples can be seen not only in the silk paintings of women unearthed at Mogao's Sutra Cave Library, Dunhuang, but also in Zhou Fang's painting of aristocratic ladies, "Beauties with Flowery Hairpins", and in the pottery figurines unearthed from two tombs of the Southern Tang period. The aristocratic ladies depicted in "Beauties with Flowery Hairpins" are the most characteristic. They have flowery hairpins for hair ornament and wear transparent gauze costumes without any underwear, except for a thin piece of gauze covering their bodies.

168

b

sides and an opening on the right side or both sides. After the World War II, the Ch'i-P'ao began to closely follow Western fashion. Fashion designers today in Taiwan find new ways to freely combine modern fashion trends with traditional Chinese symbols, motifs, patterns, constructions, colors, and materials. Most fashion designers today concentrate on modernizing traditional Chinese styles to represent the new perspectives of Chinese aesthetics (Figure C).

## Contemporary Chinese Consumer Behaviors

The raise of global communication in the 20th century has imposed more uniform standards of both fashion and physical beauty through the world than existed in earlier times (Mazur, 1986). Global communications has resulted in a preference for Western standards (Berscheid & Walster, 1974; Gitter, Lomranz, Saxe & Bar-Tai, 1983). However, variations still exist in aesthetic preferences and definition of beauty among diverse cultures. When considering color preference for leisure wear, Taiwanese subjects preferred bright colors, while U.S. subjects preferred dark colors (Hsiao & Dickerson, 1994). Cultural difference may be retained when immigrating to another country. Comparing Americans and Chinese-Americans residing in the United States, cultural differences in beliefs and values (Feldman & Rosenthal, 1990) and apparel shopping orientations (Ho, 1991) still existed between these two cultural groups. Values related to responsibility to family, the interdependence of family members, and conformity to rules of good behavior were the most important for those from the Chinese culture, whereas values related to needs, rights, and achievements of individual were more important for U.S. culture (Feldman & Rosenthal, 1990) Consumer research should examine the effect these values have on differences in aesthetic preferences for apparel.

## References


Berscheid, E. & Walster, E. (1974). Physical attractiveness. In L. Berkowitz (Ed.), *Advances in experimental social psychology* (pp. 158–215). New York: Academic Press.

Cheng, C. (1994). *Perceptions of physical attractiveness: A comparison of American and Chinese college students.* Unpublished master's thesis. Utah State University, Logan.

Feldman, S.S. & Rosenthal, D.A. (1990). The acculturation of autonomy expectations in Chinese high schoolers residing in two Western nations. *International Journal of Psychology, 25,* 259–281.

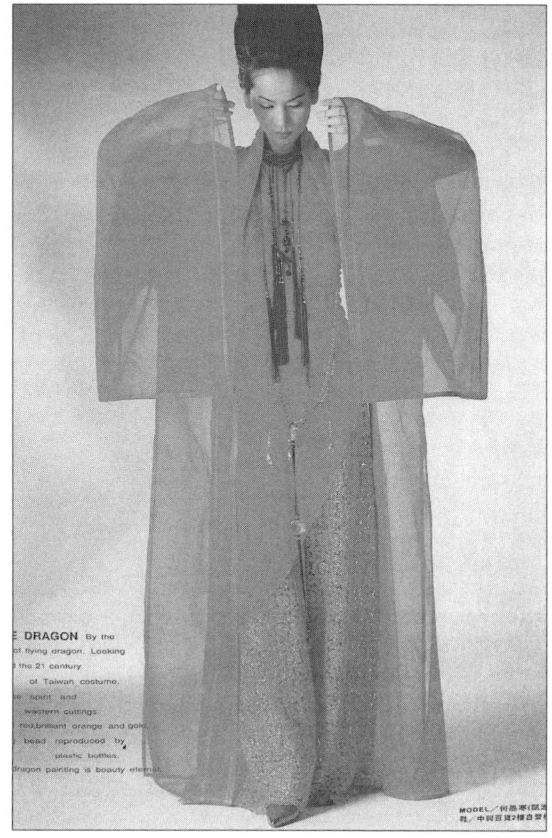


c

c. An example of contemporary fashion from Taiwan illustrating the influence of traditional Chinese costume. The aesthetic has evolved into a more modern interpretation.

Gitter, A.G., Lomranz, J., Saxe, L. & Bar-Tai, Y. (1983). Perceptions of female physique characteristics by American and Israeli students. *Journal of Social Psychology, 121,* 7–13.

Ho, S.A. (1991). *A comparative study of apparel shopping orientations between Asian-Americans and Anglo-Americans.* Unpublished master's thesis, Oregon State University, Corvallis.

Hsiao, C. & Dickerson, K. (1994). Taiwanese and U.S. students in a U.S. university: evaluative criteria for purchasing leisure wear. *International Textiles and Apparel Association Proceedings,* 59. Monument: ITAA.

Hsu, F.L.K. (1981). *Americans and Chinese: Passage to differences.* Honolulu: The University Press of Hawaii.

Mazur, A. (1986). U.S. trends in feminine beauty and overadaptation. Journal of Sex Research, 22, 281–303.

Rowland, B. (1964). *Art in East and West: An introduction through comparison.* Boston: Beacon Press.

Sullivan, M. (1989). *The meeting of Eastern and Western art.* Los Angeles: University of California Press.

Thakerar, J.N. & Iwawaki, S. (1979). Cross-cultural comparisons in interpersonal attraction of females toward males. *Journal of Social Psychology, 108,* 121–122.

Zehou, L. (1991). *The path of beauty: A study of Chinese aesthetics.* Beijing: Morning Glory Publishers.

## READING 4.4

# Different Strokes: Target 'Micromarkets' Its Way to Success

G. A. Patterson

**Phoenix**—Shoppers searching for such diverse goods as religious candles, bicycle trailers, and portable heaters need only visit a local Target store.

But there's a hitch: The Target store on Phoenix's eastern edge sells prayer candles, but no child-toting bicycle trailers. The Target fifteen minutes away in affluent Scottsdale, Arizona, sells the trailers but no portable heaters; those can be found twenty minutes south in Mesa.

Confusing? Perhaps, but it makes perfect sense to Target, the 623-store discount chain owned by Minneapolis-based Dayton Hudson Corp. Target is a master at what retailers call "micromarketing"—a consumer-driven, technology-packed strategy to tailor merchandise in each store to the preferences of its patrons. It is a big reason that Target is growing rapidly even as things slow for its top competitors.

America has more racial, ethnic and lifestyle diversity than ever, and micromarketing aims to satisfy the resulting panoply of consumer preferences. It used to be that U.S. consumers, no matter their origins, gravitated toward a mid-American monolith, says John Costello, senior executive vice president of Sears, Roebuck & Co. Not anymore. These days, he says, "Consumers are interested in preserving their culture."

### Powerful Advantage

What's more, micromarketing allows retailers to stand out in an increasingly crowded marketplace. After crushing smaller competitors with lower prices, big retailers like Target and Wal-Mart Stores Inc. now are using micromarketing to battle each other.

"I can't think of a more powerful advantage," Target President Ken Woodrow says of the company's micromarketing.

Under Mr. Woodrow, Target has spent millions of dollars on the sophisticated computer system needed to stock thousands of different items in each store. It has weaned its buyers off the notion that the best purchases are big purchases. And it has strong-armed sometimes reluctant vendors into providing Target with specialized merchandise to make its new strategy work.

Target's push into micromarketing seems to be working. Target last year recorded an impressive 7 percent same-store sales gain and an 11 percent boost in operating profit. And the sixty-five new stores Target plans to open this year far exceed any other chain, including rival Kmart Corp. and Wal-Mart.

### Leading a Pack

Though micromarketing isn't the sole source of Target's success—its sunny decor and smart clothing assortments also contribute—it is the one area where Target really stands out from its competitors. "Hardly any retailer is as far along with micromarketing as Target," says Chicago retail consultant Sid Doolittle.

Though ahead of the pack, Target isn't alone on the micromarketing path. Wal-Mart sells silky, first Communion dresses in stores that serve Hispanic communities. Many Nordstrom Inc. department-store buyers also work the selling floor to ferret out local tastes. Sears carries Essence brand hosiery, made in colors and sizes that are more appealing to African-American women, in stores with a large black clientele.

"Everybody is trying to crack the [micromarketing] code, particularly national retailers," says Robert Giampietro, the Target vice president who leads the effort. "It comes down to having the right merchandise in the right store at the right time."

### Some Reluctance

That is easier to say than to do. Kmart and Venture Stores Inc. have struggled with their respective micromarketing programs. Part of the problem is that Kmart, which still is wrestling with getting its basic marketing programs into shape, is reluctant to plunge whole-hearted into the more complicated world of micromarketing. "We try not to get caught in too many one-store projects," says Richard Pellino, Kmart's divisional vice president for women's wear.

Target's own micromarketing initiative was born out of embarrassment. In September

Reading 4.4 Patterson, G.A. (1995, May 31). Different Strokes: Target 'Micromarkets' Its Way to Success; No 2 Stores Are Alike. *Wall Street Journal*, pp. A1, A9.

1989, Target opened its first Florida stores while conducting a nationwide marketing effort with Wil Steger, the first person to cross Antarctica on dog sled.

That fall, Target's Florida stores brimmed with parkas, gloves, and sweaters. They didn't sell. And Target told Mr. Giampietro to start the micromarketing program.

Early efforts focused mainly on obvious climatic differences, things like keeping heavy coats out of Southern California and laying on the rain gear in Seattle.

After initial experiments succeeded, Target in 1992 began investing heavily in new computer equipment. And it began working with its buyers to get the new type of merchandise it needed. Some vendors resisted. Hallmark Cards Inc. and American Greetings Corp., Mr. Giampietro says, were slow to present Target with the black and Hispanic greeting cards and wrapping paper it sought. So, Target hooked up with another card supplier that could provide the merchandise. Some eighteen months later, the two big card companies brought out their own ethnic lines —and got back some of the Target business.

Target's micromarketing also faced internal hurdles. Buyers resisted micromarketing because they figured their success lay in making big, profitable deals yielding brisk sales through all the stores, and they eschewed buying smaller lots.

But the watershed event came from Target's success at selling team-logo athletic apparel in the same markets where their fans lived. That business grew from almost nothing in 1991 to $100 million last year, according to insiders. Now, the buying staff, "clearly understands why there is a need to do business this way," says Target spokeswoman Susan Eich.

Target requires its 150 Minneapolis-based buyers to visit the stores for which they buy as well as their competitors. Moreover, Target gives its stores the ability to add merchandise without gaining approval from buyers.

The other key to Target's success is a complex computer-driven combination of buying, planning, and store operations that works like a cafeteria. Buyers create merchandise assortments that fit the racial, ethnic, and age features of different clumps of customers. Then planners, treating each store the way a diner fills a lunch tray, match the merchandise to the community profile. Managers at the store level refine the model from what they know about local tastes and practices.

Target uses its flexible system to do things it couldn't before, such as display children's dolls in ninety-six variations—all depending on demand at individual stores.

The industry adage that "retail is detail" is ever more true in micromarketing. In practice, attending to details for Target means carrying local favorite Jays potato chips in Chicago but stocking Saguaro brand chips in Phoenix. It also means sending more one-piece bathing suits to its stores on Florida's western coast, where the crowd is older, while packing off extra bikinis to the younger patrons of the state's eastern stores.

The sum of different products carried in any of its stores is only 15 percent to 20 percent, but the mix is different in almost every store. Target's goal is to increase the proportion of goods contoured to local tastes to 30 percent, according to Bart Butzer, a regional manager. "Then we will truly be micromarketed," he says.

On top of all this, Target continually feeds actual sales and profit tallies for each square foot of space. Target uses the results in the battle among products for space on its shelves, a process called "space wars." Successful performance by hunting gear one month likely will lead to more space, and perhaps less for fishing equipment, if it lags.

Two Phoenix-area stores illuminate Target's approach. The Arcadia Crossing store in east Phoenix and the store five miles away in Scottsdale opened in the past eight months. They are the same size and have identical layouts. Health and beauty products, housewares, sporting-goods, and electronics line the outside walls, while apparel assortments take up the middle. Every worker wears a red shirt or blouse and khaki pants or skirt.

But a walk through the Scottsdale store with manager Ellie Bernards shows how differences among the two stores' patrons yields differences in their merchandise. Ms. Bernards makes one of her first stops in the sporting-goods department where both sides of a twenty-four-foot aisle are stacked nearly ten feet high with in-line skates and accessories. The merchandise sells briskly to Scottsdale's young, affluent families who have fifty miles of paved pedestrian paths nearby. The store in Phoenix—whose buyers have an average household income 42 percent below those of the Scottsdale store—carries only half as much skating merchandise.

## READING 4.5
# African-American Aesthetics of Dress

G. O'Neal

Historically, preferences for certain colors, styles, and forms of clothing and adornment that did not conform to dominant cultural values, were viewed as barbaric rather than aesthetic. It was thought that these expressions could not be deliberate aesthetic expressions, possessing intrinsic value or beauty. Such attitudes were based upon the notion that the aesthetic judgements of the dominant culture were only valid judgements of aesthetic taste. This attitude formed the basis for negative stereotypes of African Americans.

While an African-American aesthetic of dress is neither African or American, it is shaped by unique "cultural" experiences resulting from being of African descent and living in America. In the last several decades scholars (Asante, 1980; Hacker, 1992; Zirimu, 1973) have drawn attention to the fact that African Americans have been and continue to be a nation within a nation. "They have been a distinct society especially in their authentic creative work" (Zirimu, 1973:59). Thus, African Americans have come to define for themselves aesthetic value and worth.

An African-American aesthetic of dress reflects the basic nature of descendants of African people dispersed to the New World (Asante, 1980). The self definition of "African Americans" is believed to be derived from several cultural and philosophical premises shared with "tribes" from the coastal belt of West Africa and the Congo (Herskovits, 1970; Asante & Asante, 1990; Curtin, 1969; Holloway, 1990). While differences existed among the various tribes, there were underlying similarities in the "experiential community" of African peoples. A "collective consciousness" or spiritual disposition of oneness with nature and the importance of survival of one's people superseded "tribal" differences. In addition, individuals were believed to be made by the community and were thought to be a unique expression of a common spirit. Collins (1989) noted that unity or oneness with nature also meant collective kinship and individual expressiveness.

In an effort to give voice to African Americans in defining their aesthetic of dress, O'Neal (in press) interviewed African-American women and asked: "Is there an African-American aesthetic of dress?" and "If so, how might it be manifested?" She found that African-American aesthetic preferences are centered in African cultural modalities and are expressed in several ways: 1) Individual expression or "style"; 2) The notion of unity or oneness; 3) Preferences for fabric with improvisations or off-beat patterns, i.e., multiple rhythms; and 4) The vast use of "loud" or "high affect" colors. While these elements were expressed by the majority of the participants, they do not suggest an essentialist notion of such an aesthetic. One participant stated:

> [A]esthetic of expression is what I think is to be identified as African American. The spectrum of African America is going to explore every possible aesthetic. Just look at us, we are everything possible.

Individual expression or "style" was noted consistently by participants. This aesthetic expression refers to "the tradition of artfully embellishing movement, speech, and appearance . . . into a product or action" (Semmes, 1992:131). A participant stated:

> It's something about the way a black woman puts a hat on her head. . . . It's not so much what you do, but it's the attitude and the spirit with which you do it

Another stated:

> It is . . . not only just putting the object on but bringing that style to it. . . . You have to have some passion to dress this way.

The notion of unity or oneness was evident but seemed more difficult to express and was closely related to other elements as can be seen in the following expression:

> I think it is not only in one's dress because dress is a part of one's being. It goes back to this spirituality we were talking about. So it is in clothes but it is

Reading 4.5 O'Neal, G. (1950). African-American Aesthetics of Dress. Written by O'Neal for this textbook.

> also in the way one wears the clothes and also in the way one talks.

In explaining preference for fabric with improvisations or off-beat patterns, a person stated:

> I remember when I was doing art as an undergraduate and in high school. When we learned about patterning, you always learned that you put a circle here and a space, and you put a circle here and a space and there was that consistency of the pattern because that was what was acceptable. Now we have all these wonderful random patterns. There is a kind of rhythm, but it is a kind of rhythm of its own. Not a consistent rhythm that was taught in the past. Now these ideas of random patterns have been within the African context for eons. The so-called clashing colors were part of the African context for eons.

The phenomenon of "off-beat" patterns in African textiles has been documented by many researchers, and has been found in African-American art forms, e.g., painting, sculpture, dance, music, and quiltmaking. These multiple rhythms are often created by the use of color and off-beat patterns.

The preference for "high affect" colors and large bold patterns is a negative historical stereotype of African Americans. Yet all of the women interviewed stated a love for "high affect" colors and fabrics with multiple rhythms:

> What is coming to be identified as maybe having Africanisms in the African-American community I think, is rich color combinations, atypical use of garment combinations, bold colors, sometimes subtle colors but in lots of combinations. I think that part of that aesthetic is also the way we express ourselves, what we do with our nails, the whole notion of our nails being multicolored and designed and patterned and so forth. That's part of the aesthetic too. And when I look at some of the nail patterns for example, they look just like cloth that comes from the mother land which are highly patterned. . . . I'm beginning to see that it comes together. It's not always conscious because folks who are doing hair and nails are not necessarily saying I'm going to do this because it looks like something from the Continent. It just peaks our imagination.

Not only African Americans, but marketers and large apparel retailers are beginning to accept and validate an African-American aesthetic of dress.

## References


Asante, M. K. (1980). *Afrocentricity: The theory of social change.* Buffalo: Amulefi.

Asante, M. K. & Asante, K.W. (Eds.). (1990). *African culture: The rhythm of unity.* Trenton: African World Press.

Collins, P. H. (1989). The social construction of Black feminist thought. *Signs. Journal of Women in Culture and Society, 14* (4). 745–773.

Curtin, P. (1969). *The Atlantic Slave Trade: A Census.* Madison: University of Wisconsin Press.

Hacker, A. (1992). *Two Nations: Black and White, Separate, Hostile, Unequal.* New York: Ballantine Books.

Herskovits, M. J. (1970). *The Myth of the Negro Past.* Gloucester: Peter Smith.

Holloway, J. E. (1990). The origin of African-American culture. In J.E. Holloway, (Ed.). *Africanisms in American Culture* (1–18). Bloomington: Indiana University Press.

Semmes, C. E. (1992). *Cultural hegemony and African American Development.* Westport: Praeger.

Zirimu, P. (1973). An approach to Black aesthetics. In A. Gurr and P. Zirimu (Eds.). *Black Aesthetics* (pp. 58–68). Nairobi: East African Literature Bureau.

# READING 4.6
# Aesthetics of the Homosexual Market

Nancy A. Rudd

We create our appearances and continually appraise them in comparison to cultural standards of attractiveness. These standards are learned through socialization, a process whereby one learns expected demeanor, expression, and behavior of the group. Homosexual men, as a consumer culture, are often assumed in popular opinion to have distinctive modes of appearance. Frequently the assumption is that homosexual men may prefer fashion innovative appearances or spend extensive amounts of time on grooming and other details of appearance management. However, little support for any of these assumptions is found in the sparse literature, suggesting that such assumptions are little more than erroneous stereotypes.

In an attempt to examine the existence of any particular aesthetic operating among homosexual men, the aesthetic responses to fourteen style categories of apparel and three fragrance categories were compared between homosexual and heterosexual men (Rudd & Tedrick, 1994). Significant differences were found in certain style categories, but not in others. Innovative, trendy styles of dress pants, dress shirts, outerwear jackets, ties, socks, and casual shoes were preferred by homosexual men, while casual, relaxed (sporty) variations were preferred by heterosexual men. Both groups preferred classic or traditional jeans, casual shirts, casual pants, underwear, and coats. In sports coats, sweaters, and dress shoes, preferences for both groups were split among innovative, sporty, and classic variations. Fragrance aesthetics were more conclusive. Not only did homosexual men report using cologne more frequently, but they preferred floral, sweet fragrances and oriental, spicy fragrances, while heterosexual men preferred woody, green fragrances. Thus, it would appear that distinctive appearance aesthetics may operate for certain aspects of appearance management. This suggests that appearance may be more important in socialization for homosexual men than for heterosexual men, and in fact, the literature on homosexual identity supports this idea.

Appearance is an important factor in homosexual socialization (Marmor, 1980), serving both attraction and communication functions. Various aspects of appearance such as body build, grooming, attractiveness, and dress are highly valued (Kleinberg, 1980; Lakoff & Scherr, 1984), because they may be perceived to be associated with sexual behavior (Hagen, 1979). Other reasons contributing to this valuation may be the conditioned attraction of some homosexual men to a narrow range of body builds, resulting in a greater focus on physical attractiveness rather than on other personal characteristics (Silberstein et al., 1989), and potential social rejection if a man does not live up to a socialized standard of attractiveness (Sergios & Cody, 1985/1986). This sexual objectification may explain greater body dissatisfaction among homosexual men than among heterosexual men, and an increased predisposition to eating disorders (Siever, 1994).

Because appearance is a cultural sign system that serves to communicate, it may be used to structure interactions based on those impressions and to create specific impressions. Do homosexual men prefer to interact socially with other men that resemble their own appearance styles? Not necessarily; men equally preferred to interact with other homosexual men dressed similarly to themselves as with those dressed differently. Is there any consistent meaning of certain aesthetic characteristics in clothing among homosexual men or is aesthetic meaning time and context dependent. A trendy appearance with many fashion details garners a wide range of social acceptance among homosexual men. This appearance led to more positive and more negative social impressions than other appearances (Rudd, 1992).

From a marketing point of view, aesthetic preferences are no more or less consistent within the homosexual population than they are within any other consumer population. Rather than targeting all homosexual men as one market segment with similar lifestyles, attitudes, and aesthetic tastes, it makes sense to recognize that a variety of homosexual

Reading 4.6 Rudd, N. A. (1995). Aesthetics of the Homosexual Market. Written by Rudd for this textbook.

subcultures may exist within particular geographic or social parameters, each having a distinctive value system and mode of expression. Some may be organized around recreational or social activities, such as clubs and bars, performing groups, or political activist groups. The activities and the norms of each subculture will help to establish aesthetic expectations for appearance, as for example among female illusionist pageant contestants, members of a literary club, or patrons of a "leather" bar. Market research firms can be helpful in identifying particular demographic and lifestyle characteristics of any target market segment for retailers who wish to offer appearance products (apparel, fragrance, cosmetics, accessories) and services (hairstyling, facials, aromatherapy, wardrobe planning) to homosexual men.

### References


Hagan, R. (1979). *The bio-sexual factor.* New York: Doubleday.

Kleinberg, S. (1980). *Alienated affections: Being gay in America.* New York: St. Martin's Press.

Lakoff, R. & Scherr, R. (1984). *Face value, the politics of beauty.* Boston: Routledge & Kegan Press.

Marmor, J. (1980). Clinical aspects of male homosexuality. In J. Marmor (Ed.), *Homosexual Behavior.* New York: Basic Books.

Rudd, N.A. (1992). Clothing as signifier in the perceptions of college male homosexuals. *Semiotica, 91* (1/2), 67–78.

Rudd, N.A. & Tedrick, L.S. (1994). Male appearance aesthetics: Evidence to target a homosexual market? In M. DeLong & A.M. Fiore (Eds.), *Aesthetics of Textiles and Clothing: Advancing Multi-Disciplinary Perspectives* (pp. 200–211). Monument, Co: International Textiles and Apparel Association.

Sergios, P. & Cody, J. (1985/1986). Importance of physical attractiveness and social assertiveness skills in male homosexual dating behavior and partner selection. *Journal of Homosexuality,* 12 (2), 71–84.

Siever, M. (1994). Sexual orientation and gender as factors in socioculturally acquired vulnerability to body dissatisfaction and eating disorders, *Journal of Consulting and Clinical Psychology,* 62 (2), 252–260.

Silberstein, L., Mishkind, M., Striegel-Moore, R., Timko, C. & Rodin, J. (1989). Men and their bodies: A comparison of homosexual and heterosexual men. *Psychosomatic Medicine,* 51, 337–346.


## READING 4.7
## The Secret Life of the Female Consumer

B. Kanner

Reading 4.7 Kanner, B. (1990, December). The Secret Life of the Female Consumer. *Working Woman,* pp. 69–71.

Women who drink General Foods International Coffees take their ads light and sweet. Scenes that show best friends chatting do well. So do images of women relaxing with their husbands and kids. And women respond favorably when soft, relaxing music plays in the background.

How does General Foods know all this? Because the executives who market the brand conduct extensive tests that tell them how far they can push your hot buttons. They know, for instance, that high-tech images, blue light, or a close-up of an ice cube moving along a woman's neck will turn you off. They also know that you'll react warmly to an ad showing a man canceling a golf game to be with his wife, or one that shows a mother having a heart-to-heart with her daughter.

Scoff if you like, but the touchy-feely approach works. Between July 1989 and July 1990, sales of General Foods International Coffees (GFIC) were $115.9 million, an 11 percent rise over the same period a year earlier. This is startling when you consider that sales in the instant-coffee category as a whole, estimated to be worth $1.1 billion, are off by 9.4 percent. In fact, nearly all supermarket brands are down, the victims of rising health concerns about caffeine, the gourmet-bean trend, and morning cola consumption.

But GFIC isn't like other coffees. It's presweetened and positioned as a specialty product, not a commodity. This gives it a designer image. GFIC is also aimed at women, who have been the brand's biggest consumers since its introduction in 1974 (although there is talk now of targeting men).

"GFIC is the closest coffee comes to the fashion or perfume business," says Tom Pirko, president of Bevmark Inc., a Los Angeles consultancy. "It's selling the sizzle as much as the steak."

As one of the largest consumer-products companies in the world, General Foods has long depended on consumer research to market its brands. But as the roles of American women have changed, it has become more difficult to peg female consumers. Today it is important for marketers to define not only who consumers are but also who they would like to be. Increasingly, women, like men, buy products because they identify—or strive to identify—with the kind of people they think use them.

"This has confused many food companies," says Carol Brandy Blades, president and chief operating officer of The Softness Group, a New York-based consultancy that specializes in marketing to women. "Many shoot for a hot, contemporary feel in the ads but overlook the fact that women need to identify with the actress. If your female audience doesn't empathize with her, you've lost them."

To make sure that doesn't happen, GFIC's marketers stress an emotional benefit—"more the feeling than the function" says Nancy Wong, director of marketing for General Foods' Maxwell House division, located in White Plains, New York. And that feeling? When it comes to GFIC, it's self-indulgence and traditional values represented by a series of emotional moments in commercials.

### What do women want? Ask them.

The team behind GFIC is headed by Wong, 48, who supervises all aspects of selling the brand, including product development, packaging, advertising, and promotion. To determine what women want from the brand, the team stages hundreds of focus groups each year and mails out thousands of questionnaires. Reporting to Wong is Cathy Ko, 36, the brand's senior product manager, who monitors product development, consumer research, and media planning, and is the team's liaison with the advertising agency. David Hirschler, 29, also an associate product manager, oversees the budget, business analysis and planning, and sales coordination. Margaret Block, 32, is in charge of GFIC's consumer promotions.

Over the years, GFIC's research techniques have become more complex as its audience has grown more sophisticated. It is no longer enough to ask, "What do you like about the taste?" While the GFIC team does not hire anthropologists or sociologists to study the cultural environment of the brand's consumers, as some companies do, it does employ psychologists to run the focus groups. They draw out and interpret women's feelings about coffee and the brand.

"How do you feel before you've had a cup?" the psychologist might ask. "And after?" He or she then might direct women to draw pictures illustrating the transformation. "If you were having a dream in which GFIC played a part, what would it be?" There are even questions to tease out the brand's "personality": "How old is GFIC?" "Is it male or female?" "What music does it listen to?" "What kind of car does it drive?" Women are also given stacks of photographs and asked to create a collage using pictures of ordinary people who they think would consume the brand.

During these sessions, the women might be asked to fill in balloon captions of cartoon characters or "read" their feelings into a picture, a technique called a "thematic appreciation test." This reveals not just what consumers think about the brand but how they feel about everything.

From the research, the team has determined that the typical consumer is a baby boomer or younger, earns a middle income, is warm, friendly, and drinks coffee on a regular basis. And although she works, research reports, she's not obsessed with her career.

Research also tells General Foods how to position existing products—and when to launch new ones. In keeping with the times, sugar-free versions appeared in 1984 and decaffeinated ones were introduced in 1989. Last year single-serving envelopes were rolled out after women said they especially like curling up with a cup when traveling. The newest variety, Hazelnut Belgian Cafe, was added in July. The team decided on the name because hazelnut is a popular gourmet-bean flavor and in Belgium hazelnut is often used in pastry.

### Turning research into ads

Once GFIC's marketers know what turns women on, they create a series of test ads. These are shown to focus groups to learn what might work in ongoing campaigns. "Because we're dealing with image advertising," Wong says, "we have to continuously check the tone and manner to be sure it's effective."

The GFIC team won't discuss details of the findings, but advertisements for the brand provide insight into their thinking. In the most recent television commercial, "Home Movies," a thirty-something couple is shown sitting in their living room, sipping from mugs of Hazelnut Belgian Cafe. They're watching a black-and-white home movie of a back-packing trip they took to Belgium some years ago. Phoebe Snow's earthy voice is heard in the background.

"The ad works because it's comforting, not patronizing" says Blades, of the The Softness Group. "It acknowledges that it's late in the feminist age. While the woman is shown with a man, she's in control, the product works for her."

Young & Rubicam, the agency that created the advertisement, has worked on the brand since it was introduced. Back in the early 1970s, actress Carol Lawrence was GFIC's spokeswoman. Lawrence, best known as Maria in the Broadway version of *West Side Story,* was chosen for her European looks. At the time, the General Foods marketers working on the brand wanted to emphasize its international personality. College-age women, the target audience, had traveled abroad or intended to, and the coffee stirred up their wanderlust.

Bill Burgess, a former member of the original GFIC team and now a principal with Weston Group, a Westport, Connecticut, consulting firm, recalls, "With Lawrence we were tapping into the heartbeat of the prime prospect at the time—homebodies who kaffeeklatsch, who are nurturers, who wanted to use this as an experience to treat themselves as they would company."

By 1980 the brand's marketers felt that Lawrence should be replaced by unknown actors playing consumers in real-life situations. The ads positioned the brand as the coffee to drink when bonding with family, friends, or co-workers. But that wasn't the only change. Men, who had always appeared in the ads, were given more prominent roles in the late 1980s. In one ad, a woman pauses in the kitchen while drinking a cup of GFIC to watch her husband and child snuggle in the living room. *It's a laugh, it's a cry . . . all the moments that you want to celebrate . . . You don't need an invitation,* croons Snow.

The team is now studying ways to attract larger numbers of men without triggering a rebellion among loyal female consumers. "We're not going to do macho stuff," says Wong. "We have to take it slow. We need to know more about the way they feel, but we have to be careful. Men don't always open up as easily when we ask our type of questions."

# READING 4.8
# Aesthetics and Special Needs Populations

Nancy A. Rudd

Special needs populations refer to various groups of consumers who may have physical characteristics, as well as psychosocial concerns, that necessitate specialized apparel. Some of these groups include those with physical disabilities, those with facial or bodily characteristics that appear or function out of the norm, chemotherapy patients experiencing hair loss, and women who have undergone mastectomies to combat breast cancer. To the extent that certain appearances are devalued by the dominant culture, people with such appearances may be or feel excluded from complete social participation, thereby causing negative self-feelings and disempowerment. Clothing and appearance management behaviors play a key role in the presentation of self to others, contributing to physiological comfort, social acceptance, and psychological satisfaction. The goal in studying special needs populations is to develop strategies to enhance feelings of self-esteem and perceived quality of life, regardless of the particular physical or psychosocial concerns.

Breast cancer is a very real risk for women. It affects about one in eight women (total lifetime odds), or approximately 182,000 women every year (Cancer Facts and Figures). The most commonly recommended treatment is mastectomy or surgical removal of the breast, although lumpectomy is considered an equally viable treatment in many cases. Each case is unique from the standpoint of individuating factors such as heredity, size and location of the tumor, and overall health risk.

Mastectomy often carries with it both negative physiological and psychosocial outcomes. Physiological effects may include tenderness, scarring of chest and/or underarm, sunken areas in chest/underarm, limited arm movement, lymphedema (swelling) of arm on the operative side, figure imbalance, and posture changes (Meacham et al., 1986). Psychosocial consequences may include trauma to self-esteem, related to feelings of overall attractiveness, desirability and sexuality. How a woman copes psychologically with the loss of one or both breasts may depend on the emotional investment she has in her breasts. Furthermore, if a woman undergoes chemotherapy after surgery, which is the most common means of eradicating any remaining cancer cells or controlling the spread of cancer, she may experience an additional threat to her sense of self—alopecia, or hair loss. If a patient has lost both breast and hair, the effect on her body image can be devastating. Considering the social significance attributed to the female breast in Western culture, and the importance of attractive hair, it is critical to a patient's overall recovery to address aesthetic needs with respect to clothing (Feather & Lanigan, 1986; Rudd et al., 1988), headcoverings (Rudd & Johnson, 1989), and total appearance (Feather et al., 1988; Mulready & Lamb, 1985).

Data from in-depth interviews revealed several basic design criteria that post-mastectomy women expect in their clothing: provides ease in movement, fits comfortably with no binding or tight seams to irritate the operative area, hides any sunken or scarred areas, accommodates limited arm movement or lymphedema, focuses attention away from the breasts, and eliminates the worry of a gaping neckline (Rudd & Dodson, 1985). A survey of post-mastectomy women indicated specific garment selection criteria that are important: attractiveness of garment, fit, overall garment appearance, comfort, care requirements, cost fashion, and distinctiveness (Meacham et al., 1986). Many of these criteria are no different from the criteria that the average consumer uses in making aesthetic judgements about apparel (Morganosky & Postlewaite, 1989). However, particular concerns are indicated by post-mastectomy women with respect to swimwear, eveningwear, suits, and dresses. These include necklines that are not too revealing or gaping, greater coverage in chest and armhole areas, adequate support to hold the prosthesis (man-made breast shape worn in a bra or held in a swimsuit), sleeve or armscye area that is not too snug, and fashionable choices (Rudd et al., 1988).

Reading 4.8 Rudd, N. A. (1995). Aesthetics and Special Needs Populations. Written by Rudd for this textbook.

Specific apparel design solutions that may be found in ready-to-wear, or which may be custom-produced by dressmakers, should include attention to both physiological concerns and self-enhancement. Raglan or kimono sleeves can accommodate lymphedema; blouson styles, gathers over the bust, and free-falling styles from the shoulders can conceal lack of breast symmetry and sunken areas; higher necklines can cover scarring; attention can be drawn to other parts of the body through the use of color, texture, or line; inner support structures can hold a prosthesis firmly in place in swimwear or eveningwear; soft fabrics may be more soothing to the touch if tenderness is a problem; front opening, slip, and wrap styles can accommodate limited arm movement. Examples of design solutions that address these aesthetic concerns are as follows:

Headwear problems commonly experienced by chemotherapy patients include wigs that are hot, irritating to the scalp, or not well secured; skull caps or dust-ruffle caps that are too snug; scarves that are clammy and do not stay secured (Rudd & Johnson, 1989). Design solutions that are currently available or which have been improvised by chemotherapy patients include turbans with bangs attached to them, lightweight wigs with an airy mesh base and no-slip elastic bands, cotton scarves, a wide variety of hats, and even wearing one's baldness with pride.

By examining the aesthetic needs of any given special needs population in relation to both physiological and psychosocial concerns, and by remembering that these individuals still have the same cultural desires for fashionable and attractive appearances, we can provide aesthetic solutions that may play a vital role in the adjustment and recovery of women who have undergone mastectomies. After all, this is life-sustaining surgery and chemotherapy is life-promoting post-operative treatment. Quality of life is an important consideration to anyone's overall happiness, and is particularly critical to one's ability to cope with adverse circumstances such as cancer.

## References

Cancer Facts and Figures (1995). Atlanta: American Cancer Society, Inc.

Feather, B. & Lanigan, C. (1986). Mastectomy, clothing and self-image. *Association of College Professors of Textiles and Clothing Proceedings: Combined Central, Eastern & Western Regional Meetings, 1985,* 69.

Feather, B., Kaiser, S. & Rucker, M. (1988, December). Mastectomy and related treatments: Impact of appearance satisfaction on self-esteem. *Home Economics Research Journal, 17* (2), 127–129.

Meacham, E., Kleibacker, C., Pitts, N. & Rudd, N.A. (1986, December). Clothing designs for mastectomies. National Endowment for the Arts Grant Report No. 52–4232–0029, The Ohio State University Research Foundation.

Morganosky, M. & Postlewaite, D.S. (1989). Consumers' evaluations of apparel form, expression and aesthetic quality. *Clothing and Textiles Research Journal, 13,* 12–20.

Mulready, P. & Lamb, J. (1985). Cosmetics therapy for chemotherapy patients. In M. Solomon (Ed.), *The Psychology of Fashion.* Lexington: Lexington Books, 255–263.

Rudd, N.A. & Dodson, S. (1985, June). Special needs: Clothing for women who have had a mastectomy. Research Abstracts, American Home Economics Association, 115.

Rudd, N.A. & Johnson, J. (1989, June). Headdress for female chemotherapy patients: Implications and recommendations. In K. Holloway & B. Ledwith (Eds.), *Proceedings, On the Cutting Edge: Computer Applications in Clothing Design for People with Special Needs,* Saratoga, CA, 39–41.

Rudd, N.A., Pitts, N., Meacham, E. & Snezek, L. (1988). Apparel designs for women following mastectomy. *Proceedings: 4th National Conference–Clothing for People with Special Needs,* 16–26.

PART TWO

# Aesthetic Aspects of the Apparel Product and Environment

CHAPTER 5

# Visual Elements of Design

## Objectives

- Understand the elements of design as they comprise an aesthetic product, specifically apparel and textile products
- Recognize the elements of color, lighting, line, and shape as they influence perception and appreciation of aesthetic products and environments
- Become aware of the formal, expressive, and symbolic qualities of color, lighting, line, and shape
- Analyze the visual elements of design and apply them to the design and presentation of apparel products

Suppose that while on a trip to New York, you have the opportunity to attend the fashion show for the Calvin Klein fall collection. You attend and have a wonderful time. When you get back to school, you are excited and want to describe the show and the collection to your roommate. What would you talk about? Where the clothes were manufactured? Maybe. What size they were offered in? Only if your roommate wanted to buy something without seeing it. Fiber content and care instructions? No, these are not the types of things that would likely interest your roommate. Instead, you would want to describe the colors, silhouettes, and styles of the garments shown in the collection. You would describe the fabric patterns and textures, how the garments looked on the models as they walked down the runway, and the dramatic effect created by lighting and music. The specific information about color, style, fabric, lighting, and music describes the elements of design.

The **elements of design** are the basic perceivable units of a form. These elements are perceived through any of our senses—sight, sound, smell, touch, and taste—and can describe a product or experience. Design elements are the building blocks of aesthetic products and environments. The individual elements operate in conjunction with each other. So while we will discuss each of the elements individually in order to describe and fully understand it, remember that each must be considered as part of a total whole.

We will begin this chapter with the elements of design that are perceived only through vision—color and light. Then we move on to line and shape. These are elements perceived primarily through vision, but three-dimensional forms may also be felt. Each element of design has formal, expressive, and symbolic qualities. For each element, we will explore these qualities in detail.

**Layout, surface, and light structure of apparel, body, and environment.** Elements of design making up apparel, body, and environment forms can be attributed to layout, surface, and light structure. **Layout structures** are due to the three-dimensional, physical manipulation of the materials of apparel (DeLong, 1987), body, and environment. Lines, shapes, and textures are created by the processes of cutting, sewing, and other processes of apparel production. Seams, darts, pleats, and gathers create layout lines. Garment parts such as sleeves, bodices, skirts, pockets, and collars contribute layout shapes. Shirring or gathering fabric can affect textural appearance. Cutting, braiding, and perming the hair can affect layout shape, line, and texture of the body. Construction of architectural spaces and furnishings contributes layout shapes, lines, and textures. **Surface structures** are the contributions made by surfaces of fabrics and trims (DeLong, 1987), the body, and materials used to create the environment. Surface structures include texture of fabrics, skin, hair, and building materials; color from dyes, cosmetics, stains, and paints; shapes and lines from fabric prints, knit or weave structure, and trims. **Light (and shadow) structure** are the elements contributed by the light source of the environment (DeLong, 1987). Light interacts with layout and surface affecting elements of design. For example, light reflecting off a shiny surface gives the appearance that the object is the color of the light. One must consider the interaction of the three structuring sources because the combinations can blend parts (e.g., matching plaid at seams), create parts or focus (e.g., solid white collar against print shirt to create focus), reinforce parts (e.g., chevron pattern of fabric following pointed shape of yoke), and create unity from similarity (e.g., rectangular shapes of print repeating the shape of pockets and standing collar). As you will see in Chapters 13 and 14, layout and surface are good concepts to use to analyze fashion trends.

## COLOR

Color is frequently rated the most important aesthetic criteria for preference of many aesthetic forms, including apparel (Eckman, Damhorst & Kadolph, 1990). Color has perhaps the greatest impact on our perception. When we observe things, we almost always identify color simultaneously with form. Color has rich symbolic and expressive potential as well. This is evident in the way we frequently speak of things. A "shiny sports car" just doesn't have as much impact on our imagination as a "shiny *red* sports car." Color is very important to aesthetic appreciation of products and environments.

## FORMAL QUALITIES OF COLOR

If every person in class were to take a set of paints and mix "pink," "fuschia," "seafoam green," and "baby blue," we would have as many colors as people in class. The problem would not be that anyone's color was "wrong," just that these color names are not specific and systematic enough to be precisely defined and duplicated by each member of the class. We each have an idea what pink is, but there are an infinite number of tints that we would correctly identify as "pink." To address this problem, various color systems have been developed that allow us to systematically identify color.

### Color Notation

**Color wheel.** **Color wheels** organize color relationships according to hue, value, and intensity of color. There are a variety of color wheels in existence, but the most widely accepted, traditional color wheel has twelve colors as shown in Color Plate 1. This color wheel is derived from pure pigment colors; other color wheels and color systems are based on colors from refracted light or on how colors are perceived by the eyes and brain.

The colors in the traditional color wheel consist of **primary, secondary,** and **tertiary** colors. Table 5.1 shows these colors and how they are derived.

**Hue.** **Hue** is the name of a color on the color wheel. There are relatively few actual color hues. Hues are based on pure pigment colors and equal mixtures of pure pigments. Red, orange, green, and blue-green are examples of hues. Mauve, plum and avocado are not hues; they are color names that do not accurately specify colors.

**TABLE 5.1** Primary, secondary, and tertiary colors.

| *Primary* | *Secondary* | *Tertiary* |
|---|---|---|
| Yellow | Green | Yellow-green<br>Blue-green |
| Blue | Purple | Blue-purple<br>Red-purple |
| Red | Orange | Red-orange<br>Yellow-orange |

*Primary + Primary = Secondary color*
*Primary + Secondary = Tertiary color*

**Value. Value** is the lightness or darkness of a color as compared with white or black. Pure hues have different values. Yellow is the lightest value whereas blue and purple are the lowest values on the color wheel. The value of each color can be raised along an incremental scale by mixing the color with white, increasing the amount of white until it is indistinguishable from white. Similarly the value may be lowered by mixing the color with black. The resulting value scale can be compared with an incremental scale ranging from white to black (Color Plate 2).

**Intensity. Intensity** is the purity, brightness, or saturation of a color. Pure pigment colors on the color wheel are saturated colors. The intensity of a saturated color can be lowered in two ways. First, it can be lowered by mixing the color with its complement—the color directly opposite on the color wheel, such as red and green. Brick red, created by mixing red with a small amount of green, has a lower intensity than pure red. Second, intensity is lowered by mixing the hue with gray of the same value.

When values are altered by mixing a color with the neutrals white or black, intensity is also lowered. Tints are colors mixed with white, resulting in higher values. Tones are colors mixed with grays. Shades are colors mixed with black, resulting in lower values. Tints, tones, and shades have lower intensity than pure hues. Color Plate 3 demonstrates the range of tints and shades and varying intensities of color for the hue red. Mixing red with white lowers the intensity and raises the value. The resulting pink color is called a tint of red. In the same way, mixing red with black lowers the intensity and lowers the value. The resultant burgundy color is called a shade of red.

**Color warmth.** The pure hues from the color wheel can be divided into warm colors and cool colors. **Warm colors** include the range of colors from red-violet through red, orange and orange-yellow. **Cool colors** comprise the other side of the color wheel from blue-violet through blue, green, and yellow-green. When individual colors are mixed from pure pigment, minute amounts of a warm or cool color may influence the cast or *undertone* of the color. For instance, many colors of purple can be created from red and blue. The balance of the pigments may differ, creating a range of purples. A purple with more red will appear warmer. As one moves further away from pure hues in color mixing, more complex colors can be created. A peach color is a mixture of red, yellow, and white, but its intensity has been lowered through mixing with complements or gray. This mixing further influences the cast of the color, yielding warm peach (when intensity was lowered with warm grays) or cool peach (when intensity was lowered with cool gray, green, or purple). Color Plate 4 shows how the warmth of the color can differ and still be within the general color description.

**Color relationships. Color relationships** or color schemes are established patterns of color combinations based on their positions on the color wheel and on value and intensity levels. The most common color schemes are simple relationships from the color wheel (Color Plate 5). **Monochromatic colors** are multiple tints, tones, or shades of a single hue. **Analogous colors** are two or three colors side-by-side on the color wheel. Blue, blue-green, and green is an analogous color group. **Complementary colors** are those colors directly across from each other on the color wheel. Blue and orange, red and green, and blue-violet and yellow-orange are examples of complementary colors. There are variations on complementary relationships, such as a double complementary (two adjacent hues and their complements), adjacent complements (complementary hues and one hue next to one of the complements), and single split complementary (one hue and the hue on each side of its complement). **Triad colors** include three colors of equal distance from each other on the color wheel. There are many other color relationships and sophisticated color schemes that designers and colorists have devised and explored (c.f., Lauer, 1985; Zelanski & Fisher, 1984). Remember from Chapter 4 that set color relationships may be intentionally disregarded in post modern fashions.

Different apparel market categories rely on certain color schemes for basic or classic goods. For example, trendy styles often employ more complex color schemes than basic goods. Formal wear often relies heavily on monochromatic color schemes. And the triad relationship of primary colors is an often used scheme in children's wear.

### Colors of the Body

The body itself is also a source of color that must be considered. Hair, skin, and eye colors can be defined according to color notations of hue, value, intensity, and undertone. The colors of apparel and the environment surrounding the body may influence and interact with body colors. Thus, all three elements—the body, apparel, and the environment—must be considered together when discussing color relationships.

### Color Systems

Understanding color notation can help industry professionals communicate about color, but they need a standard system of reference for communication to be effective. Color systems combine exact notations of hue, value, and intensity to specify an individual color. Color systems for mixing pigments, such as Munsell (Color Plate 7) or Pantone specify individual colors based upon a formula such as the percentages of hues combined and the value level. The Pantone color system for mixing pigments is widely used in the textile and apparel industries, allowing more exact color formulations for fabric dying and printing, as well as color matching in the selection of coordinates and trims for apparel and home furnishings. In the Pantone system, the first two digits specify the value of the color as compared with white (10) and black (19). The second two digits specify the location on a color wheel divided into a range from 1 to 64. One denotes yellow green and 32 denotes its complement. The last two digits specify the saturation level of the color, which can range between 0, specifying white, gray, or black, and 64, specifying the most intense. Color Plate 6 demonstrates these three dimensions of value, hue, and intensity in the Pantone system. Other color systems are used for formulating dyes and printed materials (cyan, magenta, yellow, black) and light images such as TV and computer screens (red, green, blue).

| | |
|---|---|
| **ACTIVITY 5.1** | Using the Pantone color system selections shown in Color Plate 6, how would you describe the colors noted as: 13-1764, 1-3005, and 18-6160? Which is darkest value? Which is least intense? Which is bright green? |

Such precision in color system notation is necessary both to fully employ current technology and to reduce error. Without some color notation, we could not order fabrics without samples, because there are so many colors possible. Research estimates that the human eye can distinguish approximately 17,000 different colors (Palmer, 1985). Computer-aided-design technology now puts all those colors within easy reach of designers and merchandisers. The Pixelpaint computer-aided-design software system provides standard palettes, but by manipulating the value, and intensity of a color, users can customize the system to exact specifications of colors for design purposes.

### Optical Color Effects

**Optical color effects** are interactions between colors during the process of perception that appear to alter colors or create new colors. Have you ever stared at the words on a page and looked up quickly to see a light shadow of those words on the wall? This is called an *afterimage.* The words don't appear on the wall for a moment through magic, they are perceptual effects that are due to chemical activity on the retina of the eye. Many such aftereffects can occur with colors, various geometric patterns, and moving objects that are viewed for a long period of time. They are all conditions that occur when the neurons of the retina and along the optic nerve adapt to what is perceived for a period of time. When the scene before the eyes change, it takes a moment for the retina to readjust. During that moment, some aspects of the earlier perception remain (Favreau & Corballis, 1976). Many "op-art" fabric print patterns popular in the late 1960s and 1970s and used in apparel and home furnishings employed optical effects.

**Optical color mixing. Optical color mixing** occurs when small dots of colors appear to the eye as the blended color of the two pigments. For instance, a painting using small dots of blue and yellow will appear to be more green than yellow or blue, although upon closer inspection, there is no green paint used. This effect was used by the Impressionist painters and is called *pointillism.* Optical color mixing can occur when small patterns of color are used in fabric prints. A gray houndstooth check suiting fabric may not be gray at all, but small squares of black and white that appear gray.

**Simultaneous contrast effects. Simultaneous contrast effects** occur when the differences in value, intensity, or warmth/coolness of two colors, placed next to each other, are emphasized. If you place a medium value color on a high value background such as white, and a low value background such as black, the color may appear darker against white and lighter against black. This will occur if a medium value color is placed in the center of each stage in its value scale as well. Similarly, the intensity of a color will appear to change based on the intensity of its background color. And the warmth of a color will appear to move towards greater contrast with the warm or cool background color. Color Plate 9a, b and c demonstrates several simultaneous contrast effects in which the sample color appears to change in value, warmth, and intensity.

**Simultaneous contrasts between the body and apparel.** The simultaneous contrast effect can occur between the body and clothing. After spending the summer working hard on that golden tan, what color shorts do you pull from your drawer to show off the tan? Pale gray? Olive green? Or bright white? Obviously you've chosen bright white to emphasize the contrast between the dark tan and light color. This is an example of simultaneous contrast.

Many wardrobe advisors and personal color analysts (e.g., Jackson, 1980) have developed various systems to help their clients make color choices in clothing and make-up that harmonize the color relationships between their skin, eyes, and hair. These systems assert that individuals' natural coloring can be categorized as having either warm gold or cool blue "undertones." Color palettes appropriate for each category of warm or cool are then organized according to their intensity and value. By avoiding simultaneous contrast of undertones between skin and clothing, the unappealing bluish or yellow undertones are underplayed.

## Color Forecasting

In the apparel and home furnishings industries, color forecast associations provide subscriber members with trend directions and predictions about color palettes that will be popular in upcoming seasons. Designers at all levels of the industry, from fabric designers to apparel and accessory designers, need to be aware of these trends. The Color Marketing Group and Color Association of the United States (CAUS) are two examples of these forecasting organizations. Reading 5.1 is the CAUS Color Forecast for Menswear for the Fall and Winter 1996/97 season. It discusses the trends that influence color selection.

## Formal Qualities and Apparel

Let's follow a line of children's activewear from design through purchase. We will see how formal qualities of color are an important component of line planning at each level of the apparel process and to illustrate how the use of a color system makes life easier for apparel professionals. The color forecast for Spring/Summer children's wear included bright, jewel-tone colors in medium values and pure intensities. Color schemes that are predicted include complementary and triads combined with white or black.

Using the Pantone system and the forecaster's advice, a children's wear designer selects a palette of exact colors to use in planning a line of play clothes. Let's assume the colors are bright, intense blue, purple, green, and red-violet. The fabric dyers and print designers (who have also followed the forecasts) use Pantone color designations to identify their lines. So the fabric buyer and the trims buyer match the designer's color specifications with those from fabric suppliers. Fabrics are ordered and sent to the manufacturers. The garments are produced and all the colors match very well.

Meanwhile, the sales reps present the line to buyers. The children's wear buyer for a major department store may decide to purchase only certain garments from the line. She or he buys from several manufacturers and must make sure that items from the different companies' lines can be combined into groups to be sold in the store. Several children's wear companies are following the same trends in color. Using the Pantone color designation, the buyer can be confident that items from various lines will be compatible. The merchandise is ordered and shipped to the stores.

The visual merchandiser receives a description of the merchandise that is arriving soon and begins to plan the display and furnishings to accompany the groups. When the merchandise arrives, the floor plan and displays are ready to go. Sales associates arrange the merchandise on the selling floor in time for the big spring promotion.

The customer (who doesn't feel very confident about her skills in selecting colors that look good together) arrives in the store looking for a gift for her nephew's second birthday. His mother told her his size and said he likes bright colors. The customer selects an adorable shirt and shorts as well as a romper and matching socks. She remarks to the salesclerk as she makes her purchase, that "It's amazing that all these things are different brands, yet they match so well! Picking matching outfits was easy!"

## EXPRESSIVE QUALITIES OF COLOR

Perhaps more than any other element of design, color has powerful expressive potential. The expressiveness of color comes through physiological and psychological responses. Physiological responses to color may include changes in blood pressure, heart rate, and respiration, muscular tension or relaxation, and brain wave activity due to the perception of warmth or coolness, value, and intensity of color. However, these responses are subtle and consistent research data is often lacking (Pile, 1988). Psychological or emotional states influenced by color include the three dimensions—pleasure, arousal and dominance.

### Physiological Responses to Color

Color intensity and warmth or coolness have measurable effects on the physiological systems of the body. Red was found to be more stimulating to the brain and nervous system than green (Wilson, 1966). Higher intensity of colors may raise blood pressure and may contribute to physical tension and agitation. On the other hand, various cool colors, blue in particular, may lower blood pressure and encourage relaxation in the body's systems. Neutral tones of browns and grays also may slow down body systems, but very low-value, low-intensity colors can depress mood if not relieved by some contrast.

Researchers have found several trends in the relationships between color preferences and personality and mental states. In general, one's personality may influence preferences for colors because of their physiological stimulation. Introverts—people who are shy and reserved—have been found to prefer low-stimulus colors and combinations of colors with low intensity and little contrast. Extroverts—those who are more outgoing—may seek higher levels of stimulation; they generally prefer colors of higher intensity and combinations of higher contrast (Eysenck, 1981). Whereas personality is a fairly stable and unchanging psychological pattern, even the more temporal mental states can influence color preferences during a particular moment. If a person is anxious, he or she will be less likely to select physiologically stimulating colors in a preference test (Ireland, Warren & Herringer, 1992).

Interior designers often use these physiological color effects when planning color palettes for residential and commercial spaces. Hospital interiors are usually painted with high-value, low-intensity to medium-intensity colors from the cool range in order to enhance relaxation and lift energy. Sports complexes and active wear apparel, on the other hand, are usually designed with higher intensity, medium value colors with contrasts of warm and cool colors, particularly primary colors. These color schemes enhance the physical energy and vitality of the sport activities and may enhance individuals' performance.

In a study of the effects of color in retail store design, researchers concluded that the level of physiological stimulation and warmth of color were very important for the retail environment (Bellizzi, Crowley & Hasty, 1983). Warm colors may tend to help bring a customer into a store and may enhance impulse purchases for special displays. Colors in general areas of stores where shoppers deliberate over purchase decisions should be cool colors. When there is a high level of tension involved in purchase decisions, color of store design should not further agitate customers.

## Psychological and Emotional Responses to Color

In addition to the physiological stimulation caused by colors, the emotional pleasure, arousal, and dominance are influenced by color characteristics of hue, value, and intensity color relationship. Researchers have found that blues, blue-greens, and purples may induce the most pleasure while yellows and yellow-greens are least pleasurable. Greens, green-blues, and green-yellows are the most arousing, and green-yellow may induce the greatest feeling of dominance (Valdez & Mehrabian, 1994). When children and adults were asked to connect colors with emotions and then to rank both the colors and emotions, there were significant relationships found between the pleasantness of the emotion and the preference for its associated color (Terwogt & Hoeksma, 1995). Monochromatic and analogous relationships are more calming than complementary and triad relationships.

The degree of value contrast also directly influences the types of expression found in an aesthetic work (Zelanski & Fisher, 1984). Higher contrasts between values of color tend to be more dynamic or vigorous, thus high in arousal and dominance. Such combinations can express power, exuberance, or joy. Lower contrasts of value are lower in arousal and less dominant. Low contrasts are more harmonious, calmer, and peaceful, but no contrast at all can express boredom or depression.

Another characteristic of color that has potential for expression is the warmth or coolness of a color. Warm colors are those on the red—yellow side of the color wheel and cool colors are the blues and greens. Purple may be either warm or cool, depending on the influence of red or blue in the shade. There are a host of psychological associations between feeling states and physiological temperature that can be expressed through color warmth (Bevlin, 1989). Physical warmth and warm colors may indicate happiness, security, and affection. Passion, fear, love, and hate are "hot" emotions often expressed by intense reds. A "little red dress" has become a cliché for expressing one's sexuality and the desire to be perceived as attractive. Coldness is often perceived in "icy" high-value blues, and white or gray. Cold emotions may include detachment, disdain, or despair. Gray business suits may express the detachment of business decisions and activities from emotion.

### SYMBOLIC QUALITIES OF COLOR

Color symbolism arises from nature and from social convention (Lauer, 1985). Symbolic aspects of color are often connected to the color of objects in nature. For example, red can be used to symbolize blood and life. Color in nature also indicates the health of living objects. Green is a sign of health and growth in plants, and may be used to symbolize such things in other objects.

Color symbolism is also developed over time through social convention. When the use of a color for specific items or events becomes traditionally accepted among a group of people, the color begins to function as a symbol in that context. There is no reason for the color selection outside of choice and convention. Therefore, among a different group, the color symbolism may be different. Reading 5.2 gives some examples of color symbolism among different cultures.

Finally, color symbolism can add meaning to a product or experience. Consider the symbolism in the names given to color swatches in color charts or presentations. When a shopper selects "misty mauve" lipstick or "flaming flamingo" active wear, she may be responding to the meaning from the color name as well as the appropriateness of the color for her complexion.

## LIGHT

Apparel professionals use the element of lighting as an important tool in the visual design of environments to enhance the presentation of apparel products. Lighting not only facilitates visual perception of products and environments, but it can stimulate the consumption of and aesthetic satisfaction from those products and environments.

Qualities of lighting can affect what we see, how easily we see, and how we respond, although consumers may not always be aware of lighting's effects. We have certain expectations about lighting that influence our reactions. We can't imagine shopping in a darkened theater, or having a class lecture complete with colored lights, a spotlight, and flashing strobes. If your instructor were to lecture while using strobe lights, you would be surprised and amused. But if you did not have enough light to see your notebook as you took notes, you would complain.

Lighting has the potential to contribute to aesthetic experience in a variety of situations. One goal of the interior designer in selection of lighting to provide adequate lighting for *visibility,* or ensuring enough light in homes and offices for activities to be easily carried out. But lighting can also create different moods and perceptions of space in buildings. The mood that lighting creates is important to our being ready to work in an office, play in a recreational center, and relax in a bedroom. Stage lighting designers consider visibility only a minor criterion in their lighting plans. Many of the stage designer's criteria for lighting choices are based upon reinforcing or contributing to the aesthetic nature of the play or musical performance (Palmer, 1985).

Lighting considerations for apparel professionals such as visual merchandisers and store designers may fall somewhere between the practical and the theatrical. A fashion show coordinator may select lighting to light the runway, which allows the models to move effortlessly, directs the focus of the audience, and enhances the softness of the apparel forms presented.

## FORMAL QUALITIES OF LIGHT

Whether in a home, office, or retail store, the first provision of lighting is ambient or general lighting. **Ambient or general lighting** serves the practical need for light to perform activities. **Accent lighting** calls attention to specific, small areas or objects. In a home, an accent light might focus on a piece of art or a grouping of plants. In a retail store, the accent lighting adds visual impact to special displays. **Perimeter lighting** lights boundaries of a space. Small yard lights defining a landscaped garden path provide perimeter light. Perimeter lighting in a retail setting focuses on walls and wall displays.

Whatever the lighting purpose, there are several objective qualities of light that we will consider. These include intensity, color, diffusion, form, and visibility. These characteristics are influenced by the source and type of light available.

### Intensity

**Intensity** is the amount of light energy that is reflected in an area. Intensity is the brightness or dimness of the light. Intensity is influenced by the light source, the type of light, and the size of the light or distance between the source and the object seen. Sources of light include the sun, the light bulb in your desk lamp, even the dials and dots on your stereo. We don't recommend reading by the light of the stereo, however!

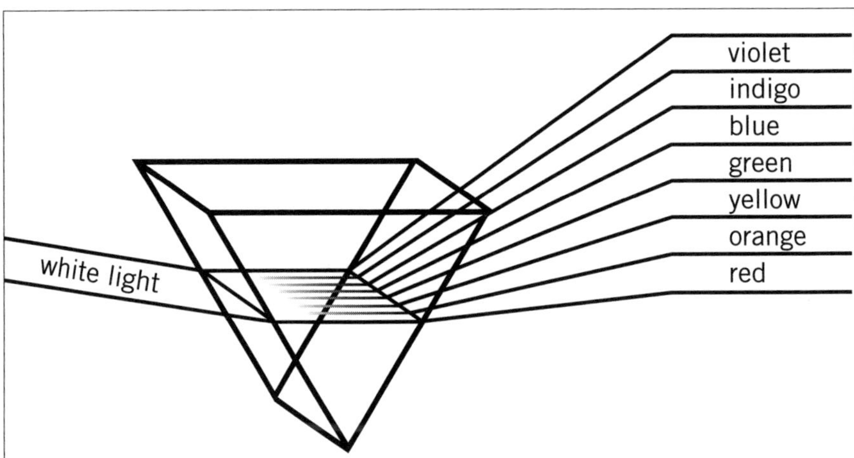


Figure 5.1. The visible spectrum of light refracted by a prism.

## Color

Only a small portion of all light waves is visible to the human eye. Other light waves that we cannot see include infrared, ultraviolet, and x-rays. The visible spectrum of light is the portion of light waves that can be discerned by the human eye. This spectrum includes refracted light of various colors. Refracted light creating the visible spectrum can be demonstrated when a ray of white light passes through a prism. This spectrum ranges from red through orange, yellow, green, blue, indigo, and violet as shown in Figure 5.1. Light can be white—an equal mix of all colors, or it can have a higher proportion of one color than others from the spectrum.

## Diffusion and Form

**Diffusion** is the concentration and direction of the light rays. Light can be passed through filters, shades, or lenses that scatter or concentrate the light beams. The light from the sun is diffused or scattered in all directions by the elements (air and clouds) in the atmosphere. A laser beam is highly concentrated and focused by magnifying lenses. A lampshade on a table lamp diffuses the light rays through the material of the shade, depending on its materials and color. Light beams may also be magnified and concentrated through the use of lenses. Spotlights at fashion shows pass light through lenses—and possibly colored filters—and direct the light beams toward the models on the runway.

**Form** in lighting, is the shape of individual pools of light created by the lighting source(s). Spotlights create visible lines through the darkened room and a circular pool of light around a stage figure. Shapes can also be found in reflections and shadows resulting from the interaction of light with layout and surface structure. Light reflecting off draped satin can create organic shaped reflections and shadows. Geometric shapes may be formed by reflections and shadows from lapels or pleats. The reflected light from a mirrored "disco" ball on a dance floor creates many tiny forms of light.

### Artificial Light Sources

Thomas Edison revolutionized the world when he invented the light bulb. This allowed humans to change their work habits, releasing us from dependence on the sun and oil lamps. **Artificial light** is produced by the combustion of some consumable fuel by fire, by passing electrical energy through a filament (incandescent), or by the creation of an electrical charge among certain gasses (fluorescent). The light sources differ slightly in the portion of the visible spectrum of light that they reproduce.

**Combustion** or flame produces a warm orange-colored light. Candles are a very low-intensity light source and produce a significant amount of heat relative to the amount of light produced. We often use candles or fireplaces to produce a warm, cozy atmosphere.

**Incandescent light** is from the yellow portion of the spectrum, and gives a warm glow to objects that are seen in it. Incandescent bulbs are the most commonly used in homes for *ambient*, or general light, and are similar in color and warmth to the light from the sun.

**Fluorescent light** comes from the blue area of the spectrum. Fluorescent bulbs are more efficient and economical to use, and they generate intense light with much less accompanying heat. Therefore, large spaces of discount stores are most commonly lit through the use of fluorescent lighting. However, there is more distortion of the apparent color of objects under fluorescent light. Colors will often appear to be more blue or violet than with incandescent bulbs.

### Formal Qualities and Apparel

In the presentation of apparel products, lighting intensity, color, and form can affect the perception of the product. Lighting intensity and color affects the perception of colors in objects. An interaction between lighting color and object color can distort our perception of the true color. Violets may appear more blue or reds may appear more orange. This color distortion can cause inaccurate color matching in the selection of coordinating items, ultimately leading to customer dissatisfaction.

Lighting intensity and color can affect how body and apparel coloring is perceived as well. Medium intensity, diffused, warm light is important in dressing rooms to encourage positive evaluations of garments on the body. Very intense, cool lighting in a dressing room can be very unflattering to customer's skin and hair coloring, causing them to look or feel bad when they try on garments.

## EXPRESSIVE QUALITIES OF LIGHT

While we are often unaware of it, light has the potential to express or influence energy levels and moods. The lightness or darkness of our surroundings is a signal to our physical bodies of time for rest and relaxation or work and play. Bright lights are not only necessary in stores to see by, but may excite the consumer.

The color of light or dominant area of the spectrum reproduced by a light source influences our perception of temperature. White light can range from warm yellow to cool blue. The color of light has similar physiological and psychological effects as color. Warm light makes us feel warmer than cool light, even when actual air temperatures are the same. Warm colored light may be the type of lighting that best makes people feel good and enhances productivity (Baron, 1990).

The intensity and dispersion of light beams creates impressions of softness or harshness. Greater intensity and concentration of light creates hard beams of light that can seem harsh or even glaring. *Glare* is too much light in our eyes and it causes discomfort (Palmer, 1985). Soft light is comfortable to our eyes, and thus encourages a sense of overall well-being. A particular brand of light bulb purports to provide softer light at the same wattage as other bulbs by using a frosted coating on the glass, diffusing the light.

In visual design, lighting considerations include more than just the types of light fixtures used in homes, offices, and stores, but also light "within" a form. When light is reflected off a surface of a form, an illusion can be created that the light comes from within the form (Myers, 1989). A bride in her white gown or a woman in a shiny, glittery evening gown may be told she is "positively radiant." This is not only because she is happy, but because the reflection of light by the fabric surface creates the illusion that she is glowing or giving off light. Store furnishings and displays that reflect light may also present the illusion of light within a form. Mirrors may be used to line the bottom of a display case and add glow to small objects such as jewelry or fragrance bottles.

Lighting is an important element in the creation of mood. Suppose you are planning a romantic dinner and you are selecting lighting to enhance the mood. Which of the following would you choose? (a) 150-watt bulbs in a ceiling fixture dangling on a wire with no shade? (b) portable generator and search lights? or (c) soft candlelight placed in front of mirrors? (If you've selected a or b, this might explain why you have a hard time in the dating scene.)

## SYMBOLIC QUALITIES OF LIGHT

Aside from being the necessary ingredient in visibility allowing us to see other symbolic elements such as line and shape, light itself has the power to communicate a message. The lightness of the outdoors helps us to gauge the time of day and the weather.

Lighting also communicates to us where we ought to turn our attention or where we ought to go. Who can resist visually following a spotlight at a rock concert or a fashion show? The intensity of light suggests importance of the individual person on stage or runway.

### Expressive and Symbolic Qualities and Consumer Behavior

As you recall from Chapter 4, an important element in the aesthetic appreciation of apparel products and environments is feeding fantasy. A consumer must be able to imagine himself or herself wearing or using a product. The lighting used in the promotion of apparel products creates mood and fosters the fantasies of "what could be." Fashion shows use lighting effects to create drama and enhance the fantasy of being "on the cutting edge" in the latest fashions. The setting of photographs of models in a Victoria's Secret catalog are often evocative of a large country mansion with dark furnishings and low lights (Figure 5.2). This fosters a soft, romantic mood and is supposed to engage customers in their own romantic fantasies. Purchase of the lingerie ensues as customers decide that the apparel can help them make their fantasies come true.

## Lighting the Apparel Product Environment

Light creates the impression of welcoming people into stores. Lighting at store entrances is very important to bring customers inside. Lighting should focus attention on window displays and on items several feet inside the doors to attract attention inside. If you've ever watched window shoppers, you know that people don't walk in a straight line. People meander along, walking toward products and displays that attract their visual attention. So lighting that calls attention to objects inside a store helps to draw customers into the store.

All the qualities of light discussed may be important in stores, fashion shows, catalog presentations, and advertisements. Reading 5.3 discusses the important features of lighting for retail store design. Types of lighting and lighting needs vary from store to store, depending on the merchandise, the store type, i.e, discount to up-scale specialty store, and the store image.

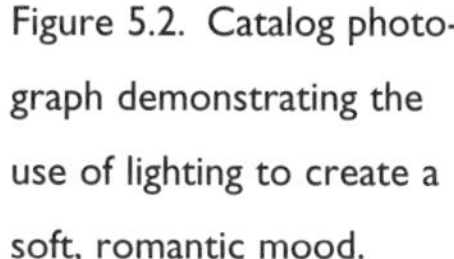

Figure 5.2. Catalog photograph demonstrating the use of lighting to create a soft, romantic mood.

**ACTIVITY 5.2** Lighting in stores can contribute to the shopping experience and the store image. In order to investigate lighting uses in the retail setting, take a trip to your local shopping mall. Consider yourself a lighting designer on a fact-finding mission to scope the competition. Visit at least two department stores. (You may want to review the information from Reading 5.3 before you go.)

1. Jot down some notes about the types of general, accent, and peripheral lighting used.
2. Also note the type of store image conveyed through merchandise selection and store furnishings.
3. Describe the formal qualities (color, intensity, diffusion) that are used.
4. How does the lighting affect the color rendering of products in the stores?
5. What is the mood of the lighting in the stores? Does this differ by department?
6. Evaluate the effectiveness of the lighting in different areas of the store. Is lighting used as an effective contributor to a successful retail environment?

# LINE

## FORMAL QUALITIES OF LINE

Let's begin with a practical definition of line: **Line** is a form that has a significantly greater length than width, such that we generally perceive only its length to be important (Lauer, 1979, p. 123). The formal qualities of lines are those that can be described in objective terms such as the type of line, the size and quality of the line, and the direction of the line.

### Type of Line

There are generally two types of lines: actual lines and implied lines. **Actual lines** exist in space. They are woven in or printed on fabric, created by the joining of planes or surfaces such as garment parts, or created by folds or pleats in fabrics. An actual line can be traced over, as can the lines in Figure 5.3a. The seam down the leg of your jeans is an actual line. So is the edge of a sofa or the beam of light in a laser light show.

**Implied lines** do not actually exist in space but we "see" them because of visual or psychological processes. We see a straight succession of dots as one continuous line, such as the row of buttons down a shirt. In our mind's eye, we connect the dots. The lines indicated by the dashes and dots in Figure 5.3b are implied lines. Such implied lines are illusions in which our mind "fills in the blanks" (Walker, 1988). Psychological lines are those such as the path of a moving ball or the line we draw in the air when we point at an object (Figure 5.3c). Following a psychological line is a learned behavior. An infant will not understand and follow a pointed finger to find a toy until he learns the meaning of pointing to objects sometime around twelve to eighteen months of age.

Figure 5.3. (below) Illustration of several examples of actual lines (a) and implied lines (b and c).

Figure 5.4. (right) Advertisement for Paloma Picasso handbags showing an implied line created by the Xs on the products.

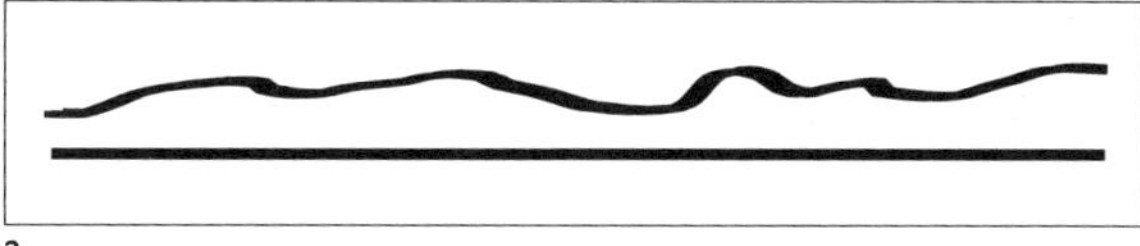

a

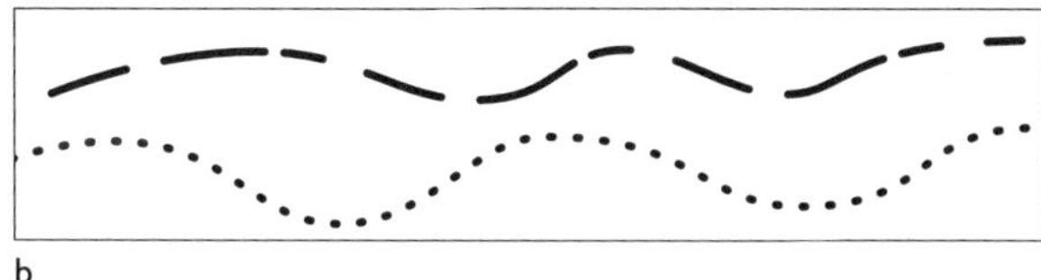

b

c

Implied lines in clothing may help to create the illusion of an ideal figure. By placing a row of buttons down a coat-dress, a vertical line is implied that emphasizes the vertical dimension of the figure. Stylists who arrange products such as shoes and handbags in an advertising layout may create implied lines, such as the diagonal lines connecting the Xs on the handbags in Figure 5.4. This implied line serves to reinforce the concept of matching products, thus coaxing the consumer to purchase several items from the grouping.

## Qualities of Line

The qualities of a line are created by its characteristics of length, width, visual weight, uniformity along its length, and direction. Different ways of creating lines in apparel yield different potential qualities.

**Length.** Every line has a specific, measurable *length*. When the eye perceives a line, it has a tendency to follow the line from beginning to end. Short choppy lines break up the flow of the eye through a product or environment. Long, flowing lines carry the eye along their length. A jacket printed with short broken lines breaks up the view of the torso, while the long lines of the jacket's silhouette and pants carry the eye smoothly down the wearer's hips and legs (Figure 5.5).

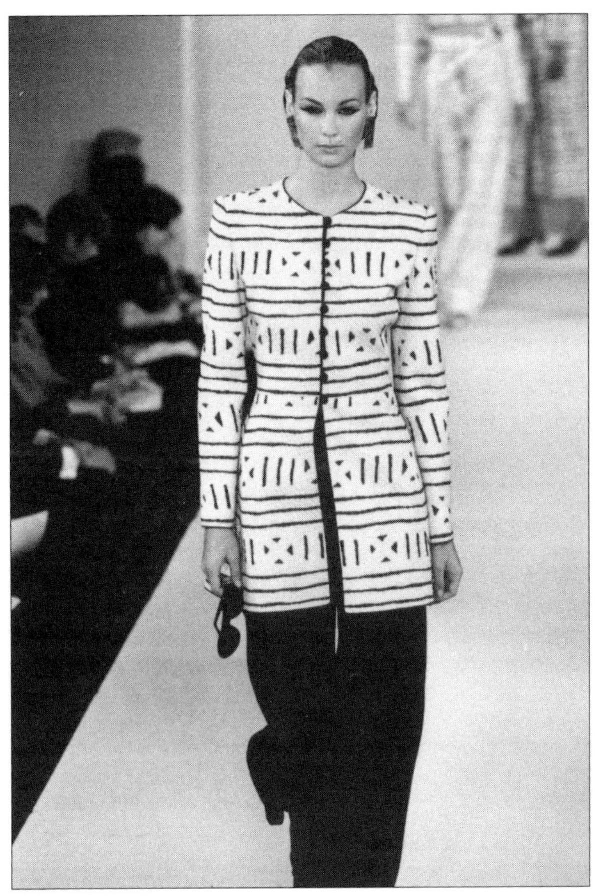

Figure 5.5. Ensemble with short, broken lines in bodice and long flowing lines in silhouette and pants.

**Width.** A line can be thick or thin, depending on how it was created it or how often the line is repeated side-by-side. The stripes on a rugby shirt are very wide lines. Pinwale corduroy is a succession of very thin lines. The lines in a "broomstick" skirt are generally thin, but because the pleating is not orderly, there is some variety among their widths.

**Weight.** Line has a *visual weight,* or apparent heaviness. Weight is due to a combination of line size, darkness, and opacity or transparency. A line can be heavy and solid such as dark, printed stripes on white fabric, or light and feathery such as a line created by brushed-on dye in a hand-painted fabric. In the lighter weight line, the background color tends to show through the line.

**Uniformity.** The uniformity of a line refers to the similarity of it's width and weight along the length of the line. Lines may be created that have the same thickness all along their length, or the thickness may change. Figure 5.6 demonstrates lines that are uniform and varied in their width and weight.

**Direction.** Finally, lines have movement in some *direction.* The general direction of a line can be horizontal, vertical, or diagonal. Lines move in these directions either in a direct or meandering manner. A direct line is relatively straight between two

Figure 5.6. Illustration of uniform and varied line widths, weights, uniformity, and direction.

points across a surface. A meandering line changes direction any number of times, such as an undulating wave of a circle skirt hem, the zig-zag of a handkerchief skirt hem, or a freshman finding her or his way to class on the first day. Abrupt changes in direction create angular lines, whereas gradual changes in direction result in curved lines.

## Lines of the Body

Lines are created by the body, the apparel, and the environment. Lines are evident in the contours of the face, the body, and hair. The lines of the body are in constant motion as the body changes position. Many lines of the body can be purposely arranged. Long straight hair worn loose and brushed smooth creates straight lines down from the head to the shoulders. The same hair could be worn up in a loose knot, creating rounded and spiral lines around the head.

As the body moves, the direction and length of garment lines on the body may change. And the body moves through various environments that can have different line effects. Sitting among the cushions of a plump sofa and walking along a sidewalk are two opportunities for different types of lines to surround the body.

## Formal Qualities and Apparel Products

**Lines in apparel. Outer lines** create the edge between the apparel, body, and the environment. These lines have a specific length, width, weight, uniformity, direction, and angularity or curvilinearity. **Inner lines** divide the apparel and body into smaller parts or embellish the surface. Print fabrics, such as stripes and florals, add inner lines to bodices, sleeves, and skirts. The braided trim around a Chanel jacket

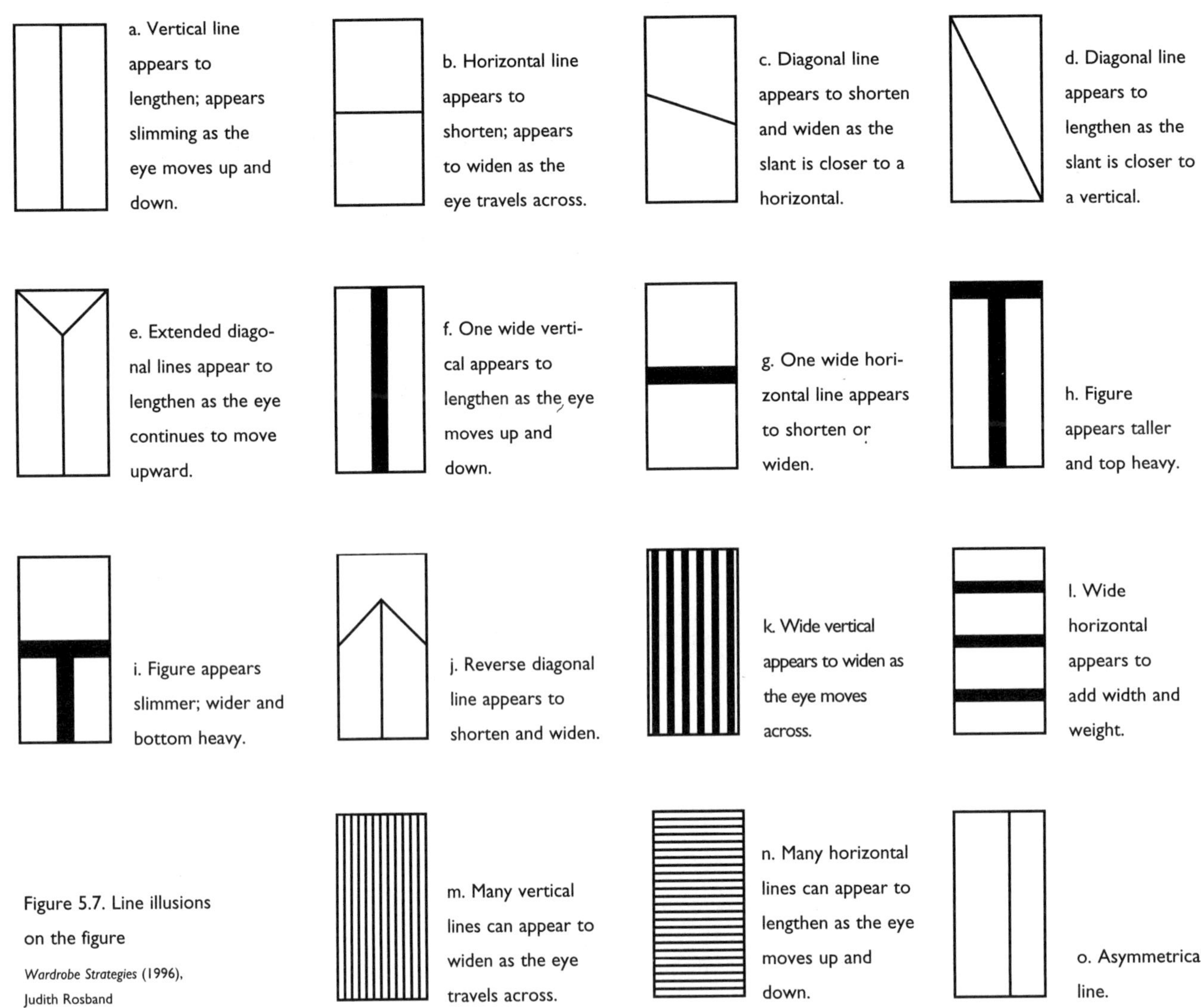

a. Vertical line appears to lengthen; appears slimming as the eye moves up and down.
b. Horizontal line appears to shorten; appears to widen as the eye travels across.
c. Diagonal line appears to shorten and widen as the slant is closer to a horizontal.
d. Diagonal line appears to lengthen as the slant is closer to a vertical.
e. Extended diagonal lines appear to lengthen as the eye continues to move upward.
f. One wide vertical appears to lengthen as the eye moves up and down.
g. One wide horizontal line appears to shorten or widen.
h. Figure appears taller and top heavy.
i. Figure appears slimmer; wider and bottom heavy.
j. Reverse diagonal line appears to shorten and widen.
k. Wide vertical appears to widen as the eye moves across.
l. Wide horizontal appears to add width and weight.
m. Many vertical lines can appear to widen as the eye travels across.
n. Many horizontal lines can appear to lengthen as the eye moves up and down.
o. Asymmetrical line.


Figure 5.7. Line illusions on the figure

*Wardrobe Strategies* (1996), Judith Rosband

front and hem is an embellishment near the edge of the garment that helps to emphasize the silhouette or outer lines.

Lines can be combined to create a variety of optical illusions in apparel. The effect of a line is due to the amount of time spent perceiving it. Thus, longer lines take more time to follow than short lines, and can therefore appear even longer. Repeated vertical and horizontal lines reinforce the emphasis of single lines, making a form appear longer or wider, based on the direction the eye moves. Wardrobe management consultants analyze individual body forms and suggest techniques for the use of layout and surface lines to help create a visual illusion of an ideal body figure—a tall, slim hourglass shape for women and a broad-shouldered, tapered hip line for men (see Figure 5.7). The use of line, along with other elements of design, to create an ideal body figure will be explored in greater depth in Chapter 12.

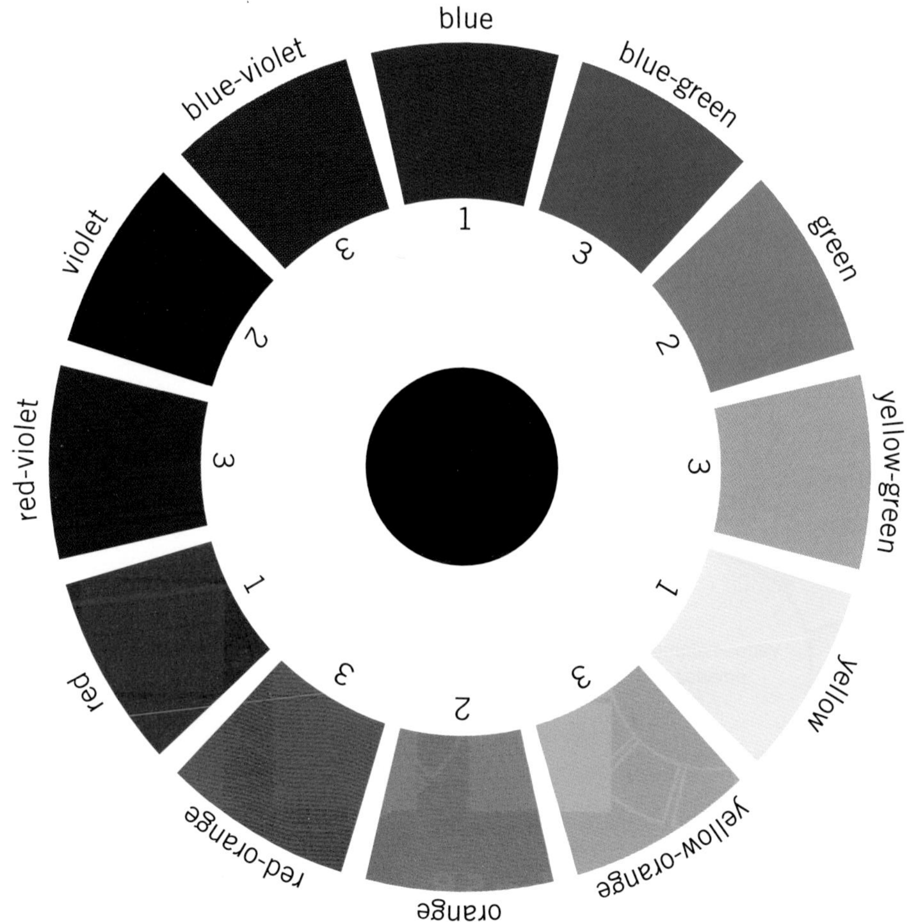


**Color Plate 1** Basic color wheel with designations for primary (1), secondary (2), and tertiary (3) colors.

**Color Plate 9**

Low, medium, and high levels of value contrast in colors of the body.

Dark

Medium

Light

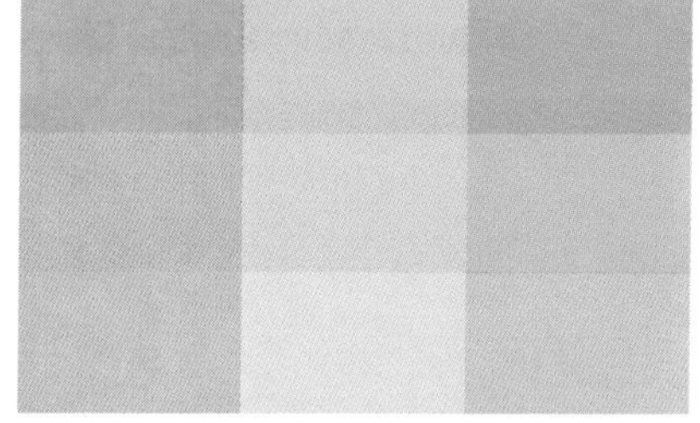

**Color Plate 10**

Coat by Ana Lisa Hedstrom.

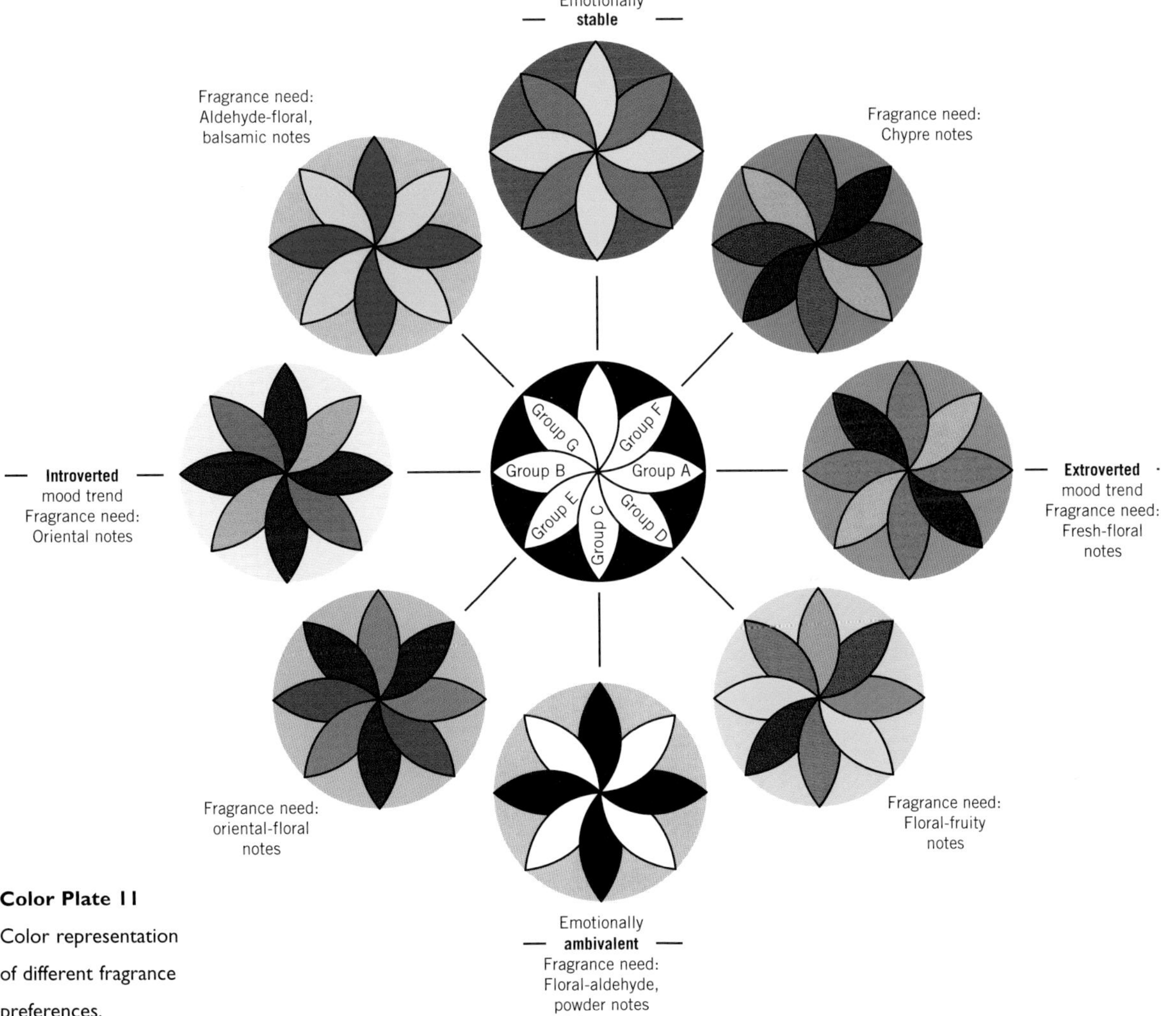


**Color Plate 11**

Color representation of different fragrance preferences.

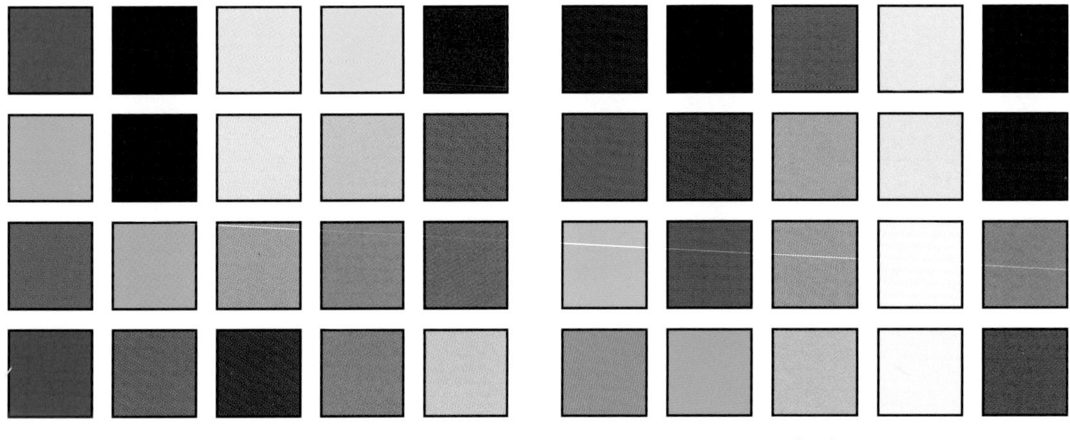


**Color Plate 12**

Warm and cool undertone swatches.

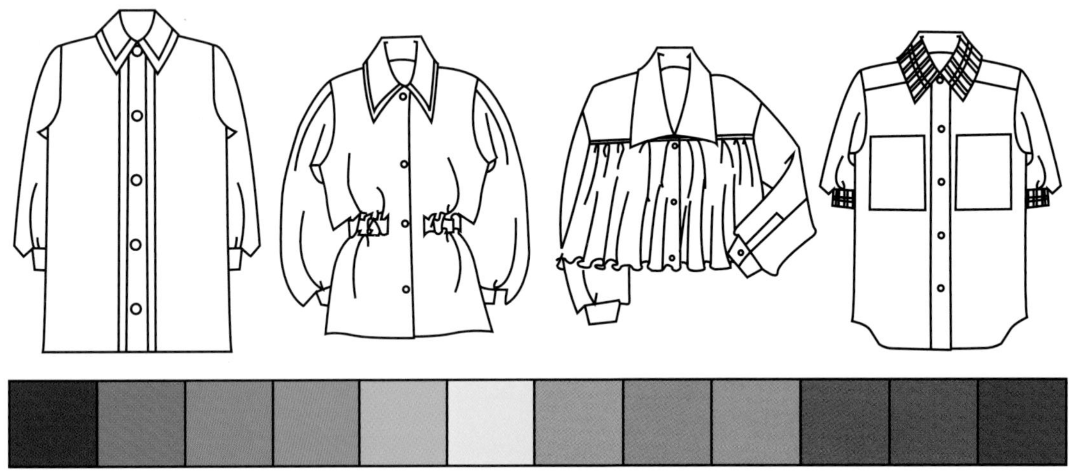

**Color Plate 13**

Elements from a presentation board including a color palette and four uncolored flats.

Figure 5.8. (below) Children's sportswear with angled and diagonal lines to express energy.

Figure 5.9. (right) Bed linens with simple stripe pattern that creates a more calming effect.

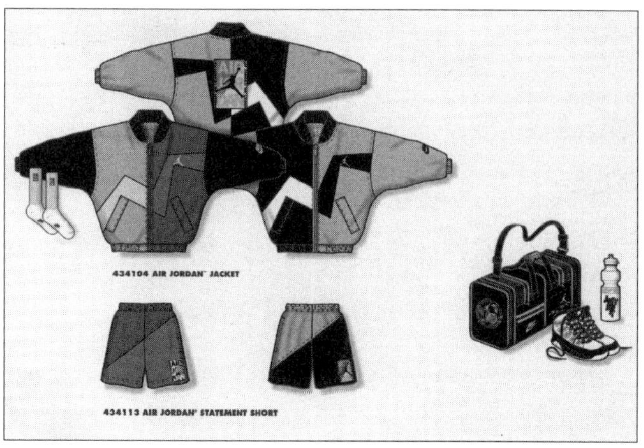

## EXPRESSIVE QUALITIES OF LINE

Let's continue with a second definition of line: A **line** is the visual depiction of movement and energy across a surface. This definition allows us to take up the expressive nature of line. A line is created by energy—the tension between gravity and the powerlines bringing electricity to every house, the effort of a sea turtle dragging himself onto the beach and leaving a curious pattern of footprints and lines from his shell in the sand, even the movement of your hand as you pull a pencil across the page to take notes takes energy. Do you have enough to keep going?

The direction of line influences the type of movement and energy expressed. Horizontal lines appear stable and at rest, as if they have succumbed to gravity. In apparel, they may create an emphasis on the width of the body. Vertical lines appear a little more forceful; they are able to withstand the pull of gravity. Vertical lines in apparel emphasize the length of a figure. Diagonal lines are the most dynamic lines—as if they are moving from a vertical to a horizontal position due to gravity. Thus, they create a sense of movement and energy.

The qualities of line contribute to the dimensions of pleasure, arousal, and dominance in an emotional experience. The qualities of the line may contribute pleasure to the senses. If the eye is led by the line in an interesting manner through a form, pleasure and satisfaction may result. The lines of high-heeled shoes lead the eye around and over the foot, contributing a pleasant sense of gracefulness.

Arousal and dominance are affected by the degree of energy expressed by line. This energy or movement can be described as *dynamic* or *static*. For instance, a heavy, varied line that has frequent and abrupt changes in direction will be perceived

**ACTIVITY 5.3** There are many emotions that can be communicated through line. Take a moment and try to imagine how you might express each of the following emotions through line in dress. First, draw lines that you think express the emotion. Then make a simple sketch, find examples from magazines, or describe the design you would create.

- Happiness
- Sadness
- Excitement
- Fear

as dynamic, active, and moving. It may help the viewer feel more aroused, active and "get going." Children's activewear often has many shapes and seamlines that create short, moving lines and can express the energy children expend during play activities (see Figure 5.8). On the other hand, a line that is fairly uniform, straight, and horizontal will tend to be perceived as static, stable, or at rest. Bed linens often have simple, repeated lines to help settle oneself for sleep (Figure 5.9). Uniformity and variation of lines affect the dominance of the emotional experience. When uniform lines are repeated, a greater level of control and order is expressed. If a form does not have enough repetition or similarity in the lines, it may seem frenetic and out of control. If one cannot find some degree of order among a group of lines, one will be overwhelmed and dissatisfied.

The expressiveness of line may complement the purposes of the product or environment. Consider the delicate, curved, and flowing lines of a lacy, beaded wedding gown. The lines are cascading around the figure, suggesting lightness and effervescence (Myers, 1989). The line in the lace, in the context of the marriage ceremony, expresses the emotion of love and the joy of the event. Love and joy are just two of the many emotions that can be expressed through the use of line and its qualities.

## SYMBOLIC QUALITIES OF LINE

As you recall from Chapter 1, symbolic qualities culminate in meaning or content, communicating an idea about the world. We can create our own meanings or interpret the ideas of others through symbols. A line becomes a *symbol* when there is a specific meaning attached to it (Bevlin, 1989). Symbols may or may not have physical resemblance to the object or activity symbolized. For instance, the flowing, diagonal swish-stripe on a pair of Nike™ tennis shoes is a symbol that stands for the brand, with no resemblance to the brand name. However, the flowing diagonal line represents the movement of athletic activity—fluidity, grace, and swiftness.

Many discount and department stores put lines or "walks" through their stores to tell customers, "come in, walk around this way." Many times, these walks are simply wider aisles that divide areas of the store. But some stores such as Kmart put tile designs on the floor that emphasize the walks around the floor plan of the store. Reading 5.4 provides an example of a store that used line effectively not only to outline the "walks" in the floor plan, but also to communicate the store's image.

Symbolism becomes standardized when a symbol and its meaning are accepted by members of groups or society at large. The most standardized symbols are lan-

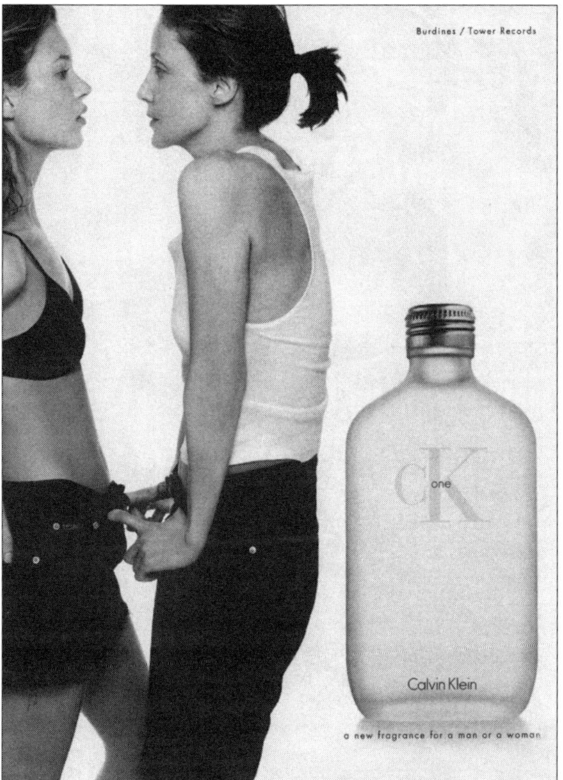


a

b

Figure 5.10 a and b. Examples of consistency between product image and logotype style.

guage. We use language to express thoughts and ideas accurately to others. Language can be used on apparel, as in T-shirts with slogans or cartoons on the front. Advertising also often uses tag lines (catchy phrases) to emphasize the emotional feeling or meaning of a product. Television ads for Nike shoes and apparel include a line that reads, "Just do it." These words are supposed to communicate the forceful, aggressive attitude consumers might find satisfying in the performance of athletic activities.

The very symbols in language—letters and alphabets—have become arts as well. Calligraphy is the art of hand lettering, exploring the grace and movement of line within a prescribed letter form. Typography is another such art, but the letter sets are mechanically produced, rather than hand lettered. When an apparel designer prepares a storyboard in the line planning process, calligraphy or typography styles may enhance the feeling of the collection and help express the essence of the clothing styles that are being proposed.

Symbolic and expressive features of typography are very important to the design of signage (labels, packaging, and advertising materials). The style of a logo or product name must harmonize with the feeling of the product or company image. The logotype for Calvin Klein products always includes very clean, simple letter forms. This is harmonious with the overall aesthetic style of all Calvin Klein designs (see Figure 5.10a). Compare the Calvin Klein style with that of Claude Montana in Figure 5.10b. What differences in expressive quality do you find due to the quick, slashing signature?

**ACTIVITY 5.4**

Team logos are carefully designed to represent the image of the university and the athletic program. For instance, the Iowa State University team logo was recently redesigned in order to enhance the vitality and aggressiveness of the athletic department's image. In Figure 5.11, you see the wimpy "before" Cyclone logo and the aggressive "after" Cyclone logo.

1. Do you think the redesign was successful?
2. Why?
3. What are the formal qualities of the lines that have enhanced the logo?

a

b

Figure 5.11 a and b. Old (a) and new (b) "Cyclone" logos for the Iowa State University Athletic Department.

### Expressive and Symbolic Qualities and Consumer Behavior

The expressive and symbolic nature of the many sources of line in apparel (e.g., outer silhouette lines and inner lines from seams, darts, pleats, fabric patterns) combine to create an overall effect. The expressive features of line may reinforce abstract and standard symbolism.

Look back at the children's activewear in Figure 5.8. The lines of the jackets are short, active lines expressing energy and movement. This dynamic quality is reinforced by the symbolic message of the "Air Jordan" logo. The Air Jordan trademark represents the athletic achievement and celebrity of Michael Jordan. Activity 5.4 will allow you to consider types of line, their expressive and symbolic qualities in another sports team logo.

## SHAPE

Whereas the most significant dimension of a line is its length, shapes have both length and width, and sometimes depth if the form is a three-dimensional object. Shapes also have formal, expressive, and symbolic potential. Sources of shape in apparel include the shapes of the body, the layout of garments and garment parts, and the surface shapes in patterned fabrics.

## FORMAL QUALITIES OF SHAPE

There are many ways to describe shapes. We can talk about the boundary of the shape and what it is like, or the surface and interior. A shape has a certain size and occurs in space. The shape has a relationship of proportion to other things around it. If there are multiple shapes in a form, then there are various relationships created between them.

### Types of Shapes

Shapes have an overall character or type that can be described as geometric or organic. **Geometric shapes** are generally characterized by straight, angular lines or simple forms. Squares, rectangles, triangles, and circles are common geometric shapes. **Organic shapes** usually have curvilinear lines and are similar to objects found in nature. Patterns created by oil on water or the shapes created in marbled prints are organic.

### Arrangement of Shapes in Patterns

Many shapes can be arranged together to create larger shapes or patterns. When shapes are interspersed at regular distances from each other in uniform positions, **ordered patterns** are created. Shapes that are arranged with no uniformity or regularity in their distance or placement create **random patterns.** A balanced plaid or checked fabric is geometric and completely ordered. An abstract tie-dyed fabric includes organic shapes in a planned placement. An animal print creates an organic and random pattern. (See Figure 5.12.)

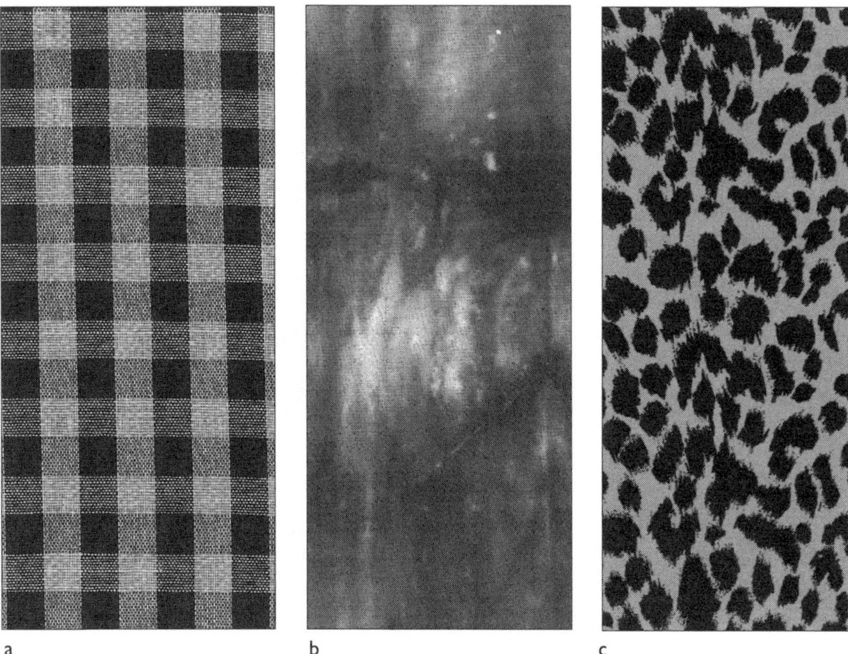


Figure 5.12. Examples of types of shapes and arrangements: (a) geometric, ordered checked fabric; (b) organic, ordered tie-dyed (c) organic, random animal print fabric.

Figure 5.13. Examples of the hourglass, bell, tubular, A-line and wedge silhouettes found in Western and non-Western cultures.

Figure 5.13a.
A-line Silhouette

- A garment that falls from shoulder in diagonals extending to hem.
- No indentation at waist.
- Examples: A-line dress popular in 1960s or trapeze coat.

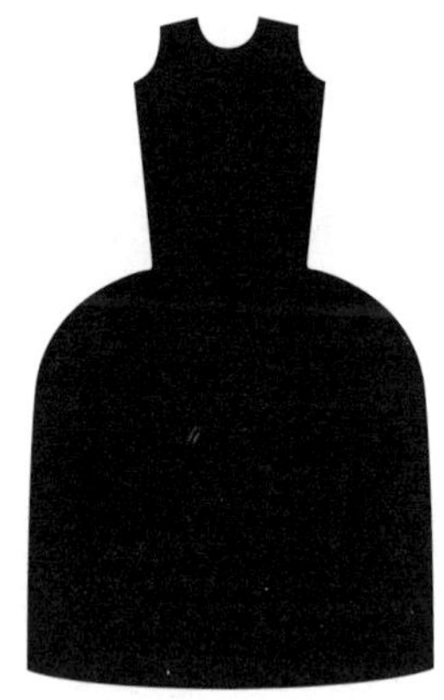

Figure 5.13b.
Bell Silhouette

- Indented waist with full, gathered, or pleated skirt adding fullness in hip and falling straight to floor.

Figure 5.13c.
Tubular Silhouette

- Narrow, cylindrical form with little indentation for waist or curve of bust or hip.

Figure 5.13d.
Wedge Silhouette

- Greater width in upper body than lower with diagonal/vertical lines; V-shape.

Figure 5.13e.
Hourglass Silhouette

- Balanced or equal shoulder and hip with obvious waist indentation.

a

b

Figure 5.14 a and b. (a) A figure with open, amorphous, boundaries between the apparel and (most of the) body and the environment. (b) Figure with closed, distinct boundaries between the apparel and body and the environment.

Right: photo by Wayne Maser.

## Boundaries of Apparel and the Body

The boundary of the entire apparel and body form is considered its **silhouette.** Silhouette is frequently used to define the outer shape of the apparel ensemble alone. These silhouettes are given the terms hourglass, tubular, bell, A-line, and wedge (Figure 5.13a-e). Popular silhouettes differ according to changing fashion trends through time.

The **boundary** of a shape is its apparent outline, border, or edge. These boundaries are created by line, color, shadow, or texture. An **open boundary** is formed when elements of design of apparel and the body blend with the elements of design of the surrounding environment (DeLong, 1987). Open boundaries are amorphous and blurry with no clear demarcation of the silhouette. A **closed boundary** clearly separates the apparel and body from the surrounding environment due to differences in design elements. Closed boundaries isolate the form from the background with a distinct edge. When paging through a fashion magazine, you might notice that photographs are designed to make the silhouette of the body less distinct. Through similarity of the elements of design of the apparel and body with the formal elements of the environment, the figure appears to blend in with the environment. In other photos, the shape of the body and the clothing is markedly different from the environment making it clearly defined and distinct. Figure 5.14 a and b illustrate the contrast between shapes that are clearly bounded and those that are more amorphous. Try Activity 5.5.

**ACTIVITY 5.5** Find three color figures that represent an open, closed, and in-between open-closed images. Place them on a continuum with open boundaries on one end and closed boundaries on the other end. What are the similarities and differences between the formal qualities of the apparel, body, and the environment that contribute to the types of boundaries perceived? How does the position and movement of the body contribute to boundaries seeming open or closed?

**Example of open boundary.** Similarities or differences between the apparel and body and the environment:

1. ____________________

2. ____________________

3. ____________________

4. ____________________

**Example of boundary that is somewhat open and somewhat closed.** Similarities or differences between the apparel and body and the environment:

1. ____________________

2. ____________________

3. ____________________

4. ____________________

**Example of closed boundary.** Similarities or differences between the apparel and body and the environment:

1. ____________________

2. ____________________

3. ____________________

4. ____________________

### Dimensionality

The **dimensionality** of a shape describes its apparent occupation of two- or three-dimensional space. When shapes occur in three-dimensional space, they are usually referred to as **forms**. The dimensionality of shapes or forms can be *actual or implied*. A three-dimensional shape has actual dimensionality. Implied dimensionality gives the illusion of depth when none actually exists, or de-emphasizes the actual depth of a form. A two-dimensional drawing of a three-dimensional figure, such as a fashion illustration, implies that the figure is three-dimensional. This is illusory; in fact, the figure is as flat as the piece of paper it is drawn on. Apparel professionals work with actual three-dimensional forms, but may create illusions of greater or less depth to create an ideal figure such as decreasing or increasing the fullness of the bust.

a

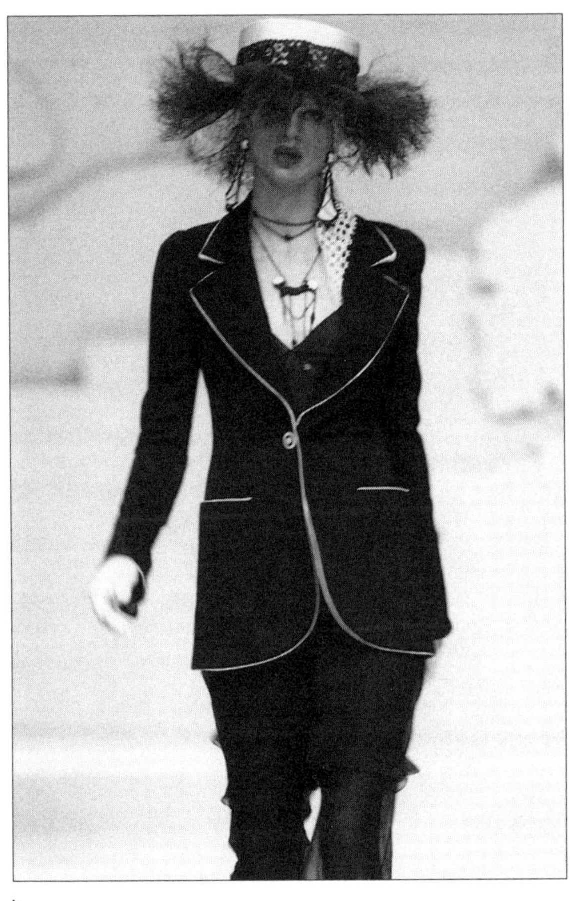

b

Figure 5.15 a and b.
(a) Ensemble displays a rounded effect that looks three-dimensional, assisted by shadowing and reflective qualities of fabric.
(b) Suit displays a flat effect that looks two-dimensional even though curved lines are obvious in jacket trim.

The body is a three-dimensional form occupying space. Apparel can enhance or de-emphasize the body's dimensionality. This interaction between the body and clothing is described as a flat-rounded continuum (DeLong 1987). A **flat effect** occurs when the three dimensional nature of the figure is de-emphasized and the silhouette becomes the most important visual feature. Apparel that has simple lines, a distinct silhouette that hangs away from the body, and a non-reflective surface can make the body appear more flat (Figure 5.15 a). A **rounded effect** emphasizes the cylindrical nature of body parts rather than the silhouette contours. Form-fitting garments with shiny surfaces and lines that extend around the body will emphasize the wearer's body curves and make it appear more rounded. When a body faces a viewer in a static pose, the effect may be one of flatness. Viewing a figure from one

**ACTIVITY 5.6**

Find examples of a flat effect and a rounded effect in a magazine or catalog.

1. Describe the characteristics of the garment layout and surface in the flat example that contributes to the perception of flatness.
2. How does the flat example differ in formal characteristics from the rounded example?
3. Does body position influence roundedness or flatness in your examples?

a

b

Figure 5.16 a and b. (a) Figure with many garment shapes that appear to advance and recede in space, creating planar separation. (b) Figure with shapes that appear to lie on the same plane, creating planar integration.

side or when the body is in motion increases the effect of roundness. Lighting also affects the apparent roundness of the body form because of the increase or decrease of reflection or shadow on the surface of the form. Explore your ability to identify flat and rounded effects in Activity 5.6.

Dimensionality can also be enhanced by overlapping shapes and through the use of a combination of color, lines, shapes, or texture that appear to be closer or further from each other and from the viewer. This apparent variability in distance of planar surfaces is called **planar separation** (DeLong, 1987). The different shapes appear closer and further from the viewer. Planar separation can enhance the visual dimensionality of the figure creating a visual focus. **Planar integration** occurs when the shapes in a form appear at the same distance from the viewer. Planar integration decreases the apparent dimensionality of the wearer. Figure 5.16 a and b demonstrate how planar separation can enhance or minimize a figure's apparent depth.

## EXPRESSIVE QUALITIES OF SHAPE

The expressive qualities of shape are partially derived from the qualities of the lines or surfaces that comprise the shape. A hard-edged square made with bold heavy lines will emphasize similar feelings of weight and clarity as the lines themselves

**ACTIVITY 5.7** Find five magazine ads with full-length figures which have various numbers of shapes.

1. Arrange them along a continuum with the examples showing planar separation effects at one end and integration effects at the other.
2. Describe the characteristics of the two examples you have placed at the extreme ends of the continuum. List which characteristics cause garment shapes to appear to lie on planes at varying differences from the viewer and on planes at similar distance from the viewer.

*Characteristics that create separation:*

1. ______________________________

2. ______________________________

3. ______________________________

4. ______________________________

*Characteristics that create integration:*

1. ______________________________

2. ______________________________

3. ______________________________

4. ______________________________

might. In addition, the quality of the boundary or edge expresses an attitude toward the surrounding environment. The quality of a shape's edge—hard or soft—expresses a tendency to yielding to pressure or weight.

There is a "directed tension" or visual dynamic that is expressed through shapes (Arnheim, 1986). This dynamic expresses the balance between forces inside the shape pressing out and the forces of gravity and objects around a shape pressing in. Consider the example of a balloon: A tension exists between the force of air inside and the stretch of the rubber balloon. Too little air pressure and the balloon deflates; too much and it will explode. Geometric shapes express greater dominance than organic shapes because geometric shapes express physical forces such as gravity, weight, and centripetal force. Thus they express power and control. Organic shapes are less dominant because they evoke the yielding and adaptive nature of biological things such as cells and organisms.

The size of shapes also contributes to dominance and arousal with larger shapes generally being more dominant and arousing. Size and scale relationships can express feelings or attitudes between the subject and the wearer or viewer. Compare the two floral shape prints in Figures 5.17 a and b. For the print union suit, the flowers are decorative, ornamental, and simply create a pattern. The arousal created

Figure 5.17 a and b. Floral prints with different size and scale relationships and different expressive qualities.

a

b

by the print is low. But the flowers in the bedding are more significant in size and may be used to create an overwhelmingly romantic setting.

## SYMBOLIC QUALITIES OF SHAPE

Just as lines can communicate specific meaning, shape also takes on symbolic qualities within the stylistic conventions and traditions of a particular culture (Parker & Deregowski, 1990). Organic shapes symbolize objects from nature. Geometric shapes may communicate concepts such as regularity and predictability, due to their origins in geometric systems (Hagen, 1986). For instance, squares symbolize the completeness of the four directions, solidity, correctness, and conformity. Triangles have dynamic potential, the tension of an uneven number of sides, and all the mystical and spiritual associations with the number three. And the circle symbolizes perfection, completeness, and unity (Myers, 1989).

These shape meanings may be carried into the design of store display. Furnishings to display businesswear for men often are comprised of simple, geometric shapes such as polished cubes in steel or wood. Activewear displays often include combinations of geometric shapes, including sports equipment. Furnishings and display equipment in a bridal and formal wear boutique often include more complex and organic shapes such as wrought iron or wicker chairs and soft cushions and pillows. These shapes carry meanings that enhance the meanings associated with the garment shapes and the contexts in which the apparel is worn. These meanings arise through the inherent nature of the shape as well as the acceptance by society of the meanings of these elements.

When shapes become standardized symbols, they become widely understood, just like symbols using line. Standard symbols are often highly geometric

**ACTIVITY 5.8** Find three fragrance ads from a magazine. Using a piece of tracing paper, trace the shapes created by the bottle, the cap, and any shapes created by details present on the surface of the bottle or cap. What types of shapes are created? Are they primarily organic or geometric? Are there many shapes in relationship to each other, or are there only a few? What is the overall feeling the different bottle shapes express? Any symbols included? How are the shapes emphasized through the design of the ad?

in shape, aiding recognition of the symbol and recall of its meaning. Traffic signs are made up of geometric shapes so we don't have to think "How many curves in a stop sign or a yield sign—I always forget?" Recognition of geometric shapes is immediate. Walk through an airport in any country in the world and there are certain symbols that you are bound to recognize. Although the specific shape of the male or female figure may differ somewhat among countries, you will likely be able to distinguish the men's and women's restrooms by their gender symbols.

Other common uses of shapes as standardized symbols include company logos, media features such as the Monday Night Football logo, and commemorative designs, such as the symbol for the Olympic Games. The use of logos on apparel is big business. For example, the Olympic games logo and Ralph Lauren's Polo logo are selling points for T-shirts and sweatshirts.

Reading 5.5 shows how various cultures use shapes to represent the turtle and the meanings of the turtle. Note how Patagonia has created a print using the turtle symbol to add meaning to the garments.

## SUMMARY

The elements of design are the building blocks of products and environments. The elements of design discussed in this chapter are color, lighting, line, and shape. The elements of color and lighting are perceived through vision, whereas three-dimensional lines and shapes may also be felt or touched. Each element can be analyzed in terms of its formal, expressive, and symbolic features. These features often operate unconsciously to contribute to an overall aesthetic experience. However, when one attends to these elements and consciously considers them, appreciation of the experience is deepened and enhanced. As future apparel professionals, you must understand and utilize the elements of design to enhance apparel products and environments.

The elements of design are integral to all aspects of the apparel and textile industries from design to retailing. At every point in the process, consideration of the elements that comprise the product or environment can help apparel professionals develop a more successful product or environment for consumers.

In Chapter 6 we will continue with the analysis of elements of design, taking up the elements of texture, space, kinesthetics and movement. Once again, we will find that each element has its own language of form that influences our aesthetic appreciation of objects and environments.

**LAB ACTIVITY 5.1**

You have now covered the elements of line, shape, and color. Its time to put what you have learned into practice. The formal, expressive, and symbolic aspects of line, shape, and color must be integrated to produce a successful apparel product.

In Color Plate 13 you see a presentation board that several designers have been planning. The designers have selected these four ladies blouses for inclusion in a line. But the designers were called to a meeting, so you, as a design assistant, are asked to make final decisions about this product line.

1. Color selections need to be made. The palette must be cut down to three colors per style body, with a total of no more than eight colors used.
2. Give names to the colors in the palette that are consistent with the expressive and symbolic feeling of the garment layouts.
3. The product plan also needs to have colors assigned to the style bodies.
4. Explain why you selected the colors you did. How are the colors, color names, and garment layouts consistent in expressive and symbolic nature?

## KEY TERMS AND CONCEPTS

accent lighting
actual dimensionality
actual line
afterimage
ambient or general lighting
analogous colors
artificial light sources
boundary
closed boundary
color
color notation
color relationships
color warmth
color wheel
combustion
complementary colors
cool colors
diffusion (of light)
dimensionality
direction
elements of design
expressive qualities of color
expressive qualities of light
expressive qualities of line
expressive qualities of shape
flat effect
fluorescent light
form
form (of light)
geometric shapes
hue
implied dimensionality
implied line
incandescent light
inner line
intensity (of color)
intensity (of light)
layout structuring
length
lighting
lighting the apparel product environment

line
monocromatic colors
open boundary
optical color effects
optical color mixing
ordered patterns
organic shapes
outer shape
Pantone color system
perimeter lighting
physiological color responses
planar integration
planar separation
primary colors
psychological and emotional color responses
random patterns
rounded effect
secondary colors
shade
shape
silhouette
simultaneous contrast effects
surface structuring
symbol
symbolic qualities of color
symbolic qualities of light
symbolic qualities of line
symbolic qualities of shape
tertiary colors
tint
tones
triad colors
undertone
uniformity
value
visibility
visible spectrum of light
visual weight (of line)
warm colors
width

## SUGGESTED READINGS


Davis, M. (1980). *Visual design in dress.* Englewood Cliffs, NJ: Prentice-Hall, Inc., pp. 48–51.

Myers, J. F. (1989). *The language of visual art: Perception as a basis for design.* Fort Worth, TX: Holt, Rinehart and Winston, Inc., pp. 161–182.

# READING 5.1

## Color Forecast for Menswear, Fall and Winter

Reading 5.1 Color Association of the U.S. Color Forecast for Menswear, Fall and Winter, 1996/97.

"Color (is) the most relative medium in art." Josef Albers

For 1996, a presidential election year, projected men's wear shades are tonally rich and a little ambiguous in cast. Men are seeking security in deep, resonant colors—wine reds, steely blues, and other rich shades whose exact hues are sometimes hard to pin down. An important trend is the growing influence from women's wear not only in color but also in fabrication. Menswear will move towards heavier, softer, and more easily draped fabrics in clothing with less construction and a softer outline. There is a strong emphasis on surface textures, which may range from high-tech coatings and glazes to weaves with a strong visual interest, such as the classic Harris Tweed. Interesting visual effects can be generated by opposing natural and synthetic fabrications, or draped and structured constructions.

Black and white are constant, particularly for the dressier looks. The Forecast's dark, 'aged' colors, most useful for suitings, jackets, and outerwear, include moss greens, smoky taupes, and steely blues. Browns are directional, as they are in women's wear, but the chocolates of the previous year have been entirely displaced by a striking collection of wine tones (the redish browns of column III) and by brolive, or a browned olive. A blued direction in the greens is also noteworthy.

The quirkiest colors are the slightly metallic tones of column IV. These colors of urbanized technology are appropriate to a younger, recreational market for tailored sportswear. These are deep colors with a sheen and rich depth that in chenille and mohair blends can also make a sweater glow. Grays, as in column I, are also becoming darker and cooler, tending toward deep smoky tones, such as an elegant taupe. In common with all the dark tones, however, they have the richness of velvet.

The pales of column V have a translucent quality and are also a little grayed, although less than on the Women's Forecast. Brown is directional, with the pale ecru being one of the most important colors. Wrinkle-free treatments will continue to grow and add to the appeal of pale dress shirting shades.

The accent colors shown in column VI, the Safe Brights, are slightly altered primaries with a frosted appearance. Royal blue, cherry red, and bright yellow return with little variation, but emerald and orange have been replaced by an old gold and a reddened blue. The effect is to make a group that is less sporty and more painterly—dramatic shots of color that vivify the more traditionally inspired tones of the rest of the forecast.

As a whole, the Forecast indicates a growing polarization between the light and dark ranges. Contrasts of soft and strong colors, or the sober accented by the striking, are a leading story. Nevertheless, the focus is solidly on the deeps with interesting color alliances including rich browns with spruce greens, and brown with gold orange. The forecast has a traditional elegance with an edge of sophistication that will appeal strongly in the late 1990s.

## READING 5.2
# Color Symbolism

D. Lauer

*"Don't worry, he's true blue."*

*"I caught him red-handed."*

*"So I told her a little white lie."*

*"Why not just admit you're too yellow to do it?"*

We frequently utter statements that employ color references to describe character traits or human behavior. These color references are *symbolic*. The colors in the above statements symbolize abstract concepts or ideas: fidelity, sin, innocence, and cowardice. The colors do not stand for tangibles like fire, grass, water, or even sunlight. They represent mental, conceptual qualities. The colors chosen to symbolize various ideas are often arbitrary, or the initial reasons for their choice are so buried in history we no longer remember them. Can we really explain why green means "go" and red signifies "stop"?

Reading 5.2 Lauer, D. (1985). Color Symbolism. From *Design Basics* (2nd ed.), p. 212. New York: Holt, Rinehart, and Winston.

A main point to remember is that symbolic color references are cultural: They are not worldwide, but vary from one society to another. What is the color of mourning that one associates with a funeral? In our society one would say black, but the answer would be white in India, violet in Turkey, brown in Ethiopia, and yellow in Burma. What is the color of royalty? We think of purple (dating back to the Egyptians), but the royal color was yellow in dynastic China and red in ancient Rome (a custom continued in the cardinals' robes of the Catholic Church). What does a bride wear? White is our response, but yellow is the choice in Hindu India and red in China.

Different eras and different cultures invent different color symbols. The symbolic use of color was very important in ancient art for identifying specific figures or deities to an illiterate public. Not only the ancients used color in this manner. In the countless pictures of the Virgin Mary through centuries of Western art, she is very rarely not shown in a blue robe over a red or white dress.

Symbolic color designations are less important in art than they once were. Still, they linger on and can help an artist to create designs on specific themes.

## READING 5.3
# Lighting Design

Reading 5.3 Lighting Design. (1992, December). *Chain Store Age Executive*, pp. 22–23.

Lighting, a key element of any successful retail design, can be a formidable weapon in keeping ahead of the competition. Good, well-designed lighting enhances merchandise appearance, calls attention to special displays, and contributes to overall ambience. Without the correct lighting, the article on display, be it a high-end luxury item or a fresh cut of meat, arouses little interest.

"When used correctly, lighting is a merchandising tool that is extremely effective in making products more desirable to shoppers," says lighting consultant Frank LaGiusa, Illuminations Plus, Cleveland.

Lighting also plays a key role in establishing store image. The interior is (or should be) a reflection of the sales and marketing strategy. Consequently, the lighting should be in harmony with the overall merchandising philosophy. Value-minded shoppers will often pass right by a store that "looks" expensive.

"It's important that your lighting doesn't send out mixed signals about what kind of store you are operating," explains LaGiusa. "Use the most efficient source that is consistent with the image that you want to project. Continuous rows of bare strip fluorescents, for example, clearly communicate a discount image."

## General Lighting

There are three main sub-systems of retail lighting: general lighting, perimeter lighting, and accent lighting. General lighting, the building block for any retail illumination system, establishes basic visibility by providing sufficient quantity, distribution, and color of light. It allows for clear evaluation of all merchandise.

Retailers should also keep in mind that the correct quantity of light is dependent on store type. Mass market, self-service environments (discount stores, drug store chains, etc.) require the highest general illumination levels, usually seventy to 100 footcandles or more. At the other end of the spectrum are high-end stores, which typically have a twenty to thirty footcandle range. The lower lighting level is offset by dramatic highlighting of featured displays.

All store types benefit from good color-rendering lamps and controlled glare.

## Accent Lighting

Accent lighting or highlighting (localized illumination using beamed or concentrated light) brings visual impact and adds sparkle to key displays. It attracts attention and can stimulate sales. In order to be effective, however, accent lighting must be used selectively.

"If you highlight everything, you end up highlighting nothing," says LaGiusa. "Too many people equate general lighing with accent lighting. Accent lighting is the headline—it's what captures your attention. Overuse it, and destroy its effect."

David Apfel, vice president and director of lighting design, HTI/Space Design International, New York, agrees that caution should be exercised when using accent lighting.

"Specialty stores tend to over-accent merchandise," he says. "They have rows and rows of track lighting on the ceiling, but it's not doing anything for them."

Most lighting designers agree that, as a general rule, featured displays should be illuminated five times the level of their surroundings. While the 5–1 ratio is typical, a 3–1 and 10–1 range is sometimes used in large, upscale stores.

Distance is important in accent lighting. The greater the distance, the smaller the effect and the greater the area illuminated. The effectiveness of light sources for accent lighting depends upon the intended degree of contrast. Incandescent lamps of low-voltage halogen lamps provide good accents in an upscale interior with subdued general illumination. More powerful general lighting, however, requires high intensity, high-wattage accent lamps for a noticeable contrast.

## Perimeter Lighting

Perimeter lighting (the lighting of vertical surfaces) adds visual excitement to wall displays and brings added attention to merchandise. In addition, strong perimeter lighting helps establish ambience and define the total space. Although all light sources can be used to light walls, fluorescent systems, which are linear by nature, are perhaps best suited to the task. Wall mounted lighting brackets (valences) that emit both uplight and downlight illuminate merchandise displays while defining the space. Hidden light sources are also useful.

## Glare Control

It's for good reason that glare is often called the enemy of good lighting. Reduced glare or good brightness control makes for a more comfortable store environment. And it helps keep shoppers' attention on the merchandise.

Direct glare from a lamp/luminaire combination is frequently caused by the incorrect positioning of the unit. Properly shielded luminaries can prevent this annoying distraction. Direct visual contact with the lamp/-luminaire combination should always be avoided. Indirect glare is usually caused by lamp light that is reflected off mirrored surfaces. The problem, while not as noticeable as direct glare, can be equally annoying. It can be eliminated by ensuring that the differences in brightness within the immediate area are not that great.

Mirrors and high-gloss metal panels and similar surfaces should always be used with caution. Forward-tilting surfaces reduce the chance of reflection. The mirror effect in a glass showcase can be softened by a high lighting level in the case.

### Light Color

The image that a store or an individual department conveys is partially dependent on the color of the light. All lamps do not emit the same color of light. Warm light from incandescent lamps, for example, suggests a feeling of intimacy; cool lighting can make a store seem larger than it actually is.

The color temperature (or chromaticity) of a light source is measured in Kelvins (K). The warmer the appearance, the lower the number; the higher the number, the bluer or cooler the color. The average color temperature of an incandescent lamp is about 2800K (generally referred to as warm-white). The color temperature of daylight (bluish-white) is about 5000K.

Designers should choose lamps that complement the store's product and overall image. Low lighting levels and warm white colors are generally preferred for intimate environments where ambience is a priority. A high general lighting level with a cool light color will help reinforce a low-price or discount image.

### Color rendering

The other way to describe the color of the light source is by its color rendering index (CRI), which measures how well it renders colors of objects. The maximum value of the CRI is 100, the point at which all colors are equally well rendered, such as with daylight or incandescent lamps. The higher a light's CRI number, the better the colors will appear under the lamp's light.

Values above 90 indicate excellent color rendering above 80 very good. Lamps with moderate color rendering properties (CRI lower than 80) should be used in areas where the quality of the color rendering is not a top priority.

## READING 5.4
# Finish Line Scores with Flooring Imprint

Reading 5.4 Finish Line Scores with Flooring Imprint (1995, March). *Chain Store Age Executive,* p. 74.

Few stores have combined flooring with ceiling treatments as effectively and for such high impact as Finish Line. The 7,500 sq. ft. athletic superstore prototype in North Riverside, Illinois, features a variety of surfaces that work together to create a sense of motion that practically propels customers through the space.

"We used flooring and ceiling treatments to convey movement. The materials create the store's energy and sense of action," says Gretchen Heinle, senior designer, Jon Greenberg & Associates, Southfield, Michigan, which executed the project for the Indianapolis-based retailer.

The tension between the free-form ceiling treatments and corresponding floor surfaces not only makes for an exciting and fun design, but also helps identify key departments.

The entry is marked by a wide marmoleum title aisle that wiggles through the store, front to back. The meandering aisle is reflected overhead by a wave-like ceiling form that undulates toward the rear of the space.

"To create tension and energy, the flooring and ceiling appear as if they are moving contrary to each other," Heinle adds.

A highly stylized graphic, representing Finish Line's "running man" icon figure, has been cut into the floor at the leaseline. Four different color tiles were used to fashion the graphic.

"The icon is used as a decorative element in different locations around the store, including behind the cashwrap," says Heinle.

The curving aisle, done primarily in light taupe, effectively splits the narrow store in half lengthwise as it pulls shoppers to the rear. It is flanked on either side by multicolored carpeting that echoes the hues used throughout the store. Tile is set into the carpet at various points. A striking orange tile triangle, for example, sets off the outdoor shoe department.

A charcoal-colored circular graphic is cut into the aisle three fifths of the way toward the rear of the store. The circle marks the entry to the licensed goods department. A high-profit category for Finish Line, the area is designed as a store-within-a-store.

The main aisle proceeds from the graphic in a light blue shade through licensed goods, where it is flanked on either side by imitation wood flooring (made of vinyl). Overhead, the high ceiling is fitted with a drop ceiling grid frame minus most of the panels.

## READING 5.5

# Turtle Symbolism For Various Cultures Adding Meaning to Surface Design Shapes of an Apparel Product

### Bearing the Universe on its Back

A common thread weaves through many myths of the world's diverse cultures. Our earth, these myths say—perhaps the entire universe—rides on the back of a turtle.

The Chinese tortoise divinity Kwei created the universe and stocked it with a long line of helpful turtles. One such turtle once slipped under a falling pillar to save the universe from collapse. In Mayan and Hindu legends the turtle is the universe itself. Sky and stars arc inside its carapace; its sturdy legs support land and ocean.

People in the Marquesas, Hawai'i, Fiji, Vanuatu and other islands of Oceania admired the turtles ability to dive to great depths. When they ate the turtle, they did so with rites that honored its sacredness. In Japan the turtle symbolizes peace, good fortune, and success. Native Americans spin intriguing tales of turtles involved in creation. In Wyandot myth, bits of soil on a turtle's back became the island that grew to be the world. For the Navajo the turtle is a warrior, and many Pueblos wear turtle shell rattles on their leggings during ceremonial dances. Turtle motifs appear in ancient rock art all over the world.

It's not surprising that mankind gave the turtle such extraordinary wisdom and responsibility. This is a creature of true dignity and patience, grace and imperturbable will.

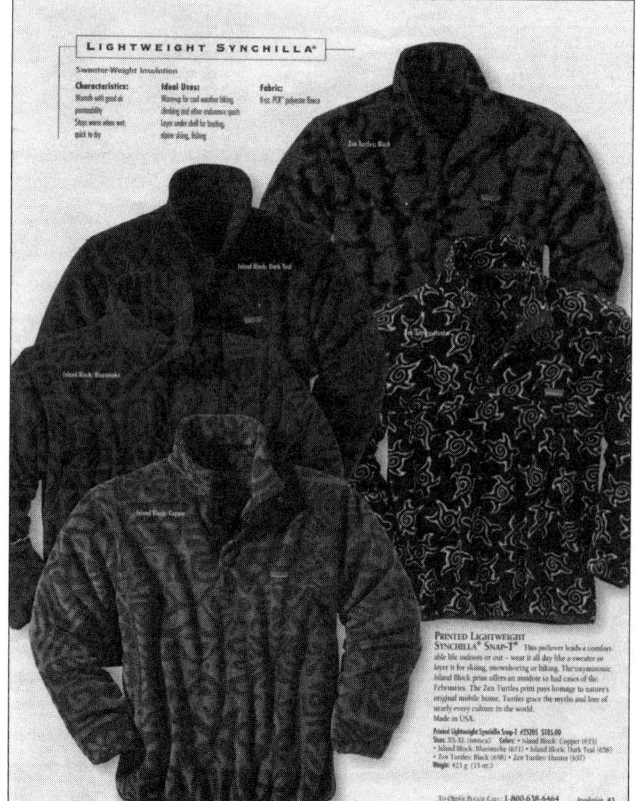


Reading 5.5 Turtle Symbolism For Various Cultures Adding Meaning to Surface Design Shapes of an Apparel Product, (1995). From Patagonia Fall/Winter Catalog.

CHAPTER 6

# Visual and Tactile Elements of Design

## Objectives

- Recognize the physiological processes that contribute to tactile sensation
- Understand and appreciate the dimensions of apparel forms that elicit the sense of visual and tactile textures
- Understand the concept of space on and around the body and in the near environment
- Appreciate the qualities of space that enhance apparel products and aesthetic experiences
- Recognize the kinesthetic sensory nature of the interaction between the body and the near environment, particularly through clothing
- Recognize the significance of tactile and kinesthetic senses to aesthetic appreciation of apparel and textile items
- Integrate visual, tactile, and kinesthetic elements of design in the planning and presentation of apparel products and environments

Suppose you were asked to put on a blindfold and try to identify your favorite sweater from a group of five sweaters. You would be allowed to touch the sweaters and try them on, but not see them. Do you think you could choose your sweater? You probably could, especially if it is a favorite because of the way it feels. The feel of a sweater to the hand and on the body is one of its most important aesthetic features. Without the ability to see and judge by visual features, one becomes more aware of tactile features of apparel. Apparel professionals must realize that the tactile elements of design are just as important as the visual design features in consumers' appreciation of textile and apparel products and environments.

In Chapter 5, we began to explore the various elements of design that are important to the design and presentation of apparel products. We discussed color, lighting, line, and shape. These are elements that are perceived mainly through our visual senses. In this chapter, we will continue with the elements of design, exploring texture, space, kinesthetics, and motion. These elements are multisensory elements of design. They are perceived through the sense of vision and the sense of touch. Thus, texture, space, and kinesthetics are considered visual and tactile elements of design.

## TEXTURE

**Texture** describes the uniformity or variation of the surface of an object. Texture is a description of the actual or implied characteristics of surfaces. Every surface has texture, whether it is smooth or rough, shiny or dull. Texture makes a significant contribution to the aesthetic satisfaction derived from textile and apparel products (Brand, 1964; Eckman, Damhorst & Kadolph, 1990). In addition to contributing sensory information about surfaces, texture also aides in the perception of three-dimensional form (Todd & Akerstrom, 1987).

Fabrics and garment construction details are the main sources of texture in apparel and textile products. Fiber content, yarn and fabric structures, and fabric finishes contribute textural qualities to apparel and furnishings. Construction details, such as seams, gathers, or pleating, alter the surface of the fabrics to create new textures. Findings and trims such as buttons, lace, and braid are additional sources of texture that may enhance a product. Take a moment to notice the variety of textures contributed by fabrics, trims, and findings on the apparel worn by those around you.

Texture can be actual or implied. **Actual or tactile texture** is due to variation or lack thereof on a surface that can be felt by the skin. **Implied or visual texture** is that which we "see" due to various visual design techniques, but cannot be physically felt. For instance, patterns of lines or small shapes might imply texture, but the this texture could not be perceived through touch. Implied texture is sometimes called "visual texture." However, we will use the terms actual texture and implied texture because actual texture is perceived through both the visual and tactile senses.

### TACTILE PERCEPTION OF TEXTURE

The tactile perception of texture occurs when individuals actually touch objects. When a person caresses a fur coat, or the smooth polished wood of a dining table, the hands and fingers "feel" the texture. Objects in the near environment can be touched whereas visitors are usually not allowed to touch a painting, sculpture or fiberart in a museum. Thus, the body, clothing, furnishings, work and study environments, and outdoor environments provide many experiences for tactile appreciation of texture.

The perception of tactile texture results from the activation of our sense receptors in the skin, not only in the hands but all body areas, through contact with some surface. There are three types of sensation that provide information to the brain about what we are feeling against our bodies. These types of sensation are *pain, touch, and temperature* (Heller, 1991). Touch is most closely related to texture. All three sensations can be activated by contact with apparel and other objects in our environment. When we caress an angora sweater, we perceive the touch of the surface, the tickle of the fiber ends, and the warmth of the fabric. Likewise, if we were to caress a steel-wool scouring pad in a similar manner, we would perceive the touch of contact, the prick of fibers, and the impression of temperature.

Our aesthetic appreciation of these two touch encounters are different because the *tactile thresholds* of the two contacts differ. A tactile threshold is the point at which a stimulus is strong enough to be perceived or produce a response. Tactile thresholds include the *intensity* or pressure of the contact, the *duration* of the contact and the *vibration* between the surface texture and the skin (Heller, 1991). Caressing the sweater may be pleasurable because the intensity of contact is low as we move our hand across the surface quickly and lightly. There is a tickle of vibration between our hand and the sweater. The same intensity of touch on the scouring pad is scratchy and unpleasant because the vibration between our hand and the stiffer metal fibers is greater, thus activating our pain receptors and causing us to pull our hand away.

## VISUAL PERCEPTION OF TEXTURE

When we cannot touch a surface to "feel" it, our sight becomes a substitute for the sense of touch. Through experience, we learn to recognize different textures and to make assumptions about how they will feel. Young children are avid about touching objects around them (while often incurring their mother's frustration with grimy fingerprints everywhere). Children touch things out of curiosity and the desire to learn about their environments. They store impressions of how different surfaces and textures look and feel. Adults do not have to run through the house touching everything; data in memory is used to relate the visual and tactile impressions of surface textures.

Although the correspondence between the visual and tactile senses is learned early, individuals continue to seek confirmation of visual perception of texture through touch. Research has found that individuals sometimes depend more heavily on either visual or tactile sensory cues, depending on the dimension of texture (e.g., density or roughness) that is being judged. However, the information from both sensory channels is integrated into the tactile impression and neither information from vision or touch is considered more important than the other (Lederman, Thorne & Jones, 1986). This is because the correspondence between vision and tactile senses is not perfect. The eyes sometimes play tricks, as in the perception of implied textures. The eye suggests that a snake's skin might be slick and slimy, but when touched, the surface is dry and smooth. Thus individuals do not rely solely on vision for

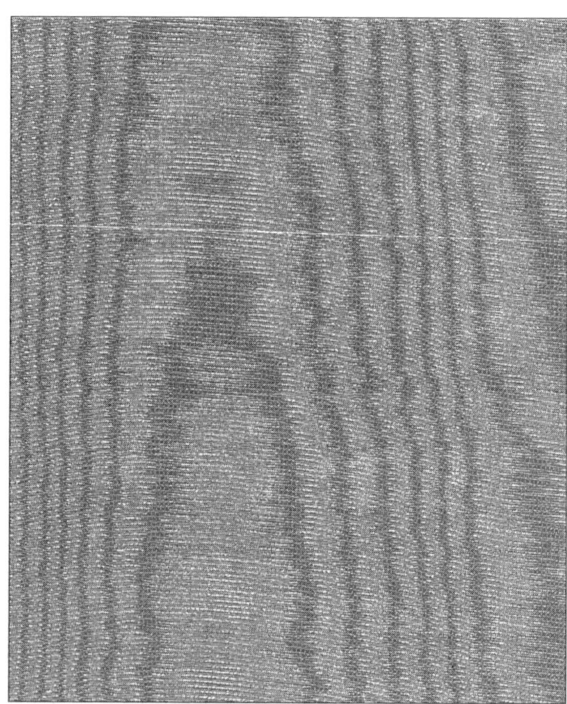

Figure 6.1. Fabric with visual texture that differs from its tactile texture.

texture information. Figure 6.1 demonstrates that fabric may feel different than the visual texture suggests.

Adult shoppers often touch and caress clothing as they sort through items in a store with as much interest and curiosity as children. First, people touch fabrics for the sheer pleasure of perceiving sensations of texture. Shopping activities feed the senses, including touch. Second, the tactile impression of the garment is important to determining preference and making purchase decisions. If an individual were to trust a visual impression of a wool jacket that looked soft and smooth only to later discover it was scratchy and rough, then he or she would be dissatisfied with the jacket. The inability to confirm the visual perception of texture through touch is a limitation of catalog and television shopping. These marketers must be aware of this problem and address it through various means, including accurate, high quality close-up photography and verbal descriptions of fabrics. Figure 6.2 shows an example of copy used to describe the feel of a pullover jacket, explaining how the jacket fabric will perform in keeping the wearer warm and dry.

## FORMAL QUALITIES OF TEXTURE

In the apparel and textile industry, fabric *hand* and *drape* (Kadolph, Langford, Hollen & Saddler, 1993) are important aspects of fabric texture. **Fabric hand** describes the way a fabric feels to the sense of touch. **Fabric drape** is the manner in which a fabric falls or hangs over a three dimensional form. The hand and drape of fabrics are classified according to objective features of the fabrics that are listed in Table 6.1. These qualities of texture are usually described according to a continuum between two extremes for each dimension.

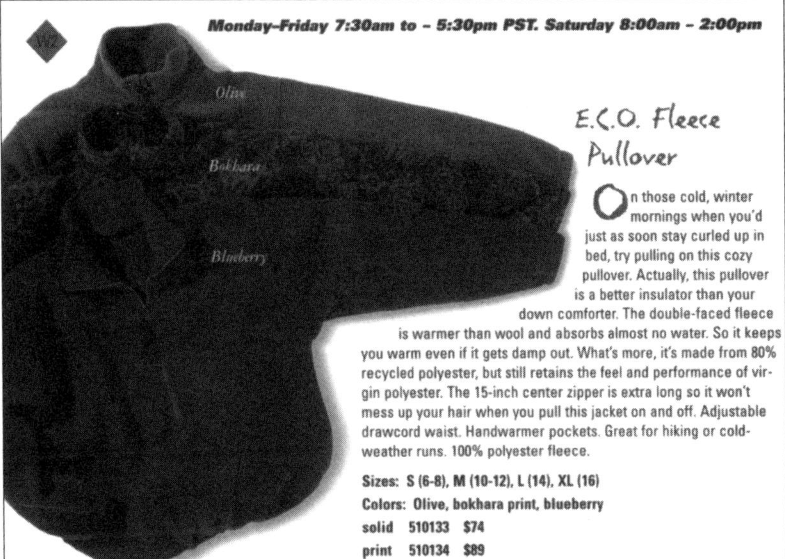


Figure 6.2. Photo and copy describing a fabric texture in detail.

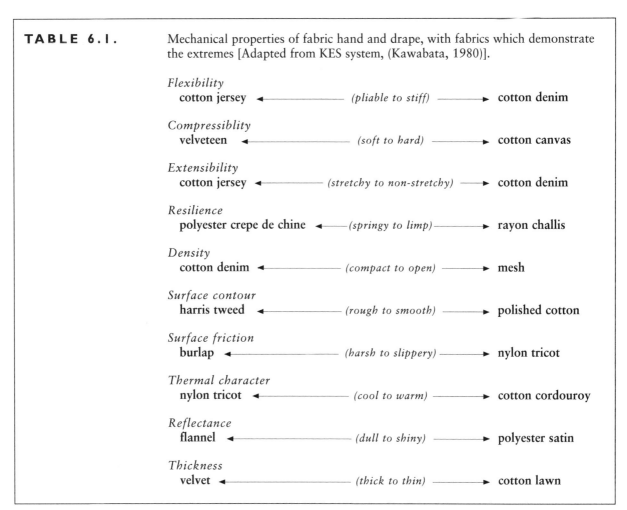

**TABLE 6.1.** Mechanical properties of fabric hand and drape, with fabrics which demonstrate the extremes [Adapted from KES system, (Kawabata, 1980)].

| Property | Extreme | Range | Extreme |
|---|---|---|---|
| *Flexibility* | cotton jersey | ← *(pliable to stiff)* → | cotton denim |
| *Compressiblity* | velveteen | ← *(soft to hard)* → | cotton canvas |
| *Extensibility* | cotton jersey | ← *(stretchy to non-stretchy)* → | cotton denim |
| *Resilience* | polyester crepe de chine | ← *(springy to limp)* → | rayon challis |
| *Density* | cotton denim | ← *(compact to open)* → | mesh |
| *Surface contour* | harris tweed | ← *(rough to smooth)* → | polished cotton |
| *Surface friction* | burlap | ← *(harsh to slippery)* → | nylon tricot |
| *Thermal character* | nylon tricot | ← *(cool to warm)* → | cotton cordouroy |
| *Reflectance* | flannel | ← *(dull to shiny)* → | polyester satin |
| *Thickness* | velvet | ← *(thick to thin)* → | cotton lawn |

These properties are *objective* features of fabric texture. They may be measured or consistently described through a variety of methods or tests by various individuals. These dimensions of hand have impact on aesthetic perceptions (Brand, 1964; Elder, 1977; Paek, 1979; Paek 1985). However, consumers may use descriptive or evaluative terms that are less objective or encompass more than one objective dimension. Explore this idea in Activity 6.1. For instance, research often assesses consumers' perception of fabrics based on the four dimensions of smoothness, stiffness, bulk or compactness, and thermal characteristics (Burns & Lennon, 1994).

Within the textile and apparel industry, the purchase of fabrics is still dependent for the most part, on the use of samples that designers and buyers directly see and feel—subjective decision-making. The standardization and use of the objective descriptors such as the KES system, may allow researchers and industry specialists to specify fabrics more precisely and make better use of computer technology (Hearle, 1993). These objective measures could be systematized in the same way color systems such as Pantone and Munsell have standardized color-related aspects of design and production through computer and communications technology. Such developments might aid manufacturing and retailing industries in increasing efficiency in the production of apparel and textile products which successfully meet consumers' preferences for texture.

## SOURCES OF TEXTURE

Texture in textile and apparel products is created at various levels of the design process from fabric design through apparel design. Texture in apparel comes from fabric surfaces, fabric prints or patterns, manipulations of the surface in garment construction, and variance in the tone or light on the surface. Textures are present in the surfaces of the body. Body textures can be enhanced or diminished by apparel and other products. Texture can be emphasized and enhanced in the presentation of those products in advertising and store display. Texture in textile and apparel products can be due to characteristics of the fibers, yarn structure, fabric construction, finishes, and surface design (Kadolph, et al. 1993).

### ACTIVITY 6.1

The properties listed in Table 6.1 are referred to as objective properties—they are measurable or quantifiable facts about fabrics. Consumers often use more subjective terms to describe fabrics and textures. The following is a list of subjective terms that might describe textures.

1. What objective properties are involved in these subjective descriptors? (Hint: some terms might be influenced by more than one objective property.)
2. Name at least two common fabric names (e.g. corduroy, satin) that might fit each subjective descriptor.

- silky
- lofty
- crisp
- sheer
- glossy
- spongy
- delicate
- scratchy
- cozy
- creamy

## Textures in Textile and Apparel Products

**Texture due to fibers.** The fiber used in a fabric may determine the textural qualities of the surface of the fabric. The length and surface contour (convolutions, scales, etc.), pliability, diameter, and cross-sectional shape of the fiber determines how it can be spun into yarn and influences the texture of fabrics created by the yarns (Kadolph, et al. 1993). For instance, silk fibers are long and smooth and most often yield smooth fabrics. Wool fibers are short and crimped. When the wool is spun, the crimp and the fiber ends contribute a softness or roughness to a surface.

**Texture due to yarn structure.** There are many types of spun yarns that have different textural properties. A two-ply worsted yarn is usually much smoother than a novelty yarn such as a slub yarn or a boucle yarn. The novelty yarn will create more surface interest and is most often used in a less dense fabric than the smooth yarn.

**Texture due to fabric construction.** The means of constructing fabric from fiber and yarn is another source of variation in texture. Patterns due to various knitting or weaving combinations used to produce fabric yardage yield different textures. For example, satin fabric has a smooth texture due to long floating yarns across the surface. Dense, loopy knits used for winter hats and scarves are thick and lofty.

**Texture due to finishes.** Various thermal, mechanical, and chemical treatments are often employed to alter fiber and fabric properties. These finishes may also influence textures. For example, the mercerization of cotton yarn or fabric creates smoother cottons. Crimping polyester—passing fiber or yarn between heated textured metal rollers—adds resilience, minimizes the clammy feeling, and adds spring to fibers used in sweaters, carpets, and other furnishings. Laundry practices such as stone washing and the use of starch and fabric softener also subtly alter fabric stiffness or softness.

**Texture due to surface design.** Further manipulation of fabrics can add textures. Printing designs with paint or dye on fabric adds pattern. Small repetitive patterns printed on fabrics may create implied texture. Other patterns may be embossed (imprinted) in the fabric surface to create textural interest. For example, velour upholstery fabric may have texture added when it is embossed with decorative patterns.

The perception of patterns of shapes on the surface of fabrics *as texture* is dependent on the *size* of the shapes and the *distance* from which the viewer perceives the shapes. There is a threshold between perceiving patterns as individual shapes or as a surface texture. When shapes are large, they may more likely be seen as individual shapes, such as large polka dots. When shapes are smaller, they are more likely to be perceived as texture. Similarly, when a viewer is very close to the surface, the individual shapes are distinct, but as the viewer moves away, the eye takes in more shapes at once and the shapes lose definition. Thus, small individual shapes are perceived as a textural surface element.

a

b

Figure 6.3 a and b. Figures demonstrating (a) determinate and (b) indeterminate surfaces.

The apparent thickness or visual clarity of the surface is called the determi- :y of a surface (DeLong, 1987). **Determinate surfaces** are definite, sharp, and clear. Shapes on the surface are perceived as clear figures. The lines in the surface are often straight and angular. The uniformity and size of shapes influence the perception of those shapes as a clear pattern rather than as a texture. Contrasting, rather than blended colors and simple, smooth surfaces contribute to the perception of determinate surfaces. Fabrics such as wool gabardine or cotton broadcloth would likely be perceived as determinate surfaces. **Indeterminate surfaces** are characterized by a lack of clarity and an apparent visual thickness. There are many levels of figure and ground in the pattern on an indeterminate surface. Small, organic shapes in random organization and reflective surfaces tend to create indeterminate surfaces and more visual texture. Again, the distance between the viewer and the surface will contribute to the clarity or determinacy of the tactile surface. In viewing an indeterminate surface, visual cues may be inaccurate or provide insufficient information about the nature of the surface. Indeterminate surfaces invite the viewer to touch them and confirm or disprove the visual perception of the surface. Examples of indeterminate surfaces could include boucle and angora sweater knits and fur. Figure 6.3 a and b illustrates the visual differences between a determinate and an indeterminate surface. Try Activity 6.2.

| **ACTIVITY 6.2** | Find two examples that represent either indeterminate or determinate surfaces.<br>1. Which ensemble shows determinate surfaces? Which one is indeterminate?<br>2. What are the formal qualities of the apparel and body surfaces that contribute to determinacy? |
|---|---|

**Texture from product design.** Textile and apparel designers select fabrics based on their inherent textural qualities; designers also manipulate fabrics in the design process to enhance the inherent textures or to create new textures. The smoothness of satin can be enhanced by using few seams and no surface embellishment in a flowing silhouette. Or the smooth satin can be manipulated to create texture by pleating or gathering the fabric and by embellishing it with thread, trim, sequins or beads.

The texture of the fabric surface and layout design considerations must be considered simultaneously. The surface of the fabric will influence the effect created by layout design. Changes in the hand, drape, and visual texture of a fabric will change the look of a design. Imagine the differences between a simple cape or shawl in silk chiffon and the same style garment made up in fake fur. Or even, as Figure 6.4 suggests, consider a cape made of carpeting!

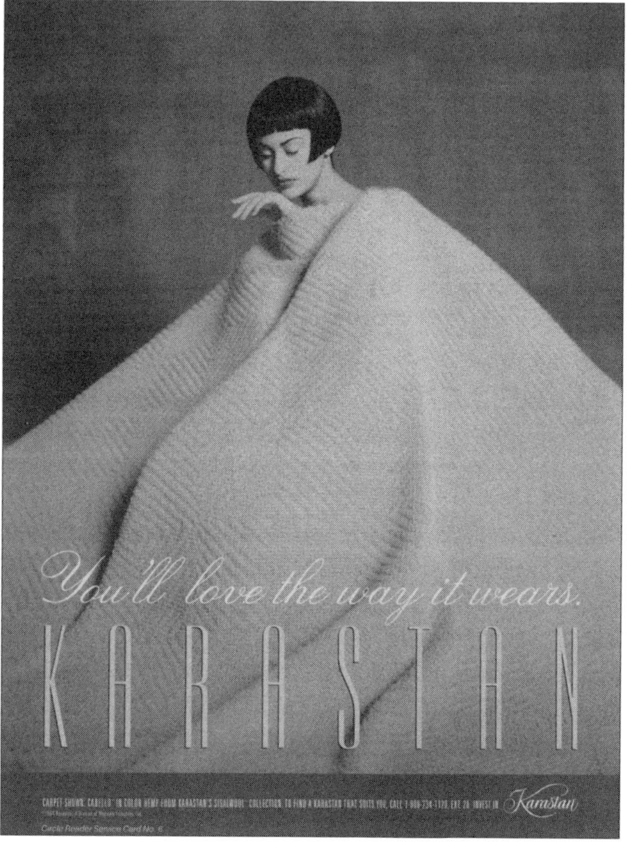


Figure 6.4. Hand and drape influence the effects created by layout considerations.

**Texture from light on the surface.** Finally, variation in the amount of light cast on or reflected by a surface can increase or decrease the perception of texture. The amount of ambient light present in an environment affects our visual perception of actual texture. Light affects our ability to see differences in color or tone created by reflected light and shadow on a surface. Intense light eliminates much of the shadow created by surface texture. Low levels of light or inadequate light does not create strong shadows or allow the eye to differentiate shadow from lighter surface areas. Medium light creates the highest degree of contrast in light and shadow, thereby enhancing the visual perception of texture (Myers, 1989).

The amount of light reflected or absorbed by a surface is influenced by its color value. Low value hues like black or navy absorb light, whereas high values reflect it. The same fabric texture in high and low values would tend to be more easily perceived in the higher value, light-colored fabric. Practice identifying sources of texture in Activity 6.3.

### Textures of the Body

Skin and hair are surfaces of the body that have textures. In Western culture, smooth skin is an ideal to be sought. Consumers pursue a smooth look for skin and want to feel soft and smooth to touch and be touched. Creams, lotions, and other cosmetic treatments are applied to the body in order to add moisture and soothe the skin. Blemishes and imperfections in skin are smoothed and concealed either with make-up or surgery. Touching smooth objects with rough hands creates contrast and may decrease sensory enjoyment of the smoothness.

Fashions in hairstyles depend not only on shape, but also on the texture of hair. Long, straight hair styles and those with short, tight curls provide different textures for hair. Products are available to straighten or add body and curl to hair, depending on fashion and individual taste. The textural effects vary by

**ACTIVITY 6.3**

Recall that at the beginning of this chapter, we suggested that you are probably able to identify your favorite sweater without being able to see it. Let's test this assumption. Each student should bring a sweater from home for the activity. Form groups among the students in class (seven to ten students per group).

1. Blindfold each student and pass the sweaters around in random order, one at a time.
2. Pass the sweaters until each student believes he or she has her/his own sweater.
3. Once each student has found their own sweater, each should describe the textural cues used to identify it.
4. Remove the blindfolds and see if everyone has the correct sweater. How easy was it to perform the activity?
5. What tactile dimensions most contributed to the ability to identify the sweaters?

Figure 6.5. Products that perm or straighten hair change its natural texture.

style and by individual. Figure 6.5 shows some different textural effects in hairstyles for African-American women.

## Formal Qualities, Apparel Design, and Consumer Behavior

The texture and hand of fabrics is important to the design of apparel and textile products. The emphasis on textural qualities changes as fashion trends change. At one time, color and pattern variations might be important for a particular market segment; other times, texture variations may become the focus of fashion trends. Designers need to be aware of texture as a source of interest and an element that is combined with line, shape, color, and pattern. According to a recent trade journal article (Taylor, 1995), interest in texture was "considered a major influence for the holiday and spring men's wear" lines for 1996 through 1997 according to a fabric buyer. The buyer for another company said, "Texture and color are important . . . I also have an eye out for prints. Mixing texture and prints is something we're trying to work out." These statements demonstrate how the elements of design are emphasized or create the focus for new styling in apparel design. Note the interaction of textural and other design elements in the trends in children's outerwear discussed in Reading 6.1.

Fabric hand is always important to consumers. Regardless of whether texture is an important design focus in apparel, consumer satisfaction includes appreciating the feeling of the fabric to the hand and on the body. Reading 6.2 demonstrates another textile product—bath towels—through which consumers seek satisfaction from texture. In this reading, we see that aesthetic satisfaction from texture often drives a purchase.

Textures of apparel products can be emphasized through the manner of presentation in apparel product environments. As we pointed out earlier, medium light is the most effective light condition for perceiving texture. The effect of ambient and accent lighting on products for which texture is an important design feature is important to consider. Consider the lighting in a fashion show; it should be carefully designed to show the textural interest in a designer's collection.

Textures of apparel products may also be emphasized through similarity or contrast with the textures of display furnishings in stores. Glass, steel, and wood furnishings and display units are often highly polished and reflective surfaces. These might emphasize a smooth texture through their similarity, or contrast with a rough texture. Other types of surfaces include faux granite, smooth or rough plastics, and plaster.

## EXPRESSIVE QUALITIES OF TEXTURE

The expressive nature of texture may arise through associations with the surface contour, flexibility, and thermal character of the fabrics. Smoothness and roughness (surface contour) are evocative of emotional soothing or irritation. Smoothness is a pleasurable sensation and contributes to peaceful effects. Pajamas are usually smooth textured, to soothe the nerves of the body and contribute to emotional calming and rest. Stiffness and resilience, on the other hand, can be arousing. Consider the sturdy surface of a vinyl rainslicker. Not only does it keep the wearer dry, its stiffness and resilience echoes the buoyant feelings and determined attitude of the wearer to "beat the elements."

Highly flexible or yielding textures such as soft sweater knits or velours may be expressive of pleasurable, low arousal and high dominance, emotional states such as comfort and relaxation. On the other hand, stiff fabrics such as starched cotton shirts and firm jackets are more dominant and may be expressive of activity rather than repose.

The perception of warmth in a fabric can enhance the expression of emotional comfort and warmth. A stiff, heavy fabric made of Kevlar™ Aramid (which is used in firemen's protective suits) might keep one warm enough, but its stiffness and density doesn't feel cozy, as soft wool sweaters do. Similarly, one could curl up with a book on a sofa covered with tin foil, but metal doesn't evoke warmth as soft leather would. The perception of warmth may come from social traditions as well as tactile qualities. Quilts are expressive of physical warmth due to the tactile weight of the fabrics and they are also expressive of affection between individuals (Cerny, 1994). Warm, cozy fabrics may make people feel loved.

### SYMBOLIC QUALITIES OF TEXTURE

Textural qualities may have symbolic meanings connoting formality or status. Texture may be due to some variation in the materials of a surface. Refinement is the process of removing irregularities or impurities from a substance or a surface. A refined surface is smooth and polished. Refinement and polish, as personal or social characteristics, indicates a person with fine or elegant manners. Hence, surfaces that have less variation, are more smooth or shiny and are often symbolic of elegance and status. In apparel, women's formal eveningwear generally employs smooth, silky, or shiny fabrics rather than rough, nubby wools or lofty knits to communicate elegance. This may be a meaning carried on from the days when wealthy classes wore fine silks and poor laboring classes wore clothing made from coarse homespun woolens and cottons.

The symbolic and expressive elements of texture are highly related. These meanings arise through cultural conventions and change over time. For instance, the meaning of velvet in women's apparel in the early twentieth century centered on images of wealth and luxury due to the cost of producing the fabric. But over time, velvet has come to also encode images of femininity and sensuality, meanings that arose through associations of meaning with the sensory qualities of the fabric's surface (Lutz, 1994).

The uniformity of body surfaces may also imply perfection. In the classical Greek sculptures, the ideal for physical beauty included a concern with perfecting the form and the surface of the body. This smoothness and perfection of body surfaces continues to be part of an ideal beauty today in Western cultures. Smooth textures in skin and hair are symbolic of perfect, classical beauty. To further consider the formal, expressive and symbolic aspects of texture, try Activity 6.4.

## SPACE

Have you ever been in an elevator with someone who is claustrophobic? Or are you claustrophobic yourself? People who are claustrophobic are afraid of being in small spaces. On the other hand, people who are agoraphobic are afraid of wide open spaces. Regardless of which extreme causes anxiety, some people have a very heightened awareness of the concept of space. Apparel professionals should cultivate an awareness of space because it affects the way consumers perceive and appreciate apparel products and environments.

**Space** is all the available area within a given boundary. In the visual arts, the picture plane or the visual field define the space available for paintings or

**ACTIVITY 6.4**

Find three magazine ads in which the apparel ensembles include three or more textures on fabric and other surfaces (don't forget skin, hair, and accessories).

1. Create a chart similar to the one below for the examples identifying the source of the textures and the formal qualities of the textures. Are these objective or subjective descriptors?
2. What are the expressive and symbolic effects of the apparel ensembles? How do the textures evident in the ensembles contribute to these effects?

| | *Sources of Texture* | *Formal Qualities* | *Objective or Subjective?* |
|---|---|---|---|
| *Example 1* | | | |
| 1 | | | |
| 2 | | | |
| 3 | | | |
| 4 | | | |
| *Example 2* | | | |
| 1 | | | |
| 2 | | | |
| 3 | | | |
| 4 | | | |
| *Example 3* | | | |
| 1 | | | |
| 2 | | | |
| 3 | | | |
| 4 | | | |

sculpture. The arrangement of elements within that space is the composition. Apparel professionals develop an awareness of space in two ways: the composition of space occupied by the body and apparel, and the composition of space in apparel product environments.

Space is not itself an element of design, but it is controlled and defined through the use of the elements of line, shape, color, texture, and lighting. In designing apparel and body relationships, the space occupied by, and directly surrounding, the body is broken up into shapes, textures, etc. and organized into a coherent visual image. As the body moves, it interacts with the space in the near environment. We will focus here on the space of the body, and consider the aesthetic experiences of apparel through kinesthetics and movement in the next section. But the reader should keep in mind that space and movement of the body are intimately related.

The space inside a retail store or other product environment is also divided into smaller areas and shapes to create and organize the consumer's experience with products. Lines, shapes, patterns, and textures are created through store layout and interior design, furnishings, display equipment, signage, and the products themselves. These elements are designed and organized within the available space to create pleasing shopping experiences.

## FORMAL QUALITIES OF SPACE FOR APPAREL AND THE BODY

Space is created and organized on the body through the placement of lines, shapes textures and patterns on the surface and the layout of the apparel. These elements create the visual effect of filled or unfilled spaces. There are also visual relationships created between the space occupied by apparel and the body.

### Filled versus Unfilled Space

The space occupied by the body and apparel can appear to be filled or unfilled. The consideration of filled or unfilled space must include both two-dimensional surfaces and three-dimensional forms. **Filled or unfilled space** describes the relationships between figures (ie., lines, shapes) and the ground (ie., surface) of apparel and within the apparel layout. Filled spaces have many figures created by pattern or texture and little or no apparent ground surface. Unfilled surfaces have few or no figures on the surface. Filled space in the three-dimensional form may include the perception that the body fills or takes up all the space created by the garment forms. Unfilled three-dimensional forms may be larger or more voluminous than body forms, there is more space inside the form than the body can potentially occupy.

Spatial relationships between the apparel product and the body are perceived through visual, tactile, and kinesthetic senses. One can see the patterns of shapes filling a space when observing another clothed body in a photograph (2-D) or in person (3-D). One can also feel the spatial relationships of the apparel, body, and environment as a wearer.

**Size of elements.** The size of the elements in a pattern or texture affects the perception of filled or unfilled space. On apparel surfaces, patterns composed of larger shapes might create an effect of filled space more than small shapes placed at similar distances. But when placed closer, small shapes may have a more filling effect, covering more background area. Small, all over textural effects often have a more filling effect, taking up all surface and leaving no clear

a

b

Figure 6.6 a and b. Two sweater knit ensembles that differ in their perception of filled (a) or unfilled space (b).

background. Larger, organized patterns create a sense of figure and ground. Compare the two sweaters in Figure 6.6. The sweater in Figure 6.6 a has a linear textural pattern composed of small areas of many colors. There is no clear background color or area. In Figure 6.6 b, the black stripes appear to be figures (lines) on the white ground of the sweater. Thus, the surface of the sweater does not appear as filled as the sweater in Figure 6.6 a.

**Placement of elements.** The placement of elements (lines, shapes, etc.) on the surface in random or ordered patterns and the density of the patterns can influence the perception of filled or unfilled space. An ordered placement of elements may create the effect of a more filled surface than would the random placement of the same elements. The spacing or distance between surface elements is the **density** of the print or pattern. Patterns that are densely spaced create a filled effect, whereas patterns that are more spread out on a surface create an unfilled effect. Figure 6.7 shows two fabric surfaces that differ in their appearance of being filled or unfilled.

The placement of three-dimensional forms on the body also influence the perception of filled or unfilled space. In Western dress, there are standard forms of organizing body shape including the fitted bodice, tubular sleeves and pants, and the use of the waistline to divide the figure into top and bottom. These standard garment forms divide and organize the space of the body in the silhouettes described in Chapter 5. In other cultures, these forms may not be as

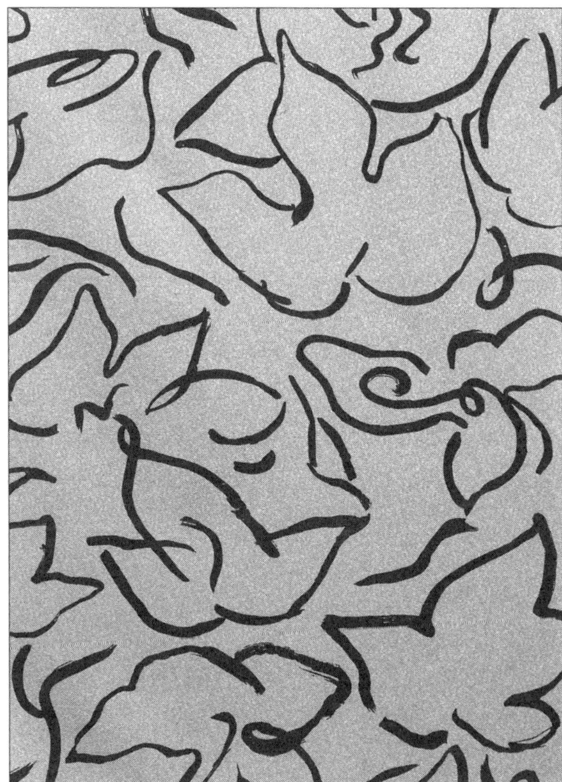

Figure 6.7. Filled (left) and unfilled (right) fabric surfaces.

prominent. For instance, the traditional Japanese kimono organizes the body into rectangular sleeves and a tubular body shape. These shapes are less conforming to the shapes of body parts (i.e., arms, legs) than Western dress, and carry different feelings of filled space. The kimono sleeve hangs from the arm in a flat plane; the interior of the sleeve is not filled by the arm as a tailored shirt sleeve might be.

## Relationships between Apparel and the Body

The relationships between shapes in apparel and shapes of the body influence perception of space. First, the additional size and space created in a garment beyond the physical dimensions of the body is called the *ease* and *fit* of the garment. Second, shapes of apparel can either conform to, contrast with, or extend the natural body shapes. The effect created by shapes of apparel, along with color and texture, places visual emphasis either on the 3-D clothing or the body.

**Ease and fit.** Clothing is designed with a certain degree of ease or "room" in the garment, which is dictated by style, movement, and fit considerations. Style ease is a design consideration for apparel; the amount of style ease incorporated in garments is dictated by style and fashion trends. For instance, baggy "grunge" styles of the 90s include shirts and jeans with a great deal of ease. The amount of ease in a design affects the degree to which bodies fill the 3-D space available in garment forms.

a

Figure 6.8. Shapes, surfaces, and patterns of apparel create (a) body primary or (b) clothing primary emphases.

b

Fit ease allows for expansion and movement of the body. Fit affects both the aesthetic appeal and the practical concerns for comfort. As an aesthetic criterion, if a garment fits too snugly, there may be a distortion of the intended shapes created by apparel on the body. When garments are too large, the shapes may collapse.

**Emphasis on the body or the apparel.** The 3-D space created by apparel or body shapes can conform to the natural contours of the body, or create space with new contours. In addition, colors and textures can enhance the visual importance of apparel or body shapes, creating a primary emphasis on either clothing or the body. This is called a body-primary or clothes-primary effect (DeLong, 1987). A **body primary** ensemble creates a visual focus on the body shapes, surfaces, and contours. Body primary ensembles tend to have 3-D space filled by body shapes (such as knit garments, or slim tailoring), and unfilled 2-D space with muted colors that do not create focus. A **clothing primary** ensemble may conceal body contours through unfilled 3-D space of the garment and create visual focus surface on elements of the clothing itself. Clothing primary ensembles might include large shapes extending beyond or hanging from the body, and surfaces comprised of interesting colors, patterns and textures. Compare the visual emphasis on the body and the clothing in the ensembles in Figure 6.8. Practice identifying body and clothing primary ensembles in Activity 6.5.

**ACTIVITY 6.5** Select four clothing ensembles from a magazine or catalog that demonstrate a variety of visual design characteristics.

1. Arrange the examples on a continuum ranging from most body primary on one end and most clothing primary on the other.
2. Do the shapes of the ensembles conform to body curvatures or conceal them?
3. How do the characteristics of line, color, and texture further influence the visual importance of the body or clothing in your examples?

## FORMAL QUALITIES OF SPACE IN APPAREL PRODUCT ENVIRONMENTS

### Filled versus Unfilled Space

In the apparel product environment, similar concepts of filled or unfilled space can be applied. The types of surfaces and the number, size, and placement of shapes and forms within the two-dimensional or three-dimensional environment creates filled or unfilled space. In addition, the scale relationships between the size of the product environment and human size creates different spatial effects. We will focus in this section on the retail setting. You should also keep in mind that the concepts may also be applied to two-dimensional environments such as catalogs, print advertisements, or television.

**Types of surfaces.** In the apparel product environment, surfaces include flooring, wall, and ceiling surfaces as well as surfaces of display units and furnishings. These surfaces can be filled or unfilled through pattern or texture. When filled surfaces are used in a three-dimensional environment, the surfaces contribute a greater sense of filled space in the total area. Compare the two interiors for Cole Haan Shoes in Figure 6.9 a and b. In store b, the physical dimensions of the selling floor are larger than in store a, and there are less furnishings taking up space in the center of the area. Even so, the space seems to be filled by the patterned flooring and chairs. The use of the same patterned flooring in the smaller store a might create a sense of overcrowding.

**Number and size of elements.** Three dimensional forms created by display units, merchandise, and furnishings occupy space inside the product environment. The number and size of these elements also contribute to the visual effect of filling the space in the environment. Obviously, more elements and larger elements fill more space.

**Placement of elements.** Three-dimensional elements can be placed randomly, in groupings, or at regular intervals throughout a space. The more random the placement of objects throughout a space, the more the space will seem filled and cluttered.

**Scale of elements.** An object's size relative to the human body is referred to as **scale.** The physical dimensions of product environments are perceived in relationship to human size. Product environments can have a very large, grand scale

a

b

Figure 6.9 a and b. Differences in the visual appearance of filled and unfilled space in Cole Haan stores at Rockefeller Center, New York City (a), and Boston, Massachusetts (b).

Photos by George Heinrich.

or a small, intimate scale. An environment that is in very large scale includes a good deal more space than customers can potentially occupy. Compare the scale of the environments created in the Neiman Marcus store on Union Square in San Francisco, and the Broadway store in Northridge, California, in Figure 6.10. The height of the ceiling above a customer in Neiman's creates a very different perception of unfilled space than the moderately scaled ceiling height in the Broadway store.

a

b

Figure 6.10 a and b. Differences between size and scale of retail environments shown by Neiman Marcus, Union Square, San Francisco, CA (a), and Broadway, Northridge, CA (b).

Photos by Paul Bielenberg, Bielenberg Associates.

## Customer Interactions within a Product Environment

The organization of filled or unfilled space in a product environment has its impact on the way customers might interact in a space. The goal of store designers and visual merchandisers is to control the flow of shopper traffic and create an overall aesthetic feeling within the store space. The types of merchandise displays will dictate the desired type of customer interactions within a store's space.

These goals may be achieved, in part, through placement of the elements within an environment. For instance, are there aisles or walkways created between the elements in the store? Are these aisles wide and orderly, creating a clean, formal atmosphere? A trendy apparel boutique might use clear mannequins or other plexiglass fixtures to display products, creating a clean, spare, and spacious environment. The customer can select products without lingering long within the space because merchandise presentation is very direct. Or does merchandise "close in" around the shopper, creating a more festive environment? The amount of unfilled space and the organization of elements affects formality and festivity, as well as the ease with which a customer can walk around and browse in a store. A vintage clothing store may use a dense, cluttered arrangement of merchandise. There may be little room to move through the space. But this closeness may encourage a customer to slowly peruse the racks and piles of one-of-a-kind items, leisurely comparing the items. Compare the different arrangements of space in Figure 6.11.

a

b

Figure 6.11. Two retail environments differing in the use of visual space: (a) An unfilled, formally arranged store display in Marshal Field, State Street, Chicago, IL, and (b) a more densely filled, festive store display, Rich's, Atlanta, GA.

Courtesy of FRCH Worldwide.

## EXPRESSIVE QUALITIES OF SPACE

The space occupied by the body and clothing can be expressive of emotional states and feelings such as physical freedom or restriction. Physical freedom of the body in its occupation of space may be considered more pleasurable than constriction. At the end of the work day, people often "slip into something more comfortable" which can include looser, softer fabrics that allow the body to relax and occupy more space. The extension of the boundaries of the body through apparel expresses a feeling of freedom to expand and extend oneself.

Apparel that constricts or limits the space of the body may exert dominance or control over body postures. Although facial expression is the strongest bodily cue showing the expression of emotional states, it has been suggested that posture reinforces the expression and indicates the intensity of the emotion (Bull, 1983). Clothing that is restrictive and controlling of posture may contribute to expression of the reserve or withholding of oneself emotionally from others. Tailored, close-fit businesswear enhances the image of control over emotion that may be seen as necessary in the business setting. Similarly, costumes for theater and dance are meant to enhance the expression through body posture or movement. We will take up the expressiveness of the body in further detail in the next section on kinesthetics and movement.

In the apparel product environment, the amount of filled or unfilled space also may contribute to feelings of pleasure, arousal, and dominance. Filled spaces provide many elements, which can elicit sensory pleasure and lead to greater arousal. Toy stores might fill every available surface within a space in order to stimulate and arouse the customer (Figure 6.12).

The scale of the space can create a mood and lead to arousal and dominance. Larger scale spaces may be awe-inspiring or overwhelming to a viewer. Take a look back at the interior of Neiman Marcus in Figure 6.10a. The scale of this space is intended to express elegance and grandeur because of its sense of dominance. Small scale spaces are more intimate and cozy; there is greater potential for people to come together. Smaller spaces in a retail environment are often being structured to set a mood similar to that which people create in their homes—relaxed and casual. Reading 6.3 is a segment of a survey of visual merchandisers and store designers which suggests that the move away from abstract and trendy environments toward "homey" environments is a trend of the 90s.

## SYMBOLIC QUALITIES OF SPACE

Space occupied by apparel and the body can be symbolic of personal power and the spirit or ethos of a particular era. Space might be considered a commodity item; control or ownership of space costs money or power. The amount of space one can command for oneself is an indicator of one's personal power. Henry the VIII, King of England dressed in apparel that greatly expanded the amount of space that he physically occupied. The extensive sleeve padding and elaborate dress of the king symbolized his power as a royal monarch. The padding in business suits suggests a similar meaning in contemporary society.

The figure ideal for any particular period in history defines the desired shape of the body and the space that a body should occupy. Mannequins are idealized three-dimensional forms of the human body, which demonstrate the culturally appropriate alignment of the spine and distribution of weight that define posture. The interaction of body ideals, space, and fashions is evident in the evolution of mannequin styles and postures that are used to display and

Figure 6.12. Filled spaces stimulate high arousal as shown by the Marvel Comics Boutique at FAO Schwartz.

Courtesy of Amtico.

promote fashion (d'Aulaire & d'Aulaire, 1991). In the twentieth century, these figure ideals have changed along with fashion trends and the *zeitgeist*—the spirit of the times (Danielson, 1989).

In the 1980s, apparel forms often consisted of many layers with elaborate surfaces. These filled spaces on the body communicated an element of luxury, grandeur and consumption consistent with the contemporary economic mood of expansion and growth. In the 1990s, apparel forms are simpler, cleaner shapes and surfaces. The 90s spirit, which is communicated through apparel and other trends, includes awareness of environmental and social issues engendered by individual and mass consumerism. Practice applying the concepts of space we have discussed by trying Activity 6.6.

**ACTIVITY 6.6**

Try this activity to see if you can apply the concepts of space we have discussed in an analysis of different apparel product environments. Make a visit to your local shopping mall or downtown business district where you can visit three different apparel stores. (They don't all have to cater to the same consumer market segment.)

1. Note the formal elements of space in the environment. Do you get a sense of filled or unfilled space as you enter the stores? What elements contribute to this feeling (i.e., describe the surfaces, and the size, number, and placement of elements)?
2. What type of customer interactions are encouraged in the space? Do customers linger over displays, sorting through merchandise or do they glide by?
3. What mood is set by the space? What contributes to this feeling?
4. Evaluate the space in the stores. Do you think the store interiors and displays are successfully designed?

# KINESTHETICS AND MOVEMENT

Suppose you are planning to go to the Homecoming dance with several friends. You stare into your closet wondering what you would like to wear. After evaluating several items, you come down to the following choices: (a) the T-shirt, jeans, and tennis shoes you wore to class; (b) a bodysuit, jean jacket and slim miniskirt with sandals; or (c) a fringed satin blouse and full skirt with boots. Which outfit might contribute the most to your enjoyment of the dance? If you chose c, you may already understand that the movement of apparel and the body enhance aesthetic experience. The fringed blouse and the full skirt will swing and sway with your movements and the boots will emphasize the stomping beat of your feet as you dance.

**Kinesthetics** is the aesthetic satisfaction derived from the movements of one's own body. Kinesthetics is an appreciation of the "way it feels to do something." Kinesthetic satisfaction from apparel comes to the *wearer* through the sensory experience of interaction between one's own body movement and apparel. Satisfaction can also result from a *viewer* appreciating the *movement* of apparel and the body of another person.

As we said earlier, space and movement are intimately connected concepts. Movement takes place within space, but during movement activity, the body's occupation of space constantly changes. "Movement shows the difference between space and time, and simultaneously bridges it" (Ullman, 1984, p. 36). Thus, when we consider the movements of the body, we may refer to the space occupied by the body and changes that occur through those movements.

## FORMAL QUALITIES OF MOVEMENT

The qualities of movement affect how consumers perceive and appreciate apparel as a wearer and as a viewer. In an apparel product environment, the movement of apparel on the body of a model in a fashion show or advertisement may enhance satisfaction and stimulate the purchase of apparel.

### Type of Movement

Movements of the body may be described according to the type of action that is performed. Types of movement include *stretching* the trunk or limbs, *extending* the body and limbs in space, and *bending* limbs or trunk to create an angle. When a person reaches for something overhead, he or she stretches muscles in the legs and torso and extends an arm. The body may be extended to its greatest potential in order to grasp the object.

*Opening* and *closing* movements define the placement of the limbs in relation to the torso of the body. Arms hanging down or reaching outward from the body are open. Arms held in front of or folded across the torso are closed. Similarly, crossing one's legs in a sitting position is a closing movement. Models in advertisements are often shown in a moment of action, performing an activity that may include these various types of movements.

### Direction

Body and limb movements are directed through horizontal and vertical planes in space. Movements can follow upward or downward, forward or backward, side-to-side, or in some combination of these directions. Various activities include movement in different directions sequentially. Walking or running has primarily a forward direction, but the process involves upward and downward motions of limbs in sequential and rhythmic patterns. The heel-to-toe step of runway models causes an exaggerated swing of their hips from side to side.

### Force

Movements of the body are performed using varying degrees of *force*. The **force** of a movement is the strength or energy expended in the muscles to overcome any resistance. Resistance may come from gravity, wind resistance, or any additional weight (including clothing) that the body must carry or push against. The force of body movements may or may not be adequate to overcome the resistance. Most people can easily muster the force to overcome gravity to walk, but few can clear a five-foot bar in a high-jump competition. Force can also be an excess of strength required to overcome resistance. If a person closes a door with excessive force, it will slam shut and create the (desired) effect of a loud bang.

### Flow

Movement of the body rarely occurs as a single, isolated event—except for the couch potato who rarely exerts him or herself to any more movement than that required to breathe! Usually, body movements occur in succession, such as one foot-step after another for a walker, or the rapid tapping of a writer's fingers across a keyboard. The succession of body movements is called the **flow**.

Flow of movement has a **tempo,** which is the timing or speed of repeated movements. As walking speed increases to a run, the tempo of footsteps increase. The flow of movement will include more forceful steps, and the coordination of steps with the swinging or pumping of the runner's arms will increase. Runway models move at different tempos depending on the style of apparel, music, and the theme of the show or collection.

The uniformity or variation among movements of various body parts in succession creates **pattern.** Dance steps can create elaborate patterns of arm, leg, and torso movements. Consider the many patterns created by steps and arm movements in the various Country Line dances that have become popular. Even a movement as universal as walking creates patterns that can vary. There is a pattern of movement that is specifically defined for the wedding march—step-together-pause, step-together-pause.

## Interaction between Apparel and Body Movement

The movement and flow of the body must be considered in the design and promotion of the apparel product. As the body moves, apparel on the body moves with it. This interaction creates awareness of the presence of the apparel, from the movement of the apparel items, and from relationships between the movement of the body and of clothing.

The movement of apparel in response to body movement may create or reinforce for a wearer or viewer the simple awareness of the presence of those apparel items. This awareness may be considered pleasing or annoying and thus affect aesthetic satisfaction. Dangling earrings that touch the face or neck with every move of the head are difficult to ignore. The presence of such earrings might remind the wearer of how the earrings look, that they are a favorite pair, and that the touch feels sensual. On the other hand, the awareness of the item might be an unwanted distraction for the wearer during activities that require concentration, such as reading or at work.

As the body and apparel move together, that movement may be pleasurable for the wearer to feel or the viewer to see. A long skirt creates an s-curve line as the wearer moves. It may be sensual for the wearer to feel the fabric move against the legs with each step. The graceful curve is also pleasant to the viewer. Thus, the aesthetic appreciation of the body's movement is reinforced through the movement of the apparel as well.

The layout of a design, the ease and fit, and the hand and drape of the fabric affect the way apparel will respond to body movement. The body interacts with apparel in appreciation of movement (DeLong, 1987). The range of apparel movements includes *correspondence, anticipation, restriction, and lag.* In corresponding movements between the body and apparel, both move together smoothly and equally. The most corresponding apparel ensemble might be a leotard; the garment maintains the same relation to the contours of the body as the body moves.

Figure 6.13. Stiff fabrics and rigid shapes anticipate body movement.

*W*, Isaac Mizrahi, September 1995.

A stiff, heavy fabric or shapes that extend the boundaries of the body might anticipate body movement, moving forward as the body does. For instance, the full, petticoated skirt in Figure 6.13 is forced forward ahead of the wearer's legs as she walks. The skirt is stiff and does not conform to the contours of the legs as she moves, rather it holds its own shape but precedes the legs through space in the same direction. The repeated contact of the skirt with the legs of the wearer reinforces the rhythmic pattern of walking.

Garments that inhibit or slow movement are restricting. Restriction might be due to the hand of the fabric (e.g., weight and flexibility) or the cut of the garment. Stiff or heavy fabrics may restrict or slow movement. A narrow skirt will shorten the stride of the wearer, producing more graceful steps.

Finally, garments may lag behind as the body moves. This lag occurs when light, flowing fabrics move outward from the body and are slowed by air resistance. Think of a child wearing a very full, flowing skirt and spinning in a circle. The fabric will flow out around her, drag through the air, and come to rest in its original position a moment after she stops. A designer may use fans when fitting garments on models in order to ensure that the style creates a pleasant effect through movement of the fabric. Fans are also used in photo sessions to stimulate movement.

## EXPRESSIVE QUALITIES OF MOVEMENT

Movement of the body has very strong expressive potential. Individuals may gain satisfaction from the expression of emotion through body movement. Viewers can "read" this emotion through the movements of others as well (Watts, 1977). Researchers have found that particular movement features can be accurately interpreted as specific emotions such as joy, admiration, surprise, interest, contempt, anger, fear, grief, shame and sympathy (de Meijer, 1989). Emotion can often be identified from very little visual information, such as the movement of points of light attached to specific points on the body (Walk, 1984). The degree of pleasure, arousal, and dominance of emotional experience may be communicated by the type of direction, force, and flow of the movement. For example, joy might be expressed by movements of stretching or opening upward and forward such as if a person were to fling his or her arms outward and upward from the body while stretching toward the sun. Pattern and tempo are also important to expression, as evidenced by children's "dance of joy" when they receive something they want. If children's clothing was restrictive of the emotional expression through body movements, mothers might go deaf when children would resort to more vocal expressions!

Models are frequently called upon to convey an emotion such as happiness or leisure during a photo shoot for magazine layouts and advertisements. They do this not only through facial expression, but through continuous movement of the body while the photographer snaps frame after frame. The photographer will later select the frame that best captures the sense of movement and emotion.

When one becomes conscious of the interaction between movements of the body and apparel, it may increase the expressiveness of movements of the wearer. This unity of expressive intent and movement might be termed grace (Moore & Yamamoto, 1988). If clothing is dominant over body movements, as in anticipatory or restrictive apparel, a feeling of control may be created. A wearer may submit to this feeling, altering movements of the body into a harmonious relationship with the apparel. For instance, flowing garments may make a person want to move smoothly, encouraging the apparel into that flowing pattern. Restrictive garments may hamper body movement and consequently make a wearer conscious of a feeling of stateliness in his or her movements. Such is the case of a bride in a long wedding gown. The anticipation of body movement evident in the full skirt along with the lag in veil and train behind the bride enhance a feeling of solemnity and celebration for the occasion.

The degree to which the body movement is visible or camouflaged by apparel may enhance or detract from movement's expressiveness. For instance, an ice skater might wear a costume that exposes the length of the limbs, and lags behind her as she twirls in order to enhance the expressiveness of her movements in her skating routine. This can be very important because artistic expression, along with technical performance, is evaluated by judges in skating competition. Activity 6.7 will continue to explore the expressiveness of clothing and body movement.

**ACTIVITY 6.7**

Examine several fashion show segments on videotape. (These may come from various television programs such as CNN's *Style or fX's* Fashion TV. *Check your local listings for offerings in your area.)*

1. Describe the movements of the models in the various shows. (Include types of movement, direction, force, and flow).
2. What types of interaction are created between the apparel and movements of the body?
3. What was pleasing about the movement of the body and the apparel?
4. Were the models effective in showing off the features of the garments?

## SYMBOLIC QUALITIES OF MOVEMENT

Culturally determined patterns of movement can be symbolic forms. The most common is dance. Dance is a complex pattern of movements of the body, usually set to music or rhythm accompaniment. When dance patterns are planned and directed, they are *choreographed.* Anthropologists have shown that in various cultural contexts, choreographed dances may symbolize religious, social, political, and aesthetic meanings (Ness, 1992). Dance elements may be symbolic of visual images associated with a movement, such as fighting (a balanced, spread stance and swinging fists) or growing (rising and stretching the torso and arms upward), as well as musical images of rhythm or melody (Watts, 1977). Dance costumes may be important contributors, reinforcing the symbolism of movements of the body.

## SUMMARY

Tactile and kinesthetic design elements are important—though often overlooked—aesthetic features contributing to satisfaction derived from textile and apparel products and environments. These elements include texture, space, kinesthetics, and movement. These elements are perceived through the senses of touch and vision and thus are considered multi-sensory elements of design.

The tactile elements of design are perceived both visually and through actual touch of objects. Visual and tactile texture cues may reinforce each other. Texture is created by variation of a surface and/or pattern. The dimensions of tactile texture in fabrics are described as the hand and drape of fabrics. Body surfaces such as hair and skin also contribute textures. These textures can be emphasized through similarity or contrast with apparel textures.

Space is an important consideration for both the design of apparel and apparel product environments. Space can be perceived as filled or unfilled. The perception of filled space is influenced by the number, size, and placement of elements on a surface or within a three-dimensional form. The body and apparel interact to create different spatial relationships. Customers also interact within the space of product environments.

Kinesthetics and motion influence the satisfaction gained by wearing clothing. Kinesthetics is an appreciation of movement of the body and the way

**LAB ACTIVITY 6.1**

This lab activity is intended to bring together concepts from this chapter and give you a chance to apply your understanding of the aesthetic aspects of tactile and kinesthetic experiences brought about through the wearing of clothing. You will analyze the aesthetic experience of clothing through interviews with three individuals in a market segment, determine tactile and kinesthetic preferences for this group, and make suggestions for the design and marketing of apparel that would successfully meet these consumers' preferences for tactile and kinesthetic elements of apparel.

1. Identify three individuals who are likely to be members of the same market segment (e.g., three teenagers or three career women of similar age and lifestyles, etc.) who would be willing to be interviewed. (They should not be college-aged consumers.)
2. During an interview, ask the consumers to talk about the visual and tactile dimensions of clothing. Some questions you might use include: (a) What kinds of clothes do you like to wear specifically because of how they feel on your body? (b) Describe an outfit which is a favorite because of the way it feels to wear it (ask about style and fabric). (c) Describe the way clothing makes you feel emotionally. (d) When you select clothing for particular activities that include a lot of movement of the body, what do you choose and why?
3. Create a chart that describes the tactile, spatial, and kinesthetic sensations that are pleasing to members of this market segment (e.g., soft, flowing vs. tight fitting, corresponding). What are the types of apparel products that satisfy this preference?
4. Based on your findings, what suggestions would you incorporate into the design of apparel that might increase consumers' satisfaction with apparel products based on tactile and kinesthetic dimensions? Can you also make any suggestions for marketing such products?

apparel feels to the wearer. Motion of the body and apparel can also be appreciated by a viewer. Kinesthetic satisfaction derives from the formal qualities of movement and the relationships created between body movement and apparel.

Apparel professionals should strive to consider the visual and tactile elements of design in the planning and presentation of apparel products and environments. These elements can contribute to increased consumer satisfaction with these products.

## KEY TERMS AND CONCEPTS

actual texture

anticipation

body primary

choreography

clothing primary

correspondence

customer interactions within a product environment

density

determinate surfaces

direction of movement
duration of contact
ease
expressive qualities of movement
expressive qualities of space
expressive qualities of texture
fabric drape
fabric hand
filled or unfilled space
fit
flow
force
implied texture
indeterminate surfaces
intensity of contact
kinesthetics
lag
objective features of textures
pattern
posture
restriction
scale
space
symbolic qualities of movement
symbolic qualities of space
symbolic qualities of texture
tactile thresholds
tempo
texture
texture of the body
type of movement
types of sensation
vibration
zeitgeist

## READING 6.1
## Outerwear '96

L. M. Johnson

Reading 6.1 Johnson, L. M. (1996, January). Outerwear '96. *Children's Business. 11*(1), pp. 30–31.

Give fall '96 outerwear a hand; manufacturers certainly have. They have created coats and jackets in a myriad of textural finishes, ranging from dry, crinkled surfaces to slick, high-gloss coatings. Nylon, by far, is the fiber of choice, and it has many incarnations. Ripstop, oxford, twill and Taslan nylons are out front in styles that are inspired by the slopes. Cinched-waist parkas are the most popular models for girls, while boys are offered boxy, retro-styled jackets or those with shirttail bottoms, which has become a look synonymous with snowboarding. In addition to perennial black and fashion-forward brown, the color palette goes vibrant this season with shades of yellow, orange, red and royal. Because many styles are clean and simple in design, there is a greater emphasis on linings and trims. Look for bright contrasting linings often in polar fleece or quilted flannel, and you won't miss the many silver linings that lend a high-style, high-tech look to jackets. As for details and trims on sporty nylon models, get ready for industrial-strength rubber zipper pulls and patches, sturdy silver zippers and snaps, reflective patches and taping, and quilting . . . More novel finishes for fashion outerwear this fall include polyurethane-coated cottons, shiny pvc patents, coated cottons made to look like oil cloth, and "sparkled" nylons and velvets . . . Wool dress coats also get textural interest, primarily via collars and cuffs in faux furs, such as Persian lamb, and piles like berber . . . Technical polyester fleece, meanwhile, takes on new textural characteristics, such as faux sherpa, while offering a weight that works for warmer climes . . . Lighter weight outerwear, in fact, has received a lot more attention because fickle Mother Nature has been delivering much warmer temps in the winter. The trenchcoat with a removable lining, therefore, has become a favorite.

## READING 6.2
## Necessary Luxuries

Reading 6.2 Bath Towels. (1995, January). Necessary Luxuries. *Stores,* pp. 58–590.

Bath towels are a necessity, but many Americans also treat them as if they were one of life's little luxuries. Attracted by the feel of soft, lofty cotton against their skin and enticed by seasonal white sales that offer domestics at bargain prices, shoppers buy bath towels frequently—and they buy in bulk.

Those are the findings of the latest study conducted by Chicago-based Leo J. Shapiro & Associates, a market research firm that tracks consumer purchasing intentions toward a number of products.

The research, derived from a nationwide telephone survey of more than 450 households, shows that nearly one third, 29 percent of those surveyed, bought towels less than six months ago and almost two thirds, 64 percent, have purchased towels within the last year. On average, consumers bought bath towels more than a year and a half ago, which makes this category one of those household items that are frequently replaced.

Most often six towels are bought at once—a figure that probably comes as no surprise to retailers who routinely sell two bath towels, two hand towels, and two washcloths at a clip.

When asked if their household was in need of some new bath towels, 74 percent said "no" while only 24 percent answered "yes." Yet, when they were asked the likelihood of actually purchasing towels in the coming twelve months, 43 percent claimed that they would do so.

Perhaps the reason so many Americans want to buy bath towels, even though they don't really need them, is that people want towels to be thick, thirsty, and luxurious. Most would agree that a towel feels best when it's new.

An overwhelming majority, 81 percent of prospective shoppers, say the most important consideration when purchasing bath towels is how the towel feels against their skin. Though towels are used for decorative purposes in the bathroom, the appearance of the towel is mentioned as a top priority by only 15 percent of those surveyed. Considering American's partiality toward towels with a soft hand, it is not surprising that 83 percent of consumers prefer their towels to be cotton. Only a small proportion (14 percent) are in the market for towels that are a cotton/polyester blend.

Solid-color towels are preferred over patterned styles by a margin of seven to one, according to the study. Only 12 percent prefer a bath towel with a pattern; 85 percent opt for solid colors.

Solid colors are easily adaptable to different decorative motifs and are perceived by the consumer to be more pure. Patterns, on the other hand, are believed to be more limiting decoratively and not quite as comfortable.

The most sought-after color is America's favorite, blue, which was picked by 31 percent of those polled. Shoppers also show a strong preference for green (14 percent), a "hot" color for the past few years, and white, picked by 12 percent.

## READING 6.3
## The World Is Your Living Room

Reading 6.3 "The World Is Your Living Room." Excerpt from A is for Attitude. (1995, June). *Visual Merchandising and Store Design,* p. 50.

Several designers expressed an interest in materials that would help them create warm, inviting, and at times downright residential enviroments. It is reflected in a renewed interest in fabrics, in texture over color, and in residential-style fixtures and furnishings.

"Warm and welcoming is one of the things we feel really strongly about in terms of retail," says Kiku Obata of St. Louis-based Kiku Obata & Associates. "In this crazy world, we're looking for a secure environment. Retail can give people that."

These ideals translate to spaces that tend to be clean, light, fairly neutral, and adaptable, she says—environments that encourage people to come together and be more expressive. "People like being around other people, even if not to talk," adds Obata. "It's just nice to be out there in humanity, someplace that's safe and desirable today."

Chris Visconti, of Oakland, New Jersey–based Visconti Interiors, works extensively with women's apparel specialty stores, and notes another variation on the "cocooning writ large" *zeitgeist.* "The clients we are serving are seeing a big response toward a more homey feel in stores," he says. "This product isn't something for a sterile environment." He's also doing considerable work for manufacturers, who want to represent their merchandise in a marketing environment they feel best represents their customers.

CHAPTER 7

# Auditory and Olfactory Elements of Design

### Objectives

- Understand the importance of auditory and olfactory aspects of the apparel product/body and environment in aesthetic appreciation of these products or environments
- Recognize how the formal, expressive, and symbolic qualities of music can contribute to product or store image
- Apply knowledge of these qualities to selection of music to enhance the product image
- Understand how music affects consumer behavior
- Recognize fragrance notes
- Understand how formal, expressive, and symbolic qualities are involved in aesthetic appreciation of fragrance
- Understand how fragrance affects consumer behavior

## MUSIC

When you think about aesthetic experience coming from auditory stimuli or sound, you probably think about music. As we will discuss, pleasure is derived from sensory, as well as emotional, and cognitive responses to music (Lacher, 1994). The pleasure produced by music is similar to pleasure produced by other forms of stimulation, such as texture or movement. These sensations all produce chemical and electrical changes in the body. Research (Ackerman, 1990) has shown the chemical nature of pleasure from music. People who usually receive shivers of delight ("goose bumps") from a certain piece of music were given an endorphin-blocking drug. The shiver-producing music was played and this time the person felt no rapture. Thus, pleasure from music is linked to the physiology of the body.

Trace the activities of your day. When is music present? Music may fill the air the moment the alarm goes off and continue through the drive or walk to class, during meals, and accompany studying, work, or social activities. Special events in life usually include music. Birthdays, holidays, weddings, funerals, parties, and graduations include music. The pervasive nature of music in daily and special events suggests that music is an important aspect of human experience. If you are still not convinced, consider the amount of money you spend on music, including stereo components, CDs, and concert tickets. This suggests the importance of music to your life.

Music is important to apparel product environments. Music is commonly found in apparel retail stores, fashion shows, and advertisements to provide pleasure and promote an image of the product. MTV's *Fashionably Loud* combines music and the latest designer collections in a new form of promotion of both music and fashion. Music is also an important element of the physical store environment because it contributes to store image (Baker, Levy & Grewal, 1992). Many national retailers, such as JCPenney, develop a uniform physical environment to give a consistent store image throughout the store and from store to store. Thus, it is essential to consider music as an apparel professional because of the prevalence of music in promotion of apparel products.

Apparel products themselves create sounds that can inhibit or provide pleasure. Squeaky or clomping shoes and corduroy pants that swish as one walks are examples of sound negatively affecting the aesthetic aspects of the product. A subtle form of pleasure can also come from sounds made by items worn on the moving body. For instance, pleasure can come from rhythmic tapping of shoes, chattering beads on clothing or jewelry, musical jingle of bangles or bells on a child's playsuits, rustling of taffeta evening wear, and snapping of a cotton sports uniform. The positive aspects of sound of the product are important because these aspects contribute to the overall appreciation of the product.

## FORMAL QUALITIES OF MUSIC

You can probably name your favorite musical artist or your favorite song. However, you will likely have a more difficult time describing why it is your favorite. What is it about the sound of the artist or song that makes it your favorite? Knowledge of the formal elements could help you describe music. This chapter provides some of the basic elements of music. These formal qualities or elements of music can be divided into three categories: time or duration, pitch, and texture (Bruner, 1990). Music moves through time and is made up of sounds varying in pitch and texture.

The formal elements of music should be carefully considered when selecting music for environments, such as retail outlets, fashion shows, and advertisements. These elements should complement or echo the visual qualities of the product. For instance, Japanese designer Jun Takahashi explained the connection between his Fall 1995 collection and the music that inspired and accompanied this collection in his fashion show. Takahashi stated he used the hard-edged music of Nirvana for his show to accompany the hard-edged fabrics of leather,

Figure 7.1. (left) Small, sharp-edged triangles and short horizontal lines spaced apart to show ground would be complemented by staccato notes.

Figure 7.2. (right) Long, smooth, blending lines of the neckties down the front of the bust are reflective of smooth legato notes.

rubber, and a rough bonded wool, and primary colors. Many fabrics were shiny. He also described the shapes as strong. Hard edges were given to the body through plastering the hair with wet, brightly colored baking powder and by using heavy, dark eye makeup. Table 7.1 provides some of the connections between design elements of apparel and music. Visual examples of these connections will be included in the present section.

## Time or Duration

Articulation, rhythm, and tempo are three aspects of music that relate to how individual sounds or an arrangement of sounds occupy or move through time.

**Articulation. Articulation** is how the sound is made, determining the length of time a note sounds. *Staccato* notes often sound for a short period of time, whereas *legato* notes sound until the next note sounds. Staccato notes have an abrupt, sharp sound; whereas legato notes have a connected, smooth sound. The violins in the *William Tell Overture* (the theme for *The Lone Ranger*) is an example of music using staccato notes whereas ballads and folk songs tend toward legato notes. Articulation may reflect the size or transition of visual and tactile elements of apparel. For instance, the sharpness of staccato notes may complement small, sharp-edged shapes and short lines (Figure 7.1). Whereas long, overlapping shapes in apparel surfaces may be best reflected by legato notes (Figure 7.2).

**Rhythm. Rhythm** is the recurring pattern of pulses (notes) and rests (silences or pauses). The ability to recognize rhythms starts early in life; this ability is even

**TABLE 7.1** Interrelationships among some visual and tactile aspects of the apparel product, body movement, and elements of music (Developed by A.M. Fiore & J. Prater)

| Elements of Music | Individual Elements | Surface Design | Ensemble Layout |
|---|---|---|---|
| **TIME** | | | |
| Articulation | | | |
| staccato | short lines; small sharp shapes; succinct movements of the body; crisp textures | much ground (space) between figures of surface | clear edges among ensemble parts; smaller size parts |
| legato | long lines; large curved shapes; extended movements of the body; silky textures | overlapping figures filling surface | blending edges among ensemble parts; larger size parts |
| Rhythm | | | |
| firm | distinct movements of the body; contrasting colors | hard edges of figures on ground | clear pattern among edges or inner lines of ensemble parts |
| flowing | flowing movements of the body; blending colors | soft edges of figures on ground | obscured pattern among edges or inner lines of ensemble parts |
| pattern | pattern in movement and rests of body similar to music | pattern in surface design similar to pattern in music | pattern of inner lines of layout similar to pattern of music |
| Density | | | |
| thick | thick, irregular, opaque surfaces; dark rich colors | many figures in small area | many inner lines |
| thin | thin, regular, transparent surfaces; light pale colors | few figures in small area | few inner lines |
| Tempo | | | |
| fast | fast movements of body; rapid changes of color | rapid repeat of figures | rapid repeat in inner lines |
| slow | slow movements of body; slow change of color | slow repeat of figures | slow repeat in inner lines |
| **PITCH** | | | |
| Harmony | | | |
| consonant | blending lines, shapes, colors, and textures; analogous colors; coordinated, graceful movement of body | unity of figures | unity of parts |

**TABLE 7.1** Continued

| Elements of Music | Individual Elements | Surface Design | Ensemble Layout |
|---|---|---|---|
| dissonant | disjointed lines; irregular shapes; unrelated color combinations; disjointed movement of body | disunity of figures | less unity of parts |
| Mode | | | |
| major | up-turned or wavy lines; clear colors; freedom of movement | — | fullness at top of silhouette |
| minor | down-turned or straight lines; somber colors and movement | — | fullness at bottom of silhouette |
| Melody | | | |
| simple | straight lines; simple geometrics; natural movements of body | simple, ordered repeat; determinate surface | simple silhouette with few inner lines |
| complex | meandering lines; complex shapes; complex movements of body | complex, random repeat; indeterminate surface | complex silhouette with many inner lines |
| **TEXTURE** | | | |
| Volume | | | |
| loud | intense colors/light; large shapes, thick lines exaggerated movements of body | bold, high contrast figure/ ground | exaggerated size and shape of silhouette |
| soft | soft colors and light gentle movements of body | blending figure and ground | proportional size and shape of silhouette |
| Timbre | | | |
| thinness of flute | light, transparent textures; thin lines; light colors; soft light | blending figure and ground | small parts |
| brassiness of trumpet | shiny, crisp textures; bold lines; bright colors/light | contrasting figure and ground | large parts |
| sonorous saxophone | dense textures and lines; dark, rich colors | blending figure and ground | |
| brittleness of xylophone | thin, crisp textures; intense colors | jagged hard edges of figure | jagged lines of layout |

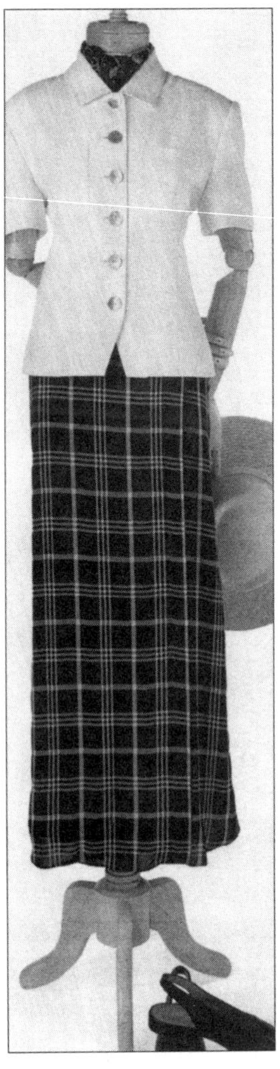

Figure 7.3. The regular three line, one line alternating pattern of the windowpane plaid suggests a three note, rest, one note, rest regular pattern in musical rhythm.

present in infancy (Winner, 1982). The rhythm of the heart can be thought of as two beats, rest, two beats, rest. Think of the rhythms of the secret door knocks you did as a child. Knock twice, pause, knock three times, pause, knock twice again. Music includes rhythm, but the rhythm is often more complex. Rhythm may be *firm* with clear patterns of pulses and rests (e.g., marches) or may be *flowing* with less articulation between pulses and rests (e.g., lullabies). Rhythm can also be described as regular or irregular. *Regular* rhythm produces repeated patterns (e.g., two beats, pause, one beat, pause then repeat with two beats, pause, one beat, pause). An *irregular* rhythm might instead end with three beats. Changes in patterns of visual and tactile elements may coordinate with the changes in pulses and rests. Imagine lines in a plaid representing notes and rests; the pattern of notes and rests may coincide with the same regular pattern in the number and order of lines (Figure 7.3). Movement of apparel on the body may create a rhythm, such as the rhythm of a full skirt whipping back and forth as the wearer walks.

**Density. Density** is the number of notes in a given amount of time. Music may be perceived as having a *thick* density due to a large number of notes with few rests played in a given amount of time. Rap music generally has a thick density. Thick density is perceived as more intense. *Thin* density has a small number of notes and many rests per given time. Thin density is perceived as more calming.

**Tempo. Tempo** is the speed or rate at which the pulses move. Tempo can move from very slow to very fast. Metronomes (those ticking, pyramid shaped devices with a moving arm, generally placed on pianos) are used to help the musician play at the prescribed tempo. Seventy-two beats per minute (bpm) is comparatively slow and frequently used in contemporary music. Marches have a much faster tempo at 120 bpm. The same piece of music may be played at different tempi (plural of tempo), just as the heartbeat can increase or decrease in tempo, but still maintain the same two beats, rest rhythm. A piece of music that has changes in tempo is called *rubato*. The tempo of music may relate to the rate of change in elements of the visual form, with more frequent change in visual elements complementing a more rapid tempo.

## Pitch

The category of pitch contains organizations of notes. These organizations are described according to their relationship in pitch or frequency of sound. **Pitch** in music refers to the number or frequency of vibrations of sound per second (Sporre, 1989). Pitch is described along the continuum of high to low. An increase in frequency per second produces a perceived increase in pitch. High pitch sounds are represented by bright and small visual qualities, whereas low pitch sounds are reflected by dark and large visual qualities (Marks, 1982).

By convention, the frequency spectrum for music is divided into registers (ranges) called octaves. In Western music each octave is subdivided into twelve half steps (Figure 7.4).

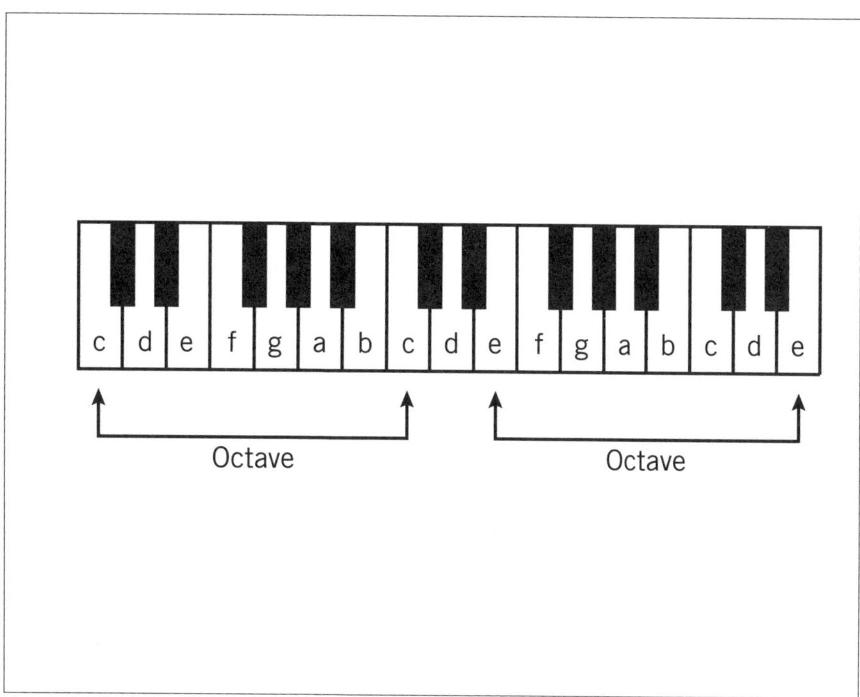


Figure 7.4. Piano keyboard showing octaves and twelve half steps.

**Harmony. Harmony** is a group of notes of two or more pitches sounded *simultaneously.* Harmony refers to a quality of the organization of notes. In Western music, consonant harmonies sound stable and dissonant harmonies are often tense and unstable (Sporre, 1989). Certain musical groups, such as Boyz II Men are known for their creation of consonant harmonies. The beginning of *Chopsticks* is an example of a dissonant harmony. The organization of elements in apparel may coincide with the level of harmony of musical notes. The elements of apparel may be perceived as consonant or dissonant. Apparel products (parts of an ensemble) may be perceived as stable or "going together" (Figure 7.5). A dissonant ensemble requires more effort to find order or stability (Figure 7.6). Evaluation of harmony may vary by individual. As you recall from the earlier discussion of modern and post modern characteristics of apparel, modern fashions tend to emphasize harmony and post modern fashions are more likely to emphasize intentional destruction of harmony.

**Mode. Mode** refers to a series of notes that provides the substance of a musical piece. There are major and minor modes. You have probably heard the notation of music "played in the key of C major." This means many of the notes in the song are in the key of C major and the song likely starts and ends on the key of C major. Major modes are more common than minor modes in present day Western music (Dowling & Harwood, 1986). Major modes are perceived as more optimistic than minor modes. Minor modes have a dreamy, mystical, dark feeling. A somber visual form may be reinforced by a musical piece written in a minor mode. We will discuss the expressive qualities associated with formal elements in detail in an upcoming section.

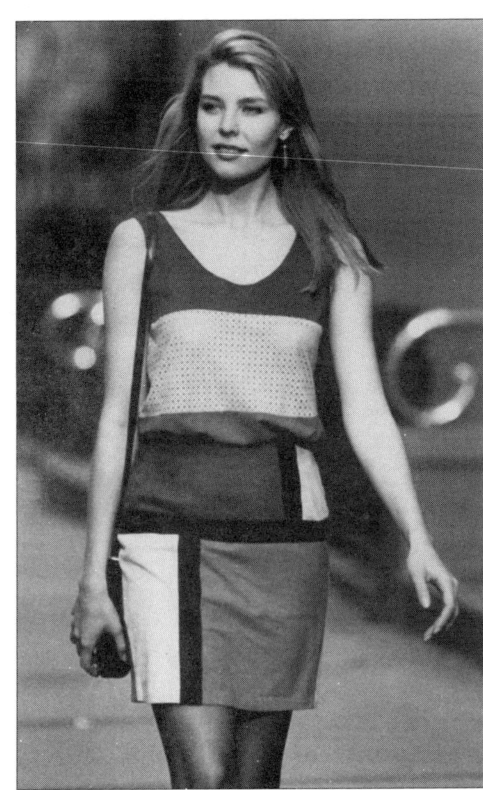

Figure 7.5. (left) Consonant ensemble that has similarity of color, curved lines of layout and surface, and soft texture leading to unity among the parts.

Figure 7.6. (right) Dissonant ensemble with unrelated colors segmenting the garment.

**Melody. Melody** is the organized series of tones sounded *successively.* The notes of a melody ascend (raise) or descend (drop) in pitch. Contours are the up and down patterns of pitch of the melody. Some organizations of melodies are *simple,* having gradual changes in pitch. While other melodies are *complex* and have sweeping changes in pitch. There are different shapes or contours to melodies such as arc (down, up, down) or wavy (down, up, down, up). Contour is important in identifying musical pieces (Winner, 1989). Simple melodies may represent simple surface and/or layout designs (Figure 7.7). Complex melodies may represent apparel that contains many, changing elements in surface and/or layout (Figure 7.8).

## Texture

**Volume. Volume** is the perceived loudness or softness of the sound. It is also referred to as intensity or dynamics. A crescendo gradually become louder and decrescendo gradually becomes softer. **Volume** relates to the amount of energy used in producing musical sound. Intensity or size of visual or tactile elements of apparel may be best reflected by volume of music. For instance, research shows that loudness of sound is associated with brightness of light (Marks, 1982). Loud music is associated with bright light.

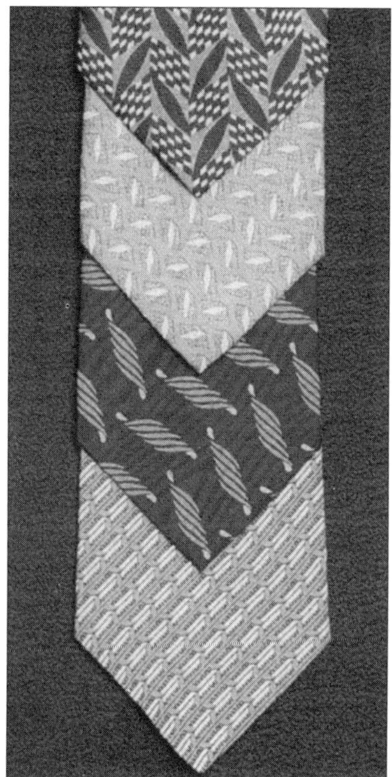

Figure 7.7. (above) Neckties with simple repeats reflecting simple melodies.

Figure 7.8. (right) Neckties with complex, changing surface designs reflecting complex melodies.

**Timbre.** Timbre (pronounced tamber) is the distinguishable quality or "color" of the different musical instruments. The sensations that come from the notes played on a violin differs from the sensations that come from the same notes played on the piano. The timbre of a note may suggest particular visual or tactile elements. For instance, the thinness of the high notes of a flute (White, 1992) may suggest light or high value colors and thin, transparent textures. The brassy nature of a trumpet may suggest bright color, crisper texture, or a bold print. The sonorous (rich and full) notes of a saxophone may best reflect deeper value colors and dense, plush textures.

Try Activities 7.1 and 7.2 to hone your abilities to identify formal qualities of music and apply this knowledge to developing an environment that reinforces the product.

**ACTIVITY 7.1**

Activity 7.1 will give you practice analyzing formal qualities of music. This activity will also allow you to examine the level of similarity of formal qualities of instrumental and vocal components of music.

Select two pieces of music that have both instrumental and vocal aspects. Your instructor may select music for the class to analyze. Using the following table of formal qualities, analyze the overall nature of formal qualities of the musical selections as a class.

| *Instrumental* | *Music Selection 1* | *Music Selction 2* |
|---|---|---|
| Articulation | | |
| Rhythm | | |
| Density | | |
| Tempo | | |
| Pitch | | |
| Harmony | | |
| Melody | | |
| Volume | | |
| Timbre (type of instrument) | | |

| *Vocal* | *Music Selection 1* | *Music Selection 2* |
|---|---|---|
| Articulation | | |
| Rhythm | | |
| Density | | |
| Tempo | | |
| Pitch | | |
| Harmony | | |
| Melody | | |
| Volume | | |

ı are the display artist for a boutique that is featuring the jacket design in lor Plate 11. You need to select music for the store environment. Using the ments listed in the chart in Activity 7.1, describe the elements of music that ›uld best reflect the design

Think about the music that played during a significant event in your life (e.g., winning an award, first kiss or slow dance, loss of first love, graduation, wedding, funeral). As you hear the music play in your head, try to identify the emotion you are feeling or remembering. Could you recall the emotion felt during the significant life event? Is there a strong association between the music and the emotion you felt during the significant life event?

### Formal Qualities of Music and Consumer Behavior

Formal qualities of music affect consumer behavior and sales volume. For instance, tempo of music had an effect on the pace of in-store traffic flow and dollar sales volume in a supermarket (Milliman, 1982). Similar results were found in the length of stay and number of drinks purchased by restaurant diners (Milliman, 1986). A longer stay and higher sales volumes were found with slower tempo music. Loudness of music also affects consumers. Consumers spent significantly less time in a store when the music was loud compared to when it was soft (Smith & Curnow, 1966). Sound pitch and volume have been considered the main auditory dimensions of the retail atmosphere (Kotler, 1973-1974). However, music is made of a combination of the above formal qualities that should be considered in selecting music for apparel environments.

## EXPRESSIVE QUALITIES OF MUSIC

Music arouses and expresses emotions. This emotional component is considered the primary ingredient in appreciating music (Sloboda, 1985). Unraveling the specific nature of the emotional component of aesthetic experience is a hot pursuit of philosophers (e.g., Goldman, 1995; Ripley, 1995; Robinson, 1994; Sparshott, 1994 ). Philosophers conclude that emotions are affected by a number of aspects of music including the expressive qualities of the formal elements of music. Second, expressive qualities of music include words from titles or lyrics that affect moods and cognitions. Third, because music may be associated with emotional experiences, a particular song may conjure up emotion-rich memories. Music can propel the listener back in time, to feel the emotions of that past experience. Try Activity 7.3.

The formal qualities of instrumental and vocal components of music are associated with emotions. Formal qualities combine to create various expressions. Tables 7.2 and 7.3 summarize emotional expressions of instrumental music. Emotional expressions of vocal aspects of music add to the expression

**TABLE 7.2** Characteristics of instrumental music producing emotional expressions. Table 3 from Bruner, G.C. (1990). Music, mood, and marketing. *Journal of Marketing, 54*(4), 94–104.

| Musical Element | Emotional Expression | | | | | | | | |
|---|---|---|---|---|---|---|---|---|---|
| | Serious | Sad | Sentimental | Serene | Humorous | Happy | Exciting | Majestic | Frightening |
| Mode | Major | Minor | Minor | Major | Major | Major | Major | Major | Minor |
| Tempo | Slow | Slow | Slow | Slow | Fast | Fast | Fast | Medium | Slow |
| Pitch | Low | Low | Medium | Medium | High | High | Medium | Medium | Low |
| Rhythm | Firm | Firm | Flowing | Flowing | Flowing | Flowing | Uneven | Firm | Uneven |
| Harmony | Consonant | Dissonant | Consonant | Consonant | Consonant | Consonant | Dissonant | Dissonant | Dissonant |
| Volume | Medium | Soft | Soft | Soft | Medium | Medium | Loud | Loud | Varied |

**TABLE 7.3** Characteristics of instrumental music producing emotional expressions. Table 1 from Bruner, G.C. (1990). Music, mood, and marketing. *Journal of Marketing, 54*(4), 94–104.

**Time-Related Expressions**

1. Duple rhythms produce a rigid and controlled expression in comparison with triple rhythm, which is more relaxed or abandoned.
2. The faster the tempo, the more animation and happiness is expressed.
3. Even, rhythmic movement can represent the unimpeded flow of some feelings; dotted, jerky, uneven rhythms produce more complex expressions.
4. Firm rhythms suggest a serious mood whereas smooth-flowing rhythms are more playful.
5. Staccato notes give more emphasis to a passage than legato notes.

**Pitch-Related Expressions**

1. "Up" and "down" in pitch not only correspond to up and down in the physical world, but can also imply "out-and-in" as well as "away-and-back," respectively.
2. Rising and falling pitch can convey a growing or diminishing intensity in a given emotional context.
3. Songs in higher keys are generally considered to be happier than songs in lower keys.
4. Music in the major mode expresses more animated and positive feelings than music in the minor mode.
5. Complex harmonies are more agitated and sad than simple harmonies, which are more serene and happy.

**Texture-Related Expressions**

1. Loudness can suggest animation or proximity whereas low volume implies tranquility or distance.
2. Crescendo (soft to loud) expresses an increase in force whereas diminuendo (loud to soft) suggests a decrease in power.
3. The timbre or brass instruments conveys a feeling of cold, hard force whereas reed instruments produce a lonely, melancholy expression.

**TABLE 7.4** Characteristics of vocal music producing emotional expressions. (Based upon Goldman, 1995; Sundberg, 1982).

| | Happiness or joy | Sorrow | Anger | Fear |
|---|---|---|---|---|
| Tempo | medium/fast | slowest | fast | fastest |
| Pitch | high | monotone, low descending | high wide range | low sudden peaks |
| Articulation (phrasing) | medium | slow long | excessively distinct | precise |
| Volume | medium | medium to soft | loud | soft |

of the music. Table 7.4 lists expressions of vocal aspects of music. Notice the similarity of characteristics between the instrumental and vocal aspects of the same emotion. The emotional response to formal qualities of instrumental music resembles the response to similar formal qualities of the voice (Goldman, 1995). Return to Activity 7.1. How would you describe the emotional expressions of the instrumental and vocal aspects of each musical selection?

### Expressive Qualities of Music and Consumer Behavior

The importance of the emotional component of music is used to distinguish among market segments; this component is particularly important to a consumer segment populated by college students (Shulman, 1980). Music is an important means of expressing emotions for this segment. Other market segments use music for its functional value, such as high school-aged consumers using music to gain social status and influence peers.

Retail settings have used background and foreground music to influence consumers. These two different types of music in a store setting created different emotional responses in consumers (Yalch & Spangenberg, 1990). Music is considered *background* when played softly and consumers are not consciously aware of its presence. **Background music** is not only lower in volume, but frequently is orchestrated to eliminate the attention-getting details. For instance, in the development of *Muzak* for stores, offices, and other public spaces, high pitches of the music may be replaced with middle range pitches, and a stimulating trumpet will be replaced with a less stimulating flute. Lyrics are removed. Muzak "is meant to be heard but not listened to" (Rosenfeld, 1985, p. 56). According to research using supermarket shoppers, a majority of consumers (77%) desired background music while they shopped (Milliman, 1982). Background music may be used in textile and apparel product related stores. Large retailers, such as Lord & Taylor, have background music fed to all stores by

**ACTIVITY 7.4** This activity will provide opportunity to consider the effect of expressive qualities from formal elements of music, words of titles or lyrics, and memories associated with emotional experiences. Your instructor may provide you with an advertisement to be used for this activity. Or you may be asked to listen to an ad on the radio or television using instrumental and vocal music. (It may be best to record the ad to refer back to it as you are completing this activity.)

1. Use the chart in Activity 7.1 to describe the formal qualities of the music.
2. Determine the emotional expression created by the music. Refer to Tables 7.2 and 7.3.
3. Determine if words or lyrics, or emotional memories attached to the song influence the emotional qualities of the music and the image of the product. For instance, how do the expressive qualities from the words in the song reinforce the product image of excitement or comfort?
4. Discuss whether the music is successful in reinforcing the image of the product.

satellite. This helps the retailer create a consistent store image across the country. Background music helped the furniture store shopper "stroll from room to room immersed in a positive feeling towards furniture and Colby's [a furniture store] (Kotler, 1973-1974, p. 56.)."

Music is considered **foreground** when played more loudly in order for the consumer to pay attention to it. The consumer is conscious of its presence. Foreground music may be preferred in certain retail environments, including apparel stores. Consider, for instance, the use of music videos of popular artists in junior's clothing departments. This music draws the young consumer into the department and provides the consumer with a pleasurable (auditory) environment. The pleasure is partly due to the aesthetic appreciation of the music itself. The pleasant experience is also due to *familiarity* with the environment. This is called "extexturing" or providing a familiar sensory environment to produce psychological and physical comfort (Rubinstein, 1989). Reading 7.1 provides an example of a retail store owner using foreground music to create the right emotional state among consumers.

The three dimensions of emotional experiences (pleasure, arousal, and dominance) relate to music as well as visual and tactile elements of design. Music and lighting, in conjunction with number and friendliness of store employees, affected the perceived pleasantness of the store environment (Baker, Levy & Grewal, 1992). Number and friendliness of store employees, alone, influenced arousal. Evaluation of the store environment may affect evaluation of the store's products. Higher levels of the emotional dimensions of pleasure and arousal from the store environment enhanced the respondents' willingness to buy products from the store. Thus, music plays a role in a consumer's willingness to buy from a store.

Music in ads may have a significant impact on moods and purchase intentions, without necessarily affecting cognitive assessment of the advertised product. Music may affect the emotional response to the product in the ad without altering thoughts about the product (Alpert & Alpert, 1990). The overall emotional expression of the music should reinforce the emotional feeling of the product. Complete Activity 7.4.

## SYMBOLIC QUALITIES OF MUSIC

Formal, expressive, and symbolic qualities are intertwined. Instrumental music may create symbolic images because formal qualities of music may represent aspects of an object or event. For instance, descending pitch and increasing volume followed by increasing pitch and decreasing volume within the piece may create the image of a passing storm. Both contain the same building, tension-filled beginning followed by a slow transition to calm.

As stated, images and memories may be evoked by music (Lacher, 1994). These images may reinforce the image of clothing. For example, Anna Sui's spring 1995 line included "rock star/gangster looks." Music from the movie *Pulp Fiction,* an off-beat story about modern-day gangsters, was used in her fashion show to reinforce the off-beat gangster image of the clothing. Re-experiencing music may trigger personal emotion-laden memories of the initial experience (Dowling & Harwood, 1986). The symbolic qualities of the song in this case may have little correlation with the formal or expressive qualities of the music itself. Instead, the symbolic qualities come from the associations between the song and the external situation. For example, Bruce Springsteen's sad song *Philadelphia* may be playing at a party when one meets a person who becomes very special in one's life. When hearing the song a year later, one may be filled with thoughts of the kindness and passion experienced with that special person.

Philosophers disagree on the amount of information provided by the formal qualities of instrumental music alone (Robinson, 1994). Some philosophers believe that only general emotions can be expressed, while particular events cannot be communicated. For example, instrumental music may express the general feeling of fear, but cannot communicate the specific fear caused by forgetting to study for a test, being followed by a stranger, or sky-diving for the first time. These specific feelings or images require the aid of words from a title or lyrics. For example, lyrics of the song, *Philadelphia,* tell a haunting story about the fear and suffering of a man with AIDS. As one listens to the words, one imagines the experiences of this man.

### Symbolic Qualities of Music and Consumer Behavior

Meaning associated with types of music (e.g., classical, pop, jazz, heavy metal, Indian, "nature sounds") used in the retail environment may enhance the symbolic quality of the product or the store image. For instance, classical music is generally perceived as more conservative and restrained than jazz, which is seen as more "off beat" and individualistic. Thus, jazz may be a better fit with a fashion-forward, individualistic apparel product line. "Nature sounds" may complement a store image emphasizing its concern for the natural environment and specializing in products made from natural fibers. Live classical piano

**ACTIVITY 7.5** Return to Activity 7.4. This time discuss the symbolic qualities of the music incorporated in the ad. How does the music influence the image you have of the product? Is the symbolic content of music due to similarity of formal qualities between the music and the object, images or memories associated with the song, or from words of the song? If the music in the ad doesn't appear to have symbolic qualities, select music that has symbolic qualities that would complement the message of the ad.

music adds to the aesthetic environment of an upscale department store, reinforcing the store image. In Reading 7.2, a retail executive talks about the design of a shoe store environment, including music, to create the experience of a Victorian English club. Can you come up with an example where the symbolic qualities of music are successful in reinforcing a product or store image?

Music in ads may have an effect on mood that, in turn, affects thoughts about the product. Music-induced mood may influence information processing and response to the product (Alpert & Alpert, 1990). Mood affects what we think about and remember. A positive mood evokes more positive thoughts and memories. A negative mood evokes more negative thoughts and memories. Thus, music in an ad that puts one in a positive mood may result in thinking about the positive attributes of the product.

Music is said to intensify pictures and enrich the key message in the ad (Hecker, 1984). Mood may be influenced by the *fit* between the impressions of the music and the visual message of the ad. A poor fit may have a negative effect on remembering the ad (Kellaris, Cox & Cox, 1993) and on the emotions of the consumer (MacInnis & Park, 1991). This effect on emotion may be particularly true when consumers have high affective and low cognitive involvement with the product; this is generally the case with apparel, jewelry, and cosmetics (Bruner, 1990). Thus, one must be careful when combining music with apparel products in retail settings or ads. Try Activity 7.5.

## FRAGRANCE

If you had to lose one of your senses, which would it be? Which would be the last sense you would want to lose? Take a public vote in the class. Many would give up their sense of smell, believing that smell contributes little to their ability to negotiate the world. (You may think, "What's the worst to happen? . . . I may end up drinking milk gone sour.") Vision is probably the last sense to be given up. The perceived importance of vision over the sense of smell is particularly true in Western societies due to their dependence on visual forms of communication (e.g., books, newspapers, TV, computer communication). The importance of vision within these societies is also due to their focus on cognitive abilities (Van Toller, 1988). Vision is thought to gather information for cognitive processing whereas other senses are thought to deal with the sensual and emotional. Yet, without a sense of smell, one may miss signs in the environment that warn of danger such as fire, natural gas leaks, and rotten food. Quality of life decreases for those who lose their sense of smell; these individuals often become depressed (Wilkie, 1995).

Vision is even thought to be more relevant than the other senses to aesthetic appraisal in Western societies. This belief in these societies is due to the perceived importance of cognitive insight from symbolism of art (McQueen, 1993). However, it should be apparent to the reader of this textbook that sensual (formal) and expressive qualities are vital to aesthetic experience of products and environments. The sensual and expressive qualities of the smell of a product may be particularly important for individuals of non-Western cultures. Some of these cultures are known to place more importance on information from senses other than vision, affecting their conception of the world and aesthetic experience (Classen, 1993).

As we have discussed in Chapter 2, sensual and emotional aspects of aesthetic experience are influenced by stimulation of all the senses. The smell or fragrance is a vital contributor to aesthetic experience. For example, the human body is anointed with perfumes, colognes, and other "beauty care" products to provide sensual pleasure and to enhance attractiveness. These fragrances may also be used to affect the emotions of the wearer. The overall fragrance trend now is towards fresh and light to provide a fun, uplifting experience (Wilkie, 1995). Fabrics for clothing can be coated with a finish of micro-encapsulated fragrance. The micro-encapsulation cells open as the wearer of the garment moves, emitting a pleasant fragrance that augments the sensory experience from clothing.

Fragrance is a growing part of aesthetic experiences of environments such as homes and retail stores. For instance, fragrances are added to an architectural space by interior designers to create an evocative and memorable environment. This, as defined in Chapter 2, is environmental fragrancing (Figure 7.9) and is a growing trend among retailers (McCarthy, 1992). People are also insisting on beautiful, interesting fragrances, not to mask odors, but to add an extra sensory dimension to their homes (Steele, 1992). Activity 7.6 will give you a chance to examine the effect of fragrances on aesthetic appreciation of products and environments with which you have come in contact. Try Activity 7.6.

## FORMAL QUALITIES OF FRAGRANCE

While there is general consensus about the visual and tactile elements of design and formal elements of music, we have not been able to identify sources describing the formal elements of fragrance. Individual ingredients may be thought of as formal elements, but fragrances are usually a combination of ingredients. The fragrance industry uses a classification system of notes that may be thought about as describing the formal qualities of fragrance. **Notes** are distinctive characteristics of a fragrance. These notes can be thought about as formal qualities because the notes constitute the composition of the product, provide pleasure to the senses, and have symbolic meaning (Fiore, 1993). The six notes are floral, oriental, chypre, lavender, fougère, and citrus. These notes are broken down

## ACTIVITY 7.6

List eight products (of any type) where the smell or fragrance of the product was an important factor in your decision to purchase or not purchase the product. Determine if these products are appearance related (are they applied to the body)?

| | Product (e.g., shampoo, fruit) | Appearance related (yes or no) |
|---|---|---|
| 1. | | |
| 2. | | |
| 3. | | |
| 4. | | |
| 5. | | |
| 6. | | |
| 7. | | |
| 8. | | |

List five environments (of any type) where the smell or fragrance in the environment affected its aesthetic appeal. Also determine the source of the smell.

| | Environment (e.g., theater) | Source (e.g., popcorn) |
|---|---|---|
| 1. | | |
| 2. | | |
| 3. | | |
| 4. | | |
| 5. | | |

As a class tabulate the percentage of responses where the *product* was appearance related.

## ACTIVITY 7.7

Examples of women's and *men's* fragrance products representing the notes are given in brackets. To sharpen your ability to distinguish among the notes, once you have reviewed the notes, visit a fragrance department and smell the fragrances listed for each note. Try to differentiate among the notes. Ask the sales associate to identify other fragrances with different notes and test your ability to correctly identify the notes. Warning: This skill takes practice. Your instructor may decide that a class trip to the fragrance counter may save the sales associates in the area the onslaught of students' repeated requests to smell particular fragrances.

further into subgroups such as fresh, fruity, green, leathery. So there may be a fragrance that is floral-fresh and another fragrance that's floral-fruity.

We will emphasize the six notes, as they are sufficient for the purposes of understanding the role of fragrance in products and environments. Also, it is difficult for most untrained consumers to distinguish among these six notes (Jellinek, 1992). Try Activity 7.7 after reading about the notes. Examples of women's and men's (in italics) fragrances are given in brackets for each note.

### Floral

**Floral notes** are made primarily from floral ingredients such as rose, jasmine, ylang-ylang, narcissus, tuberose, iris, and carnation (*H & R Fragrance Guide,* 1989). Many women's fragrances are classified as floral. These fragrances are broken up into subgroups of floral-green, -fruity, -fresh, -sweet, and -aldehydic (a synthetic ingredient with a powerful, pungent, but powdery smell). [Charlie, Giorgio, Liz Claiborne, White Shoulders]

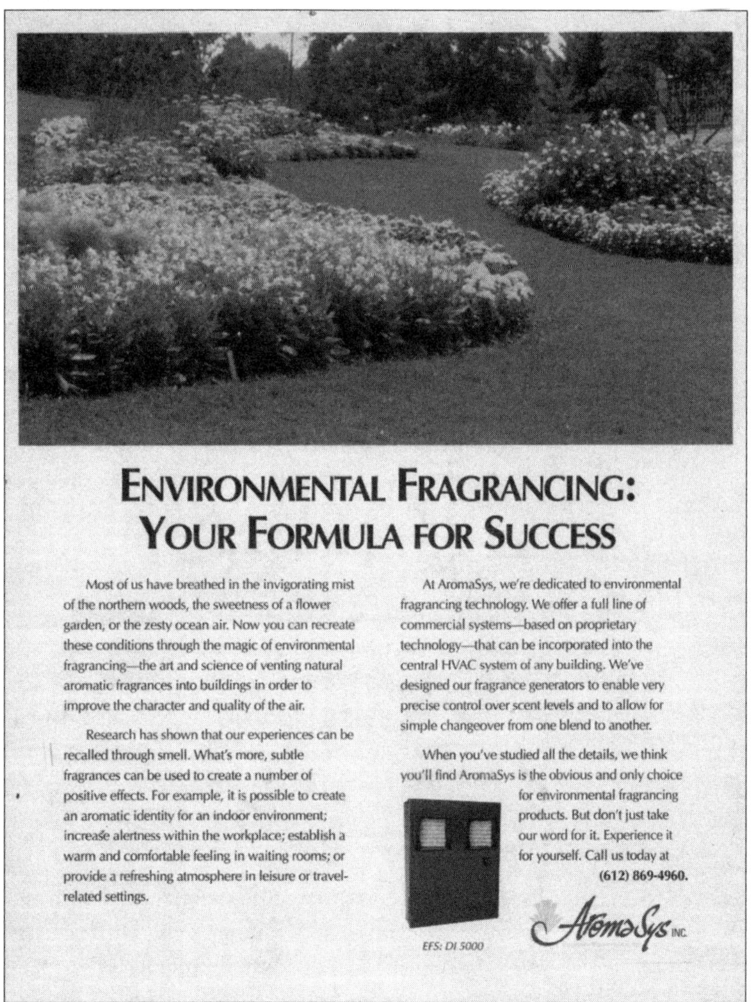


Figure 7.9. AromaSys brochure selling environmental fragrancing equipment affecting the sensual, expressive, and symbolic environment.

## Oriental

**Oriental notes** have a heavy sweetness from the sweet balms and resins of Arabia and the spices from India (*H & R Fragrance Guide,* 1989). Resins are solid or semi-solid plant secretions that contribute a warm richness to the fragrance. Some of the spices commonly found in women's oriental fragrances are vanilla, nutmeg, clove, and cinnamon. Marjoram, coriander, and pepper are found in men's oriental fragrances. Depending upon the overall effect of the fragrance, oriental fragrances are subdivided into oriental-sweet or oriental-spicy. [*Black Suede, Chaps, Old Spice,* Opium, Shalimar, Youth Dew]

## Chypre

**Chypre notes** (pronounced sheepra) are characterized by a contrast between a fresh (bergamot) citrus and dry-woody oak moss accord (*H & R Fragrance Guide,* 1989). In addition, patchouli (an herb in the mint family with a earthy-woody scent) is an indispensable ingredient in chypre notes. Fragrance materials for chypre notes come from Mediterranean countries. Hence, chypre is named after the island of Cyprus. Like oriental notes, chypre notes are common in women's and men's fragrances. There are many different interpretations such as chypre-fruity, -floral, and -aldehydic for women and chypre-woody, -leathery, and -coniferous for men. Women's and men's fragrances are also classified as chypre-fresh, and -green. [*Aramis, Drakkar Noir, Fahrenheit,* Intimate, Passion, *Polo*]

Selection of the appropriate fragrances note must be considered when worn with visual and tactile aspects of apparel products or when incorporated into an apparel environment. Research using women's (floral, oriental, and chypre) fragrances showed that associations are made between the olfactory notes of fragrance and the visual and tactile elements of fabrics worn on the body (Fiore, 1993). These associations may affect what is perceived as appropriate fragrances for different forms of apparel. As a sales consultant, one may find the associations presented in Tables 7.5 and 7.6 helpful in creating successful appearances for the consumer or in suggesting products that the consumer may accept.

## Lavender

**Lavender notes** are characterized by a dominating freshness due to the predominance of lavender oil (*H & R Fragrance Guide,* 1989). Lavender has a dry-fresh, herbaceous smell. Lavender is particularly common in men's fragrances. It's the basis for many refreshing splashes. Subgroups consist of lavender-fresh and lavender-spicy. [*English Lavender, Halston 101, Lavender*]

## Fougère

**Fougère notes** (pronounced foochair) are based upon the interplay between lavender, oak moss, and coumarin (a plant extract with a sweet, herbaceous smell) with a herbaceous-woody quality (*H & R Fragrance Guide,* 1989).

Fougère notes were originally intended to serve as women's fragrances, but are now acknowledged as men's fragrances. Fougère-fresh, -floral, -woody, and -sweet are the subgroups for this note. [*Brut, Iron, Paco*]

### Citrus

**Citrus notes** have a freshness produced through citrus ingredients such as lemon, bergamot, tangerine, and orange blossom (*H & R Fragrance Guide,* 1989). These number among the oldest creations in the history of perfumery and were used as refreshing splashes. While considered a men's fragrance note, some are so light and lively that they are characterized as being unisex notes. Among the citrus notes are citrus-floral, -fresh, and -green. [*Armani, English Leather, Lacoste*]

### Formal Qualities of Fragrance and Consumer Behavior

Understandably, sensual pleasure provided by perfume is of central importance for consumers. Consumers differ in the notes they find pleasant. However, there is a tendency for a consumer to prefer fragrances with a particular note. For instance, a consumer may prefer a range of chypre fragrances over oriental, citrus, or lavender fragrances. This tendency is said to be based upon the physiology of the individual (Mensing & Beck, 1988) as discussed in Chapter 4. However, intensity of the fragrance may affect preference (Henion, 1971). The same fragrance may be pleasant at one level of intensity, but become less pleasant as the intensity increases. In general, American consumers prefer less intense eau de toilettes or colognes over more intense perfumes, whereas consumers in Saudi Arabia prefer strong perfumes (LeNorcy, 1988). The importance of the pleasantness of the smell extends to other products used for the body (e.g., face soap) and apparel (e.g., laundry detergent) and was found to be more important than other product features such as texture and price in determining product preferences (Byrne-Quinn, 1988). While many consumers find the addition of fragrance to products to be desirable, there is a growing number of fragrance-free products entering the market to meet consumer demand for such products.

Pleasant scents may be added to apparel to enhance the desirability of the product. Whereas micro-encapsulated fabric is a recent method for adding a pleasant fragrance to apparel, the effect of a pleasant scent on desirability of apparel products has been known for some time:

> In an early experiment, Laird (1932) tested the effect of scent on product quality perceptions. Subjects evaluated four pairs of hosiery, differing only in scent. Although researchers did not ask the subjects to smell the hose, 50% of the subjects preferred the narcissus scented hose while only 8% of the respondents preferred the unscented hose. Respondents attributed their preferences for the scented hose to nonfragrance attributes such as durability, sheen, and weave (Gulas & Bloch, 1995, p. 88).

**TABLE 7.5** Description of visual and tactile aspects of fabrics associated with women's fragrances. Table 2 from Fiore, A. M. (1993). Multisensory integration of visual, tactile, and olfactory aesthetic cues of appearance. *Clothing and Textiles Research Journal, 11*(2), 45–52.

| | Fragrance | | |
|---|---|---|---|
| | Chypre | Oriental | Floral |
| *Color* | | | |
| value | | | light |
| intensity | low | low | medium to high |
| *Color in prints* | | | |
| value contrast | high | high | low to medium |
| intensity | low | low | medium to high |
| contrast | | | |
| *Texture* | | | |
| thickness | thin to medium | thin to medium | thin to medium |
| tactile texture | silky or nubby | silky to smooth | |
| *Line in prints* | | | |
| straightness | straight | straight | |
| direction | | | |
| softness | soft | | |
| order | ordered | ordered | |
| *Shape in prints* | | | |
| size | small | small | |
| shape | geometric | geometric | organic |
| softness | soft | soft | soft |
| order | ordered | ordered | random |
| determinacy | determinate | medium to determinate | indeterminate |

Fragrance is becoming a part of the retail environment with the intention of increasing sales. While there are more and more retailers using fragrance (Kleinfield, 1992), research supporting the profitability of using fragrance in the retail environment is just beginning. There are some encouraging findings, however. It appears that consumers linger longer in a fragranced environment. A floral fragrance, incorporated into a jewelry store, led to consumers spending more time in the store. Although, it didn't affect their buying decision at the time. In a research experiment, a floral fragrance affected willingness to purchase and the amount respondent's were willing to pay for a product. Comparing an

**TABLE 7.6** Description of visual and tactile aspects of fabrics least associated with women's fragrances. Table 3 from Fiore, A. M. (1993). Multisensory integration of visual, tactile, and olfactory aesthetic cues of appearance. *Clothing and Textiles Research Journal, 11*(2), 45–52.

| | Fragrance | | |
|---|---|---|---|
| | Chypre | Oriental | Floral |
| *Color* | | | |
| hue warmth | | mix | |
| value | light to medium | light to medium | medium to dark |
| intensity | medium | | low to medium |
| value contrast | low | low | medium to high |
| *Texture* | | | |
| thickness | medium to thick | medium to thick | medium to thick |
| tactile | smooth or fuzzy | smooth or fuzzy | |
| visual | matted | matted | |
| *Line in print* | | | |
| straightness | straight | straight | straight |
| softness | soft | soft | |
| order | ordered | ordered | |
| *Shape in prints* | | | |
| size | | | medium to large |
| shape | | geometric | geometric |
| softness | soft | soft | soft |
| order | ordered | ordered | ordered |
| determinacy | indeterminate | indeterminate | medium determinacy |

"unscented" sales room with a floral scented sales room for Nike athletic shoes, people were more likely not only to buy, but to pay a higher price for athletic shoes in the floral scented room (Anderson, 1992). Even when the floral fragrance was so light that it was undetected, it still affected increased willingness to purchase and the amount willing to be paid in the same way (Steele, 1992). Research (Fiore & Yan, in progress) with a pleasant and appropriate fragrance added to a display of sleepwear found that fragrance-enhanced respondents willingness to buy the product and the amount they would pay for the product. Reading 7.3 provides other examples of retailers using fragrance in the attempt to affect consumers.

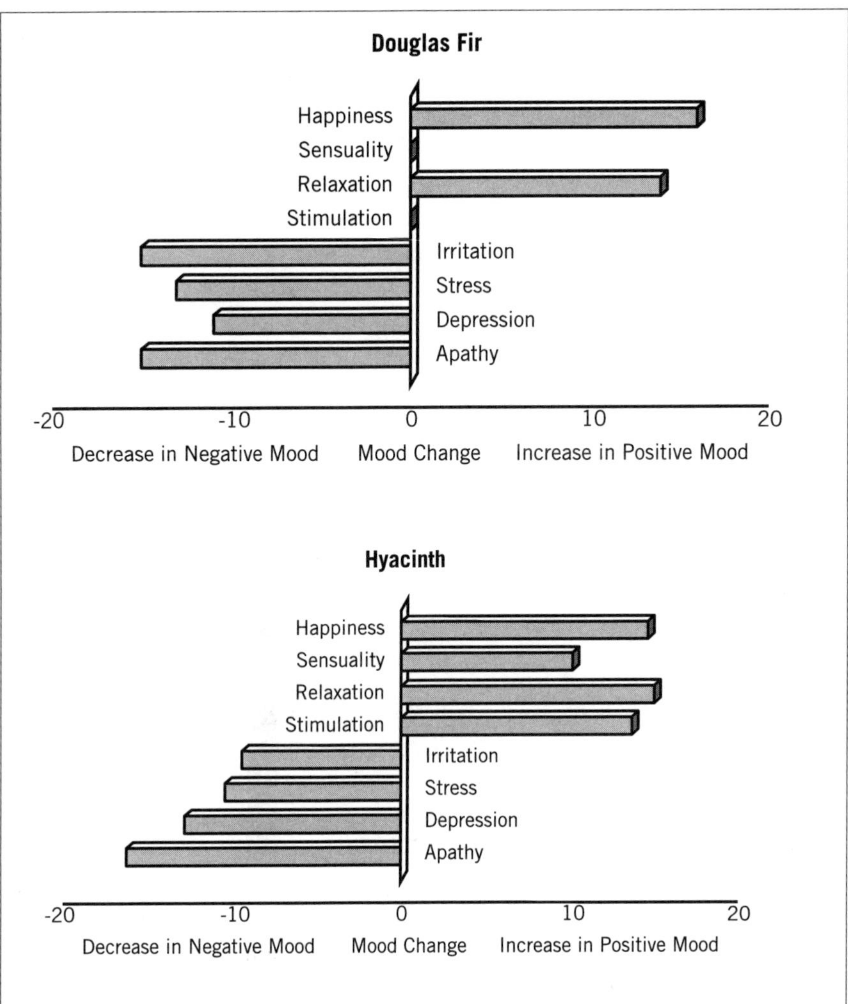


Figure 7.10. Profiles of self-reported mood change caused by Douglas fir and hyacinth.

Adapted from Warren C. & Warrenburg, S. (1991, November). Mood benefits of fragrance. Paper presented at the meeting of Aroma-Chology: The Impact of Science on the Future of Fragrance (sponsored by Olfactory Reassert Fund, Ltd.), New York, NY.

## EXPRESSIVE QUALITIES OF FRAGRANCE

Odors are said to have a powerful effect on stimulating emotion. Researchers (Engen, 1982; Van Toller, 1988) believe this powerful connection is due to the fact that both emotion and olfaction are processed in the same (limbic system) section of the brain. This perspective is supported by measurable changes in this section of the brain when smelling different fragrance ingredients (Lorig, Herman & Schwartz, 1990; Lorig & Schwartz, 1988; Torii, Fukuda, Miyanchi, Hamauzu & Kawasaki, 1988). Each ingredient may affect mood in an unique way. For instance, Figure 7.11 provides examples of self-reported mood change caused by two fragrances (Douglas fir [evergreen] and hyacinth).

Fragrance ingredients have differing effects on the arousal component of emotional states. Some ingredients produce calming effects to one's emotional state, whereas others produce an excited emotional state (Green, 1993; Lorig, et al., 1988; Torii, et al. 1988). Still others both calm and excite at the same time [called calm vitality] (Warren & Warrenburg, 1991). Some ingredients

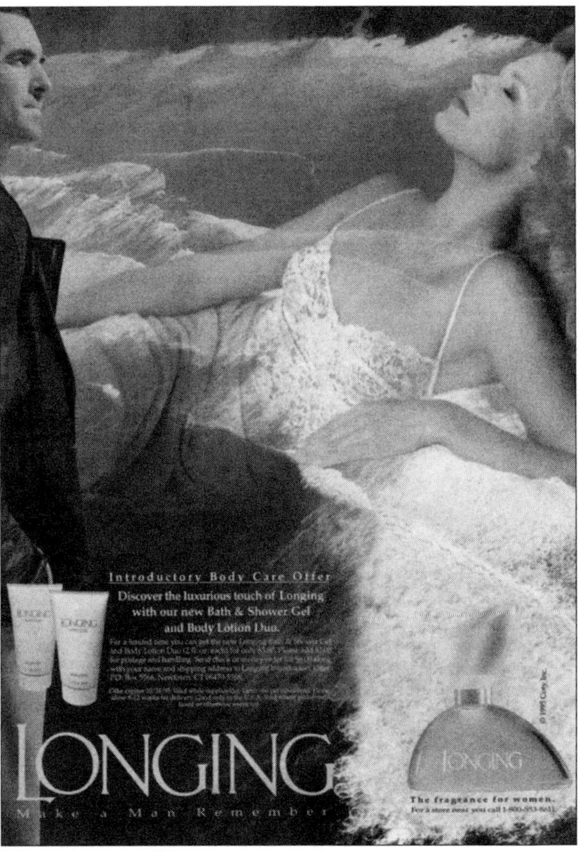


Figure 7.11. Ad for the fragrance, Longing, can help usher in memories; "Make a man remember."

with definite calming effects are: bergamot (spicy citrus), chamomile, lemon, marjoram, sandalwood. Whereas others with definite stimulating effects are: basil, clove, neroli (orange blossom), nutmeg, peppermint, rose, and ylang ylang (flower).

## Expressive Qualities of Fragrance and Consumer Behavior

Fragrances are worn for a variety of aesthetic and instrumental reasons. From their late teens to age 50, women report wearing fragrance for the instrumental reason of attracting men. Women also wear fragrance for aesthetic reasons. In their late teens and twenties, women use fragrances for the expressive and symbolic qualities (to feel feminine, fresh, and happy). Women in their forties state that pleasing themselves is an important reason for wearing fragrance (Wilkie, 1995).

Retailers are warned that care must be taken in selecting a fragrance for the particular product or store image. The mood evoked by fragrance should coordinate with the image of the product or store. A light, citrus fragrance is incorporated into men's sports departments because the smell connotes energy and excitement, whereas a more soothing woody musk scent is used in an area selling men's conservative business attire (McCarthy, 1992). A badly selected fragrance, however pleasant, may inhibit spending. This is due to the mood and thoughts evoked by the particular fragrance. Frederick's of Hollywood followed the lead of Victoria's Secret and introduced a sweet floral scent to its stores. While this scent worked well for Victoria's Secret, it was associated with decreased sales for Frederick's. A fragrance researcher provides a reason for the difference:

> The failure resulted from a misunderstanding of the customer base. Victoria's Secret targets female buyers with a soft, pink boudoir lighting and flattering night wear. A sweet floral smell worked well there. But the provocative Frederick's attracts men shopping for women and the lingerie is somewhat more the male fantasy of women's undergarments. In such an atmosphere, the sweet scent backfired. . . . If men were the primary customer . . . perhaps they didn't want to be reminded of their mothers. It could be that the smell wasn't matched with the customer. . . . Basically it comes down to evoking the proper mood in customers at the moment they're considering particular purchases. Perhaps Frederick's should try "Risqué," Technical Concepts' "sensual" fragrance (McCarthy, 1992, pp. 86-87).

## SYMBOLIC QUALITIES OF FRAGRANCE

Symbolic qualities of fragrance are comprised of widely accepted cultural meanings, associations attributed to the fragrance through personal experience and imagination, and product images created through promotion. One cultural meaning ascribed to fragrances is gender. Certain notes are feminine and others are masculine. The fragrance industry divides fragrances into feminine and masculine notes. Floral notes are seen as feminine and herbaceous notes are seen as masculine.

The sense of smell has been tied to regions of the brain responsible for memory (Howes, 1991). Smells, more than visual or verbal cues (Rubin, Groth & Goldsmith, 1984), have a powerful ability to usher in a flood of rich memories of persons, places, and events (King, 1988; Lyman & McDaniel, 1986; Richardson & Zucco, 1989). The ad for the fragrance, *Longing,* even states that a fragrance can affect memories, as it can "Make a man remember" (Figure 7.11). These thoughts or memories represent personal associations. In this ad the man's associations are between the perfume and romantic feelings for the wearer or the perfume and events involving the wearer. Smells may also spark indirect associations [the smell of cedar associated with a street name, Cedar Avenue] (Kenneth, 1927).

Multi-million dollar advertising campaigns are common in the perfume industry to promote the image of the fragrance, which strongly affect the sale of the product. Reading 7.4 discusses symbolic qualities promoted through the names and taglines of fragrance products. Visual images of the ad also help create the symbolic meaning attached to the fragrance. Fashion models, for example, are carefully selected to enhance the symbolic meaning of the ad. To test this, a research study (Solomon, Ashmore & Long, 1992) had eighteen fashion

Figure 7.12. Examples of six beauty types: a) classic beauty/feminine, b) cute, c) sex kitten, d) sensual/-exotic, e) girl next door, and f) trendy.

The Image Bank: photos a, b, f, Regine M.; c, David de Lossy; d, Nancy Brown; e, Simon Wilkinson.

editors select fashion models that would best fit ads for different fragrances. The fashion editors chose models from six beauty types: classic beauty/feminine, cute, sex kitten, sensual/exotic, girl next door, and trendy (see Figure 7.12). There was a consensus on the type of model suited to three of the five fragrances examined. The classic beauty/feminine type was chosen for Chanel. Editors agreed that the girl next door type was bad for Poison, but a good choice with White Linen. The trendy type was considered a bad choice for White Linen. This suggests that advertisers differentiate images of fragrance products and reinforce these product images through visual aspects of the ad.

### Symbolic Qualities of Fragrance and Consumer Behavior

As discussed in Chapter 2, the pleasurable experience created by products and environments can be due to fantasies. The symbolic qualities of the product or environment feed fantasies and altered states of reality. Fragrances may be especially powerful in stimulating mental processes of visual imagery and fantasy (King, 1988; Wolphin & Weinstein, 1983). For instance, fragrance may help catapult the wearer into a romantic fantasy when trying on lingerie. Fantasy is said to be an important influence on consumer behavior (Hirschman & Holbrook, 1982). Research (Fiore & Yan, in progress) shows that fragrance added to a display of sleepwear apparel could affect fantasy images. These fantasy images were connected with a more positive attitude toward the product and more willingness to buy the product.

## SUMMARY

This chapter examined auditory and olfactory aspects of the aesthetic product and environment. Apparel products themselves create sounds that can inhibit or provide pleasure. Music is commonly found in apparel retail stores, fashion shows, and advertisements to provide pleasure and promote an image of the product and the store. Formal, expressive, and symbolic qualities of music affect consumers.

The formal qualities or elements of music can be divided into three categories: time or duration (articulation, rhythm, density, tempo), pitch (harmony, mode, melody), and texture (volume, timbre). These qualities can be related to visual and tactile aspects of the apparel product and body movement. Emotions and symbolic images are affected by a number of aspects of music including the formal elements of music, words from titles or lyrics, and associated experiences. The formal, expressive, and symbolic qualities of music should be carefully considered when selecting music for environments to complement or echo the qualities or image of the product or store image.

The smell or fragrance is a vital component to aesthetic experience of products and environments. Formal, expressive, and symbolic qualities of fragrance affect consumers and should be carefully considered when combined with apparel on the body or in advertisements or retail settings. Fragrances can be divided into six notes: floral, oriental, chypre, lavender, fougère, and citrus. These notes can be thought about as formal qualities because the notes constitute the basic building blocks of the composition of the product, provide pleasure to the senses, and have symbolic meaning. Odors are said to have a powerful effect on stimulating emotion. Symbolic qualities of fragrance are comprised of widely accepted cultural meanings, associations attributed to the fragrance through personal experience, imagination, and product images created through promotion.

## LAB ACTIVITY 7.1

Form groups of three to act as a team of advertisers. Your group is responsible for a new mode of advertising, incorporating music with print ads posted in public areas, such as bus and train stations. The print ads have already been developed (Figures 7.13 and 7.14). Your group must select music to complement these ads and "pitch" your concept to ad managers and executives from the companies advertised in the ads. (This group is represented by other members of the class.)

1. Define the formal, expressive, and symbolic qualities of the print ad.
2. Determine how these qualities may be represented in music for the ad. For instance, the indeterminate print fabrics in an ad may suggest a more blended melody with a smooth contour. The expressiveness of the horizontal lines may suggest music with a calming effect. The use of pedigree Great Danes as props may call to mind music that is written by an aristocratic composer such as Mozart.
3. Gather music from CDs, cassette tapes, recordings off the radio, etc. that can be considered for the ad.
4. Select a piece of music that would complement the print ad.
5. Explain to the group of managers and executives how the formal, expressive, and symbolic qualities of music will complement the formal, expressive, and symbolic qualities of the print ad.
6. Compile a written report for steps 1 through 5. Be sure to include your music selection.

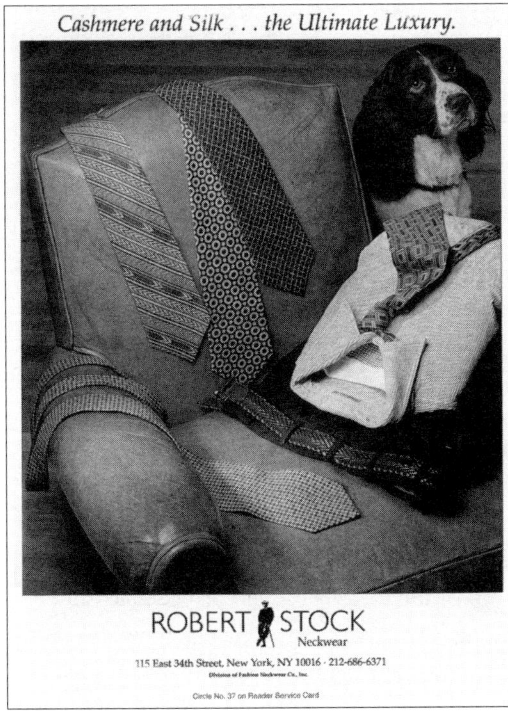


Figure 7.13. Advertisement for Robert Stock.

Figure 7.14. Advertisement for Vanilla Fields.

## KEY TERMS AND CONCEPTS

articulation

aspects of time or duration

background music

density

effects of fragrance on consumer behavior

effects of music on consumer behavior

expressive qualities of fragrance

expressive qualities of music

foreground music

formal qualities of fragrance

formal qualities of music

fragrance notes

harmony

interrelationships among elements of apparel, body, and music

melody

mode

Muzak

pitch

rhythm of music

six types of fragrance notes

symbolic qualities of fragrance

symbolic qualities of music

tempo

timbre

volume

## SUGGESTED READINGS

Green, A. (1993, March-April). The fragrance revolution: The nose goes to new lengths. *The Futurist,* pp. 13–17.

Gulas, C. S. & Bloch, P. H. (1995). Right under our noses: Ambient scent and consumer responses. *Journal of Business and Psychology, 10*(1), 87–98.

Kotler, P. (1973-74). Atmospherics as a marketing tool. *Journal of Retailing, 49*(4), 48–64.

### For Advanced Levels

Alpert, J. I. & Alpert, M. I. (1989). Background music as an influence in consumer mood and advertising responses. *Advances in Consumer Research, 16,* 485–491.

Classen, C. (1993). *World of senses.* London: Routledge.

## READING 7.1
# Sense of Place in the Retail Context or "It's the Feeling That Counts."

Reading 7.1 Sense of Place in the Retail Context or "It's the Feeling That Counts" (p. 435–436). In McGrath, M. S. (1989). An Ethnography of a Gift Store: Trappings, Wrappings, and Rapture. *Journal of Retailing, 65*(4), 421–449.

In the gift shop venue, owners and employees constantly rearrange merchandise in the course of a selling day. Consistent with attention to the visual and spacial, the display areas are "totally taken apart" every two weeks, which involves moving the display pieces into different areas, and reconstructing new presentations. An illusion of newness is created by having the same items displayed in new locations and in the contexts of different adjoining items.

"We may add a few things, but in general, we fool them."

There is a decided effort to make the store itself a gift to its customers. The store is visually stimulating, but has an overall calming atmosphere. Music is played to manipulate the feeling within the store; when the store is relatively busy, Judith tends to play a classical tape "to calm things down." The relatively tranquil atmosphere of the store is mentioned by some customers as a haven not only from the bitter-cold winter elements surrounding the first Christmas season, but also from the frantic Christmas shopping found in many stores. The retail ambience, calculated to be calming, visually pleasing, and forever new, is noted and appreciated by customers. Several aspects of the setting have been touched upon by other researchers. A gallery perception is maintained by merchandising what Hirschman and Wallendorf (1982) label "high Culture"; duplicates of an item are stored rather than displayed. The owners seek to manipulate what Kotler (1974) has described as the atmospherics of the store in order to influence purchase behavior. The importance of the emotional reactions of customers to the dimensions of arousal and pleasantness in the store environment has been stressed as important by Donovan and Rossiter (1982). This parallels the owner's intuitive strategy—to study the lesser understood emotional response of consumers to such changes, to architectural forms, and to objects in general.

## READING 7.2
# Excerpts from Atmospherics as a Marketing Tool

P. Kotler

Reading 7.2 Kotler, P. (1973–74). Excerpts from Atmospherics as a Marketing Tool. *Journal of Retailing, 49*(4), p. 55.

Through most of history, shoes were bought to protect one's feet. As long as this motive prevailed, the rate of demand matched very closely the rate of population growth. In recent times, shoe manufacturers have attempted to increase demand by creating a fashion interest in shoes through new styles, colors, and materials. The new thinking is reflected in the following statement of Francis C. Rooney, a modern shoe executive:

"People no longer buy shoes to keep their feet warm and dry. They buy them because of the way the shoes make them feel—masculine, feminine, rugged, different, sophisticated, young, glamorous, 'in.' Buying shoes has become an emotional experience. Our business now is selling excitement rather than shoes."

Rooney has redefined shoes away from a *utilitarian* concept to a *pleasure* concept. Once this view takes root, it spreads to the whole shoe-buying experience. Nunn-Bush shoes recently opened a chain of men's shoe stores called the Brass Boot. A Brass Boot store recreates the atmosphere of "a Victorian English club."

"Customers relax in leather-covered seats beneath tinkling chandeliers. Goblets of red wine and piped-in sitar music stimulate the buying hormones . . . Orgiastic collection (of shoes) . . . designed to blow your mind." The atmosphere is designed to give the buyer the feeling of being rich, important, special . . . and that he deserves the very best in shoes.

## READING 7.3
## Perspectives: Sensory Engineering

Reading 7.3 Excerpts from Anderson, P. K. (1992, April). Perspectives: Sensory engineering. *Visual Merchandising and Store Design,* p. 1.

For years, Lord & Taylor has sprayed fragrance at the entry to its New York City flagship in the interest of capturing noses racing up and down the Avenue. Giorgio in Beverly Hills actually takes smell to the streets, scenting the sidewalk out front for some olfactory action.

Certainly The Limited Inc. has known about the power of pleasing smells—your nose and your clothes take the scent of Victoria's Secret floral potpourri with you when you leave. And now The Limited has "Bath & Body Works" shops inextricably linked with its Express operations. You keep smelling; you keep shopping. JC Penney recently got into smells as well. At some of the retailer's intimate apparel shops, scent machines occasionally send wisteria wafting through the air. And have you walked into Knot Crazy stores lately? Have you smelled their "masculinity"? Scented pellets throughout the store emit subtle odors of tobacco, leather, and wood.

There's some serious smelling and selling going on these days. Just ask J'Amy Owens, president of Retail Planning Associates' Seattle office. In fact, the made-to-order odor at Knot Crazy was Owens' idea. She now includes a customized fragrance in every store plan she prepares. Says Owens, "Retail Planning Associates believes that a custom designed scent not only will differentiate your store, but will leave a positive subliminal reminder . . ."

## READING 7.4
## Names that Smell

Reading 7.4 Names That Smell. (1995, August). *American Demographics,* p. 48–49.

When Coco Chanel was alive, she simply numbered her perfumes. Even today, Chanel No. 5 evokes an image of luxury. But new perfumes cannot make a name for themselves if they go by the numbers. Today, perfume names and taglines are an important piece of the product's marketing strategy.

Women's perfumes often promise their wearers happiness, freedom, and celebration. "Breathe in happiness," says Parfum d'Etè by Kenzo of Paris. Amarige by Givenchy is "a celebration of laughter . . . love . . . and intense happiness." Sunflowers by Elizabeth Arden is "a celebration of life." Safari offers "a world without boundaries," while Vivid creates "a spirit that will not be denied."

Foreign names are appealing, if not always immediately comprehensible. It took several department stores to find a salesperson who knew that Lancome's Tresor means "treasure." It is easier to relate to Yves Saint Laurent's Champagne; some words need no translation. But if Borge's I l Bacio didn't specify that *baci* means "kiss," one might guess that it means "a batch of stuff in a bottle."

Perfumes from this side of the Atlantic also range from the romantic to the unintelligible. Some sport adjectives plucked off the cover of the latest bodice-ripper, such as "Passion" and "Knowing." Some focus on their natural origins. Dune by Christian Dior offers "total serenity for body and soul," and "only nature could inspire so perfect a fragrance" as Vanilla Fields. More confusing is Calyx. The word, which may be pronounced kay-licks, kay-leeks, kalicks, or ka-leeks, refers to an outer set of leaves that make up the external part of the flower. When presented with such a name, most people, botanists aside, would be as likely to think "acne medicine" as "flower."

In contrast, Liz Claiborne seems to understand American women with Realities. This perfume could be worn just about anytime. A different Liz goes for the opulent. White

Diamonds is "the fragrance dreams are made of," for all those women who have ever envied Elizabeth Taylor's legendary beauty—or at least her jewelry.

The men's fragrance scene is a study in the gender politics of language. The names of these colognes and eaus de toilette—don't call them perfumes—are down-to-earth, literally. Gravity is "more than a fragrance, it's a force of nature." Minotaur is apparently for those who want to smell like a mythical bull, and Farenheit is for those who want to turn up the heat. Even wimps can splash on fragrances like Boss or Tsar to feel more dominant.

Men's scents also appeal to the stronger sex's inner self. Guilt for Men, advertised in a catalog called *The Territory Ahead,* is "as necessary as it is inevitable." The message here seems to be that you know you're going to do bad things anyway, so you might as well go all out and smell good, too. But the name that says it all, perhaps, is Chanel's Egoiste—for the man who has everything, and knows it.

CHAPTER 8

# Complexity, Order, and Novelty

## Objectives

- Understand the importance of complexity, order, and novelty to the aesthetic form
- Understand how level of complexity, order, and novelty affect preference for apparel products and environments
- Recognize how categories of apparel differ in levels of complexity and order
- Apply components of complexity and order to alter apparel products and their arrangement

You are now steeped in the basic elements of design. However, apparel products and environments are not an accidental mix of colors, textures, lines, sounds, smells, etc. The elements of the product or environment can be carefully combined or orchestrated to create an aesthetic experience. This chapter will begin to outline factors used to create or analyze the organization of the elements of design within the product or environment. In aesthetics, the concepts of complexity, order, and novelty are used to understand organization of the design elements. We'll get to definitions of these concepts in a minute.

The desire for complexity, order, and novelty is common to many aspects of life, not just aesthetic experience. Before we focus on aesthetic experience, let's use an inescapable experience of college students (reading a textbook) to show how complexity, order, and novelty are desirable. You want the textbook to offer many interesting ideas that require some thought (that's complexity). Otherwise, the book would be very boring and not hold your interest. Parallel to this, you want the ideas to be understandable, organized, and well connected to one another (that's order). If the ideas are not well organized and connected, then you cannot make sense of the book and again you lose interest. In addi-

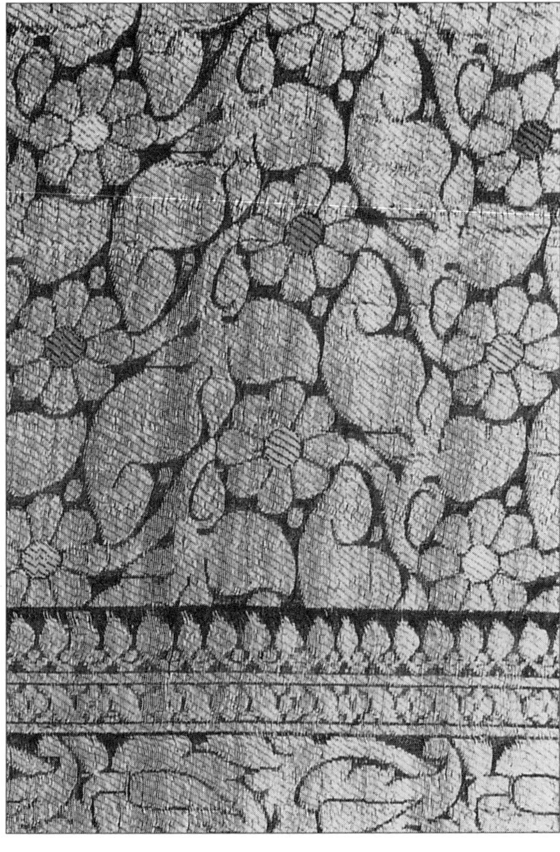
a

b

c

Figure 8.1. Complexity and order in aesthetic objects (textile designs) from a traditional society (a), a developing nation (b), and an urban area of an industrialized nation (c). Fabrics from 19th-century France, India, and Guatemala, respectively.
Costume and Textile Collection of the Department of Textiles and Clothing, Iowa State University.

tion, you would like new ideas to be presented in different chapters of the textbook (that's novelty). If the same ideas were presented over and over again then you would be bored silly. Too little complexity, order, and novelty produce the same result—the only redeeming quality of the book becomes its ability to cushion your head from hitting the table as you fall asleep reading.

Now for a few definitions. A **unit** is an identifiable part of the form. **Complexity** (and order) relates to the degree of stimulation from the number and physical quality of units, the degree of dissimilarity of units, and the level of organization in the arrangement of units (Day, 1981, p. 33). We will provide a thorough discussion of the interrelated concepts of complexity and order. We will then provide the definition of novelty later in this chapter.

## DESIRE FOR COMPLEXITY, ORDER, AND NOVELTY IN THE AESTHETIC FORM

Complexity and order are important to aesthetic experience. Complexity and order (unity) have been described in philosophy as universal criteria for judging aesthetic objects (Beardsley, 1958). These concepts have been used to describe many aesthetic forms including architecture (Venturi, 1977), music (Burke & Gridley, 1990 Holbrook & Huber, 1983), and paintings (Hekkert & van Wieringen, 1990). Taking fragrances used on the body as an example, these products are made up of a large number of ingredients (e.g., sandalwood, musk, rose, lilac, citrus oil) that add to complexity of the fragrance. As you appreciate a fragrance you find that these ingredients blend together, but you can also discriminate among "layers" of heavy base notes, lighter middle notes, and very volatile top notes. These layers are perceived as order within the product that leads to aesthetic pleasure from the fragrance.

Complexity and order affect aesthetic preferences around the world. The importance of complexity and order to aesthetic preference is found within traditional (small-scale) societies (Child & Siroto, 1971; Hirschfeld, 1977), within rural areas of lesser-developed nations, and urban areas of industrialized nations (Berlyne, Robbins & Thompson, 1974). While complexity and order are present in the aesthetic forms of these societies, *the ways* of representing complexity and order vary by society (Figure 8.1).

This apparent universal nature of complexity and aesthetic preference makes sense in light of our discussion in Chapter 1. As you should recall from Chapter 1, stimulation of the nervous system and brain is needed for proper physical and psychological development. If the form is too simple (not complex or novel), then attention is not maintained and the brain is not challenged for proper development to occur. Too much complexity or novelty may diminish aesthetic pleasure as well. Aesthetic pleasure comes from *successful* recognition and discrimination of sensory stimulation by the brain. When the brain cannot recognize the sensation or create order out of the sensations, then pleasure is diminished. Complexity and novelty provide the needed stimulation to the nervous system while order aids recognition and discrimination. Examine the figures in Activity 8.1 and determine the effect of complexity and order.

The role of many apparel professionals is to provide order in complexity for the consumer. For instance, order may result from the designer repeating design lines within an apparel product (Figure 8.5), a stylist coordinating products with the aesthetic qualities of the body, or a department manager arranging products in a retail setting (Figure 8.6). Providing order requires that the elements of design, discussed at length in Part 2 of this book, are carefully considered when developing a product or environment or when arranging products on the body or in a promotional setting.

## PREFERRED LEVEL OF COMPLEXITY AND ORDER

The nineteenth century was said to be marked by attempts to create a "science of art." The era was comprised of defining rules that govern use and arrangement of design elements, such as color, to create pleasing art forms (Brett, 1986). The scientific approach to aesthetics initiated during the 19th century has influenced present-day research of aesthetics, including studies by Daniel Berlyne. Berlyne is the founder of modern day experimental aesthetics (Cupchik, 1988) and his work will form the backbone of this chapter. In experimental aesthetics it is assumed that understanding aesthetic pleasure or preference can come from breaking down aesthetic forms into measurable parts (variables) for scientific study. For instance, to understand aesthetic preference for shapes one may study the number of angles in geometric shapes (e.g., Boselie, 1984).

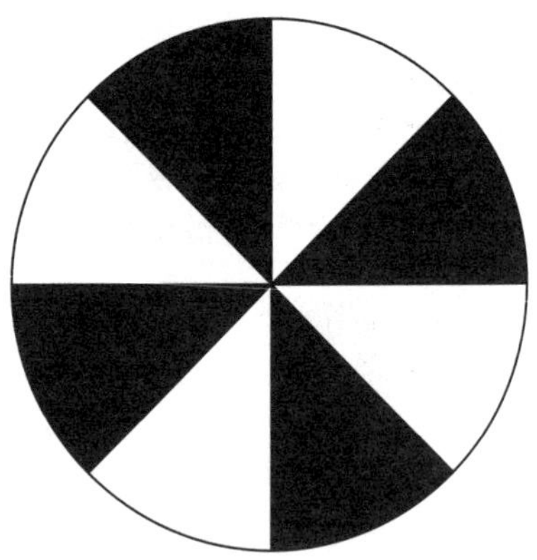

Figure 8.2. Simple geometric shapes randomly placed.

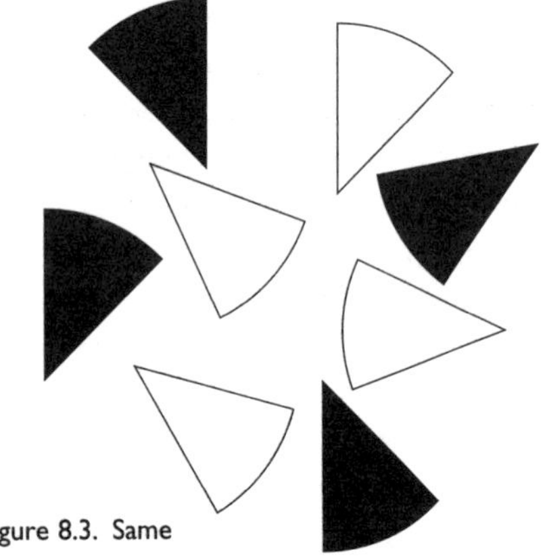

Figure 8.3. Same geometric shapes placed in an ordered pattern.

Figure 8.4. M. C. Escher's drawing of *Sky and Water I* showing the effect of complexity and order.



**ACTIVITY 8.1**

Figures 8.2, 8.3, and 8.4 show how order can influence what is perceived to be pleasing. Examine Figures 8.2 and 8.3. Determine which you find most pleasing. As a class, tabulate which was found to be most pleasing. Both Figures 8.2 and 8.3 contain the same numbers and types of shapes, but in Figure 8.3 these shapes are arranged in a pattern that provides a clearer order. If order influences pleasingness, then most in the class would say that Figure 8.3 is more pleasing than Figure 8.2.

Note your emotional response to Figure 8.4. What is your emotional response when you first look at Figure 8.4? What is your emotional response when you recognize the interconnectedness of the forms (ducks and fish) in M. C. Escher's artwork? The degree of visual interest of the forms and the number of the forms add to complexity. The interconnectedness of the forms, how the edge of the duck is also the edge of the fish, helps give order or organization to the units of the form. Thus, complexity and order provide pleasure for many appreciators. Do you think this piece of art would still be pleasing if there was no interconnectedness of the ducks and fish? Does the interconnectedness add to the pleasingness of the form?

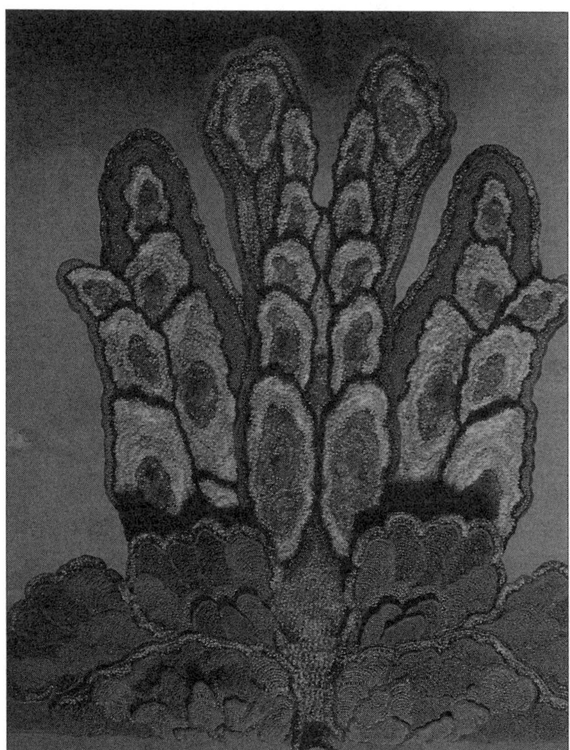

Figure 8.5. (left) Order within products.

Figure 8.6. (right) Order among products in a retail setting.

Berlyne and his colleagues (Berlyne, 1974 Day, 1981) worked with visual (e.g., simple geometric forms and fine art paintings) and auditory forms (music) as aesthetic objects in their experiments. Berlyne and fellow researchers wanted to determine the underlying factors affecting pleasingness of form. Berlyne and many of his colleagues believed that level of complexity of the parts of the form contributed to pleasingness of and preference for the aesthetic form in a predictable manner.

An inverted-U relationship was proposed to describe this predictable relationship between level of complexity and pleasingness of and preference for the aesthetic form. This **inverted-U relationship of pleasure** states that a medium level of complexity leads to a higher level of pleasure, than do low or high levels of complexity (Walker, 1981). It is given the name *inverted-U* because when the relationship between complexity and pleasure is graphed, it makes an upside down or inverted U shape (Graph 8.1). Looking at the graph, moving up vertically denotes increased pleasure. Moving to the right horizontally denotes an increase in complexity. If one tracks the curved relationship between these two variables of pleasure and complexity, one sees that low complexity is related with low pleasure. As complexity increases to a moderate level, pleasure is at its highest point. Then pleasure diminishes as complexity continues to increase. Low levels of complexity offer little stimulation and are boring and less pleasing than moderate levels of complexity. High levels of complexity are too confusing and also result in lower levels of pleasure.

Graph 8.1

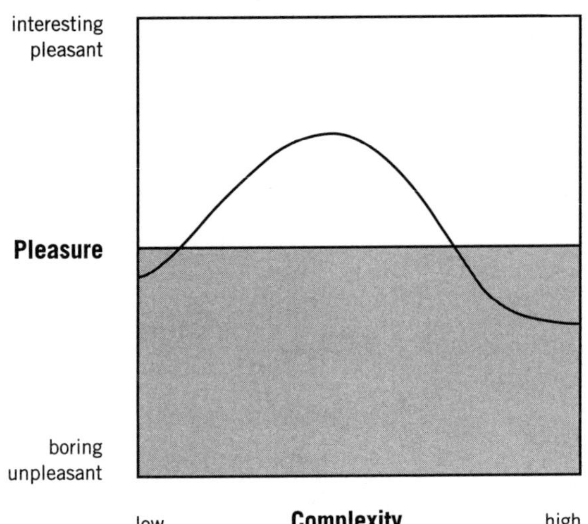


Graph 8.2

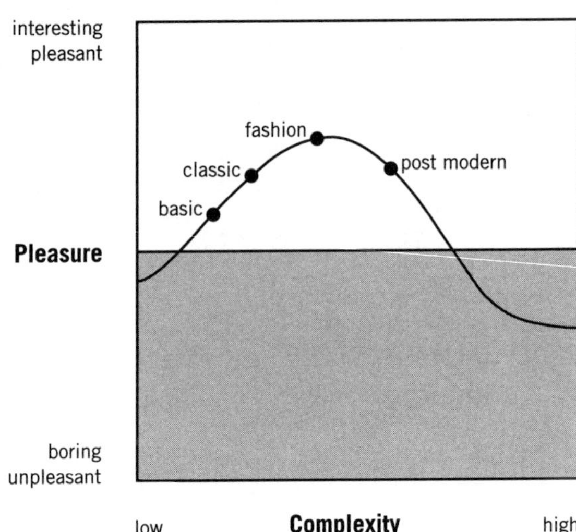


Graph 8.1. Inverted-U relationship of pleasure

Graph 8.2. Placement of categories of apparel on the inverted-U graph.

## Complexity and Order Applied to Apparel

The concepts of complexity and order are relevant to describing categories of apparel products. On a general level, basics, classics, fashions, and post modern designs may be placed on the inverted-U graph to understand each of the categories and their relationship to one another (Graph 8.2). You will notice that all are within the mid to upper range of the pleasure variable. However, basics and classics are less complex than fashions and post modern designs.

**Basic goods** are products with little demand for change in their simple styling (Glock & Kunz, 1995). Men's white briefs, undershirts, and athletic tube socks are a few examples of basic goods. Basics are not generally purchased because of their arresting aesthetic appeal. (When was the last time you raved about the attractiveness or aesthetic appeal of your white athletic tube socks or white briefs?) **Classics** are stable styles with integrity of design and versatility, coordinating easily with other apparel products. Classics are more interesting than basics because of the higher level of complexity. A classic lies between a basic and fashion good. The sheath dress, trench coat, and pleated-front trousers are examples of classics. **Fashion goods** are products with more complex styling that experience frequent change. The appearance of fashion products may change rapidly, but the underlying level of complexity remains somewhat intact. Women's and children's dresses are examples of fashion goods. Changes in fashion products means that order is now produced in a new way, but an order is still apparent. For instance, a new fashion may use similarity of reflective texture instead of similarity of hue to provide order. **Post modern** styles are generally more complex, exaggerated styles usually containing planned organization among the parts, though the organization may be less apparent. Post modern styles, while most appealing to a portion of consumers in Western culture, are not as broadly accepted as modern fashions. Figure 8.7 shows a post modern style with a high level of complexity.

Figure 8.7. Design by Christian Lacroix, 1992.

## Defining the Preferred Level of Complexity

The inverted-U relationship may be applied to apparel products and environments in a general way. A product or environment that is too far on either end of the complexity range will be less aesthetically appealing to the majority of consumers. However, a wide range of complexity levels may lead to pleasure. Research (Dember & Earl, 1957; Eisenman & Rappaport, 1967) shows that individuals have a preferred level of complexity. This preferred level of complexity may be used to help predict aesthetic preferences of products or environments.

Understanding the preferred level of complexity and order of a product or environment is important to the processes of designing, production, and promotion. For instance, a design assistant may have her designs rejected if she or he doesn't realize the classic nature (lower complexity) of designs that is the signature of that designer. It would be detrimental to the product if the production specialist decided to cut the cost of production by tinkering with the complexity of design lines (e.g., converting the curved hem of Figure 8.5 into a straight hem). A low complexity product attracting little attention by consumers may be made more interesting and profitable by displaying the product in an ensemble with a multitude of accessories.

It is many times easier to determine that "something is not right" with the design, ensemble, or environment, than it is to determine "*what's* not right with" or "how to fix" the design, ensemble, or environment. Considering the concepts of complexity and order of the product or environment may be of assistance in determining what's not right and how to alter it. The first thing to do is consider the level of complexity and order that is preferred or appropriate. It is important to remember that this level may be based upon personal preference, the aesthetic set forth by the creator, and/or the appropriate look for a situation. Secondly, one should determine how that level of complexity is or could be achieved. Thirdly, one should apply this information to attain the level of complexity and order. This process requires an understanding of the component parts of complexity and also an understanding of principles that affect complexity and order.

In the following section of this chapter we will discuss the component parts of complexity and principles affecting complexity and order. Then you will practice applying these components of complexity and principles to attain the specified level of complexity and order.

## COMPONENTS OF COMPLEXITY AND ORDER

To repeat the definition of complexity: **complexity** (and order) relates to the degree of stimulation from the number and physical quality of units, the degree of dissimilarity of units, and the level of organization in the arrangement of units (Day, 1981, p. 33).

Thus, complexity is affected by the components of:

- number of units
- degree of interest of the units
- cohesion among the units

To *increase* complexity

- increase *the number of units*
- increase *the degree of interest of the units*
- decrease *the cohesion among the units*

### Number of Units

As stated earlier, a **unit** is an identifiable part of the form. For instance, a unit can be a color, a stripe in a print, or a shape created by garment layout. Input to any of the senses may be broken into units. For instance, a piece of music can be broken into units of sounds from different instruments or different notes. The number or types of instruments used or notes found in the musical selection can be thought of as the units.

Number of units refers to the number of identifiable parts of the form. Complexity increases with the increase in the number of units. The forms on the left Figure 8.8 are less complex than the similar forms on the right. Though similar in formal qualities, the forms on the left are less complex than the forms on the right because there are fewer units. Applying this concept to apparel, garments increase in complexity as they move to the right of Figure 8.9 because the number of units from layout increase.

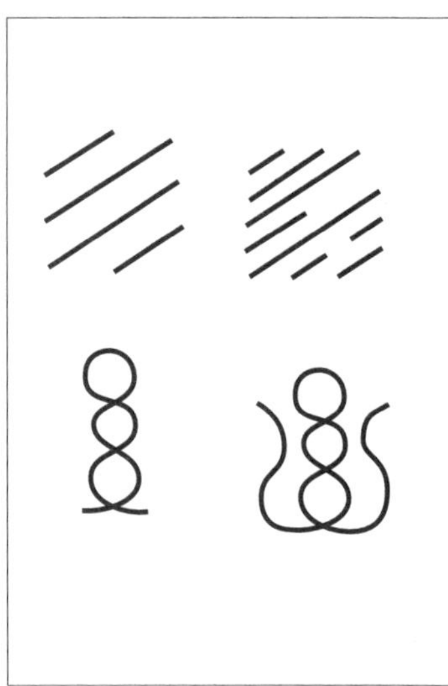

Figure 8.8. (left) Simple patterns showing the effect of number of units on complexity. Lower complexity is found in forms on the left of the pairs.

Figure 8.9. (right) Tops that increase in complexity due to an increase in number of units.

## Degree of Interest of Units

Some units are more interesting than others because of the amount of stimulation provided to the nervous system. The nervous system is stimulated when there is less regularity *within* the unit. The more the nervous system is stimulated the more interesting the unit. Simple geometric shapes are of less interest than irregular shapes such as organic shapes. Smooth, matte textures are less stimulating than textures offering variation in visual and tactile surfaces, such as damasks or tweeds. Curvilinear lines and diagonal lines are more complex than straight and vertical or horizontal lines. Intense colors are more stimulating than neutral colors. Figure 8.10 provides examples of irregularity of shape. The more regular forms on the left are less complex than the forms on the right of the exhibits. Try Activity 8.2 to define how degree of interest affects complexity.

## Cohesion of Units

**Cohesion of units** refers to the sameness of units and regularity of arrangement of these units. Regularity comes from orderly placement of units. (We will discuss regularity of arrangement in more detail in the following chapter.) Sameness can be found in any of the aspects of formal elements. For instance, Figure 8.11 shows examples of different levels of sameness of shape and line. Again the forms on the left are less complex than the forms on the right. The number of units is the same from left to right, but the cohesion due to similarity or sameness of units is also different, affecting complexity. Cohesion due to regularity of arrangement of units is also seen in Figure 8.11. The remaining examples show comparisons of regularity of arrangement. Figure 8.12 shows an increase in complexity due to surface design. The print increases complexity. When a form consists of a number of units with little cohesion, it may be con-

**ACTIVITY 8.2**

Which is least complex? Describe at least two features (color, texture, size, line, and shape) of each of the four graphic designs for "Summer Sale" that contributed to its level of complexity.

**Summer Sale** *Summer Sale* Summer sale Summer Sale

1. ____________________

2. ____________________

3. ____________________

4. ____________________

Figure 8.10. Simple shapes showing the effect of regularity within the unit on complexity. Lower complexity is found in forms on the left of the pairs.

sidered a part relationship. A **part relationship** consists of units that, when initially viewed, separate out from each other because of differences in the units and their arrangement (DeLong, 1987) (Figure 8.13a). On the opposite end of the continuum is a whole relationship. A **whole relationship** is marked by an initial blending of the units due to the sameness of the units and the regularity of arrangement (Figure 8.13c). In general, part relationships describe forms that are more complex and whole relationships describe forms that are less complex. Activity 8.3 provides you with an opportunity to analyze forms as part or whole relationships. Activity 8.4 helps you apply components of complexity and order.

While we have focused upon complexity of the product, Reading 8.1 shows that complexity and order can affect the shopping experience. Welcome Home's disarray has been replaced with a more orderly layout. As you read the article, you see that the number of units did not change but the cohesion among the units has increased through fully merchandised, separated areas of the store. This has decreased complexity resulting in the consumer staying in the store longer and increased sales. Remember, however, that some consumers may prefer shopping environments that consist of a higher level of complexity than what might be found in a "typical" department store. As you recall in Chapter 2, the marketplace or retail shopping environment can vary widely in level of formality and festivity. Informal, festive shopping environments may be preferred by consumers who appreciate a higher level of complexity. These environments may offer a variety of items that have high degrees of visual interest and little cohesion except grouping by category of product (i.e., shirts, coats, dresses on separate racks). The fastidious shop owner who insists on organizing the overstocked surplus store or bulging vintage clothing shop may be destroying the complex environment that consumers enjoy (Figure 8.15).

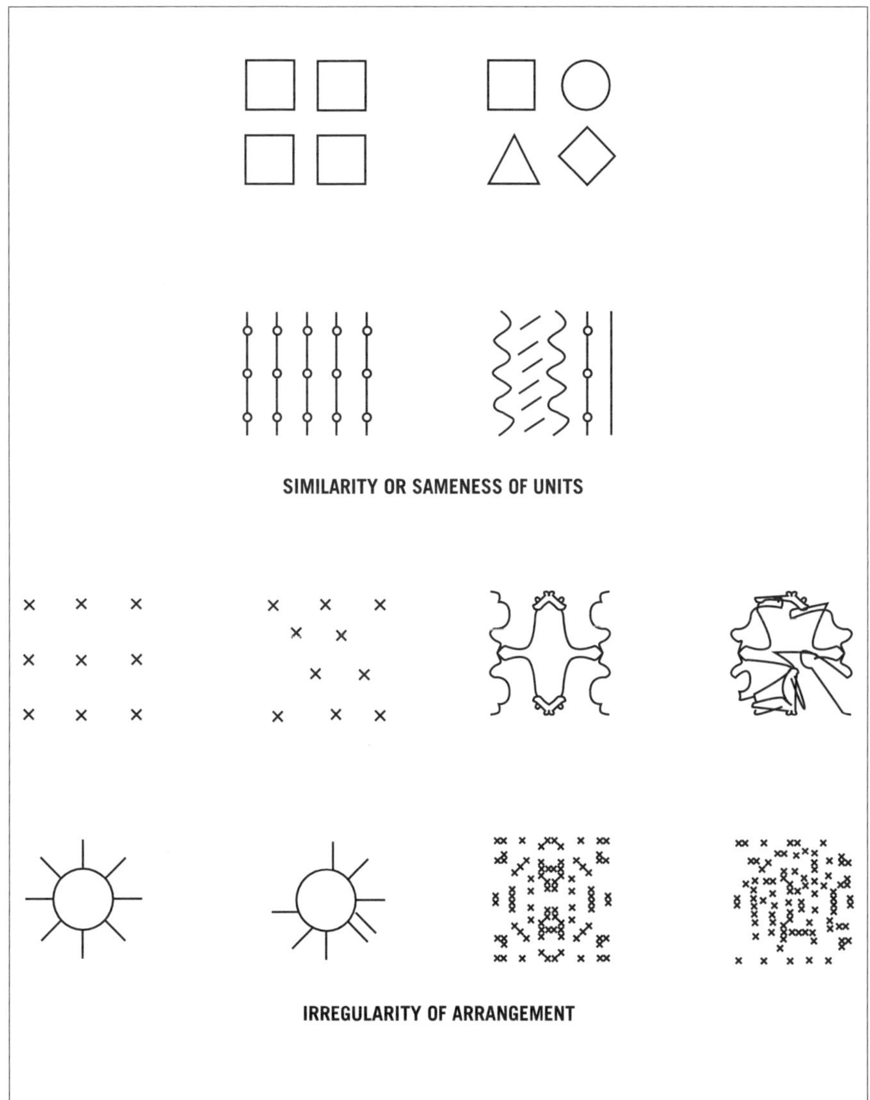


Figure 8.11. Simple patterns showing the effect of cohesion among the parts on complexity. Less complexity is found in forms on the left of the pairs.

## PREFERRED LEVEL OF NOVELTY

The product and environment is pleasurable because of complexity and order. According to Berlyne, novelty of the product or environment also affects pleasure. **Novelty** is the perceived newness of the units and their organization, based upon comparison of the present form with forms of past experience. The inverted-U relationship of pleasure applies to novelty just as it did to complexity. This **inverted-U relationship of pleasure** states that a medium level of novelty leads to a higher level of pleasure, than do low or high levels of novelty (Walker, 1981).

Pleasure derived from everyday experiences, from food to romantic relationships, is affected by novelty. Take your favorite food (let's say its Snickers

a

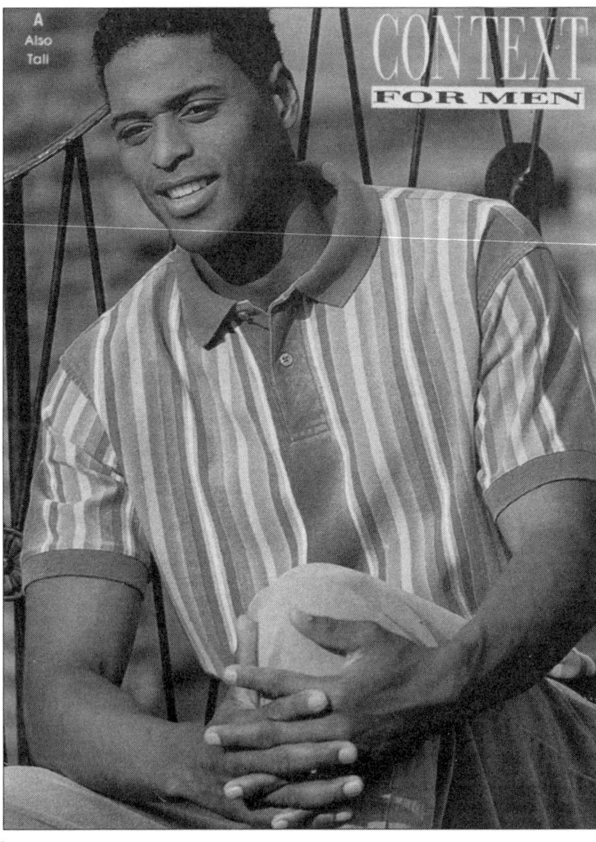


b

Figure 8.12 a and b. Garment that increases in complexity due to the surface design. (a) A simple layout and solid fabric is lower complexity than (b) the same layout using a mix of solid and stripes.

bars). Snickers bars will begin to lose their appeal after a steady diet of nothing but Snickers bars for a week. After a while you become bored with Snickers bars and begin to think of new ways to consume Snickers bars—you try freezing them, chopping them up and adding them to cookie dough, and melting them down as ice cream topping. (When all this fails to provide novelty to Snickers bars, you feed them to the squirrels.) Thus, the same form may be pleasurable one day and less pleasurable the next day because of a decrease in novelty. High levels of novelty, forms that have little connection to past forms, may not be pleasurable as well because it is difficult to make sense out of the new form. The perceiver's brain doesn't have the mental structure in which to "fit" the new form if there is nothing like it in past experience. Consider a new style that you see for the first time. The style may be too novel and thus disliked, but after seeing the style in fashion ads and on the street, it may lose some of its novelty and become more appealing to you. The importance of novelty is reflected in the statement of the author's auto enthusiast friend raving about the new Corvette model, "The corvette is totally redesigned, but easily recognizable as a Corvette!" The design is new, but still fits with the mental structure for a Corvette.

Culture has an effect on the level of novelty desired in the aesthetic form. In Western cultures, newness or originality is desired and is an important component in defining what is perceived to be "good art" (Hausman, 1981;

**ACTIVITY 8.3**

Figures 8.13 a, b, and c show continuum with a part relationship on one end and the whole relationship on the other end. Describe the differences in the units that help them separate for the part relationship. Then describe the similarities that help the units create a whole relationship. Remember to consider many aspects of the visual elements of design and to consider the body as a component of the form.

Figure 8.13a = Example of part relationship

Part relationship due to differences of _______ between (among) which parts of the form:

1. ______________________________
2. ______________________________
3. ______________________________
4. ______________________________
5. ______________________________
6. ______________________________
7. ______________________________

Figure 8.13b = Example of the middle of the part-whole relationship

Figure 8.13c = Example of whole relationship

Whole relationship due to similarities of _______ between (among) which parts of the form:

1. ______________________________
2. ______________________________
3. ______________________________
4. ______________________________
5. ______________________________
6. ______________________________
7. ______________________________

Osborne, 1979). To insult an artist's work in these cultures, one might say "the work is derivative of another artist," which means it lacks a high level of newness or originality that is necessary for professional acclaim in Western cultures. Knocking-off, or closely replicating, the creative work of another designer or company in the apparel industry is a common business practice. While knock-offs are accepted, they are also generally perceived as being of lower quality

a

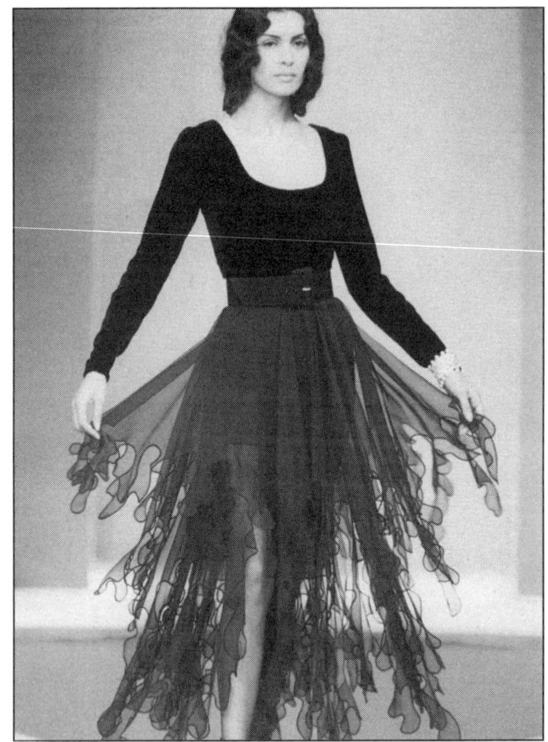

b

Figure 8.13a, b, and c. Variations in layout and surface creating a part relationship (a), a mid-level in the continuum (b), and a whole relationship (c).

c

**ACTIVITY 8.4**

If something is not considered aesthetically appealing, it may require the addition or subtraction of complexity to create the desired aesthetic. Identifying the level of complexity and what creates the complexity and order in a product helps one analyze the desired aesthetic. The product can be analyzed using the components of complexity identified by Berlyne. The factors that affect complexity can be used to increase or decrease complexity to help provide the desired aesthetic. Let's try to use the three components of complexity (number of units, degree of interest of units, and cohesion of units) to create classic and post modern designs.

Figure 8.14 shows a fashion product with a middle level of complexity. Using the three components of complexity, suggest *six* changes to make the design more aesthetically appealing to consumers looking for a classic style. (Remember, classics require a decrease in complexity.) To create a classic the following changes could be made:

1. ________________________________
2. ________________________________
3. ________________________________
4. ________________________________
5. ________________________________
6. ________________________________

Figure 8.14

Using the same three components of complexity, work again with the fashion product found in Figure 8.14 and suggest *six* changes to make the design more appealing to consumers desiring a more complex, post modern aesthetic. To create more of a post modern aesthetic the following changes could be made:

1. ________________________________
2. ________________________________
3. ________________________________
4. ________________________________
5. ________________________________
6. ________________________________

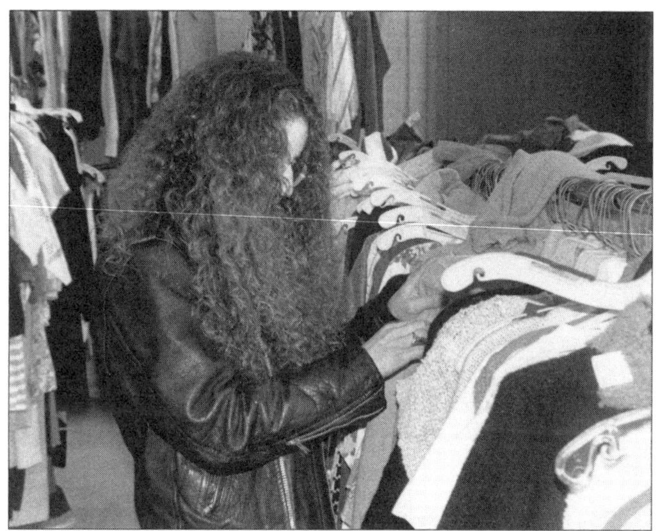

Figure 8.15. Bulging clothing shop containing items with little cohesion among the items on the rack except for category of apparel product.

mainly due to the practice of using lower-cost materials and production methods (Glock & Kunz, 1995), but also because there is less originality involved in the design of a knock-off.

In other cultures, originality or newness is less important in determining the value of the aesthetic form. Other cultures, such as the Ashanti of West Africa have firmly established stylistic conventions (Silver, 1981). Here, newness is not a primary factor in determining value of aesthetic creations. Artists in these non-Western cultures produce occasional innovations within the firmly established stylistic conventions, but quality of aesthetic creation with these cultures is more often based upon technique or skill in production, or symbolism of the aesthetic form. In these cultures, the most prized textile or apparel product may be the one that has been handed down through the generations, not the newest design.

Apparel professionals walk a fine line between offering novelty to keep the consumer interested, but not offering styles that are so novel as to alienate the consumer. Fashion is an *evolution,* which means a moderate level of novelty is built into the product or environment for slow change to occur. If there is too much novelty then fashion becomes a *revolution,* leading to confusion on the part of the consumer. More novelty may be found in fashions and post modern styles than in basic and classic styles, because fashions and post modern styles change more quickly and radically. Yet, even a classic, when first introduced, can be considered novel. For instance, leggings were seen as novel in comparison to woven, looser fitting pants styles during the 1980s, but are now considered by some firms to be a classic style that is included in new merchandise assortments.

As if life wasn't challenging enough for the apparel professional, both complexity and novelty must be considered in tandem. Research (Berlyne, 1970) suggests that the most pleasurable experiences come from simple yet novel forms or complex yet familiar forms. Forms that are simple and familiar or complex and novel are less pleasurable (Graph 8.3).

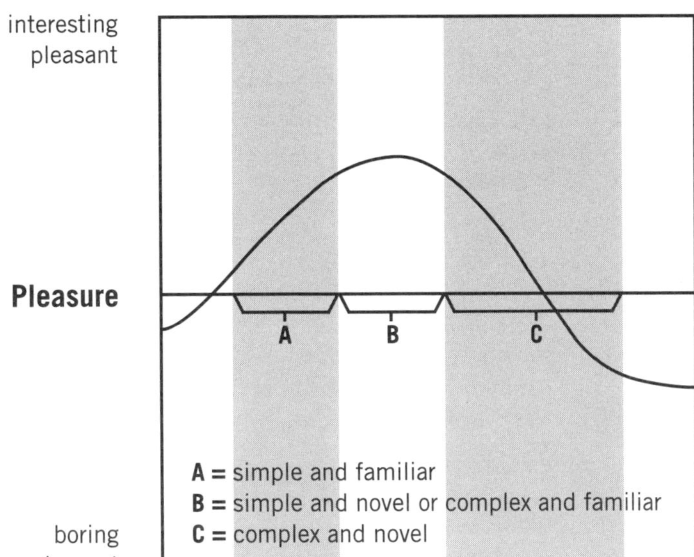


Graph 8.3 Inverted-U relationship of pleasure for complexity and novelty.

Just as consumers prefer different levels of complexity, consumers vary on the level of preferred novelty. Some consumers may seek novelty, while others will purchase a style only after that style has become widely accepted. It is the responsibility of the apparel professional to understand and meet the preferred level of novelty of the target consumer.

The concepts of complexity, order, and novelty are found in retail practices. Examples of retail practices used to entice the consumer include the following:

- **Catch the eye.** Retailers believe consumers are more apt to buy clothes that appear in full size and color assortments. Therefore, they put their most complete lines at eye level where shoppers see them first. Lower racks show broken assortments that are missing some colors and sizes. A change in color also signals that fresh merchandise has arrived.
- **Shock 'em with the new.** Stores make the most money on new clothes that haven't been marked down. Retailers also know that new, fresh fashions grab the consumer's attention. Therefore, new lines are always in the front of the store or the department, where they will be spotted first.
- **Make 'em see red.** If you see red, you're probably reading a "sale" sign. Red excites; stores maintain it stimulates buying. Consumers see it used sparingly in upscale stores, and blaringly among discounters. Warm pinks, peaches, and corals make people feel good about themselves and are often found in dressing rooms.
- **Give 'em the rack.** That sale rack at the discount-store entrance was meant to stop consumers in their tracks. At a more image-conscious store, consumers might have to search for the sale racks. It's no accident that by the time they find it in the back, they've had to pass by display after display of attractively arranged, full-priced merchandise.

Cohesion among units is important in catching the eye, and tempting consumers with attractively arranged goods; novelty is important in shocking them with the new, and degree of interest of the units is important in making them see red. Apparel professionals must consider the concepts presented in this chapter to offer products and environments that have a positive impact on consumers.

## SUMMARY

The desire for complexity, order, and novelty is common to many aspects of life, including aesthetic experience. *Complexity* (and order) relates to the degree of stimulation from the number and physical quality of units, the degree of dissimilarity of units, and the level of organization in the arrangement of units (Day, 1981, p. 33). Thus, complexity is affected by the components of

- number of units
- degree of interest of the units
- cohesion among the units

Novelty is the perceived newness of the units and their organization, based upon comparison of the present form with forms of past experience.

The role of many apparel professionals is to provide complexity, order, and novelty for the consumer. It is important to remember that the preferred levels of complexity, order, and novelty may be based upon personal preference, the aesthetic set forth by the creator, and/or the appropriate look for a situation. However, in general, an inverted-U relationship is proposed between level of complexity or novelty and perception of pleasingness of and preference for the aesthetic form. This inverted-U relationship of pleasure states that a medium level of complexity or novelty leads to a higher level of pleasure, than do low or high levels of complexity or novelty (Walker, 1981). Basics, classics, fashions, and post modern designs may be placed on the inverted-U graph to understand what defines each of the categories and their relationship to one another (see Graph 8.2). All four design classifications are within the mid to upper range of the pleasure variable. However, basics and classics are less complex than fashions and post modern designs. The apparel professional must consider complexity and novelty in tandem. According to research findings, the most pleasurable experiences come from simple yet novel forms or complex yet familiar forms.

## KEY TERMS AND CONCEPTS

basic goods
classic styles
cohesion of units
complexity and order
components of complexity and order
experimental aesthetics
fashion goods
inverted-U relationship of pleasure
novelty in different cultures
part-whole relationship
post modern styles
preferred level of complexity and novelty (combined)
preferred level of complexity and order
preferred level of novelty
units
ways of increasing complexity

**LAB ACTIVITY 8.1**

1. Each student should bring six images (two of each level of complexity: high, medium, and low) to class.
2. In class: Put your images into three groups of high, medium, and low complexity.
3. As a class, determine if any of the images need to be rearranged into other groups.
4. Form groups of three students based upon alphabetical order of your last name (your instructor will give you information on which group you are in).
5. As merchandise display teams, you need to create a store display using images from the three groups of complexity. Choose six images–two using each level of complexity for your window display.
6. Define the level of complexity of each image–high, medium, or low complexity. (In other words, how the elements of design lead to that level of complexity.) Make sure to be as comprehensive as possible in this description.
7. Arrange the images in an aesthetic manner on foamcore board.
8. Explain what criteria you used to select your images for the group of images. This means finding similarity of elements of design discussed in chapters 5 and 6.

## SUGGESTED READINGS


Beardsley, M. C. (1958). *Aesthetics.* New York Harcourt, Brace, & World, Inc.

Gombrich, E. H. (1979). Introduction (pp.1–16) to *Sense of order.* Oxford, England Phaidon Press.


### For Advanced Levels


Crozier, W. R. & Chapman, A. J. (1984). The perception of art: The cognitive approach and its context. In W. R. Crozier & A. J. Chapman (Eds.), *Cognitive processes in the perception of art* (pp. 3–23). New York: Elsevier Science.

Martindale, C., Moore, K. & Borkum, J. (1990). Aesthetic preference: Anomalous findings for Berlyne's psychobiological theory. *American Journal of Psychology, 103*(1), 53–80.

Wentworth, N. & Witryol, S. L. (1983). Is variety the better part of novelty? *Journal of Genetic Psychology, 142,* 3–15.

## READING 8.1
# Welcome Home's Warm Glow

M. Wilson

Comfortable and homey are the words that best describe the new prototype for Welcome Home. With its soft lighting and residentially-styled fixtures, the design has apparently struck the right note with shoppers. "The three stores we have remodeled are all experiencing high double digit sales increases over last year. We have also opened twelve new stores with the redesign." says Ed Kleiger, president, Welcome Home, Wilmington, N.C., which operates 143 off-price home decor stores averaging 2,400 sq. ft. each.

Welcome Home features some 10,000 skus, ranging from napkins to framed art. In keeping with the home-related merchandise, the overall goal behind the redesign was to evoke the ambience of a residential setting. "The chain's identity is totally reinforced via the store design," explains Amie Gross, president, Amie Gross Architects, New York, which executed the project. The warm, domestic ambience of the redesign differs from Welcome Home's previous look, which was reminiscent of a traditional factory outlet shop. "There wasn't much design and the traffic flow was poor," says Gross. "Shoppers were bypassing whole areas of the store."

The store also had an image problem. "We found that the customer's first impression on entering the store was one of confusion," explains Gross. "The range of product being sold was unclear." By contrast, the redesign makes a strong opening statement. Products representing the full range of merchandise carried by Welcome Home are displayed on loose fixtures carefully positioned in the entry area of the store. The items are then fully merchandised within their own area of the store.

In keeping with the main theme, the display fixtures look more like residential furniture than standard cases. Porcelain and other fragile items, for example, are displayed in a hutch-like unit with glass shelves; hard goods are showcased in a fixture styled after a curio stand. The domestic imagery continues at the cash/wrap, which resembles a chest of drawers. Dump bins for impulse merchandise are built into either side of the unit.

Low-price and mid-price goods are housed in the middle of the store. Dubbed "The Emporium," the space is made up of three kiosks, shelving units, and end-caps designed to look like wicker baskets. Small, boutique-like niches are positioned at either end of the store's rear. The cozy spaces allow for specific category merchandising. "Putting the niches at the end of the aisles promotes the customer to shop the entire store," adds Gross.

**Maximize space:** The prototype allows Welcome Home to display 20 percent more merchandise than had previously been displayed in the same space. "We reevaluated how they utilized space," says Gross. "Previously, all the shelves were eighteen inches deep, even though the merchandise was less than twelve inches deep," explains Gross. "To save space, we reduced shelf space to the minimum depth required by the product. And we made the units along the perimeter higher, bringing the product up to the ceiling line."

The new layout also helps maximize space. "We created a strong circulation path that takes shoppers throughout the entire store," says Gross. "It ends in the higher-priced framed art department, which is merchandised on the wall gallery-style."

Welcome Home's management says the design is living up to its promises. "The traffic flow has improved considerably and merchandise categories are better defined," says company president Kleiger. "People stay in the store longer and our average transaction has risen."

Reading 8.1 Wilson, M. (October 1993). Welcome Home's Warm Glow. *Chain Store Age Executive.* 69(10), pp. 142–143.

CHAPTER 9

# Principles of Design

## Objectives

- Recognize the Gestalt principles that influence the processes of perception
- Understand how Gestalt principles of similarity, proximity, closure, and continuation affect the complexity or order perceived in an apparel form
- Recognize the principles of design used to organize the elements of design
- Understand how design principles of rhythm, proportion, balance, and emphasis affect the complexity or order perceived in an apparel form
- Apply the Gestalt and design principles to manipulate the complexity and order of apparel products

In Chapter 8, you learned that the success of an apparel product may be affected by its appropriate or satisfactory level of complexity (and order) for the target consumer. Recall the inverted U-shaped curve which indicates the relationship between pleasingness of the form and its degree of complexity. You know that a medium range of complexity is more pleasing for the majority of people than very low or high levels of complexity. If the apparel form is not complex, the consumer may find it boring and reject it. If the product exhibits too much complexity, the consumer may not be able to find order within the form, and again will reject the product. By creating products with a moderate level of complexity, designers increase the likelihood of success of the apparel product. In this chapter, we will explain the guiding principles that can be carefully applied to the creation of apparel products and environments to achieve the desired level of complexity.

There are two groups of principles that can be used to understand or analyze the arrangements and combinations of elements of design in apparel forms. First, the Gestalt principles of perceptual organization explain processes through which the brain interprets certain patterns of visual information. Gestalt principles influence the level of complexity and order by decreasing the numbers of units and increasing similarity. Second, design principles of organization refer to the visual effects of arrangements of design units affecting cohesion. The usual goal of the apparel professional in the application of principles of organization is to create a pleasing arrangement of elements, providing moderate complexity and order.

## GESTALT PRINCIPLES OF PERCEPTUAL ORGANIZATION

During the early part of the 20th century, a branch of psychology, known as Gestalt psychology, focused on the principles underlying how we see or the processes of perception. Gestalt psychologists are primarily concerned with how perceiving the whole obscured perception of the component parts. "The whole is greater than the sum of the parts," is a fitting motto for this approach to psychology. That is, Gestalt psychology studied the effect of *relationships* among units within the configuration or form and not just the units themselves. Gestalt principles (Koffka, 1935) were developed to explain certain underlying processes of perception. Researchers have applied these principles to the study of aesthetics of visual and musical forms. DeLong (1987) has described the visual appearance of the clothed body form using Gestalt principles. We believe that these principles can be used to modify the visual complexity of the product (clothed body) and environment. We will examine a few of the Gestalt principles and then discuss their importance to complexity and order.

### Use of Gestalt Principles to Achieve the Desired Level of Complexity and Order

The Gestalt principles of similarity, proximity, closure, and continuation have an impact on perception of the number of units, the degree of interest of units, and the cohesion among units of the form. In the process, organization among the units is altered. The consideration of Gestalt principles in the process of product development or creating an environment is a sign of sensitive awareness of the form. Consideration of the Gestalt principles results in a more refined product or environment because the interrelationship among the parts is considered. In many professions such as design, styling, or display, a sensitive awareness of the interrelationships within the form is important to successful products or environments.

### Similarity

**Similarity** of the units refers to the grouping of units due to their sameness. As you recall, the sameness of units contributes to increased cohesion of units. Thus, similarity of units can result in a decrease in complexity of the apparel

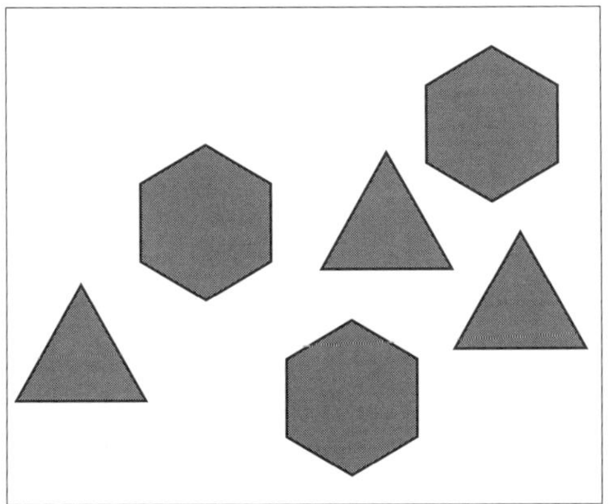

Figure 9.1. (left) Similarity leading to a decrease of complexity due to cohesion and fewer number of units.

Figure 9.2. (right) Similarity between silhouette of hair-style and apparel products found within each model and ensemble combination.

form. Similar units are viewed as groups rather than individual units, which also decreases the number of units in the perceptual process. Describe what you see in Figure 9.1. Do you perceive the configuration as six forms or two sets (triangles and hexagons)? When the configuration is perceived as *two* sets rather than *six* forms, complexity has decreased because the number of units have decreased from six to two.

Figure 9.2 shows how similarity between the body and apparel was used to bring order to the advertisement. Compare the shape of hair style silhouette (or outer shape) with the silhouette of the ensemble worn by each model. Do you see the similarity of shape between the body and apparel product worn by each of the three models? The fashion stylist made a deliberate decision to create similarity through shape of silhouette to add order to the advertising layout.

## Proximity

**Proximity** of the units refers to grouping of units due to their sameness *and* closeness in space. When there is sameness of units and these units appear close to each other, the perceived number of units decreases and cohesion increases, again resulting in a decrease of complexity. How do you describe what you perceive in Figure 9.3? Do you view the configuration as two groups or six units? Many will see the configuration as two groups, grouping the three units close to each other. This is proximity at work.

Figure 9.3. (left) Proximity of units decreasing complexity by decreasing the number of units from six to two.

Figure 9.4. (right) Proximity of buttons decreases complexity by decreasing the number of units from four to one.

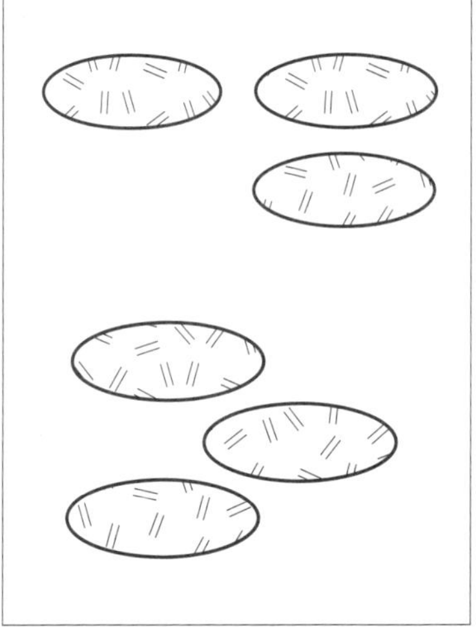

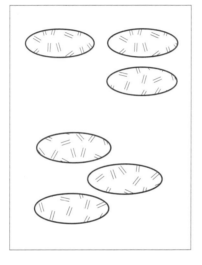

When units in apparel are grouped together by the eye, proximity is at work in the form. When units are grouped they may become a focus area for the eye, providing order for the viewer. In Figure 9.4, the vertical line of the opening is grouped with the adjacent line from the vent creating a focus.

## Closure

**Closure** is the perception of implied shapes that are not actually enclosed or complete forms. Closure results in completed *shapes.* In Figure 9.5 the mind completes the shapes to create a square and a heart-shape even though these shapes are not physically complete. Instead of perceiving four or ten separate units the mind decreases the number of units to one implied shape.

Once these shapes are perceived, cohesion can be increased by finding similarity between this shape and other shapes. The buttons of Figure 9.6 close off to create a shape that is similar to the bodice shape that is wider on top. Thus, complexity is decreased due to closure. The number of units decreases and cohesion increases.

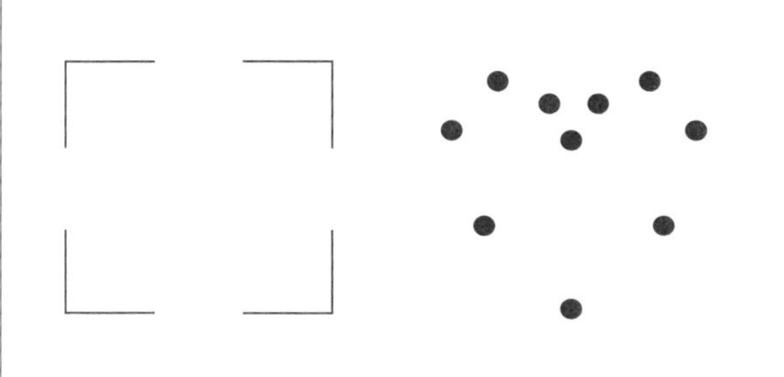

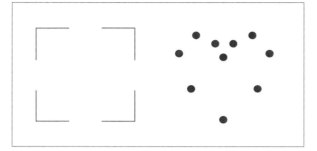

Figure 9.5. (above) Closure of units into shapes, a square and heart-shape, resulting in a decrease of number of units.

Figure 9.6. (right) Closure of units (buttons) into a shape (rectangle) leading to a decrease in the number of units and the increase of cohesion found among rectangle formed by buttons and other rectangular shapes.

## Continuation

**Continuation** is the following of a direct path or line through an interruption or break. The result of continuation is *line,* whereas the result of closure is *shape.* Trace how your eye observes the form in Figure 9.7. Does the eye travel all the way along the curvilinear line even though it is interrupted by the angular line? If the eye does travel uninterrupted, then continuation of line has occurred. Complexity is affected by continuation. Lines created by continuation decrease the overall number of lines in a form, connecting separate line segments into one line. These created lines may be related to other lines of similar length in the form, increasing cohesion. The line produced through continuation can also add to order by allowing the eye to move smoothly along units that are different, such as trousers and a shirt made of different colors and textures.

The ensemble in Figure 9.8 is an example of continuation apparent in the apparel form. The line created by the edge of the wrap skirt follows along the dart of the jacket, which connects to the jacket opening. Continuation allows the mind to dismiss the break in the lines created by the jacket's hem. Practice using all the Gestalt principles in Activity 9.1.

Figure 9.7. (left) Continuation of curvilinear line, dismissing the interruption of the angular line.

Figure 9.8. (right) Effect of continuation—following the lines of jacket and skirt edges through the break of the jacket hem.

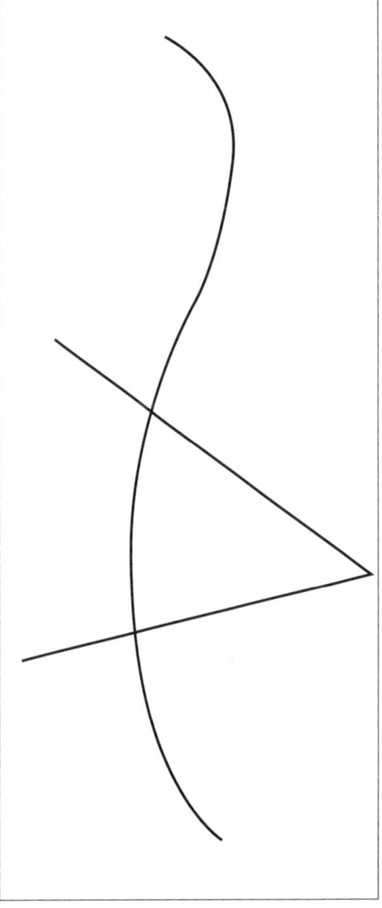

**ACTIVITY 9.1**

Use the Gestalt Principles of similarity, proximity, closure, and continuation in creating ensembles with a high degree of order.

1. Start with basic silhouette shapes traced from products in fashion ads or create your own basic silhouettes to produce an ensemble.
2. Use Gestalt principles when adding details to the illustration such as button style, button placement, pleats, pockets, and hems. (If you have the software package, SnapFashun, you could use the program to create an ensemble.)
3. Select a fabric swatch(s) or create a surface design(s) with a pattern. Consider how the surface can add order to the form.
4. Explain your selections in terms of the effect on order produced by the Gestalt principles. For instance, order may be produced through similarity of diamond shaped buttons and pointed pocket style and handkerchief hem of the ensemble. Consider proximity, closure, and continuation as well.
5. Change one styling detail such as cut of the sleeve or closures to decrease order.
6. Record how the use of Gestalt principles affected order in the form.
7. Describe the change in level of complexity in terms of number and interest of the units and cohesion of the units.

## PRINCIPLES OF DESIGN ORGANIZATION

The principles of design are related to the arrangement of the units affecting cohesion of the form. Variations within these organizational principles also affect the level of complexity within the form due to their impact on the similarity, number, and interest of units in the form. The principles of design that organize visual elements include rhythm, proportion, balance, and emphasis (Lauer, 1985).

The principles of organization of rhythm, proportion, balance, and emphasis are important for many apparel professionals such as designers, product developers, sales representatives, visual merchandisers, and stylists. Consideration of visual organization of products and environments can help textile and apparel professionals successfully develop and promote the product.

Designers and product planners generate a large volume of ideas for apparel products that must be culled into a coherent line. The principles of design can be used to evaluate individual sketches or samples, determine a direction for a collection and select items for the collection or group. The principles may be applied to fine-tune and modify items, strengthening the theme and essence of the collection.

Let's explore this fine-tuning in an example. The product is promoted internally in the company, and wholesale and retail to buyers and consumers through such activities as sales presentations, fashion shows, and advertising campaigns. Suppose that the dominant organizing principles for a line of men's suits are an emphasis created by contrasting colors and a new proportion. Emphasis and proportion of the collection can be accentuated by the display or mannequins used in the designer's showroom where merchandise is presented to buyers. These features (emphasis and proportion) become central in the planning of a fashion show. Lighting, background setting, and the sequencing of garments are designed to show the color contrast. Proportions of the ensemble will guide the selection of models to reinforce the freshness of the designer's collection. The visual merchandiser will coordinate the important features of the suits with the store's visual image through the use of various types of displays to promote the product to the consumer. Finally, understanding the importance of the proportional relationship will help the stylist and the fashion photographer capture that feature through model selection, set-up or props in the scene, camera angles, etc.

### Rhythm

**Rhythm** is created by the movement of the viewer's eye across repeating units in a form. Rhythm in visual design is quite similar to rhythm in music; a series of units are repeated in a specific manner. In apparel, rhythm can be created through the repetition of units (lines, colors, shapes, and textures) in the layout or surface design. Stripes, the sequence of buttons, or a series of pleats create different rhythms.

The elements incorporated in the rhythm may vary. For instance, units in the ensemble contributing to rhythm may include one type of line with two col-

Figure 9.9. Rhythms created through repetition of color, stripes, buttons, rounded edges, and directional lines.

ors and textures. The more varied the units contributing to rhythm, the more complex the design. The use of a polka dot print and round buttons would be less complex than a rhythm created by the repetition of several varied textures and colors (Figure 9.9). The complexity and effect of rhythm varies according to the pace and pattern of the repetition.

**Pace.** The number of units used and the distance between them creates the **pace** or an impression of speed or action implied in the repetition of units. Rhythms that have small units repeated often and closely spaced seem faster than those which use larger units and fewer repetitions. The quicker the pace of the rhythm, the less complex it may appear.

**Pattern.** The **pattern** of a rhythm is the sequence of the units. Rhythmic patterns are either *alternating* or *progressive.* Alternating rhythms are created through repetition of a regular, predictable sequence. The most basic alternating rhythm is the on-off pattern of a basic two-color stripe. There is a regular occurrence of stripe, space, stripe, space. An alternating rhythm makes use of consistent units and similar intervals of occurrence. The pattern can become more complex, such as stripe, stripe, space, stripe, space, stripe, stripe, space, stripe, space, but its occurrence is regular and once the pattern is established, the pattern group will be repeated uniformly. Because the pattern is predictable, alternating rhythms are lower in complexity.

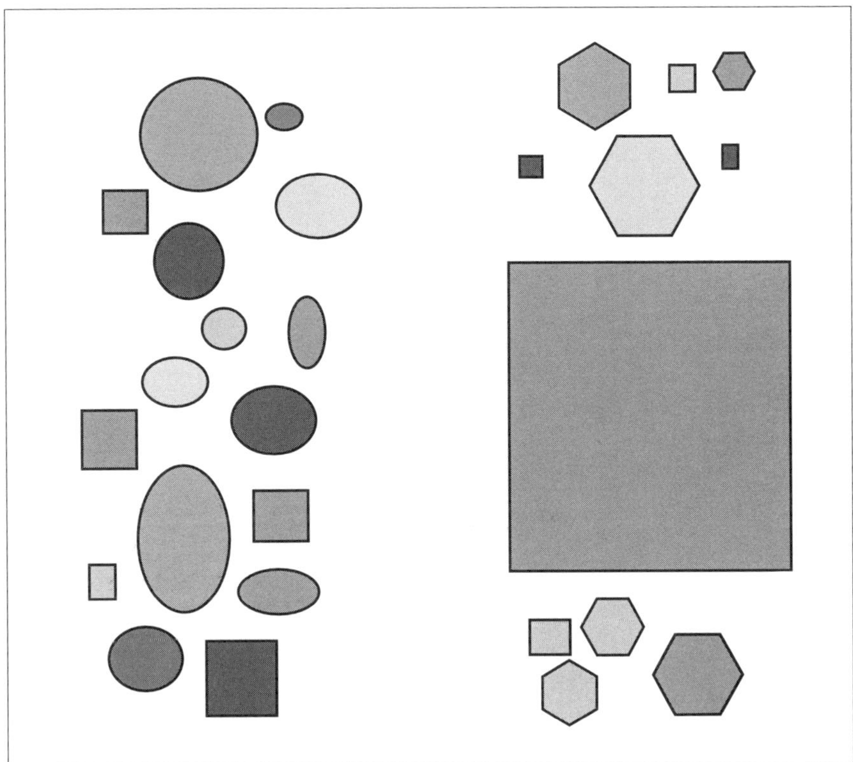

Figure 9.10. Shapes in and out of proportion with each other due to similarity or difference in size.

Progressive rhythms also include the repetition of units, but within a sequence that contains a gradual change in size or placement of the units. The ripples created by a stone dropped on a smooth pond are progressive; there is an increasing size of each unit (ripple) and an increasing distance between each unit in the sequence. Other progressive units may have a pattern of increasing and decreasing spacing or size of units. A gradual change from one color to another or gradual change in intensity of color also provides progressive rhythms. Changes in the intensity of color or texture occurring gradually through the form also produce progressive rhythms. For example, hand-dyed fabrics often employ slow color changes in which value or intensity gradually becomes lower.

Progressive rhythms contribute more complexity to a form than the regular, alternating rhythm pattern. The gradual change in units and/or spacing of units of a progressive rhythm creates a more complex pattern.

## Proportion

**Proportion** is the relative size and scale relationship between the various units within the apparel layout and surface structures and between the size of those units and the body. Units are "in proportion" with each other when they are similar in size or have pleasing size changes. Figure 9.10 shows a group of shapes with relatively similar proportions and another group in which one shape is vastly out of proportion with other shapes around it.

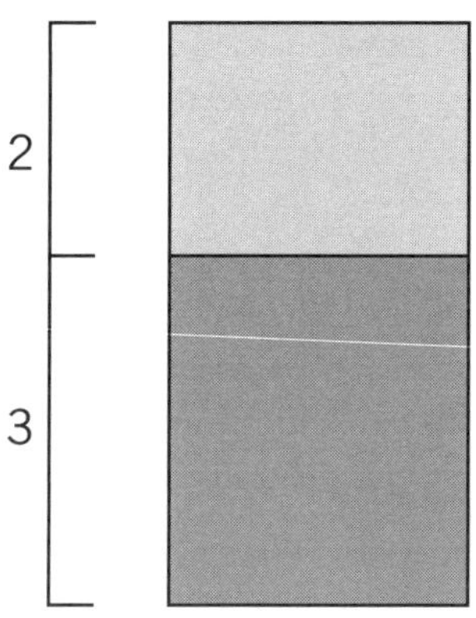

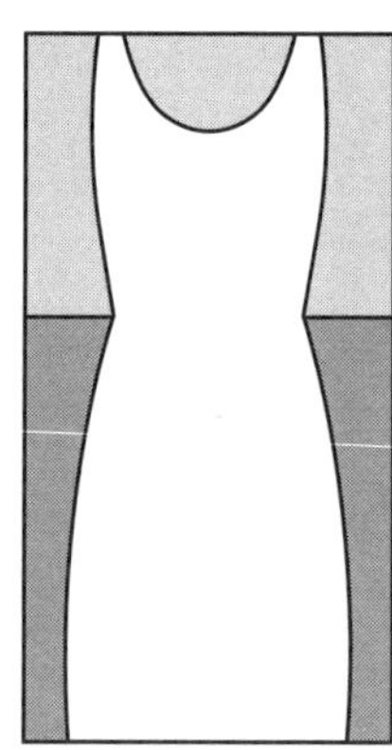

Figure 9.11. Examples of the golden section proportional relationship.

Certain proportional relationships, such as those made up of units of equal size (Arnheim, 1986) and those which exhibit "the golden section" (McWhinnie, 1987) are more pleasing than others. The "golden section" defines relationships with a proportion of approximately 3:5. In other words, a shape is divided into two smaller shapes with one shape being 3/5 and the other 2/5 of the larger shape. In another example, a line would be divided into two lines at a point 3/5 of its original length. Figure 9.11 shows several figures that demonstrate the golden section proportion.

Proportional relationships exist between all the units (lines, shapes, textures) created in an apparel ensemble. For instance, the size of an individual shape can be compared to other shapes within the ensemble, such as pocket and button size compared to lapels and cuffs. The size of shapes can also be related in the overall silhouette. When asked to describe what makes a new collection unique or special, designers often cite changes in proportional relationships created by the silhouette of a new style. For example, the proportions popular in women's suits in the mid-1990s are created by the combination of natural shouldered, upper hip-length jackets and short, slightly flared skirts. This is a very different proportional relationship than the broader, longer jackets and knee-length skirts of the mid-1980s (Figure 9.12).

Proportional relationships can also be influenced by the *scale* of the units in the ensemble. **Scale** is the relative size of one object compared to some standard measure. The standard size can be the size of the human body or the size of the environmental space. The size of units in apparel ensembles are often scaled or adjusted for different body types. For instance, a design in a misses size will be altered to maintain the same scale in a petite size. The scale of units of layout structures and surface features such as pattern or texture must be considered. The size of surface designs and layout details will be made smaller to be in scale with the petite figure. Small floral prints would provide pleasing scale relationships for the size of children. Thus, small prints are more often used in little girls' dresses than are larger "Hawaiian prints" or "cabbage roses" in order to maintain a pleasing scale relationship with the wearer. The larger florals are considered out of proportion with little girls' bodies, but appropriate for teens and adult women. Figure 9.13 shows the large scale of the "whale"

a

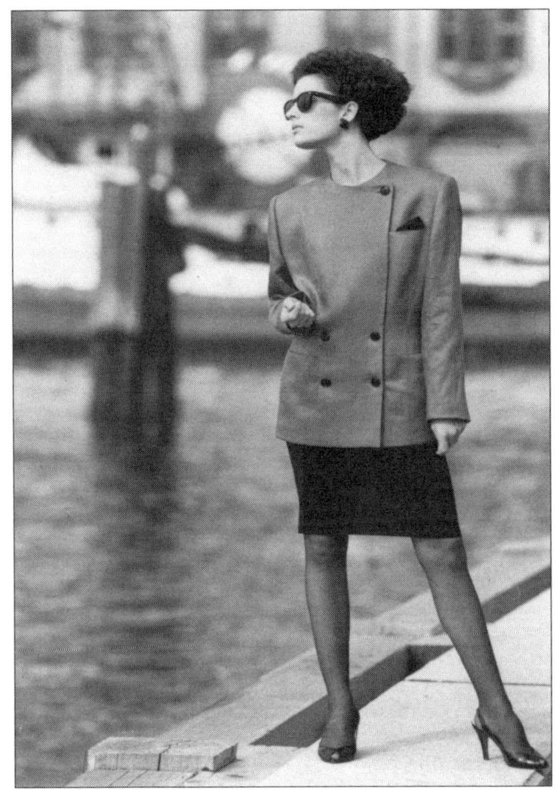

b

Figure 9.12 a and b. Evolution of proportion in women's suits over the past decade. (a) Marc Eisen, 1994 and (b) Donna Karan and Louis Dell'Olio for Anne Klein, 1985.

print to be in proportion to the large layout shape of the dress and the size of the tall model.

Similarity of size of units or similar scale of units to the body increase cohesion and decrease the complexity of the form. Proportional relationships with dissimilar sized units or units in an unrealistic scale can increase complexity, requiring more visual attention to "figure out" the relationship.

## Balance

**Balance** is the distribution of visual weight within a form. Very early in life, children develop a kinesthetic sense of balance in the body, and quickly learn that balance (standing, walking, sitting) is preferable to imbalance (falling). Vision contributes to the perception of balance within the body; in order to maintain balance, a person continually evaluates visual information and adjusts weight accordingly. For instance, watching a film of a tightrope walker who looses her/his balance creates a sense of tension in one's own body. The viewer will shift her or his weight to "keep from falling." Visual balance is the sense that the objects seen are stable rather than unstable or precarious. In the apparel form, balance among the units is preferable to make the body seem stable.

Balance in apparel considers the weight of units relative to the axis of the body. When a form is perceived, the viewer feels the existence of the horizontal and vertical axes in the body. The weight of units are balanced against each

Figure 9.13. Large scale print that is appropriate in scale and proportion to the model and the layout.

other on either side of the axes. Consider a see-saw—the center of the see-saw is the axis and in order to make the see-saw work, there must be equal weight distribution on each side. However, these weights may not necessarily be equal distance from the axis; a heavier weight can be moved closer to the axis in order to balance a lighter weight on the other side. Balance can be achieved through the use of symmetry, asymmetry, radial balance, and all-over pattern (Lauer, 1985).

**Symmetrical balance. Symmetrical balance** consists of similar units in the same positions on either side of a central axis. In symmetrical balance, each side of the body is a mirror image of the other. The axis dividing the two symmetrical halves of the form can be vertical and/or horizontal, although vertical balance between the right and left sides is generally more important to the apparel form. (It would be hard to create true horizontal symmetry on one's body unless you can paint a face on one's shins and create shoes that also double as a hat!)

Symmetrical balance is perhaps the most common form of balance in apparel ensembles. Symmetrical balance is the least complex manner of creating visual balance, thus it is evident in many basic and classic goods. Most skirts and trousers, jeans and shorts, t-shirts, sweaters, etc. have the same major shapes and details on the left and right sides of the form. A store facade that has a central entrance with display windows on either side is another example of symmetrical balance.

**Asymmetrical balance.** **Asymmetrical balance** combines dissimilar units that have equal visual weight or interest. Balance may be achieved through the use of units with different degrees of visual weight or interest due to shape, color, texture, or value (Lauer, 1985). The careful placement of the units of different weight is essential to creating asymmetrical balance. Remember, on the see-saw, heavy weight close to the axis is balanced by lighter weight farther from the axis. The amount of interest of the unit influences its visual weight. For instance, more intricate shapes have more visual interest than simple shapes, thus small intricate shapes can balance a larger simple shape. Similarly, small areas of brighter colors or higher values can be used to balance larger areas of dull or dark color.

Asymmetrical balance is evident in apparel ensembles such as in surplice or wrap bodices, sarong-style skirts, and scarves draped over one shoulder. In Figure 9.14, the surplice front closure is asymmetrical, but visual balance is achieved between the diagonal lines moving the eye to the right and the intricate shapes detailing the waist bringing the viewer's focus back to the left. The use of asymmetrical balance adds complexity and interest to the form. The balance of dissimilar units may not be immediately evident, thus it requires a higher level of sensitivity on the part of the viewer to understand and appreciate the form. High costs of production (due to cutting two different pattern pieces, separate procedures for finishing, etc.) can limit the use of asymmetrical balance in apparel.

**Radial balance.** **Radial balance** is the arrangement of units around or originating from a central point. Lines, shapes, colors, and textures directed outward—radiating from a focal point creates the feeling of equal weight distribution around the center. This central focal point may or may not be on the central axis of the body, however. Radial balance also contributes greater complexity and interest to the apparel form than simple symmetrical balance (Figure 9.15). Look back at the rotunda of the Neiman Marcus store in Figure 6.10a. This space employs radial balance as all the elements are arranged outward from the center. The circular product display on the lower level reinforces this radial design.

**Allover pattern.** An **allover pattern** provides visual balance by incorporating units of equal weight or interest throughout the form. An allover pattern appears to have no beginning or end, nor any particular focal point. The pattern is not necessarily read from left-to-right or top-to-bottom, thus there is no need to balance one side against another. When you decorate your Christmas tree, your goal is an allover pattern with evenly spaced lights and ornaments.

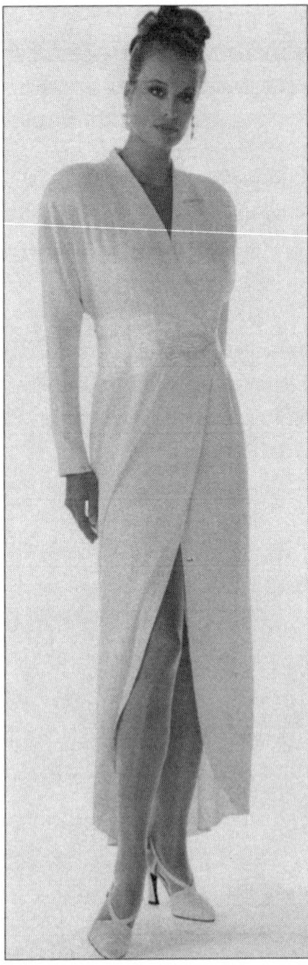

Figure 9.14. (left) Balance is created between the asymmetrical front closure and the intricate shapes detailing the waist.

Figure 9.15. (right) Radial balance exemplified by lines originating from central point.

Allover pattern is most common in surface design for fabrics. Allover patterns are more versatile and economical than border or other prints for garment construction. An allover pattern decreases complexity through the repetition of the same or highly similar units.

## Emphasis

**Emphasis** is an area that attracts viewers' attention and becomes a focal point. Emphasis is often the result of a strong use of rhythm, proportion, or balance in the apparel form. One point of emphasis can be used, or one main emphasis can be used with several lesser points of interest called accents (Lauer, 1985). Emphasis, the use of a unit or units with strong visual interest, decreases the complexity of the visual form by differentiating the units in the form and creating an order for the eye to follow. A point of emphasis can be created through contrast of units, isolation of a unit from others, and the placement of a unit within the form.

**Contrast.** Contrast of size, shape, color and/or value of units in a form can create a visual point of emphasis. When placed in combination with large and simple shapes, small and irregular shapes can become more visually interesting,

Figure 9.16. (left) Contrast of color and texture creates emphasis in apparel.

Figure 9.17. (right) Isolation of a unit increases the visual emphasis of the unit.

drawing the attention to the intricacy of those shapes. Similarly, color and value contrasts can attract attention. In Figure 9.16, the stark contrast of black and white draws immediate attention, creating a focus in the center of the upper body. This emphasis decreases complexity and creates order by leading the eye through the form in a predictable and regular manner.

**Isolation.** Units that are placed apart or separate from other groups of units become a point of emphasis. Because of the isolation of the unit, it has a stronger visual interest. This is the opposite of proximity; because the unit is isolated, it draws more attention. In the little girl's ensemble in Figure 9.17, the plaid puppy figure is isolated on the vest from the other plaid figures in the blouse fabric, thus creating a stronger point of emphasis.

**Placement.** The placement of a unit in a prominent position within the form lends emphasis to the unit. Often, this prominent placement reinforces the horizontal or vertical axis of the body. For instance, if a shape or texture area is placed near the center and upper half of the apparel form, the area will become

**ACTIVITY 9.2**

Find at least five ensembles that illustrate a designer's collection for a particular season. (You might look for a multi-page spread of advertising in *Vogue* or *Harper's Bazaar* or collect several ads from the same designer in consecutive months.) You are going to use this collection to practice analyzing the organizing principles of design and to understand how they contribute to complexity of the form.

1. What are the dominant principles organizing the collection? For instance, is there a specific use of rhythm through all the pieces, or emphasis created by contrast? Also consider proportion and balance.
2. What level of complexity is fostered by the organization of the units in the form?
3. If you wanted to target this collection to a more sophisticated consumer who is looking for more complexity and visual interest in the form, how would you use the organizing principles to achieve more complexity? Be specific in suggesting changes. For instance, you might consider lengthening the skirt to change proportion, or changing the front closure style and adding details on the opposite side to create an asymmetrical balance.

a focal point. Jewelry and accessories often create emphasis through their location in the center of the body. A pendant or a belt buckle becomes a focal point because of its prominent placement in the center of the body. Another form of emphasis due to placement occurs when the unit is the origination point for directional lines (such as in a radial balance design). As the viewer's eye moves around and through the form, the lines direct the eye back to that unit, creating emphasis in that area.

Reading 9.1 is a fashion review for fall 1995. See if you can find references to the principles of rhythm, proportion, and emphasis. Then practice using the principles of design organization in Activity 9.2.

## SUMMARY

The elements of design are not randomly combined in the creation of successful apparel products and environments. Consideration of the Gestalt principles of perception and the principles organizing units of the form is necessary for the development and promotion of apparel products and environments. Sensitivity to the resulting order and complexity of the form must be cultivated by professionals in the textile and apparel industries in order to successfully develop and promote the product.

The Gestalt principles of similarity, proximity, closure, and continuation affect how the viewer perceives complexity and order within the apparel form. Similarity is the perception of like units as a group rather than individual units. Proximity is the grouping of units close together into fewer units. Closure is the perception of complete, bounded shapes from implied lines. Continuation is the perception of a continuous line through a small break or interruption. These Gestalt principles serve to decrease the complexity in the form through decreasing the number of units perceived in the form and increasing the cohesion of the units.

**LAB ACTIVITY 9.1**

With a group of three or four students, review the collections used in Activity 9.2. Select one student's designer and increase the number of examples of that designer's collection to seven or eight ensembles. Assume that your group has been hired as consultants to that designer to plan the promotional strategy for the collection.

1. Describe the Gestalt principles and the organizing principles of design that are evident in the examples. Assess the level of complexity achieved in the forms. What type of consumer would this level of complexity appeal to? (Review Chapter 8 if necessary.)
2. Make suggestions for promoting the collection through the fashion system using
   a. fashion shows
   b. wholesale showroom displays
   c. advertising
   d. and retail visual merchandising.

Make these suggestions specific techniques for layout, presentation, props, or settings for these various promotional avenues. Make model selections and any other suggestions you think may be important for professionals promoting this collection to the consumer.

The principles of design may be used to create an appropriate level of order and complexity in the apparel form. Rhythm, proportion, balance, and emphasis should be considered in the organization of units within the form. Rhythm is created by the pace and pattern of the repetition of units. Proportional relationships of size and scale exist among the units in the form and between the units and the body. Balance is the equal distribution of the apparent visual weight of the units throughout the form. Emphasis on a specific unit in the design can be created through contrast, isolation, and placement of the unit. These visual devices can be manipulated to increase or decrease the complexity of the form.

## KEY TERMS AND CONCEPTS

allover pattern
alternating rhythm
asymmetrical balance
balance
closure
continuation
contrast
emphasis
Gestalt principles
golden section
isolation
pace
pattern
placement
progressive rhythm
proportion
proximity
radial balance
rhythm
scale
similarity
symmetrical balance

## SUGGESTED READINGS


### For Advanced Levels

Koffka, K. (1935). *Principles of Gestalt psychology.* New York, NY: Harcourt, Brace & World.

McWhinnie, H. J. (1987). A review of selected research on the golden section hypothesis. *Visual Arts Research, 13*(1), 73–84.


## READING 9.1
## Best Styles From Fall and Winter

Sandra Betzina

Readings 9.1 Betzina, S. (1995, January). Excerpts from The Best Styles From Fall and Winter. *Threads,* p. 32.

If you liked last season's soft, flowing, layered fashions, you'll see more of the same this season. This time around, it's soft pants, loose tops, and vests in lightweight wools and soft knits. The secret to successful layering is drapey fabric, which is why you'll see so many lightweight, all-knit multilayers this season. Layering proportions look freshest when a short layer is worn over a long one, for example a short vest over a long blouse, or when a really long layer is worn over a short one, for example, a full-length coat with a short skirt.

The number-one wardrobe essential for this season is the long white shirt, about knee length, often with interesting cuffs. An essential companion for the white shirt is the short boxy vest. If you already own a few pairs of loose, fluid pants, add a slimmer, close-to-the-leg pant to your wardrobe. A long, voluminous coat will not only keep you warm this season, but also adds a longer layer that's good over a wide variety of styles.

What's the word on shoulder pads? They're back (for most of us, they never left). Last season's natural-shoulder looks are being replaced by rounder, not overly substantial pads. But as always, choose the pad that's right for you.

If you love brown, this is your season. For a fresh approach, combine it with violet blue or shades from the red family. Head-to-toe ensembles in cream are interesting if textures and flat weaves are combined; subtle harmony is created with neutral shades. While fashion experts claim that brown is the new black, you can bet there will be plenty of real black around, as always. If monochromatic looks seem too boring for you, pick them up with a shot of color on a blouse, a mohair sweater, a T-shirt worn under a jacket, or a pair of socks worn with pants. Transparent layers of fabric worn over each other create subtle new shades of color.

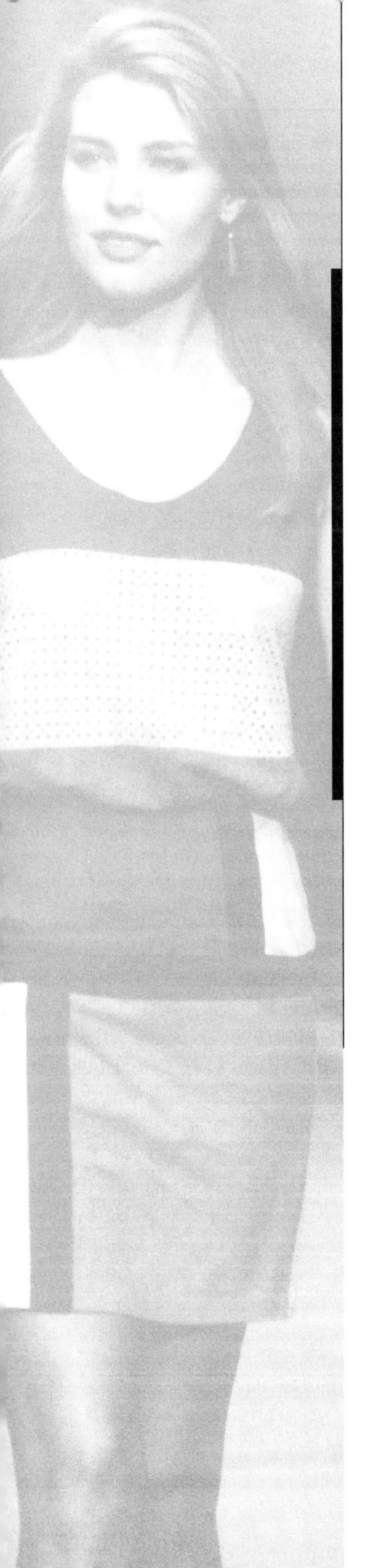

PART THREE

# Aesthetics Related Skills and the Apparel Professional

CHAPTER 10

# Creative Activities and Skills

## Objectives

- Understand the activities involved in the creative process
- Recognize the creative activities of apparel professionals in various positions in the industry
- Understand the skills of perceptual analysis, forecasting, consumer preference analysis, finding inspiration, developing and advancing a concept, and communication that apparel professionals employ in the development, selection, and promotion of apparel products and environments
- Cultivate these skills as apparel students

The **creative process** is the term used to describe the conceptual steps involved in the development of innovative solutions to problems. Frequently the solution developed in the creative process is a physical aesthetic product, such as an apparel ensemble, an ad campaign, or a visual display. Sometimes the creative solution is not a tangible object but an idea or approach to some problem, such as a business or marketing plan. Apparel professionals must cultivate the skills that are employed during various stages of the creative process.

The broad activities involved in the creative process include (1) defining the problem; (2) gathering and analyzing information; (3) synthesizing of information; (4) generating ideas; and (5) formulating, evaluating, and implementing solutions. (Although different authors may break the process into more stages with various names, these five activities will suffice for our discussion.) The creative process is often diagrammed as a step-by-step progression from one stage to the next with the option of returning to, and repeating, previous steps in the process (Lamb & Kallal, 1992; Watkins, 1988). While these models imply that the activities involved in the process are completely logical, it must be acknowledged that all creative actions and decisions are not necessarily so. Imagination, unconscious mental processes, emotional states, and spiritual responses, which are also involved in creativity, are not easily represented in step-by-step models, but they are vitally important as well (Fiore, Kimle & Moreno, 1996; Kato, 1994; Kimle, 1994).

Defining the problem includes setting goals and specifying the criteria necessary to develop a satisfactory solution. For most apparel professionals, the problem is defined in terms of some aspect of the development, selection, or promotion of apparel products and environments. The problem will largely be defined by the functions each professional performs in their particular firm. A forecaster's problem is the generation of predictions about future trends. A designer will define the problem in terms of generating new fashion products. A buyer's problem definition will focus on the selection of a successful merchandise mix for the retail store. Each professional will begin with his or her own set of problems to address with creative solutions.

Next in the creative process is the activity of gathering and analyzing information. At this stage, all relevant information that can be used to provide the background or "set the stage" for new ideas is collected or generated. This information is often used to establish criteria for evaluating the ultimate solutions. The synthesis of information from widely different sources and the generation of ideas are the stages in which new product ideas or problem solutions begin to develop. At this point, inspiration helps generate new ideas. Synthesis means the bringing together of forms that were previously separate. The creative person is able to find similarities among formal, expressive, or symbolic qualities that had previously not been associated (Tijus, 1988; Winner, 1982). By combining previously unrelated ideas or drawing on internal emotions and symbolism, the creative activity results in something new or unique (Fiore, Kimle & Moreno, 1996).

Finally, the creative solutions are formulated, evaluated, and implemented. The many ideas that are generated must be evaluated according to the criteria established in the earlier stages. Some ideas are accepted, perhaps after being modified and perfected; whereas other ideas are rejected. The final solutions are implemented and put into use.

There are skills that are representative of specific activities of this creative process. In the apparel industry, various career options require particular skills reflecting specific activities of the creative process. These skills include perceptual analysis, forecasting, consumer preference analysis, deriving inspiration, developing and advancing a concept, and communication. Figure 10.1 demonstrates how particular skills are closely associated with specific creative activities. As you read from left to right in Figure 10.1, you will notice that the activities and skills involved result in the creation of the apparel product and environment. Also, as one moves from one skill to the next, there is a building process, later skills and activities build upon previous ones. As we discuss each of the skills of apparel professionals, we will describe how they relate to activities of the creative process and functions within the industry.

## BASIC PERCEPTUAL ANALYSIS

Perceptual analysis skills are necessary for the information gathering and analysis activities of the creative process and underlie all the processes of developing, selecting, and promoting products and environments. Perceiving the aesthetic form underlies the ability to forecast new products, understand current consumer preferences, derive inspiration, move new ideas forward, and communicate those ideas. Perceptual analysis entails perceiving what exists in the aesthetic form, then examining and understanding similarities and differences among forms.

### Perceiving Forms

Perceiving the form occurs when analyzing an individual sensory product or environment. This can include analysis of one ensemble or body form. Individual elements and the interrelationships among the elements of the apparel product are identified. Analysis can also include individual bodies, as when a wardrobe consultant works with a client determining wardrobe recommendations to enhance the individual's body form.

### Abstracting Across Products

**Abstracting across products** is the process of identifying the underlying similarities of the products. The abstracting process begins with the skill of perceiving forms, but this perception and analysis is applied to many sensory products or environments. In the abstracting process, *comparison* among forms occurs. Apparel professionals, such as sales consultants, must cultivate their perceptual skills to summarize what is available in the current apparel market. They compare many options existing in the store's stock. This becomes the basis for suggestions of styles for consumers seeking advice.

Figure 10.1. Model of the creative activities and skills employed by apparel professionals.

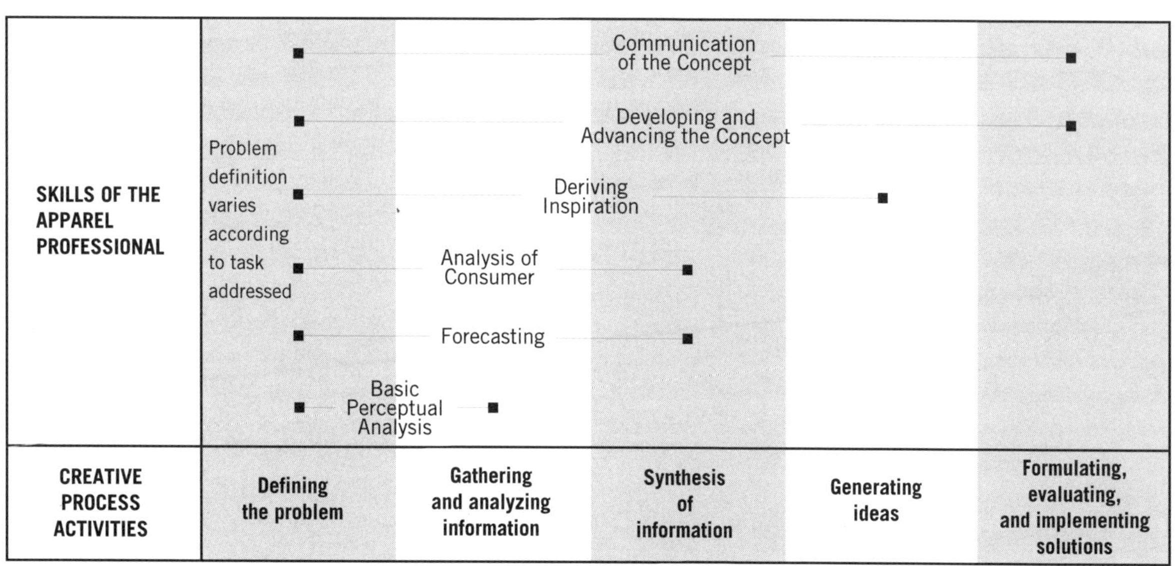

Fundamental to the skill of perceiving and abstracting across forms is the continual seeking out of information about apparel products and trends. For instance, designers, product developers, or merchandisers will likely spend a great deal of time "shopping the stores" (the competition). Shopping the stores is the process of absorbing information about products in the current market. This information is then used as a point of comparison to identify important fashion trends that might be capitalized upon within the firm's own line.

Perceiving the form is an ongoing process for the apparel professional. One's awareness is heightened; an apparel professional becomes a "sponge" soaking up information from many sources. Such information comes from general and trade newspapers and magazines, entertainment, sports, and other media events, as well as fashion as it is worn "on the streets."

## FORECASTING TRENDS

Fashion products are *evolutionary* in nature in that they change slowly from season to season or year to year. These changes are generally gradual for fashion products. In the apparel industry, there are professionals whose primary emphasis is understanding this evolutionary nature and forecasting or predicting the changes in new products. The process of forecasting trends includes understanding the direction and rate of change of products. These trends are based upon analysis of transition in the product over time. In addition, changes in the product coincide with or reflect broader socio-cultural changes. These socio-cultural forces may affect the product's selection and use. Forecasting activities parallel the creative process phases of collection and analysis of information and synthesis of information.

### Forecasting: Abstracting across Products over Time

In abstracting across products, similarities are identified among products. However, in forecasting, abstracting across products over time focuses on transition or change in the form *over time.*

Some forecasters and designers are able to conduct this process of abstraction internally, holding information in memory about styles and previous trends as well as awareness of current forms and trends. This is a mental skill that requires a great deal of experience and the cultivation of sensitivity to fashion products over many years. For the student and beginning professional, we recommend a more concrete process of abstracting using a systematic approach such as that explained in Chapter 14. By selecting many examples and abstracting from actual information, professionals can be sure not to place undue emphasis on any particular bit of information or personal inclination in the process of identifying and forecasting future trends.

In the apparel industry, there are several forecasting services. The main element of forecasting is color, although style trend forecasts are also available. Two color forecasting services include the Color Association of the United States (CAUS) and the Color Marketing Group (CMG). The Color Marketing

Group is an industry association with over 1,400 members representing firms in the textile, apparel, and home furnishings industries. These professionals meet twice yearly to develop a color forecast for upcoming seasons in product categories such as apparel, home furnishings, and cars. These professionals each provide their analyses of the current market and ideas on future trends at the annual meeting. In the discussion of this information and the development of the CMG's forecast, the abstracting process occurs *writ large.* In other words, these professionals who have abstracted across product information present their ideas that are again abstracted to summarize the broad industry trends that all members believe will be important. This process of color selection for forecasts is driven by consumer preferences; CMG members are attempting to anticipate public demand, thus facilitating design and merchandising decisions in the industry (Jacobs, 1994; Lane, 1992).

In addition to color forecasting groups, there are companies that develop forecasts of style trends and sell them to clients at various levels in the industry. These forecasters identify and synthesize trends occurring in society and the marketplace. The forecasts highlight concepts on which designers, manufacturers, and retailers can capitalize. For more about fashion forecasting services, Reading 10.1 highlights the activities of the Doneger Group, a large buying office and their forecasting service called $D^3$.

### Interpreting the Socio-cultural Context

The apparel professional understands that products reflect the socio-cultural context. Broad social patterns shape the socio-cultural context in which consumption occurs. In addition to collecting and analyzing information about the form, forecasters also collect and analyze information that helps them define and understand the socio-cultural context. Uncovering the nature of the socio-cultural context of the product requires observation and interpretation of current issues or events. An example of the socio-cultural context reflected in products may be the awareness and concern for the environment prevalent in the media as the "spirit of the 90s." This value may influence aesthetic preferences for products that symbolically represent nature. An example of a product line that has been successful in reflecting environmental awareness is home furnishing textiles that are produced with natural dyes rather than chemical dyes (Figure 10.2). The consumers who select this product may find the colors more pleasing because of their association with "natural" colors.

## ANALYSIS OF CONSUMER PREFERENCES

In order to effectively develop, select, and promote apparel products and environments, apparel professionals need to understand the customer. Apparel professionals can focus product development, selection, and promotional efforts through analyzing various types of information about consumers. A detailed understanding of consumer preferences is necessary because individual consumers will respond differently to various apparel products and environments.

Figure 10.2. Eco-ordinates products using natural dyes.

Without understanding consumer preferences, the most an apparel company can do is produce goods and toss them into the market hoping that *someone* might trip over them and decide to purchase them.

Analysis of consumer preferences further aids in the creative process activities of defining the problem, the analysis of information, and synthesis of information. Defining the problem includes setting criteria for a successful solution. These criteria include responding to consumer preferences. For instance, if information is available about color preferences, successful new designs will meet these color demands. Analysis of consumer preference information is also used in evaluating and implementing solutions, as when consumer feedback is used to improve products.

## Consumer Market Segments

Consumers are often categorized into market segments in order to analyze preferences and to target marketing efforts toward certain consumers. Market segmentation divides the heterogeneous mass market (all consumers with their characteristics and preferences), into smaller subgroups of consumers who have certain homogeneous (similar) characteristics such as their fashion preferences, lifestyle and demographics, shopping habits, and purchasing behavior (Solomon, 1992). Segmentation of the consumer market defines groups of consumers

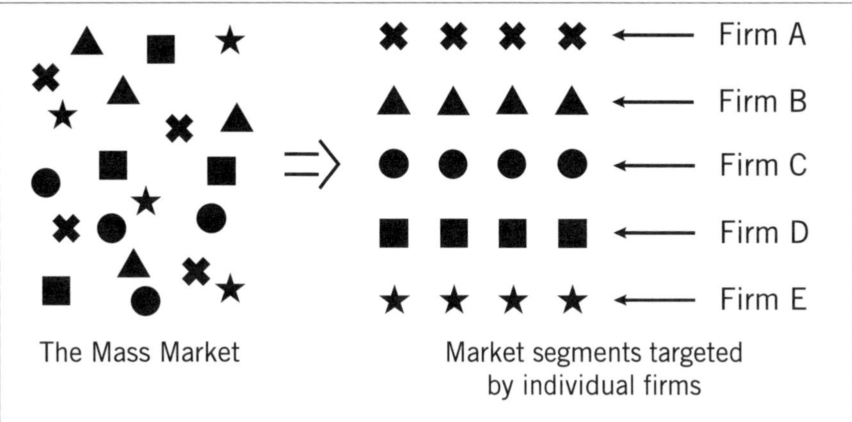


Figure 10.3. Market segmentation based on similarity of consumer characteristics.

whose purchasing needs may be targeted by the individual firm (Jarnow & Guerreiro, 1991). In Figure 10.3, the mass market is represented by the group of shapes on the left. Market segmentation divides the mass market into groups of consumers who are similar in some way. Firms may then decide to target these groups.

Although market segments can be large—such as the baby-boomers, or small—such as cycling enthusiasts, targeting a consumer market segment is most effective when the segment can be defined as narrowly and specifically as possible (Jarnow & Guerreiro, 1991). Thus, factors of age, gender, body form, income, lifestyle, demographics (e.g. geographic location), and shopping and purchasing patterns are some of the items that define market segments. For instance, a market segment such as suburban female teens provides product developers, selectors, and promoters with a great deal of focus and direction. By focusing on this juniors market segment, producers and retailers limit the range of consumers who might purchase the product. However, they also use the information about that consumer group's aesthetic preferences to design products and environments to successfully satisfy the demands of consumers within that market segment. In a trade publication ad, the VF Corporation makes special reference to the means by which they focus on the junior market and the information they gather about consumer preferences; VF claims "We know what she wants. We asked her." To identify consumer market segments and consumer product preferences, information about consumers is collected through the processes of content analysis of qualitative and quantitative information.

## Content Analysis

**Content analysis** is a technique for determining the values, themes, and other elements of culture from objective materials produced by people (Engel & Blackwell, 1982). Content analysis can be performed on any visual or verbal information to determine the meaning contained in that information. Content analysis about consumer behavior is necessary to understand the success and failure of various products in the marketplace. Information for this type of analysis can come from both qualitative and quantitative data.

**Qualitative information.** Qualitative information includes the subjective opinions of consumers. Informal qualitative information can come from sales staff, retail managers, and buyers who listen to customer concerns and preferences. These apparel professionals can share such information with sales reps, other merchandisers, and design teams, allowing them to refine products to better serve the customer.

More formal qualitative information can also be solicited from consumers through research activities such as surveys and focus groups (Solomon, 1992). Surveys involve an individual consumer answering a set of specific questions. Surveys can collect qualitative statements by participants or quantitative responses to direct questions. Surveys may be conducted with customers in stores, by telephone, or through the mail. Consumer response is best in the face-to-face store intercept situations. But this method taps only a limited range of consumers—those who shop in a particular store at the time of the survey.

Focus groups involve a group of consumers discussing attributes of the product prompted by a few broad questions such as "What do you like about the product?" Focus groups are being used by researchers and apparel marketers alike in order to understand consumer behavior in general, as well as consumer responses to specific apparel products. Lands' End company recently sponsored research exploring how consumers evaluated the quality of certain apparel styles (Abraham-Murali & Littrell, 1995). They identified specific features consumers associated with quality products.

**Quantitative information.** Quantitative information that can be used to analyze and understand consumer preferences includes data (usually numerical) specifying facts about consumer segments and past consumer activities using a large number of consumers. For instance, quantitative information includes demographic data about the consumer such as age, income, location, and family composition that can be used to classify individuals into market segments (Engel & Blackwell, 1982). Information about past consumer activities includes sales figures and information from credit records such as credit card purchases. Telephone and mail surveys usually collect quantitative data through a preset response format (e.g., yes/no answers, rating scales, questions about number of purchases).

Through analyzing the combination of qualitative and quantitative information regarding individuals in specific consumer market segments, apparel professionals are better able to specify the needs and wants of their target customer. Firms are becoming more and more detailed in the type of consumer information they collect. For instance, when customers use a store credit card or pay by check, their names and addresses can be placed in a database and future purchase activities can be recorded. When companies record information about a past purchase, the consumers are more easily targeted with promotions for related products. For instance, if a customer purchased a women's size dress through a mailed catalog, her mailbox might then be flooded with catalogs for women's size clothing, shoes offered in wide widths, and "cooking light" magazine offers. In Activity 10.1, you will apply the methods we have outlined to carry out a consumer preference study.

**ACTIVITY 10.1** Focus groups are effective ways for marketers to find out about the "whys" behind consumer preferences. In this activity, you and a partner will conduct a mock focus group in class with five to seven people and explore preferences for appearance care products. One person will lead the discussion and the other will take notes on what is said in the focus group.

1. Decide on the appearance care product you will focus on in your focus group (cosmetics of a particular brand, hair care products, shaving products, or hand lotions are some possibilities). Arrange to have sample products on hand that the group can try. (You can bring products you have on hand or perhaps you know a sales consultant who can provide samples.)
2. Begin by asking everyone what products they use and why they like them.
3. Find out if there are any drawbacks to those products or reasons why the group may or may not like certain products. (Allow the group to talk with each other and "bounce ideas" around. But you may need to encourage all members of the group to participate. As leader of the discussion you might bounce an idea around with a shy person who might not otherwise say much.)
4. Pass out the samples and ask the group to evaluate the test product.
5. What information was gathered regarding the product you selected?
6. What recommendations would you make to product developers and marketers regarding this product based on the group's findings? What features of the product stood out? What were the reasons for evaluations?

## DERIVING INSPIRATION

Once the problem has been defined, the information gathered and analyzed, and the criteria for success specified, the creative process needs a spark. The next activity is the generation of new ideas. This requires a leap from what *is* to what *could be*. Sometimes this flash of inspiration may come from the individual's imagination. More often, inspiration comes from the seeking out of other forms (e.g., other products or the arts). Finding similarities in different forms and bringing them together in new combinations is called "**divergent thinking**" (Tang & Leonard, 1985). This leap into the realm of ideas is what separates creativity from rote work processes.

The direction for new apparel forms is affected by currently popular items and the evolutionary changes forecasted for those products. But the direction for the evolutionary change may be accommodated by ideas from cultural or historic apparel forms, aspects of the physical environment, or multi-sensory experiences that have some similarity to the direction of current trends.

### Cultural Forms

Cultural forms in apparel are those items that have a long-standing tradition within specific socio-cultural groups. Ethnic and national folk costume can provide inspiration for apparel designs. Folk costumes can be used as a source of inspiration for details such as fabrics, styles, or trims used in the design of new apparel.

Another cultural pattern or form that often provides inspiration for apparel forms is the concept of gender. Most cultures have certain apparel and other art forms that symbolize gender differences. In Western culture, certain aspects of apparel forms are strictly reserved for one gender, while others are more unisex. For instance, skirts are commonly worn by women while pants are more commonly worn by men and women. Some forms are ambiguous. Ties are worn by men, but occasionally women might wear modified versions of this item. Menswear frequently serves as inspiration for women's apparel in Western cultures. On the other hand, women's appearances less frequently inspire menswear in Western culture. When gender-specific apparel forms are borrowed or modified by the opposite sex, it is referred to as "gender bending."

## Historic Forms

Just as cultural forms can be used as inspiration for new apparel ideas, fashions and styles from previous historical periods can be "revived" to serve the present fashion spirit. Many designers collect historic costume references for use when they seek inspiration. Generally, the important style features such as the silhouettes, fabrics, or colors that defined the earlier era are preserved, but the styles will also be "updated" in some way to create novelty within the form. Creative "divergent thinking" might bring an old silhouette together with today's new "high tech" fabrics. Consumers often consider it "fun" to revive old ideas, but without some aspect of change and modernization, the old design might be perceived as dated and inappropriate for today. The socio-cultural context of the product has changed from it's original usage to the present, requiring change in the form.

While design inspiration often comes from a revival of a particular era, the post modern approach to design employs the combination of style details from many different cultural and historical eras into one new cultural form. The post modern approach finds significance in the combinations of styles and meanings of elements from past settings, leaving the new meaning open to interpretation by each individual perceiver (Gitlin, 1989). Mixing design details from different cultural and historic references is often the fuel for the creativity of post modern designers such as Jean-Paul Gaultier and Christian Lacroix. Gaultier's exotic headdressing for his Spring 1994 show was described as "the combination of high-tech silver shine with an earthy, cross-cultural primitiveness" (Astley, 1994, p. 392). Figure 10.4 demonstrates this post modern combination of the ethnic traditions of the African Masai, Indian culture, and modern, high-tech metal.

## Physical Environment

Inspiration for apparel forms can be derived from formal features of many aspects of the physical environment, including nature and the outdoor environment, architecture, interior design, and technology. Formal qualities of the physical environment often provide inspiration for apparel items. For instance, surface designs inspired by nature could incorporate organic shapes and bark-

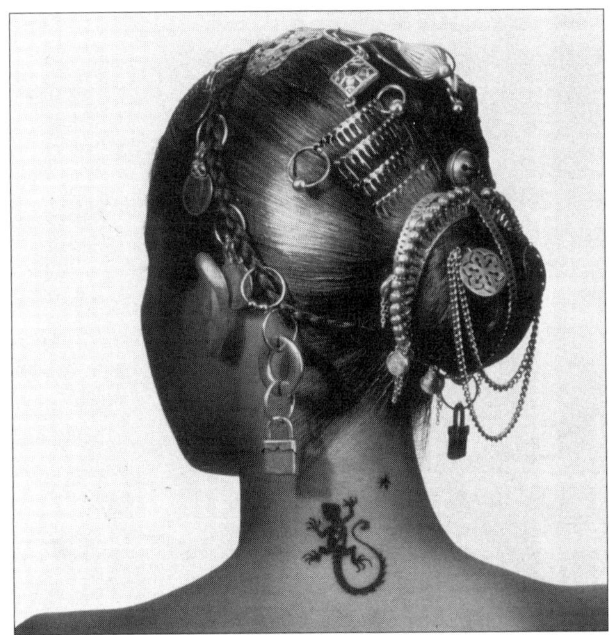

Figure 10.4. Jean-Paul Gaultier's headdress is a mix of cultural references.

Photo by Irving Penn. Courtesy *Vogue*. Copyright © 1994 by Condé Nast Publications, Inc.

like textural interest whereas designs inspired by computer technology might have more geometric, hard-edged, smooth qualities. Formal qualities of objects from the physical environment can be represented in a realistic, stylized, or abstract manner.

**Realism.** A realistic representation of an object reproduces the object's features as closely as possible to the way the object appears in the environment. Realism in presentation shows objects or images as they "really are" or as a camera would record them. The recognition of the object is important in a realistic approach. An illustration that uses a realistic presentation uses recognizable images of a body and clothing details. The viewer would not only recognize a figure with fairly natural proportions, but would be able to identify details of the apparel ensemble (Figure 10.5a).

**Stylization.** Stylization in presentation employs elements of the object that have been distorted either through mild simplification or exaggeration. Stylized objects maintain some resemblance to real objects, but they are not as real or life-like in presentation. Emphasis in a stylized presentation is placed on the formal qualities of the design rather than on the object as found in the environment (Richardson, Coleman & Smith, 1984). The formal qualities may be exaggerated in order to enhance the expressiveness of those formal features. Stylization of the body was the most important focus for the famous illustrator and costume designer, Erté (Figure 10.5b). Erté elongated the body beyond realistic proportions and incorporated many flowing, curvilinear lines.

**Abstraction.** In an abstract presentation, the formal and expressive elements of the object are simplified and become the subject rather than the original object. Abstract presentations employ extreme simplification of the form and there is

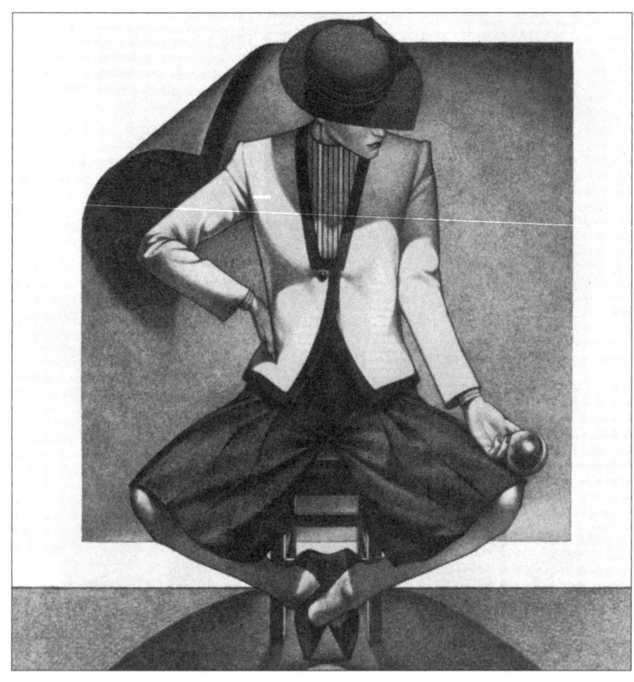

a

Figure 10.5. Realistic fashion illustration (a) by George Stavrinos showing natural body proportions and specific apparel details. (b) Stylized fashion illustration by Erté showing exaggerated body proportion and apparel details. (c) Abstract fashion illustration by Gianfranco Ferré with vague and distorted body proportion and apparel details.

b

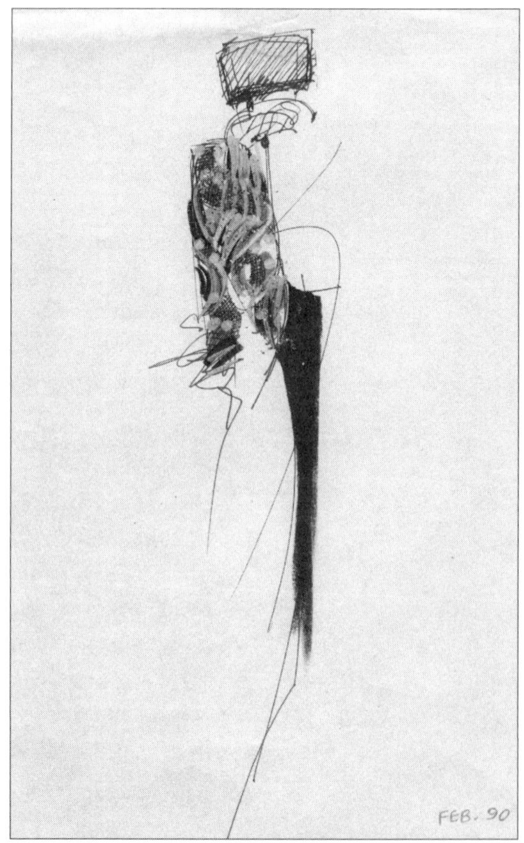


c

little attempt to maintain the resemblance to any object. The formal elements themselves, rather than the content of the form is important (Richardson, Coleman & Smith, 1984). Simplification of the formal elements of the object often results in more regular, geometric shapes. The abstract presentation seeks to distill the essence of the form, eliminating extraneous details. Form, texture, and color become more important than content or object references. In the fashion illustration by Gianfranco Ferré in Figure 10.5c, there is little resemblance to an actual body and very little specific product information.

### Multi-Sensory Stimulation

In Chapters 5, 6, and 7, we discussed the formal features of visual and tactile forms, sound, and scent. By now, you should understand that similarities can be found between expressive and symbolic qualities of forms that are perceived through different modalities (sensory channels). People can match the qualities of one form, such as scent or music, to qualities of visual forms (Smets & Overbeeke, 1989). Students designed sculpture that corresponded to various scents and designed cassette players evoking different musical styles. Not only could students convert olfactory and auditory cues into visual form, but others were able to match the sculptures and cassette players with the scents and the music that inspired them. These researchers concluded that "patterns in the stream of energy striking the senses" can be transposed from one sense to another.

Apparel designers can use these multi-sensory relationships as inspiration for new apparel forms. Apparel can be designed with inspiration from the sounds of 1950s B-Bop, heavy metal, or blues music as well as spicy, oriental, or earthy, outdoorsy fragrances. Design using auditory or olfactory stimulation as inspiration requires heightened sensitivity to the formal features of the object and the visual form in order to create patterns that effectively translate the same aesthetic.

## DEVELOPING AND ADVANCING THE CONCEPT

Once inspiration has struck, a multitude of ideas may be generated. Development and advancement of the concept involves pulling multiple ideas together into a coherent whole. Individual ideas must be evaluated, eliminated, modified, or selected. The development and advancement of the concept involves the last two stages of the creative process.

Grasping and maintaining the idea is difficult when the product does not yet exist. Turning an idea into an actual product takes the ability to maintain a vision within one's mind of the concept, while the development of this reality takes place. This process requires the ability to maintain a focus while being open to many options in developing the product. At each turn, whether in choosing fabrics for a line, in planning an assortment, or in designing an ad campaign, the apparel professional must determine if the intended concept is coming through.

## Distilling the Essence of the Product

While generating ideas, the "essence" or theme for the product should emerge. The theme may be identified at the beginning and stimulate product ideas, or it may evolve out of similarities among a group of product ideas. Creative activity includes evaluating individual ideas based upon how well they embody this theme. The theme is demonstrated through similarity of form, expression, or meaning in the products. For instance, many ideas generated by a designer might have a similar silhouette that provides the theme. In a collection of women's blouses, the essence or spirit of the collection might center around the expressive nature of feminine and frilly embroidery details. Not all ideas will communicate the essence as effectively as others. Thus, the evaluative process involves culling coherent and viable features from a multitude of ideas.

## Building a Line or Collection

After identifying this emergent essence or theme of the product, the creative process requires the elimination of all extraneous ideas and building the items up into a collection. For instance, using the theme as the organizing feature, a designer creates a line of products that include some variety in color, style, and detail. The designer or product developer must capture the essense of the aesthetic product while eliminating details or production methods that are not central to the aesthetic of the product's theme.

The line must have enough variety to appeal to a wide number of buyers, but it must maintain enough similarity and coherence to communicate the theme. The number of pieces and groups in a line will vary from one design firm to another.

## Knock-offs and Private Labels

The close reproduction of one designer's concept by another company, usually using less expensive materials and production methods, is called a **knock-off.** The apparel business is fueled by the practice of reducing popular up-scale designers' styles to lower-cost products for moderate and budget markets. By taking inspiration from successful designs and trends in the marketplace, manufacturers of lower-cost goods make the same general aesthetic available to larger consumer segments. Although this is a wide-spread practice, it does raise ethical questions about intellectual property and copyright issues.

**Private label merchandise** is produced exclusively for one retailer and the brand used is owned by the retailer (Jarnow & Guerreiro, 1991). Retailers develop contracts with various manufacturers to produce their private label merchandise. A retailer may use many different manufacturers for a wide variety of products, including basics such as jeans, innerwear, and socks as well as fashion goods such as sportswear. A buyer or merchandiser for the retail firm must capture the essense of the product to be emulated in the private label product. The merchandiser works with the design team and manufacturer to determine the products that are selling well in the market and uses this information as a basis for the new private label product lines.

Private label merchandise is carried not only in the large department stores such as JCPenney (whose labels include Worthington and Hunt Club), but more and more discount chains are finding private label merchandise to be profitable ventures (Agins, 1995). For instance, Target Stores carries their own Trend Basics line; Kmart has the Jaclyn Smith Collection; and Wal-Mart has the Kathie Lee Gifford line. Private label merchandise is a very effective way for retailers to develop and maintain a unique image in the marketplace.

### Cutting Production Costs While Maintaining Aesthetic Integrity

In the development of products, including knock-off and private label products, the designer and production manager strive to cut the production costs yet maintain the overall aesthetic appeal of the product. The use of less expensive fabrics and trims, slightly smaller patterns to use less fabric, fewer production steps such as eliminating seams or pattern matching, and the use of less expensive construction techniques all decrease the production cost and, ultimately, the retail cost of the garment. But each of these changes can alter the integrity of the original product idea, and possibly lessen its appeal. A balance must be maintained between cost-cutting measures and the fashion and aesthetic features of the garment. In Reading 10.2, you will see how one young designer pays careful attention to each penny in materials and production costs so that some construction details that enhance the product can be maintained, while producing a budget-level product. Next, practice what you have learned in Activity 10.2.

### Stocking the Store

In the selection of merchandise for the stores, the buyers must keep in mind the store's overall aesthetic image and creatively work within those boundaries.

**ACTIVITY 10.2**

In this activity, you will consider the "essence" of a line and how you would carry the idea into a discount mass merchandiser's private label line.

1. Select several examples of a current line of apparel from a designer label (such as Calvin Klein, Donna Karan, Escada, St. John). Your line should include three to five items that exemplify the same theme. You may find these items in current fashion magazines or catalogs.
2. What is the overall theme or essence of the line? What formal, expressive, or symbolic features define or create this theme?
3. Make some suggestions about how this theme might be used for a private label line for a large retailer such as Target or Kmart. What details might be eliminated or changed in order to produce the garment(s) at a lower price point? What features must be retained in order to maintain the aesthetic integrity and appeal of the product?
4. Develop this product into a group of five to seven items that could be merchandised for the mass market retailer.

The store's image is specified as a part of the business plan for the retail organization. Such images include descriptions such as up-scale, moderate, trendy, or classic. The store's image is intended to appeal to target consumer market segments with certain income and lifestyle factors.

The merchandise made available at a given time by the apparel firm is called the **assortment plan** (Rupe & Kunz, in review). In determining the assortment plan for the retail store, buyers must not only consider the appeal of the product, but also the visual effect of merchandise in the department. The merchandise should be displayed in a manner consistent with the store's image. For example, if the store in question is an exclusive boutique decorated with marble and fine hardwood furnishings, athletic team logo jackets would look out of place.

Within the framework of the store image, buyers must select merchandise that will successfully appeal to the consumer. This includes maintaining a balance between the selection of items that are new and those that are familiar to the customer and could coordinate with past purchases. Providing a pleasing selection of options for the customer is a must. This depends on the merchandiser's ability to present merchandise from the same or different manufacturers in coherent groupings. Merchandise groups should exhibit similar aesthetic qualities such as color, texture, or layout in order to maintain or expand coordinating possibilities and encourage multiple purchases.

## COMMUNICATING IDEAS

The result of the creative process is a solution that can be implemented. In the apparel industry, this solution is usually the apparel product or environment. Implementation of the new product entails communication about this product to the appropriate audience so that it can be adopted. Communication about the apparel product generally emphasizes or reinforces the formal, expressive, or symbolic features of the product. Communications about apparel products frequently involve situating the product within an environment to create a context for that product's future usage. Those who develop communications need to foster the skills involved in identifying features of the product to enhance and develope imagery that will increase the product's appeal.

Communication about apparel products and environments takes place within apparel firms, among different firms providing goods and services to each other, and between the industry and consumers. The goal of communication is to create or raise awareness of the product's features among a target audience. The target audience depends on the firm doing the communicating: a forecasting service communicates with their clients who subscribe to their services; a designer may create communication for use among the product development team; the sales representatives communicate with buyers; and advertisers communicate with consumers.

Communication can include visual and verbal information about product lines. The visual representation of the product is usually achieved through drawings, photographs, or video. The verbal information is any text or spoken

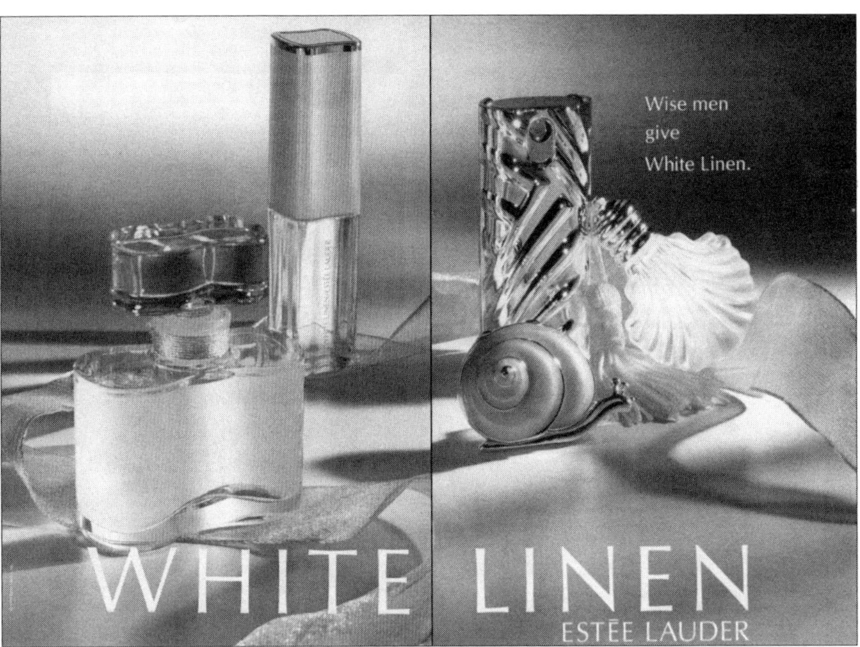


Figure 10.6. Ad for White Linen that stimulates the senses, the mind and the emotions.

word included. This verbal information can be simple factual information (e.g., designer names, description of features of product, retail sources) and/or an appeal to the consumer. A background or context can also be added to the communication to enhance the appeal through photos and graphics as well. Most communication about apparel products will combine images of the product with visual context and verbal information.

Consumers may choose a product through a rational, problem-solving approach in which they weigh the facts about a product, or they may make choices based on a hedonic (pleasure-seeking) response (Hirshman & Holbrook, 1982). The **hedonic response** affects the choice to purchase or use a product because it satisfies the need for emotional expression or feeds fantasy. Advertising communications often use imagery—words and pictures which stimulate mental thoughts, feelings, and sensory experiences rather than rational decisions—to invoke the hedonic response (McCracken, 1987; Rossiter, 1987). Imagery in promotional materials targeted to the consumer is intended to increase the appeal. Imagery may enhance the sensory stimulation offered by the product, arouse the emotions, or activate thoughts or fantasies. These imagery processes can be illustrated by the ad for White Linen fragrances in Figure 10.6. The sensory stimulation by the product is increased in the photo layout, through the use of lighting to enhance the shine and emphasize the colors and textures of the product and packaging. The verbal phrase "wise men give White Linen" stimulates the mind, making reference to the traditions of gift-giving at Christmas. And since this is a magazine targeted to female consumers, the viewer may feel emotional and fantasize about receiving this gift from her own special "wise man."

## SUMMARY

Creative activities are evident in professionals' tasks throughout the apparel industry. Creativity requires a special set of skills that are important for various aspects of the development, selection, and promotion of apparel products and environments. The activities of the creative process include (1) defining the problem; (2) gathering and analyzing information; (3) synthesis of information; (4) generating ideas; and (5) formulating, evaluating, and implementing solutions. Various skills employed by apparel professionals focus closely on different creative activities.

The skill of perceptual analysis of the form is used in analyzing the apparel form and abstracting across forms. This basic perceptual analysis skill underlies all further apparel processes. Forecasting trends begins with the skill of perceptual analysis, but expands the focus to changes in the apparel form over time. Forecasters must consider the transitional change in the form of the product as well as the socio-cultural context that can influence the selection and use of apparel products.

Sources of information for defining market segments and consumer preferences are varied, including such sources as lifestyle and demographic data, customer feedback, and credit histories.

After the collection of information that defines the problem and provides direction for idea generation, the creative process may include the use of outside source material for inspiration. Inspiration for new apparel forms may come from cultural traditions, historic apparel forms, the physical environment, and other sensory information. To fully develop the creative concept and move it forward, the professional must focus on the concept while making aesthetic decisions about the product. Moving the concept forward occurs through the development of product lines, in the development of knock-off and private label merchandise, and in the process of stocking the store.

Creative solutions in the apparel industry generally result in an apparel product or environment. Implementation of the solution entails communicating the new ideas to the appropriate audience such as client firms, colleagues, or consumers. Communication about apparel products combines verbal and visual information about the product. Communication directed to the target consumer uses imagery to enhance the formal, expressive, and/or symbolic features of the product in order to increase the appeal of the product.

## KEY TERMS AND CONCEPTS

abstracting across products

abstracting across products over time

abstraction

analysis of consumer preferences

assortment planning

building a line or collection

communicating ideas

consumer market segments

content analysis

creative process

cultural forms as inspiration

cutting production costs

defining the problem

deriving inspiration

developing and advancing a concept

divergent thinking

forecasting trends

formulating, evaluating, and implementing solutions

gathering and analyzing information

generating ideas

hedonic response

historic forms as inspiration

interpreting the socio-cultural context

knock-offs

multi-sensory stimulation as inspiration

perceiving forms

perceptual analysis

physical environment as inspiration

private label merchandise

qualitative information

quantitative information

realism

stocking the store

stylization

sythensizing information

## SUGGESTED READINGS

Agins, T. (1995). Why cheap clothes are getting more respect. *The Wall Street Journal,* Oct. 16, 1995, pp. B1, B6.

### For Advanced Levels

Smets, G. J. F. & Overbeeke, C. J. (1989). Scent and sound of vision: Expressing scent or sound as visual forms. *Perceptual and Motor Skills, 69,* 227–233.

## LAB ACTIVITY 10.1

In this activity, you should become more aware of the creative process of developing, selecting and promoting a new fashion product. Divide the class into a number of groups that are a multiple of three (e.g., three, six, nine). One of the three will do the developing, the second will do the selecting, and the third will do the promoting of the product as outlined below.

**Developing**

*Analyzing consumer segments*

1. Define your target market. Describe some of the characteristics of your target consumer. For instance, is the target consumer a serious skier vacationing in a ski resort town or a novice skier visiting the local slopes? Are these products purchased by those who ski frequently and have a whole wardrobe of skiwear already or those who seldom get to the slopes and see the product as general purpose, versatile winter wear? How old are they? Are these products designed to be unisex or do your consumers desire different products for males and females? Are these fashion forward consumers?

*Building a line or collection*

2. Once your target consumer is identified, explain how the target market will affect specific features of the product such as fabric, color, sizes, functional or style features.

**Lab Activity 10.1 (continued)**

3. Working with *one* of the manufacturers' lines found under company names in Figure 10.8—Mountaineer, Sky Top Inc., Slippery Slopes, or Downhill Racer—suggest how to incorporate the features identified in step 2 into your product line. In particular identify the fabrics used, surface patterns and colors, size range, and any changes to the layout. Present this information as a presentation board.

**Selecting**

*Analyzing consumer segments*

1. Separate from what the developers have determined about their target consumer, describe some of the characteristics of the *target consumer for your retail store*. For instance, is the target consumer a serious skier visiting your store while vacationing in the ski resort location or a novice skier visiting a local store far from any ski slopes? Are these upscale consumers who ski frequently and have a whole wardrobe of skiwear already or do they seldom get to the slopes and see the product as general purpose, versatile winter wear? How old are they? Do you see your customer as traditional, expecting different products for males and females rather than unisex products? Are these fashion forward consumers?

*Stocking the store*

2. Describe how your target market will affect the products you will buy for the store or department? Describe the products and the range of products you will purchase. For instance, if your customer is looking for a versatile jacket to be worn with many items, you will stock more basic colors. What size ranges will you need to carry if you have an older consumer?

3. The four manufacturers found in Figure 10.8 will present their lines to you. From these lines, select styles, colors or fabric designs, and sizes (e.g., men's, women's petites, children's, misses, tall, petite; s, m, l, xl, xxl) to create your assortment plan for your ski shop or department. Assume that you want to match jackets and bottoms and create a unified whole with your store image. You are *limited to 90 stockkeeping units* (sku's). Sku's are determined by multiplying styles by colors/surfaces and then multiplying this number by sizes (e.g., 6 styles each coming in 4 colors = 24 sku's. Then 24 sku's X 3 sizes each = 72 sku's in total). So you see you have to limit your selection.

4. Present the assortment plan as a presentation board.

**Promoting**

1. Describe the interior features of the store such as the interior space, the interior decor and the merchandise display fixtures. These should all coordinate to communicate a consistent and pleasing store image for the target customer defined by the retailer.

2. Plan the visual merchandising strategy for display in the store. How might the assortment plan be divided into groups and arranged for display?

3. Finally, what will be the promotional strategy for communicating the store's concept and this new merchandise to the target consumer? Design an ad campaign for the local newspaper for the next 2 weeks (one ad per week). Each ad should be similar enough to be recognized as representing the same store, but with enough variety to stimulate interest. (For example, you may use the same layout, your store name or logo [e.g., Figure 10.7] and different merchandise items and copy each week.) Develop a presentation board with the display and two ads.

Figure 10.7. Store logos.

Figure 10.8. Merchandise lines from four manufacturers.

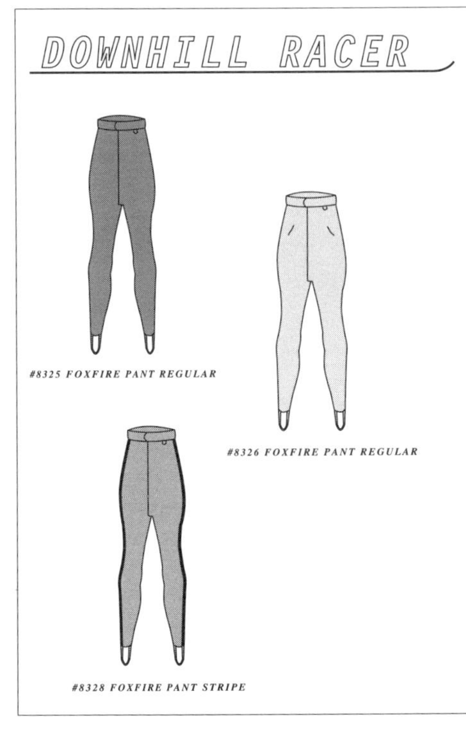

## READING 10.1
# Fashion Forecast: $D^3$, From Visionaries to Visuals

Reading 10.1 Fashion Forecast: $D^3$, From Visionaries to Visuals. (1995, June). *Visual Merchandising and Store Design,* pp. 38–42.

"Retailers today want to know what is happening at all levels," says Abbey Doneger, president of The Doneger Group, one of the largest resident buying-office companies. "People who shop at Nordstrom or Wal-Mart also shop in department stores or outlet malls," Doneger says. However, he quickly adds that such information alone is not enough unless it's accompanied by insight to evaluate the facts and provide advice.

That's one reason why just over three years ago The Doneger Group began its $D^3$ division (Doneger Design Direction). Explains Gae Marino, $D^3$'s vice president of fashion marketing and managing director, "When $D^3$ started in January 1992, it was the first time a buying office offered a fashion forecasting service to the industry."

What Doneger sensed was a way to combine fashion-forward forcasting with the reality of retail and market information provided by its buying office. As a resident buying office, the company represents 850 clients with worldwide retail sales in excess of $25 billion in over 7,000 retail locations. The firm continues to provide the same service and information fundamentals as when Abbey Doneger's father Henry started the business in 1946.

What has changed over the near fifty years Doneger has been in business is the diversity of clients representing all aspects of retailing at every price point; the expansion of classifications in women's wear, men's wear, children's wear, home furnishings, large sizes, off-price and newsletter, international and designer divisions; the development of private-label merchandise; and the expansion of its services, notably $D^3$ and HDA International, the import/export division of the company. Doneger foresees broadening assistance to clients in product development, sourcing, advertising, and marketing.

David Wolfe is creative director for $D^3$. He makes predicting and analyzing fashion sound simple. "I make the leap from what exists now to what fashion leaders will do," says Wolfe. "I get inspiration from old movies and at museums. I look at Michelangelo and think, 'Oh, that makes a great swipe.'" The trick, he explains, "is to see the image in a new context." The bottom line? It's up to Wolfe to accurately assess emerging fashion for the economic benefit of $D^3$ clients.

Wolfe explains, "When I present the actual European and American collections, they serve as confirmation of the trends we predicted. In June '94 we forecast 'uptight conservative chic' and people laughed. By November anyone looking at the election results would know this would happen."

Creating a better bottom line for its clients is another reason why $D^3$ offers extensive trend forecasting services. However, anyone in the fashion industry can attend a $D^3$ trend presentation. "Our forecast shows are open to the general market. Anyone in the industry may purchase tickets without being a $D^3$ client." The logic behind the move is twofold, as Wolfe explains: "First, we want to introduce people to our thinking. Second, it spreads the gospel. The more we guide, the more wide-spread our influence."

Marino continues, "We report on what is selling today and what will be important tomorrow from all price levels and consumer market segments." Marino has also found that color forecasting has become more important over the years. "Mass merchants even have a color focus now. Color information is used for the product development, to set up displays, and for arrangements of merchandise in stores," she says.

## READING 10.2

# From Couture to Elastic Waistbands: A Designer's Journey

Reading 10.2 From Couture to Elastic Waistbands: A Designer's Journey. (1995, October 16). *Wall Street Journal,* pp. B1, B5.

As a design intern for Yves Saint Laurent in Paris, Anthony Mark Hankins learned to craft buttonholes and stitch hems by hand on garments that sold for as much as $20,000.

Now Mr. Hankins runs his own design studio in Dallas. But he mostly works with elastic waistbands and inexpensive rayon fabric, turning out mass-produced women's clothes that sell for as little as $14.99.

Designing machine-washable, budget clothes would be anathema to many young designers. But Mr. Hankins, twenty-six years old, knows he stands a better chance of making a name for himself this way—even if it is as the Calvin Klein of the coupon-clipping set. The budget business is growing fast, while the market for expensive clothes is depressed and crowded.

Already, his one-year-old company, Anthony Mark Hankins, Inc., designs moderately priced collections bearing his own label for Dayton Hudson Corp.'s Target Stores, J.C. Penney & Co., and Federated Department Stores, Inc. The company also designs children's clothing for Vogue/Butterick Patterns.

Mr. Hankins, who learned to sew in grade school, knows all about budget clothes. He grew up in a blue-collar neighborhood in Elizabeth, New Jersey, where his mother dragged him back-to-school shopping at discounters like Bradlees. Back then, "no one was designing the right colors or the latest styles in that price range," he recalls.

After attending the Pratt Institute in Brooklyn, New York, for two years, he studied fashion design at the Chambre Syndicale in Paris. Although Mr. Hankins once dreamed of being a couture designer, he quickly changed his mind after working in Paris where "gratification came from making only a few" garments for the handful of elite customers, he says.

While working as a design assistant on Seventh Avenue for designer Adrienne Vittadini, he answered an ad for J.C. Penney to work as a quality control inspector. There, he honed his skills in producing inexpensive apparel.

Mr. Hankins recently headed out to the Los Angeles garment district to meet with Wanda Saleem, a buyer for Target Stores, at the headquarters of Tops of California Inc., a budget apparel contractor that produces his Anthony Mark Hankins Authentics line for Target.

In a tedious, all-day session, Mr. Hankins presented sample garments for the Christmas selling season for Target to consider. He also displayed sketches and fabrics for next spring's line.

In turning out a designer collection for Target customers, Mr. Hankins says he is challenged to create styles that use his trademark bold ethnic prints, but still flatter large-size women.

"When women choose prints, they are expressing their individuality," he says. "Just because it is a big print doesn't mean that it has to look cheap."

The art of making inexpensive apparel is in adding details that make shoppers feel as though they're getting clothing that's both chic and cheap. Mr. Hankins knows that many budget shoppers love nice looking "twofers," or tops that look like a jacket and a blouse, but are actually one piece.

During Mr. Hankins's presentation, Target's Ms. Saleem seems impressed with his holiday group of dressy apparel in black rayon velour, white rayon, and crinkly gold polyester—which will sell for less than $20. "Just look at this blouse," Mr. Hankins brags, pointing out the eight black and gold enamel buttons down the front. But hidden on the cuffs are plain white buttons that cost less than a penny each and saved Mr. Hankins fifteen cents per blouse. Such subtle scrimping allows him to splurge on covered shoulder pads and interfacing, a stiff lining, down the front and inside the collar of the blouse, which gives it a crisp finish.

CHAPTER 11

# Developers, Gatekeepers, and Promoters of Textile and Apparel Products

## Objectives

- Understand the roles of textile and apparel professionals as developers, gatekeepers, and promoters of aesthetic products
- Be able to categorize activities of textile and apparel professionals as those of developers, gatekeepers, and promoters of aesthetic products
- Examine responsibilities of successful textile and apparel professionals as related to the aesthetic product
- Examine educational backgrounds and career paths of successful textile and apparel professionals

Let's start this chapter with an activity. As a class, complete Activity 11.1. Your initial decision to enter the textiles and clothing-related major may have been influenced by your interest in fashion of textile and apparel products. Students commonly enter the major with the desire to obtain one of three career positions, designer, buyer, or store manager. Was this the case with your class? Yet, there is a cornucopia of career options in the textiles and apparel industries that require similar skills to these three positions. Thinking more broadly, identifying career options based upon required skills, may help you see the flexibility of your potential career opportunities. A designer that develops a knock-off, a production manager who maintains the aesthetic integrity of the product when cutting costs, a buyer who helps develop private label merchandise, and an advertiser who emphasizes the important qualities of the product all depend upon the ability to distill the essence of the product. Whereas moving among these positions would require preparation for new duties, the skill of distilling the essence of the product is transferable from one career position to another. This allows for more flexibility in thinking about a future career path; hence, the reason Chapter 10 was built around skills of the apparel professional. The

**ACTIVITY 11.1**

1. Individually record the career position(s) you hoped to obtain upon graduation when you first declared the major. If you had no idea of the career position, then say "none."
2. As a class, develop a listing of career positions and the frequency of response for these positions.
3. Are there some positions that were more commonly selected than others? What were they?

purpose of Chapter 10 and the present chapter is not to pinpoint the exact career position for you, but rather to broaden your perception of options within the textile and apparel industries.

## DEVELOPERS, GATEKEEPERS, AND PROMOTERS OF AESTHETIC PRODUCTS

Another way of thinking flexibly about career options is to consider the similarity in roles of various professionals in industry. Textile and apparel professionals affecting the aesthetic product may be categorized as: (1) developers; (2) gatekeepers (selectors); and (3) promoters. The present chapter will examine career opportunities as developers, gatekeepers, and promoters of aesthetic products.

### Developers

**Developers** are professionals involved in the creation of the product, from initiating and contributing ideas, presenting the ideas, through perfecting the design, and ending with the completion of production. Table 11.1 provides some of the developer options.

### Gatekeepers

**Gatekeepers** are professionals who influence which existing products reach the consumer based upon criteria such as fashionability, salability, and/or quality. Gatekeepers may affect which physical products or representations (verbal or visual) of the product reach the consumer. Many gatekeepers provide information about fashion or sales trends, affecting the products selected for retail sale. Gatekeepers do not have a vested interest in forwarding particular products; they are not paid by firms representing the particular product. In cases where the gatekeeper is paid by the firm representing the particular product (e.g., quality assurance positions within a firm), this gatekeeper is selective about which items from those produced by the firm will be passed on to the consumer. Table 11.2 suggests gatekeeper options.

### Promoters

**Promoters** are professionals who emphasize and enhance an aesthetic product's value through verbal communication and/or design of the sensory qualities of

**TABLE 11.1** Developers of textile and apparel products.

| | |
|---|---|
| *Apparel Designer* — | Develops creative, appealing apparel designs/lines |
| *Buyer* — | Oversees private label development |
| *CAD Artist/Technician* — | Creates artwork and patterns on computer |
| *Colorist* — | Creates color combinations for fabrics |
| *Consumer or Market Researcher* — | Identifies consumers' impressions of product, used to create the product |
| *Creative Director* — | Sets design direction for firm |
| *Culture Broker* — | Provides information about preferences of foreign consumers to product developers of more traditional societies |
| *Fit Analyst* — | Perfects fit of the product |
| *Fit Model* — | Assists in perfecting fit and styling of the product |
| *Product Manager* — | Ensures product line is consistent in image, differentiated from other makers, and has sales appeal |
| *Patternmaker* — | Develops flat pattern based on sketch or muslin |
| *Piece Goods/Trim Buyer* — | Researches and acquires product materials |
| *Product Developer/Merchandiser* — | Develops product lines; heavily dependent upon sales information |
| *Production Managers* — | Defines production methods, balancing cost and design integrity |
| *Sketcher* — | Artistically illustrates designer's ideas |
| *Sourcing Specialist/Materials Buyers* — | Identifies best supplier of needed goods/services meeting price, aesthetic and quality standards |
| *Specifications Developer* — | Technically draws and accurately describes materials, design, and production methods for product |
| *Textile Artist* — | Develops creative, appealing textile designs/lines |
| *Textile Dyer* — | Formulates dyes and oversees dying of yarns and fabrics |

the environment. Promoters have a vested image in promoting particular products. These professionals are paid to promote particular products, such as an advertiser paid to develop a persuasive ad campaign. Examples of promoters are found in Table 11.3. Once you have examined the three tables, try Activity 11.2.

## INTERVIEWS WITH SUCCESSFUL TEXTILES AND APPAREL PROFESSIONALS

Successful textiles and apparel professionals from coast to coast as well as Europe have been interviewed. Interviews with these successful professionals will provide insight into actual responsibilities of developers, gatekeepers, and

**TABLE 11.2** Gatekeepers of textile and apparel products.

| | |
|---|---|
| *Buyer* | —Analyzes past sales and selects product lines for retail sale |
| *Fashion Director* | —Identifies trends and sets seasonal fashion direction for buying office and stores |
| *Fashion Editor/Journalist* | —Researches and communicates trends to the trade or lay public |
| *Fashion or Color Forecaster* | —Supplies firms with predicted fashion trend information |
| *Independent Wardrobe/Color Consultant* | —Suggests or selects products for the consumer |
| *Market Representative* | —Analyzes and supplies buyers with fashion and sales trend information |
| *Quality Assurance Manager* | —Ensures products meet quality standards, affecting aesthetic integrity |
| *Store Manager* | —Defines store image, affecting merchandising of store |

**TABLE 11.3** Promoters of textile and apparel products.

| | |
|---|---|
| *Art Director* | —Develops ad concept and integration of ad elements |
| *CAD Technician* | —Creates or enhances images for visual ads |
| *Copywriter* | —Develops creative text and scripts for ads |
| *Educational Representative* | —Disseminates promotional message for trade association or firms |
| *Fashion Illustrator* | —Produces artistic drawings for advertisements |
| *Fashion Photographer* | —Shots artistic photos for advertisements |
| *Fashion Show Coordinator* | —Plans and executes fashion shows |
| *Marketing Specialist* | —Plans and implements promotional activities for product at trade shows |
| *Market Researcher* | —Identifies consumers' impressions of product, used to develop ad |
| *Packaging Designer* | —Designs creative packaging for products |
| *Photo Stylist* | —Assists photographer by creating ambiance through props, hairstyles, makeup |
| *Sales Consultant* | —Promotes products to buyers in a showroom or to consumers in a store |
| *Sales Representative* | —Travels to present line(s) of products to designers or retailers |
| *Store Designers* | —Design interior elements of stores according to store image, to complement products |
| *Visual Merchandiser* | —Arranges in-store and showroom displays |

**ACTIVITY 11.2** Activity 11.2 will help you become more familiar with how career opportunities are categorized into developers, gatekeepers, and promoters of aesthetic products.

1. Your instructor will divide the class into three separate groups and will photocopy and enlarge Tables 11.1, 11.2, and 11.3. The forty-two boxes in the three tables representing different career opportunities will be cut apart and shuffled.
2. Each of the three groups will be given fourteen of the boxes.
3. The three groups will compete against each other in assigning the careers into the right categories of developers, gatekeepers, and promoters.
4. The group with the most correct responses is the winner!

**ACTIVITY 11.3** As you read the interviews with the developers make a list of the responsibilities that would be considered as part of the role of a developer. For example: assistant designer does design variations of basic bodies. Refer to the definition of a developer to guide your selection of representative responsibilities. Identify at least ten responsibilities. Save this list for Lab Activity 11.1.

promoters. It should become apparent from the interviews, successful professionals interact with many different people in the industry. Not only do they need to know about their job, but they have to understand the perspective or role of other apparel professionals. Downsizing of companies, a cross-functional team approach, and the development of private labels have generated more multi-task professionals (where one professional is capable of performing a variety of tasks). For example, the description of a merchandiser's responsibilities at J. Crew is part developer and part gatekeeper. These interviews will also exemplify the educational backgrounds and career paths of a range of textiles and apparel professionals. Notice how many of these professionals have educational backgrounds and opportunities similar to you. The range of professional interactions, the variety of tasks performed on the job, and the non-linear career paths suggest that an integrated program of courses, exposing you to a variety of aspects of the industry, should better prepare you for your career. This section focuses on entry level and intermediate level career positions, of relevance to students soon to become full-time textiles and apparel professionals. Before you read the interviews of developers, gatekeepers, and promoters, note the tasks identified in Activities 11.3, 11.4, and 11.5 respectively.

### Developer: Sarah Rye, Assistant Designer of Misses Dresses, Clues, New York, New York

**What are your typical responsibilities?** I am an assistant designer for a moderate dresswear company, Clues. Their product is geared towards the mass market, selling to a wide audience. The owners of Clues also own other labels,

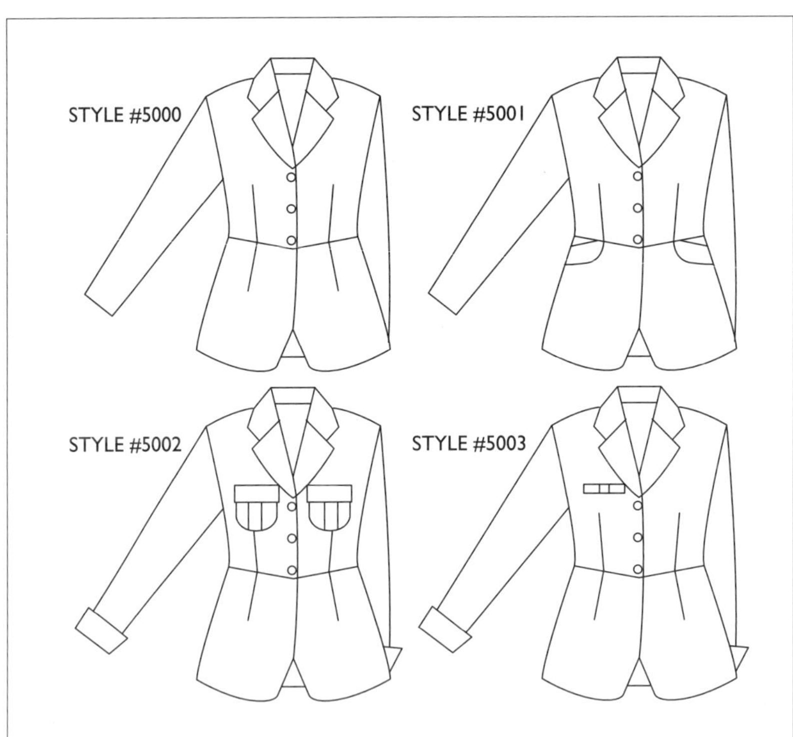


Figure 11.1. Flats from style books showing style variations for a basic body.

Oberon, which is a higher-priced label and Isadora, which is a really hot contemporary label right now.

Sometimes I do variations of best-selling garment bodies [i.e., a basic garment layout}. I draw a lot of flats. I might be asked to draw three versions of one body, then four versions of another body. So rather than having patch pockets, I might put in slash pockets. Rather than having buttons down the front, I'd put them down the side. It sounds silly, but sometimes that's all you do. Once the style changes are made you select new fabric and trim. We commonly keep the same body and just change the details and fabric. For example, we have a sleeveless jumper that's a v-neck and it buttons down the front. In it's original incarnation, it had princess seams down the back with tabs that buttoned on each princess seam to pull in the waist a little bit. We've made other back variations, such as smocking in the back and ties in the back. We've also done it in prints, solids, in chambray, leno-check, solid crepes, and on and on.

I help the designer find fabrics. I keep track of trim and sample yardage. I do cost sheets. I swatch my brains out. Every time a buyer comes in and likes certain fabrics, you swatch and send the swatches to the buyers. I keep track of style books. That is, for every new style that we do, every new garment, we give it a number. I then draw a flat of it, swatch fabrics, and we take a picture of it too. We put the 4900 bodies in one book, the 5000 bodies in the next, etc. The salespeople show these books to the buyers when they come in. It's a quick way to look through a lot of styles without having to pull out samples. It's a good way to remind the buyer of a previous order and show the new style based on the same body.

One of the responsibilities that I really like is "shopping the stores." When you're shopping the stores you are looking for information about what's new and what other designers are doing. You look for designs that you like, designs that are salable, styles that relate to designs we have been working on. I look for new trims and fabrications, prints, and colors. If the garment strikes you, you buy it or draw it for reference. You need to scout what's hot from other manufacturers, so that you can produce your own variation of that hot style. Most buyers come in and want to know that this is our version of, say, a Donna Ricco body that she blew out the doors. The buyers want to know that Jones New York did it, or that Seville did it, and that it sold really well.

You have to be really good at picking out what's new, at knowing this designer, this designer, and that designer are doing this, even if they are not merchandised together on the floor. An assistant designer should have a good memory; if you show her or him a garment the assistant designer could probably tell you who did it, because you see it so much and you are aware of different looks by different designers. Recognizing the basic differences among designers helps you make sense of all the styles that you see. A Tahari doesn't look like an Ellen Tracy.

**What paved your way to this position?** I had a design internship at Stephanie Quellar, who manufacturers missy sportswear. I loved the company and I had a wide variety of design related experiences. My first job in New York was at Item-Eyes, where I designed for their private label division. I had a wide variety of experience, because I had a year of doing just about everything there. I did cost sheets to packing. Here in the dress market, the assistant helps the head designer sometimes knock things straight off and other times make adaptations or maybe come up with something new.

**How did your education prepare you for this position?** The pattern making was important, because when you look at the stores and want to do a version of something, you need to know how a pattern is made or put together. In addition, sometimes assistant jobs require pattern making, and people end up going the pattern-making route. Any course is important if it helps you see and describe what's going on in the product, such as textiles science or aesthetics because it gives you a vocabulary to communicate with. I loved history of costume. This is especially relevant, as every single season, there are styles that reflect historic forms. What are they showing this year? Forties and Mod styles. They are doing an updated twist of the historical forms.

The design internship was really helpful, just day in and day out of how things operate in the industry. The field study (study tour of the New York garment industry) was really helpful because it took out the intimidation factor of coming and working in New York. Being at a midwestern university, it's easy to get intimidated about moving to Los Angeles or New York, or anywhere you are going to move to, especially if you come from a small town in the Midwest. The field study definitely helps because you lose the intimidation factor.

**What publications and resources do you use to keep current professionally?** I read *Women's Wear Daily.* I subscribe to *Allure,* but that's because I sold cosmetics and I still love cosmetics. *Vogue, Glamour, Marie Claire, Harper's*

*Bazaar, In Style,* and *US Magazine,* which I know isn't a fashion magazine but people in there are wearing clothes, celebrities, so I subscribe to that. I don't have to buy European magazines because we have them in the office. They are filled with page after page of photos. I also look at catalogs.

## Developer: Jaana Seppä, Apparel Designer of Junior Sportswear, Lutha, Ltd., Helsinki, Finland

**What are your typical responsibilities?** My area of specialization is designing for the young and one of my main responsibilities is creating new collections. The products are designed for international markets and we sell them all over Europe. My tasks as a designer include choosing fabrics (together with the production manager) and creating collections. This involves the analysis of consumer segments and market situations. In some cases the design solution is totally intuitive and can be very difficult for me to explain to people responsible for marketing. On the other hand, some products are very carefully planned to fulfill the needs and expectations that already exist in the consumer market. I am also responsible for drawing the collection and discussing it with the sample maker, and looking over the prototypes for appearance and fit. In addition, I work with the stylist in designing the brochures, and take part in fashion fairs (trade shows).

As a designer, one must be aware of the needs and preferences of the consumer when creating new ideas and try to fit the designs to the product profile of the company. To take full advantage of your potential as a designer, you have to be technically talented and aware of all the technical potential of the company. While it is important that the designer be allowed to concentrate on creative work and let assistants and other professionals handle the rest, it is also important that the designer know every detail of the product development process so that she or he can cooperate effectively with others.

**What paved your way to this position?** I worked as an assistant to a designer during my school years. As an assistant I was involved in marketing, paper work, and drawing. After graduation I got the chance to design my own collection, and two years later I was appointed designer.

**How did your education prepare you for this position?** Before I studied fashion design, I went to a technical college. The most important and useful subjects in the design school were the classical art subjects such as Life Drawing, Drawing, Painting, Visual Design, and 3D Form. The opportunity to take part in international design contests and my graduation (senior) project also provided valuable experiences. My graduation project was creating a collection for a company operating in the fashion industry.

**What publications and resources do you use to keep current professionally?** I look at different European periodicals, magazines, and trend predictions. The whole culture including architecture, films, literature, and art exhibitions are a source of inspiration.

## Developer: Brecca Farr, Women's Petite Fit Model, Ford Fit Division, New York, New York

**What are your typical responsibilities?** In any fit session, which is the primary place that a fit model performs most of her (or his) functions, a fit model helps evaluate the fit of garments. This role entails putting on a sample garment. This garment can be made of muslin, the final fabric, or a similar fabric; all variations from the actual fabric to be used must be taken into account when evaluating the fit. The fit would then be evaluated in relation to the firm's target market. For example, as a women's petite model, if the target market is the mother of the bride, the expected fit of the garment would be very different than if the target market was a college student. As a fit model I was twenty-five years old and, being twenty-five years old, proverbial gravity hasn't yet taken effect. I have a higher bust line; I have a definite contoured backside. If I were fitting for a mother of the bride, I'd have to take those things into consideration. In terms of the back, due to the normal aging process, the height of where the first curve of the backside occurs is probably going to be lower on a fifty-year-old woman, mother of the bride, than on the college student.

Specifically, as a fit model, I would work with a variety of individuals. With a manufacturer, I might work with a patternmaker, technical or fashion designer, a line coordinator, account representatives, general merchandisers for a line, as well as production management individuals. Occasionally the owners

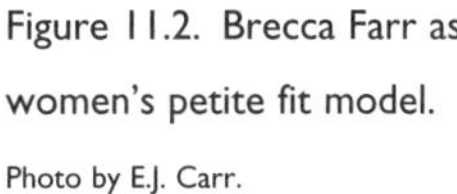

Figure 11.2. Brecca Farr as women's petite fit model.
Photo by E.J. Carr.

or vice-presidents of the manufacturer would be present at a fit session. Also within a fit session, if I'm working with a retailer, I might be working with their version of a quality control person, a technical designer, a buyer (in a retail setting), or divisional merchandise managers. Let me give a few examples of what these people might be looking for.

With the production folks, the sequence of operations would be important. Say we had to change a closure for drape front crossover blouses. If you are working with women's or women's petite, where the general bust is going to be somewhere from 38 to 50 inches, the closures at the bust are more critical than in other size ranges. In the petite and misses size range, where the blouses had initial popularity, there would be enough fullness in the drape so that the fabric would stay in place if the closures were only on the sides or lower down in the front. However, in the women's and women's petites, because you didn't have the same ratio of fabric to the bustline, you typically had to put a closure right at the bust point. What that closure might be would be an issue for the production management people. Would a facing be necessary, or would they have to put in a button? Production people are also going to be very aware of the capabilities of their contractors, the limitations of their factories.

If I were working with a buyer, one of the things that would be paramount on her or his mind would be how this garment is going to sell; questions such as would taking in the waist one inch preclude a large part of the target market from being able to wear the garment, thus leaving a large inventory behind at the end of the season. Some other things that a buyer might be interested in is design coordination. In other words, if we are working with a blouse manufacturer and we have an embroidered point collar, an embroidered notch collar, and an embroidered peter pan, and the peter pan is just not working out because of the configuration of the collar and the slope or other things, the buyer might have the tendency to scrap it. Yet if that garment is supposed to be part of an ensemble with a pants manufacturer and a sweater manufacturer, the buyer may not have the option to drop the garment even though the fit is much more difficult to achieve.

From my personal experience, I had several different firms where they would present me with ten styles and say that for women's petite they would want to choose three or four styles to offer with some depth of assortment and ask which I would recommend. So we would sit down and figure out to whom they were trying to sell, meaning the retailers, and who is the target market, such as mother of the bride, professional, or college student. This information would be combined with the various available fabrics. So we would look at the combinations of styles and fabrics; if we did this style, let's do it in these fabrics for this reason. The one thing I was always asked was "Why?" It's not just "I like this." It was "Personally I like this, but this other might be a better choice for the following reasons . . ." such as vertical eye movement or horizontal eye movement, due to broken and unbroken line, shape, size of print, or line direction.

In addition, for eight to twelve weeks of the year I worked in a showroom, not as their fit model, but as a women's petite model where I worked with buyers and line representatives and divisional merchandise managers basically selling petites. A lot of this would be explaining how the fit differs, why the women's petite customer required a different fit than a women's customer. So much of my job was to go over the technical issues or answering why certain styles did not work well conceptually in women's petites.

**What paved your way to this position?** After graduation, my first job was for a corporate buying office located in the New York garment district. At the firm I worked as an associate buyer-buyer trainee, then I was promoted into a position that would be considered nowadays more product development. The firm I worked for had a solely owned subsidiary that contracted most of its ladies private label sportswear. My job functions were evaluating fit and helping buyers write the specs for these private label programs. A number of the buyers that had been with the company did not have extensive spec writing background. So one of the aspects of that job was "flat specing" the garments, where you lay a garment on a flat surface, so that it is laying flat without being in any way dimensionally unstable. You have key measurements that you take such as shoulder point to shoulder point, bust so many inches down from high shoulder point, neck width, sleeve length, wrist opening, etc. It was a way to dimensionally represent a garment with numbers. It obviously did not take into account the curvature, which is why we followed up with a fit session. We had a combination of employees within the firm that were used as ad-hoc in-house fit models for certain lines. But fortunately for other lines I hired professional fit models. A connection was made and one of the professional fit models asked if I had ever considered doing women's petites. A few days later I got a call from the Ford modeling agency, and one month later I quit my job and started modeling.

**How did your education prepare you for this position?** I have a Bachelor of Science degree in fashion merchandising from a state university in the Midwest. I studied product analysis, merchandising concepts, marketing, economics, accounting: all of the business-related areas. So I was very familiar with the textile and apparel industry going into it from my formal education. Also, developing communication skills was very important. Part of that was family experience; communication, reading, and writing were all very important in my family, especially to my mother.

**What publications and resources help you keep current professionally?** I would listen to what the sales associates said about their customers' likes and dislikes, compliments or general complaints. You are constantly sponges of information. You have to maintain accurate records for what each company does; you have to maintain information regarding trends, keep up on *Women's Wear Daily* or some of the fashion magazines. Even if *Vogue* is not indicative of trends in women's petite, petite customers read *Vogue,* therefore I read *Vogue. Allure* was a good publication, as it got into hair and make-up concepts as well as image. *Glamour* has run a number of articles targeted to consumers on their different size shapes and good styles for different shapes. If you as a fit model are trying to be a good voice for the consumer, you have to be familiar with what the consumer is reading. I would say trying to keep up on general things, the *New York Times* or *Wall Street Journal,* to keep up on what is going in the New York garment district. They would occasionally run articles on new technologies, on industry changes that the industry execs are reading. You have to keep current.

### Gatekeeper: C. Shane Santi, Merchandiser of Men's Wear, Roffé Accessories, Inc., New York, New York

**What are your typical responsibilities?** I have a variety of responsibilities. While I am responsible for many merchandising aspects of the product, I also design ties using CAD (computer-aided-design). Because of my computer knowledge I get involved in sourcing computer-related products when the company is thinking of purchasing new items. Right now we are looking into purchasing a new CAD system.

In terms of my other functions, I am in charge of a new line we have acquired called "Duckhead," getting the showroom ready for presentations to buyers. I am also the EDI coordinator, consulting with both clients and our sales people, trying to keep them up-to-date on the different aspects of EDI. EDI stands for Electronic Data Interchange. It's the electronic connection between, for example, a manufacturer and a retailer so that everything involved with order taking to sending the order to the retailer is sped up. It allows the retailer and manufacturer to communicate much more efficiently and quickly. It uses point of sale information to tell what styles are selling so that the manufacturer can get prepared to ship those styles in order to quickly replenish the store. At present we aren't using EDI to track information about pattern and color trends of the best selling products, but if we were to track pattern and color information of the product, we could use it to design new yet similar styles, a sister set, based upon the popular styles.

I communicate with a variety of people. I communicate with buyers and assistant buyers. Buyers want to know about a specific style, if it is selling well, when they order that style. So I need to know or be able to retrieve information on the sales figures. Other times, I'll deal with our factory. They produce samples for us; I'm in charge of samples. They send customers and buyers samples. So I talk to distribution people, production, and the samples people.

**What paved your way to this position?** Internships were advantageous. One summer I was a fashion merchandising intern with Gap in Houston, Texas. Another summer I did an internship in design with Mary McFadden, in New York. Both of these were great experiences because they were close to the job I was going to have after graduation. So internships can directly expose you to what you are going into. You gain an enormous amount of information from doing internships.

**How did your education prepare you for this position?** The communication courses, such as English Composition, I had in college prepared me to effec-

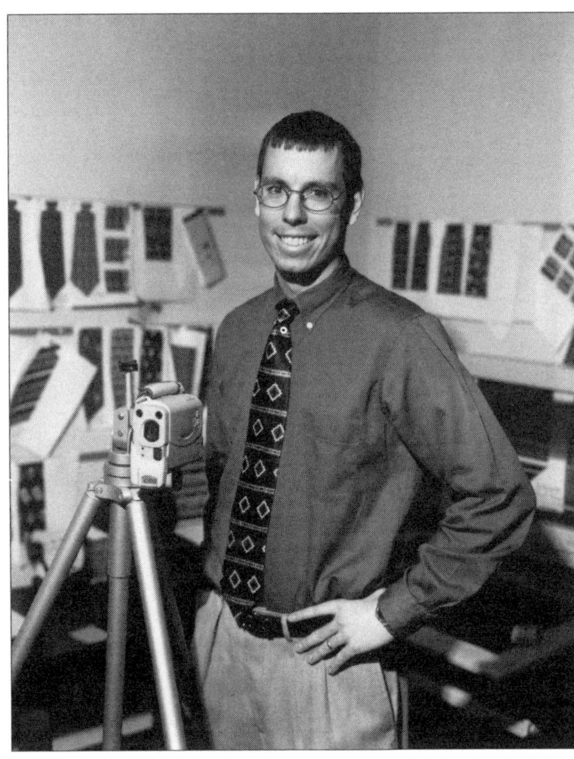

Figure 11.3. Shane Santi in the Roffé showroom with the Duckhead line.

**ACTIVITY 11.4** As you read the interviews with the gatekeepers, make a list of the responsibilities that would be considered as part of the role of a gatekeeper. For example: Warehouse manager sends products through quality control to be inspected for any defects affecting aesthetics of the product. Refer to the definition of a gatekeeper to guide your selection of representative responsibilities. Identify at least ten responsibilities. Save this list for Lab Activity 11.1.

tively communicate with others in the industry. Effective communication is vital when you are writing letters to your customers and when sending memos to the sales staff. I had computer-aided-design in college, which is important to my current position as well. My design training taught me how a design goes through a process. You don't just sit down and draw a design; you have to have an idea of where you are going with that design, what your final customer wants, what's selling. The classes taught me that you have to go out and research before you start designing.

**What publications and resources help you keep current professionally?** Everyone around here reads *DNR* (*Daily News Record*). We subscribe to and advertise in *MR, Men's Retailing*. This is the New York garment center; there are always trade shows around here. There's an upcoming CAD expo, and they have one of those every three or four months. There are always trade shows that are color oriented, trend oriented, style oriented. Other than that, the biggest source of information is from the buyer.

### Gatekeeper: Christopher Kolbe, Merchandiser or Merchant of Men's Wear, J. Crew/Clifford and Wills, New York, New York

**What are your typical responsibilities?** I am a merchandiser for J. Crew. This company does all the buying internally; we develop the products, source the products, and we sell the products so it is a little bit different than the traditional buying sense. But, the bottom-line responsibility of my job is to make sure that I get the right product to the floor or to the customer at the right times and the right price. I manage my inventory so I am totally responsible for the bottom line of the business.

I spend a lot of my time working with people from different departments of the company, design and production. The concept and the direction come from design. They actually present story boards, fabrics, and color palates. So they set the direction, but then as a merchant or merchandiser in our company I have a lot of say in what the product finally looks like. We are presented with this huge, great opportunity of options where we can go in thousands of different directions. Then the merchant comes in and does editing and changing. For instance, design will present thousands of different plaids. We might pick out different plaids that we think we would rather have. Then we will take those plaids and maybe recolor them, maybe change the scales, or maybe change the fabric. So we have impact on the actual result of a plaid or color way. Merchants have the ultimate power as far as what we really end up doing. Merchandisers are looking for what sells and is profitable. This means something safe. The designer wants to push the envelope in different directions a lot of the times. It is a com-

Figure 11.4. Chris Kolbe, merchandiser of men's wear, considering design changes to a product at J. Crew.

promise, working with design, making sure that they give us exactly what we need. I have, at times, developed something not presented by design. If I don't get what I need, I have to just create what I think I should have.

Production handles most of the manufacturing and sourcing. My job is to work with them and make sure that production can get me the costing, the right quality, and delivery that I need to sell the goods. We start with a very wide assortment in the design line then we start costing it out to figure if we can afford to do all these different sweaters or whatever at the price we need. Things fall out along the way. For example, we may run into "up charges" because we can't make the cut minimum for an item, so then the item falls out. Unfortunately there is a 20 percent fallout of styles. That is, we'd develop ten styles and maybe only eight of them would really hit the floor. That's bad if you plan to do a business with ten styles and you only have eight, then obviously you fall short of your business plan. In a nutshell, I am supposed to pull it all together and make sure that it runs smoothly and efficiently and profitably. As a merchant you have to think creatively as well as in a business way.

As a merchant my job is to constantly be shopping stores, looking at the market, reading magazines, and just watching where things are going. I shop every weekend in stores. I'm always out circulating in the city, going to SoHo, going to boutiques, and there's a certain handful of boutiques that we spend a lot of time in, seeing what they're doing, and we translate that. If we go out shopping on a weekend and find something to consider, we buy it and we're reimbursed. We have samples laying around everywhere. I take the direction and marry it with what sells for us and what our customer really wants. It is taking little pieces from everywhere and then trying to pull it into something new for our customer for next year.

We draw conclusions about what's selling. We speak to our stores a lot. Our store managers will tell us that they love the color, or fit, or they hate the color or fit, or the quality is not up to standard. We get a lot of grassroots information from our stores. We can talk to mail order and find out what they are doing well with. Merchandisers also get together for trend meetings. Here, we pull out and hang up all the styles that are doing well and take a look at them. Then we pull out all the things that aren't doing so well. From this we can draw conclusions on what is doing well. That customers are responding to plush texture and warmth, for instance. We might find that one stretch sweater blows out the door, but its the only stretch sweater that we have on the floor; so maybe we should have four.

**What paved your way to this position?** I had retail sales experience in men's wear during college. When I came to New York I entered the Saks Fifth Avenue training program. It was good because I got a broad introduction to the retail business of a big company. It is a very structured corporate company. The program was broken down into vocations. So I worked in different offices and saw a wide variety of things. I got a good general idea of what goes on in a buying office. From there I worked for the catalog division of Saks for almost two years. There I got more into the planning side of things, more into the numbers, doing elaborate spreadsheets, and really analyzing and managing a business. I really learned the analytical, the mathematical end of looking at a business, which really wasn't my strong point. So I really developed it there. But it became too one-dimensional and too non-creative for me. It really wasn't taking me in the right direction because everybody wanted me to become a planner. The notion of becoming a planner was pretty boring to me because you deal with numbers all day. You have less time to work with the product itself. A planner is the one who tells the buyer what he or she can spend and when merchandise should be marked down. I learned how a mail order business runs versus a retail store business. Most people don't realize there is a drastic difference between how the two businesses are run; I learned both sides.

I work for J. Crew, which is a mail order company with a small retail division. Because of my Saks experience, I understood both sides going into J. Crew and it helps me in working with all the people involved in mail order. I had to force my way into this position; I told people that I would not accept anything related to planning, which is automatically where all headhunters wanted to place me because of my past experience. In this job I am able to take my prior analytical experience and merge it with my creative experience. It was a tough road during the first six months, but I found it came more easily to me than to others with no prior experience. It is a tough adjustment to come into a company like J. Crew and just hit the ground running because it is so different in the way the company is set up and the way they operate.

**How did your education prepare you for this position?** I think the thing I got out of my education was exposure to technical aspects. When I am sitting with a designer and we are going over different fabric qualities, I can understand what the different types of yarns or weaves mean. I can understand the benefits of having 100 percent wool versus an acrylic blend. I can understand more intrinsic properties [e.g., aesthetic, quality, durability] of a product than maybe somebody who didn't have that background. Most people who work in industry do not have that background, they learn it as they go. I worked with people who didn't understand the difference between a yarn dyed fabric and a printed fabric. That is pretty scary because it is pretty basic. Some people just never had that technical exposure. I think I also learned to look at clothing in a more nonpartisan way. I think you have to train yourself to look at things more objectively. Some of the classes taught me to look at the aesthetics of the product in a more technical way, other than just I like it or I don't like it.

**What publications and resources do you use to keep current with the industry?** I get *Daily News Record* delivered to my desk everyday. I read a lot of magazines. I personally get a lot of magazines at home and I peruse more magazines at work. I get all the basics like *GQ*, also European issues of *Vogue* and *GQ*, rock music magazines, men's health magazines, anywhere you find little elements of fashion. Even more important than magazines is shopping the market, seeing what is out there because in magazines you get an edited perspective of what is being done. Whereas if you go to stores you get everything and obviously in New York you see a lot of different people in one afternoon; by just walking the streets you get a really good feel for what is going on. I spent my whole day Friday working in one of our stores, just working the floor and working with customers and talking to salespeople. I sort of hover around, observe. I will go in and work with our visual display people, move things around in the store, but at the same time I am also helping customers and talking to our people at the register and our managers. In two or three hours I can absorb a lot of information about why a product is or is not selling well. This helps me make sense of sometimes in a sales report. Maybe a sweater was tucked in one of the back rooms on a shelf, and that is why it isn't selling. As merchants, we are looking where things are in the store, what are they sitting with; maybe that has something to do with why it is not selling and why it isn't working. We are constantly analyzing where we are at, what we are doing, where things should be, moving things around and then looking at responses. The way our company works, we give company directives as to where to position products in stores. So if we move a group of sweaters to the front of the store all of our stores will do the same thing. As a merchant it is your job to communicate that to the stores, making sure they understand how to arrange the merchandise.

## Gatekeeper: Anthony Fiore, Warehouse/Traffic Manager, Tumi Luggage, Middlesex, New Jersey

**What are your typical responsibilities?** Basically, I ensure that the merchandise is received correctly, and then passed through quality control and packers, eventually stored, and then shipped to customers, such as department stores or specialty stores. Department stores actually have quite a few specifications that must be met. They are quite specific on how they want things packaged and shipped. Most have several pieces of information on their shipping labels including their purchase order numbers, which one of their stores it's ultimately going to, which department it's for, how many cartons there are assigned to each store. The packing slip must be in a certain position on the carton. When you are dealing with department stores they have specific routing guides, depending on the weight and number of cartons, that tell you what trucker or UPS to use. We also have to attach price tickets. All department stores require everything on UPC labels that enables them to scan at point of sale, which not only tells them how much to charge the customer but deducts it from their inventory automatically.

Planning is very important to this position. Planning to receive the shipments, alotting space for it, planning on what items to pass through Q.C. (quality control) in anticipation of orders. As our own product is a high price, high quality item, we are very quality conscious. Basically, when a bag comes in, it goes through quality control to be inspected for any defects. Some defects we can fix.

I should tell you some of the things we look for during quality control checks, because they directly tie into aesthetics of the product. We rep about fifteen different lines, including our own line of leather luggage. We have ballistic,

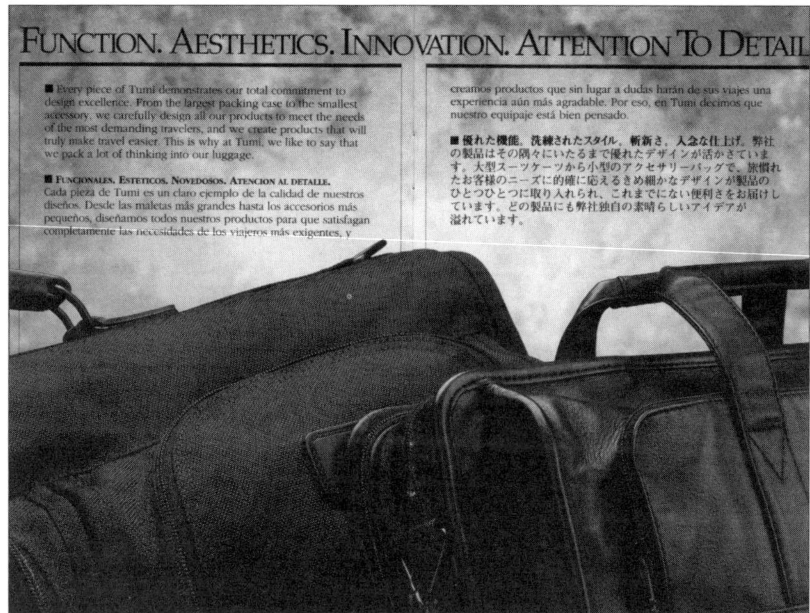

FUNCTION. AESTHETICS. INNOVATION. ATTENTION TO DETAIL
■ Every piece of Tumi demonstrates our total commitment to design excellence. From the largest packing case to the smallest accessory, we carefully design all our products to meet the needs of the most demanding travelers, and we create products that will truly make travel easier. This is why at Tumi, we like to say that we pack a lot of thinking into our luggage.
■ FUNCIONALES. ESTETICOS. NOVEDOSOS. ATENCION AL DETALLE.
Cada pieza de Tumi es un claro ejemplo de la calidad de nuestros diseños. Desde las maletas más grandes hasta los accesorios más pequeños, diseñamos todos nuestros productos para que satisfagan completamente las necesidades de los viajeros más exigentes, y creamos productos que sin lugar a dudas harán de sus viajes una experiencia aún más agradable. Por eso, en Tumi decimos que nuestro equipaje está bien pensado.
■ 優れた機能、洗練されたスタイル、斬新さ、入念な仕上げ。弊社の製品はその隅々にいたるまで優れたデザインが活かさています。大型スーツケーツから小型のアクセサリーバッグで、旅慣れたお客様のニーズに的確に応えるきめ細かなデザインが製品のひとつひとつに取り入れられ、これまでにない便利さをお届けしています。どの製品にも弊社独自の素晴らしいアイデアが溢れています。


Figure 11.5. Promotional material for Tumi luggage stressing function, aesthetics, innovation, and attention to detail. These are ensured by quality control checks.

heavy duty nylon. We have Kipling, which is a medium priced, brightly colored line, very attractive, very big in the European marketplace. We are heavy into leather. We are very concerned with the quality of leather, that it is a smooth piece of leather, not wrinkly. Sometimes we get belly leather that has stretch marks on it and that is not acceptable. Another thing is that the panels match, have the same texture. With leather there wouldn't be a 100 percent match because it is a natural product. We look at color; we do a lot of black. We also have a brown line, and these are the colors that have a tendency to vary. We have a color range that they have to meet. Being a natural product, the color will never match 100 percent, but we have a definite standard or acceptable color range. Generally speaking we don't have a problem with smell. If a product had a certain smell, a mildew smell from traveling overseas, we would reject it. Sometimes, in transportation, the leather might get dents in it from the bag sitting on top of it, at which time we will try to blow dry the dent out with hot air. Other times we will have to cream the bags to give them a better finish. Or we will take a leather dye and touch it up. Another thing is the stitching, making sure it's proper, that it's put together right, with all the proper pockets.

Then comes packing, another important aspect of the aesthetics of the luggage. Stuffing it really increases the appearance of it. If you look at a flat piece of luggage it looks blah, but once you put your belongings in it, or in our case we will stuff it with paper, it really increases the appearance 100 percent. It also shows off the features. When we are stuffing it we have to take into account the features that we don't want to hide, like inside pencil slots. We will attach various hang tags to highlight different features, such as carry-on capability or stress features. We also have to attach a UPC code in an accessible location.

**What paved your way to this position?** Prior to this I was a production manager, involved with receiving and shipping of lighting fixtures. Prior to that I was involved in the textile industry, in marketing and purchasing, so I am familiar with these aspects of the product and how they would relate to warehouses. I worked with hospital textiles, which included towels, sheets, garments rather than fashion products.

**How did your education prepare you for this position?** My education is not in this area, but rather in engineering. In engineering they teach you how to plan for things, just the way of thinking, how you have to plan. The particulars to this industry I picked up on the job.

### Gatekeeper: Natalie Perr, Color and Fashion Trend Forecaster, Self-Employed Consultant, (Member of the Color Association of the United States)

**What are your typical responsibilities as a color forecaster?** Looking at the world around us, being aware of anything happening around us that could influence color: whether it be cultural factors, whether it be political factors, technological updates, market research, knowing the market that one is forecasting the color for and then also having the right gut instinct, putting it all together and deciding what colors will sell either one year or two years in advance. These colors are swatches and made into a color card. The reason that I say one year or two years in advance is, usually that the forecasting for the market is a year in advance, deciding what color to put in a collection. However, for something like the CAUS (Color Association of the United States) color card, we have to work two years in advance for the textile market and the fiber producers. So we work two years before the product hits the shelves.

I work independently with individual clients, but CAUS colors are done by committee. The CAUS card is done through a consensus of colors predicted by a range of people from the fibers, textiles, apparel, and interior design industries. In general, these colors have got to go to a number of different products and price ranges. So we have to think of them selling across the whole country. There can be some hits and misses because we are trying to be forward enough but also play it safe.

Good instinct is something that you really have to have, you can't learn it. A forecaster needs a good eye for color, the ability to see fine differentiations in color, in shades, and intensities. A forecaster needs a good color memory, where one can look at a shade and almost be able to match something to the shade that is only a picture in one's mind. Not everybody has a good color memory.

**What paved your way to this position?** The responsibility that I had as head of design at Jones New York helped. I was in charge of developing, designing, and overseeing the Jones New York line, a very large collection. If you don't select the right shades then the merchandise will not sell. When you are dealing with product retailing, the first thing that a customer generally sees when she goes into a store is the garment sleeve or part of a garment. Because you have all these racks of jackets or sides of skirts, what pulls her over to that rack has got to be color, that's the first thing. So if the color doesn't hit her eye, she is proba-

Figure 11.6. CAUS member, Natalie Perr, examining sources of inspiration for color predictions.

bly not going to go over to the rack and touch the garment and feel the fabric, which is next, or pull it off the rack and check for style and fit. So the responsibility of doing a line that had to sell at least 120 million dollars a year put me into the position of having to be an accurate forecaster as a part of my job.

After Jones New York, I was Design Administrator at Macy's. Because our organization was so large and because of the number of labels, as well as the wide range of products from career to sportswear to jeans and activewear, it was essential that we had our own forecasted color card for the different Macy's departments. So I really got involved then in actually producing a color card just specifically for our programs. Not only predicting and forecasting but getting it done one time so that it could be used in a timely manner. I would say, for the most part, running Per Sé, a separates line business targeted to the specialty store market, was a similar experience. I don't think that I gained anything new from that, except for the fact that my own money was on the line. And then as a consultant, I have branched out into more areas. I have gotten involved in a little bit of men's wear. I've been asked to give color direction to the paper industry. So along the line I'm still learning new markets.

Understanding one's market is very important. Fashion trends in clothing influence other products. Interior design tends to be influenced by apparel fashions more than fashion is affected by interior design. Other products for the home are strongly influenced by clothing fashion, especially with more and more designers, like Guess Jeans opening up Guess Home. These home products have a look influenced by the Guess label. And Adrienne Vittadini sheets and towels look like Adrienne Vittadini clothing; one has to have something to tie

**ACTIVITY 11.5** As you read the interviews with the promoters, make a list of the responsibilities that would be considered as part of the role of a promoter. For example: Visual display selects the correct mannequin for the style. Refer to the definition of a promoter to guide your selection of representative responsibilities. Identify at least ten responsibilities. Save this list for Lab Activity 11.1.

them together. Cars, a little more difficult. Yes they sometimes do correlate with clothing trends. But people don't change cars quite as frequently. Now we are starting to see cars go into a cycle of purples and shades of deep, dark, subtle berry tones with some iridescent colors. There is some sort of a correlation because we are seeing a lot of purples forecasted in the clothing business as well. Yet cars take a lot longer in the planning stage and the cycles last a lot longer.

**How did your education prepare you for this position?** I have a Bachelor of Science in Fine Arts and Design. I don't think that I was really taught anything specific about forecasting. Probably one thing in my education that really helped me was a teacher who gave quizzes to make sure we were aware of the world around us. She might have asked us a question about Jackie Kennedy Onassis, or about a popular move, or some event that she went to that really didn't relate to anything that we were studying; she would throw in a question like that just to catch us off-guard and make sure that we were aware of what is happening in the world around us.

**What publications and resources do you use to keep current professionally?** I try to get and look at as many things as possible. I subscribe to every single American fashion magazine just about. Of course, I buy *Women's Wear Daily, W,* and European magazines periodically. I get almost all of the European magazines during the key months. Textile View has their own color forecast and it's a very inspirational magazine. I think it's published in Amsterdam but it's available here. Basically, besides the fashion and textile magazines, when putting together a forecast or presentation, I try to look for inspiration in other kinds of magazines, just for things that might tie in with what I am thinking of. Architecture magazines, photographs of interior designs, even food sometimes. Movies and music can also influence my thinking about trends.

### Promoter: Lynn Amos, Sales Representative, Maressa Sales, Los Angeles, California

**What are your typical responsibilities?** As a sales rep, I travel to accounts with samples of lace, trims, and piece goods from the manufacturers that I represent. I show the customer (usually the designer or design assistant) new products, leave samples for them to consider, take their orders either at my visit or after they have had time to determine the amount needed for production, and make sure their deliveries are on time.

A sales rep has got to be selective in the products shown to the customer. I cannot bombard the customer with the hundreds of samples I rep. I have got

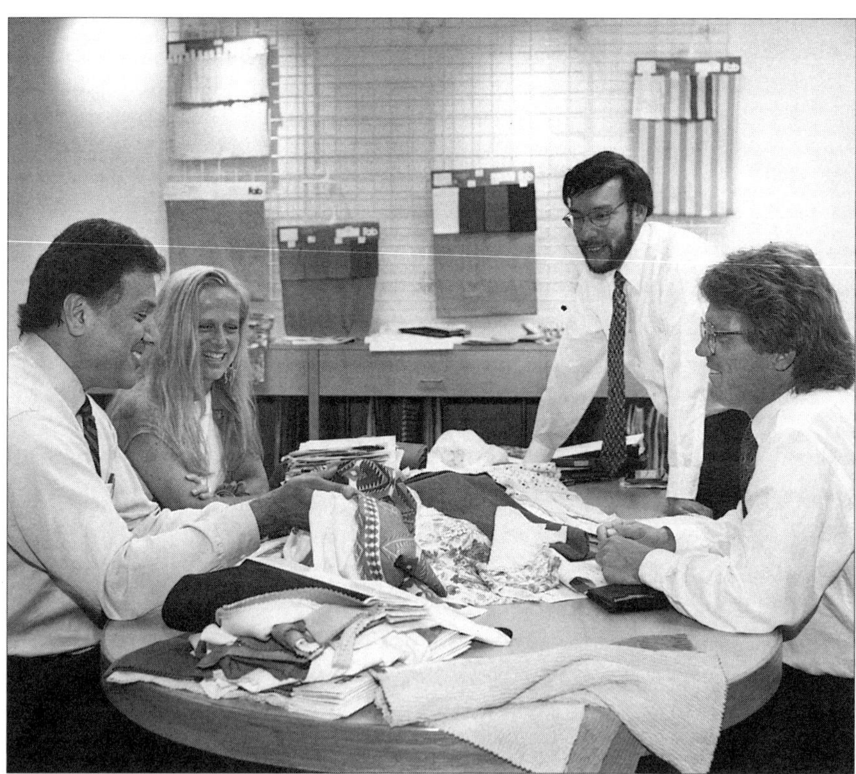

Figure 11.7. Sales representatives and designers reviewing sample books of fabric.

to consider their needs. Every company and every division has their own needs based on their customer and what works for them. Sometimes designers request to see particular products, such as embroideries; other times they don't have specific requests. Either way, this means I have to research their company. I need to identify whether it is missy or missy contemporary, identify their trends and style, then show selective samples that I think will be of interest. I have got to be aware of the styles they have on the market, so I pay attention when I am in stores and listen to what others in the industry can tell me.

I need to know their price point. I was at an account today, XOXO, and they purchased fabric that I knew my next account couldn't buy because it was too costly for their price point. I need to know what kinds of prints or trims they work with, and then match these needs with samples that I think they would be interested in seeing. I have an account that designs for a young, hip, trendy consumer. They recently bought an embroidered butterfly in blue and orange and in purple and neon green. While their selection of embroidery wasn't *my* taste, I showed it because I thought it was right for the customer. I was at another account today and saw two designers. One was in the dress division, the other was in the sportswear division. The sportswear designer sampled interlock knits and the dress designer sampled batik patterns. So you have to be very aware of who's doing what.

I also need to let my accounts know what is happening in the market, what's hot and really selling for me. I make suggestions as they flip through the samples and let them know what is popular. I am going to an appointment tomorrow morning and she wants to see stretch laces, but I know with their line and what I've been selling that they should be doing embroideries as well. So I will take my embroidery samples with me and if they don't want to see them then I don't push the issue. Everybody wants to know what everybody else is doing. I can tell them that a certain item, heart appliqués for instance, is really selling for children's. If they put me on the spot and ask who is running this pattern, I would tell them other children's accounts. I wouldn't give them specifics of my other accounts. I won't tell them, "Well, Jonathan Martin has this print on a line and they are doing it with this print." When I was a designer it bothered me when sales reps would say "Oh this company is doing this," because you knew that same sales rep was also telling the competition what my company was doing.

**What paved your way to this position?** Before my sales rep position, I was a designer for a sportswear company in Los Angeles. There, I was the one meeting with sales reps, sampling fabrics for the line. Because I was a designer, I understand the limitations and concerns of my customers better. I understand their time constraints and the importance of showing them items that suit their needs in terms of price point and style. I have a sense of what certain designs cost to produce, which might limit the price they can afford for fabric or trims. As a designer, I shopped the stores to see what the competition was doing. I would examine who was doing what styles and details, how certain companies constructed a garment to be similar in style to another company, but end up much lower in price. This gives me a good basis for working with my accounts, because I have a sense of their style and the kinds of fabrics and trims they use. I am also able to make suggestions to the designers about how they might use a more expensive trim or fabric but still stay within the price range for the garment. This knowledge makes me more efficient; it helps me pinpoint the designers needs and what I should be showing them. I know the importance of providing good customer service, being there when the designer wants to see samples and following through to make sure the order arrives on time.

**How did your education prepare you for this position?** Having a four-year degree teaches you about the industry, but at the time you may not realize the importance of it. When I was on study tour for instance, we would see lace machines, but I thought, "why would I need to see lace machines when I am in design?" Now I am a sales rep for lace products, so it helps me better understand and explain the special nature of the product to my accounts. All the information you get in college adds up to a better understanding of the product and the industry. Everything is interrelated. As a designer, I might not make lace fabric, but knowing how it is produced helps me understand its properties, which is important for designing with and selling the product.

**What publications and resources do you use to keep current with the industry?** All the fashion magazines, *Women's Wear Daily,* and *California Apparel News* are really good for knowing what is happening in the market. With *WWD,* I usually flip through and read articles about the companies I work with. *WWD* also talks about store sales and trend forecasting. When I was a designer, my company subscribed to a forecasting service, called Here & There. They do color, fabric, and trend forecasting. They send slide presentations and have a library of images of trends that designers could review. So a designer could see all the jackets for the season.

### Promoter: Lisa Williams, Visual Display Assistant, Lord & Taylor, Chicago, Illinois

**What are your typical responsibilities?** My position is to keep all displays and windows updated, creating displays that will grab the eye of the customer and add interest to the store so it doesn't look like a sea of garment racks. Every month we are provided information on what's hot and we use this information in merchandising the store displays to stress the Lord & Taylor look.

I work in all departments of the store. However, I work much of the time in men's wear, where we use bust forms (upper torso forms) for displays. I look at the new merchandise that has been picked out for each fixture and pull together ensembles incorporating these products. We like to use at least three layers in an ensemble, such as a T-shirt, a buttoned-down shirt, and a sweater for impact and to show customers how things may be combined. With posable mannequins, I may pose them (e.g., put the hand on the hip) to show off the layers of the ensemble. With the rigid mannequins, I have to select the right mannequin for the product image. One of the poses is called the thinker, a much more serious pose. Other mannequins are lying down, some are sitting. You have to really think where to put them and what type of fixtures you have and the mood that you want to set. For instance, a mannequin sitting on a table

a

b

Figure 11.8 a and b. Mannequins differ in image. Visual display artists must consider the image of the mannequin used in displays to effectively promote products. Mannequins: our fantasy figures of high fashion.

Photos by Chad Slattery.

### Visual Merchandising Specific Objectives to Create

- Shopping Enjoyment. We should make certain that every customer at JCPenney finds the store to be an enjoyable place to shop. If our customers enjoy their shopping experience, they will be back again.
- Personal Satisfaction. Customers want to feel that we understand their needs and our department layout and merchandise mix is a reflection of their needs.
- Theater/Entertainment. No customer wants to go into a dull, unexciting shopping environment. They want to feel good about where they shop; they want displays, merchandise and visual affects that say "Excitement."
- Convenience/Value. We don't want our customers to have to search for the items they want. Effective store signing communicates value by assisting customers to use their shopping time more effectively. Visual merchandising helps our merchandise communicate the value story to every customer.

Figure 11.9. Visual merchandiser's objectives for JCPenney consist of creating an aesthetically pleasing and convenient shopping experience.

is in a lounging, sexy pose making it appropriate for eveningwear or intimate apparel. We have mannequins, we call "Pucci girls", that we use all the time for Liz Claiborne and Jones New York Sport because they have a less dramatic, casual look. Because of our up-scale clientele, cost is not a factor in creating the ensemble. That's of less concern for our clientele; they want to know what's new and how to pull things together.

A visual merchandising manager will also do floor plans. Tomorrow my manager is working on a new floor plan for the area because we just received a large quantity of new merchandise. We will have to arrange the T-stands and four-ways while making sure the department layout is balanced and strollers and wheelchairs can move freely.

**What paved your way to this position?** I have not worked in visual display before this, so I am lucky to have this position. I worked as a sales associate in a number of stores, where I would help arrange visual displays. I have also done a design internship. These have provided experiences to develop my fashion sense and my eye for presentation.

**How did your education prepare you for this position?** My design major has really enhanced my creativity and my ability to work out ideas to the final physical product, which is basically what you do in visual display. You start with a creative idea and actually produce a physical product. My classes that required drawing and working with various fabrics have really helped me through the creative process and being able to physically manipulating the fabric and hair on the mannequins.

**What publications and resources do you use to keep current with the industry?** Basically, I keep current through fashion magazines such as *Vogue* and *W*, catalogs, and fashion shows. Some of the trade publications good for visual merchandising are *Display & Design Ideas, Lighting Dimensions,* and *Visual Merchandising and Store Design* (*VM&SD*).

### Promoter: Pamela Holt, Marketing Manager, Helly-Hansen (NA), Inc., Redmond, Washington

**What are your typical responsibilities?** My responsibility as a marketing manager is to handle all the different marketing functions related to the product line. Activities consist of putting together our buyer's guide catalog, developing visual merchandising displays for the trade shows and point of purchase sales, creating hang tags, and working on other sales promotions. The company makes specialty outerwear, such as sailing clothing, climbing clothing, and skiwear. We sell mainly to specialty stores (e.g., ski shops) and big sporting goods retailers.

Let me expand a bit on some of the responsibilities. The buyers' guide is a color catalog that the retail buyer uses to select what to order for their outdoor store. So the buyer's guide doesn't go to the end customer. I work with our

Figure 11.10. Helly-Hansen buyer's guide promoting the product line through page layout, vivid visual images, and verbal descriptions.

graphic designer, our printer, and our product development folks within the company, to bring all of the pieces together to create an effective buyer's guide that shows off the product to the best advantage. I need a good eye to make sure the guide is attractive and works well for the buyer. I have to apply the same principles when we work on the hang tags. I work with the ad agency to make sure the layout of the hang tags, the sketches, and the callouts are presenting the best image of our product. A callout is an enlarged image (sketch) and a description of a design feature, such as underarm zippers to stay cool, used in promotional materials such as buyers' guides.

I also do some work with point-of-purchase displays, promotional displays for use in the store. These show off a product, making sure the display isn't too high or wide and is also within our budget. It has to look good, because if it doesn't look good, stores won't use them and then the company wasted a lot of money. At trade shows I determine how the booth should look. This means I determine what kind of visual images we want in the booth, where we want the mannequins, what kind of story we are trying to tell to the buyer, and how to lay out the booth so that people could move through it. Product managers tell me what products should be promoted. I figure out how to position it, to best get the message across at the show.

**What paved your way to this position?** I was with US West Communications for five years and when I finished there I was a marketing manager. It's the same title as my job at Helly-Hansen, but the tasks are not the same. I was in a different industry, but managers of Helly-Hansen thought I had the right skills and I could learn the specifics of the active sportswear industry. I left US West to go back to graduate school. While in graduate school I worked as a retail sales associate at Nordstrom's in their women's activewear department. Mainly, I assisted women in selection of products. I had to know the product and what product would work best for the customer. I had to select the right garment for the women's body and budget and then communicate to the customer what made a particular product right for her. This position made me more aware of how to merchandise apparel, how to best present the product to the customer.

**How did your education prepare you for this position?** I have an undergraduate degree in marketing and I am working on a Master's degree in textiles and clothing. My education has enhanced my analytical skills. I learned how to determine what is the essence of the problem and how it can be solved most efficiently and effectively. I remember in a Global Issues course we would critically analyze articles by professors or people in the industry who were well known in their fields. We talked about why their statements did not make sense. This helped in my ability to analyze a situation. At Helly-Hansen there is really no one to direct me; it is all upon me to figure out how to solve a problem. So I would say problem-solving skills are very important skills that my education helped develop. Another thing that helped me was the technical writing skills I gained. Being able to compose and write clearly so things aren't misinterpreted is very important. Aesthetics played a role too, when working with a graphics designer or advertising.

**What publications and resources do you use to keep current with the industry?** At Helly-Hansen there are a number of trade publications that I read, including *Outdoor Retailer, Sports Trend, Sportstyle,* and *Skiing Trade News*. I get all the ski magazines, all the outdoor magazines, Sierra Club magazines, canoeing, paddling, and biking magazines that go to the end consumer. I go through them so I can see what is going to the consumer and see the competitors ads and see how they positioned their products. I would also read marketing research about the competition.

## SUMMARY

Textile and apparel professionals affecting the aesthetic product may be categorized as: (1) developers; (2) gatekeepers (selectors); and (3) promoters. *Developers* are professionals involved in the creation of the product, from initiating and contributing ideas, presenting the ideas, through perfecting the design, and ending with the completion of production. *Gatekeepers* are professionals who influence which existing products reach the consumer based upon criteria such as fashionability, salability, and/or quality. Gatekeepers may affect which physical products or representations (verbal or visual) of the product reach the con-

### LAB ACTIVITY 11.1

In this Lab Activity you are going to identify how your college curriculum could provide you with knowledge and experience that will prepare you for a position as a developer, gatekeeper, or promoter. Bring a course catalog of your academic institution and your curriculum program for the textiles and clothing-related major to class.

1. As a class, form three separate groups. One group each for developers, gatekeepers, and promoters.
2. As a group combine and edit your ten responses from Activity 11.3 (developers), 11.4 (gatekeepers), or 11.5 (promoters) into a more complete list of responsibilities.
3. Add any other responsibilities that you feel are important to the role, but were not mentioned in the interviews.
4. Each group should have at least one course catalog for the academic institution and the curriculum program for the textiles and clothing related major.
5. For each entry in the combined list of responsibilities from steps 2 and 3, identify which course(s) inside and outside your major will provide the knowledge and experience needed. For example, an introduction to marketing course in business may define market segments. Through a social psychology of dress course offered by the textiles and clothing department you may identify needs of different market segments.
6. Identify any responsibilities that are not covered by the curriculum.
7. Propose ways that knowledge and experience of these responsibilities may be gained, such as adding to a course already offered, creating a new course, or developing an internship with a particular type of business.

sumer. *Promoters* are professionals who emphasize and enhance a product's value through verbal communication and/or design of the sensory qualities of the environment. Promoters have a vested image in promoting particular products. The present chapter examined the varied responsibilities, career paths, and educational backgrounds of a sample of developers, gatekeepers, and promoters. The chapter also examined the trade publications and popular press resources used by the professionals to stay current with the industry.

## KEY TERMS AND CONCEPTS

- assistant designer responsibilities
- buyer's guide
- callouts
- CAUS (Color Association of the United States)
- color card
- color memory
- considerations in creating visual display
- developers
- EDI (Electronic Data Interchange)
- ethical concerns in sales representation
- factors affecting samples shown by sales rep
- factors considered in color forecasting
- fallout of styles
- fit model responsibilities
- fit modeling
- "flat specing"
- floor plans for merchandise
- forecaster responsibilities
- garment bodies
- gatekeepers
- integrated program of courses
- marketing manager responsibilities
- merchandiser responsibilities
- point of sale information
- point-of-purchase displays
- promoters
- "Pucci girls"
- quality control checks
- relationship of apparel trends to other products
- sales representative responsibilities
- "shopping the stores"
- sister set
- style books
- swatching fabric
- visual display assistant responsibilities
- warehouse/traffic manager responsibilities
- women's and women's petite sizes

## SUGGESTED READINGS

Fiorito, S. S. & Fairhurst, A. E. (1993). Comparison of buyers' job content in large and small retail firms. *Clothing and Textiles Research Journal, 11*(3), 8–15.

Folse, N. M. & Henrion, M. (1981). *Careers in the fashion industry.* New York, NY: Harper & Row.

Gaskill, L. R. (1992). Toward a model of retail product development: A case study analysis. *Clothing and Textiles Research Journal, 10*(4), 17–24.

Glock, R. E. & Kunz, G. I. (1995). *Apparel manufacturing: Sewn product analysis.* Englewood Cliffs, NJ: Prentice-Hall, pp. 122–128.

Lamb, J. & Kallal, M. (1992). A conceptual framework for apparel design. *Clothing and Textiles Research Journal, 10*(1), 42–47.

PART FOUR

# Application of Aesthetics Related Skills Used by the Apparel Professional

CHAPTER 12

# Perceiving Form: The Body and Apparel

## Objectives

- Understand the importance of perceiving the form for the apparel professional
- Identify color, texture, and proportion of the body
- Understand how formal qualities of apparel interact with the body's formal qualities to enhance appearance
- Select apparel to enhance appearance

Listening to consumers trying on apparel in the dressing room can provide insight into the importance of the interaction between apparel and the body in the apparel purchase process. One of the authors has collected statements made by consumers in dressing rooms from students employed as retail sales consultants and from our personal experiences. Here are a few statements of how interactions between apparel and the body have negatively or positively influenced perceived attractiveness and subsequent purchase decisions:

*Negative influences*

- The color washes you out.
- The cuffs shorten my legs too much.
- Green is not your color. *But this dress is yellow* No, I mean the color it turns your skin.
- Against that shiny texture, I'm not sure if I'm looking at my hair or a bale of hay.
- The suit makes you look like Arnold Schwartzenegger... in the movie *Junior.*
- If this exercise bra were any tighter, I would indent.

*Positive influences*

- That color creates a striking contrast with your skin and hair.
- The color shows off my tan.
- The texture blends with the softness to your skin.
- The skirt emphasizes your small waist.
- Stripes show off my lats (back muscles).
- Is that cleavage!

## IMPORTANCE OF PERCEIVING THE FORM FOR THE APPAREL PROFESSIONAL

The body consists of colors, textures, and proportions that interact with the formal qualities of apparel. These aspects of a body become considerations in development of apparel products for different segments of the market, selection of apparel by sales consultants or wardrobe consultants for an individual consumer, and promotion of the product using fashion models or mannequins to display apparel to its best advantage. Thus, apparel professionals must be sensitive to the effect apparel has on the appearance of the body. Brecca Farr, the fit model interviewed in Chapter 11, discusses the importance of understanding proportion and developing apparel to fit the proportion of the body:

> **Farr:** When palazzo pants became popular again, a lot of people said that women's petite couldn't wear palazzo pants. I thought that women who are a size range of women's petite can not "pull off" palazzo pants if they are not proportionate, but there is no reason that a short body cannot wear pants as long as they are in proportion. So understanding conceptually what are key elements to creating attractive styles for your size range, such as vertical eye movement, horizontal eye movement, broken and unbroken line, shape, size of print, line direction is essential. Line is probably the most critical; basically do you have vertical eye movement. What I'm referring to is unbroken line, easy eye movement, where the body isn't chopped in half. Does there seem to be a disproportion between size of top and size of bottom, either by color, shape, or texture.
>
> There can be trouble when a manufacturer takes a style that was popular in juniors or another size range and decides that it should be done in women's petite. Particularly when you are talking a new size range for them, whether it's women's petites or petites or women's, or branching from juniors to misses or vice versa. Inevitably one of the ways they do that is to take their most popular styles and try to translate them into the new size range. A lot of times you have people who are knowledgeable about the initial size range, but they haven't a clue about the new size range. I was amazed with the number of people who would look at me when I came in as a women's petite model and said, "Well why can't you just take a different size in women's?" Well, I'm four to six inches shorter. I would come out in the original gar-

ment and say, "Look at me. This does not fit. My pants are down around my ankles. My shoulders are huge." We would go through step by step, revising the sample, pinning, marking, and ripping the sample; by the time we got to the end; there was a remarkable difference.

> Sometimes they would translate concepts that I would be very skeptical about. One dress in particular that I can remember, (I'm 5'2". My target market is 5'4" and under) the target market for the original style was a taller market. Their samples were geared for women who were 5'6" to 5'7", so you are talking an immediate four-inch difference just in body length between me and their sample size. The dress was bright red knit, with a huge cowl neck (huge—the length of the turn on the cowl neck was about fourteen inches); it was a 3 by 3 rib and it would go into a fine gauge with a six-inch rib cuff. And they said, "Well, you can turn it back." Great, now I have a three-inch double thick 3 by 3 rib cuff. It had a balloon style bottom. They still translated it. It was just hideous. But it didn't matter, they had an order for it.

Figure 12.1. A personal care product that enhances skin color and texture, producing even-toned, soft skin.

Reading 12.1 discusses another reason why apparel professional should be sensitive to the effect of apparel on appearance of the body. Appearance may have a significant effect on self-esteem of the consumer. An apparel professional should offer products that enhance attractiveness for consumers of all ages and proportions, because attractiveness of appearance is of importance to this wide range of consumers.

Computer and video technology aids the analysis of the body form and helps visualization of the interactions of apparel on the body. Technology analyzes color or shape of the face and then video screens project the person's image with computer suggested cosmetics or hair style options. Similar technology projects an image of the whole body in selected apparel styles. Reading 12.2 shows how technology aids the custom design of swimsuits to enhance the interaction of apparel on the body. Thus, perceiving the body form can become extremely important before apparel is designed or selected. The success of the apparel product, ultimately, rests on the combination between the body and the product. We will address perceiving the body form and how apparel interacts with the body to enhance appearance.

## ANALYSIS OF THE BODY FORM

### Color

Products are developed to enhance the color of skin, hair, and eyes. Skin is lightened (Figure 12.1), blushed, and bronzed; hair is dyed and bleached; and eye color is changed with contact lenses. Color consulting, a rage in the 1980s, focuses on enhancing appearance through the interaction of color of the body and apparel. Color of apparel placed on the body can have a major impact on the body's attractiveness. Value contrast, intensity, and undertone (warmth or coolness) of body colors are many times considered in selection of apparel.

**Value.** Values of the body may be measured using a value chart (Color Plate 9) divided equally into light, medium, and dark values. Value contrast among skin, hair, and eyes can be considered low, medium, or high. Value contrast is determined by the similarity of value levels of the body. If values of skin, hair, and eyes all fall within the same value level (e.g., dark value), then the value contrast is low (Figure 12.2a). If the values of the body fall within two adjacent levels (i.e., light and medium, medium and dark values), then the value contrast is a medium level. A mixture of light and dark body values creates a high level of value contrast (Figure 12.2b). One may also consider the distance among the specific body values to determine the level of value contrast. A dark eye value may be directly next to the division point between medium and dark, while skin and hair occupy the value immediate to the right of the division point. In such case, the value contrast level may be considered low.

**Intensity.** Intensity of natural body colors does not cover the full range of intensity presented in a Munsell chart. Body colors are generally low to medium in intensity. Intensity is commonly increased through personal care products such as cosmetics and hair dyes. Contacts and hair dyes may even create higher

Figure 12.2 a and b. Low, and high levels of value contrast in colors of the body.

a

b

a

b

Figure 12.3 a and b. Differences in intensities of skin, hair, and eyes. (a) Blonde-haired model represents higher intensities, than the (b) brown-haired model who represents lower intensities.

**ACTIVITY 12.1** Skin, hair, and eyes vary along the continuum of intensity. Color Plate 9 provide examples of a low and high intensities for skin, hair, and eyes. Complete a chart using examples of skin, hair, and eyes from print sources to create a range of body intensities.

1. Each person in the class should collect three examples of intensity; find one head example for skin, the second head for hair, and the third head for eyes. Make sure the eye examples are large enough; an eye should be at least 1/2" long. (See Activity 12.2 and 12.3 if you want to collect examples needed for these activities at the same time.)
2. As a class, sort the examples of hair into piles by color such as blonde, gray, brown, red for hair; and blue, green, brown for eyes. All skin examples can remain in one pile.
3. Divide the class into groups according to the number of piles found in step 2 plus one. Each group will select one of the piles. Two groups should merge to work with the skin examples.
4. Within the group, place the examples along the continuum of intensity. (Note that brown hair and eyes will lean towards the side of lower intensity.)
5. As a class, verify the order of intensity in each continuum. Once it's agreed upon by the class, cut a sample of skin and hair at least one inch square. Cut out an entire eye in a rectangular shape.
6. Affix the rows of examples to a board as a reference of intensity of the body. Try to match up level of intensities vertically. For instance, the blue, green, and brown eyes of the same intensity should be in a straight vertical column.
7. Divide the continuum into three parts and label them low, medium, and high intensity.
8. Working with a partner, define the intensity of the partner's skin, hair, and eye colors by comparing them to the charts.

Save this information for use in the Lab Activity 12.1.

intensities than normally found in the body. Intensities may be described as low, medium, or high (Color Plate 9). Carry out Activity 12.1 to create skin, hair, and eye charts that show a range in intensity. To determine body color intensities, the body may be compared against the chart of intensities for skin, hair, and eyes developed in Activity 12.1.

**Undertone.** Warmth and coolness of body undertones can be determined by placing swatches of fabric or paper representing warm and cool undertones (Color Plate 12) against the body. A blended effect between either the warm or cool swatches and the body color suggests the body's warmth or coolness of undertone. Generally, the skin, hair, and eyes have the same undertone, but cosmetics, dyes, and contacts may alter the undertones of the body. Color Plate 12 shows examples of blending between the warmth or coolness of the body and apparel undertones. In Activity 12.2, the class will develop another chart for undertones similar to that found in Activity 12.1. The chart developed in Activity 12.2 can be used to determine undertones of skin, hair, and eyes.

### Texture

If the package for a hair care product said, "makes your hair look like brillo," would you purchase it? Probably not, unless of course a pot needs scouring. Many personal care products are designed and purchased to enhance the texture of the skin (Figure 12.1). The packaging of personal care products will likely state the resulting improvement in body texture from use of the product. For instance, looking at the packaging of hair care products, one might find statements such as, "locks in longer-lasting softness, flexibility, and shine" or "creates natural movement and shine without stiffness or weight." A cosmetic product such as pressed powder might read, "helps make pores less visible so the skin looks soft and smooth." These products are offering enhancement of texture of the body to achieve the perceived cultural ideal. Enhancing the texture of the body through apparel is frequently overlooked. However, apparel products may enhance the visual effects of skin and hair through contrast of texture of apparel and the body. Yet, seldom is apparel advertised as enhancing the texture of the body.

Two aspects of body texture that seem to pervade the development of personal care products in Western culture are shininess and smoothness (even textured). The ideal skin texture in much of Western culture is matte or pearl and smooth. The ideal hair texture commonly is shiny and smooth or evenly textured. Skin and hair may be analyzed along the continua of shiny-matte and smooth-coarse (Figure 12.5). Complete Activity 12.3. It will lead to the development of a chart of these visual continua of skin and hair textures.

### Proportion

Apparel products are frequently developed and purchased to alter the perceived body proportion to attain the cultural ideal. In general, the ideals for women and men in Western culture are a thin or muscular body, respectively. Apparel

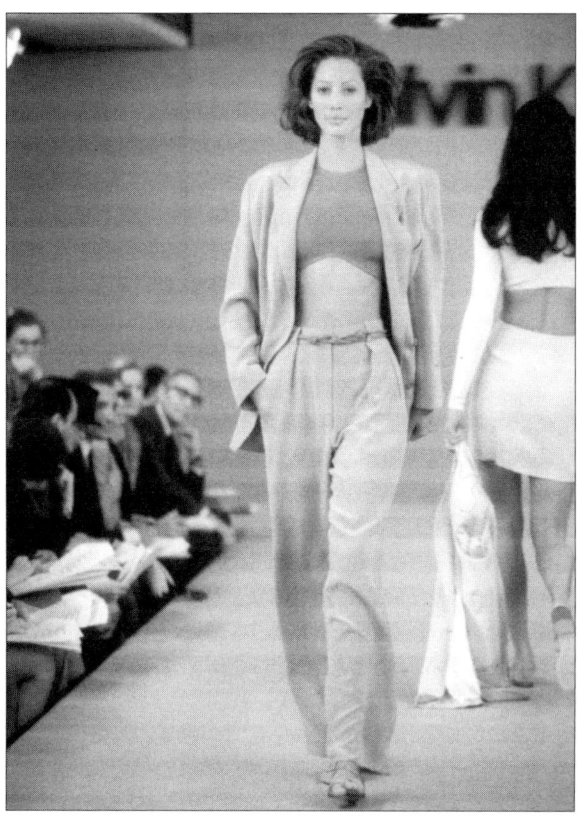

Figure 12.4. Blending between the warmth or coolness of the body and apparel color undertones.

**ACTIVITY 12.2** Skin, hair, and eyes vary according to undertone. Color Plate 12 provides examples of warm and cool undertones for skin, hair, and eye. Complete a chart using examples of skin, hair, and eyes from print sources to create groupings of warm and cool undertones.

1. Each person in the class should collect three more heads; find one head example for skin, the second head for hair, and the third head for eyes. Again, make sure the eye examples are large enough; an eye should be at least one-half inch long.
2. Create three piles for all the skin, hair, or eyes examples.
3. Divide the class into three groups, one group each to work with skin, hair, or eyes.
4. Sort the examples by warm or cool undertones. (You may want to work in subgroups with a few examples then report back to your whole group.)
5. As a class, verify the placement of examples into warm or cool undertones. Once it's agreed upon by the class, cut a sample of skin and hair at least one inch square. Cut out an entire eye in a rectangular shape.
6. Affix the examples to a board as a reference of undertone of the body.
7. Label them warm and cool undertones.
8. Working with a partner, define the undertone of the partner's skin, hair, and eye colors by comparing them to the chart.

Save this information for use in the Lab Activity 12.1.

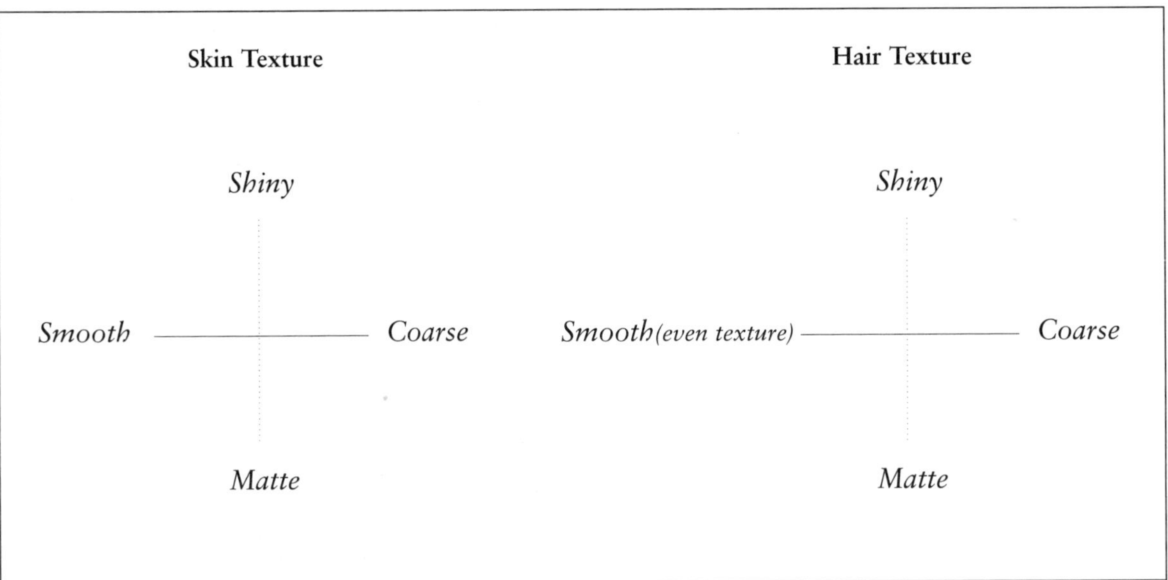


Figure 12.5. Continua for textural analysis of skin and hair.

**ACTIVITY 12.3** Skin and hair vary along the continua of shiny-matte and smooth-coarse. One may become more aware of differences in body texture if a number of visual images are compared. This activity will result in a chart of textures for use by the class.

1. Each person in the class should collect four images of faces with visible hair on the head. Texture should be apparent, so choose a large head image, at least two inches by two inches.
2. As a class, label four piles: skin (shiny-matte), skin (smooth-coarse), hair (shiny-matte), and hair (smooth-coarse).
3. Each person should randomly place one of the images in each of the four piles.
4. Divide the class into four groups. Each group will select one of the four piles.
5. Within the group place the visual images along the continuum, such as from shiny hair to matte hair.
6. As a class, verify the group's continuum of visual images.
7. Once it's agreed upon by the class, affix the images to a board as a reference of visual textures of the body. Use only the part of the body (skin or hair) needed for the chart.
8. Label the group (e.g., skin: shiny-matte).
9. Working with a partner, use the texture chart to determine the partner's skin and hair texture along the two continua.

Save this information for use in the Lab Activity 12.1.

| **TABLE 12.1** | Analyzing the Proportion of the Body | |
|---|---|---|
| | *Designator* | *Description* |
| *Front View Width* | A | wider hips with narrow waist and shoulders |
| | V | wider shoulders with narrow hips, waist may be same width as hips |
| | X | shoulders and hips are the same width with narrow waist |
| | H | shoulders, waist, and hips similar in width |
| | O | waist wider than shoulders and hips |
| *Side View Width* | i | little protrusion of the bust |
| | r | full bust, out of proportion |
| | b | stomach fullness forming an exaggerated protrusion |
| | d | buttocks fullness forming an exaggerated protrusion |
| *Front Length View* | W | distance between shoulder and waist is noticeably shorter than between waist and hip; generally coincides with longer legs |
| | Y | distance between shoulder and waist is noticeably longer than between waist and hip; generally coincides with shorter legs |

may have some influence on creating the appearance of these ideals, such as control top panty hose "thinning" the body. However, apparel products are better able to alter the perceived body to attain the ideal *proportions*. Focusing on proportion instead of size or weight is preferable because apparel is effective in altering perceived proportion of the body, providing a sense of satisfaction to individuals who do not fit the cultural ideals of size or weight.

When analyzing the proportion of the body it is important to consider the front and side views. (See Table 12.1.) Both width and length proportions of the body are examined. For front width proportions, the width of the shoulders is compared to the width of the waist and hips. The resulting proportions can be given letter designators A, V, X, H (August, 1981) or O which represent the general proportion. The shape of the letter coincides with the proportion of the frontal view of the body (Figure 12.6). The present ideal in much of Western culture is the X proportion for women and the V proportion for men.

Side views are examined for prominence of upper (bust) and lower body (stomach or buttocks) widths. The ideal is frequently seem as gentle curves, rather than fully rounded or flat forms. While each person is given a frontal view width designator, a person with gentle curves is not given a side view width designator. The side view designators are i and r for the bust for women only and b and d for the stomach and buttocks, respectively (August, 1981). Figure 12.8 is an example of a body that would be considered an i and d. Again, the shape of the letter coincides with the proportion of the side view of the body (Figure 12.7).

Length proportion is determined by comparing the front length between the shoulders and waist with that between the waist and the hips. Equal length mea-

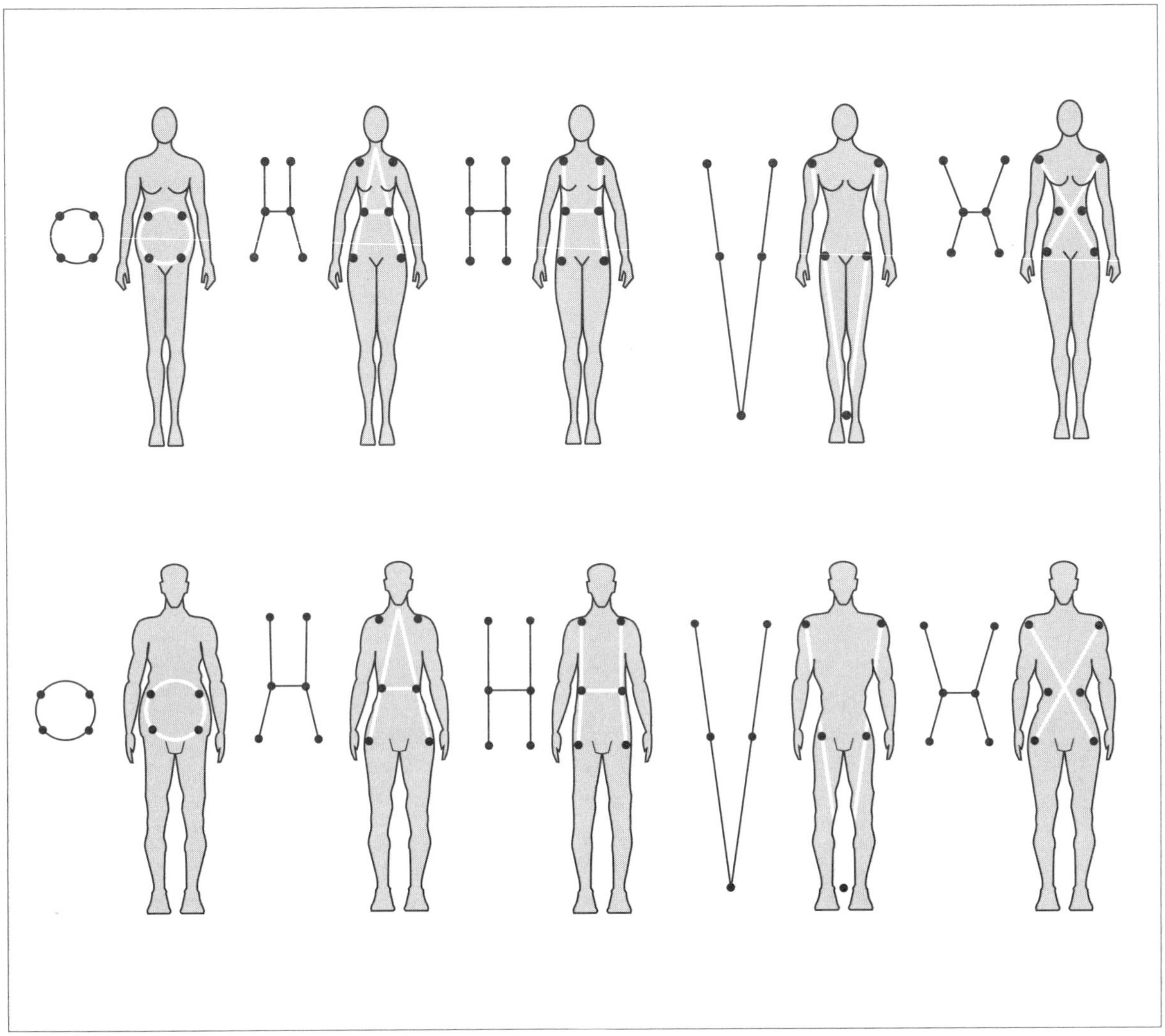

Figure 12.6. (above) Frontal view width designators for women and men.

Looking Thin (1981), Bonnie August with Ellen Count.

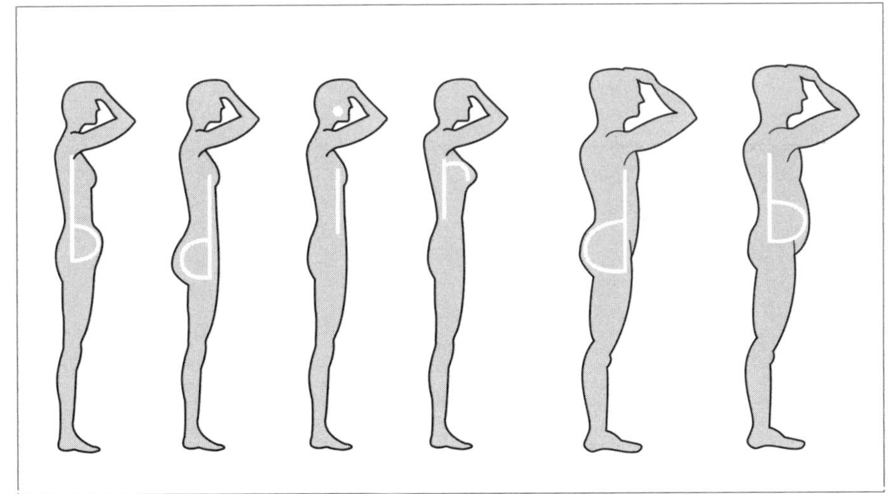

Figure 12.7. (right) Side view width designators for women and men.

Looking Thin (1981), Bonnie August with Ellen Count.

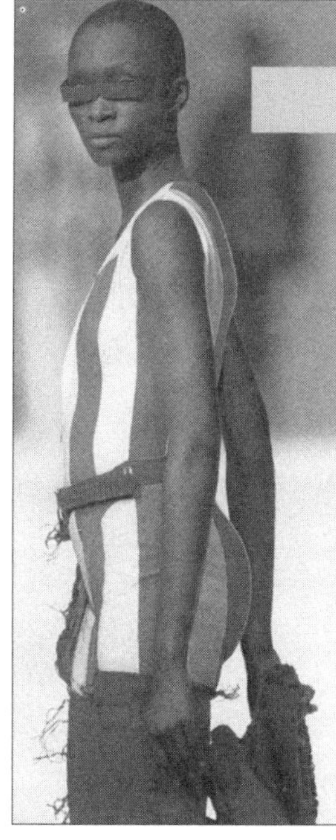

Figure 12.8. This model's body would be considered an i and d.

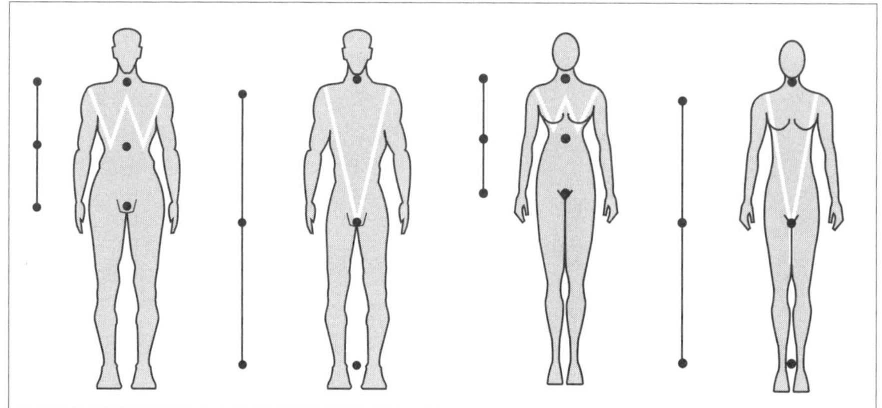

Figure 12.9. Front length designators for women and men.

surements is generally considered the ideal in Western culture. The length designators are W and Y (Figure 12.9). As with the side view designators, an individual may not be given a length designator because she or he has equal length measurements. Try to determine the body proportions of partners using Activity 12.4.

## INTERACTIONS BETWEEN APPAREL AND THE BODY TO ENHANCE APPEARANCE

Perception of the features of the body form—color, texture, and proportion—can be influenced by the formal qualities of apparel placed on the body. This influence can be positive when the influences lead to the perception of an ideal body form. In Western cultures, the ideal is generally a thin body form for women and a muscular body form for men. Apparel can be used strategically to create illusions that the body is closer to this ideal than it actually is. These illusions are created through the use of unity, contrast, balance, and proportion between the body features and apparel.

### Color

Apparel colors can influence the perception of body colors, especially the complexion of the skin. The interaction of apparel and body color occurs through similarity and contrast effects of value, intensity, and undertone. Generally, a

**ACTIVITY 12.4** It is difficult to determine the body proportion of models in print ads because apparel affects appearance of proportion. Identifying the proportion of class members will help you become more sensitive to body proportions.

1. To determine proportion, one should wear form-fitting apparel and stand against a wall while two class members examine the front and side views. A wall with a grid helps identify the proportions more easily, but with practice one is able to "eyeball" the proportions fairly accurately.
2. The two class members should determine the front view width designator of the other member.
3. The two class members should determine if side view width or front length designators are appropriate. Remember for the i, r, b, d, W, and Y designators, a prominent or exaggerated proportion is required.

Save this information for use in Lab Activity 12.1.

medium level of contrast between value, and intensity creates a pleasing result (Rasband, 1996).

**Value.** When color values are similar, with low to medium contrasts created between body color and apparel, there is a pleasing effect, creating a "whole." For instance, a person with high value body coloring might employ similar high value apparel to create unity. On the other hand, contrast of color value can be used to create emphasis within the body form. Contrast between facial coloring and clothing is effective in bringing attention to the face. Contrast color value within an ensemble may emphasize a proportional relationship on the body, such as the torso/leg length proportions.

**Intensity.** The intensities of skin, hair, and eyes may be similar or varied, creating high or low contrast. When low intensities exist among one's body coloring, higher intensity colors may be introduced in apparel to create pleasing color relationships (Rasband, 1996). Cosmetics may be used to intensify the colors of the body. The use of brighter colors adds interest and energy to personal appearance. However, high intensity apparel against low intensity body colors can also create a relationship of color where the "clothing wears the person."

**Undertone.** Recall that a simultaneous contrast effect results in the apparent differences of value, intensity, and undertone being emphasized when two colors are placed next to each other. In selecting apparel for the body, one is primarily concerned that unpleasant simultaneous contrast effects in undertone are not created between body colors and apparel colors. Simultaneous contrast effects that increase the apparent sallowness (yellow) or blueness of skin tone are considered undesirable. For instance, warm colors in apparel worn by a person with cool body undertones will contrast and create the impression of a more blueish skin tone. Rather, a blended effect between similar undertones will de-emphasize the undesirable blue or yellow undertones in body coloring. Use hue, value, intensity, and undertone in Activity 12.5.

### Texture

Similarity and contrast also affect interactions between textures of the body and apparel. Contrasts will emphasize differences, pushing different textures to the extremes of smooth or coarse and shiny or matte. Similarity leads to the blending of all surfaces toward a similar degree of texture. For instance, similarly smooth and shiny textures in skin, hair, and apparel can reinforce each other, creating a unified whole as in Figure 12.10. Contrasts between skin, hair, and apparel can also be created. Contrasts perceived as pleasing emphasize the smoothness of the body through contrast with coarse apparel textures. Consider the texture in Figure 12.11. There is a similar coarseness of textures in the hair and the sweater. Together, these surfaces appear in contrast with the skin, making it appear smoother.

### Proportion

Perceived proportion of the body can be influenced by the placement of apparel forms on the body with attention to the outer shape of the silhouette, the direction and placement of inner lines due to garment parts, and surface prints or patterns. These layout and surface characteristics of apparel can be used to emphasize the ideal proportion or downplay prominent or exaggerated proportions.

**Outer shapes.** Emphasis on a body part can be created through bringing attention to and perhaps increasing the apparent size and shape of the body area through the outer shape or silhouette of the garment. Outer shapes may extend beyond the natural contours of the body, changing the apparent size and thus influencing proportional relationships. Puffed sleeves or padded shoulders could

**ACTIVITY 12.5**

Color of apparel can influence the perception of body coloring. Working in groups of three students, each person should find three to five figures in magazines or catalogs with different personal coloring and apparel. Try to find figures of approximately the same size and pose.

1. Cut out the figures from the backgrounds. Cut the heads off the photos and paste them onto a blank piece of paper (white or cream color). Note which head was originally wearing each outfit.
2. Try the different outfits together with each of the different heads. Compare the effects of different color ensembles on the appearance of the models.
3. Did certain outfits look better with the different model's faces?
4. What interactions of model and apparel coloring looked best? Worst? Why?

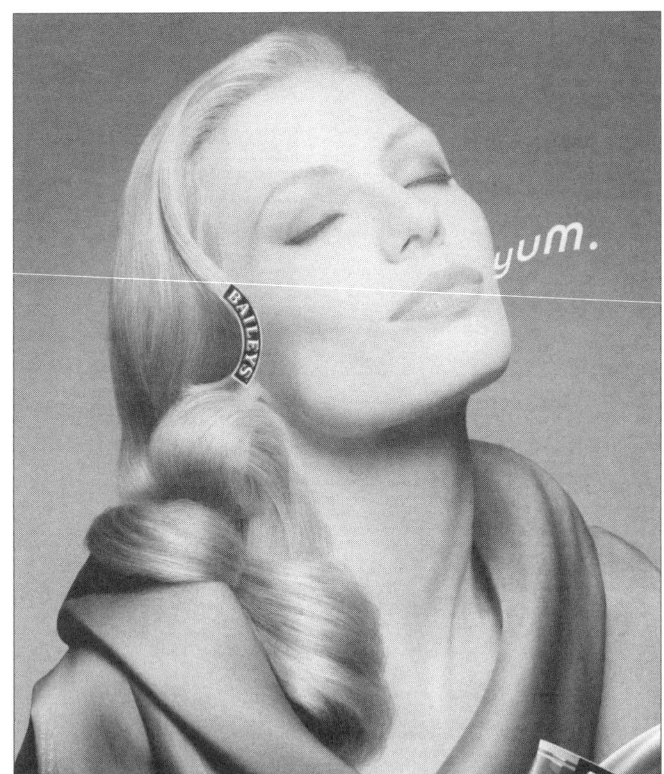


Figure 12.10. (right) Similar textures in hair, skin, and apparel create a unified whole.

Figure 12.11. (below) Contrast between hair and sweater textures with the skin emphasizes the smoothness of the skin.

| **TABLE 12.2** | Techniques for Enhancing Body Proportions. | |
|---|---|---|
| | *Designator* | *Balancing Techniques* |
| *Front View Width* | A | Emphasize upper body or enlarge shoulder width |
| | V | Emphasize lower body or enlarge hip width |
| | X | Accentuate small waist |
| | H | De-emphasize waist, emphasize upper or lower torso |
| | O | De-emphasize waist, emphasize upper or lower torso |
| *Side View Width* | i | increase dimension of the bust area; create horizontal or curved lines at bust level |
| | r | reduce fullness at bust; create vertical lines down center front |
| | b, d | avoid emphasizing the difference between the waist and full hip or abdomen |
| *Front Length* | W | focus interest below the waist through fabric surface; divide the body with horizontal line below natural waist |
| | Y | focus interest above the waist; divide the body with lines above the waist |

provide an outer shape that is larger than the natural body shape in the shoulder area. Silhouette shapes discussed in Chapter 5 affect apparent proportion of the body. For example, A-line or bell silhouettes would increase perceived hip width, suitable for a V proportion. A wedge silhouette would emphasize shoulder width, but for an A proportion.

**Inner lines.** Inner lines created by layout details such as seams, hems, and collars or surfaces such as stripes or ordered prints can also be used to attract attention in specific areas of the body. The direction of inner lines changes the perceived proportional relationships of the body. For instance, a V-shaped yoke seam extending to the shoulder point can increase width of shoulders. Vertical lines lengthen and divide the body, adding height and decreasing the perceived width of an area. Horizontal lines shorten the body and add width. Curved lines add roundness and increase visual weight. Diagonal lines take on the property of either vertical or horizontal lines, depending on the angle of the diagonal.

**Surface.** The surface characteristics of the fabric can increase visual weight or focus in an area of the body through color, texture, or print. Weight is increased by (1) bright, warm, or light colors; (2) shiny, bulky, fuzzy, or coarse textures; and (3) bold, busy, or multi-dimensional prints. Visual weight can be increased in areas of the body that need to be emphasized or can be decreased to de-emphasize an area.

In order to balance proportions, the proportional width consistent with the ideal become a focus whereas a prominent or less-than-ideal proportional width

Figure 12.12. (left) Shoulder pads in the jacket raise and extend the shoulderline, balancing shoulder and hip widths.

Figure 12.13. (right) Ensemble adding width at the hip to balance shoulder width.

is de-emphasized by creating focus in an area opposite the undesirable feature. Table 12.2 lists techniques for enhancing the front view proportions.

For an A type figure, one should create the illusion of shoulder width. For instance, in Figure 12.12, the jacket layout with shoulder pads raises and widens the shoulderline bringing emphasis to the upper body and making shoulder width equal to that of the lower body. Vertical patterning in the skirt also help to decrease the apparent width of the hips.

The V type, with wide shoulders and narrower waist and hips is the ideal type for men. Women of this type would balance shoulder width by adding width or emphasis at the hip. The ensemble in Figure 12.13 would achieve this effect through the long, flared skirt and intricate surface detail, which brings attention to the lower torso. The horizontal line at the hip adds width while the vertical lines created by the fabric surface and fringe carry the eye away from the shoulder down through the form.

The X proportion is commonly thought of as the Western ideal for females. This type would want to emphasize this proportion by accentuating the small waist and emphasizing the contrast between waist width and shoulder and hip

Figure 12.14. (left) Wide shoulder and horizontal emphases contrast with narrow waist, highlighting the X figure.

Figure 12.15. (below) Color and pattern of surfaces bring emphasis to the upper and lower body and de-emphasize the waist for an H type.

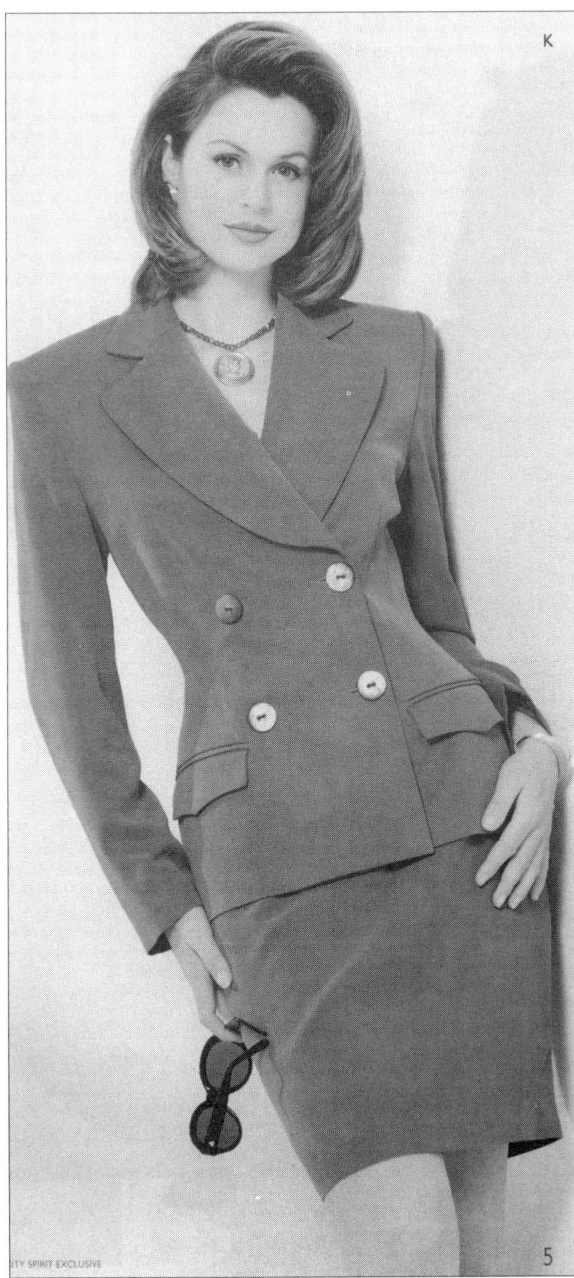

Figure 12.16. Jacket emphasizes shoulder and hip, balancing an H or O proportion.

**ACTIVITY 12.6** Practice applying different apparel ensembles to enhance the body and achieve the appearance of the ideal proportions.

1. For each frontal view proportion—A, V, X, H, and O—find two more examples of ensembles that emphasize or create the figure proportions.
2. Explain how each ensemble interacts with the body to achieve the desired effect.

widths. The directional lines created in the wide lapels and the padded shoulders in the suit in Figure 12.14 provide emphasis to the waist by contrast. The hip width is also emphasized through horizontal lines in the pockets, double-breasted closure, and hipline hem. The waist is emphasized through contrast with the wide shoulder- and hemlines.

The H body type and the O body types have waist widths equal to or larger than shoulders and hips. In these cases, the waist should not be emphasized through any waistline features such as belts. Emphasis on the upper and lower body should become the focus instead. In Figure 12.15, there are no lines that emphasize the waist area. The yellow color, interesting neckline detail, and the patterned lower garment create interest in the upper and lower body and the patterned buttons carry the eye in a vertical line. This example would be

Figure 12.17. (left) Fullness of the bust increased through diagonal lines and textural interest..

Figure 12.18. (right) Strong contrast in color creates vertical lines down the center front to bisect the area.

appropriate for an H body type. The O type could be similarly treated. In Figure 12.16, the natural waistline is concealed with a sweater and hip-length jacket. The oversized jacket with dropped shoulder seams adds width to the shoulders and skims the mid-torso. The horizontal line of the hem creates a focal point at the hipline, thus emphasizing top and bottom while de-emphasizing the waist.

For the i type, the addition of fullness will create the illusion of a fuller bustline. This fullness could be added through gathers or tucks above or below the bust, layering of fabrics, or the application of trims. The dress in Figure 12.17 would achieve the desired illusion through the layering of draped fabric and the creation of diagonal lines across the bust. The luxurious surface of the velour fabric also increases the visual weight of the figure.

Minimizing emphasis at the bustline would be the goal for an r type figure. This is achieved by avoiding horizontal or curved lines in the bust area and by creating vertical lines down center front to bisect and lead the eye away from the area. The color contrast and lines created by the jacket and blouse at the center front in Figure 12.18 achieves this effect.

Figure 12.19. This ensemble is effective in concealing a prominent abdomen.

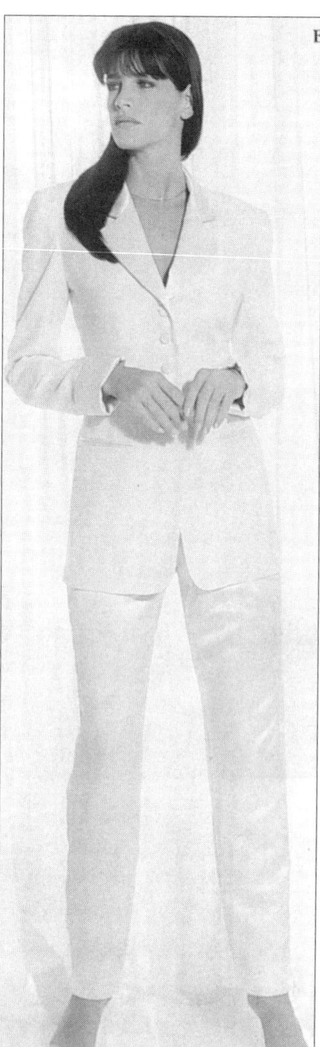

Figure 12.20. W proportion balanced by a low horizontal line and visual interest below the waist created by fabric surface.

Figure 12.21. Y proportion balanced by raising the waist and creating focus above the waist.

Both the b and d types have a prominent curve below the waist, in the front or back of the body. In order to conceal these body features, one should avoid emphasizing any contrast between the dimension of the waist and the hip. Cinched belts and skirts or pants fitting tightly through the hip would not be recommended. Instead, longer jackets, straight lines, and skirts or pants with some added fullness would conceal the roundness. The ensemble in Figure 12.19, conceals a prominent abdomen due to the loose flowing fabric and the surface design unrelated to body contours.

The W proportion type is short-waisted. In order to balance this proportion, an illusion needs to be created that divides the body into more balanced lengths, suggesting a lower waistline. This is achieved through creating a horizontal line below the natural waist and bringing visual focus to the lower torso, as in Figure 12.20. Adding visual weight to the upper torso will increase the short-waisted affect and should be avoided.

The Y proportion is the opposite of the W; the torso is long and legs appear short. This type can be balanced by raising the apparent waistline and directing visual focus to the upper torso. Figure 12.21 achieves this effect through the high waistline and upper body interest created by the detailing in the overalls. Shorter garment hems, creating lines just above the waist, are effective for a Y proportion. Try Activities 12.6 and 12.7.

## SUMMARY

The body consists of colors, textures, and proportions that are influenced by the formal qualities of apparel. Body coloring can be analyzed in terms of the value, intensity, and undertone in skin, hair, and eyes. Textures of skin and hair may vary between smooth and coarse, and between shiny and matte. The textures and colors of the body can be influenced by textures and colors of apparel and beauty care products. The influence of apparel occurs through perception of similarity and contrast effects.

The proportions of the body can be classified according relationships among body width and length measurements. Designators A, V, X, H, and O are used to specify types of proportional relationships created by the front width of shoulders, waist, and hips. The current ideal proportions for women and men in Western culture are X and V, respectively. Prominence of upper or lower body widths in side views are given designators i, r, b, and d. The propor-

### LAB ACTIVITY 12.1

In this activity, you will use the information you have collected in the chapter activities to make wardrobe selections appropriate for a client.

1. Collect your findings about a partner's personal coloring and proportions. (Intensity was determined in Activity 12.1, undertone in 12.2, skin and hair texture in 12.3, and proportions in 12.4.)
2. Using this information, develop a set of recommendations about wardrobe selection criteria for your partner. Include recommended colors, textures, silhouettes, and styling details (inner lines and surfaces) appropriate for the partner's personal characteristics.
3. Find three ensembles that exemplify the recommended wardrobe.
4. Develop a presentation board with these ensembles and background information about the client.
5. Describe how or why these wardrobe selections enhance the partner's attractiveness.

**ACTIVITY 12.7** Continue finding examples of balancing techniques.

1. For the types i, r, b, d, W, and Y, find two examples of ensembles that would balance or conceal the less-than-ideal proportion.
2. Explain how each ensemble interacts with the body to achieve the desired effect.

tional relationships between the length of the upper and lower torso and the leg are designated W or Y.

The apparent proportional relationships within the body can be altered through the placement of apparel forms on the body. This can be achieved through bringing visual focus to an ideal proportion or correct a proportion by creating a visual focus opposite the negative feature. The outer shapes, inner lines, and surface of apparel can be consciously manipulated to create these emphases.

## KEY TERMS AND CONCEPTS

A V X H O body proportions

balancing techniques

color consulting

color intensity of the body

color values of the body

color value contrast of body

ideal texture in Western culture

inner lines

interactions between apparel and body to enhance appearance

outer shapes

perceiving the apparel body form

surface

technology aided image analysis

texture of body

undertone of body

visual continua of skin or hair texture

## READING 12.1
# Aesthetics and Body Image

Nancy A. Rudd

We cannot overlook the importance of the body in our daily presentation of self through our appearance. The body is a major component of appearance, and in Western culture, is often the source of great dissatisfaction. This dissatisfaction may prompt us to devote extensive time, effort, and money to altering the body, either temporarily or permanently, in the name of achieving some aesthetic ideal. These aesthetic ideals are culturally determined guidelines of beauty; they are narrowly defined and arbitrary, yet they serve as the standard against which many of us measure our appearance. *Body image* refers to the mental image we hold of our bodies, both perceptually and emotionally (Fallon, 1990).

The Western standard of ideal beauty in the late 20th Century may be described as one of thinness, attractiveness, and fitness (Cash et al., 1986; Freedman, 1986). These expectations may be more critical for women than for men, primarily due to the historically traditional definition of the female gender role as one of beauty. However, current research shows that body size and weight are considered by women to be the most important aspects of their physical attractiveness (Cash, 1989); about 75 percent of American women are dissatisfied with their bodies (Cash et al, 1986). Furthermore, women are more likely than men to be defined by their aesthetic value, and more likely to be defined by aesthetic value than other social or personal values (Freedman, 1986; Hatfield & Sprecher, 1986).

Satisfaction with our bodies contributes to overall self-esteem (Lennon & Rudd, 1994; Streigel-Moore, Silberstein & Rodin, 1986). We employ *social comparison* in our evaluations of personal attractiveness, which means we compare our appearance to media images of others or to real people and come to some evaluation of where we stand. If we believe we are more attractive, self-esteem increases; if we believe we are less attractive, self-esteem decreases. Because of this importance of the body to Americans, many industries exist to help us modify our appearance through weight loss, exercise and weight training, cosmetics and cosmetic surgery in order to come closer to meeting the cultural norm.

Rudd & Lennon (1994) explained how social comparison operates as individuals construct their appearances in relation to the cultural ideal and then assess their personal aesthetic value. The cultural ideal is perpetuated through media images such as beauty pageants, supermodels, film and television stars, and beauty advertisements, yet it excludes many body types, textures, colors, and other typical "packaging" that humans come in. Each person internalizes this ideal differently. However, we are bombarded with messages that we can achieve these narrow standards of beauty by simply trying hard to achieve them. Thus, many people come to believe that with enough time, effort, and willpower, we can shape the body into nearly any desired shape. We learn to engage in appearance management behaviors that we believe, or that others believe, will enhance our attractiveness and bring us close to the cultural norm. These behaviors may include food monitoring (from counting fat grams to anorexia or bulimia), exercise (mild to obsessive), body shaping (from wearing control-top pantyhose to surgical implants), body coloring (from cosmetics, hair dye, and tanning to permanent tattooing of lip color or eye liner), body texturing (from shaving to dermabrasion), grooming (cleaning, styling, odorizing, and deodorizing), and apparel and accessory selection.

Once we construct our appearance, we gauge how others respond to it and come to some conclusion about our relative aesthetic value. If we believe we approximate the ideal and think others respond well, our self-esteem tends to increase. If we believe we do not come close or if we think others do not respond well, we may develop strategies for dealing with these negative evaluations. Some strategies are more positive than others (i.e., modifying our personal standard to be more accepting and less critical), and some strategies could lead to hazardous behaviors and lowered self-esteem (i.e., accepting the dominant standard and trying harder to reach it, through disordered eating, obsessive exercise, or abuse of substances such as diet aids, laxatives, diuretics, and steroids).

Reading 12.1 Rudd, N. A. (1995). Aesthetics and Body Image. Written by Rudd for this textbook.

Adolescents often struggle the hardest with body image concerns, not only because their bodies undergo dramatic change in physical attributes, but also because physical appearance plays a key role in establishing relationships and in developing independence. Peer pressure can be a motivating force in sanctioning appearance standards and in reinforcing both routine and hazardous appearance behaviors. Dieting behavior often begins in early adolescence or even in preadolescence, as does onset of disordered eating (Moore, 1993). Dieting behavior is more common among girls than boys; one study reported that 63 percent of high school girls and 16 percent of high school boys were currently dieting (Rosen & Gross, 1987). During puberty, weight gain for girls is based on fat gain in breasts, thighs, hips, and buttocks, but for boys it is based on muscle gain; thus, as boys mature, they come closer to the cultural ideal, while girls deviate more from the ideal. Other factors contributing to body image concerns and predisposition toward hazardous body modifications include the American world view of controlling one's destiny (including appearance), sports participation, teasing by others, dieting history, and traditional gender role ideology.

Because body image dissatisfaction and related hazardous behaviors are so prevalent, there are many stakeholders who could play important roles in changing popular opinion about ideals of beauty. Among these groups are advertising agencies, manufacturers of beauty products, and publishers of fashion magazines who could offer more diverse images of beauty. Apparel professions could affect change in the present culturally restrictive images that influence both children and adults to engage in behaviors that may compromise health and well-being.

### References


Cash, T. F. (1989). Body-image affect: Gestalt versus summing the parts. *Perceptual and Motor Skills, 69,* 17–18.

Cash, T. F., Winstead, B. A. & Janda, L. H. (1986, April). The great American shape-up. *Psychology Today,* pp. 30–37.

Fallon, A. (1990). Culture in the mirror: Sociocultural determinants of body image. In T. F. Cash and T. Pruzinsky (Eds.), *Body images: Development, deviance, and change* (pp. 80–109). New York: The Guilford Press.

Freedman, R. J. (1986). *Beauty bound.* Lexington: Lexington Books.

Hatfield, E. & Sprecher, S. (1986). *Mirror mirror: The importance of looks in everyday life.* Albany: State University of New York Press.

Lennon, S. J., & Rudd, N. A. (1994). Linkages between attitudes toward gender roles, body satisfaction, self-esteem, and appearance management behaviors in women. *Family and Consumer Sciences Research Journal, 23,* 94–117.

Moore, D. (1993). Body image and eating behavior in adolescents. *Journal of the American College of Nutrition, 12*(5), 505–510.

Rosen, J. & Gross, J. (1987). Prevalence of weight reducing and weight gaining in adolescent girls and boys. *Health Psychology, 6* (2), 131–147.

Rudd, N. A. & Lennon, S. (1994). Aesthetics of the body and social identity theory. In M. DeLong and A.M. Fiore (Eds.), *Aesthetics of textiles and clothing: Advancing multidisciplinary perspectives* (pp. 163–175). Monument, CO: International Textiles & Apparel Association.

Striegel-Moore, R., Silberstein, L. & Rodin, J. (1986). Toward an understanding of risk factors for bulimia. *American Psychologist, 41,* 246–263.


## READING 12.2
## Computer-designed Swimwear

Reading 12.2 Computer-designed Swimwear. (1991, September-October). *The Futurist,* p. 6.

Computers are now coming to the aid of sun worshipers who dread the annual trial of trying on swimsuits. A manufacturer in Ellicott City, Maryland, offers the latest fashions, designed to enhance an individual's best features and downplay the "not-so-best." The company, Suited for Sun, uses computer and video technology to measure up to 28 different vital body statistics; specially trained designers assist clients in selecting the ideal combination of styles and colors for a custom-made suit that complements their unique shapes.

CHAPTER 13

# Abstracting Across Products Within Collections

### Objectives

- Identify aesthetic similarities among apparel products
- Recognize aesthetic similarities within French, Italian, U.S., and Japanese apparel designs
- Differentiate among various designers' aesthetics

You have just been given a list of gift ideas for a sibling's birthday. One of the items on the list is "shirt." There are a myriad of possibilities of shirt styles there are camp shirts, Hawaiian shirts, woven shirts, baseball shirts, T-shirts, and dress shirts. Shirts also come in an array of shapes, sizes, prints, colors, and textures. How do you select a shirt that your sibling would like? You could buy a shirt that *you* like and, after a while of the shirt hanging unworn in the closet, justify using the shirt yourself because your sibling isn't going to use it. At that point your sibling is probably glad to get rid of the hideous shirt taking up valuable closet space. A more considerate gift-giving strategy would be to analyze the aesthetic of the relative and purchase a shirt that reflects that aesthetic. To analyze the aesthetic, you could examine the similarity of aesthetic characteristics of shirts in your sibling's closet next time you're in there to "borrow" something. Analyzing the similarities of your sibling's clothing is an example of abstracting across products.

## ABSTRACTING ACROSS PRODUCTS

**Abstracting** across products within a collection means identifying the underlying similarities (or transitions) of the products. The result is a general description of the aesthetic similarities (or differences) of a majority of the forms. Abstracting across products is a skill required by many apparel professionals. Designers and product developers abstract across garments within a collection to ensure new designs reflect the established aesthetic. Wholesale sales representatives abstract across a product line to communicate the new aesthetic to the store buyer. Fashion journalists may also summarize broader aesthetic trends by abstracting across the work of many designers for the new season. Likewise, forecasters summarize broad trends by abstracting across past seasons and the present season to predict trends for the future. Marketing specialists and buyers may abstract across products that sell well or not sell well to determine consumer preferences or to identify styles to develop into private label merchandise. Sales consultants may abstract across a client's wardrobe to better predict the client's liking for new stock items. In this chapter we will abstract across products within designers' collections across the seasons. This is done to illustrate the process of abstracting and to also provide insight into the aesthetics of different designers.

The designers presented in this chapter have had a major influence on the fashion industry. However, they represent only a few of the designers with whom you should become familiar. There are valuable resource books (e.g., Stegemeyer, 1995) for those who are interested in biographical information on many influential designers of the fashion industry. We also suggest that you cultivate your ability to recognize the aesthetics of different designers by trying to identify the designer of the styles seen in publications such as *Harper's Bazaar* and *Women's Wear Daily*, in the stores, or on the streets. We are cognizant of the creative contributions of designers from many countries, including Great Britain and Spain, but we do not have space to discuss individual designers from all countries.

## AESTHETIC SIMILARITIES WITHIN FRENCH, ITALIAN, U.S., AND JAPANESE DESIGNERS

### French and Italian Designers

French (Paris) and Italian designers are at the center of production of the finest materials and are supported by a steady supply of the best craft persons. This results in products that are markedly different from the products of American designers. French and Italian designers many times use more exquisite, custom fabrics. Many designers have long-standing relationships with the fine fabric houses of Europe and develop custom fabrics for use in their apparel collections. The highly skilled craft persons allow designers to produce apparel consisting of fine handwork and fit.

Paris designs are known for their complex layout and surface designs with three-dimensional shape accentuated within the garment. Frequently, these garments closely contour the body shape, facilitated by traditional tailoring methods (inner fabric layers and stitching for structure). Handwork (e.g., beading) is common. More intense and contrasting colors are found within Paris designs, as compared to Italian designs. Italian designers, by comparison, tend to use less intense colors, blended color combinations, and thicker yet supple fabrics. Italian designers make use of the fine leathers and suedes of their country. Fabrics with a supple

Figure 13.1. (left) Italian design with a softer, look. Giorgio Armani, 1996.

Figure 13.2. (right) French design with a sharper fitted shape—a more geometric edge. Strelli, 1995.

hand, a looser fit, and unconstructed tailoring result in more organic Italian designs, whereas Paris designs have a sharper, geometric edge (Figures 13.1 and 13.2). The Italian design aesthetic is increasing in favor among Paris consumers and will likely influence Paris design (see Reading 13.1).

## U.S. Designers

U.S. designers are noted as masters of comfortable, more casual, and functional apparel products. U.S. designers are the leaders in sportswear design. The styles of these designers reflect the need of U.S. consumers for apparel that accommodates their busy professional and recreation filled lives. The impeccable tailoring of many European designs is replaced by a more relaxed, softer construction.

Figure 13.3 (left) Issey Miyake blends functionality with creative expression.

Figure 13.4. (right) Japanese designer, Yohgi Yamamoto, wraps and ties apparel around the body.

Navajo, grunge, and the country/western looks are a few influences percolating from groups within the United States that have affected these designers.

## Japanese Designers

The Japanese designers discussed here work in Paris, but also sell in Japan. The styles of some Japanese designers are frequently more experimental and classified as wearable art. In **wearable art** the wearer is only the carrier of the creative design. The functional needs or beauty of the wearer may be blended with or be secondary to the creative expression. The voluminous shapes of a Issey Miyake design (Figure 13.3) may not be functional for one's lifestyle; how do you close the car door without catching the garment? In addition, the symbolic qualities of the product may be more important than formal aspects. Clothing may become a metaphor for the designer's view of the world. For instance, Rei Kawakubo's torn, layered, "poor" look during the mid-1980s was to communicate the aesthetic philosophy of Zen (Koda, 1985).

Japanese designers blend their aesthetic heritage with their training in Western traditions. These designers are not stifled by the construction traditions of Western apparel where fabric is cut and sewn into shapes that contour the body. For instance, fabrics may be wrapped and tied around the body (Figure 13.4), resembling the application of a traditional Japanese kimono and obi, to give shape to the garment. Pattern pieces are looked at with a fresh eye; collars may transform into shawls, or hems and seams may be left unfinished. Japanese designers have a penchant or fondness for subdued color palettes. Texture adds interest and complexity to many of their designs.

Table 13.1 provides the underlying similarities of aesthetic for French, Italian, United States, and Japanese designers. When we could not identify an underlying similarity for a design element, we used a dashed line following the element.

## AESTHETICS OF FRENCH DESIGNERS' COLLECTIONS

The following pages outline the aesthetic of individual designers. We looked for general similarities within collections across the past seasons to identify the underlying aesthetic of the designer. Some elements of surface and layout vary widely across the seasons, limiting the elements that describe the underlying aesthetic of the designer. The aesthetics of French designers are discussed first.

**TABLE 13.1** Comparative aesthetics of French, Italian, U.S., and Japanese designers

| | French | Italian | U.S. | Japanese |
|---|---|---|---|---|
| **Surface** | | | | |
| Color | higher intensity | muted, warm | — | subdued, cool |
| Texture | thinner, flat | thick, more interest | less interest | unusual, mixed |
| Line or Shape | determinate | indeterminate | — | — |
| **Layout** | | | | |
| Line | harder edged | softer edged | softer edged | — |
| Shape | geometric | organic | softened geometric | complex, organic |
| **Integration of Surface & Layout** | surface emphasizes parts | blended parts | blended parts | blended parts |
| **Other Features** | fitted, contours body | looser fit | looser fit | looser fit, intricate cuts |
| | fine tailoring | more draping | sportswear | wearable art |

Figure 13.5 Yves Saint Laurent, 1991.

Figure 13.6 Yves Saint Laurent, 1993.

## YVES SAINT LAURENT

Saint Laurent started designing for Christian Dior in 1957. In 1962, he opened his own couture house (Stegemeyer, 1996). His designs over the years have maintained their sense of geometry from fine tailoring.

*Surface*

- Color—high intensity used with neutrals; contrast, black
- Texture—thin, smooth; e.g., worsted wools
- Line or Shape—variety of bold prints

*Layout*

- Line—hard, thin
- Shape—geometric
- Integration of Surface and Layout—different surfaces used to create part relationship
- Other Features—fine tailoring, beading; follows contours of the body

Figure 13.7 Claude Montana, 1993.

Figure 13.8 Claude Montana, 1993.

## CLAUDE MONTANA

Claude Montana is similar to Saint Laurent in the use of contrasting color and thin fabrics. Montana, however, exaggerates the shapes of layout and has a penchant for black and white rather than high intensity color.

*Surface*

- Color—high value contrast; black and/or white
- Texture—thin, smooth, and resilient
- Line or Shape—little use of print or woven surface design

*Layout*

- Line—thin
- Shape—exaggeration of shapes; often pointed or angular details
- Integration of Surface and Layout—focus on layout aided by simple, crisp surfaces

Figure 13.9. Karl Lagerfeld, 1993.

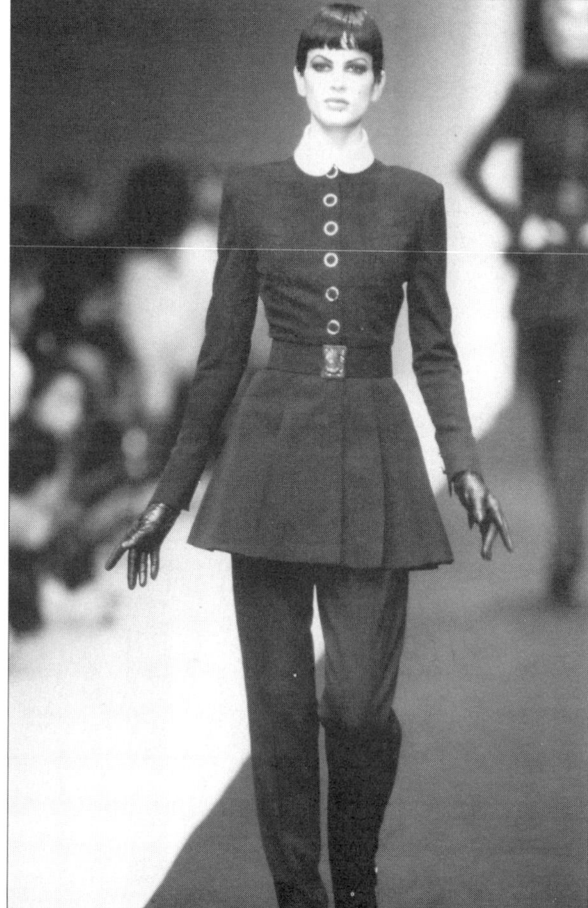

Figure 13.10. Karl Lagerfeld, 1994.

## KARL LAGERFELD

Karl Lagerfeld is a prolific designer who has designed for a number of top European fashion houses including Patou, Chloë, Fendi, and Chanel. He designs his own collection, which we will describe here. His aesthetic is similar to Montana's in the use of black and white, and the use of thin, simple surfaces that emphasizes layout over surface. A closer body contouring differentiates Lagerfeld's aesthetic from that of Montana.

Figure 13.11. Chanel suit and accessories designed by Lagerfeld, 1992.

*Surface*

- Color—high value contrast; black and white
- Texture—thin and resilient
- Line or Shape—little use of print or woven surface design

*Layout*

- Line—thin; few curvilinear inner lines
- Shape—flat, but emphasizes an X-shape silhouette
- Integration of Surface and Layout—focus on layout aided by simple, soft surfaces
- Other Features—details (e.g., button and buckle) create focus and are placed symmetrically; models have high value contrast skin and hair

Karl Lagerfeld has designed for Chanel since 1984 (Stegemeyer, 1996). Even though he has designed a number of collections simultaneously, his Lagerfeld collection is very different from the Chanel collection. He has invigorated the trademark "Chanel suit" and costume jewelry. The Chanel suit consisted of a boxy collarless jacket and straight skirt made from soft jersey or tweed fabric and often trimmed with braid. Long pearl and gold chain necklaces or belts accompany the suit (Figure 13.11).

Figure 13.12. Emanuel Ungaro, 1993.

Figure 13.13. Emanuel Ungaro, 1994.

## EMANUEL UNGARO

In comparison with Paris designers discussed thus far, Ungaro has the softest, most complex aesthetic. Prints, particularly floral prints, are combined with complex layouts produced by draping onto the dress form. Shirring with supple fabrics adds to the softness.

*Surface*

- Color—multi-colored prints with intense colors
- Texture—soft, drapable
- Line or Shape—organic prints (e.g., florals)

*Layout*

- Line—curvilinear from shirring, seaming, and draping
- Shape—accentuates roundness
- Integration of Surface and Layout—various prints combined to create parts

Figure 13.14. Christian Lacroix, 1992.

Figure 13.15. Christian Lacroix, 1994.

## CHRISTIAN LACROIX

Lacroix has a post modern flavor to his designs. He draws heavily upon cultural and historical influences, mixes surfaces in unusual ways, and exaggerates shapes to the point that only the most fashion forward women would feel comfortable in his designs. His work has a feminine feel, similar to Ungaro, but Lacroix's shapes can be much more elaborate and his historical inspiration is more literal or apparent.

*Surface*

- Color—multi-colored prints or wovens
- Texture—varies within the same garment
- Line or Shape—large shapes in prints or wovens

*Layout*

- Line—complex, many
- Shape—exaggerated shapes, unrelated to the body
- Integration of Surface and Layout—mixes surfaces to create parts

**ACTIVITY 13.1** Examine the five Figures (13.16-13.20) and determine which is the work of the five Paris designers discussed in the chapter. Give the aesthetic cues used to identify the design as the work of the particular designer. For instance, do you see the similarity between the size of the print used in the design and the provided description of the designer's aesthetic?

*Saint Laurent*

1______________________________

2______________________________

3______________________________

4______________________________

*Montana*

1______________________________

2______________________________

3______________________________

4______________________________

*Lagerfeld*

1______________________________

2______________________________

3______________________________

4______________________________

*Ungaro*

1______________________________

2______________________________

3______________________________

4______________________________

*Lacroix*

1______________________________

2______________________________

3______________________________

4______________________________

The answers are found after the summary of this chapter, but don't start flipping pages until you have made an honest effort to answer the questions above. This activity is to give you practice at identifying the designer's aesthetic; you are graded for your effort not for coming up with the correct answer.

Figure 13.16.

Figure 13.17.

Figure 13.18.

Figure 13.19.

Figure 13.20.

## AESTHETICS OF ITALIAN DESIGNERS' COLLECTIONS

Many of the Italian design houses are located in Milan. The Italian designers we will discuss are Mario Valentino (not to be confused with the designer who just goes by "Valentino"), Fendi, Giorgio Armani, Missoni, and Versace.

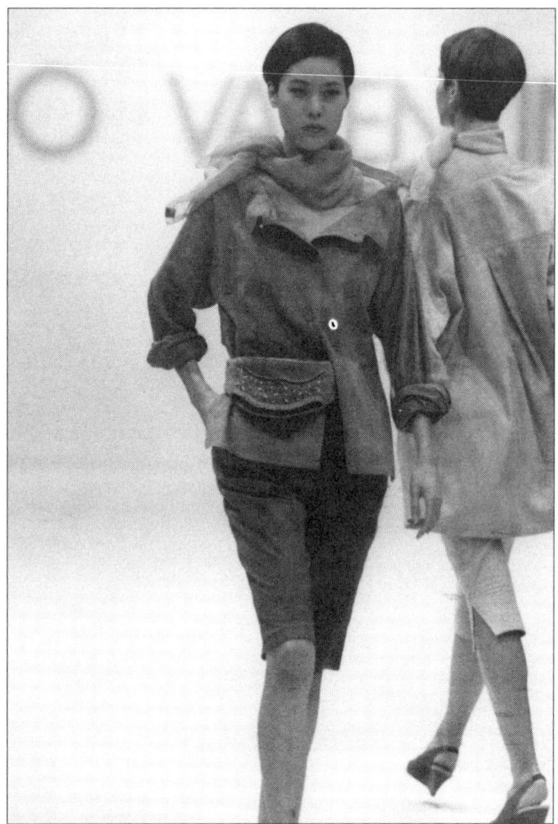

Figure 13.21. Mario Valentino, 1985.

Figure 13.22. Mario Valentino, 1989.

### MARIO VALENTINO

Mario Valentino is known for his leather. His work epitomizes the Italian aesthetic of thick, wonderfully supple leather, more organic shaped layout, and a more relaxed fit.

*Surface*

- Color—warm and rich or neutral
- Texture—thick, supple (e.g., leathers and suedes)
- Line or Shape—organic from animal skin patterns

*Layout*

- Line—soft from draped suede
- Shape—exaggerated, softened geometric or organic
- Integration of Surface and Layout—mixed textures to create parts
- Other Features—not body contouring on top

Figure 13.23. Fendi, 1992.

Figure 13.23. Fendi, 1993.

## FENDI

Fendi is run by the five Fendi sisters, but Karl Lagerfeld has recently been responsible for much of the design. As Mario Valentino is known for leathers, Fendi is known for fur. The aesthetic of Fendi and Mario Valentino is similar with plush textures, softened drape, and warm or neutral color palette.

*Surface*

- Color—warm and rich or neutral
- Texture—thick, supple (e.g. furs)
- Line or Shape—soft lines created from joined pelts

*Layout*

- Line—soft
- Shape—softened geometric or organic, loosely contours body
- Integration of Surface and Layout—whole relationship
- Other Features—unusual pelts (e.g., squirrel) innovative construction techniques with fur

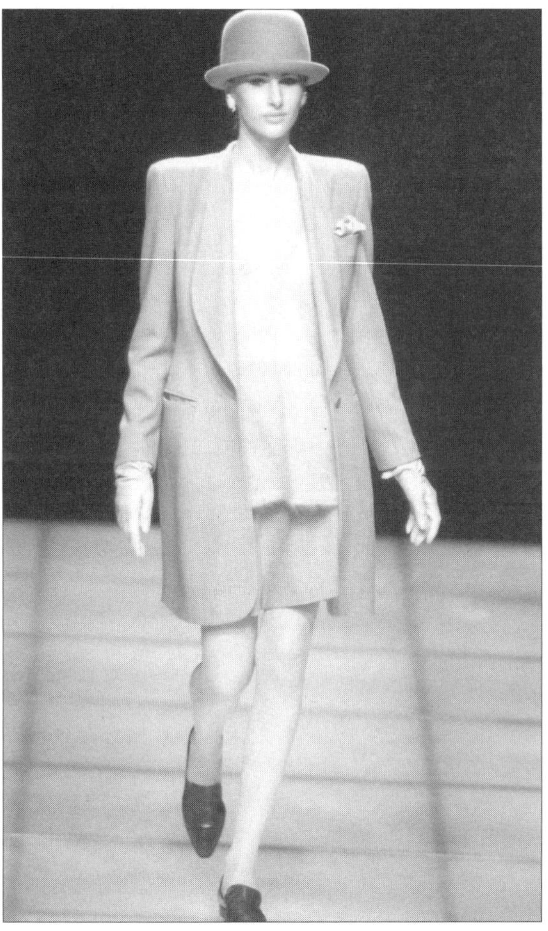

Figure 13.25. Giorgio Armani, 1992.

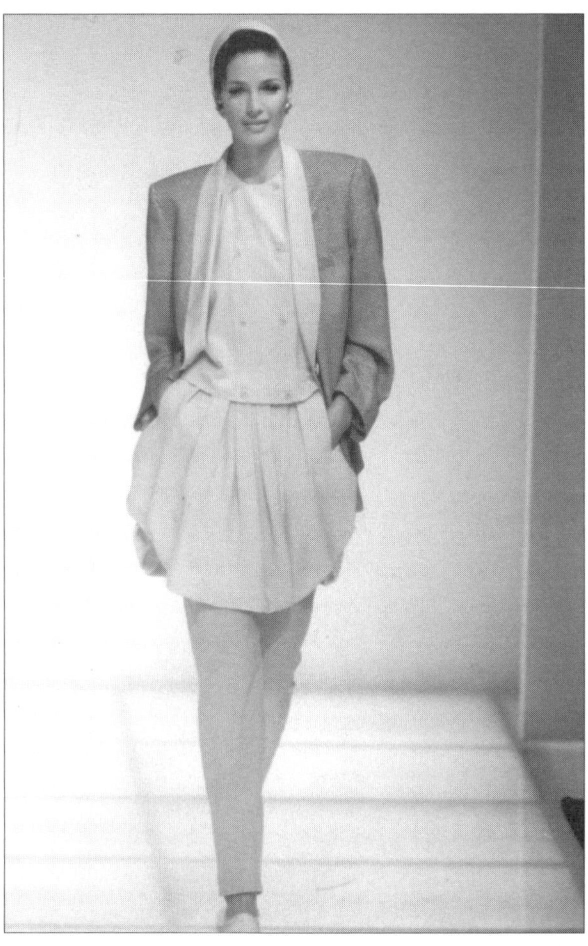

Figure 13.26. Giorgio Armani, 1993.

## GIORGIO ARMANI

Giorgio Armani started out in men's wear and was recognized for his unconstructed tailoring. This unconstructed tailoring and men's wear inspired fabrics (e.g., plaids and checks) have been applied to women's wear.

*Surface*

- Color—soft, lower intensity or neutral
- Texture—supple, soft, drapable
- Line or Shape—indeterminate linear wovens (e.g., plaids and checks), geometrics or florals

*Layout*

- Line—long, moderately curvilinear
- Shape—simple, softened geometric
- Integration of Surface and Layout—slight differentiation of parts; blending of parts

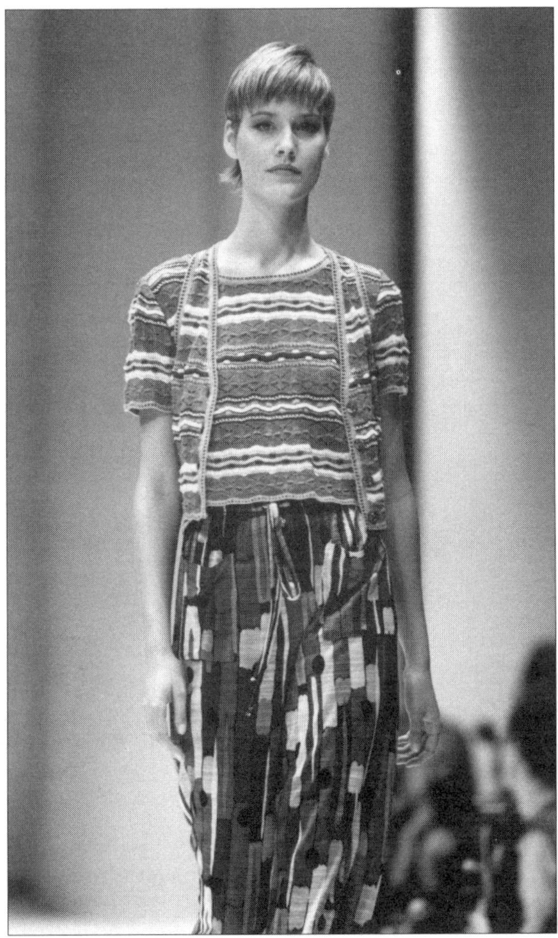

Figure 13.27. Missoni, 1994.

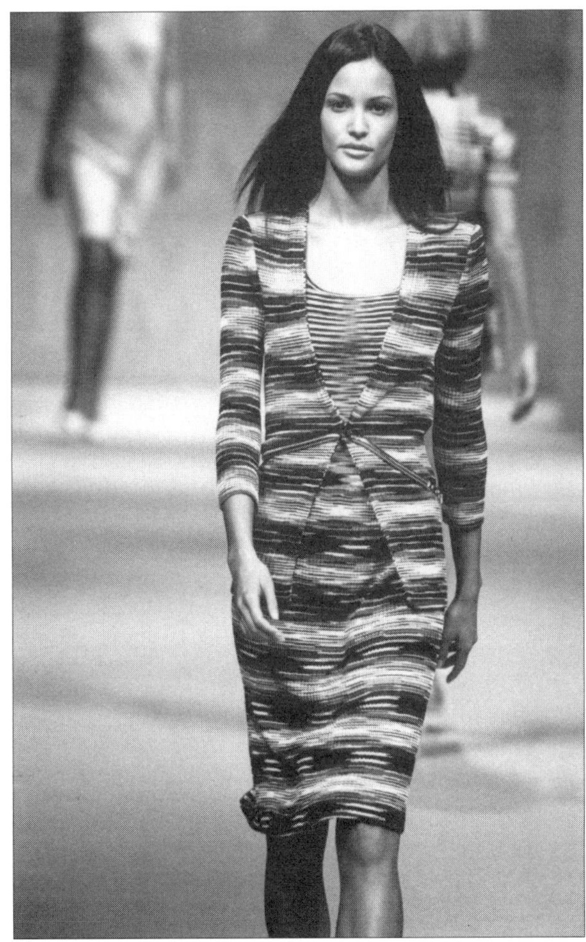

Figure 13.28. Missoni, 1996.

## MISSONI

A husband and wife team known for their complex knitted surface patterns. Softness and ease, the trademarks of Italian design, is accomplished in Missoni's designs through knit fabrics and a loose fit.

*Surface*

- Color—rich, multi-colored prints or knits
- Texture—soft, flexible
- Line or Shape—indeterminate, irregular pattern, random placement of shapes

*Layout*

- Line—simple, few
- Shape—softened geometric boxy
- Integration of Surface and Layout—simple layout to balance complexity from surface

Figure 13.29. Gianni Versace, 1992.

Figure 13.30. Gianni Versace, 1993.

## GIANNI VERSACE

Like the Paris designer Lacroix, Versace has a post modern flavor to his designs. His designs are youth oriented and popular among music and motion picture stars. His designs are a mixture of blatant sexuality and exaggerated detail.

*Surface*

- Color—neutral and intense colors
- Texture—
- Line or Shape—strong, large

*Layout*

- Line—curvilinear
- Shape—closely contour body, emphasizes X-shaped silhouette
- Integration of Surface and Layout—surface interest creates parts and accentuates shapes in clothing
- Other Features—use of decoration (e.g., beading, studding)

Figure 13.31.

Figure 13.32.

Figure 13.33

Figure 13.34.

Figure 13.35.

**ACTIVITY 13.2** Examine the five Figures (13.31–13.35) and determine which is the work of the five Italian designers discussed in the chapter. As in Activity 13.1, give the aesthetic cues used to identify the design as the work of the particular designs.

*Mario Valentino*

1____________________

2____________________

3____________________

4____________________

*Fendi*

1____________________

2____________________

3____________________

4____________________

*Giorgio Armani*

1____________________

2____________________

3____________________

4____________________

*Missoni*

1____________________

2____________________

3____________________

4____________________

*Gianni Versace*

1____________________

2____________________

3____________________

4____________________

Answers are again found after the summary of this chapter.

When the designer's aesthetic depends upon inspiration, an outlined description is not provided.

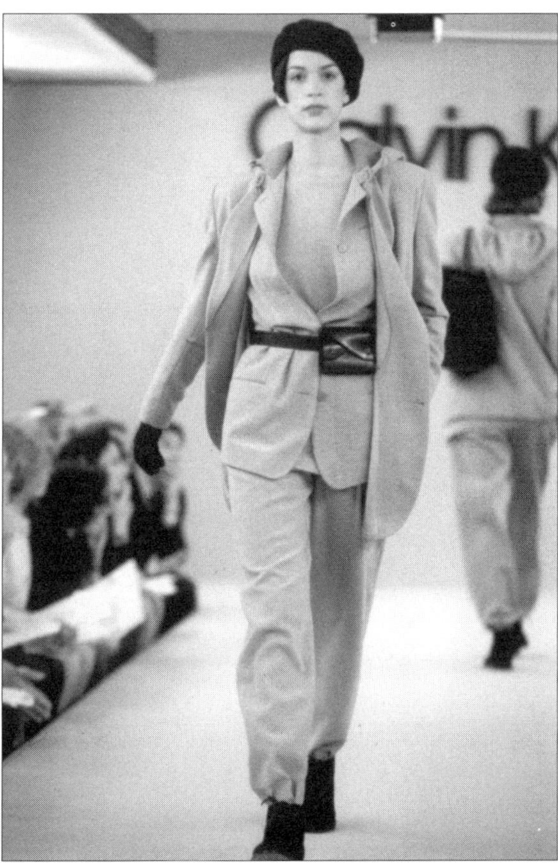

Figure 13.36. Calvin Klein, 1992.

Figure 13.37. Calvin Klein, 1995.

## CALVIN KLEIN

There is a similarity between the aesthetic of Calvin Klein and Giorgio Armani. Both produce simple layouts that skim the body made from neutral or low intensity colors and men's wear inspired fabrics. Klein's silhouettes are more geometric and the fabrics used have a firmer hand and less surface interest. Klein frequently works with solid fabrics.

*Surface*

- Color—lower intensity or neutral
- Texture—soft, yet firm hand
- Line or Shape—simple linear prints or wovens

*Layout*

- Line—long, straight, or slightly curvilinear
- Shape—simple, softened geometric, rectangular silhouette
- Integration of Surface and Layout—blending of parts, simple surface and layout

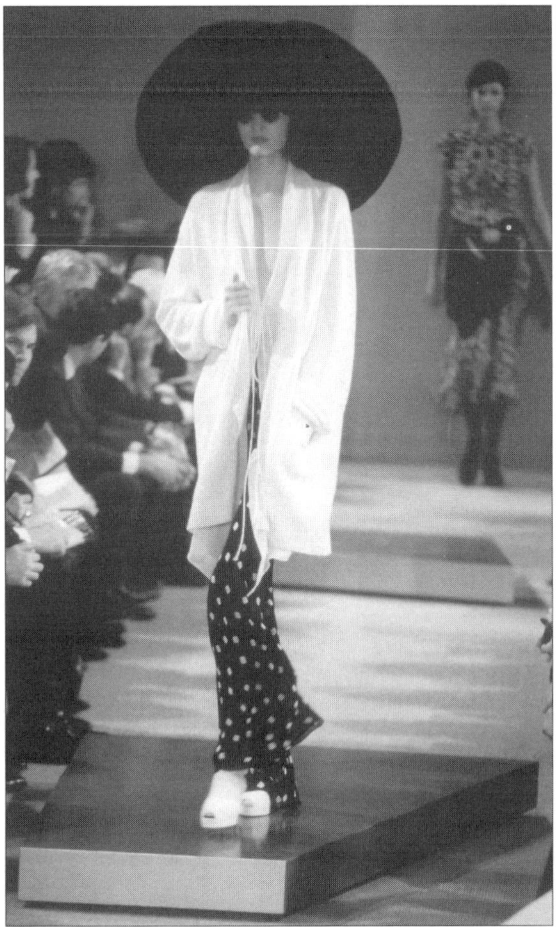

Figure 13.38. Donna Karan, 1993.

Figure 13.39. Donna Karan, 1994.

## DONNA KARAN

Both Donna Karan and Calvin Klein use neutral colors, solid fabrics, and simple layouts. Karan produces softer, more diagonal, curved lines in her designs and a more body-contouring fit. Jersey knit is a more commonly used fabric for Karan than Klein.

*Surface*

- Color—lower intensity or neutral, monochromatic
- Texture—soft, drapable
- Line or Shape—little use of print or woven surface design

*Layout*

- Line—diagonal (e.g., from radiating pleats), curvilinear
- Shape—simple, softened geometric, X-shaped silhouette
- Integration of Surface and Layout—blending of parts, simple surface and layout
- Other Features—simple accessories or closures to create focus

Figure 13.40. Ralph Lauren, 1990.

Figure 13.41. Ralph Lauren, 1990.

## RALPH LAUREN

It is difficult to identify the underlying formal similarities of Ralph Lauren's work. However, it is many times easy to spot a Ralph Lauren style because of his literal translation of inspiration. For instance, he has collections that contain clearly identifiable nautical, English gentry, or country/western influences. Because the aesthetic varies with the season's inspiration, an outlined description of the underlying aesthetic will not be provided. The focus is on symbolism of the form.

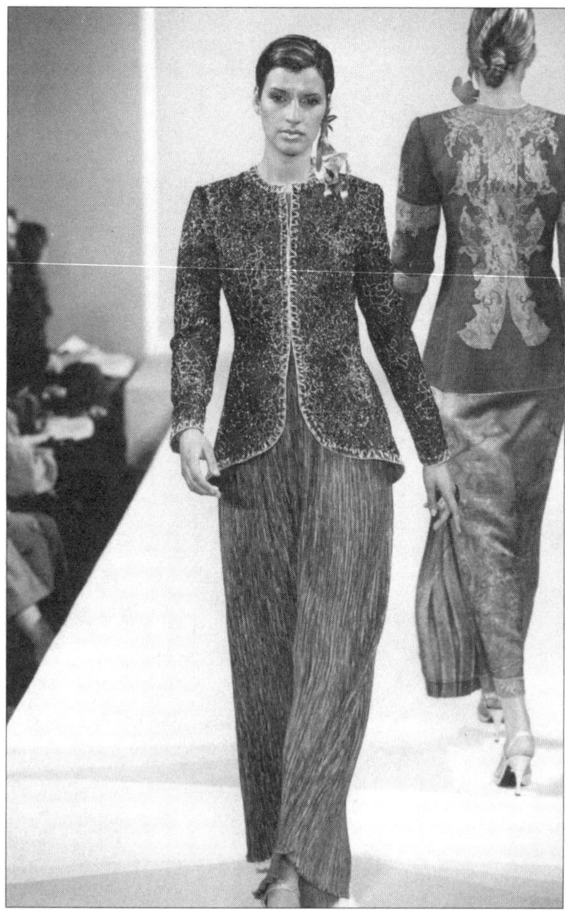

Figure 13.42. Mary McFadden, 1994.

Figure 13.43. Mary McFadden, 1995.

## MARY MCFADDEN

Mary McFadden, like Ralph Lauren, designs very close to the source of inspiration. McFadden's source of inspiration tends to be from farther back in history. The source of inspiration is generally used for the surface design while the layout is kept rather simple.

Along with her signature surface designs, McFadden is known for her pleated fabric.

*Surface*

- Color—multi-colored, intense colors
- Texture—reflective surfaces, drapable
- Line—indeterminate and small (e.g., from pleats or beads)
- Shape—indeterminate, ordered pattern

*Layout*

- Line—crisp or softened, curvilinear
- Shape—accentuates X-shaped silhouette
- Integration of Surface and Layout—mixed surface designs to create parts
- Other Features—surface design follows layout of garment piece

Figure 13.44. Anna Sui, 1992.

Figure 13.45. Anna Sui, 1992.

## ANNA SUI

Anna Sui's designs, like Lacroix and Versace, have a post modern flavor. Many of her collections have a vintage look crossed with a contemporary flair. Again, because her aesthetic depends upon her source of inspiration for the season, an underlying aesthetic description is not provided. If the garment looks like it has been pulled from a old chest in an attic and remade by someone from SoHo in New York City, then it resembles an Anna Sui design. The layout may vary but surface designs are usually complex, made from plush textures and prints.

**ACTIVITY 13.3** You probably know what we are going to suggest. Examine the five Figures (13.46–13.50) and determine which is the work of the five American designers discussed in the chapter. As in Activities 13.1 and 13.2, give the aesthetic cues for Klein, Karan, and McFadden or specific style details (e.g., gold buttons) for Lauren and Sui used to identify the design as the work of the particular designer.

*Calvin Klein*

1____________________

2____________________

3____________________

4____________________

*Donna Karan*

1____________________

2____________________

3____________________

4____________________

*Ralph Lauren*

*Mary McFadden*

1____________________

2____________________

3____________________

4____________________

*Anna Sui*

Answers are again found after the summary of this chapter.

Figure 13.46.

Figure 13.47.

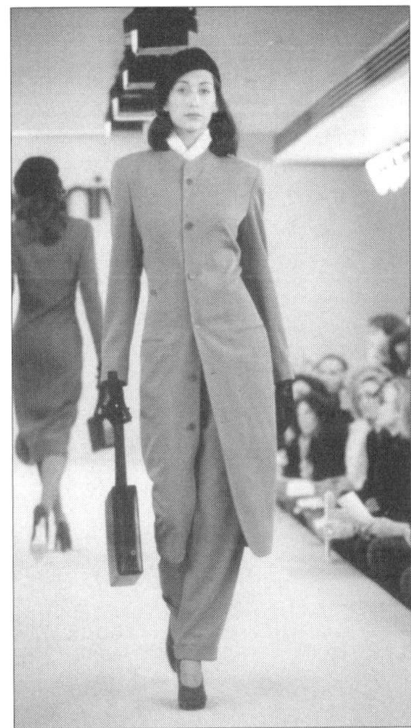

Figure 13.48.

Figure 13.49.

Figure 13.50.

**ACTIVITY 13.4** Collect two examples of any of the designers discussed in this chapter. Label the back with information of source title and issue, page number, and designer featured. Put all the photographs collected by the class on a table and number each photograph. Number lines on a piece of paper to coincide with the number of examples. Try to identify the designer of each work. Check your responses with the names on the back of the pages.

## SUMMARY

Abstracting across products is a skill required by many different apparel professionals. To abstract across products, the underlying similarities of the products are identified. The result is a general description of the aesthetic commonalities of a majority of the forms. Aesthetic similarities within designers' collections of France, Italy, United States, and Japan were discussed. In this chapter we also abstracted across products within a designer's collection across the seasons. We outlined the aesthetic of individual designers.

## ANSWERS FOR ACTIVITIES 13.1, 13.2, AND 13.3

### Activity 13.1

Figure 13.16. Christian Lacroix.
Figure 13.17. Emanuel Ungaro.
Figure 13.18. Claude Montana.
Figure 13.19. Karl Lagerfeld.
Figure 13.20. Yves Saint Laurent.

### Activity 13.2

Figure 13.31. Giorgio Armani.
Figure 13.32. Gianni Versace.
Figure 13.33. Mario Valentino.
Figure 13.34. Missoni.
Figure 13.35. Fendi.

### Activity 13.3

Figure 13.46. Anna Sui.
Figure 13.47. Donna Karan.
Figure 13.48. Calvin Klein.
Figure 13.49. Ralph Lauren.
Figure 13.50. Mary McFadden.

## LAB ACTIVITY 13.1

The underlying design aesthetic should be refined with passing seasons. The purpose of this activity is to practice abstracting across products. You will collect more recent examples of the designers work and revamp the aesthetic descriptions.

1. Divide into groups to cover all of the designers, except Lauren and Sui (these two do not have descriptions).
2. Once you have been assigned a designer, begin to collect examples of the designer's recent *Fall season* creations from trade publications such as *Women's Wear Daily* or fashion publications such as *Vogue or L'Official.* Gather at least four examples.
3. Label the back of the page with designer, year, publication title and issue, and page number of the publication.
4. As a group, analyze the new examples using the categories listed in the chapter (surface color, texture, line, or shape, etc.). Provide a written analysis of each example in chart form.
5. Abstract or summarize across the examples to come up with the underlying aesthetic, still using the categories provided. This could be a summary column in your chart.
6. Compare the aesthetic characteristics listed under the designer with your summarized aesthetic characteristics of the new examples.
7. Record the status of each characteristic in the chart; note if it should be changed or remain the same. For instance, under Mary McFadden the characteristic for surface shape is *indeterminate, ordered pattern.* If patterns are now determinate, state that a change is needed for the *surface shape* characteristic.
8. Develop a new chart for that designer. If a change is needed, then develop a new description for that characteristic. It might be best to distinguish the items that remain the same and the changes, e.g., with different colored inks or different fonts. This way the change(s) will be easily recognized.
9. Hand in the examples with your written analysis and new chart. You may be asked to develop a presentation board out of the new examples.

## KEY TERMS AND CONCEPTS

abstracting across products

aesthetic similarities within a designer's collection

aesthetic similarities within French designers

aesthetic similarities within Italian designers

aesthetic similarities within Japanese designers

aesthetic similarities within United States designers

comparative aesthetics among French, Italian, United States, and Japanese designers

how abstracting may be used by apparel professionals

wearable art

## SUGGESTED READINGS

Who's who in fashion (Stegemeyer; 1996) contains an impressive bibliography of books providing information about current and historic fashion and about individual designers. We suggest that you peruse the bibliography for the topic or designer in which you are specifically interested.

**READING 13.1**

# Parisians Accept a Style Lesson

A. Lobrano

Reading 13.1 Lobrano, A. (1992, October 3–4). Parisians Accept a Style Lesson. *International Herald Tribune,* p. 20.

Paris—Every so often an Italian or two crosses the Alps and surprises the French with a lesson in style—Leonardo da Vinci, for instance, whose multifaceted genius awed the French court; Marie de Medicis, wife of Henri IV, who vastly improved French cuisine; and more recently, a flock of Italian fashion designers and clothing manufacturers.

These latest arrivals, including Giorgio Armani and Franco Moschino, Dolce & Gabbana, MaxMara, and Genny, are increasingly winning the hearts and racks of Parisian retailers, who rejoice not only in the unflagging salability of Italian clothing during the current recession, but also report solid sales increases for their Italian labels. Some feel that this is perhaps because the Italians have a more accurate reading of the needs of contemporary women.

After years of phenomenal success in London, New York, and Los Angeles, Giorgio Armani is just now beginning to enjoy recognition from hard-sell Parisians, who are buying and wearing his clothing in large numbers. His popularity has been growing steadily ever since the lavish "debut" dinner he staged at the Musee Rodin in September 1989 for the city's beau monde and press community.

Much of what appeals to Parisian women about Armani's lines is characteristic of what Parisian retailers like about Italian clothing in general.

"The Italians produce very modern, practical clothing that especially appeals to the working woman," says Christine Ducani, owner of a boutique by the same name in the upscale Paris suburb of Neuilly. Ducani, whose best-selling label is Mani, one of Armani's more moderately priced labels, says that Mani sells well because "it's chic, elegant and *jamais de trop* [never too much], and it works perfectly around the clock."

Like many Parisian retailers, Ducani is a great fan of Italian fabrics and sees them as a major selling point.

"My clientele is very B.C.B.G. [*bon chic, bon genre,* the Parisian equivalent of American preppies or British Sloane Rangers] and they love the look and comfort of the supple fabrics the Italians do so well."

The reach-out-and-touch appeal of Italian fabrics is considered to be very important by Parisian department stores, too.

"We find that women are fascinated by Italian fabrics—they really notice the material—and that this sort of sensual response, the desire to touch something, makes this clothing easy to merchandise," says Agnes Vigneron, chief department manager for women's wear at Galeries Lafayette.

"Of course, along with fabrics, the other great strength of the Italians is their color sense. Their earth tones—beiges, greys, reds, and browns—make perfect backdrops for the accessory dressing that is today more than ever the key trend in Paris." Vigneron works closely with CFT, the huge Turin-based clothing manufacturer.

Asked why the Italians are faring so well during tough times in a city that has historically preferred its own designers, Vigneron said, "Women today don't want to be overwhelmed by their clothing—no one wants the dress to attract more attention than they do—and the Italians have a fine understanding of the aesthetic."

She also mentions what every other Paris retailer mentions—the fabrics, the colors, the simplicity of line in much of the clothing, the quality of the manufacture and the reliability of deliveries.

Putting all of this in perspective, the owner of a well-known Paris boutique, who does not wish to be named, commented on why sixty percent of his merchandise is of Italian design or manufacture.

"The quality of French ready-to-wear is generally rather poor, and this is after French industry has been trying for years to pull itself together. On top of this, the deliveries are frequently ragged and French-made clothing is often much too expensive in terms of the quality of the finish and the fabrics used in fabrication."

From a creative point of view, the French find the Italians interesting, too. During the crucial *rentree* season at the beginning of September when Parisians return to town from their August vacation, the leader-of-the-pack boutique Victoire featured Franco Moschino's Cheap and Chic lines and Dolce & Gabbana in its windows.

Francoise Chassagnac, owner of boutiques, says: "We buy slightly avant-garde clothing, and the Italians, such as Moschino, Dolce & Gabbana, Romeo Gigli, and Callaghan, are very strong in this niche right now. It's clothing that's different without being threatening."

For this season, Chassagnac is especially pleased with the new line of clothing from Loro Piana, the Italian cashmere house. "Their blazers and coats are delicious," she says, and then, commenting more broadly on the appeal of the Italians, "Simplicity is hard to find in France, and when you do find it here it's often overly intellectual, whereas in Italy it's sensual and soft and happy, and this is what I think we need right now."

Maria Luisa, of the Maria Luisa boutique in the rue Cambon, admires the Italians, but has dropped Moschino's Cheap and Chic because "my clientele would buy it once as a joke, but not a second time. I also have a suspicion that a lot of the people who buy this clothing don't even know that there's a joke going on."

She has also dropped Romeo Gigli—"His beautiful baroque mood just isn't in sync with the times anymore"—but is very enthusiastic about Costume Nationale by Ennio Capasa.

"Wild elegance is the style of this line, a black crepe dress, completely simple, worn with a leather jacket, for example," Maria Luisa said.

Doing a large business in Genny and Moschino, among other Italian designers, Parisian retail maestro Jacques Samson, the director of four Paris fashion boutiques including A La Ville du Puy and Light, said, "Look, it's simple. Their factories are superb, the quality is outstanding, and the fabrics are beyond compare. That's the real bottom line on Italy."

CHAPTER 14

# Fashion Trend Forecasting

## Objectives

- Understand the evolutionary nature of the product
- Identify the transition in aesthetic form of products over time
- Interpret the social context affecting the product
- Predict future preferences based upon transition of aesthetic form and social context

Think about the criteria you used in the decision to purchase a recent apparel product. Did the criteria include what you thought would be popular next year? Moving from consumer to apparel professional frequently requires a change in mind-set. What are consumers going to purchase *next year*?—is a central question for many apparel professionals. The answer to this question is facilitated by recognizing the transition of aesthetic form from the past through the present to the future. A consumer is also likely to think about the present and the past—"What do I want to wear now and how does it work with what I purchased in the past." However, seldom do consumers evaluate the transitional nature of the change in the product across time.

The present chapter stresses recognizing the *transition* (gradual change) in products over time. (Whereas Chapter 13 emphasized finding aesthetic *similarities* across products.) There is continuity in fashion change, where new fashions evolve from previously established fashions (Blumer, 1969). Recognizing the transition of the product can help predict the future direction of the aesthetic form. For instance, examination of the change in shoulder shape of suits from the early 1980s to the present shows that strong, angular, exaggerated shoulders were replaced by more unconstructed, softly rounded, exaggerated shoulders, then progressed to an even softer, less exaggerated slouching shape, only to begin to move back towards a slightly structured, angular, but natural sized

Figure 14.1. Transition in shoulder shapes of men's suits from 1980 to 1995. (a) strong, angular, exaggerated; (b) softer, exaggerated slouched shape; (c) unconstructed; (d) structured slightly extended angular, line.

The Fashion Association (a, b, d) and Dan Lecca / NYT Pictures (c).

a

b

c

d

shape (Figure 14.1). This transition suggests that future shoulder shapes might become more structured, angular, and slightly exaggerated.

As introduced in Chapter 4, the product is a reflection of the socio-cultural context. Thus, recognizing gradual change in aesthetic form and understanding the socio-cultural context go hand in hand when predicting or forecasting aesthetic characteristics of a future product. The change in shoulder shape, for example, should reflect the socio-cultural context. Social trends of less aggressive business strategies, slower business growth, and focus on a more balanced life between work and leisure are reflected in the relaxed dress codes for professional dress (e.g., casual Friday wear). This suggests that shoulder shapes will not take on the exaggerated proportions of the 1980s. Instead, the shoulders, while becoming more structured, will remain close to natural proportions.

Many apparel professionals will encounter forecasting as either producers of forecasts or as users of forecasts to make decisions regarding the product. The process of forecasting changes in the product is of major importance to developers and gatekeepers of textile and apparel products. It is common for it to take a year for a designer's sketch to become a garment on the store rack. Hence, developers such as designers and product developers must create product ideas that meet the consumer's future preferences. Textile manufacturers must work even farther ahead of the time the product reaches the consumer. Fabric manufacturers must determine colors and fabrications that will meet the desires of designers and, ultimately, the consumer. A primary skill of gatekeepers of the product, such as forecasters, stylists, fashion editors, and fashion directors, is predicting the future direction of the consumer preferences. Buyers use past sales figures and information about future trends to determine products and quantities to purchase for the upcoming season.

## NOVELTY AND CONSUMER ACCEPTANCE OF FASHION

As you remember from Chapter 8, **novelty** was defined as the perceived newness of the units and their organization, based upon comparison of the present form with forms of past experience. The **inverted-U relationship of pleasure** states that a medium level of novelty leads to a higher level of pleasure, than do low or high levels of novelty (Walker, 1981). High levels of novelty, forms that have little connection to past forms, may not be pleasurable because it is difficult to make sense out of the new form. The perceiver's brain doesn't have the mental structure in which to "fit" the new form if there is nothing like it in past experience.

The changing level of acceptance of a fashion by consumers and its relationship to novelty is seen in the diffusion of fashion across the categories of consumer adopters (Graph 14.1). Forms that have just been introduced commercially are novel to most consumers. The novel forms are accepted by a small portion of consumers. These early adopters (e.g., fashion innovators) of the form generally prefer higher levels of novelty. These wearers provide others the chance to repeatedly perceive the form, making the form less novel. The lowering of novelty leads to acceptance by a larger segment of consumers (mass mar-

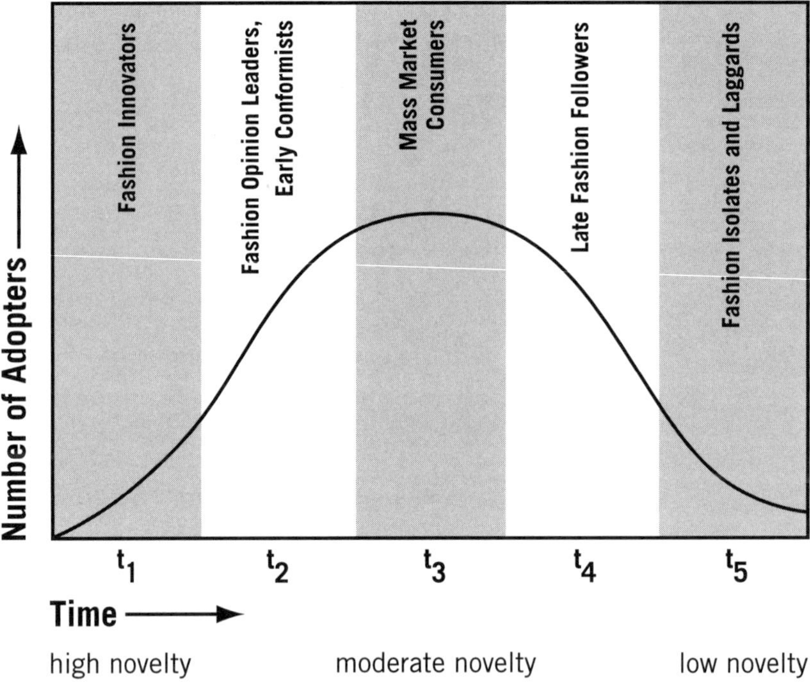


Graph 14.1. Category of consumer adopters from Sproles, G.B., and Burns L.D. (1989). *Changing appearances: Understanding appearances in contemporary society.* Fairchild Publications, p. 99 [with the addition of the high novelty, moderate novelty, and low novelty under t1, t3, and t5 respectively]

ket consumers). However, soon after this point it appears as if "everyone is wearing it," leading to a further decrease in novelty for many consumers. Consumers may begin to grow weary of the form and the form may decline in pleasure. The form is then picked up by smaller segments of consumers (e.g., late fashion followers) who may require a lower level of novelty.

## NOVELTY AND EVOLUTION OF DESIGN

Preference for medium levels of novelty coincides with the evolutionary nature of modern fashion. Elements in the aesthetic product change slowly from year to year making modern fashion a steady transition or an *evolution.* A moderate level of novelty is built into the product or environment, resulting in a slow change. High levels of novelty would result in a more rapid change of the aesthetic form. Apparel professionals provide novelty to keep the consumer interested, without alienating the consumer because of too much novelty. This moderate level of novelty is advantageous for the apparel firm because the bodies or styles that were successful last year can be utilized again for future products. Costs associated with fitting, pattern making, and assembly processes, for instance, may be minimized.

There are also functional reasons why consumers should prefer slow change in apparel products. Rapid change in fashion would result in a wardrobe that becomes obsolete quickly. A product that changes slowly over the years can be accepted as fashionable for a longer period of time than a product that changes drastically from year to year. Consumers generally build a wardrobe, slowly adding products to what is already owned. Slow change in fashion allows for the utilization of products already owned. Designers are beginning to recognize and cater to consumers who build a wardrobe slowly. For instance, designers use the same color from year to year to allow the consumer to match new pieces to what's already owned.

## ABSTRACTING ACROSS PRODUCTS OVER TIME

Forecasting future trends in the aesthetic product requires one of two things: a phone call to 1-(900)-Psychic or a systematic analysis of the product from year to year. We will, for obvious reasons, focus on a method of systematic analysis of the product over time. When abstracting across time, a sampling of products is examined from consecutive years. As a fashion forecaster, forecasting for the entire (e.g., apparel or interiors) industry, one may abstract across a range of product categories by analyzing products available in the marketplace and fashion publications. Trends within particular product categories may then be identified, as shown in Reading 14.1.

However, if one were to work for a retail design, product development, or manufacturing firm, attention would also be given to the company's past seasons' sales. Thus, the company's product lines would be carefully analyzed, looking for the underlying aesthetic of best selling items. New styles would then be purchased or developed to meet the evolving aesthetic preferences of the company's target consumer. Table 14.1 shows that apparel and interiors manufacturers depend upon a blend of past season's sales (e.g., tradition and last season's sales), information about their target consumer (e.g., function and age of the consumer market), and trends in the broader market (e.g., color forecasts and trade publications) when making color decisions for their upcoming product lines.

## PROCEDURE FOR ABSTRACTING OVER TIME

Examining *at least* three consecutive years will help one see a trend. For purposes of simplicity, select a product category, such as belts, suits, or blouses. Once the sample items are collected for each year, a systematic analysis can begin. This analysis consists of recording descriptions of the product's characteristics and their frequency of occurrence. The descriptions will be facilitated by a chart that lists aspects of the aesthetic form. The chart should draw upon elements and principles discussed in previous chapters. For instance, one may develop a chart for line from layout and surface using the concepts in Chapter 5. The chart would contain length, width, weight, uniformity, and direction of line for layout and surface (see chart in Activity 14.1). An overall feeling of the characteristic is identified or abstracted for each sample, then a mark is placed in the chart for each aspect. Remember that abstracting is a means of extrapola-

**ACTIVITY 14.1** Chapters 5, 6, 8, and 9 contain aspects of the aesthetic form that should be examined for change over time. Create chart using concepts from these chapters. We have provided an example below of how elements of design may be developed into a chart and we have developed the chart entry for Chapter 8. Note that degree of interest is not included from Chapter 8 because this aspect is encompassed in the description of the elements of design. We suggest that more than three sample items be included for each year. Only three items for each year are included in the example chart due to space limitations of the page.

**Trend Analysis Chart**

| YEAR | 1993 | 1994 | 1995 | 1996 |
|---|---|---|---|---|
| SAMPLE | 1 2 3 total | 1 2 3 total | 1 2 3 total | 1 2 3 total |
| Line | | | | |
| Layout | | | | |
| Length<br>long<br>medium<br>short | | | | |
| Width<br>wide<br>medium<br>narrow | | | | |
| Weight<br>heavy<br>medium<br>light | | | | |
| Uniformity<br>uniform<br>varied | | | | |
| Direction<br>vertical<br>diagonal<br>horizontal | | | | |
| Surface | | | | |
| Length<br>long<br>medium<br>short | | | | |
| Width<br>wide<br>medium<br>narrow | | | | |

**ACTIVITY 14.1** Continued

| YEAR | 1993 | 1994 | 1995 | 1996 |
|---|---|---|---|---|
| SAMPLE | 1 2 3 total | 1 2 3 total | 1 2 3 total | 1 2 3 total |
| Weight<br>heavy<br>medium<br>light | | | | |
| Uniformity<br>uniform<br>varied | | | | |
| Direction<br>vertical<br>diagonal<br>horizontal | | | | |
| Complexity | | | | |
| Layout | | | | |
| Number of units<br>many<br>medium<br>few | | | | |
| Cohesion<br>high<br>medium<br>low | | | | |
| Surface | | | | |
| Number of units<br>many<br>medium<br>few | | | | |
| Cohesion<br>high<br>medium<br>low | | | | |
| Part/whole<br>part<br>mid-level<br>whole | | | | |

**TABLE 14.1** Factors considered by apparel and interior manufacturers in color decisions for upcoming product lines. From Stark, S. & Johnson-Carroll, K. (1994, July). Study finds color choices far from random. *Bobbin, 35*(11), pp. 16, 18, 19.

| Force | Mean: Apparel | Interiors | Total | Standard Dev. |
|---|---|---|---|---|
| 1. Tradition | 4.08 | 3.62 | **3.898** | 1.050 |
| 2. Last season's sales | 3.98 | 3.39 | **3.751** | 0.266 |
| 3. Function of your consumer market | 3.33 | 3.50 | **3.419** | 1.354 |
| 4. Age of your consumer market | 3.55 | 3.00 | **3.312** | 1.453 |
| 5. Geographical area of your consumer market | 3.29 | 3.25 | **3.278** | 1.223 |
| 6. Trade publications | 3.12 | 2.97 | **3.082** | 1.328 |
| 7. Competition | 2.88 | 3.15 | **2.969** | 1.349 |
| 8. American apparel collections | 3.35 | 2.34 | **2.925** | 1.361 |
| 9. Consumer fashion magazines | 3.21 | 2.55 | **2.918** | 1.239 |
| 10. Color forecasts from fiber manufacturers | 2.95 | 2.79 | **2.876** | 1.364 |
| 11. U.S. street fashions | 3.46 | 1.92 | **2.853** | 1.444 |
| 12. European apparel collections | 3.24 | 2.21 | **2.821** | 1.288 |
| 13. Color forecasts from color firms | 2.84 | 2.74 | **2.769** | 1.491 |
| 14. European street fashions | 3.34 | 1.84 | **2.736** | 1.429 |
| 15. Trade shows | 2.58 | 2.82 | **2.670** | 1.432 |
| 16. Other apparel or interiors markets | 2.19 | 3.25 | **2.663** | 1.484 |
| 17. Fashion forecast reports | 2.69 | 2.29 | **2.478** | 1.239 |
| 18. Interior design magazines | 1.79 | 3.29 | **2.454** | 1.414 |
| 19. The economy | 2.05 | 2.38 | **2.198** | 1.202 |
| 20. New technology | 1.80 | 2.72 | **2.182** | 1.170 |
| 21. Entertainers | 1.91 | 1.50 | **1.763** | 1.026 |
| 22. Political trends | 1.55 | 1.62 | **1.579** | 0.856 |

Note: Mean scores were based on 5=highly important, 4=important, 3=somewhat important, 2=not very important, 1=not important at all.

tion or estimation. For example, lines in a calf-length circle skirt may be considered *long* because of the large number of lines from folds of fabric fullness, even though a number of shorter lines are created by pockets and the waistband. In this case a mark is placed in the chart on the row for Line-Layout-Length-long. One should also look for the dominant feature of the sample. A strong diagonal line created by a cross-over garment opening may dominate the garment's vertical lines created by darts. Thus, a mark would be placed on the row for Line-Layout-Direction-diagonal.

You might find in the process of abstraction that some of the aspects of the element do not relate. For instance, there may be no surface design to analyze for surface-length of line. Disregard the aspect for that item(s). In this case, no mark is made under line length for that item. Once this process is completed, each category row is totaled for each year. Activity 14.1 provides the opportunity to develop the chart as a class. Use the example chart entry as a model for the other elements and principles. Don't forget to include concepts such as flat-rounded.

Once all the data is gathered, abstracting across time can begin. The totals are examined for patterns of change. There are three major aspects of change that one should explore in abstracting across time: (1) direction; (2) rate; and 3) breadth of offerings. Predictions for upcoming styles are based upon these three aspects.

## Direction of Change

**Direction of change** refers to directional movement from one style characteristic (category row) to another. The direction may be linear, moving in one direction. For example, line length may steadily move from long to medium to short. The direction may arc, where line width moves from wide to medium to wide again. (See Table 14.2.) One may more safely predict the future trend of a linear direction of change; it will likely move in the same direction, or gradually move in the opposite direction. An arcing pattern is more difficult to predict.

## Rate of Change

**Rate of change** describes the speed by which the concentration (majority or trend) shifts among style characteristics (category rows). A rapid rate of change suggests a rapid shift in concentration from one category row to another (Table 14.3). Below the concentration in number of units moves from many to few within two years. This pattern may make predicting future trends difficult unless there is a repetitive nature to the pattern, such as a repeated shift from one category row to another. Certain apparel categories may routinely exhibit rapid rates of change. Trends of young girls sportswear undergo rapid changes (Figure 14.2). The rate of change for many apparel categories is gradual (Table 14.2, layout length). Whereas other categories may change at a snail's pace. Men's dress shirts may be an example of an apparel category exhibiting a very slow rate of change. The subtleties of style are very important to recognize with a very slow rate of change.

**TABLE 14.2** Linear movement of direction of change in line length and arcing movement in line width.

| YEAR | 1993 | 1994 | 1995 | 1996 |
|---|---|---|---|---|
| SAMPLE | total | total | total | total |
| Line | | | | |
| Layout | | | | |
| Length | | | | |
| long | 8 | 5 | 4 | 1 |
| medium | 2 | 4 | 1 | 3 |
| short | 2 | 3 | 7 | 8 |
| Surface | | | | |
| Width | | | | |
| wide | 9 | 5 | 3 | 8 |
| medium | 2 | 5 | 7 | 3 |
| narrow | 1 | 2 | 2 | 1 |

**TABLE 14.3** Shift in concentration reflecting a rapid rate change.

| YEAR | 1993 | 1994 | 1995 | 1996 |
|---|---|---|---|---|
| SAMPLE | total | total | total | total |
| Layout | | | | |
| Number of units | | | | |
| many | 10 | 5 | 1 | 1 |
| medium | 0 | 3 | 1 | 0 |
| few | 2 | 4 | 10 | 11 |

### Breadth of Offerings

**Breadth of offerings** refers to the level of concentration (majority or trend) within a style characteristic category (e.g., Direction—vertical, diagonal, or horizontal). The breadth of offerings may be described as narrow to wide. Narrow breadth of offerings designates that there is a concentration within a category row. A narrow breadth of offering permits one to say there is a strong trend. A wide breadth of offerings designates that items are scattered among the category rows in no particular pattern. (See Table 14.4.) Essentially a "trend" does not exist in this case.

**TABLE 14.4** Narrow and wide breadth of offerings for line direction.

| YEAR | 1993 | 1994 | 1995 | 1996 |
|---|---|---|---|---|
| SAMPLE | total | total | total | total |
| Layout | | | | |
| Line | | | | |
| Direction | | | | |
| vertical | 10 | 9 | 11 | 11 |
| diagonal | 1 | 2 | 1 | 1 |
| horizontal | 1 | 1 | 0 | 0 |
| Surface | | | | |
| Direction | | | | |
| vertical | 4 | 5 | 4 | 5 |
| diagonal | 5 | 3 | 4 | 3 |
| horizontal | 3 | 4 | 4 | 4 |

## INTERPRETING THE SOCIAL CONTEXT

As you can see, one may look at the product to help determine the direction of change in the product. The direction of change provides insight into the future aesthetic of the product. Yet, the validity of these predictions may be enhanced by knowing the social context, because the product is a physical manifestation of the social context. The popularity of the color green, organic cotton, and subtle colors from natural dyes are a manifestation of the focus of recent times on protecting the environment, or the "greening of America."

Social context may provide literal influences on aesthetic forms, such as the popularity of Barney, the purple dinosaur, on the color and decoration of children's clothes. Natalie Perr, the color forecaster introduced in Chapter 11, explained that a brown and white polka dot dress worn by Julia Roberts in the film *Pretty Woman* popularized brown in women's dresses. Notice that the influences of social context may be selective to particular product groups, such as children's play wear or women's dresses.

The influence may also be less direct, such as the "feeling of the times" manifested in the expressiveness of the form. Consider the three aspects of emotional experience (pleasure, arousal, dominance) when defining the feeling of the times. The 1980s were considered a time of economic prosperity for many Americans. The 80s were filled with individuals who "worked hard and played hard." Focus was on the rich and famous, those with power. Thus, the social context of the 80s resonated a feeling of intense pleasure, arousal, and dominance. The aesthetic form of the 80s expressed this feeling. Intense colors and

## BEST SELLERS

(From the New York Times)

### FICTION

**1 PRIMARY COLORS,** by Anonymous. (Random House, $24.) The progress of a certain Southern governor and his wife on their way to the White House.

**2 IN THE PRESENCE OF THE ENEMY,** by Elizabeth George. (Bantam, $23.95.) Two British celebrities contend with the kidnappers of their secret love child.

**3 MONTANA SKY,** by Nora Roberts. (Putnam, $23.95) Tensions, barbaric acts and romance beset three half-sisters who must live together for one year before they can inherit their father's multimillion-dollar ranch.

**4 THE HORSE WHISPERER,** by Nicholas Evans. (Delacorte, $23.95.) A troubled woman seeks solace for herself, her daughter, and their horse from a wrangler in Montana.

**5 THE CELESTINE PROPHECY,** by James Redfield. (Warner, $17.95.) An ancient manuscript, found in Peru, provides insights into achieving a fulfilling life.

**6 AND THIS TOO SHALL PASS,** by E. Lynn Harris. (Doubleday, $23.95.) A Chicago lawyer defends a star football player falsely accused of sexual assault.

**7 ABSOLUTE POWER,** by David Baldacci. (Warner, $22.95.) Political intrigue in Washington's high circles.

**8 FIRST KING OF SHANNARA,** by Terry Brooks. (Del Rey/Ballantine, $23.50.) War between the Druids and the monsters: prelude to "The Sword of Shannara."

**9 MCNALLY'S PUZZLE,** by Lawrence Sanders. (Putnam, .. $24.95.) The private eye Archy McNally probes the murder of a wealthy widower on Florida's Gold Coast.

**10 GUILTY AS SIN,** by Tami Hoag. (Bantam, $21.95.) The ordeals of an assistant district attorney as she prosecutes a college professor for kidnapping his neighbor's child.

**11 THE RETURN,** William Shatner with Judith and Garfield Reeves-Stevens. (Pocket, $22.) Captain Kirk of "Star Trek" returns to take part in a cosmic war.

**12 THAT CAMDEN SUMMER,** by LaVyrle Spencer. (Putnam, $23.95.) A divorced woman, returning to her hometown, finds scorn, harassment, and romance.

**13 FIVE DAYS IN PARIS,** by Danielle Steel. (Delacorte, $15.95.) A chance encounter between two Americans at the Ritz changes their lives forever.

**14 INTENSITY,** by Dean Koontz. (Knopf, $25.) On a weekend visit to a Napa Valley farm, a young woman contends with a serial killer.

**15 SPRING COLLECTION,** by Judith Krantz. (Crown, $24.) Family secrets, intrigue, and rivalry in the fashion world on the runways of New York and Paris.

### GENERAL

**1 IN CONTEMPT,** by Christopher A. Darden with . Jess Walter. (Regan Books/HarperCollins, $26.) The life of a member of the Simpson trial prosecution team, and his view of that trial.

**2 BLOOD SPORT,** by James B. Stewart. (Simon & Schuster, $25.) A journalist reviews the Whitewater case and the roles of President and Mrs. Clinton.

**3 RUSH LIMBAUGH IS A BIG FAT IDIOT,** by Al Franken. (Delacorte, $21.95.) A television comedian's comments on the current political scene.

**4 UNDAUNTED COURAGE,** by Stephen E. Ambrose. (Simon & Schuster, $27.50.) The story of how Thomas Jefferson sponsored the exploration of the American West by Meriwether Lewis and William Clark.

**5 IT TAKES A VILLAGE,** by Hillary Rodham Clinton. (Simon & Schuster, $20.) The first lady's quest for ways to help children create a better society.

**6 HOW COULD YOU DO THAT?!** by Laura Schlesinger. (HarperCollins, $22.) A condemnation of self-indulgent morality.

**7 MIDNIGHT IN THE GARDEN OF GOOD AND EVIL,** by John Berendt. (Random House, $23.) The mysterious death of a young man in Savannah, Ga.

**8 EMOTIONAL INTELLIGENCE,** by Daniel Goleman. (Bantam, $23.95.) Factors other than IQ that contribute to a successful and happy life.

**9 100 YEARS, 100 STORIES,** by George Burns. (Putnam, $15.95.) From New York's Lower East Side to show business stardom, the late centenarian recollects his past.

**10 YOU'LL NEVER MAKE LOVE IN THIS TOWN AGAIN,** by Robin, Liza, Linda, and Tiffany, as told to Jennie Louise Frankel Terrie Maxine Frankel, and Joanne Parrent. (Dove, $22.95.) Four Hollywood prostitutes recall their professional experiences.

**11 ENTER WHINING,** by Fran Drescher. (Regan Books/HarperCollins, $22.) The memoirs of the star of "The Nanny."

**12 LONGITUDE,** by Dava Sobel. (Walker, $19.) The story of John Harrison, the 18th-century Englishman who invented the chronometer.

**13 (B) REASONABLE DOUBTS,** by Alan M. Dershowitz. (Simon & Schuster, $20.) Why the jury in the O.J. Simpson case reached the verdict it did.

**14 MOUNTAIN, GET OUT OF MY WAY,** by Montel Williams with Daniel Paisner, (Warner, $16.95) From Baltimore's ghetto to television stardom: a memoir.

**15 INTO THE WILD,** by Jon Krakauer. (Villard, $22.) The life of a young man whose obsession with the wilderness has a tragic end in Alaska.

### ADVICE, HOW-TO, MISCELLANEOUS

**1 (B) MEN ARE FROM MARS, WOMEN ARE FROM VENUS,** by John Gray. (HarperCollins, $20.) Ways to improve communication and relationships between the sexes.

**2 (B) SIMPLE ABUNDANCE,** by Sara Bah Breathnach. (Warner, $17.95.) Advice for women seeking to improve the way they look at themselvs in the world.

**3 (B) THE SEVEN SPIRITUAL LAWS OF SUCCESS,** by Deepak Chopra. (Amber-Allen/New World Library, $12.95.) How to "generate wealth in all its forms."

**4 (B) THE WAY OF THE WIZARD,** by Deepak Chopra. (Harmony, $15.95.) Spiritual lessons for "creating the life you want."

**Rankings reflect sales figures for the week ending March 23, 1996. The listings are based on computer-processed sales figures from 3,985 bookstores and from representative wholesalers with more than 50,000 retail outlets, including newsstands, variety stores, supermarkets, and bookstores. These figures are statistically weighted to represent sales in all such outlets across the United States.**

**An 'X' indicates that a book's sales are barely distinguishable from these of the book above. A 'B' indicates that some bookstores report receiving bulk orders for a book.**

Figure 14.4. Best Sellers List.

high levels of value contrast; crisp, shiny, and hard surfaces; determinate surfaces; crisp edges, enlarged geometric shapes, such as expanded shoulders, express this collective emotional experience. The 1990s show a movement towards more conservative aspirations in terms of pleasure and arousal. A balance is being struck between work and personal life. The glitz of the 80s is replaced with family and home entertainment. The desire for dominance has also decreased. There is a shift to letting go of control, such as the resurgence in religion where one "gives control" to a higher power. The shift in aesthetic form of apparel reflects these changes. Colors have become less intense with less value contrast. Tactile textures take on a softer, drapable hand and surfaces have become more indeterminate. Smaller, organic shapes and garments that follow the natural shape of the body dominate in the 90s as a manifestation of the changing social context. Reading 14.2 provides further examples of the influence of social context on aesthetic form.

Uncovering the nature of the social context requires observation and interpretation. The sources for defining the social context are literally all around. Observation of the social context includes examining current issues or events in the government and economy, sports and entertainment, the arts, world and national news, science and technology, health, religion, and lifestyles and demographics. Newspapers, magazines, electronic communications, and personal experiences can be drawn upon when defining the social context. One should become a sponge, soaking up every aspect of the social context. Activity 14.2 will provide practice in analyzing an aspect of the social context. The list of best sellers (Figure 14.2) shows what is being read by a large number of individuals across the United States. One may look at the subject matter that is attracting readers to get a sense of current interests. Complete Activity 14.2.

**ACTIVITY 14.2**

1. Divide into groups of four to six students.
2. Examine the best sellers list. Read each of the book titles and summaries.
3. As a group, describe *three* trends you uncover in the topics or themes. For instance, you may notice that there is a focus on the soul or spiritual aspect of a fulfilling life (*Celestine Prophecy, Emotional Intelligence, Seven Spiritual Laws of Success, Way of the Wizard*). This reinforces that the trends toward a lower level of dominance and less materialism should still exist in the mid 1990s.
4. As a class, gather all trends and group them to come up with a list of *at least five* overriding trends.
5. Describe how these trends will be manifested in aspects of the aesthetic form. For instance, the focus on the spiritual rather than the physical may be manifested in less body-primary forms. The movement towards less materialism might suggest less ornamentation and more classic styles.

## PREDICTION OF FUTURE TRENDS OR PREFERENCES

Once abstraction of the forms and interpretation of the social context are complete, this information must be synthesized or combined to predict future trends or consumer preferences. The abstracted predictions are examined in relation to the trends of social context. Predictions are reinforced when they align with social trends. For instance, Natalie Perr predicted soft yet golden midtones based upon analysis of trends in the product. She reinforced this prediction with a social trend, the quickly growing popularity of olive oils and new pasta products in the same midtones. This connection was utilized in commercial forecasts developed by Color Association of the United States (CAUS) for the apparel and interiors industries. Lab Activity 14.1 provides opportunity to predict future preferences based upon a synthesis of abstracting across time and interpreting the social context.

## SUMMARY

There is continuity in modern fashion change, where new fashions evolve from previously established fashions (Blumer, 1969). Preference for medium levels of novelty coincides with this evolutionary nature of modern fashion. Recognizing the transition of the product can help predict the future direction of the aesthetic form. The social context must also be considered in predicting the future direction of the product, because the product is a physical manifestation of the social context. Recognizing gradual change in aesthetic form and understanding the social context go hand in hand when predicting or forecasting aesthetic characteristics of a future product.

Forecasting future trends in the aesthetic product requires abstracting across time. This is completed through a systematic analysis of a sampling of products from year to year. Descriptions of the product's characteristics and their frequency of occurrence are recorded and summarized for each year. Change in the frequency

**LAB ACTIVITY 14.1**

This activity has three parts. The first consists of abstracting across aesthetic forms. The second requires interpretation of the social context. The last part asks you to synthesize the information to forecast trends. Groups of four or five students should work together.

1. Select an apparel product category, such as men's suits, women's dresses, children's daywear. Collect at least seven items from a variety of fashion-forward sources for each of three consecutive years. Each year should have the same number of items and represent the same season (fall or spring).
2. Follow the procedure for abstracting across time, as described in the chapter. Use the chart developed in Activity 14.1.
3. Examine the social context. Gather at least two examples of current issues or events for each of the following:
   a. government and economy
   b. sports and entertainment
   c. the arts
   d. world and national news
   e. science and technology
   f. health
   g. religion
   h. lifestyles and demographics.
4. Look for and define at least four overriding trends among the social context information (e.g., emphasis on family, return of the 1950s, embracing multi-cultural society).
5. Determine what the aesthetic form for the upcoming year will be based upon the synthesis of abstracted form and interpreted social context (e.g., crisper textures, organic print, especially animal prints). Cover all aspects in the chart from Activity 14.1.
6. Explain in writing your reasoning behind the upcoming trends (e.g., more hourglass outer shapes of dresses to reflect the return of traditional women's roles).
7. Develop a presentation board representing the upcoming trends. Include a color palette, fabric swatches to show texture and surface design, trims, and drawings of layout including fashion details.

of occurrence is examined. There are three major aspects of change that one should explore in abstracting across time: (1) direction; (2) rate; and 3) breadth of offerings. Predictions for upcoming styles are based upon these three aspects.

Social context may provide literal influences on aesthetic forms. The influence may also be less direct, such as the "feeling of the times" manifested in the expressiveness of the form. Uncovering the nature of the social context requires observation and interpretation. Observation of the social context includes examining current issues or events in the government and economy, sports and entertainment, the arts, world and national news, science and technology, health and religion, and lifestyles and demographics. Newspapers, magazines, electronic communications, and personal experiences can be drawn upon when defining the social context. Once abstraction of the forms and interpretation of the social context are complete, this information must be synthesized or combined to predict future trends or consumer preferences. The abstracted predictions are examined in relation to the trends of social context.

Many apparel professionals will encounter forecasting as either producers of forecasts or as users of forecasts to make decisions regarding the product. The process of forecasting changes in the product is of major importance to developers and gatekeepers of textile and apparel products.

## KEY TERMS AND CONCEPTS

abstracting across time

advantages of moderate level of novelty

breadth of change

consumer adopters

direction of change

evolution of design

fashion trend forecasting

forcasting factors considered by manufacturers

interpreting the socio-cultural context

inverted-U relationship of pleasure

novelty

procedure for abstracting across time

rate of change

## SUGGESTED READINGS

(1993, January/February). Color predictions. *Communication Arts,* p. 70–73.

Perna, R. (1987). *Fashion forecasting.* New York, NY: Fairchild Publications.

Sproles, G. B. & Burns, L. D. (1989). *Changing appearances: Understanding appearances in contemporary society.* Fairchild Publications, p. 287–295.

## READING 14.1
# Classification News

Reading 14.1 Classification News. (1995, April/May). *RTW Review,* p. 4.

### Suits . . .

Suit and dress sales are still on the up and up. In January, suit business rose twenty-eight percent and dresses jumped five percent in comparison to sales figures from the same period last year. Success has been attributed to current key trends such as fitted jackets paired with skirts, pants, or dresses; day-to-dinner dress looks; a renewed waist emphasis; and softer colors.

While boxier jackets are beginning to emerge, the smartest suits for fall still feature shapely silhouettes. *Cut, carved, and conservatively chic* is the prevailing look for fall 1995 . . . Masculine tailoring has not disappeared; you will find it in double-breasted jackets and trousers in a variety of tweeds, plaids, pinstripes, and buffalo checks . . . In some cases coats have replaced jackets, reaching far over the hips and paired with ultra slim "drain pipe" pants. As pant legs narrow, belts are widening.

Skirted suits are ranging in length from mini, to above the knee, to exactly at the knee, and often sport pleats and panels for a feminine flair . . . Armholes are getting higher and sleeves are inches above the wrist, leaving plenty of room for "lady like" gloves—a must-have accessory for the new season.

The suit color palette contains a number of fresh new subtleties . . . Brown continues to remain a staple and looks newest when teamed with shades of lilac as a refreshing accent. Expect deeper shades of plum, wine, and burgundy to emerge . . . Pink remains a craved color whether it's pale pink, salmon, powder, or neon bright. Warmer shades of yellow, orange, and red—matte or shiny—are important, along with lime and lilac.

### Dresses . . .

The vast array of dress options available has catapulted the dress to the forefront of fashion for fall 1995. Jacket and coat dress combinations remain a strong career look, while knit cardigan dresses are being tested for the latter part of the season. The *sleeveless sheath* will replace the slipdress as fall 1995's prominent style, exemplifying infinite layering possibilities. Retro-inspired tailored shirtdresses and sheaths in ladylike florals and pastels will carry over, as will denim jumpers and bibstyle dresses. New looks include lace or crocheted pullovers topping knit tank dresses and jersey knit dresses. Lace will be a key look throughout the dress classification this season.

The response to body conscious fit and sculpted looks has been phenomenal. Cuts remain close to the body creating a very feminine silhouette . . . Waistlines are all over the place—from high above the waist to just below the hips and everywhere in between . . . Wool, cashmere, tweed, and cotton knits appear in the season's prominent dress colors . . . easy going neutrals, pink, red, charcoal, navy, and of course, black.

### Coats . . .

Active outerwear marks a rising trend in the outerwear area once again this season. Fashion with function—zip-out liners and collars in shearlings and faux fur, detachable hoods, cargo pockets, and water-repellent finishes will all be important features. Top styles include down-filled anoraks, fleece-lined jackets, casual cloth coats, and *Blue Collar* jackets inspired by firefighters and lumberjacks that have a workwear feel. The success of these styles is derived from the combination of versatility, durability, warmth, and value. Years of women buying their coats in the men's department has been a major contributing factor to the growth of this category. Lightweight nylons, canvas, denim, wool, and microfibers are the season's key fabrics. Classic shades of black, red, navy, along with playful brights like turquoise, lime, and hot pink give the season its color.

More traditional coat looks are falling to the knee in wrap, trench, clutch, overcoat, and cape styles . . . Tweeds are important, as are wool, cashmere, and faux fur . . . Cuts are close and curves are sharp. Watch for the season's newest coats that are hip belted below a fitted waistline . . . Double breasted details are resurging on again . . . the color palette runs the gamut from neutrals like gray to a range of reds, and an abundance of browns. "Life is like a box of chocolates ..."

An item to watch for future development is the *packable raincoat.* The lightweight polyester and microfiber coats are sold with a matching carrying case ... the perfect option for women who travel or anyone who doesn't want to get caught in the rain.

### Sportswear . . .

Fall 1995 will be an item driven season ... longer fitted jackets, belted looks, jumpers, vests, crisp white shirts, slim "drain pipe" pants, and sweater sets all will make their mark this season. A more fitted silhouette began to emerge this spring and it is evolving further as we head on into fall 1995. This time it's more modern in appearance. The retro feel is still evident, but the season's newest looks take on a more streamlined silhouette. It's almost more "Star Trek—The Next Generation" than it is Audrey Hepburn-ish.

## READING 14.2
## Color Predictions

Reading 14.2 Color Predictions. (1994, January/February). *Communication Arts,* p. 92.

The draugtmanship of colourists is like that of nature; their figures are naturally bounded by a harmonious collision of colored masses. Pure draughtsmen are philosophers and dialecticians. "Colourists are epic poets," wrote Charles Baudelaire. The 19th century French poet, literary and art critic was on to something. The natural environment continues to be the major inspiration for forecast colors. "The colors are not high contrast, they are more soothing, recognizing the harmony and balance that exists in nature," says Nada Napoletan Rutka, president of the Color Marketing Group (CMG) and principal of Nada Associates, a color, design and marketing consulting firm in Pittsburgh, Pennsylvania. "Not only are the color directions nature-inspired, but the looks of the pigments are also nature-derived," she says. "When you get color from vegetation it is not as highly pigmented; that's where we get the softening of the palette. The environment is also important because so many of the new environmental rules and regulations mean consumers don't want products that will add pollution in their processing—that's where the acceptance of the vegetal dye appearance comes from."

The next group of colors that will continue to grow is the orange family, Rutka claims. "We'll see bright orange used in communications as well as worldly and earthy oranges" including the colors of saffron, sunflowers, butterscotch and what she terms "kilim or vegetal dye colors."

Color directions are dependent on price points, the goals and objectives of marketing and other variables. Future color directions will come from more primitive areas, including Africa, the Middle East and Indonesia. The influences drawn from barks, henna, batiks and spice tones will be seen in higher-end products. "The metallics have gone from high shine and sparkle to accents of metals that have been around for a while, burnished looks, things with a patina of age: coppers and pewters, aged brass and bronze," Rutka says. From an ethnic standpoint, a long time ago people didn't shine objects made of metals, they were allowed to age and tarnish. "Part of the beauty of the object was the ever-changing visual," she explains. She cites Van Gogh as having brought about the current sunflower revival, with his paintings fectching record-breaking prices at auction, and she sees the sturdy flower as a symbol. "Consumers are looking for a life!" Rutka says, with a laugh. "A desire for simplicity, harmony and balance. A sunflower is regenerative. You can eat it and put it back in the ground for mulch; it's part of nature. It's real and authentic." Another art influence is the recent Matisse retrospective at New York's Museum of Modern Art, which inspired many designers to use combinations of blue and yellow, as well as to draw from Matisse's surprisingly contemporary amorphous shapes.

Colors must be interpreted for specific products and will continue to be less gender specific. Nada sees purple as a surprise color, and thinks it has a place, especially in communications. "Purple is artistic and attention getting, it's not a typical color. It's a gender neutral color that's never been taken that seriously. When atypical colors come about you can't just spring them on the population, they have to be eased in. Depending on what you're trying to say, you'll still see bright catalyst colors, canary yellows, fuschias and tropical corals; we call it 'tropical punch,'" says Rutka. "Colors are yellowing—you see it in fashion and in home furnishings."

And speaking of home furnishings, Rutka, a member of the American Society of Interior Designers, says "Denim has been translated into a millon and one interior products—it's a mainstream item. My guess is the denim mills are beside themselves."

The use of neutral colors from nature seems to be a headline grabbing color trend. "The neutrals of pure white and black are sort of gone. The neutrals now are tints of white and shades of black and they have other colors in them," Rutka says. "Yellow will be influencing the neutral palette a lot more in '94; as we move into '95, taupes, sand colors and grayed browns will be influential."

And brown, which English color theorist George Field described as ". . . dirty, or the anomalous colour brown," is undergoing a renaissance. "Brown tones will be important," says Rutka. "It's a friendly, safe, warm color. Some people have negative connotations about brown—it's almost a retro color." She's not talking about plain old chocolate brown, rather a dark bark color; browns with a red influence, a deepening of the spice tones. And while standby black may still be the best hip club color, Rutka believes that graphic designers who in the past have used black for one color projects will soon be screening back to gray.

The Color Marketing Group is a 31-year-old international non-profit association of over 1,300 design and color profesionals who forecast color directions one to three years out for all industries, manufactured products and services. These include: residential; commercial and consumer products; transportation; architectural/building products; communications/graphics; fashion; recreational, retail, hospitality; office and health care environments.

If you'd like to find out more about the forecasting of color contact the Color Marketing Group, 5904 Richmond Highway, Suite 408, Alexandria, Virginia 22203. (703) 329-8500; fax (703) 329-0155. Those wishing to join CMG are first approved by the Executive Committee to ensure that all members are color professionals.

CHAPTER 15

# Communication to Promote Apparel

## Objectives

- Recognize the importance of communication in the promotion of apparel products
- Consider the communication skills involved in promotional aspects of the apparel industry through industry communication such as presentation boards, catalogs, advertising, store display, fashion shows, and portfolios
- Understand the importance of a portfolio to personal professional development in the apparel industry
- Prepare for a professional future by planning your portfolio

Imagine sweet, five-year old Jenny has just been to the movies, and has seen the latest Disney hit, *The Hunchback of Notre Dame.* She is transformed into a different child. Her parents are ready to file for bankruptcy because Jenny has become a *rabid, crazed consumer*—she wants Quasimoto and Esmerelda sheets and T-shirts and stuffed toys. She wants to visit a certain fast-food chain to collect the movies' action figures! How has this happened? Through the magic of promotional communication. Children (and their hapless parents) are the targets of much promotional effort introducing new products and stimulating the demand for those products. Do you think this Jeckyll and Hyde transformation only happens with children? Think again. Remember the last time you saw a product you just *had* to have? The promotional efforts of marketers got to you, too.

## COMMUNICATION IN PROMOTION

Communication of information is a vital component in the process of promotion of the apparel product. Communication takes place through (1) internal promotion of product ideas among apparel professionals and (2) promotion of the product to the end consumer. Communication about the apparel product, to ultimately generate sales, occurs through advertising, visual merchandise displays, catalogs, print or TV arts, and publicity events such as fashion shows. Communication also occurs through the use of portfolios to promote one's own abilities rather than a product. Portfolios encourage professional development and advancement.

The goal of promotional communication aimed at the end consumer is to increase the salability of the product. To achieve this goal communication should raise awareness of the product and increase the perceived value to stimulate demand for the product. Raising awareness of the product entails communication to notify an audience about new products or remind them about current products. Increasing the perceived value or appeal occurs through enhancement of the aesthetic and instrumental value of the product. One way to increase perceived value is by adding meaning to the product (McCracken, 1986; 1987; White, 1959). Meaning includes the aspects of the socio-cultural context that are represented through the product. Consumers who want to participate in the aspect of culture represented through the object will be likely to purchase and use the product (McCracken, 1986). For example, wearing celebrity endorsed basketball shoes allows teenagers to participate in the popularity of basketball and dream of someday playing professional ball.

Recall from Chapter 10 that the consumer's decision-making process involves logical decisions and hedonic (pleasure-seeking) responses. Promotional communications appeal to the consumer through logical appeals and by stimulating the hedonic, emotional reaction to the product. The logical appeal is based on the presentation of "the facts" which make a product desirable. The hedonic appeal generates feelings and fantasies the consumer can participate in through the selection and use of the product. These two types of appeals can be combined in promotional communications, although many communications depend more heavily on one approach or the other.

Promotional communications appeal to the viewer through communication of factual information about the product's features, through the development of imagery associated with the product, and through fostering greater depth of experience with the product. The features of the product are usually presented in a drawing or photograph. Generally, information about layout and surface features are visible in the image of the product. Text information, which accompanies an image, may further describe the product's features as well as contribute to the imagery (Figure 15.1).

**Imagery** is the visual and verbal representation of sensory experiences and emotions fostered by the product environment. Imagery information stimulates in the viewer's imagination or memory thoughts that are often not explicitly expressed in the communication. Imagery draws the audience "in" on an emotional level. Imagery invokes a hedonic (pleasure-seeking) response rather than logical decision-making response. Imagery that results in non-verbal product-related thoughts has been found to influence consumer preference and product evaluation more than analysis provided by a logical or rational description of product features (Oliver, Robertson & Mitchell, 1993). The emotional nature

Figure 15.1. Advertisement combines image of the product with explanation of the fabric and price.

of imagery may be significant as a motivational factor, leading to purchase (Holbrook & O'Shaughnessy, 1984).

Imagery created by the product environment enhances the formal, expressive, and symbolic features of the product. Imagery is supported by visual and verbal information beyond the mere presentation of product features. The visual image of the product may be enhanced by the setting, the model, and the graphic design elements of the layout (e.g., borders, typography, logos). The environment is intended to increase the imagery associated with the product and can include references to the times or the product's use.

The use of verbal imagery (words that create pictures and sensory experiences in the mind) can supplement visual imagery. Two types of language imagery that might be used include metaphors and similes. A metaphor is a figure of speech in which one thing is described with reference to or as another thing. In a recent editorial feature in *Harper's Bazaar,* summer sportswear was described as an "L. A. afternoon, fresh and simple". The clothes are not an afternoon, but an image of California summer is called to mind by the text. A simile makes a more direct comparison using the terms *like* or *as;* "smooth as silk" or "like spun gold" are similes. Both metaphors and similes are descriptive phrases that can be used to create an image or picture in one's mind.

Imagery encourages the potential consumer to experience the product vicariously—through imagined participation with the product, substituting the self in place of the models using the product. This is the highest level of *audience involvement* with promotions of the product (Greenwald & Leavitt, 1984). The experience with the product can become closer to reality in promotional environments where the product is "live," as in a fashion show, or "up close, and personal," as in a store display. Audience involvement may be increased through more multi-sensory-based experiences, such as the inclusion of music or the opportunity to touch a product. Involvement is also higher when the consumer chooses the experience. For example, choosing to watch a fashion show or shop in a catalog demonstrates greater involvement with a product than "accidentally" seeing an advertisement while watching a tv program. Thus, the communication becomes a personal experience for the consumer.

## INTERNAL PROMOTION

Internal promotions are communications about an apparel product within or between firms. Internal promotion communicates information about the product's features through a visual image of the product, accompanying verbal information and context, such as a showroom environment.

Apparel product images may take the form of sketches and photographs, or samples of the actual product, if available. Designers' sketches serve to communicate ideas early in the product development process as no physical product is yet created. Depending on the end use for the image, various levels of "finish" or polish can be applied to the drawing (Figure 15.2). For instance, quick sketches often serve to communicate an initial idea within the firm. Flats are simple, clear drawings of apparel presented with accurate proportion and all construction details. Flats may be accompanied by swatches or they may be "colored in" to represent the fabrics used in the garment. The flats of garments produced by a firm may be organized into a line book or style book with identifying numbers. Specification drawings (specs) are even more technically accurate than flats. Specs include all information that would be necessary to produce a pattern for the garment, such as length of seams and width of hems.

An illustration is a stylized, rendered drawing (many times filled in with fabric and color) which may be used for promotional purposes. Illustrations include a representation of a model posed in the garment. In the past, fashion illustrators were frequently employed to develop stylized images of apparel products for trade publications such as *WWD* and for retail advertising campaigns. However, in recent decades, photos of the actual product are most frequently used for these communications (Danielson, 1986; Kimle, 1991).

Promotional communications within the firm use minimal verbal information. A presentation board might include a title or short theme description. But there is little time or need to put together elaborate text and presentations within a firm; the proposed products are the focus. On the other hand, a forecaster's report may include more text accompanying visual examples of trends.

Figure 15.2. Different types of drawings serve different purposes in the industry—illustration, flat, and spec drawing.

## CATALOGS

The primary concern of most catalog promotional communication is in conveying accurate information about the product's features. Consumers must be able to perceive the characteristics of the products offered in order to make purchase decisions. Clear and accurate photography is usually used to communicate to the potential consumer. Lack of visual clarity in product representation is one of consumer's frequent complaints about catalog shopping. Experience with the same catalog company over time allows shoppers to become more comfortable in determining how accurate the visual image is (Consumer Reports, 1994).

Because of the direct sales function, catalogs employ text to a greater degree than what is usually found in fashion print ads. Verbal text is important in describing and clarifying the formal features of the product, which may not be clearly evident from the photos. Text should supplement information in pictures, although catalog companies often leave much to the shopper to interpret. A novice catalog shopper may not be able to determine which description would lead to the type of fit preferred in jeans between "loose fit," "relaxed fit," and "with ease." This uncertainty may lead to a decision not to risk shopping by mail. Similar problems occur when catalog copy-writers get a little "too creative" with color names. How can a consumer be confident choosing between the "lemon" and "butter" sweater and hope that the selection would match the "sunshine" skirt purchased previously? Catalog copy writers need to be cautious and balance the consumer's need for basic product information with the development of imagery in the text.

While communication of product information is the primary emphasis of most catalog companies, some develop considerable imagery in their presentations as well. Consider the elaborate imagery created by the descriptions of clothing items in the J. Peterman catalog (Figure 15.3). The product features are reason-

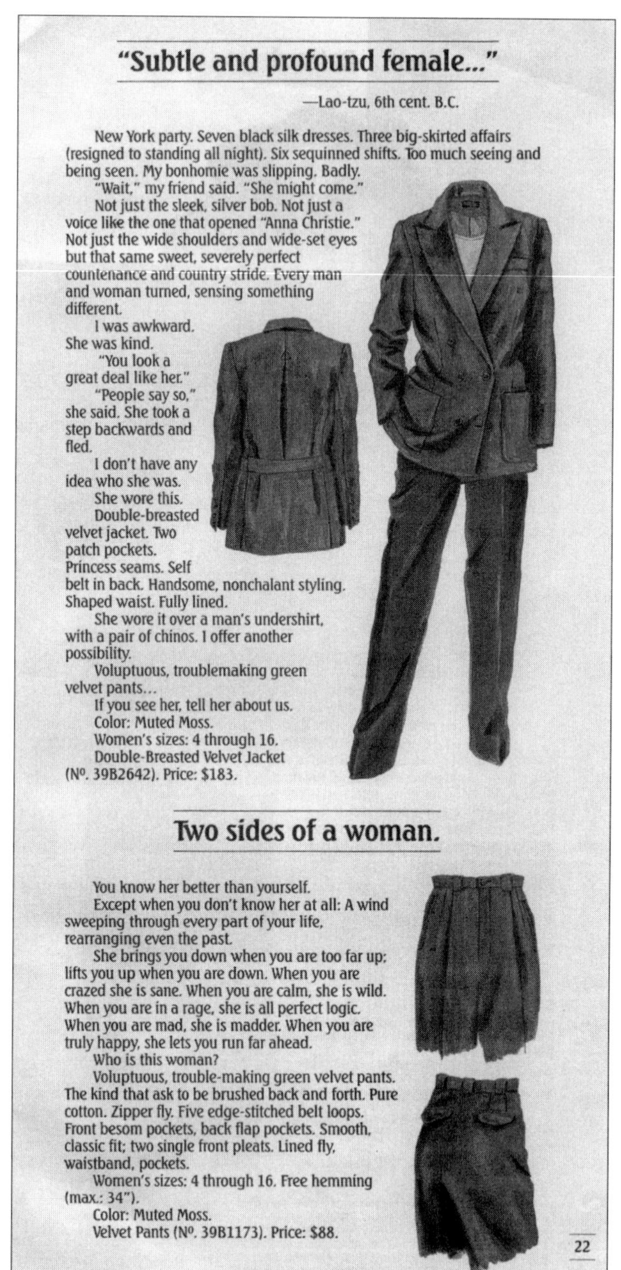

"Subtle and profound female..."

—Lao-tzu, 6th cent. B.C.

New York party. Seven black silk dresses. Three big-skirted affairs (resigned to standing all night). Six sequinned shifts. Too much seeing and being seen. My bonhomie was slipping. Badly.

"Wait," my friend said. "She might come."

Not just the sleek, silver bob. Not just a voice like the one that opened "Anna Christie." Not just the wide shoulders and wide-set eyes but that same sweet, severely perfect countenance and country stride. Every man and woman turned, sensing something different.

I was awkward.
She was kind.

"You look a great deal like her."

"People say so," she said. She took a step backwards and fled.

I don't have any idea who she was.

She wore this.

Double-breasted velvet jacket. Two patch pockets. Princess seams. Self belt in back. Handsome, nonchalant styling. Shaped waist. Fully lined.

She wore it over a man's undershirt, with a pair of chinos. I offer another possibility.

Voluptuous, troublemaking green velvet pants...

If you see her, tell her about us.

Color: Muted Moss.

Women's sizes: 4 through 16.

Double-Breasted Velvet Jacket (N°. 39B2642). Price: $183.

Two sides of a woman.

You know her better than yourself.

Except when you don't know her at all: A wind sweeping through every part of your life, rearranging even the past.

She brings you down when you are too far up: lifts you up when you are down. When you are crazed she is sane. When you are calm, she is wild. When you are in a rage, she is all perfect logic. When you are mad, she is madder. When you are truly happy, she lets you run far ahead.

Who is this woman?

Voluptuous, trouble-making green velvet pants. The kind that ask to be brushed back and forth. Pure cotton. Zipper fly. Five edge-stitched belt loops. Front besom pockets, back flap pockets. Smooth, classic fit; two single front pleats. Lined fly, waistband, pockets.

Women's sizes: 4 through 16. Free hemming (max.: 34").

Color: Muted Moss.

Velvet Pants (N°. 39B1173). Price: $88.

22

Figure 15.3. Copy and illustration of a product offered by J. Peterman.

ably presented, but the illustrations are far from accurate in every detail. The text describes the product, but also creates context for the product. Similarly, a Peruvian Connection catalog uses photographs of Central American countrysides where their products are produced to enhance the meaning and appeal of the garments (Figure 15.4). Many traditional retailers also produce their own catalogs, finding them effective marketing tools. Reading 15.1 explores the synergy that is developing between stores and catalogs for various firms. Try Activity 15.1.

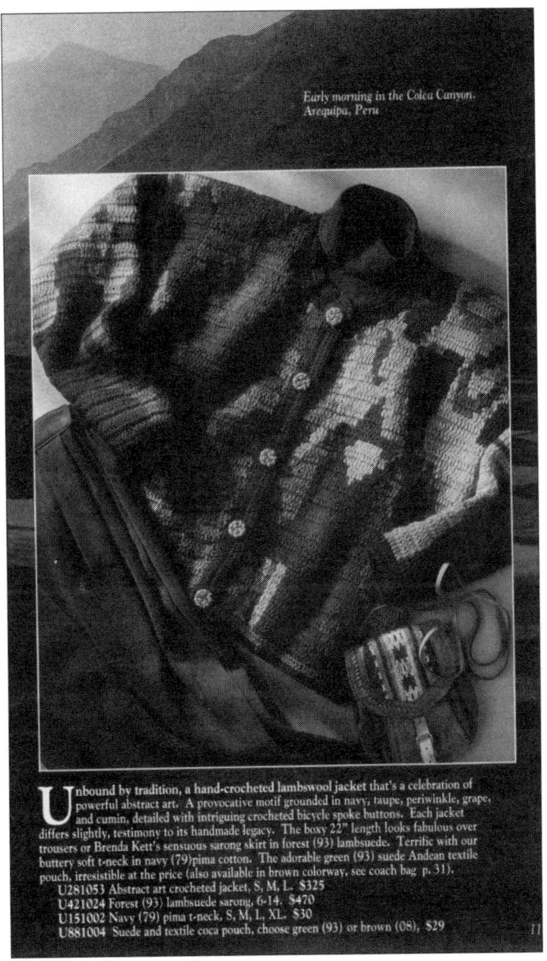

Early morning in the Colca Canyon.
Arequipa, Peru
Unbound by tradition, a hand-crocheted lambswool jacket that's a celebration of powerful abstract art. A provocative motif grounded in navy, taupe, periwinkle, grape, and cumin, detailed with intriguing crocheted bicycle spoke buttons. Each jacket differs slightly, testimony to its handmade legacy. The boxy 22" length looks fabulous over trousers or Brenda Kett's sensuous sarong skirt in forest (93) lambsuede. Terrific with our buttery soft t-neck in navy (79)pima cotton. The adorable green (93) suede Andean textile pouch, irresistible at the price (also available in brown colorway, see coach bag p. 31).
U281053 Abstract art crocheted jacket, S, M, L. $325
U421024 Forest (93) lambsuede sarong, 6-14. $470
U151002 Navy (79) pima t-neck, S, M, L, XL. $30
U881004 Suede and textile coca pouch, choose green (93) or brown (08). $29
11


Figure 15.4. Hand-crocheted sweater presented in an inset photo along with a photo of the Colca Canyon, Arequipa, Peru.

**ACTIVITY 15.1**

In this activity you will explore the visual and verbal communication involved in catalog marketing. You will critique the communication efforts of three marketers.

1. Find three catalogs from different direct marketing companies with different types of apparel and different aesthetics.
2. Evaluate the quality of a photograph (or illustration) used to represent the product. Are details clear? Can a shopper imagine herself or himself in the model's place? Do the models have "average" or ideal figures? Would a shopper be able to evaluate the fit of the styles based on the models' figures?
3. Now examine the copy for several products in each catalog. Does the text clarify the visual image or just complicate matters with ambiguous statements about fit and exotic color names?
4. Are the marketers focused primarily on product information or is there an attempt to create imagery through the presentation? Is this approach effective? Why?
5. Which catalog company do you believe is currently producing the most effective catalog? Why?

**Print advertising.** Page through a fashion magazine and look at the type of information included in the advertisements. You should notice the heavy emphasis on visual image over text in the majority of ads these days. The image of the product is carefully crafted by the stylist, the model, and the photographer to convey just the right combination of form, expression, and meaning. The image communicates about the product and enhances the meaning of the product. The imagery should allow the viewer to place herself or himself in the context of the ad, living out the mood, the mystery, or the romance that is provided by the product. For instance, Calvin Klein is (in)famous for his highly sensual and erotic images for his product lines, from sportwear, to fragrances, to underwear (Figure 15.5). This imagery, which has been established over time, is just as valuable to the promotion of the product as the formal features of the garments.

Print advertisements can be used in consumer magazines for effective target marketing. There are a wide variety of fashion and lifestyle magazines in the marketplace for fashion advertisers to consider. Most magazines have clearly defined, specific target audiences. Different editorial emphases and positioning among women's magazines has created a variety of options from which the fashion advertiser may choose. For example, the most traditional fashion flagships are still *Vogue, Glamour,* and *Harper's Bazaar,* but advertisers can also choose to place their promotions in magazines such as *Town and Country* and *Self* (Pfaff, 1986). Different types of product information and imagery may be used in different ads planned in different magazines. For example, the readers of *Vogue* are likely to be highly involved in fashion and thus fairly knowledgeable about trends. Readers of *Self* are interested in personal development. Therefore, an ad placed in *Vogue* may focus on the product's newness whereas an ad in *Self* may focus on how the product can help a woman achieve some personal goal, such as career advancement.

**Advertising copy.** The current trend in advertising is the use of very minimal verbal text. Text in most ads identifies the designer or brand name of the product, and possibly lists retailers. However, in most apparel ads, very little other text is included (Kimle, 1991). Some ads use short catchy phrases or "taglines" to grab the reader's attention and elaborate on the mental imagery initiated by the visual information. A recent trend in advertisements is the use of a casual or "conceptual" address directly to the reader. In Figure 15.6, a Levi's ad for women's jeans uses a very casual, conversational style of addressing the viewer. This is reinforced by the handwriting and "doodles" that are part of the visual presentation.

**Television advertisements.** Television advertising has the potential for stronger imagery and higher experiential involvement of the audience with the product in the ad. Television advertisements incorporate movement and the action of the model with the product. The use of live action in an ad may lead to the perception of a higher degree of excitement about the product. The nice qualities of

Figure 15.5. Calvin Klein ads for several different products all communicate the same image.

the consumer and the imagery provided in the announcement may further enhance audience involvement. The action may give the viewer a greater opportunity to imagine oneself in the situation with the product. And finally, a print ad is often viewed only for a few seconds while a tv ad might air for fifteen to thirty seconds.

Television ads may not target specific audiences as narrowly as magazine print ads do, although targeting does occur through placement of advertising during specific types of programming. Also, networks with different emphases are developing through the cable market which also encourages market segmentation among advertisers. For instance, *Lifetime* television network is specifically focused on programming for women; this might be a more effective location for an advertisement for women's apparel than other network air time. The television audience is also more likely to see the advertisement repeated rather than return to the magazine and see the same print ad again or catch another ad in the next month's issue. Thus, while the costs associated with using print versus television ads for apparel products are different, television advertising may provide more exposure.

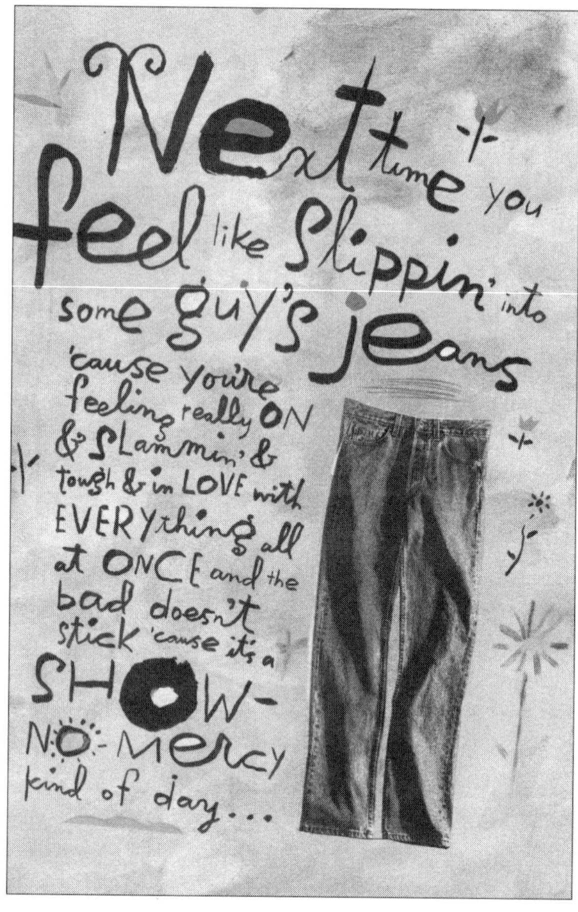


Figure 15.6. Levi's ad for guy's fitting jeans for women.

## VISUAL MERCHANDISING

Visual merchandising is used to promote the product both internally, to other industry professionals through showrooms and booths at trade shows, as well as in retail stores to the end consumer. Effective visual displays not only communicate with the viewer, they also facilitate viewer's physical interaction with the product. Buyers need to be able to examine products to evaluate them just as consumers do.

Visual merchandising in the retail setting incorporates the design of store windows and interior settings with communication and promotion in order to create opportunities for consumers to experience the product. In contrast to other forms of visual communication and promotion, store displays are three-dimensional environments. The fact that customers can move through or around a display creates a different set of opportunities to involve the customer with the imagery and encourage experiences with the product. The ways to seize these opportunities are as varied as the creativity of all the visual merchandisers and store designers in the industry. The examples in Figure 15.7 demonstrate different arrangements of merchandise, display fixtures, and props that create imagery and allow consumers to interact with the products.

Merchandise presentation must consider interactions among the product, packaging, display fixtures, signage, lighting, props, the environmental fragrance, and music to communicate the imagery and promote experience with the product. Each of these aspects may be carefully considered and designed with the product theme in mind. For instance, men's casual shirts are often hung on hangers while dress shirts are folded and neatly packaged in plastic bags. The presentation of the dress shirt, precisely folded, pinned, and packaged, adds to its level of formality. Similarly, some products have good hanger appeal—they look appealing when hung by the shoulders. Other products may not look attractive without a three-dimensional form supporting them.

Visual merchandisers must consider the amount of information that a shopper can take in at one time as he or she moves throughout a store. The retailer's concern is with the bottom line—sales per square foot of store space. But too much sensory stimulation from "busy" merchandise displays and other sensory inputs can lead to "sensory overload" for the consumer (Janiszewski, 1995; Malhotra, 1984). If there is too much sensory clutter, the shopper may develop tunnel vision or simply "shut down" in order to cope with the overload. In order to avoid this problem, merchandise displays should be arranged in groupings, with a central focus, using simple or uncluttered forms in the display (e.g., geometric shapes), and with important features at eye-level to the shopper (Philips & Bradshaw, 1993). Note the groupings evident in the examples in Figure 15.7. For instance, the Dayton's store uses isolated display fixtures so that each unit displays a group of products. The interior of the store is designed with clean, geometric forms and high-contrast color schemes.

The goal of verbal communication in merchandise presentation is the consistent and repeated use of identifiers to convey an image. Identifiers include product labels, hang-tags, and signage used in display. The repetition of the identifiers leads to the recognition of product and image (Pegler, 1995). In Activity 15.2, you will explore the use of identifiers to create and reinforce a product's image.

## FASHION SHOWS

The presentation of apparel products through fashion shows and trunk shows are often examples of communication. The presentation of the product on real models again incorporates more complexity and involvement on the part of the viewer than two-dimensional print media. Fashion shows are often targeted toward retail buyers, but they are also promotional tools reaching the general public as well. The audience for fashion shows has grown over the years as television shows such as CNN's *Style* and fX's *Fashion TV* present excerpts from designer shows for television viewers.

Although fashion shows can range from casual, informal settings to elaborately staged productions, the most common format is a runway show. Fashion shows can be held by designers and manufacturers introducing new collections or by retailers creating a special event to draw customers into the store.

The music that accompanies the model should reflect the formal, expressive, or symbolic qualities of the product and contribute to the imagery associ-

a

b

c

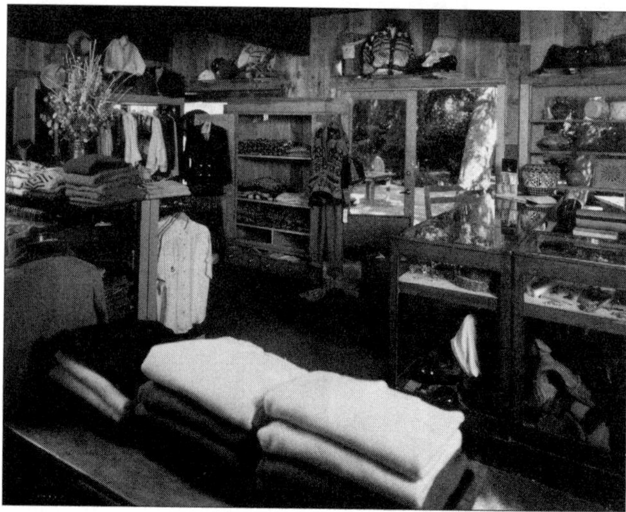

d

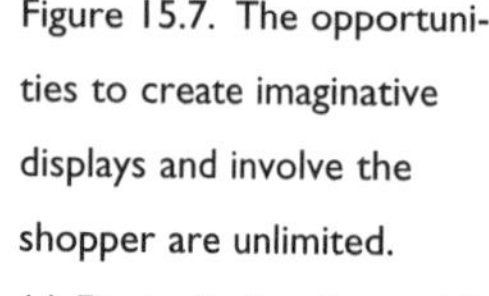

Figure 15.7. The opportunities to create imaginative displays and involve the shopper are unlimited.

(a) Dayton's, Burnhaven, MN.
Photo by Dan DuBroff;

(b) Valerie, Seattle, WA.
Photo by Doug Landreth;

(c) Out of the West.
Photo courtesy of 555 Design Fabrication Management;

(d) Sundance Resort, Sundance, UT.

ated with the product. The commentary in most shows is often minimal; it is used to communicate basic information such as fiber, fabrication, and price (Everett & Swanson, 1993). However, the script should provide variety, contribute to the imagery, and enhance the product. The simple listing of basic information for ensemble after ensemble would become tedious and boring for the listener. Commentary must elaborate on the theme of the collection, bringing the ideas to life for the audience as the models present the actual styles.

## PORTFOLIOS

Imagine yourself as a fresh graduate with your diploma in hand (we know this may seem like an event far-off in the future, but it really isn't). You are looking for a position in the apparel industry. How are you going to demonstrate to a potential employer the creative and technical abilities you would bring to their company? You need to demonstrate your skills and talents clearly and effectively during the interview. In the apparel industry, this is done through the use of a portfolio, or "book" as they're often called.

### Function of the Portfolio

A portfolio is a vital component in the job search process. The portfolio is a visual representation of a person and her or his design abilities. As you now know, aesthetics-related skills and activities are used by many professionals in different positions within the apparel industry. Professionals find it useful to prepare a portfolio to market themselves and their skills anytime their activities may be recorded visually and presented in a portfolio, usually through the use of drawings and/or photographs. This can include jobs as varied as fabric and surface design, apparel design, product development and merchandising, pattern making, styling, photography, visual merchandising, and store design.

An employer is usually aware of the type of skills and personal style they are seeking in candidates. The portfolio provides the bridge through which the abilities and personal aesthetic of the applicant are compared with the needs and the aesthetic of the potential employer. A portfolio should present both aesthetic and design skills as well as practical or technical skills. In addition, each person has an individual style or personal aesthetic which is important to convey in a portfolio.

**Aesthetic and design skills.** An individual's aesthetic sensitivity and design skills are represented through the content of a portfolio. The ability to perceive forms and glean the important characteristics, as well as an awareness of fashion timing and forecasting abilities, are demonstrated through the presentation of new product ideas. The ideas presented in a portfolio should be organized into groups. This will demonstrate an individual's skill at building a line or collection around a theme. One's color sense should come through as well. Work in a portfolio should represent an individual's creativity and mastery of design principles. Design skills can also be demonstrated through examples of an individual's ideas

Figure 15.8. Presentation board with several apparel items comprising a line.

**ACTIVITY 15.2** Figure 15.8 includes a presentation board with several apparel items. This is a portion of a line that is being developed by a new company. The company has not yet been named and the logo and signage for the products need to be developed. Working with a partner, you will help this company get started.

1. Examine the formal elements of the products. Using this information, develop a name for this company which you feel expresses the theme of the product line.
2. Develop a logo using the name of the company.
3. How might this logo be applied to the development of other signage (sewn-in product labels, hang-tags, and signage used in the store displays)? Make some suggestions or sketches.

for the presentation and promotion of products. An example of a store window planned and executed might be used to demonstrate the ability to organize products around a theme and use design principles in developing the display.

**Practical or technical skills.** Practical or technical skills that are demonstrated through a portfolio include drawing or rendering abilities, pattern-making, and garment construction skills. This will be evident in the visual material included. Work presented should indicate that an individual has high standards of quality as demonstrated through neatness, organization, and a coherent book. Portfolios should be presented to highlight an individual's strongest skills. If drawing and sketching are a strong skill, sketches should have prominent use in the portfolio. If an individual is stronger in pattern making and garment construction than drawing, perhaps it would be more effective to represent those skills through photos of previous work rather than lower quality drawings. For the entry-level or first job, the applicant will wish to demonstrate at least adequate skill in as many areas as possible.

**Presenting a certain aesthetic.** Through design and creative activities, each person has a "style" that is theirs alone. One's visual style is much like handwriting. No two people have styles that are completely alike. A designer's aesthetic is evident through fabric selection, finishing, trim, and high standards of quality, as well as the style of the product.

Design firms also have particular styles. The aesthetic product and manner in which work is carried out in different firms varies. Because of this, each firm will have a different outlook and different needs for its employees. In order to be successful, a prospective employee must demonstrate an ability to conform to and advance that aesthetic or style while performing duties satisfactorily. In the job search, one should make an effort to tailor a portfolio presentation to the needs of the company and gear the designs to a specific customer and market (price point). This will require preparation and research ahead of time. Know what the company you're interviewing with does, and what they might need from you. Try to provide this in your portfolio. Show a prospective employer what they want to see, and your chances of success will be much greater.

**Past achievements.** For the entry-level professional, it is perfectly acceptable to include in the portfolio evidence of student work and student achievements, such as awards. Later, once one has some work experience, these items may be deleted from the book and replaced with work produced at previous employment positions and major collections developed. The professional who has gained some experience will be able to demonstrate past achievements through garments featured in catalogs or ads and stating the sales generated by the styles developed. It is important to show prospective employers as many past experiences that demonstrate competence and skills as possible.

## Components of a Portfolio

"What should my portfolio look like? How should I put it together?" There is no single correct answer to these questions because portfolios are as unique and individual as their makers. But there are some general concepts you should consider in planning and developing your portfolio. These include aspects of the format, the inclusion of your resume, and the visual design of your presentation boards.

**Format considerations.** The format of a portfolio includes the size of the book, the pages, the page layout, and the number of pages included. All of these are personal decisions and must fit individual needs. When choosing a format for your portfolio, practical needs (such as portability) may influence these decisions. Portfolio binders come in a variety of styles and sizes. Binders which have removable pages are helpful for customizing a book to specific audiences. For

**ACTIVITY 15.3** What type of position do you want? What should you communicate about yourself to a company based on your abilities and the type of position you will seek? This is an ongoing question to continue to ask all along in your education, and each time you are searching for a job and updating your portfolio. Make some notes now about what you might want to communicate to potential employers in your portfolio.

many professionals, a small or medium-sized book (up to 11" x 14") is practical to carry and small enough for a viewer to open on a cluttered desk (Goldfarb, 1993).

A portfolio is a representation of work, not a life's history of work! Thus, approximately twenty pages of work should be adequate to demonstrate one's aesthetic and skills. When selecting work to include, only the highest quality should be chosen. The very best work should be placed in front and at the back to make a good impression and finish strong (Goldfarb, 1993). Work should also be organized to present a clear and logical progression from one presentation board or concept to another (Marquand, 1981). Presentations should be prepared in the most effective media possible. While different media have different effects, the tools that one is most fluent with (e.g., markers, pencils) will provide the best effect. Remember, clarity of the visual image is most important.

**Résumé.** Many professionals include their résumé in an inside pocket or as an opening page in their portfolio. A good résumé lists an employment objective, past work experience, educational preparation, and any other relevant skills and abilities which qualify an applicant for a position. As an entry-level applicant, don't forget to include internships or any practical experience you received during your education.

**Presentation boards.** The presentation of apparel product ideas in a portfolio should be organized to show the individual's ability to take an idea or product theme through the development process. The most effective manner to organize work, particularly for design or product development activities, is through the use of presentation boards (Figure 15.9). The inspiration and theme for a collection should be demonstrated. This can incorporate images from magazines, or other sources. A collage of inspiration (an inspiration board) makes an effective presentation. Several pieces from an apparel product line are demonstrated through flats or sketches, often in various color ways. Examples of fabric swatches and trims complete the line and demonstrate an ability to carry out the theme from concept through to the finishing details. Reading 15.2 provides many insights for portfolio presentation from two industry professionals.

## Helpful Hints

Always keep things neat and clean; nothing demonstrates one's attitude toward one's work more than tattered, dog-eared pages. When developing portfolio materials, keep tools and work surfaces clean.

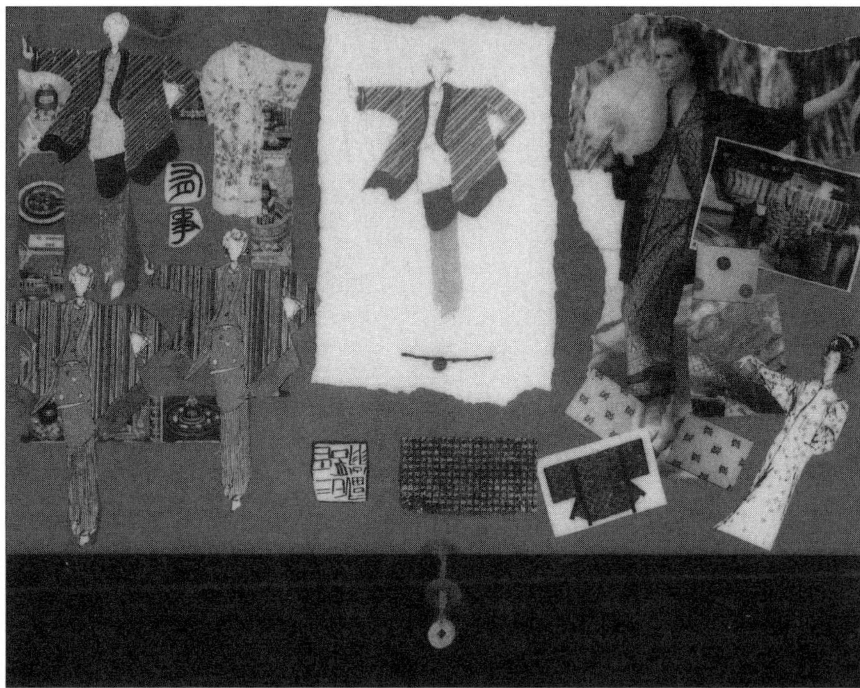

Figure 15.9. Presentation boards showing inspiration, fabrics, sketches, and flats for a product line that are appropriate for portfolio presentation. A good presentation board could also include a title, detail closeups, and background or environment.

Remember that portfolios are not static, nor are they ever finished. One's portfolio is always changing and growing just as the professional grows. A portfolio should be edited for each showing. Portfolios should be matched to the employer. For different interviews, different materials may be included or reordered in the portfolio.

Finally, have extra copies of your résumé on hand, in your portfolio. When calling on a firm to show a portfolio, always leave a resume, even if you don't interview at that time.

## SUMMARY

Communication is vital to the fulfillment of the goals of promotion. Promotion of apparel products emphasizes or enhances the product's value through communication and the design of the sensory environment for the product. The goal of promotion is to increase the salability of the product. Communication is used to achieve this goal by raising awareness of the product, increasing the perceived value and stimulating demand for the product, and adding meaning to the product. Communication promotes the product through the presentation of factual information about the product's features, the development of imagery surrounding the product, and fostering audience experiences with the product.

Within the industry, communication is used to represent the product within and between firms. The product is represented in photographs or drawings, or samples of the actual product. Different types of drawings incorporate a different amount of detail and information and are used for different purposes in the industry.

**LAB ACTIVITY 15.1**

In this activity, you should begin thinking about your future portfolio. Using information you developed in Activity 15.3, you should explore some possibilities for portfolio development.

1. What skills will be integral to a position you would seek in the apparel industry? (Reviewing Chapter 10 may help in defining the skills necessary in the desired position.) How might you represent these skills to a potential employer?
2. What type of format would be practical and effective for you?
3. Plan a presentation of a product line for a portfolio. This might include taking a project you completed in another course and develop the project into a small line based upon a theme. What is the theme for the line? Collect several visual images which demonstrate this theme.
4. Organize the information for an inspiration board.
5. Plan the presentation of your product line. Many professionals develop a consistent layout (page format, graphics, drawing media) and visual style that they use throughout a portfolio. This layout and style remains the same from page to page, even though the design concepts represented by different lines may change.
6. Make some sketches of different layouts in order to begin experimenting with different looks for your book. When you have experience in sketching or developing flats and are ready to begin your portfolio in earnest, these experiments may help you find an effective "look" for your portfolio.

Catalog presentations of apparel products also focus on the information about the product's features. This information comes from both visual images of the product and text describing the product. Consumers generally want the most explicit information possible in order to make accurate assumptions about the product.

Advertising communications move beyond the presentation of product information and build imagery associated with the product. Advertising in print and television are used to build an image for the product and stimulate interest. Advertising is most effective when it is targeted to specific market segments and audiences.

Visual merchandising and store displays are another prime opportunity to communicate with consumers about the product. Because this aspect of promotion involves presenting the actual product (as opposed to a 2-D image) in environments where the consumer can interact with the product, the opportunity for fostering experiences with the product is great. Similarly, the use of real products in a fashion show provides an opportunity to provide the audience with imagery and experience with the product that could influence future product choices.

The portfolio is a vital tool for career development and self-promotion for apparel professionals. Experience in the product development process and skills relevant to future employment are demonstrated visually through the development of the portfolio. The portfolio provides a means of comparing a prospective employee's skills and aesthetic with the needs of the apparel firm. Format considerations and the elements of the portfolio were discussed.

## KEY TERMS AND CONCEPTS

- audience involvement
- communication in advertising
- communication in catalogs
- communication in visual merchandising
- communication through fashion shows
- flats
- illustration
- imagery
- internal promotion
- metaphor
- portfolio
- presentation boards
- promotional communication
- resume
- simile
- specification drawings
- verbal imagery
- visual imagery

## SUGGESTED READINGS


Goldfarb, R. (1993). *Careers by design: A headhunter's secrets for success and survival in graphic design.* New York, NY: Allworth Press.

Phillips, H. & Bradshaw, R. (1993). How customers actually shop: Customer interaction with the point of sale. *Journal of the Market Research Society, 35*(1), 51–62.


### For Advanced Levels


McCracken, G. (1986). Culture and consumption: A theoretical account of the structure and movement of the cultural meaning of consumer goods. *Journal of Consumer Research, 13*(1), 71–84.

## READING 15.1
# Excerpts from The Mailing of America

J. Simone

*Successful catalog store roll-outs are prompting many mainstream stores to "publish or perish," confirming yet again retailing demands more than conventional marketing.*

While the overall catalog business has leveled off since the '80s, when annual growth averaged 15 percent a year, expansion today is still chugging along at 5 to 6 percent. The number of books mailed annually has dropped slightly, from 13.6 billion mailed in 1990 to 13.4 billion mailed in 1991. This suggests the market is getting crowded—which means new strategies are in order for the country's 8,000 catalog retailers.

One response to this more competitive climate is the opening of stores by firms once mail-order only, including Spiegel, Cabela's and Lillian Vernon. Even as some catalogers are opening stores in order to step outside the crowded field, a couple of daring fashion firms are joing the catalog throng.

Firms that have both catalogs and stores often use the two to bounce ideas off each other and to test merchandise. Spiegel, for example, inked a licensing agreement with Crayola and included a 16-page children's wear supplement in its Fall 1990 catalog. This evolved into a regular catalog segment, followed by free-standing Crayola Kid stores. Rob Longendyke, Spiegel's public relations manager, terms the catalog/store phenomenon a "dual-channel market," emphasizing the use of both as support systems for each other. "The catalog functions as an advertising vehicle for the stores," explains Longendyke, "while the store enables the customer to know the product line better." The stores also serve as a litmus test for new concept merchandise. If new items test well, they will generally be included in the catalog.

### Cataloging an image

Rather than being purely selling devices, today's catalogs often offer intangible yet valuable rewards. They can increase traffic in stores or build loyalty with customers, restore reputations or revamp images.

Frederick's of Hollywood, for one, used its catalog to help reframe perceptions and introduce its new act—modesty. The catalog has omitted sexual games and paraphernalia, and even the sportswear and swimwear have disappeared. It has strengthened the intimate apparel and sleepwear collections in its catalog and stores, and has renovated more than 80 percent of its 191 stores to reflect the new, more modest side of Frederick's.

Perhaps the most creative use of a catalog can be credited to Timberland, which has some 200,000 customers asking, "Is it a catalog or is it a magazine?" The company has published what it calls a "magalog," entitled "Elements: Journal of the Outdoor Experience"—an apt title considering its Fall 1991 debut issue focused on weather and the second on water. Along with merchandise for sale, the pages are filled with adventure stories and essays by writers familiar to readers of outdoors publications.

Elements is about as soft-sell in its approach as it can get. Of the two ads in its first edition, only one is for Timberland apparel and it neither identified the item nor gave a price. Elise Klysa, corporate communications manager, explains, "Elements was created mainly to emphasize the brand and to develop a deeper relationship with our existing customers—not necessarily to attract a new customer." Elaborates Ken Freitas, vice president of marketing, "We're not getting into the publications business; we are a brand business with a unique connection to our customer. Elements represents an effort to nourish that relationship."

### Designing catalog and store in synch

Not only do catalogs represent retailers' images, but they also create profound impressions of the stores, setting up certain expectations in the consumer's mind. Retailers who catalog know the book affords an opportunity to bring the store to the customer when the customer cannot get to the store. Thus,

Reading 15.1 Simone, J. (1992, November). Excerpts from "The Mailing of America." *Visual Merchandising and Store Design,* pp. 24–32.

the same sense of identity and/or exclusivity must be conveyed via the catalog.

One of Spiegel's dual-channel markets, its large-size women's apparel division, aims to present positive images in both For You stores and catalogs to customers who, in many cases, are shopping for self-esteem as well as clothing. The stores are not overmerchandised and stress assortment and breadth of fashion choices, with complete accessorized outfits displayed on face-out fixtures offering a variety of possibilities to the customer. In a similar vein, the "For You" catalog features styles and choices presented in a clear, attractive, contemporary setting. Because large-size customers can feel stigmatized in a society obsessed with runway-model-thin waistlines. For You constantly emphasizes the positive in lifestyle presentations that connote self-respect.

Ruggedness, wilderness, environment—all are catchwords these days as a spate of firms try to capture America's rampant "back-to-nature" spirit. And in order to net the adventure-minded customer, both store and catalog must bring the great outdoors to life. One such firm is outdoor sporting gear specialist Cabela's, whose 75,000-sq.-ft. store in Sydney, Neb., is virtually a three-dimensional experience for customers already familiar with the catalog. Take, for instance, the mountain Cabela's installed, measuring 40 ft. high and 80 ft. in length and featuring running streams. On display throughout the store are more than 500 trophy mounts—deer, sheep, lions, and even a full-size African elephant.

With a merchandise mix of about 60 percent clothing to 40 percent hard goods, Cabela's does 12 mailings a year and targets not just sport enthusiasts but the "20 percent of the population that won't buy direct mail," says catalog director Jim Beardsley.

In the case of Smith & Hawken, the relationship between catalog and stores is very close, except that the latter have a more sensual appeal. "The retail environment smells good in an earthy sense," says Salkin. "Our strategy is bringing the garden indoors—no cutesy antiques." A strong ecological statement is made with rocks and water, with the emphasis on a warm, comfortable environment and modular fixturing. Perhaps as part of its fashionably unfashionable image, most Smith & Hawken stores are located in rehabbed buildings. One location even sits atop a former toxic waste site cleaned up by Smith & Hawken.

Jos. A. Bank, a men's and women's clothier based in Maryland, sees itself as selling good taste at moderate prices. To call attention to the value-at-a-price credo, its 43 stores are undergoing a transformation to Shaker design, an appropriate setting as most suits fall in the $275 to $395 range and the styling is considered traditional and updated. Referring to the new look, director of creative services Peter Satten explains, "We wanted to make a statement with traditional references but we're not creating theme stores." Warm wood accents and warm color tones create a clean, welcoming atmosphere rather than an imposing one. The same simple presentations are carried through in the catalogs with straightforward visuals and copy, which again emphasize value and affordability.

An unusual synergy exists between the store and catalog formats, with both co-evolving along with the market. The more advanced catalogers are becoming more highly targeted and global in their marketing strategies where there is opportunity for expansion. Many marketers are beginning to realize the potential of catalogs to test market goods and concepts without having to make the often expensive mistake of opening another store or another branch only to find disappointment when traffic and sales don't achieve expectations.

Finally, catalogs can provide helpful direction in the store's visual environment, especially among more specialized retailers. The store is becoming a backdrop to enhance sales by providing an appropriate experience—of the great outdoors, of intimacy or playfulness, or of the sort of opulence many people dream of. It all depends on what the store and its merchandise focus represent. A good catalog helps whet the consumer's appetite for such experiences.

## READING 15.2
# Portfolio Tips For Students

Reading 15.2 Portfolio Tips For Students. Excerpts from interviews with Linda Tain, Fashion Institute of Technology, and Lisa Hendrickson, New York sportswear designer.

### How should a student approach development of their first portfolio?

**Tain:** Students should definitely focus on a particular area or market. What students notoriously do, is include a conglomeration of things—sportswear, sweaters, evening gowns, bathing suits, intimate apparel—it's like a mish-mash. And the interviewer will realize that this person is not focused in a particular area, and they become unsure whether this person would be able to capture what (the company) does. So it's very important for students to focus. Within areas, there are segments, so the student doesn't have to stick to only one thing, like in sportswear, sweater design is very important. So certainly doing a knitwear group could be very valuable with a sportswear collection. Edit out things that are not relevant to the company you're interviewing with.

### How should a portfolio look in terms of format and organization?

**Hendrickson:** It's important that a portfolio looks logical, not just random, like you took everything you've worked on and threw it in here. Pick an order for how you want your book to look. I tend to group things together, several pages at a time. Also, if you choose two categories, like dresses and sportswear, you don't want to mix them up. Put the dress sequence first, then the sportswear sequence. So, when you interview with me, I'm not interested in dresses, I'll go through that section quickly, and spend more time looking at your sportswear section.

**Tain:** We really advocate designing in groups because no one today designs just one garment. And no matter what area you work in, you really have to develop your design thinking in terms of groups. And all the items should be able to capture the thematic concept.

### Do you have recommendations for media?

**Tain:** I think people tend to work in quick media in the industry, like marker and pencil, prisma pencil, and things like that. In a certain market, like the designer market, watercolor is still done. But in most of the other markets, people like the quick media because they don't have time to do a laborious rendering, and it works for them.

Anything that's computer generated would be good. Sophisticated computer skills (such as) scanning fabrics, recolor, change scale, printing and using it in a collage type presentation for portfolio . . . That shows that the person has a certain knowledge of technology and know how to implement it.

### What do you suggest for the opening page?

**Hendrickson:** If you have a really fabulous piece of artwork, or an illustration, great. Open up with a bang. Otherwise, I would just put your resume on the first page. Have a couple so if you have to hand them out, you know you'll always have it with you.

**Tain:** I recommend students develop an art piece that represents who they are and what they are about as a designer for a first page. They duplicate it (like color copies or something) and use it as a "leave behind" piece to accompany their resume. That reinforces their image and leaves a stronger impression.

### How soon should students start developing their portfolios?

**Hendrickson:** I'd say possibly in the junior year, definitely at the start of the senior year. Whatever you have of good schoolwork, you can use, but I'm a real advocate of doing projects on your own. If you spend one day a month working on projects for your portfolio, by the time you graduate, you'll have plenty of good work to choose from. You'll be relieved. If you wait until two months before graduation and you've not done any work on your own, you're going to panic and say "I'm going to have to spend two months working on my portfolio before I can interview." If you make time to work on projects on your own, you'll really be able to spread your creative wings.

# References

A is for Attitude. (1995, June). *Visual Merchandising and Store Design,* p. 50.

Abraham-Murali, L. & Littrell, M. A. (1995). Consumers' perceptions of apparel quality over time: An exploratory study. *Clothing and Textiles Research Journal, 13*(3), 149–212.

Ackerman, D. (1990). *A natural history of the senses.* New York: Vintage Books.

Agins, T. (1995). Why cheap clothes are getting more respect. *The Wall Street Journal,* Oct. 16, pp. B1, B6.

Alexander, B. & Marks, L. E. (1983). Aesthetic preference and resemblance of viewer's personality to paintings. *Bulletin of the Psychonomic Society, 21*(5), 384–386.

Allen, P. S. & Stimpson, M. F. (1977). *Beginnings of interior environment, (6th Ed.).* New York: Macmillan.

Alpert, J. I. & Alpert, M. I. (1989). Background music as an influence in consumer mood and advertising responses. *Advances in Consumer Research, 16,* 485–491.

Alpert, J. I. & Alpert, M. I. (1990). Music influences on mood and purchase intentions. *Psychology and Marketing,* 7(2), 109–133.

Anderson, P.K. (1992, April). Perspectives: Sensory engineering. *Visual Merchandising and Store Design,* p.1.

Anderson, R. L. (1993). Cross-cultural aesthetic contrasts and implications for aesthetic evolution and change. *Empirical Studies of the Arts, 11*(1), 51–60.

Arnheim, R. (1972). The Gestalt theory of expression. In R. Arnheim (Ed.), *Toward a psychology of art: Collected essays* (pp. 51–73). Berkeley, CA: University of California Press.

Arnheim, R. (1986). *New essays on the psychology of art.* Berkeley, CA: University of California Press.

Arnheim, R. (1988). *The power of the center.* Berkeley, CA: University of California Press.

Astley, A. T. (1994, March). Quicksilver. *Vogue,* pp. 390–393.

August, B. (1981). *Looking thin.* New York: Rawson Wade.

Author and title indexes. (1993). *Clothing and Textile Research Journal, 12*(1) 1–8.

Babin, B. J., Darden, W. R. & Griffin, M. (1994). Work and/or fun: Measuring hedonic and utilitarian shopping value. *Journal of Consumer Research, 20,* 644–656.

Baddeley, A. D. (1986). *Working memory.* New York: Oxford University Press.

Baer, M. (1979). Visual recall of dress design determined by perceptual style. *Home Economics Research Journal, 7,* 292–303.

Bagly, M. K. & Supplee, K. A. (1983). Dimensions of aesthetic perception. *Journal of Psychology, 114,* 29–35.

Baker, J., Grewal, D. & Parasuraman, A. (1994). The influence of store environment on quality inferences and store image. *Journal of Academy of Marketing Science,* 22(4), 328–339.

Baker, J., Levy, M. & Grewal, D. (1992). An experimental approach to making retail store environmental decisions. *Journal of Retailing, 68*(4), 445–460.

Baron, R. A. (1990). Lighting as a source of positive affect. *Progressive Architecture, 71*(11), 123–124.

BAT shows potential of plus-size fashion. (1995, October 26). *Women's Wear Daily,* p.14.

Bath towels: Necessary luxuries. (1995, January). *Stores,* p. 58–59.

Beardsley, M. C. (1958). *Aesthetics.* New York: Harcourt, Brace, and World, Inc.

Belk, R. W. (1988). Possessions and the extended self. *Journal of Consumer Research, 15,* 139–168.

Bell, S. S., Holbrook, M. B. & Solomon, M. R. (1991). Combining esthetic and social value to explain preferences for product styles with the incorporation of personality and ensemble effects. *Journal of Social Behavior and Personality,* 6(6), 243–274.

Bellizzi, J. A., Crowley, A. E. & Hasty, R. W. (1983). The effects of color in store design. *Journal of Retailing, 59* (1), 21–45.

Berlyne, D. E. (1970). Novelty, complexity, and hedonic value. *Perception and Psychophysics, 8*(5A), 279–287.

Berlyne, D. E. (1971). *Aesthetics and psychobiology.* New York: Appleton-Century-Crofts.

Berlyne, D. E. (Ed.). (1974). *Studies in the new experimental aesthetics: Steps toward an objective psychology of aesthetic appreciation.* Washington DC: Hemisphere.

Berlyne, D. E., Robbins, M. C. & Thompson, R. (1974). A cross-cultural study of exploratory and verbal responses to visual patterns varying in complexity. In D. E. Berlyne (Ed.), *Studies in the new experimental aesthetics: Steps toward an objective psychology of aesthetic appreciation* (pp. 259–278). Washington DC: Hemisphere.

Berscheid, E. & Walster, E. (1974). In L. Berkowitz (Ed.), *Advances in experimental social psychology* (vol.7). New York: Academic Press.

Bevlin, M. (1989). *Design through discovery: An introduction to art and design,* (5th Ed.). New York: Holt, Rinehart and Winston.

Bierley, C., McSweeney, F. K., Vannieuwkerk, R. (1985, December). Classical Conditioning of preferences for stimuli. *Journal of Consumer Research, 12,* 316–323.

Bitner, M. J. (1992, April). Servicescapes: The impact of physical surroundings on customers and employees. *Journal of Marketing, 56,* 57–71.

Bleustein, J. (1995, February 8). *Changes in Harley Davidson.* Presentation at Iowa State University.

Blumer, H. (1969). Fashion: From class differentiation to collective selection. *Sociological Quarterly, 10,* 275–291.

Bone, P. F. & Jantrania, S. (1992). Olfaction as a cue for product quality. *Marketing Letters, 3*(3), 289–296.

Boselie, F. (1984). Complex and simple proportions and the aesthetic attractivity of visual patterns. *Perception, 13*, 91–96.

Boswell, T. (1992). *The costume maker's art: Cloaks of fantasy, masks of revelation.* Asheville, N.C.: Lark Books.

Brand, R. H. (1964). Measurement of fabric aesthetics: Analysis of aesthetic components. *Textile Research Journal, 34*, 791–804.

Brett, D. (1986). The aesthetical science: George Field and the "science of beauty". *Art History, 9*(3), 336–350.

Bruner, G. C. (1990). Music, mood, and marketing. *Journal of Marketing, 54* (October), 94–104.

Bryant, N. O. (1991). The interrelationship between decorative and structural design in Madeleine Vionnet's work. *Costume, 25*, 73–88.

Bull, P. (1983). *Body movement and interpersonal communication.* Chichester: John Wiley & Sons.

Burke, M. J. & Gridley, M. C. (1990). Musical preferences as a function of stimulus complexity and listeners' sophistication. *Perceptual and Motor Skills, 71*, 687–690.

Burns, L. D. & Lennon, S. J. (1994). The look and feel: Methods for measuring aesthetic perceptions of textiles and apparel. In M. R. DeLong and A. M. Fiore (Eds.), *Aesthetics of textiles and clothing: Advancing multidisciplinary perspectives*, (pp. 120–130). Monument, CO.: International Textiles and Apparel Association (special publication #7).

Bye, E. K. & DeLong, M. R. (1994). A visual sensory evaluation of the results of two pattern grading methods. *Clothing and Textile Research Journal, 12*(4), 1–7.

Byrne-Quinn, J. (1988). Perfume, people, perception and products. In S. Van Toller and G. H. Dodd (Eds.), *Perfumery: The psychology and biology of fragrance* (pp. 205–216). London, England: Chapman and Hall.

Cerny, C. A. (1994). Cultural foundations of aesthetic appreciation: Use of trope in structuring quiltmaking sentiment. In M. R. DeLong & A. M. Fiore (Eds.), *Aesthetics of textiles and clothing: Advancing multidisciplinary perspectives* (pp. 152–162). Monument CO: International Textile and Apparel Association (special publication #7).

Child, I. L. & Siroto, L. (1971). BaKwele and American aesthetic evaluations compared. In C. F. Jopling (Eds.), *Art and aesthetics in primitive societies* (pp. 271–289). New York: E. P. Dutton.

Child, I. L. (1981). Bases of transcultural agreement in response to art. In H. I. Day (Ed.), *Advances in intrinsic motivation and aesthetics.* New York: Plenum Press.

Cialdini, R., Bordon, R., Thorne, A., Walker, A., Freeman, S & Sloane, L. (1976). Basking in reflected glory: three (football) field studies. *Journal of Personality and Social Psychology, 34*, 366–375.

Classen, C. (1993). *World of senses: Exploring the senses in history and across cultures.* London and New York: Routledge.

*Color Association of the United States* Color Forecast for Menswear, Women's wear and Children's wear.

Color predictions. (1994, January/February). *Communication Arts*, p. 92.

Consumer Reports (1994, October). *Mail order shopping: Which catalogs are the best?*

Coote, J. & Shelton, A. (Eds.). (1992). *Oxford studies in the anthropology of cultural forms.* New York: Clarendon Press.

Coren, S., Porac, C. & Ward, L. M. (1979). *Sensation and Perception.* New York: Academic.

Corwin, P. (1993, May). Presentation, replenishment, and profit. *DM, 33*(5), pp. 50–54, 138, 143.

Couture to Elastic Waistbands: A Designer's Journey. (1995, October 16). *Wall Street Journal*, pp. B1, B5.)

Cowley, G. (1996, June 3). The biology of beauty. *Newsweek*, pp. 61–66.

Crane, L. L. & Hicks, R. A. (1989). Preference for the color red and activation: A test of Thayer's theory. *Psychological Reports, 64*, 947–950.

Creekmore, A. (1980). Clothing and personal attractiveness of adolescents related to conformity, to clothing mode, peer acceptance and leadership potential. *Home Economics Research Journal, 8*, 203–221.

Crowley, A. E. (1993). The two dimensional impact of color on shopping. *Marketing Letters, 4*(1), 59–69.

Crozier, W. R. & Chapman, A. J. (1984). The perception of art: The cognitive approach and its context. In W. R. Crozier & A. J. Chapman (Eds.), *Cognitive processes in the perception of art* (pp. 3–23). New York: Elsevier Science.

Csikszentmihalyi, M. & Robinson, R. E. (1990). *The art of seeing: An interpretation of the aesthetic encounter.* Malibu, CA: J. Paul Getty Trust.

Csikszentmihalyi, M. (1990). *Flow: The psychology of optimal experience.* New York: Harper & Row.

Cupchik, G. C. (1988). The legacy of Daniel E. Berlyne. *Empirical Studies of the Arts, 6*(2), 171–186.

*Daily News Record.* Source for articles on the men's wear fashion industry and trends.

Danielson, D. R. (1986). According to the artists: Professional fashion illustrators' views about their art form. *Clothing and Textile Research Journal, 5*(1), 27–33.

Danielson, D. R. (1989). The changing figure ideal in fashion illustration. *Clothing and Textiles Research Journal, 8*(1), 35–48.

Darden, W. R., Erdem, O. & Darden, D. K. (1983). A comparison and test of three causal models of patronage intentions. In W. R. Darden and R. F. Lusch (Eds.), *Patronage behavior and retail management.* New York: North–Holland.

d'Aulaire, E. & d'Aulaire, P. (1991, April). Mannequins: Our fantasy figures of high fashion. *Smithsonian*, pp. 66–77.

Davis, M. (1980). *Visual design in dress.* Englewood Cliffs, NJ: Prentice-Hall.

Day, H. I. (Ed.). (1981). *Advances in intrinsic motivation and aesthetics.* New York: Plenum.

De Meijer, M. (1989). The contribution of general features of body movement to the attribution of emotions. *Journal of Nonverbal Behavior*, 13(4), 247–268.

Degre 7 puts its best ski foreward. (1994, September). *Catalog Age*, pp. 117–118.

DeLong M. R. & Fiore, A. M. (Eds.), *Aesthetics of Textiles and Clothing: Advancing multi-disciplinary perspectives.* Monument, CO: International Textile & Apparel Association (special publication #7).

DeLong, M. R. (1977). Clothing and aesthetics: Perception of form. *Home Economics Research Journal*, *5*, 214–224.

DeLong, M. R. (1987). *The way we look.* Ames, IA: Iowa State University Press.

DeLong, M. R., Salusso-Deonier, C. & Larntz, K. (1983). Use of perceptions of female dress as an indicator of role definition. *Home Economics Research Journal, 11*, 327–336.

Dember, W. N. & Earl, R. W. (1957). Analysis of exploratory, manipulatory, and curiosity behaviors. *Psychology Review*, *64*, 91–96.

Deshpande, R., Hoyer, W. D. & Donthu, N. (1986). The intensity of ethnic affiliation: A study of the sociology of Hispanic consumption. *Journal of Consumer Research*, *13*, 214–220.

Deutsch, E. (1975). Studies in comparative aesthetics. *Monograph of the Society for Asian and Comparative Philosophy*, *2*.

Diamond, J. & Diamond, E. (1996). *Fashion advertising and promotion.* Albany, NY: Delmar Publishers.

Disney World: Putting money where the mouse is. (1991). *Chain Store Age Executive*, *67*, 202–203.

Dissanayake, E. (1984). Does art have selective value? *Empirical Studies of the Arts*, *2*(1), 35–49.

Dissanayake, E. (1988). *What is art for?* Seattle: University of Washington Press.

Domzal, T. J. & Kernan, J. B. (1993). Variations on the pursuit of beauty: Toward a corporal theory of the body. *Psychology & Marketing*, *10*(6), 495–511.

Don't make store design too posh for clientele. (1991, May) . *Chain Store Age Executive*, *67* (5), 183–184).

Donovan, R. J. & Rossiter, J. R. (1982). Store atmosphere: An environmental psychology approach. *Journal of Retailing*, *58* (2), 34–57.

Donovan, R. J., Rossiter, J. R., Marcoolyn, G. & Nesdale, A. (1994). Store atmosphere and purchasing behavior. *Journal of Retailing*, *70*(3), 283–294.

Douty, H. I. & Brannon, E. L. (1984). Figure attractiveness: Male and female preferences for female figures. *Home Economics Research Journal*, *13*, 123–137.

Dowling, W. J. & Harwood, D. L. (1986). *Music Cognition.* Orlando, FL: Academic Press.

Dubé, L., Chebat, J-C., Morin, S. (1995, July). The effect of background music on consumers' desire to affiliate in buyer-seller interactions. *Psychology & Marketing*, 305–315.

Dubler, M.L. & Gurel, L. (1984). Depression: relationships to clothing and appearance self-concept. *Home Economics Research Journal, 13*, 21–26.

Dunn, W. (1992, July). The move toward ethnic marketing. *Nation's Business*, pp. 39–41.

Eckman, M., Damhorst, M. L. & Kadolph, S. J. (1990). Toward a model of the in-store purchase decision process: Consumer use of criteria for evaluating women's apparel. *Clothing and Textiles Research Journal*, *8*(2), 13–22.

Effective visual merchandising. (1995, May). *Chain Store Age Executive*, *71*(5), pp. 145–146.

Eisenman, R. & Rappaport, J. (1967). Complexity preference and semantic differential ratings of complexity-simplicity and symmetry-asymmetry. *Psychonomic Science*, *7*(4), 147–148.

Elder, H. M. (1977). Fabric appearance and handle. *Journal of Consumer Studies and Home Economics, 1*, 171–182.

Engel, J. & Blackwell, R. (1982). *Consumer behavior*, (4th ed.). Chicago: The Dryden Press.

Engen, T. (1982). *The perception of odors.* New York: Academic Press.

Eysenck, H. J. (1981). Aesthetic preferences and individual differences. In D. O'Hare (Ed.), *Psychology and the arts* (pp. 76–101). Sussex: Harvester Press.

Fabricant, S. M. & Gould, S. J. (1993). Women's makeup careers: An interpretive study of color cosmetic use and "face value". *Psychology and Marketing*, *10*(6), 531–548.

Fallon, J. (1996, September 16). Color dazzles at Decosit. *Home Furnishing Network*, p. 38.

Fashion Forecast D3: From visionaries to visuals. (1995, June). *Visual Merchandising and Store Design*, pp. 38–42.

Favreau, O. E. & Corballis, M. C. (1976, December). Negative aftereffects in visual perception. *Scientific American*, *234*(6), 42–48.

*Fiberarts.* Source for articles on artistic weaving and surface design.

Fichner-Rathus, L. (1989). *Understanding art* (2nd ed.). Englewood Cliffs, NJ: Prentice-Hall.

Fiore, A. M. & Damhorst, M. L. (1992). Intrinsic cues as predictors of perceived quality of apparel. *Journal of Consumer Satisfaction, Dissatisfaction and Complaining Behavior*, *5*, 168–178.

Fiore, A. M. & DeLong, M. R. (1990). A personal appearance program for displaced homemakers. *Journal of Career Development*, *16*(3), 219–226.

Fiore, A. M. & DeLong, M. R. (1993). The influence of public self-consciousness and self-monitoring on participation in an effective presentation program. *Journal of Career Development*, *20*(2), 161–168.

Fiore, A. M. & Yan. X. (in progress). *Effect of environmental fragrancing on attitude and purchase intention toward an apparel product.*

Fiore, A. M. (1992). Effect of composition of olfactory cues on impressions of personality. *Social Behavior and Personality*, *20*(3), 149–162.

Fiore, A. M. (1993). Multisensory integration of visual, tactile, and olfactory aesthetic cues of appearance. *Clothing and Textiles Research Journal*, *11*(2), 45–52.

Fiore, A. M. (1994). Aesthetics: The James Dean of Textiles and Clothing. In M. R. DeLong & A. M. Fiore (Eds.), *Aesthetics of Textiles and Clothing: Advancing Multidisciplinary Perspectives* (pp. 7–12). International Textiles and Apparel Association Monograph (special publication #7).

Fiore, A. M., Kimle, P. A. & Moreno, J. M. (1996). Aesthetics: A comparison of the state of the art outside and inside the field of textiles and clothing. Part one: Creator and creative process. *Textiles and Clothing Research Journal*, 14(1), 30–41.

Fiore, A. M., Kimle, P.A. & Moreno, J. M. (1996). Aesthetics: A Comparison of the state of the art outside and inside the field of textiles and clothing. Part Three: Appreciation process, appreciator, and summary comparisons. *Clothing and Textiles Research Journal*, *14*(3), 169–184.

Fiore, A. M., Kimle, P.A. & Moreno, J. M. (1996). Aesthetics: A comparison of the state of the art outside and inside the field of textiles and clothing. Part two: Object. *Clothing and Textiles Research Journal*, *14*(2), 97–107.

Fiorito, S. S. & Fairhurst, A. E. (1993). Comparison of buyers' job content in large and small retail firms. *Clothing and Textiles Research Journal*, *11*(3), 8–15.

Flores, T. (1985). The anthropology of aesthetics. *Dialectical Anthropology*, *10*, 27–41.

Folse, N. M. & Henrion, M. (1981). *Careers in the fashion industry*. New York: Harper & Row.

Forsythe, S. M. & Bailey, A. W. (1996). Shopping enjoyment, perceived time poverty, and time spent shopping. *Clothing and Textiles Research Journal*,*14* (3), 185–191.

Fratto, T. F. (1978). Undefining art: Irrelevant categorization in the anthropology of aesthetics. *Dialectical Anthropology*, *3*, 129–138.

Freitas, A., Kaiser, S. & Hammidi, T. (in press). Communities, commodities, cultural space, and style. *Journal of Homosexuality*.

Frings, G. S. (1996). *Fashion: From concept to consumer*. Upper Saddle River, NJ: Prentice Hall.

Frost, D. (1991, January). Different smells for different shoppers. *American Demographics*, pp. 10–12.

Furukawa, T. (1995, October 6). Lighter fragrances, looser import rules spark sales in Japan. *Women's Wear Daily*, pp. 1, 4.

Gaskill, L. R. (1992). Toward a model of retail product development: A case study analysis. *Clothing and Textiles Research Journal*, *10*(4), 17–24.

Gibson, J. J. (1979). *The ecological approach to visual perception*. Boston: Houtton Mifflin.

Gitlin, T. (1989, July/August). Postmodernism defined, at last! *Utne Reader*, pp. 52–61.

Glock, R. E. & Kunz, G. I. (1995). *Apparel manufacturing: Sewn product analysis* (2nd ed.). Englewood Cliffs, N. J.: Prentice-Hall.

Golden, L.G. & Zimmerman, D. A. (1986). *Effective retailing*. Boston, MA: Houghton Mifflin.

Goldfarb, R. (1993). *Careers by design: A headhunter's secrets for success and survival in graphic design*. New York: Allworth Press.

Goldman, A. (1995). Emotions in music (A postscript). *Journal of Aesthetics and Art Criticism*, *53*(1), 59–70.

Gombrich, E. H. (1979). *Sense of order*. Oxford, England: Phaidon Press.

Gorn, G. J. (1982, winter). The effects of music in advertising on choice behavior: A classical conditioning approach. *Journal of Marketing*, *46*, 94–101.

Gould, S. J. & Stern, B. B. (1989). Gender schema and fashion consciousness. *Psychology and Marketing*, *6*(2), 129–145.

Green, A. (1993, March-April). The fragrance revolution: The nose goes to new lengths. *The Futurist*, pp. 13–17.

Greenwald, A. G. & Leavitt, C. (1984, June). Audience involvement in advertising: Four levels. *Journal of Consumer Research*, *11*, 581–592.

Gulas, C. S. & Bloch, P. H. (1995). Right under our noses: Ambient scent and consumer responses. *Journal of Business and Psychology*, *10*(1), 87–98.

*H & R book of perfume*. (1984). London: Johnson.

Hagen, M. A. (1986). *Varieties of realism: Geometries of representational art*. Cambridge, England: Cambridge University Press.

Hardin, K. L. (1988). Aesthetics and the cultural whole: A study of Kono dance occasions. *Empirical Studies of the Arts*, *6*(1), 35–57.

Hausman, C. R. (1981). Criticism and countertheses: Goetz on creativity [Review of *On Defining Creativity*]. *Journal of Aesthetic and Art Criticism*, *40*(1), 81.

Havlena, W. J. & Holbrook, M. B. (1986). The varieties of consumption experience: Comparing two typologies of emotion in consumer behavior. *Journal of Consumer Research*, *13*, 394–404.

Hearle, J. (1993, April). Can fabric hand enter the dataspace? *Textile Horizons International*, p. 14–16.

Hecher, S. (1984). Music for advertising effect. *Psychology and Marketing*, *1*(3/4), 3–8.

Hein, H. & Korsmeyer, C. (1993). *Aesthetics in feminist perspective*. Bloomington, IN: Indiana University Press.

Hekkert, P. & van Wieringen, P. C. W. (1990). Complexity and prototypicality as determinants of the appraisal of cubist paintings. *British Journal of Psychology, 81*, 483–495.

Heller, M.A. & Schiff, W. (1991). *Psychology of touch*. Hillsdale, NJ: Lawrence Erlbaum Associates.

Henderson, B. (1994). Teaching aesthetics in a postmodern environment. In M. R. DeLong & A. M. Fiore (Eds.), *Aesthetics of textiles and clothing: Advancing multi-disciplinary perspectives* (pp. 39–47). Monument, Co: International Textiles and Apparel Association (special publication #7).

Henion, K. E. (1971). Odor pleasantness and intensity: A single dimension? *Journal of Experimental Psychology, 90*, 275–279.

Hetzel, P. & Aubert, V. (1993). Sales area design and fashion phenomena. *European Advances in Consumer Research, 1*, 522–533.

Hirschfeld, L. A. (1977). Cuna aesthetics: A quantitative analysis. *Ethnology, 16*(2), 147–166.

Hirschman, E. C. & Holbrook, M. B. (1982). Hedonic consumption: Emerging concepts, methods and propositions. *Journal of Marketing, 46*, 92–101.

Hirschman, E. C. (1983). On the acquisition of aesthetic, escapist, and agentic experiences. *Empirical Studies of the Arts, 1*(2), 157–171.

Hirschman, E. C. (1984). Experience seeking: A subjective perspective of consumption. *Journal of Business Research, 12*, 115–136.

Holbrook, M. B. & Hirschman, E. C. (1982). The experiential aspects of consumption: Consumer fantasies, feelings, and fun. *Journal of Cosumer Research, 9*, 132–140.

Holbrook, M. B. & Huber, J. (1983). Detecting the differences in jazz: A comparison of methods for assessing perceptual veridicality in applied aesthetics. *Empirical Studies of the Arts, 1*(1), 35–53.

Holbrook, M. B. & O'Shaughnessy, J. (1984). The role of emotion in advertising. *Psychology and Marketing, 1*(2), 45–64.

Holbrook, M. B. & Schindler, R. M. (1989). Some exploratory findings on the development of musical tastes. *Journal of Consumer Research, 16*, 119–124.

Holbrook, M. B. & Schindler, R. M. (1994). Age, sex, and attitude towards the past as predictors of consumers' aesthetic tastes for cultural products. *Journal of Marketing Research, 31*, 412–422.

Holbrook, M. B. (1987). The study of signs in consumer esthetics: An egocentric review. In J. Umiker-Sebeok (Ed.), *Marketing and semiotics: New directions in the study of signs for sale* (pp. 73–121). New York: Mouton de Gruyter.

Holbrook, M. B. (1994). Axiology, aesthetics, and apparel: Some reflections on the old school tie. In M. R. DeLong & A. M. Fiore (Eds.), *Aesthetics of textiles and clothing: Advancing multidisciplinary perspectives* (pp. 131–141). Monument, Co: International Textiles and Apparel Association (special publication #7).

Hollies, N. R. S. (1989). Visual and tactile perceptions of textile quality. *Journal of the Textile Institute, 80*(1), 1–18.

Holt, P. W. (1996). *An exploration of the cognitive and affective responses involved in the consumption of women's swimwear*. Unpublished Master's Thesis, Iowa State University, Ames.

*Home Furnishings Network*. Source for articles on trends in interior textile products and the industry.

Horowitz, F. A. (1985). *More than you see: A guide to art*. San Diego, CA: Harcourt Brace Jovanovich.

Howes, D. (1991). *The varieties of sensory experiences: A sourcebook in the anthropology of the senses*. Toronto, Canada: University of Toronto Press.

Hull, J. (1975). *Art Deco: Decorative designs of the twenties and thirties*. San Francisco: Troubadour Press.

Ireland, S. R., Warren, Y. M. & Herringer, L. G. (1992). Anxiety and color saturation preference. *Perceptual and Motor Skills, 75*, 545–546.

Jackson, C. (1980). *Color me beautiful*. New York: Ballantine Books.

Jackson, H. O. & O'Neal, G. S. (1994). Dress and appearance responses to perceptions of aging. *Clothing and Textile Research Journal, 12*(4), 8–15.

Jacobs, D. L. (1994, May 29). The titans of tint make their picks. *New York Times* (Late New York Edition), p. 7(Sec. 3).

Janiszewski, C. (1995, October). Increasing the effectiveness of in-store displays. *Stores*, RR1–RR4.

Jarnow, J. & Guerreiro, M. (1991). *Inside the fashion business* (5th ed.). New York: Macmillan.

Jellinek, J. S. (1992). Perfume classifications: A new approach. In S. Van Toller & G. H. Dodd (Eds.), *Fragrance: The psychology and biology of perfume* [pp. 229–242]. London, England: Elsevier.

Jensen, R. (1996, May-June). The dream society. *The Futurist*, pp. 9–13.

Johnson, L. M. (1996, January). Outerwear '96. *Children's Business, 11*(1), pp. 30–31.

Jones, G. S. (1996, July). Creative assessment. *Catalog Age*, pp. 219–222.

Jones, J. L. (1991). Preferences of elderly music listeners residing in nursing homes for art music, traditional jazz, popular music of today, and country music. *Journal of Music Therapy, 28* (3) 149–160.

Kadolph, S. J., Langford, A. L., Hollen, N. & Saddler, J. (1993). *Textiles*. New York: MacMillan.

Kaiser, S. B. (1990, July). Fashion as popular culture: The postmodern self in the global fashion marketplace. *The World and I, 5*(7), 521–529.

Kallal, M. & Lamb, J. (1994). Apparel product development: meshing a consumer needs model with industry practice. *Proceedings of the International Textiles and Apparel Association*, p.131.

Kanner, B. (1990, December ). The secret life of the female consumer. *Working Woman*, pp. 69–71.

Kato, S. L. (1994). An investigation of the creative process and application to apparel design models. In M. DeLong & A. M. Fiore (Eds.), *Aesthetics of Textiles and Clothing: Advancing multi-disciplinary perspectives* (pp. 48–57). Monument, CO: International Textile & Apparel Association (special publication #7).

Kawabata, S. (1980). *The standardization and analysis of hand evaluation* (2nd ed.). Osaka, Japan: The Textile Machinery Society of Japan.

Kellaris, J. J. & Mantel, S. P. (1996). Shaping time perceptions with background music: The effect of congruity and arousal on estimates of ad durations. *Psychology & Marketing, 13*(5), 501–519.

Kellaris, J. J. & Rice, R. C. (1993). The influence of tempo, loudness, and gender of listener on responses to music. *Psychology & Marketing, 10*(1), 15–29.

Kellaris, J. J., Cox, A. D. & Cox, D. (1993, October). The effect of background music on ad processing: A contingency explanation. *Journal of Marketing, 57*, 114–125.

Kenneth, J. H. (1927). An experimental study of affects and associations due to certain odors. In S. I. Franz, H.C. Warren, M. Bentley, S. W. Fernberger, W. S. Hunter & H. S. Langfield (Eds.) *Psychological Monographs*, 64–90.

Kim, H. & Winakor, G. (1996). Fabric hand as percieved by U.S. and Korean males and females. *Clothing and Textile Research Journal, 14*(2), 113–144.

Kim, H. J. & DeLong, M. R. (1992). Sino-Japanism in Western women's fashionable dress in *Harper's Bazar*, 1890–1927. *Clothing and Textile Research Journal, 11*(1), 24–30.

Kimle, P. & Fiore, A. M. (1992). Fashion advertisements: A comparison of viewers' perceptual and affective responses to illustrated and photographed stimuli. *Perceptual and Motor Skills, 75*, 1083–1091.

Kimle, P. A. (1991). A content analysis of women's apparel advertising in Vogue, 1960–1989. *Proceedings of the International Textile and Apparel Association*, p. 140.

Kimle, P. A. (1994). *Business women's appearance management, career development, and sexual harassment.* Unpublished Dissertation, Iowa State University, Ames.

Kimle, P. A. (1994). Design education and the creative experience: A conceptual framework. In M. DeLong & A. M. Fiore (Eds.), *Aesthetics of Textiles and Clothing: Advancing multi-disciplinary perspectives* (pp. 58–68). Monument, CO: International Textile & Apparel Association (special publication # 7).

King, J. R. (1988). Anxiety reduction using fragrances. In S. Van Toller & G. H. Dodd (Eds.), *Perfumery: The psychology and biology of fragrance* (pp. 147–165). London, England: Chapman and Hall.

Kingsley, S. (1991, January). A grass roots approach to presentation. *Discount Merchandiser, 31*, pp. 66–67.

Kissel, W. (1993, June 18). Styles with a sizable difference. *Los Angeles Times*, E1-2.

Kleine, R. E. & Kernan, J. B. (1991). Contextual influences on the meanings ascribed to ordinary consumption objects. *Journal of Consumer Research, 18*, 311–324.

Kleinfield, N. R. (1992, October 25). The smell of money. *New York Times.* Section 9 pp. 1, 8.

Koda, H. (1985). Rei Kawakubo and the aesthetic of poverty. *Dress, 7*, 17–26.

Kotler, P. (1973–74). Atmospherics as a marketing tool. *Journal of Retailing, 49*(4), 48–64.

Kotsiopulos, A., Oliver, B. & Shim, S. (1993). Buying competencies: A comparison of perceptions among retail buyers, managers, and students. *Clothing and Textiles Research Journal, 11*(2), 38–44.

Kupfer, J. (1994). Clothing and aesthetic experience. In M. R. DeLong and A. M. Fiore (Eds.), *Aesthetics of textiles and clothing: Advancing multidisciplinary perspectives*, (pp. 97–104). Monument, CO.: International Textiles and Apparel Association (special publication #7).

Kwon, Y. H. (1979). Changing function of symbolism in design of Korean silk textiles. *Home Economics Research Journal, 8*, 16–26.

LaBat, K. L. & Nelson, N. J. (1996). *Contemporary Irish textiles art: The women of Annaghmakerrig.* St. Paul, Mn: Goldstein Gallery, University of Minnesota. (Exhibition catalog).

Lacher, K. T. (1994). An investigation of the influence of gender on the hedonic responses created by listening to music. *Advances in Consumer Research, 21*, 354–358.

Lamb, J. & Kallal, M. (1992). A conceptual framework for apparel design. *Clothing and Textiles Research Journal, 10*(2), 42–47.

Lane, R. (1992, April). Clash of the color czars. *AdWeek's Marketing Week, 33*, p. 18.

Langrehr, F. W. (1991). Retail shopping mall semiotics and hedonic consumption. *Advances in Consumer Research, 18*, 428–433.

Lauer, D. (1985). *Design Basics* (2nd ed.). New York: Holt, Rinehart, and Winston.

Laughlin, J. & Kean, R. C. (1995). Assessment of textiles and clothing academic programs in the United States. Part 1: Programs. *Clothing and Textiles Research Journal, 13* (3), 184–199.

Le Norcy, S. (1988). Selling perfume: a technique or an art. In S. Van Toller and G. H. Dodd (Eds.), *Perfumery: The psychology and biology of fragrance* (pp. 217–226). London, England: Chapman and Hall.

Lederman, S. J., Thorne, G. & Jones, B. (1986). Perception of texture by vision and touch: Multidimensionality and intersensory integration. *Journal of Experimental Psychology: Human Perception and Performance, 12*(2), 169–180.

Lee, D. (1987). Belief systems and art preferences. In D. Shaw, W. Hendon & C. R. Waits (Eds.), *Artist and cultural consumers* (pp. 287–290). Association for Cultural Economics.

Lennon, S. J, Fairhurst, A. & Peatross, F. (1991). Apparel and furniture attribute importance as a function of self-monitoring. *Home Economics Research Journal, 19*, 292–302.

Lennon, S. J. (1988). Physical attractiveness, age, and body type. *Home Economics Research Journal, 16*, 195–204.

Levine, J.M. & McBurney, D.H. (1981). The role of olfaction in social perception and behavior. In C. Herman, M. Zanna & E. Higgins (Eds.), *Ontario symposium: Physical appearance, stigma, and social behavior, 3* (pp. 179–217). Toronto, Canada: University of Toronto.

Levitch, G. (1993, May 17). Sensory marketing. *Marketing*, pp. 1, 3.

Lighting management. (1992, December). *Chain Store Age Executive, 68*, 13–24.

Lind, C. (1993). Psychology of color: Similarities between abstract and clothing color preferences. *Clothing and Textile Research Journal, 12*(1), 57–65.

Lindauer, M. S. (1984). Physiognomy and art: Approaches from above, below, and sideways. *Visual Arts Research, 10*(1), 52–65.

Littrell, M. A. (1980). Home economists as cross-cultural researchers: A field study of Ghanaian clothing selection. *Home Economics Research Journal, 8*, 307–317.

Littrell, M.A. (1990). Symbolic significance of textiles crafts for tourists. *Annals of Tourism Research, 17* (2), 228–245.

Lorig, T. S. & Schwartz, G. E. (1988). Brain and odor: I. Alteration of human EEG by odor administration. *Psychobiology, 16*(3), 281–284.

Lorig, T. S., Herman, K. B. & Schwartz, G. E. (1990). EEG activity during administration of low-concentration odors. *Bulletin of the Psychonomic Society, 28*(5), 405–408.

Lubner-Rupert, J. A. & Winakor, G. (1985). Male and female style preference and perceived fashion risk. *Home Economics Research Journal, 13*, 256–266.

Lutz, H. (1994). From wealth to sensuality: The changing meaning of velvet 1910–1939. In M. R. DeLong & A. M. Fiore (Eds.), *Aesthetics of textiles and clothing: Advancing multidisciplinary perspectives* (pp. 105–119). Monument CO: International Textile and Apparel Association (special publication #7).

Lyman, B. J. & McDaniel, M. A. (1986). Effects of encoding strategy on long-term memory for odours. *Quarterly Journal of Experimental Psychology*, 38, 753–765.

MacInnis, D. J. & Price, L. L. (1987). The role of imagery in information processing: Review and extensions. *Journal of Consumer Research, 13*, 473–491.

Macinnis, D. J. & Park, C. W. (1991). The differential role of characteristics of music on high-and low-involvement consumers' processing of ads. *Journal of Consumer Research, 18*, 161–173.

Malhotra, N. K. (1984). Information and sensory overload. *Psychology and Marketing, 1*(3/4), 9–21.

Marks, L. E. (1982). Synesthetic perception and poetic metaphor. *Journal of Experimental Psychology: Human Perception and Performance, 8*(1), 15–23.

Martindale, C., Moore, K. & Borkum, J. (1990). Aesthetic preference: Anomalous findings for Berlyne's psychobiological theory. *American Journal of Psychology, 103*(1), 53–80.

Mathis, C. M. & Connor, H. V. (1993). *The triumph of individual style*. Cali, Columbia: Timeless editions.

Matzer, M. (1995, January 16). Selling smell. *Forbes*, pp. 80–81.

McCarthy, C. (1992, April). Aromatic merchandising: Leading customers by the nose. *Visual Merchandising and Store Design*, 85–87.

McCracken, G. (1986). Culture and consumption: A theoretical account of the structure and movement of the cultural meaning of consumer goods. *Journal of Consumer Research, 13*(1), 71–84.

McCracken, G. (1987). Advertising: Meaning or information? In M Wallendorf and P. Anderson, (Eds.), *Advances in Consumer Research*, 121–124. Provo, UT: Association for Consumer Research.

McGrath, M. A. (1989). An ethnography of a gift store: Trappings, wrappings, and rapture. *Journal of Retailing, 65*(4), 421–449.

McQueen, D. (1993). Aquinas on the aesthetic relevance of tastes and smells. *British Journal of Aesthetics, 33*(4), 346–356.

McWhinnie, H. J. (1971). A review of selected aspects of empirical aesthetics III. *Journal of Aesthetic Education, 5*(4), 115–126.

Mehrabian A. & Russell, J. A. (1974). *An approach to environmental psychology*. Cambridge, MA: Massachusetts Institiute of Technology.

Mehrabian, A. & Russell, J. A. (1973). A measure of arousal seeking tendency. *Environment and Behavior, 5*(3), 315–333.

Mensing, J. & Beck, C. (1988). The psychology of fragrance selection. In S. Van Toller and G. H. Dodd (Eds.), *Perfumery: The psychology and biology of fragrance* (185–204). London, England: Chapman and Hall.

Milbank, C. R. (1985). *Couture: The great designers*. New York: Stewart, Tabori & Chang.

Miles, E. W. & Leathers, D. G. (1984). The impact of aesthetic and professionally-related objects on credibility in the office setting. *Southern Speech Communication Journal, 49*, 361–379.

Miller, B. E. (1984). Artistic meaning and aesthetic education. A formalist view. *Journal of Aesthetic Education,* 18(3), 85–99.

Miller, C. (1991, February). The right song in the air can boost retail sales. *Marketing News, 25*, p. 2.

Milliman, R. E. (1982, summer). Using background music to affect the behavior of supermarket shoppers. *Journal of Marketing, 46*, 86–91.

Milliman, R. E. (1986). The influence of background music on the behavior of restaurant patrons. *Journal of Consumer Research, 13*, 286–289.

Mitchell, D. J., Kahn, B. E. & Knasko, S. C. (October, 1993). There's something in the air: Ambient odor and consumer decision making. Presentation at *Association of Consumer Research Conference*. Nashville, TN.

Moore, C. L. & Yamamoto, K. (1988). *Beyond words: Movement observation and analysis*. New York: Gordon & Breach.

Morgado, M. A. (1993). Animal trademark emblems on fashion apparel. Part I. Interpretive strategy. *Clothing and Textiles Research Journal, 11*(2), 16–20.

Morgado, M. A. (1993). Animal trademark emblems on fashion apparel. Part II. Applied semiotics. *Clothing and Textiles Research Journal, 11*(3), 31–38.

Morgado, M. A. (1996). Coming to terms with *Postmodern*: theories and concepts of contemporary culture and their implications for apparel scholars. *Clothing and Textiles Research Journal, 14*(1), 41–53.

Morganosky, M. (1984). Aesthetic and utilitarian qualities of clothing: Use of a multidimensional clothing value model. *Home Economics Research Journal, 13*, 12–20.

Morganosky, M. A. & Postlewait, D. S. (1989). Consumers' evaluation of apparel form, expression, and aesthetic quality. *Clothing and Textiles Research Journal, 7*(2), 11–15.

Morganosky, M. A. (1987). Aesthetic, function, and fashion consumer values: Relationships to other values and demographics. *Clothing and Textiles Research Journal,* 6(1), 15–19.

Mueller, C. S. & Smiley, E. L. (1995). *Marketing today's fashion* (3rd ed.). Englewood Cliffs, NJ: Prentice Hall.

Myers, J. F. (1989). *The language of visual art: Perception as a basis for design.* Fort Worth, TX: Holt, Rinehart and Winston, Inc.

Names that smell. (1995, August). *American Demographics*, p. 48–49.

Nelson, J. G., Pelech, M. T. & Foster, S. F. (1984). Color preference and stimulation seeking. *Perceptual and Motor Skills, 59*, 913–914.

Ness, S. A. (1992). *Body, movement, and culture: Kinesthetic and visual symbolism in a Philippine community* [Series in contemporary ethnography]. Philadelphia, PA: University of Philadelphia Press.

Oliver, R. L., Robertson, T. S. & Mitchell, D. J. (1993). Imaging and analyzing in response to new product advertising. *Journal of Advertising, 12*(4), 35–49.

*Ornament*. Source for articles on creative design of jewelry and other crafts.

Osborne, H. (1979). The concept of creativity in art. *British Journal of Aesthetics, 19*(3), 224–231.

Paek, S. L. (1979). An analysis of sensory hand as identified by selected consumers. *Textile Research Journal, 45*, 698–704.

Paek, S. L. (1985). Effect of scaling method on perception of textiles. *Perceptual and Motor Skills, 60*, 335–338.

Palmer, R. H. (1985). *The lighting art: The aesthetics of stage lighting design.* Englewood Cliffs, NJ: Prentice-Hall.

Parker, D. M. & Deregowski, J. B. (1990). *Perception and artistic style.* Amsterdam: North Holland Publishers.

Patterson, G. A. (1995). Target 'micromarkets' its way to success: No 2 stores are alike. *Wall Street Journal*, May 31, 1995, pp. A1, A9.

Pegler, M. (1995). *Visual merchandising & display,* (3rd ed.). New York: Fairchild.

Pellet, J. (1993, October). Kiddie Couture. *Discount Merchandisers, 33*(15), 44, 47.

Pfaff, F. (1986, March). Fashion fever. *Marketing and Media Decisions*, 72–82.

Phillips, H. & Bradshaw, R. (1993). How customers actually shop: Customer interaction with the point of sale. *Journal of the Market Research Society, 35*(1), 51–62.

Pile, J. F. (1988). *Interior design.* Englewood Cliffs, NJ: Prentice-Hall.

Purcell, A. T. (1984). The aesthetic experience and mundane reality. In W. R. Crozier & A. J. Chapman (Eds.), *Cognitive processes in the perception of art* (pp. 189–211). Amsterdam, Netherlands: Elsevier Science.

Raju, P.S. (1980). Optimum stimulation level: Its relationship to personality, demographics, and exploratory behavior. *Journal of Consumer Research, 7*, 272–282.

Rasband, J. (1996). *Wardrobe strategies for women.* Albany, NY: Delmar Publishers.

Reda, S. (1995, October). That's entertainment. *Stores*, pp. 16–20.

Reda, S. (1994, August). Dollars and scents. *Stores*, pp. 38–39.

Richardson, J. A., Coleman, F. W. & Smith, M. J. (1984). *Basic design: Systems, elements, applications.* Englewood Cliffs, NJ: Prentice-Hall.

Richardson, J. T. E. & Zucco, G. M. (1989). Cognition and olfaction: A review. *Psychological Bulletin, 105*(3), 352–360.

Ridley, A. (1995). Musical sympathies: The experience of expressive music. *Journal of Aesthetics and Art Criticism, 53*(1), 49–58.

Roberts, N. (1985). *Breaking all the rules.* New York: Viking Penguin.

Robinson, J. (1994). Expression and arousal of emotion in music. *Journal of Aesthetics and Art Criticism, 52*(1), 13–22.

Rosenfeld, A. H., (1985, December). Music, the beautiful disturber. *Psychology Today*, pp. 48, 50–51, 54–56.

Rossiter, J. R. (1987). Visual imagery: Applications to advertising. In M Wallendorf and P. Anderson, (Eds.), *Advances in Consumer Research*, 101–106. Provo, UT: Association for Consumer Research.

Rubin, D. C., Groth, E. & Goldsmith, D. J. (1984). Olfactory cuing of autobiographical memory. *American Journal of Psychology, 97*, 493–507.

Rubinstein, R. L. (1989). The home environments of older people: A description of the psychosocial processes linking person to place. *Journal of Gerontology, 44*(2), S45–53.

Rubinstein, R. P. (1995). *Dress codes: Meaning and messages in American culture.* Boulder, CO: Westview.

Rupe, D. & Kunz, G. (in review). *Building a financially meaningul language of merchandise assortments.*

Sailor, P. J. (1971). Perception of line in clothing. *Perceptual Motor Skills, 33*, 987–990.

Santorelli, D. (1996, September 16). Spiegel presents Fall '97 style stories. *Home Furnishing Network*, p. 4.

Schindler, R. M. & Holbrook, M. B. (1993). Critical periods in the development of men's and women's tastes in personal appearance. *Psychology & Marketing, 10* (6), 549–564.

Schiro, A. M. (1990, April 22). Fabric, fit, and rose-tinted mirror. *New York Times*, p. 10F.

Sherry, J. F. (1990). A sociocultural analysis of a midwestern American flea market. *Journal of Consumer Research, 17*, 13–30.

Sheth, J. N., Newman, B. I. & Gross, B. L. (1991). Why we buy what we buy: A theory of consumption values. *Journal of Business Research, 22*, 159–170.

Shim, S. & Kotsiopulos, A. (1993). A typology of apparel shopping orientation segments among female consumers. *Clothing and Textile Research Journal, 12*(1), 73–85.

Shulman, J. (1980). Measuring musical tastes in popular music. *Advances in Consumer Research, 7*, 25–27.

Silver, H. R. (1981). Calculating risks: The socioeconomic foundations of aesthetic innovation in an Ashanti carving community. *Ethnology, 20*(2), 101–114.

Simone, J. (1992, November). The mailing of America. *Visual Merchandising and Store Design*, pp. 24–32.

Sloboda, J. A. (1985). *The musical mind: Cognitive psychology of music.* Oxford: Clarendon.

Smets, G. J. F. & Overbeeke, C. J. (1989). Scent and sound of vision: Expressing scent or sound as visual forms. *Perceptual and Motor Skills, 69*, 227–233.

Smith, P. C. & Curnow, R. (1966). Arousal hypotheses and the effect of music on purchasing behavior. *Journal of Applied Psychology, 50*(3), 255–256

Solomon, M. R. (1992). *Consumer behavior.* Boston, MA: Allyn & Bacon.

Solomon, M. R., Ashmore, R. D. & Longo L. C. (1992). The beauty match–up hypothesis: Congruence between types of beauty and product images in advertising. *Journal of Advertising, 21*(4), 23–34.

Spangenberg, E. R., Crowley, A. E. & Henderson, P. W. Improving the store environment: Do olfactory cues affect evaluations and behaviors? *Journal of Marketing, 60*, 67–80.

Sparshott, F. (1994). Music and feeling. *Journal of Aesthetics and Art Criticism, 52*(1), 23–36.

Spindler, A.M. (1996, October 15). Zut! British infiltrate French fashion. *New York Times*, pp. A1, B8.

Spitz, E. H. (1982). The past of illusion: A contribution of child psychoanalysis to the understanding of aesthetic experience. *Journal of Aesthetic Education, 16*(4), 59–69.

Sporre, D. J. (1989). *Perceiving the arts: An introduction to the humanities.* Englewood Cliffs, Prentice-Hall.

Sproles, G. B. & Burns, L. D. (1994). *Changing appearances: Understanding dress in contemporary society.* New York: Fairchild.

Steele, J. J. (1992). Environmental fragrancing. *International Journal of Aromatherapy, 4*(2), 8–11.

Stegemeyer, A. (1988). *Who's who in fashion.* New York: Fairchild.

Strati, A. (1992). Aesthetic understanding of organizational life. *Academy of Management Review, 17*(3), 568–581.

Sundberg, J. (1982). Speech, song, and emotion . In M. Clynes (Ed.), *Music, mind, and brain* (pp. 137–150). New York: Plenum.

*Surface Design Journal.* Source for articles on artistic design of fabrics.

Swinyard, W. R. (1993). Effect of mood, involvement, and quality of store experience on shopping intentions. *Journal of Consumer Research, 20*, 271–280.

Tang, P. C. L. & Leonard, A. L. (1985). Creativity in art and science. *Journal of Aesthetic Education, 19*(3), 5–19.

Tauber, E. M. (1995), Why do people shop? *Marketing Management, 4*(2), 58–60.

Taylor, T. (1995,January 25). Los Angeles textile show gets mixed reviews. *Daily News Record*, pp. 8–9.

Terwogt, M. M. & Hoeksma, J. B. (1995). Colors and emotions: Preferences and combinations. *Journal of General Psychology, 122*(1), 5–17.

The rainbow of toys. (1995, February). *Stores*, p. 29.

Thompson, J. A. A. & Davis, L., L. (1988). Furniture design decision-making constructs. *Home Economics Research Journal, 16*, 279–290.

Tiger, L. (1992). *Pursuit of pleasure*. Boston, MA: Little, Brown & Co.

Tijus, C. A. (1988). Cognitive processes in artistic creation: Toward the realization of a creative machine. *Leonardo*, *21*(2), 167–172.

Todd, J. T. & Akerstrom, R. A. (1987). Perception of three-dimensional form from patterns of optical texture. *Journal of Experimental Psychology: Human Perception and Performance*, *13*(2), 242–255.

Torii, S., Fukuda, H., Kanemoto, H., Miyanchi, R., Hamauzu, Y. & Kawasaki, M. (1988). Contingent negative variation (CNV) and the psychological effects of odor. In S. Van Toller and G. H. Dodd,(Eds.), *Perfumery: The psychology and biology of fragrance* (pp. 207–220). London, England: Chapman and Hall.

Trautman, P. (1996, September). Manufacturing in design: The role of technical design. *Bobbin*, pp. 148–150.

Tricks that stores use to sell. (1994, November). *Consumer Reports* , p 717.

Ullman, L. (1984). *Rudolph Laban: A vision of dynamic space*. London, England: Laban Archives in association with The Falmer Press.

Vacker, B. & Key, W. R. (1993). Beauty and the beholder: The pursuit of beauty through commodities. *Psychology and Marketing*, *10*(6), 471–494.

Valdez, P. & Mehrabian, A. (1994). Effects of color on emotion. *Journal of Experimental Psychology: General*, *123* (4), 394–409.

Van Toller, S. (1988). Emotion and the brain. In S. Van Toller & G. H. Dodd (Eds.), *Perfumery: The psychology and biology of fragrance* (pp. 122–144). London, England: Chapman and Hall.

Venkatraman, M. P. & MacInnis, D. J. (1985). The epistemic and sensory exploratory behavior of hedonic and cognitive consumers. *Advances in Consumer Research*, *12*, 102–107.

Venturi, R. (1977). *Complexity and contradiction in architecture*. Boston,MA : New York Graphic Society.

Wagner, D. & Wagner, B. (1996, February). Fashion, color dominate home textiles trends. *Textile World*, pp. 69–70.

Walk, R. D. (1984). Event perception, perceptual organization and emotion. In W. R. Crozier and A. J. Chapman, (Eds.), *Cognitive processes in the perception of art* (pp. 211–221). New York: Elsevier Science.

Walker, J. (1988). The amateur scientist. *Scientific American*, *258*(1), 96–99.

Warren C., and Warrenburg, S. (1991, November). *Mood benefits of fragrance*. Paper presented at the meeting of Aroma-Chology: The Impact of Science on the Future of Fragrance (sponsored by Olfactory Research Fund, Ltd.), New York, NY.

Watkins, S. M. (1988). Using the design process to teach functional apparel design. *Clothing and Textiles Research Journal*, *7*(1), 10–14.

Watts, E. (1977). *Towards dance and art: A study of relationships between two art forms*. London, England: Lepus Books.

Weil, J. (1986). The role of ambiguity in the arts. *Et Cetera*, *43*(1), 83–89.

Wentworth, N. & Witryol, S. L. (1983). Is variety the better part of novelty? *Journal of Genetic Psychology*, *142*, 3–15.

White, G. (1992). *Instrumental arranging*. Dubuque, Ia: Brown & Benchmark.

White, I. S. (1959). The functions of advertising in our culture. *Journal of Marketing*, *24*(July), 8–14.

Whittemore, M. (1994, December). Retailing looks to a new century. *Nation's Business*, pp. 18–24.

Wilkie, M. (1995, August). Scent of a market. *American Demographics*, pp. 40–49.

Wilson, G. D. (1966). Arousal properties of red versus green. *Perceptual and Motor Skills*, *23*, 942–949.

Wilson, M. (1993, October). Welcome Home's warm glow. *Chain Store Age Executive*, *69* (10), pp. 142–143.

Winakor, G., Canton, B. & Wolins, L. (1980). Perceived fashion risk and self-esteem of males and females. *Home Economics Research Journal*, *9*, 45–56.

Winner, E. (1982). *Invented worlds: Psychology of the arts*. Cambridge, MA: Harvard University Press.

Wolff, J. (1993). *Aesthetics and the sociology of art*. Ann Arbor, MI: University of Michigan Press.

Wolpin, M. & Weinstein, C. (1983). Visual imagery and olfactory stimulation. *Journal of Mental Imagery*, *7*(1), 63–74.

*Women's Wear Daily*. Source for articles on the women's wear fashion industry and trends.

Workman, J. E. & Johnson, K. (1993). Fashion opinion leadership, fashion innovativeness, and need for variety. *Clothing and Textiles Research Journal*, *11*(3), 61–64.

Yalch, R. & Spangenberg, E. (1990). Effects of store music on shopping behavior. *Journal of Consumer Marketing*, 7(Spring), 55–63.

Yan X. (1996). *The effect of environmental fragrancing on consumers' attitude, purchase intention, and aesthetic experience towards an apparel product*. Unpublished Master's Thesis, Iowa State University, Ames.

Zeithaml, V. A. (1988). Consumer perceptions of price, quality, and value: A means-end model and synthesis of evidence. *Journal of Marketing*, *52*, 2–21.

Zelanski, P. & Fisher, M. P. (1984). *Design: Principles and problems*. New York: Holt, Rinehart and Winston.

# Index